GERMANY
IN POWER AND ECLIPSE

THE BACKGROUND OF GERMAN DEVELOPMENT

by

JAMES K. POLLOCK, Ph.D.

James Orin Murfin Professor of Political Science
University of Michigan

and

HOMER THOMAS, Ph.D., F.S.A. Scot.

University of Missouri

WITH THE ASSISTANCE AND COLLABORATION OF

WILLETT F. RAMSDELL, M.S.F.

Late George Willis Pack Professor of Forest Land Management
University of Michigan

Wm. CLARK TROW, Ph.D.

Professor of Educational Psychology
University of Michigan

MANFRED C. VERNON, J.D., Ph.D.

Washington, D.C.

D. VAN NOSTRAND COMPANY, INC.

TORONTO   NEW YORK   LONDON

NEW YORK
D. Van Nostrand Company, Inc., 250 Fourth Avenue, New York 3

TORONTO
D. Van Nostrand Company (Canada), Ltd., 228 Bloor Street, Toronto

LONDON
Macmillan & Company, Ltd., St. Martin's Street, London, W.C. 2

PREFATORY NOTE

The preparation for World War II and the war years revealed an astonishing lack of basic data, not to mention understanding, concerning the German area and the German people. Even in several old German sources, long out of date, let alone sources in English, there was no body of essential information which added up to a well-rounded treatment of the German area and its peoples, and of how the German state and society had evolved down through the centuries. Although old, local cultural histories were available in the German language, nothing approximating a socio-economic-political survey of Germany and its integral territorial units was in existence.

Geopolitical studies of Germany, such as the Germans themselves made of other critical areas of the world, were not available when Hitler unleashed the dogs of war in 1939. Thereafter, official and private research dealing with Germany was intensified, and following the United States' entry into the war in 1941 and in the years which followed, great efforts were made to train thousands of military personnel in the general and also in the detailed facts about the German area and its people.

In connection with this training it appeared that there was an acute lack of concrete information which would be necessary and helpful to our military government personnel when they undertook to occupy and govern the country of the defeated enemy. Otherwise well-informed German specialists were without the tools with which to instruct the officers and men who were later to undertake important responsibilities all over Germany.

In this emergency situation with the help of our colleagues, we began the compilation, evaluation, and presentation of the essential facts covering the entire German area, province by province, and state by state. Some twenty-two unit studies were prepared in the course of the war and made available to the War Department and the State Department. Without any financial help from or obligation to the federal government and due to the generosity of the University of Michigan, research into all aspects of German development was undertaken to assist various agencies of the government concerned with the prosecution of the war. What value these studies had at the time will have to be stated by those who used them. But when the war was over and the vast data were still available in somewhat disparate and disorganized shape, we undertook to digest and rearrange the most essential aspects of our research into a form which we hope may be of general use and value to those who desire to acquire a knowledge and understanding of Germany as a whole, and of its various parts.

The present work has therefore resulted from extensive research undertaken during the war years and from a complete re-writing and condensation since that time. Originally intended for army use, the material has now been adapted to general use. Both a broad cultural as well as an areal approach have been used in order first to treat Germany as a whole, and then to treat it intensively area by area. Important reference material not easily available has been collected in the Appendix. Selected bibliographies are appended to each chapter. Numerous maps and charts are also included.

It is our hope that the present volume, which covers German development up to World War II, will fill a long-felt need by providing students of Germany in convenient compass with a body of essential reference material about the German area, its peoples and institutions.

The present volume is in two parts: the first deals with the evolution of the German state and society; the second treats Germany region by region in order to explain the detailed and contrasting composition of the different sections of the country. The impact of World War II on Germany together with an evaluation of German development at the point of the eclipse of German power in 1945, we have reserved for the proposed second volume which will deal principally with Germany at war and under occupation.

The completion of this survey has been made possible by the friendly assistance and collaboration of Professors William Clark Trow and Willett F. Ramsdell (now deceased), and of Dr. Manfred C. Vernon, all of whom gave many arduous days to the preparation and collation of the vast data on which this work is based. Special thanks are due to Professor Ramsdell and Dr. Vernon for the maps which supplement the text. To the Rackham Foundation of the University of Michigan we desire to express our gratitude and appreciation first for its patriotic support of our researches during the war, and second for its generous help in facilitating the completion of our work in the years since the end of the war. We were also fortunate in having Mrs. Ethlynn Sprentall as our invaluable assistant in the preparation of the manuscript.

JAMES K. POLLOCK
HOMER THOMAS

Ann Arbor, Michigan
April, 1952

TABLE OF CONTENTS

PART II. REGIONAL COMPOSITION OF GERMANY

SECTION I. EASTERN GERMANY

SECTION II. NORTHWESTERN GERMANY

SECTION III. WESTERN GERMANY

SECTION IV. CENTRAL GERMANY

SECTION V. SOUTH GERMANY

TABLE OF MAPS AND CHARTS

MAPS

Part I

EVOLUTION OF THE GERMAN STATE AND SOCIETY

Chapter 1

THE GERMAN LAND AND PEOPLE

Germany occupies the center of the European continent. It is a diversified area divided by broad navigable rivers and characterized by wide stretches of open country, highland pasturage, and wooded mountains. It extends from the North Sea across the great northern plain southward through the central highlands to the upper Danubian Basin and the snow-capped Alps. Germany's central position gives it easy access to the lands to the east, north, west, and south, with whose peoples the Germans have traded and fought for centuries.

To the east, the cold, wind-swept plains of North Germany stretch to the Ural Mountains. Across these plains the Germanic tribes of the Migration Age clashed with the Slavs, moving westward from their *Pripet* (Prêpit) marsh homeland. Reversing their march, during the early Middle Ages, the Germans began to push into eastern Europe; this movement carried them across the northern plains toward the Baltic, East Prussia (Ostpreussen), and Silesia (Schlesien), and through Austria into the lands along the Middle Danube. While the southeastern penetration was under the leadership of the Habsburgs of Austria, the northern movement into the East Elbian plains was first sponsored by the Hanseatic League and the Teutonic Knights, and later by the Hohenzollerns of Prussia. The long struggle with the Slavs for the lands between the Elbe and the Vistula has played an important part in the creation of the disciplined and militaristic ideals of the German people. These standards of conduct are the legacy of the German experience in the East.

To the north of Germany lie the Baltic Sea and the North Sea and beyond the seas the Scandinavian countries whence came the early Danish incursions, and the later Swedish conquests of Gustavus Adolphus and Charles XII. The northern cities along the Baltic and the North Sea developed a flourishing maritime trade from the twelfth to the fifteenth centuries, and upon their commercial success was built the Hanseatic League which included Bremen, Hamburg, Lübeck, Rostock, Stettin, Danzig, and Königsberg.

3

To the west, the bordering lowlands extend across the Netherlands and Belgium into the Paris Basin, bringing Germany into contact with Atlantic Europe. Farther south the eroded uplands and scarplands of Central Germany form an integral part of the ancient Hercynian Mountain Zone extending all the way from the countries along the lower Danube across Germany into France. In the two world wars of this century, it was the German movement into the Atlantic region that brought England and the United States into armed conflict with Germany. These two wars, however, were only the most recent of the many waged over this disputed borderland; hostilities in this area go back through the German victory over France in 1870, and Napoleon's conquest of Germany, to the wars of medieval times.

To the south lie the Alps, which Germany shares with France, Switzerland, Italy, and Austria. Over the Alps from the Mediterranean world came the legions of the Roman Empire, the emissaries of the Christian church, and later the apostles of the Renaissance. The German culture as it developed was, therefore, a blend of indigenous barbaric and imported classical and Christian elements. Reinforced by intimate social and intellectual cultural patterns from the West, which derived from the same Mediterranean sources, Roman elements lived on politically in the dying tradition of the medieval Holy Roman Empire in an area which embraced not only Germany but Italy, Switzerland, Alsace-Lorraine, and the Low Countries as well. Such was the German legacy from the South.

Meanwhile, within Germany, the history of political development during the early modern period is the story of territorial losses in the west, of disunity and particularism, of religious schism, and of internal strife, punctuated by periods of foreign conquest. On the other hand, the eastward movement and the subsequent rise of Brandenburg-Prussia presaged the eventual political unification of the Reich. The internal weakness of Germany from 1648 to 1871 not only enabled her neighbors to expropriate territory from the western margins of the medieval German states, but permitted the rise of the rival Prussian and Austrian states within the German land. While these states were fortifying their positions through the consolidation of their gains in the East, seeds of the French Revolution and nineteenth century liberalism found fertile soil in the western portions of Germany.

The wars of the Napoleonic era, which had brought extensive territorial consolidations within the Reich, were followed in Germany by movements for constitutional government and unity, conditioned by a growing nationalistic spirit. After the Napoleonic Wars, the Congress of Vienna, 1814-15, had left Germany under the control of an alliance of sovereigns which denied the Germans both liberty and national unity. Nor did the revolutionary movements which swept Europe in 1848 bring political unity. Middle nineteenth century

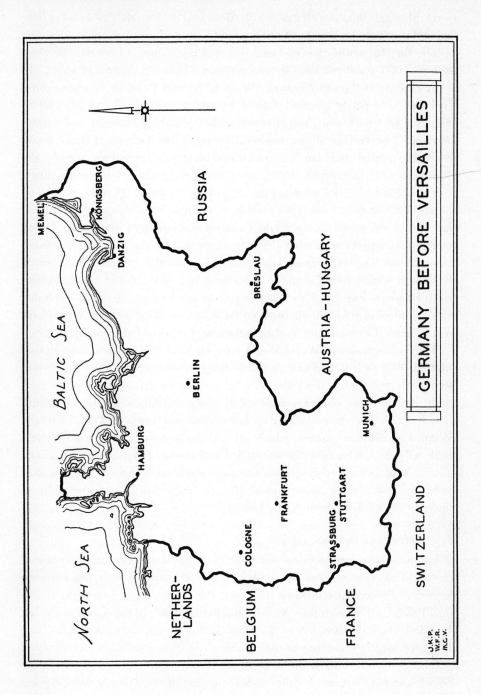

GERMANY BEFORE VERSAILLES

Germany was, consequently, politically disunited and at the mercy of strong national pressures both from the West and from the East.

The forceful unification of Germany by Prussia under Bismarck between 1862 and 1871 stabilized the German position within the European scene, but at the expense of the separation of Habsburg Austria from the German realm. This loss was partly counterbalanced by the Prussian victories of 1864 to 1871 over Denmark and France, which added Schleswig-Holstein and Alsace-Lorraine. The revival of the medieval unity of the German peoples broke down the internal trade barriers, which had been only partly liquidated by the Customs Union (*Zollverein,* 1834), movement of the early nineteenth century.

The second imperial period, extending from 1871 to 1918, was marked by the rapid industrialization of the whole of Germany through efficient utilization of natural resources. Germany's central position was responsible for an economic viewpoint somewhat different from that of the nations of Atlantic Europe, since she could easily trade not only with the industrial markets of the densely settled Low Countries and France but also with the agrarian countries of eastern Europe. This ready access to markets on all sides, combined with a control of transit trade between the East and West by the eve of World War I, made Germany the leading commercial power of the continent.

The consequences of World War I were far from disastrous to the German position. Within less than two decades, owing to the political unity which had been partly achieved, and which was reinforced by the Allies at Versailles, Germany, backed by an economic recovery in which the Allies were financial partners, was able once more to take up her nationalistic mission. True, Germany occupied an exposed position, which gave rise to illusory fears of her relatively weak neighbors who never constituted a real threat. But her position at the crossroads of Europe with its important geographical, historical, political, and economic implications might again give the Germans dominating political power in the affairs of continental Europe.

THE FRONTIERS OF GERMANY

Germany's exposed position is a consequence of its location in the center of Europe. The frontiers previous to World War II bordered no fewer than ten countries: France, Luxembourg, Belgium, the Netherlands, Denmark, Lithuania, Poland, Czechoslovakia, Austria, and Switzerland. In the course of the last thousand years, the frontiers of the state created by the German peoples have fluctuated largely according to their political unity and military strength.

The western frontier is the result of the thousand year struggle between the French and the Germans for the lands lying west of the Rhine. During the era of its medieval strength, the Holy Roman Empire extended westward to the Scheldt, Upper Meuse, and Rhone rivers, for it controlled the Low Countries,

Lorraine, Burgundy, and Switzerland. The first retraction in the western frontier came after the Thirty Years' War (1618-1648), when Switzerland and the Netherlands gained their independence from the Holy Roman Empire of the German Nation (*Heiliges Römisches Reich Deutscher Nation*). The seventeenth century brought the conquest of Alsace-Lorraine and western Flanders by the French. After the Napoleonic Wars, the Congress of Vienna (1815) placed the Austrian Netherlands, which were destined in 1831 to become the Kingdom of Belgium, under the Kingdom of the Netherlands. The next reorganization of the western frontier came after the Franco-Prussian War (1870-1871), when Alsace-Lorraine was annexed to the Reich. Further changes came after World War I, when Alsace-Lorraine and the Eupen-Malmedy area were ceded to France and Belgium, respectively, while the Saar was established as an international area subject to a plebiscite after fifteen years. These lost territories were regained by the Third Reich. The Saar was restored after the plebiscite of 1935, while Alsace-Lorraine and the Eupen-Malmedy area were re-annexed to the Reich through the victories over Belgium and France in 1940.

The northern frontier along the North Sea and the Baltic Sea is broken only by the Jutland peninsula, which is crossed by a boundary separating Germany and Denmark. Although the southern Holstein portion of the Jutland peninsula was held by the Danish crown as a fief from the Holy Roman Emperor through most of the medieval and modern periods, the Schleswig portion of the peninsula, lying to the north of the Eider River, formed an integral part of the Danish Kingdom until 1866. In that year Prussia seized all of Schleswig-Holstein by force of arms. The last reorganization of the Danish-German frontier came with the plebiscite of 1920, when the southern part of Schleswig voted to remain within the Reich.

The eastern border area is characterized by the absence of either sharp geographical or linguistic differentiation. The modern frontier was a product of the long struggle between Germans and Slavs. The northeastward expansion of the Germans, under the leadership of the Teutonic Knights during the Middle Ages, brought Pomerania (Pommern), the Polish Corridor (Pomerellen), and Prussia under German control. The strong Polish state of the late medieval and early modern period regained the Corridor area in 1466 and held it until the first partition of Poland in 1772, when it was seized by Prussia. Prussian acquisition of the Posen (Poznan) area came with the second partition of Poland in 1793. Although the Napoleonic era resulted in a considerable reorganization of the eastern frontiers of Prussia because of the establishment of the Napoleonic Duchy of Warsaw, the Congress of Vienna restored the Corridor and Posen areas to Prussia in 1815. After the conclusion of World War I these territories were given back to the restored Polish state. In 1924 the Memel area, which had been under German control since the early Middle Ages, was placed under international control and finally ceded by a Commission of the League of Nations to Lithuania (1924). These territories were seized by the Nazis in 1939.

The development of the southeastern frontiers of the German state is less complicated because until 1866 Austria, Bohemia, and Moravia formed an integral part of Germany. The only changes in this area prior to 1866 involved internal frontiers, such as those which resulted when Prussia acquired Silesia from the Habsburgs in 1742. The modern frontier of the Reich, running through the Alpine foothills, the Bohemian Forest (*Böhmer Wald*), the Ore Mountains (*Erzgebirge*), and the Sudeten Mountains, emerged after the expulsion of Austria from the German body politic at the conclusion of the Seven Weeks' War in 1866. After World War I several frontier problems arose in this area. There were protracted difficulties over Upper Silesia, which resulted in the cession of small but industrially important bits of territory to Czechoslovakia and Poland. The real troubles came after 1933 with the Nazi agitation for union with Austria and for the cession of the Sudeten area to Germany. In 1938 both of these areas were made integral parts of the German state.

The frontier development of Germany may be approached from the point of view of the spatial limitations of the German realm during succeeding phases of its development. The tradition of the medieval Holy Roman Empire, which embraced all of Central Europe and northern Italy, has long played an important role in the territorial ambitions of the modern German nationalists.

Politically, the history of Central European frontiers from medieval times may be described in terms of the break-up of the Holy Roman Empire and the emergence of Prussia as a dominant state and the establishment of rival nationalistic groups. The old Empire, an agglomeration of states and principalities under a frequently impotent emperor, maintained a tradition of unity upon which the German states occupying the major portion of the imperial territory, continued to base many of their nationalistic claims to Central Europe. Although the losses of territory in the West after the Thirty Years' War were compensated by gains of the Hohenzollerns and Habsburgs in the East, these gains did not satisfy the German desire for old western lands.

The formation of the modern frontiers of the Reich dates from the time of the Congress of Vienna in 1815. The next basic reorganization of frontiers, as has been noted above, came in 1866 with the separation of Austria from Germany. The establishment of the German Empire in 1871 on the basis of the North German Confederation and the subsequent treaties with the South-German states, fixed the frontiers of the Reich for the period extending from 1871 to 1918.

The next reorganization of the frontiers came after World War I. In this volume the German land and its peoples will be treated in terms of the frontiers after the return of the Saar in 1935. A discussion of the territories which were annexed or conquered by the Nazis during World War II will be dealt with in the second volume.

The artificial character of the frontiers of Germany is obvious. The frontiers of any particular period can only be regarded as the result of the interaction of historical forces, which must be reckoned with in terms of German political unity and military strength. The character of the frontier regions is also a product of the geographic character of the German land. The western frontier, traversing the northwest German lowlands, the Eifel, Hunsrück, and Hardt uplands, and the Rhine rift valley to Basel (Switzerland), runs through German speaking lands. The region along this frontier within the German Reich was the meeting place of French and German civilization. Influences from the Latin West gave the Rhenish culture its particular flavor. In the Northwest and North, the frontier areas have a certain Dutch or Danish atmosphere, while in the East, the German landscape has a Slavic quality. The southern and southeastern borders, however, run through the German speaking lands of Austria and Bohemia, but even here one can detect cultural elements from Southeast Europe.

The Geography of Germany

Analysis of the internal structure of the German area is complicated by its transitional character and its lack of organic boundaries. Physically, Germany is characterized by a lack of structural unity and natural coherence. The land may be divided into three large morphological regions: the northern lowlands, the central upland and valley area, and the southern plateau and Alpine region.

North German Plain

The North German Plain, which forms an integral part of the great North European lowlands extending from the Paris Basin to the Ural Mountains, consists of deposits left behind by the glaciers which fanned out from Scandinavia in Pleistocene times. The underlying rock projects above the covering glacial mantle in only a few isolated places, such as in the cliffs of the Isle of Rügen. The plain in Germany can be further subdivided into two broad geographical areas on the basis of differences in relief, climate, and flora. The northwest portion of the plain, situated between the Elbe and Ems rivers, seems to have escaped the last phase of glaciation. The northwest coastal area, which borders on the North Sea, is marked by the long narrow Frisian islands. They are separated from the marshy coast of the mainland by broad tidal flats. Away from the coastal marshes, which extend up the valleys of the Ems, Weser, and Elbe into the northwest plains, the land is characterized by large areas of bog and sandy heath. Marshes and heath extend northward beyond the Elbe into western Schleswig-Holstein. To the south the plain juts into the lower Rhenish and Westphalian (Westfalen) lowland bays.

The southern margin of the lowlands, which skirts the foothills of the central uplands, consists of a strip of rich loess soils extending from Hanover (Hannover) to Magdeburg and Leipzig. This border zone (*Börde*) is open country with a dry, warm climate. It is an area famous for its potash and lignite deposits. North of the border zone the climate of the northwest lowland becomes more humid and cool, creating conditions ideal for the dairying and livestock raising which are a notable feature of the often dreary cloud-covered plains. In the estuaries of the Ems, Weser, and Elbe rivers, which rise in the central uplands and traverse the northwestern plains on their way to the North Sea, are the only larger cities, Emden, Bremen, and Hamburg, respectively.

The northeastern portion of the plain, situated east of the Elbe and between the Baltic Sea and the Central German uplands, possesses a physical relief which was created by the retreat of the last North European glacier. The surface configuration of the northeast is based upon boulder clays of the ground moraines, mixed glacial deposits of the terminal moraines, outwash material left behind by the last glaciation, and the finely powdered loess deposited during the post glacial era. Internally, the northeastern plain may be divided into a number of regions on the basis of the arrangement and distribution of the above deposits. The Baltic coastal area, extending from eastern Schleswig-Holstein to East Prussia, consists of the Mecklenburg, Pomeranian, and East Prussian plateaus, which are separated by the valleys of the lower Oder and lower Vistula rivers. These plateaus, which rise slowly from the sandy shores of the Baltic Sea to terminate in elevated terminal moraines, are characterized by poor drainage conditions which have given rise to extensive areas of marsh and lakeland. The northern slopes of these "lake plateaus" support an important dairying industry, thanks to the cool, humid coastal climate; while the southern margins of the plateaus, characterized by a drier and warmer climate, have a moderately heavy forest cover.

Southward from the coastal area, there is a broad zone of wide valleys bordered on the north by the Baltic terminal moraines and on the south by the low hills of Fläming, Nieder Lausitz, and the Katzen Gebirge, which lies to the east of the middle Oder River. The basis of the river valley system of Northeast Germany was formed as the glaciers retreated northward. During this period broad valleys running from southeast to northwest into the North Sea formed along the southern edge of the glaciers, providing drainage for Central Germany. These valleys survive and are known as the Ancient River Valleys (*Urstromtäler*) of Northeast Germany and Poland. With the retreat of the glaciers their drainage function was transferred to the Oder and Elbe rivers, which rise in the central uplands and flow northward into the Baltic Sea and the North Sea, respectively. The land between the modern river valleys and the Ancient River Valleys consists of higher ground composed of sandy, gravelly soils. This valley area with its poor sandy soils enjoys a dry, warm climate; the winters, however, are cold, becoming more severe toward the east. Originally the low valleys were swampy, while the higher areas between the rivers were heavily forested. The German colonization of the northeast during the late Middle Ages brought the gradual clearing of the forest land and the draining of the swampy valleys. Today the swamplands of the Ancient River Valleys, now cleared for agriculture, provide natural pathways for inland water routes and railroad lines.

The northeast plain penetrates along the Oder Valley between the hills of Nieder Lausitz and the Katzen Gebirge into Silesia. The Silesian lowlands, which are hemmed in on the southwest by the Sudeten uplands and on the northeast by the southern Polish plateaus, are much like the border zone of the northwest. Although the northern and eastern portions of the Silesian plain consist of relatively infertile sandy lands, the rest of the area has a rich loess soil which has made this section one of the main cereal producing areas of Central Europe. The real wealth of the area, however, is based upon the coal, zinc, and lead deposits along the upper Oder. Such industrial towns as Beuthen, Tarnowitz, Gleiwitz, and Hindenburg, in Upper Silesia owe their rapid growth to the discovery of these deposits. The importance of Breslau and Liegnitz in central Silesia is based jointly upon agriculture and industry. Aside from these urban centers of Silesia, large cities are the exception in the Northeast.

Berlin, which is situated in the heart of the northeast plain, is the great exception in this essentially rural area. Its growth can only be accounted for in terms of its political importance and its position astride the transportation routes serving the plains east of the Elbe. The small towns of Brandenburg and Frankfort-on-the-Oder (Frankfurt-an-der-Oder) as will be noted later, are the only other important centers. The coastal zone, however, supports a number of important port cities such as Kiel, Lübeck, Rostock, Stettin, and Königsberg. The North German Plain, extending from the Low Countries on the west to the Slavic lands on the east, has long been served by excellent east-west lines of communication and contains the river routes leading into the central uplands. Its geographical features facilitated the political and territorial expansion of Hohenzollern-Brandenburg into the Prussian state.

Central German Uplands

The Central German uplands, consisting of a series of well defined massifs interlaced by innumerable valleys, stand in strong contrast to the low plains of northern Germany. Embracing the Rhine Plateau, the hills of the Weser and the Saale, and the Saxon upland, they are based upon a series of ancient Hercynian massifs, consisting of resistant slates, sandstones, and quartzites, occasionally interrupted by sporadic areas of erupted volcanic materials, such as are found near Coblenz (Koblenz) and in the upper valley of the Fulda River. This broad region, bordered by the North German Plains and hemmed in on the south by the valley of the Main, extends from the Low Countries (Ardennes) on the west to the Ore Mountains, which separate Saxony (Sachsen) from northwestern Czechoslovakia. It may be subdivided into a western and an eastern geographical region on the basis of relief.

The western or Rhenish part of the central uplands, which is drained by the Rhine and Weser rivers, connects with the Ardennes uplands of Belgium. The Rhenish and Hessian hills partially encircle the southwest portion of the North German lowland, giving rise to the lower Rhenish and Westphalian lowland bays. The Rhenish upland consists of the Hunsrück and Eifel ranges which border the Rhine on the west, and of the Taunus, Westerwald, and Sauerland ranges, which guard the eastern bank of the Rhine. The Hessian hills which lie to the east include the Vogelsberg, Spessart, Rhön, and Weser highlands, which are separated by the valleys of the tributaries of the Weser River. An extension of the Hessian hills, consisting of the Teutoburger Forest (*Wald*) and the Weser upland (*Bergland*), sweeps off to the northwest between the valleys of the lower Weser and the Ems to encircle the Westphalian bay on the north. These uplands are covered with deciduous forests, open highland pastures, and stony fields, resulting in the concentration on fodder crops and dairying. The drier and warmer climate in the valley areas within the uplands foster the cultivation of the hardier cereals and potatoes and the raising of livestock. In the broader valleys of the Rhine and Mosel, where an even warmer and drier climate is usual, orchards and vineyards dominate the landscape. The towns of the upland area, including Trèves (Trier), Coblenz (Koblenz), Giessen, and Cassel (Kassel), have attained importance only in modern times because of their strategic positions on important transportation arteries. North of the Rhenish uplands are situated the important industrial and manufacturing towns of the Lower Rhine and Westphalian areas—Cologne (Köln), Düsseldorf, Duisburg, Essen, Dortmund, and Hamm. These cities are located in the transitional zone between the North German Plain and the Hercynian uplands, which forms the major industrial area of Germany. The development of the great Rhine-Westphalian industrial area is due largely to its strategic position at the junction of the Rhine Valley and the North European Plain routes in the Lower Rhine Bay, and to the utilization of the great concentrations of coal and lignite, located along the northern margins of the central uplands.

The eastern or Saxon portion of the central area lies within the basin of the middle Elbe. The core of this area is formed by the plains of the Saxon Bay extending from Magdeburg to Leipzig. These plains, which are traversed by the Elbe and its tributaries, the Saale and Mulde, can be regarded only as an extention of the border area. They have the same basic loess soils and enjoy a similar warm, dry climate. This region is important for its large crops of cereals and sugar beets. The extensive deposits of salt and lignite, coupled with the mineral deposits of the uplands to the west and south, provide the resource basis of the industries of the Saxon area. It is this combination of a rich agrarian hinterland and important mineral resources which has made possible the development of the cities of Halle, Leipzig, and Magdeburg. To the west the lowland gives way to the Harz Mountains and the Thuringian Hills, which rise gradually into the high Thuringian Forest (*Thüringer Wald*). The economy of these highlands, which form the western frontier of the Saxon area, is much like that of the Rhenish upland to the west. The towns of the western Saxon uplands, like Erfurt and Weimar, tend to be small. Southward, the Saxon lowlands give way to the Saxon uplands (*Sächsisches Bergland*), which rise gradually into the Erz Gebirge. Although the hilly Saxon area is agriculturally unimportant in comparison to the lowland region, it has several important industrial and manufacturing areas, which include the cities of Zwickau, Chemnitz, and Zittau.

The Central German area, with its distinct Rhenish and Saxon facets, lacks the physical unity of the East Elbian or northwest plains areas. It is divided and separated by highland barriers and deep gorge-like valleys. It is only natural that this portion of Germany should have remained politically divided against itself until forced into partial political unification by the expanding Prussian state. Culturally, it remains a land of particularism, marked by sharp contrasts in its many ways of life.

South German Area

The South German area, which is characterized by elevated plateaus and scarplands, is situated between the valley of the Main and the Alps and between the Rhine and the Bohemian Forest. The valley of the Rhine, which borders the southern German area on the west, consists of a broad valley possessing wide areas of fertile land enjoying a dry, warm climate. The Rhine, which rises in the high Alps, first touches German territory after it enters Lake Constance (*Bodensee*), from which it flows westward through a deep valley to the Swiss city of Basel, standing at the head of navigation on the Rhine. From

Basel, the river flows northwards through a wide flood plain to the city of
Mainz, when it is joined by the Main. Downstream from Mainz, it flows
through a deep gorge cut in the Rhenish uplands of West Central Germany.
Dry infertile terrace lands, composed of glacial sands and gravels, border the
Rhine for some distance on either side, providing safe locations above the floods
for towns such as Freiburg, Carlsruhe (Karlsruhe), and Darmstadt. Behind
the terraces lie the foothills of the Vosges Mountains of Alsace and the Hardt
uplands of the Bavarian Palatinate (*Bayrische Pfalz*) which border the Rhine
on the west.

The eastern bank of the Rhine is dominated by the Black Forest (*Schwarzwald*) of Baden and the Odenwald of southern Hesse (Hessen). The broad
valley area created through the junction of the Rhine and Main rivers forms
one of the most important agricultural regions of Germany. Its dry, warm climate, coupled with the excellent valley soils, makes it an ideal area for vineyards and orchards. The Rhine-Main area, by virtue of its strategic position at
the junction of the Rhine route linking the Low Countries with Switzerland and Italy, and the Main route connecting Central Germany with eastern
France, has developed into one of the more important manufacturing areas
of Central Europe. The economy of the Rhine-Main area is focused upon the
city of Frankfort-on-the-Main (Frankfurt-am-Main). The Black Forest which
stands guard over the southwest corner of the German realm, is famous for its
rugged mountains covered by dense spruce and fir forests, and for its narrow
valleys dotted with small peasant farms. Eastward, the bleak Swabian and
Franconian (*Fränkische*) scarplands swing northeastward from the Black Forest in a great semi-circle to the upper valley of the Main, reaching almost to
the frontiers of Thuringia (Thüringen) and Saxony.

Between these scarplands and the western Black Forest and Odenwald lie
the eroded terrace lands of Franconia (Franken) and Swabia (Schwaben),
which are bordered on the north by the valley of the middle Main River. The
life of the Swabian terrace area is oriented toward the city of Stuttgart on the
Neckar, which is located on the major land route connecting the Rhine and
Danube, while the Franconian area is dominated by the famous city of Nuremberg (Nürnberg). The Danube River, which rises in the Black Forest, flows
northeastward along the southern edge of the Swabian and Franconian scarplands through the traditionally important towns of Ulm and Ingolstadt to
Regensburg (Ratisbon), where it turns to the southeast. North of the Danube
at Ingolstadt and to the east of the Franconian scarplands lies the valley of the
Nab. Beyond it rises the Bohemian Forest, which divides southern Germany
from Bohemia. The Swabian and Bavarian lands, located between the Danube
and the Alpine ranges, and demarcating the frontier between southern Germany and the Austrian Tyrol, may be subdivided into three distinct areas.

There is a rich agricultural zone bordering the southern bank of the Danube, which extends from Ingolstadt to Passau on the Austrian frontier. Southward, this zone gives way to the Bavarian Plateau, which forms a part of the elevated pastoral area reaching from the Upper Rhone to the Inn River. This plateau is traversed by the Iller, Lech, Isar, and Inn rivers, which rise in the Alpine mountain system bordering south Germany. Augsburg and Munich (München), the only large cities situated between the Danube and the Alps, are located within the Bavarian Plateau. The third area of the Swabian-Bavarian zone is characterized by rugged uplands intersected with deep valleys, and by lakes and moors left behind by past glaciers. The South German terrain through its physiographic structure provides the basis for five distinct political-cultural areas. The state of Baden with its characteristic culture grew up along the Rhine rift valley, while the Swabian state of Württemberg expanded to its logical limits within the Swabian terrace area, hemmed in by the Black Forest and the Swabian scarplands. It was only natural that the states of Hesse should have been located upon the integrated Rhine-Main valley area. The state of Bavaria (Bayern), based upon the Bavarian Plateau, expanded at the expense of its Swabian neighbors on the west and the Franconians of the Main Valley on the north. South Germany is essentially oriented around five cities: Badenese Carlsruhe, Franconian Nuremberg, Swabian Stuttgart, the imperial free city of Frankfort (Frankfurt), and Bavarian Munich.

It now becomes clear that, just as Germany has no historically stable political frontiers, so geographically it has neither a unifying geographical pattern nor sharp natural boundaries. Its central position in Europe has made it a crossroads, with each road leading outward to trade and conquest. To the east these roads extend along the cold wind-swept plains of Prussia, which give way imperceptibly to the plains of Poland and the Slavic world. To the northwest, they lie along the monotonous Low Saxon Plains and find their way without much change of scene into the Low Countries and Atlantic Europe. To the south, they pass through mountain lands to reach the Mediterranean world.

Not only geographically, but also culturally, the outlying areas tend to merge with the surrounding lands. While the culture of Central Germany is a creation of the German peasant and burgher, the bordering provinces bear the imprint of the Latin West and the Slavic East. The South, with its Hessian, Swabian, Franconian, and Bavarian facets, might be regarded as the meeting place of influences coming from the Mediterranean and southeastern Europe. The characteristics of all these areas are epitomized in the life and traditions of the central Saxon lands along the middle Elbe and Saale rivers.

This diverse and uncoordinated area is brought into a unified whole by the great German land and water routes. The Rhine, which flows from Switzerland through the western margins of the German realm to the North Sea, penetrates into the remote parts of both southern and western Germany through such tributaries as the Neckar, Main, Mosel, and Ruhr. While the Rhine river system links southern and western Germany, the Weser, Elbe, and Oder rivers, rising in the Central German highlands, tie the North German Plain to the Central German upland area. The Danube, on the other hand, gives Germany easy access to southeastern Europe. Supplementing the unity provided by the river systems is that of the traditional land routes on which the traffic has long moved in both directions, not only outward to the bordering states, but also inward toward the center; such movements tended, naturally, to build up the nation at the crossroads. The great west-to-east route, leading from the Paris Basin to Cologne on the Rhine and thence along the northern foothills of the central uplands via Hanover, Magdeburg, and Berlin to Frankfort on the Oder and the East, tends to unify the northern portions of Germany. The southern east-west route, running from Paris via Frankfort-on-the-Main or via Strasbourg on the Rhine, connects with the Danube, linking western and southeastern Europe. Of even greater importance are the great north-south routes, which have been utilized since Neolithic times. The route from Italy which passes over the Alps through the St. Gotthard pass on its way to the Rhine Valley makes Germany the connecting link between the Low Countries and the Mediterranean. An alternate route runs from the North Italian plain through the Brenner pass to Frankfort-on-the-Main. To the east, routes from the North German Plain pass southward along the valleys of the Elbe and Oder through the uplands to reach the Middle Danubian area. While these routes link Germany with its neighbors, they also provide for the internal integration of the land. In modern times, the traditional land and river routes of the northern plain have been supplemented by an extensive network of canals.

Although the land and water routes have tended to pull together the diverse regions of the German area, the political and cultural unification of the land, which was accomplished only in relatively recent times, was a product of the historical development of the German people. The recent emergence of a unified German state, long delayed by geographic and political difficulties, represents a nationalistic merger of particularism and sectionalism, inherent in the diverse geographical and cultural structure of Central Europe.

THE SETTLEMENT OF THE GERMANS

The Germans, forming the largest ethnic group in Europe west of Russia, numbered prior to World War II approximately 80,000,000. Although the largest group of Germans was concentrated within the frontiers of the German state, over 12,000,000 of the 80,000,000 European Germans dwelt outside the Reich in central, southeastern, and eastern Europe. Recently united by a relatively new common language and by relatively new common cultural and

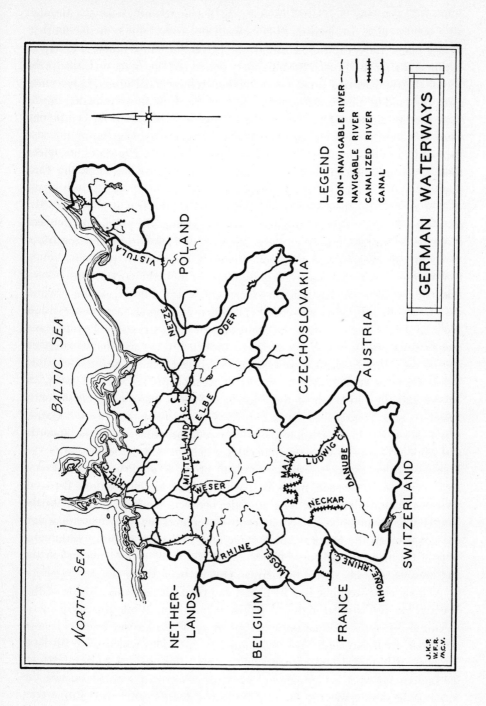

GERMAN WATERWAYS

LEGEND

NON-NAVIGABLE RIVER
NAVIGABLE RIVER
CANALIZED RIVER
CANAL

political aspirations, the Germans constitute a nationalistic group of great significance. German nationalism with its insistence upon ethnocentrism did not form a major European problem until the late eighteenth century; it emerged during and after the French Revolutionary period and has been, since that time, one of the fundamental problems of modern continental Europe. During the early and middle nineteenth century, most of the European Germans, except those dwelling in Russia and the southern Balkans, lived within the confines of German states, which were members of the German Confederation. Nor were the German minorities of western Poland forgotten by the Prussian state, while those of the middle Danubian area enjoyed the security of the Habsburg Empire.

The energies of the German nationalists during the first half of the nineteenth century were devoted to attempts to bring about the political unification of German Central Europe. The separation of the Habsburg realm from Germany proper in 1866 laid the foundations of the modern problem. While Germany had achieved a partial unification through the strong conservative leadership of Prussia, the traditional unity of Central Europe, dating back to the Holy Roman Empire, was ended. The intensification of nationalism within Hohenzollern Germany made the problem even more serious for Europe. Germany's defeat in World War I added further fuel to the nationalistic fires by cutting away from Germany such areas as Alsace-Lorraine, and the so-called Polish Corridor area. Furthermore, the destruction of the Austro-Hungarian empire and the formation of the Succession States—Austria, Czechoslovakia, Hungary, and Yugoslavia—not only revived the issue of the Austrian Union (*Anschluss*), but made possible the rise of problems concerning the Sudeten and Middle Danubian German minorities. Again, it was the formation of the Polish Corridor, through cession to Poland of the West Prussian and Posen areas, with their German minorities, which hindered the relations between these two nations during the long armistice between World War I and World War II. The termination of German control over areas with German minorities did not dampen the hopes of the Pan-German militarists to bring within the orbit of German political control all so-called "German" areas, however remote and however sparsely settled by German emigrants of earlier times.

Although the Republic had its liberal and pacifistic elements, the life of the Weimar era was also strongly colored by nationalism. While this spirit motivated the desire for internal unity and progress, it also activated ambitions for territorial expansion and foreign domination, ambitions which were justified in terms of historical and ethnographic claims based upon popular tradition. To understand what is German and what is not German, an analysis must be made of the development of German settlement within continental Europe.

History of Settlement

The history of the settlement of Central Europe by the Germans reaches back into the remote past. Although central and northern Europe were occupied by nomadic hunting and fishing peoples during the long Palaeolithic and Mesolithic epochs, sedentary settlement did not begin until Neolithic times (3000-1800 B.C.). During the early Neolithic period, when Central Europe enjoyed a moist Atlantic climate conducive to the growth of heavy forests and woodlands, peasants migrating from southeastern Europe settled along the open valleys of the Danube, Main, and Rhine. By middle Neolithic times, they had expanded northward to the open lands of the lower Rhine and Saxony. While this movement was taking place in southeastern Central Europe, people coming from the western Mediterranean via the Rhone Valley occupied western Switzerland and southwestern Germany. It was they who built the pile villages of the Alpine lakes. In the northwestern portions of Germany and in southern Scandinavia, coastal peoples coming from Alantic Europe were settled and have left behind their megalithic graves.

Toward the end of the Neolithic age, Indo-European nomads from the Eurasiatic steppe crossed Poland and followed the Ancient River Valleys into Northwestern Germany and southern Scandinavia. Their first settlements are marked by single graves covered by a simple mound and containing the typical cord-decorated pottery and perforated battle axes. In Northeast Germany these nomads had displaced the earlier hunting and fishing population. Pushing into South Germany along the valleys of the Rhine, Weser, and Elbe these Indo-Europeans conquered the peaceful peasant groups. The Neolithic, an era of movement and strife in Central Europe, thus ended with the first settlement of the Indo-Europeans.

The Bronze Age (2000-800 B.C.) opened with a marked change in climate. When the moist conditions of the preceding period gave way to cooler and drier climatic conditions, large formerly forested areas were opened up for settlement. The Indo-European settlers slowly began to differentiate into three distinct cultural groups. In the North, the ancestors of the Germanic peoples occupied southern Scandinavia and northern Germany. The Keltic peoples differentiated from the Indo-European group in western and southwestern Germany, while the ancestors of the Italic peoples occupied South Central Europe. Southeast Central Europe fell into the hands of the Proto-Illyrians. The Keltic, Italic, and Proto-Illyrian folk of South Central Europe gradually established Bronze Age cultures on the basis of a metallurgy acquired from traders and miners who had penetrated into the heart of Europe from the western Mediterranean and southeastern Europe. By 1500 B.C. the knowledge of bronze metallurgy had reached the North German Plain, where it inspired the North German Bronze cultures. Toward the end of the Bronze Age the dry-cool, subboreal climate began to wane. The advent of more moist conditions brought a rapid extension of forest and marshes, which limited the areas possible for settlement. In consequence, the Keltic peoples began to push eastward into Bavaria and Bohemia, while the northern Germanic folk expanded toward the south. Under this pressure, the Italic peoples began their migrations into Italy, while the Illyrians began a gradual movement into the Balkans.

The Iron Age of Central Europe beginning approximately 800 B.C. and comprising most of the first millennium before our era, is marked by the growth of three distinct cultural groups, each with a distinctive language, society, political organization, and material culture: the Germans in the North, the surviving Illyrians in East Central Europe, and the Kelts in South Germany. Iron metallurgy began in the South, where metallurgical influences from northern Italy inspired the Hallstatt culture, which lasted until about 500 B.C. Among the Germanic and Illyrian peoples, bronze continued to be the major material for tools and weapons until after the middle of the first millennium before Christ. During this transitional phase of the Iron Age, the Germans were slowly expanding westward to the Ems River, southward into Thuringia, and eastward to the Vistula River, while the Kelts were expanding westward into France and Spain. In the South the gradual transformation of the Hallstatt into the La Tène culture (500 B.C.-A.D. 50) was accomplished by introduction of cultural elements from Greece and Italy. While this change was taking place in the Keltic area, iron metallurgy was becoming more common in northern Germany. The widespread movements of the Keltic peoples to the west and southeast resulted in the regionalization of Keltic culture in La Tène times. The Keltic cultures of southeastern Europe were differentiated from those of southern and western Germany under the influence of the Sarmatians of the Eurasiatic steppe; and the Spanish, French, and British aspects of the Keltic La Tène culture (late Iron Age) took up separate paths of development in western Europe.

While these changes were taking place on the fringes of the Mediterranean world of the Phoenicians, Greeks, and Italians, the Germanic peoples were split into an eastern group based upon the East Elbian Plain, a northern group centering in Scandinavia, and a western group occupying the lands between the Elbe, Rhine, and Main rivers. The Iron Age was essentially a period of struggle and movement, marking the first phase of the expansion of the German peoples.

At the beginning of our era, the armies of the expanding Roman Empire conquered all of Gaul and pushed eastward to the Rhine and Danube, bringing most of what remained of Keltic Germany under their control. The arrival of

Roman legions in western and southwestern Germany produced many drastic changes, for they imposed upon the Keltic culture the ideas and ways of the Mediterranean. Villas were established in the country, while towns were founded at strategic points along the Rhine and Danube. Modern cities, such as Cologne (Colonia Ara Agrippininensis), Bonn (Bonna), Trèves (Trier, Augusta Treverorum), and Augsburg (Augusta Vindelicorum), have their origins in this period. Beyond the Roman "limes" (frontiers formed by wall and trenches), Germany was divided among the Eastern and Western German tribes.

It must be noted that by this period the Northern Germanic group, which was ancestral to the peoples of modern Denmark, Norway, and Sweden, was beginning to separate from the Germans of Germany. Here several tribal groups were slowly beginning to emerge as distinct entities. The Frisians and Low Saxons occupied the northwestern plains, and the Franks, the lands bordering the lower Rhine on the east. Central Germany was occupied by the Thuringians, while the valley of the Main was held by the Alemannians. The East Elbian plains were held by the Goths, Suevi (Swabians), Vandals, Burgundians, and Lombards. During the second century of our era, the Gothic tribes moved southeastward up the valley of the Vistula and down the valley of the Dniester to establish themselves in the western Ukraine, while the Vandals moved over the Carpathians to settle in Hungary. In the West the Franks and Alemannians were filtering into the Roman lands along the Rhine and Danube. The migration era had begun.

The era of the Migration of Peoples (*Völkerwanderung* A.D. 400-750), so named from the movement of German tribes into the declining Roman Empire, cannot be explained entirely in terms of the pressures imparted by the Hunnic tribes, which had swept in from eastern Eurasia. For the German population, which was increasing beyond the confines of its primitive economy, the only alternative to migration was to engage in the difficult task of land reclamation; migration into the declining Empire was easier and quite possible from the military and political point of view. For this reason, the German tribes began to cross the Rhine and Danube in force.

In the East, the West Goths under the leadership of Alaric and under the pressure of the Huns invaded the southern Balkans between A.D. 395-398. After a campaign in Italy, they turned westward and reached Spain by A.D. 415. Meanwhile the East Goths pushed westward to settle temporarily in western Hungary. Toward the end of the fifth century they established themselves in Italy under the rule of Theodoric the Great. The other eastern German tribes, which had remained on the East Elbian plains, also moved westward during the course of the fifth century.

The Suevi had pushed across France into Spain, while the Burgundians had migrated to the valley of the upper Rhone, where they established the ephemeral Kingdom of Burgundy. Migrating westward from their temporary home on the Middle Danubian plains the Vandals had crossed southern Germany and France to Spain, from where they moved to North Africa; this continent became their base for sea raids upon Italy and the isles of the western Mediterranean.

Nor had the western German tribes been quiescent. The Franks crossed the Rhine in force and by A.D. 425 had occupied Flanders and the lands along the Meuse (*Maas*) and Mosel rivers. Southwest Germany had fallen into the hands of the Alemannic tribes. The Hunnic tribes, pushing steadily westward during this period, began their actual invasion of Central Europe in A.D. 450. This threat to Europe from the East was routed by the German tribes under the leadership of a surviving group of Roman officers in the battle of the Catalaunian fields of Gaul, A.D. 451.

In A.D. 476 the last Roman emperor, Romulus Augustulus, was deposed by the German military leader Odovaker and the Roman Empire was finished in the West. The lands of Rome had been inherited by the barbarian kingdoms of the Germanic tribes. Spain and southern France were held by the West Goths; the Franks and Burgundians held the rest of Gaul. In Germany the land was divided between Franks, Frisians, Low Saxons, Thuringians, and Alemannians. The West Goths and the Lombards stood on the fringes of Southeast Central Europe awaiting their turns to invade Italy. The lands to the east of the Elbe, which had been under the control of the East German tribes, were slowly being occupied by Slavic peoples spreading west from the upper Dnieper basin.

Under Merovingian leadership, the Franks in the early sixth century pressed into southern Gaul, where they drove out the West Gothic rulers, and into Southwest Germany, where they established their rule over the Alemannic tribes. The tribal state of the Thuringians had fallen before Frankish arms in A.D. 530-532, and the Kingdom of the Burgundians was liquidated A.D. 532-534. While the Franks were establishing their control over these western areas, the Marcomanni of Bohemia, the ancestors of the Bavarians, pushed across the Bohemian Forests into Bavaria, leaving the lands along the upper Elbe open to the Slavs. By the end of the sixth century, the frontier between Slavs and Germans extended along a line running from Lübeck to the lower Elbe and thence along the Elbe and Saale to the Fichtel-Gebirge. From the Fichtel-Gebirge, the line continued southeastward along the Bohemian Forest across Austria into the northwestern Balkans. The German side of the frontier was held by the Saxons in the north, the Thuringians and Franks in the center, and the Bavarians and Lombards in the south.

Although the Germanic tribes ruled most of western Europe between the fifth and ninth centuries, culturally and linguistically they impressed themselves upon only a limited portion of this vast domain. The region under German settlement extended westward from the Elbe-Saale line to western Flanders and the lands along the Meuse, Mosel, and Upper Rhine. The Alpine ranges limited the German area on the south. At this point in its expansion, Germany began the first phase of its modern settlement. The more favored regions, such as the Rhine, Main, and Danube valleys, and the Thuringian Basin, had long been occupied by village centers supported by agrarian activities, but it was not until this period that these village settlements were gradually enlarged. In the Northwest, the number of isolated hamlets and farmsteads increased, while new villages were being established in the uplands of Central Germany. Merovingian Germany was essentially a land of isolated villages and hamlets tied together by primitive trade and the loose political control of the Franks.

The Carolingian era (A.D. 751-911), which began with the unification of all the Germanic holdings in France, Italy, and Germany under the leadership of Charlemagne, brought drastic changes in the settlement practices of the Germans. They turned to the gigantic task of clearing extensive areas of swamp, marsh, and forest for settlement—an undertaking which is still in progress in contemporary Germany. While the German settlers in Italy, France, and Spain were gradually being absorbed by the Latin populations of the West, conditions within Germany were slowly stabilizing. In Southern and Central Germany the peasants of the valleys moved into the uplands, where they cleared forested areas for agricultural settlements. In the Northwest the Low Saxons, who had been brought under the control of the Carolingians after several bloody campaigns, were beginning to drain the marshy river areas for occupation. Along the Rhine and Danube the old Roman towns regained their former positions as commercial and cultural centers. In Central and Northwestern Germany villages located at strategic trade and transportation junctions developed into towns, which became the political and religious centers of their respective areas. As has been noted before, such a position accounted for the origin of the modern cities of Hanover, Magdeburg, Hamburg, and Lübeck.

The political stability of the Carolingian realm was short-lived. After the death of Charlemagne, the Frankish monarchy disintegrated into a series of succession states by virtue of the dynastic divisions at Verdun in 843 and at Mersen in 870; these agreements brought about the creation of the Kingdoms of France, Italy, and Germany. The situation in Germany under the late Carolingian rulers was further complicated by the reassertion of the partial independence of the old tribal areas under the leadership of their respective dukes. At the end of the tenth century, Germany was largely ruled by the tribal Dukes of Saxony, Thuringia, Franconia, Bavaria, Swabia, and the two Lorraines. The frontier areas beyond the Elbe-Saale line were under the control of a group of Margraves or Counts of the Border.

The foundations of the modern Reich were laid during the age of the Saxon, Franconian, and Hohenstaufen dynasties (919-1254). Villages and hamlets in the old German area to the west of the Elbe multiplied in number. Trade began to revive and to nourish the growing towns. While the lands of Burgundy and northern Italy were being brought into the Empire on the west through dynastic arrangements and political maneuvers, the Germans were beginning to advance into the Slavic lands lying to the east of the Elbe. Although the armies of Charlemagne had reached the Oder in the northeast, eastern Moravia in the east, and central Hungary in the southeast, these forays had not brought the establishment of permanent German settlements. The successful colonization of the lands to the east of the Elbe and along the Middle Danube followed in the wake of German military expansion. The settlers, who came from every part of the Reich except the Swabian southwest, included nobility and knights, monks and priests, traders and burghers, and above all peasants. They moved eastward under the leadership of lay and ecclesiastical lords anxious to acquire new lands and holdings. Although this movement began in the early tenth century, it did not reach its peak until the eleventh and twelfth centuries.

The eastward migration was the result of a number of factors. Within Germany, the progress of settlement and the revival of economic life made cheap land desirable; and the Slavic East, with its sparse population and its backward pastoral economy, could offer only isolated resistance to the German advance. The plains along the upper Elbe between the Saale and Bober rivers were originally brought under control through the establishment of fortified cities, including Merseburg, Meissen, and Leipzig. These penetrations were consolidated and turned into a German area by Frankish and Thuringian settlers.

To the north, the Germans were opposed by the Danes and the Slavic Wagri tribes of Mecklenburg. The conquest of the latter group in the middle twelfth century opened the way to the Baltic Sea. The Low Saxons moved eastward across the northern plains, aided by immigrants from the Low Countries who were skilled in techniques of draining marshlands and swamps. They settled, at first, only in fortified villages because of the opposition of the hostile Slavic population. The process of Germanization along the Baltic coast went on for centuries. With control of the coastal ports, the Germans began a sea-borne invasion of the eastern shores of the Baltic. German settlements in Kurland, Livland, and Esthland during the thirteenth and fourteenth centuries were begun by the Church, but were soon inherited by the Order of Teutonic Knights. This organization won its first holdings through the conquest of East Prussia in the twelfth century. The East Prussian area, though separated from Germany by Slavic Pommerellen (later, the Polish Corridor), was more attractive to the German settler than the more remote lands of the eastern Baltic.

To the southeast, German expansion in Carolingian times had been opposed by the Avars. In the tenth century the Magyars, who had replaced the Avars in control of the Danubian plains, harassed southeastern Germany, but in A.D. 955 German forces under the Saxon Emperors put this warlike tribe to flight in the battle of the Lech (Bavaria), thereby opening the way for German expansion down the Danube. Peasants, monks, and traders followed the conquering German forces into Austria. In 1055 the Margrave of Ostmark founded the city of Vienna. Only the Czechs living behind the forested uplands of the Sudeten, the Ore Mountains, and the Bohemian Forests had escaped Germanization, although even here German settlers penetrated into the margins of Bohemia. The real German settlement of Bohemia did not come until the eighteenth century.

The Silesian area, situated to the north of Bohemia, was sporadically settled by Germans as early as the tenth century; but effective colonization did not begin until the eleventh and twelfth centuries, when the region was finally wrested from Polish control. By the middle of the thirteenth century, the major movement of Germans to the east had been completed. Except for a few isolated German settlements which had been established in Moravia (Kuttenburg), Slovakia (Zips), Hungary (Ofen, Stuhlweissenburg, and Fünfkirchen), and the Carpathians (Hermannstadt) during the twelfth and thirteenth centuries, all of the other newly settled lands had been brought under German political control.

MODERN SETTLEMENT OF THE GERMANS

The core of the late Hohenstaufen Germany consisted of Low Saxon peoples of Northwest Germany, Thuringians and Franks of Central and Western Germany, and Swabians and Bavarians of the Southwest. Colonial movements of the preceding centuries had laid the population foundations of Austria and East Elbia. With the beginning of the fourteenth century, the Germans were faced by serious domestic and foreign troubles. The great duchies of the early Middle Ages were disintegrating internally into a series of petty states ruled by an aristocratic nobility. Imperial power, which became more and more dependent upon the personal resources of the ruling family, was used to increase the possessions of a particular dynasty rather than to advance the good of the nation. The triumph of the Habsburg dynasty in 1440 brought little improvement in internal conditions, for the rulers used their royal prerogatives to carry out a program of dynastic expansion in Southeast Central Europe. Internally, Germany was ruled by the Habsburgs of Austria, the Wittelsbachs of Bavaria, the Wettins of Saxony, and the Hohenzollerns of Mark Brandenburg. Limited areas in Central and Western Germany were under control of ecclesiastical lords and

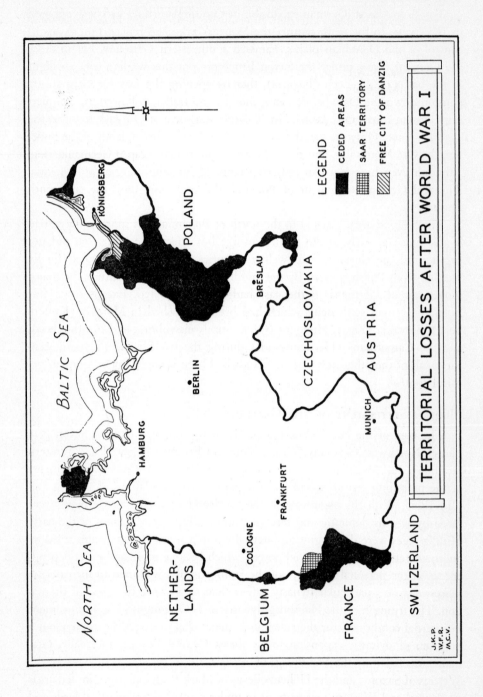

the petty nobility. The eastern frontiers were held by the Hohenzollerns of
Brandenburg, the dukes of Silesia, the kings of Bohemia, and the Habsburgs
of Austria.

The political chaos within Germany at the end of the Hohenstaufen period
had brought about a conclusion of political expansion to the east, and now a
revival of the political fortunes of the Poles and Magyars constituted an actual
threat to these borderlands. In 1410 the combined Polish and Lithuanian forces
routed the Teutonic Knights, and by 1466 Poland had regained control of the
Pommerellen area. In the Southeast, Mongol invasions, coupled with the subsequent revival of the Kingdom of Hungary, put an end to German colonization in the Middle Danubian area. The later Turkish domination of the
northern Balkans during the sixteenth and seventeenth centuries placed a further ban upon German expansion to the southeast. In the Baltic area Poles and
Lithuanians conquered the lands of the Teutonic Knights of Livland and Kurland during the sixteenth century, while the Swedes seized the holdings of the
Teutonic Knights in Esthland.

German reverses were not limited to the eastern frontiers, for the wars of
the Reformation period (1522-1618) not only resulted in further internal political disintegration, but marked the first advances of the French toward the
Rhine. In 1552, Metz, Toul, and Verdun were seized by the armies of France.
The Thirty Years' War, which made Germany a battlefield for Austrian, Danish, Swedish, Bohemian, and French forces, produced a complete social and
economic collapse of vast areas within the Reich. The Peace of Westphalia
(1648) recognized the independence of the Northern Netherlands, Switzerland,
and the Swedish holdings in Pomerania. While Germany under the leadership
of the Habsburgs, the Hohenzollerns, the Wittelsbachs, and the Wettins was
attempting the restoration of the land after the devastating Thirty Years' War,
the French under Louis XIV continued their eastward advance into Flanders
and Alsace-Lorraine.

The revival of German power in the eighteenth century under the Habsburgs and Hohenzollerns was marked by a renewal of colonization in the East.
After the Hohenzollerns had consolidated their holdings in the Northeast
through the addition of eastern Pomerania (1648), Altmark (1680), and Silesia
(1742), they took part in the three partitions of Poland (1772, 1793, and 1795),
which opened the way for the renewal of German settlement in western Poland.
This officially sponsored movement continued until the outbreak of World War
I. In the Southeast, after the conquest of Bohemia, Moravia, and Silesia in 1526,
and after the temporary setbacks of the Reformation period, the Habsburgs
took up the task of driving the Turks from the lands of the Middle Danube.
In the latter part of the seventeenth century, Habsburg forces drove the Turks
from Hungary and Transylvania and opened the way for a revival of German

colonization in the northern Balkans. The Napoleonic period brought only a temporary interruption of the German movements to the east and southeast. During the period of the German Confederation (1815-1866), Hohenzollern Prussia and Habsburg Austria continued to support the eastward movement of Germans, in order to strengthen their control in areas where the incipient nationalism of the Slavs was beginning to create an active opposition to German political control.

Throughout the nineteenth and early twentieth centuries, all German minorities implanted in eastern Europe enjoyed the protection of German political power, except those that had settled in the Baltic area during the early Middle Ages and in Russia during the eighteenth and nineteenth centuries. While colonization of the Prussian and Austrian portions of Poland continued, the Russians closed the eastern part of Poland to German settlers. The separation of Austria from the German Confederation in 1866 had no effect upon German colonial activities in the East. However, the victory over France in 1871, which added Alsace-Lorraine to the newly formed German Empire, brought a temporary revival of Germanization efforts in the West. Although the period of the Second German Empire (1871-1918) brought an intensification of settlement activities in the Polish part of Prussia, which reached their peak in World War I, they were never sufficient to Germanize completely any of the Slavic areas lying to the east of East Prussia, Pomerania, or Silesia.

The defeat of Germany and Austro-Hungary in World War I drastically altered the political status of German speaking population "islands" scattered through the lands of the Poles, Hungarians, Czechs, Slovaks, Rumanians, and South Slavs. In eastern Germany the cession of border lands to Poland and Lithuania, and the formation of the Free City of Danzig, brought about a separation of approximately 1,200,000 Germans from the Reich. It should be noted, however, that with the exception of Danzig, the Germans were everywhere in a minority, dwelling largely in village and town centers surrounded by a Slavic and Lithuanian peasantry. In the Posen and West Prussian areas, which were organized into the "Polish Corridor," the German minority represented only about seventeen per cent of the population, despite a century and a half of settlement activity sponsored by the Prussian government. In the part of Upper Silesia which came under Polish control after the plebiscite of 1921, the German minority formed less than one-third of the population, the majority being Polish. The problems of German minorities in Poland were further complicated by the fact that the Polish government attempted to evict the thousands of German settlers, who had been brought in during the course of World War I. In the Memel area, which was finally ceded to Lithuania in 1924, the Germans were a minority of considerable size.

Loss of German population and control was not restricted to the East. The

German speaking population of Alsace-Lorraine, who have long desired to gain political and cultural independence from both France and Germany, came under French control. To the north the purely German area of Eupen-Malmedy was given to Belgium. The plebiscite in northern Schleswig, where the Germans represented about twenty-five per cent of the total population, placed approximately 40,000 Germans under Danish rule. The destruction of the Austro-Hungarian Empire at the close of World War I, and the creation of the Succession States, produced a number of serious nationality problems, which were further complicated by the termination of economic unity in the Middle Danubian area. From a German point of view the creation of Czechoslovakia destroyed the political security of German speaking minorities dwelling in the Ore Mountains and Sudeten upland, in the Bohemian Forest, Budweis, Brünn, Iglau, and Pressburg areas, and in the mountains of Slovakia. In the Middle Danube, German speaking minorities fell under the control of Yugoslavia, Hungary, and Rumania. Altogether, approximately 5,500,000 German-speaking people scattered through the northern Balkans lost the political protection which had been provided by the Austro-Hungarian Empire. Although the Germans of Austria retained their independence, their political position was complicated by the *Anschluss* question.

To the east of the limits of the old German and Austro-Hungarian empires, there remained thousands of German settlers in Russia. Aside from the large group of Baltic Germans, with roots going back to the days of the Teutonic Knights, there were the German minorities which had settled in the Ukraine, in Bessarabia, and in Eastern Russia during the eighteenth and nineteenth centuries.

The last phase of German settlement and expansion came with the revival of German power under the Nazis. Their annexation of Austria and their seizure of the Sudetenland, coupled with their subsequent formation of the Protectorates of Bohemia and Moravia and their invasion of Poland, opened a way to Russia and the Balkans.

The defeat of the German effort to restore political control over areas with the slightest German coloring, has settled, at least for the present, the question of the status of the German minorities in the East and the problem of the redefinition of the eastern frontiers of the German state. The Potsdam agreement, which was signed three months after Germany's defeat in World War II, resulted in the transfer of millions of Germans who were living outside the new boundaries to a circumscribed area west of the Oder-Neisse line.

Considering all the difficulties, *the essentially German portion of Central Europe was fairly decided by the Versailles Treaty at the conclusion of World War I. German political frontiers between World War I and World War II embraced the area which had been systematically settled by the Germans since*

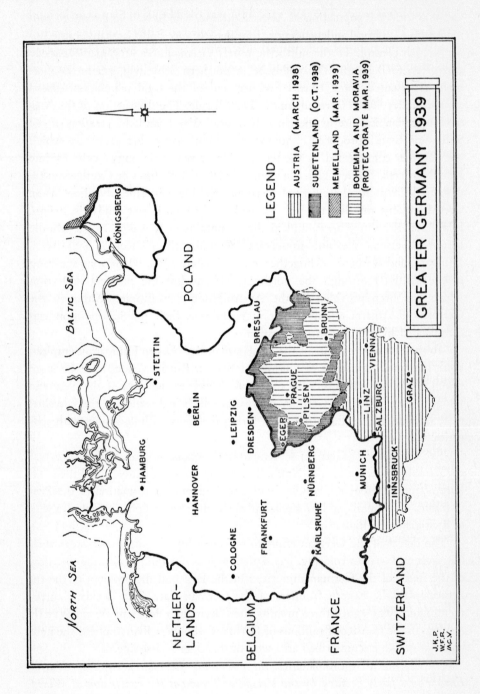

LEGEND

AUSTRIA (MARCH 1938)

SUDETENLAND (OCT. 1938)

MEMELLAND (MAR. 1939)

BOHEMIA AND MORAVIA
(PROTECTORATE MAR. 1939)

GREATER GERMANY 1939

NORTH SEA

BALTIC SEA

KÖNIGSBERG

POLAND

STETTIN

BRESLAU

BERLIN

LEIPZIG

BRUNN

HAMBURG

DRESDEN

PRAGUE

VIENNA

HANNOVER

EGER

PILSEN

LINZ

GRAZ

COLOGNE

NÜRNBERG

SALZBURG

FRANKFURT

MUNICH

INNSBRUCK

KARLSRUHE

NETHER-
LANDS

BELGIUM

FRANCE

SWITZERLAND

J.K.P.
W.F.R.
M.C.V.

early medieval times. The only exception was the Masurian Slav zone in southern East Prussia, but in July 1920, this area voted to remain with the Reich. In the West, the political and cultural differentiation of the Swiss, Flemings, and Dutch in early modern times had not only removed all nationality claims, but had destroyed the basis of any political claims on the part of the Germans to Switzerland, Belgium, and the Netherlands. Furthermore, the cultural and political reorientation of Alsace-Lorraine to the west during the eighteenth and nineteenth centuries (excepting the interlude of 1871-1919) had largely removed this area from the sphere of German influence. The western frontier defined at the Congress of Vienna in 1815 and only slightly modified at Versailles through the temporary internationalization of the Saar and through the cession of the Eupen-Malmedy areas to Belgium, fairly delimits the western border of the German cultural and political area.

In the Northeast, solid German settlement extends only to the eastern frontiers of the provinces of Pomerania and Silesia. The Germans are only a minority group in the Polish areas of Posen (Poznań) and Pommerellen (Pomorze), which separate German East Prussia from the body of the Reich. In other words, the essentially German portions of the Northeast were left within the Reich at Versailles.

The problem of the Germans in the Southeast is more complex. After the dissolution of the Austro-Hungarian Empire, Austria was the only area left with a solidly German population. Except in the case of western Czechoslovakia, where the German minority dwelt on the frontier margins adjacent to Germany and Austria, the German minorities of Slovakia, Hungary, Rumania, and Yugoslavia were scattered in widely isolated pockets. The position of the southeastern Germans in relation to the nationalism of the Germans in Germany is complicated by the fact that under the long centuries of Habsburg rule, their interests were oriented not toward the heart of Germandom, but toward southeastern Europe. Owing to this cleavage in German and Austrian interests, the impetus for the development of much of German nationalism came from those Germans dwelling within the German Reich.

THE DISTRIBUTION OF THE GERMANS

The pattern of settlement of Germany within the World War I to World War II frontiers had been achieved as early as the fourteenth century. Subsequent centuries brought only an elaboration of this pattern through gradual growth of the population. While the German settler was penetrating into eastern Europe during the early Middle Ages, German agrarian settlements and market towns were growing rapidly in size and numbers. In the old German area of Carolingian times lying between the Rhine and the Elbe and the North Sea and the Alps, numerous isolated farms and elevated marsh villages, built on mounds, were established on the plains of the Northwest by Low Saxon peasants; at the same time Franconian, Thuringian, Alemannian, and Bavarian peoples of central and southern Germany were founding nucleated villages in the open valley lands, establishing elongated villages in the forested uplands, and settling in tiny hamlets and isolated farmsteads in the more mountainous areas. Although the open plain and valley areas of the Lower Rhine, Main-Rhine, Neckar, and Saxo-Thuringian regions had been settled and worked by a peasantry going back to Neolithic times, it was not until the early medieval period, that an intensification of settlement occurred. The growth of agrarian settlement within these regions, supplemented by the development of towns and cities, has continued into our own day, making them the most densely settled zones of the German Reich.

While these developments were occurring in western Germany, the newly conquered and settled lands of East Elbia, embracing modern Mecklenburg, Brandenburg, Saxony, Silesia, and East Prussia, were slowly being settled by Germans from the west. It should be noted that in the better agrarian areas of East Elbia, such as Silesia, the land was more intensively settled by the peasant cultivator. While rural areas were being settled by the German peasants, the old Roman towns along the Rhine and Danube, the strategically located villages west of the Elbe, and the fortified centers in the formerly Slavic lands of East Elbia, were developing into towns. By 1400 Germany had over 3,000 towns, a few of which were large enough to be classified as regional centers, important politically, economically, and for their part in international trade. The towns of Cologne, Mainz, Frankfort, Ulm, and Augsburg along the Rhine and Danube trade routes of western and southern Germany were the major centers of the most highly developed urban areas of medieval Europe. Munich, Nuremberg, and Stuttgart had begun their development in the heart of the Bavarian, east Franconian, and Swabian areas. The commercial life of these towns was oriented toward Italy and the Mediterranean.

In the North, the original Hanseatic towns of Hamburg, Bremen, and Lübeck were joined from the twelfth to the fourteenth centuries by the rapidly developing towns of the North German Plains in the exploitation of commerce in the Baltic and North Sea areas. The North German towns, which had evolved from old trading points or fortified centers set up against the Slavs, tended to be smaller than those of Central and Southern Germany, although they served a larger market area. The rapid tempo of rural settlement and town development continued through the later Middle Ages into early modern times, despite the disturbing political conditions within Germany.

The first setbacks came as a result of the discovery of America, which brought a complete re-orientation of European commercial life. In the North, this commercial change, coupled with the rise of the Dutch, resulted in a marked decline of trade. The life of the northern towns began to stagnate, until in 1630 the Hanseatic League was dissolved. Subsequently, the collapse of Italian and Levantine trade in the eastern Mediterranean, as a result of the extension of Turkish power in the Balkans and Near East, brought decline to the cities of southern Germany. These commercial setbacks were followed by the political and military disasters of the Reformation and Thirty Years' War. Mercantile reverses of the sixteenth century had done much to undermine the commercial and cultural position of the German cities, but it was military action incident to the Reformation and the Thirty Years' War which brought widespread destruction of towns and villages. As commercial life sank to its lowest ebb, the once flourishing towns disintegrated under the impact of war. Vast areas of farm land were deserted and allowed to revert to forest and marsh. The wars of the seventeenth century left Germany thinly populated and exhausted.

The eighteenth century brought a gradual recovery of the German population and a revival of village and town life. Agriculture expanded rapidly in the fertile Lower Rhine, Rhine-Main, Neckar, and Saxo-Thuringian areas, which had long constituted the most densely settled portions of the Reich. In the southern and central uplands, where agrarian life recovered more rapidly than in the north, arable areas which had reverted to forest were rapidly cleared for cultivation. Revival of industries in the towns brought the cutting of traditionally forested areas for charcoal, opening up new areas for agrarian activity.

The sparsely settled northwestern river and coastal marshlands, which had been partially reclaimed from the sea through dyking, witnessed renewed reclamation efforts. In the Prussian Northeast, a government sponsored program initiated by Frederick the Great brought about the founding of numerous new agrarian settlements. The agricultural revival was accompanied by recovery of trade and industry in the towns. Although Germany had led Europe in mining and metal production during the Middle Ages, the reign of Frederick the Great brought a more extensive exploitation of the iron, silver, copper, and salt resources of the central uplands. The textile, metal, and pottery industries of the cities in the Lower Rhine, Rhine-Main, Neckar, Saxo-Thuringian, and South German areas began to revive and expand in importance.

The beginnings of the industrial revolution were foreshadowed in the eighteenth century, for coal was beginning to replace dwindling charcoal supplies in the production of iron, glass, and salt. By the middle of the eighteenth century coal mines had been opened in the Saar and Ruhr fields.

Although these craft and industrial developments were important, they were small in scale and lacked the stimulus of a large market. Trade in eighteenth-century Germany was largely local because even domestic commerce was hampered by lack of roads and hindered by the tariffs of the three hundred small states and principalities. International trade was also somewhat limited for the seas were dominated by the Dutch and British. The agricultural and commercial developments of this period, though minor in scale, were laying the foundations for the mushroom growth of the German population in the nineteenth century.

During the first half of the nineteenth century there was only a moderate increase in population. At the conclusion of the Napoleonic era, which had brought about a partial consolidation of Germany through liquidation of most of the petty states and principalities of the West, the population stood at twenty-four millions. By 1850, the gradual increase in the tempo of German agricultural, industrial, and commercial life, partly made possible by the Customs Union movement, was reflected in the expansion of the population to thirty-five millions. Although the early nineteenth century had seen remarkable industrial development, Germany was still essentially a collection of agricultural states dotted by numerous market towns with limited craft industries and narrow spheres of trade. While the Customs Union had opened the way for domestic trade, and the development of the railroad and the construction of canals had laid the foundations of a transportation system essential to industrial development, the major expansion of economic life and consequent population expansion came after the political unification of the Reich in 1871. The period of the Second German Empire was marked by rapid industrialization of the old craft towns of the Rhine-Ruhr, Rhine-Main, Saxo-Thuringian, and Silesian areas. In the South, Stuttgart, Munich, and Nuremberg became centers for numerous manufacturing establishments, while Hamburg and Bremen developed in the Northwest. Berlin, because of its strategic position in East Elbia and its political status, became the economic center of the Northeast. The population of the Reich increased from forty millions in 1871 to sixty-four millions in 1914.

The rapid growth of the German population was interrupted by World War I. Nearly 1,900,000 men lost their lives as the result of military action, and another million civilians died as the result of epidemics growing out of war conditions. The growth of population during these war years was further handicapped by a birth deficit, which has been placed as high as 3,200,000. Although there was only a limited population recovery between 1918 and 1925, at which later date the population of Germany stood at sixty-two millions, the prosperous years of the Weimar Republic were marked by the resumption of population expansion. By 1933, despite the depression years between 1929 and 1933, the population had increased to over sixty-five millions. The period of the Third Reich brought further population growth. Even though the Nazis were constantly emphasizing the problem of Germany's overpopulation, upon assuming power they, for military reasons, immediately began measures aimed at increasing the population. To stimulate the birth rate, they embarked upon an extensive propaganda campaign, which they further implemented by granting tax exemptions to large families and by making loans available to needy couples; the loans were canceled after the birth of a fourth child. It should be noted, however, that the birth rate for the boom years before the inflation exceeded that of the best years under the Nazis. The increased birth rate of the late thirties can be ascribed in part to the marriages postponed from depression years. However, the large growth in population between 1933 and 1939—an increase of 4,200,000—was only partly due to the temporarily increased birth rate. For the return of the Saar in 1935 added over 800,000 to the population of the Reich, while increasing numbers of immigrants coming largely from Austria and the Sudetenland not only counterbalanced the number of emigrants from the Reich, but supplemented the population by at least another 600,000. In 1939, Germany, including the Saar, but not including Austria, the Sudetenland, the Polish Corridor, Danzig or Memel, had a population of over sixty-nine millions.

The density and distribution of this population present several interesting features. Rapid increases in population during the last seventy-five years had, naturally, brought increasing population densities. In 1871 the population density for the German area, which, including the Saar, measured 470,000 sq. km. was 76 individuals per sq. km. By 1910, the density had increased to 124, and by 1939 to 136 per sq. km. The nineteenth and early twentieth centuries brought about great variation in the distribution of the population densities through development of the industrialized urban areas. At the beginning of the nineteenth century, when Germany was basically an agrarian country, there was little marked variation in the distribution of population. The more densely settled areas, where the population density ranged between 50 and 100 individuals per sq. km., were restricted to Rhenish, Thuringian, Saxon, and Silesian Germany. South Germany and the western and central portions of the North German Plain had a moderate population density of 25 to 50, while the Baltic coastal area, embracing Mecklenburg, Pomerania, and East Prussia, was only sparsely settled.

With the rapid extension of agricultural activity and the growth of small craft-industrial towns, the first seventy years of the nineteenth century saw marked changes. These changes, however, represented developments of the basic pattern of population distribution going back to late medieval times. There were increases in the population density of the Lower Rhine and Ruhr, Rhine-Main, Neckar, Saxon, and Silesian areas, which can be accounted for only in terms of an expanding agricultural population and a developing urban life, based on gradual industrialization. The growth of rural population was also marked in the Main Valley of northern Bavaria, while settlement policies

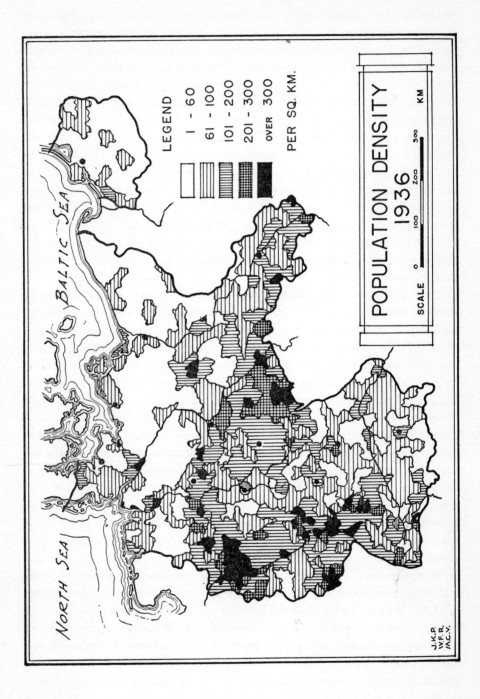

LEGEND

1 - 60
61 - 100
101 - 200
201 - 300
OVER 300

PER SQ. KM.

POPULATION DENSITY
1936

SCALE

0   100   200   500   KM

BALTIC SEA

NORTH SEA

J.K.P.
W.F.R.
IAC.V.

of the Prussian government brought population increases in eastern Brandenburg, western Pomerania, and northern East Prussia, where the increasing use
of fertilizer made possible the wider utilization of impoverished soils. The
northern cities of Bremen, Hamburg, and Berlin were already significant centers of population.

During the latter part of the nineteenth century, the impact of industrialization caused even more marked changes. Many differences in the distribution
of population densities can be accounted for partly in terms of differentials in
the natural population increase, but it is the widespread movement of population resulting from the shift of people from agricultural areas to mining, manufacturing, and commercial centers which is more significant. While all of
Germany was affected by these internal migrations, the major geographical
movement after 1870 was from the poorer agricultural districts lying to the east
of the Elbe to the industrial and manufacturing centers of Western and Central
Germany. It is interesting to note that the agrarian East continued to have a
steady natural increase of population, which was constantly drained off by domestic emigration to urban centers of the western and central portions of the
Reich. These internal changes in population distribution brought only an intensification of the older pattern of settlement, because the industrialization of
Germany took place in regions where there was already a dense agricultural
and town population. The Rhine-Ruhr area, because of its strategic position
on the lower Rhine near great concentrations of coal and lignite, became the
leading center of German heavy industry.

This industrial development brought about a significant concentration of
people. The more heavily industrialized portions of the Ruhr have a population
density of approximately 1,500 individuals per sq. km. The entire area has
a density ranging from 300 to 1,500 persons per sq. km.; it is one of the most
densely settled portions of Europe. Up the Rhine from the Ruhr industrial
area, the Rhine-Main, Saar, and Neckar manufacturing regions have moderately dense populations. The density within these west German areas, which
have been relatively heavily settled for the last millennium, increased from a
range of 100 to 200 in 1871 to a range of 300 to 500 in 1933, with a few isolated
urban centers along the Rhine possessing densities as high as 1,000 per sq. km.
The Saxon industrial and manufacturing region of Central Germany, which
has been densely settled since the Middle Ages, underwent a remarkable increase of population during the latter part of the nineteenth century. In 1933
the population density of this area ranged between 150 and 500 persons per sq.
km. The heavily settled portions of Silesia were restricted to limited areas in
central and upper portions of the province, while the areas of dense population
in Bavaria were concentrated around the towns of Würzburg, Nuremberg,
Augsburg, and Munich. On the northern plains were to be found the only other

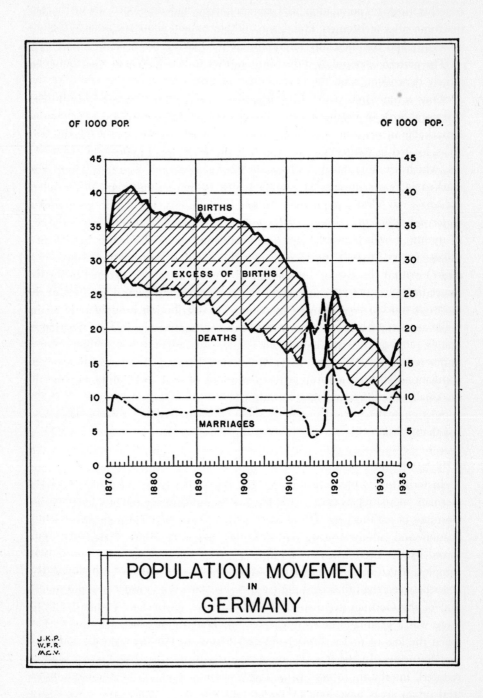

POPULATION MOVEMENT
IN
GERMANY

concentrations of population in Germany; they had developed about the old maritime cities of Bremen, Hamburg, and Stettin and about the isolated though politically and commercially important city of Berlin.

The pattern of population distribution prior to World War II was, therefore, largely dependent upon the development of urban centers in the course of the previous seventy-five years. This dependence is thrown into relief by the fact that rural areas of northern, central, and southern Germany have sustained no remarkable increase in population. It is true, however, that the better agrarian areas, located in Central Germany and along the Rhine, Main, and Neckar rivers, which are adjacent to manufacturing and commercial districts, have had marked increases in their populations. *The rise of the large commercial and industrial city with a population greater than 100,000 stands out as one of the major developments of modern Germany.* Rapid transformation of rural Germany into a highly industrialized state had thus involved the growth of major urban centers. In 1871 there were only eight such metropolitan areas (*Grossstädte*) within the Reich. The amazing urbanization of Germany during the succeeding seventy-five years raised this number to over fifty-two. In 1933 almost one-third of the German population was concentrated in these large cities, while another fifth of the population lived in the 510 smaller cities with populations ranging between 10,000 and 100,000. The small country towns, which numbered over 3,000, account for another seventeen per cent of the German population. At the beginning of the nineteenth century most Germans dwelt in the small agricultural villages, but prior to World War II only one-third of the population was scattered in the 46,000 rural communities with populations of less than 2,000.

The Composition of the German Population

In terms of its physical and cultural characteristics, the composition of the German population is extremely varied. While cultural differences between the Germans of various parts of the Reich have been reduced through political unification and administrative centralization—processes which have been reinforced by the rise of nationalism—the physical composition has become more complex. Much of this complexity can be explained in terms of growing differences between the urban and the rural populations. An analysis of sex composition of the German population reveals that during the last seventy-five years there was a gradually increasing excess of females until the first World War, when the loss of males through military action resulted in a greatly increased female surplus. In the late twenties and early thirties this surplus was sharply reduced. Interesting to note is the fact that the populations of the large industrial urban areas have long been characterized by a female excess, while predominantly rural portions of the Reich have had male surpluses.

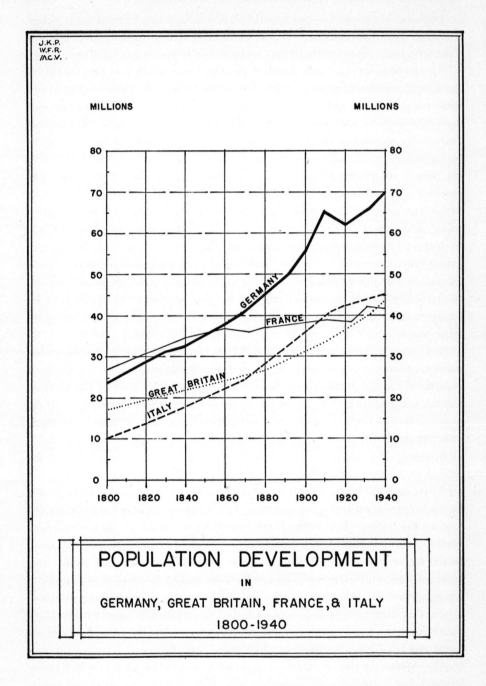

POPULATION DEVELOPMENT

IN

GERMANY, GREAT BRITAIN, FRANCE, & ITALY

1800-1940

Regional variations are also found in age composition. In rural areas where the large family has survived because of its economic usefulness, there is a statistically younger population. The statistical rise in age of the total population, which has been in process since the days of the Second Empire, is revealed by the fact that the percentage of individuals under nineteen years of age declined from forty-three per cent in 1910 to thirty per cent in 1938, while the percentage of individuals over forty increased by leaps and bounds. Although statistical evidence reveals that this tendency was retarded temporarily by the increase in the birth rate which was promoted by the Nazis, the process should continue if the trend toward urbanization is resumed after World War II. The statistical rise in the age of the German population was largely due to the steady decline of the German birth rate in urban areas, where the small family continued to supplant the large, as in all of western Europe. Germany appears to be faced with the problems of a probably declining birth rate and a further rise in the average of the population. World War II, as will be pointed out later, has only intensified German population difficulties. The loss of male population through military action, and of civilian population through bombing, will be accompanied in all probability by a drastic decline in the birth rate in the lean years following World War II.

The great shifts in population which were brought about by the industrialization and urbanization of Germany during the last seventy-five years have intensified the complexity of the biological composition of the German population. An examination of the racial composition of the German population involves the use of the techniques of physical anthropology by means of which anatomical and physiological data are obtained from living and fossil man. The anthropological study of man as a biological specimen has led to the formulation of the concept that a race consists of a large group of mankind characterized by a particular combination of physical traits of nonadaptive type, which they have derived from their ancestors, and which they transmit by reproduction to their offspring. Although the range of variation of biological traits within a racial group, such as the Caucasian, Mongolian, or Negroid races, is small, slight variations in metrical and morphological features enable the anthropologist to differentiate distinct strains within the large racial groups. Utilizing metrical (head form, face form, nose form, and stature) and morphological (pigmentation of hair, eyes, skin, and nasal profile) variations, the Caucasian race which dominates most of Europe can be broken down into a number of strains that are common in Central Europe.

The Mediterranean racial type, common among the peoples of the Latin West and of southwestern Germany, is set off from the other members of the Caucasian race by its tendency toward a long head form, a long straight nose, and a short stature, accompanied by a dark olive or brown complexion and black to brown eyes and hair. The Alpine strain, which is characterized by its round and high head form, prominent blobby nose, and short stature, is typical among the peoples of Austria and southern Germany. The Nordic stock, which was so popular with the Nazis, has a tendency toward a long head and face form, a long narrow nose, and a tall stature. These metrical features are usually accompanied by a fair complexion, long, fine, light-colored hair, and blue eyes. This strain is most common in the Low Countries, in northern Germany, and in Scandinavia. The East Baltic type, which is common among the peoples of northeastern Germany and the Baltic states, seems to be a stabilized blend of Alpines and Nordics with Mongoloid types from the East. Today, it is characterized by its broad head and face form, and by its low concave nose form. This strain is further distinguished by a fair complexion, ash brown hair, and blue or grey eyes.

The present complexity of the racial composition of Germany cannot be evaluated entirely in terms of these four racial types, because of the survival of much older racial elements. The earliest population of Germany, which dates back to the Glacial Age (Palaeolithic cultures), was made up of archaic strains of the Caucasian race, which we know today through the remains of the Cro-Magnon and Combe Capelle-Predmost types. The Alpine seems to have been the first of the modern strains to penetrate into Central Europe. Although the first Alpine men came in Mesolithic times, the major movement of this stock took place in the Neolithic period, when they may well have been the bearers of the Danubian culture, which was brought in from Southeast Europe. The Neolithic era also introduced the Mediterranean strain from the West. Long identified with the Indo-Europeans, the Nordic arrived in Central Europe from the Eurasiatic steppe toward the end of the Neolithic Age. The East Baltic type had certainly been formed by the Bronze Age. These incoming peoples not only mixed with one another, but with the surviving Stone Age population. The intermixture of strains had progressed to such an extent by the beginning of the first millennium before our era that the racial composition of Central Europe in the Iron Age was already extremely complex. Migrations of German and Slavic tribes brought additional racial intermixture, and the problem of differentiation was further complicated by the eastward movement of German peoples in the early Middle Ages and in early modern times.

Although the population of modern Germany is highly mixed as a result of the movements of peoples, the rural population of various parts of Germany exhibits a tendency toward certain types of racial affinities. In the Northwest, the peasants tend toward the Nordic type, although survival of old white strains dating back to the Palaeolithic, plus later admixtures from the South, have strongly influenced the basic Nordic type. The population of the Northwest shades off into that of the Low Countries and Scandinavia. In the north-eastern area, the Nordic strain is gradually replaced along the Baltic coast by the East Baltic type, while the Alpine strain replaces the Nordic in Branden-burg and Silesia. The southern German uplands still possess a dominantly Al-pine population, although it is influenced by Mediterranean elements in the West and by Nordic elements which filtered in from the north. The western and central Uplands have a population which has resulted from intermixture of Alpines, Nordics, and Mediterraneans on a vast scale.

The rise of the town in late medieval times and of the city in more recent times has further complicated the picture. Although town and city may draw their basic population from their immediate hinterland, much of it comes from far afield. The internal migration from farm to city during the late nine-teenth and twentieth centuries greatly accelerated this process of racial inter-mixture. In view of the fact that over fifty per cent of the German population is concentrated in towns and cities, where the racial composition is highly com-plex, even the tendency toward particular types is disappearing, except in the more remote rural areas. It is evident that the Nazi pseudo-scientific use of racial concepts to support nationalistic and political ambitions had no founda-tion, for the racial composition of the German people had nothing to do with their politics, language, religion, or culture.

The social and cultural composition of the German population, like that of any population, involves linguistic, religious, class, and occupational charac-teristics. Although linguistic differences in terms of dialect have long divided the peoples of Germany, the spread of standard German during the nineteenth and twentieth centuries has tended to wipe out many differences. This dissem-ination was brought about by education and by the easier communication made possible by political unification and the consequent growing economic and cul-tural interrelationships. Much of the deep religious feeling, which had separated the Catholic and the Protestant since the Reformation, has been overcome in modern times by the spread of nationalistic feeling. Linguistic and religious dif-ferences have become less pronounced mainly in urban areas; on the other hand, the class and occupational characteristics of the German population have grown more complex through the impact of urbanization and industrialization.

German is a development of the language of the West Germanic tribes: Sax-ons, Franconians, Thuringians, Hessians, Alemannians, and Bavarians. Dur-ing the first millennium of our era the speech of these tribes was distinguished by dialectical variations, involving marked differences in matters of phonol-ogy and vocabulary, which prevented mutual understanding between individu-als belonging to different tribes. By Carolingian times, the dialects of western Germany, which survive among the peasants of our day, had been established through stabilization of the areas of tribal settlement. The German dialects fall into three groups: Low, Middle and Upper. The latter two are commonly called High German.

Low German, which embraces Low Franconian, Low Saxon, and the East Elbian dialects, is restricted to the North German Plain. The differentiation of these Low German tribes led to the formation of Low Franconian, which developed into Flemish and Dutch through political and cultural isolation. It might be noted here that the overseas migration of the Angles and Saxons to the British Isles laid foundations for English, which is closely related to Low German. In like manner, the isolation of the Frisian tribes along the North Sea resulted in the separate development of the language of the northeastern Netherlands and the Frisian islands. While these developments were occurring in the west, the Low Saxon dialects were forming in northwestern Germany. Low Saxon colonists, who spread into Slavic territory east of the Elbe during the early Middle Ages, laid the foundations for the East Elbian dialects spoken today in Mecklenburg, Brandenburg, Pomerania, and northern East Prussia. The southern limits of modern Low German extend along the Benrather Line (*Linie*) running from Aix-la-Chapelle (Aachen) via Düsseldorf, Siegen, and Magdeburg to Fürstenwald on the Oder, although in earlier times it was spoken farther south along the middle Elbe in the Saxon Bay.

The second group of dialects, Middle German, was developed by the tribes which had settled in western and central Germany. The Franconian tribes of the lower Rhine area, centering about Cologne and Aix-la-Chapelle, developed the Riparian Franconian dialect, while the Franks to the south developed the Mosel and Rhine Franconian dialects. The latter extends into the Bavarian Palatinate, northern Baden, and southern Hesse. The isolation of the Hessian and Thuringian tribes in the central uplands led to special dialectical developments. German colonists of the early Middle Ages carried these ways of speech eastward into Saxony and Silesia and southern East Prussia, where subsequent development, coupled with elements borrowed from the Slavic language of the earlier inhabitants, led to the formation of the Upper Saxon and Silesian dialects of German in the lands to the east of the Saale River.

The third group, Upper German, consisting of the East Franconian, Alemannic, and Austro-Bavarian dialects of southern Germany, is again the product of tribal movement and settlement. The Franconian dialect of the Main Valley, extending from Würzburg to Bamberg and Nuremberg, resulted from the "southernization" of Frankish tribes, which had settled in this region after driving the Alemannic tribes off to the southwest. After their expulsion the Alemannians settled in eastern France, eastern Switzerland, and southwestern Germany. Once established, their dialect differentiated into the Swabian dialect of Württemberg and the northwest Tyrol, the High Alemannic dialect of

Switzerland and the southern Black Forest, and the Low Alemannic dialect of Alsace and the central part of the present state of Baden. While these developments were taking place in the northern and western portions of South Germany, the Austro-Bavarian dialect of southeastern Bavaria and Austria established itself along the upper Danube.

These dialects dominated the German scene until the early modern period, for there was no common language understood by everyone. Although the period before the twelfth century was marked by the production of didactic and theological works written in dialect, Latin was the language of the politician, the lawyer, and the churchman. During the thirteenth century the poets (*Minnesänger*) attempted to form a literary language on the basis of the High German Alemannic-Franconian dialects and failed; the movement, however, was accompanied by the increasing use of the German dialects in legal documents. Progress toward a standard German language began near the end of the fourteenth century, when the knowledge of writing ceased to be a monopoly of the few and spread to the burghers of the towns. Need for a uniform way of writing German was partially met by the language developed for official documents in various chanceries. The way toward a uniform language was pointed by the influential Imperial Chancery at Prague and by the Saxon Chancery at Dresden. When Luther chose the language of the Saxon Chancery for his translation of the Bible, the pattern of later development was set. The Middle High German, popularized by Luther's Bible, found immediate acceptance in Thuringia, Saxony, and Silesia and spread slowly down the Elbe to the towns of northern Germany. In the seventeenth century, Luther's language was adopted by most of the chanceries, the pulpits, and the presses of Central and North Germany.

In the South, the idiom of the Imperial Chancery of the Habsburgs at Vienna and the local dialects continued as the basis of the literary language during the seventeenth century, because of the Catholic opposition to the Protestant ways of Central and North Germany. The work of eighteenth century grammarians, backed by the literary efforts of Lessing, Schiller, and Goethe, brought the triumph of standard German in the early years of the last century. This language form spread rapidly among the educated classes of the Reich during the nineteenth century. Under the Second Empire, the developing standard German was affected by two important influences. One influence was the growth of specialized vocabularies fitted to the needs of the scholar, the scientist, the administrator, and the businessman; while the other was the influence of the speech of the Prussian civil servant. In the modern period, the tendency toward specialized vocabularies continued, and many such vocabularies were built up on the basis of newly created synthetic words suited to specialized and technical purposes. Today, the Prussian influence is gone, having given way to a tendency toward a truly national language. Not only has the language of the educated and official classes become more and more specialized and standardized, but it has become, in addition, more widely dispersed, spreading as it has throughout urban Germany. Although the impact of political unification and growing commercial integration, implemented by an expanding educational system, has given the people of the towns and cities of Germany a uniform language, the picturesque dialects, which have long divided the Germans, continue in the small towns and villages, as well as among, the lower class population in the cities.

The religious division of the Germans into Protestant and Catholic camps dates from the beginning of modern times. The Catholic Church had tended to reinforce the unity of the early medieval Empire and had served as a force for peace during the political disintegration of the late Middle Ages, but during the Reformation the politician brought about the termination of the undivided rule of the Church. In late medieval times, the break-up of the religious unity of Germany was foreshadowed by the spread of religious enthusiasm and the development of the belief that the Papacy and the Italian cardinals were primarily interested in Germany as a field for economic exploitation. When the growing rivalry of the princes, coupled with the discontent of knights and peasants was added to these divisive tendencies, ideal conditions for a religious revolt were created. The Protestant movement, which opened with Luther's attack upon abuses of indulgences in 1517, was followed by the first Protestant revolt of 1521-1525, implemented by the first political alignment of the princes of the realm on religious grounds. These political and religious developments were accompanied by a revolt of the knights in 1522 and by a peasants' rebellion in 1525, both of which were based largely upon economic discontent. In the peasant revolt, the Catholic princes joined under the leadership of the Duke of Saxony, the Electors of Brandenburg and Mainz, and the princes of Brunswick in the League of Dessau; while the Protestant princes organized the League of Torgau under the leadership of the Elector of Saxony and the Landgrave of Hesse.

Although the religious settlement of Augsburg in 1555, which permitted the princes and imperial cities to choose between Catholicism and Lutheranism, brought temporary peace, it failed because it had not granted religious toleration to the Calvinists of Hesse and the Palatinate, and because it had made unsatisfactory arrangements for the disposition of Church lands which had been seized by the Protestant princes during the wars from 1521 to 1555. These failures, coupled with the rapid spread of Protestantism into formerly Catholic areas, prepared the way for the Thirty Years' War. This war, which drew in all of Europe, made Germany a battleground not only for the forces of German Protestantism and Catholicism, but also for the Protestant armies of Sweden and Denmark and the territorially ambitious forces of France. Although the war left Germany somewhat depopulated and exhausted for a hundred years, it settled the religious division of Germany.

The geographical distribution of Catholics and Protestants within Germany has been almost the same since the Peace of Westphalia of 1648. The southern Catholic strongholds of the late seventeenth century in southwestern Germany, southern Bavaria, and along the Main River still constitute the major Catholic areas in Germany. In the West, along the Rhine and in southern Hanover and Westphalia, the Catholics are still dominant. With the exception of Catholic pockets in Upper Silesia, all of northern, eastern, and central Germany has remained Protestant. The only major Protestant area in southern Germany is located in Swabia and Franconia. In 1933 the Protestants of Germany formed about sixty-two per cent of the population, while the Catholics formed about thirty-two per cent.

The deep fissure between Catholics and Protestants has been largely healed and has ceased to be a national issue of great consequence, but it is still a potent factor in local affairs. Old suspicions have survived to influence cultural and political attitudes. Religious feeling among the lower classes is deep, still preventing the normal flow of social intercourse, nor has it vanished entirely among the more educated classes, where it still influences professional, intellectual, and cultural life.

The cultural implications of the religious division of the Germans remain important as an emotional factor in German life. In Catholic areas, the Catholic church, which is always open, and the wayside shrines are notable features in the villages and small towns; while in the Protestant North the austere Lutheran church dominates the scene. In the large towns and cities, which contain the greater proportion of Germany's population, sharp religious divisions have tended to disappear through the shifting of population in the last hundred years. The Jews, who were the only other religious group of any size, constituted only about seven-tenths of one per cent of the German population in 1933. The Nazi pogroms brought a drastic reduction in the size of the traditionally small Jewish population, which was concentrated in the towns and cities of the Reich.

The German population is further divided in terms of its occupational composition and class structure, both of which have undergone profound changes during the last hundred years. At the beginning of the nineteenth century, about eighty per cent of the population were engaged in agriculture and forestry, while the remaining twenty per cent were supported by crafts, commerce, and transportation. The economic and social life of Germany was but a step removed from medieval conditions. The peasant constituted the dominant class of the West, while the serf of the large estate formed the largest element in the population of East Elbia. The influential landed nobility, including the Junkers, the landowners of the East, and the squires of western and southern Germany, was at the height of its power. The towns, which were small and few in number, contained the limited number of middle class, composed of merchants, craftsmen, and professional people. The gradually emerging civil servant group, which exercised the will of the greater nobility—kings, princes, and dukes—was still small.

The first half of the nineteenth century was marked by drastic changes which included the abolition of serfdom and the introduction of improved methods of cultivation, as well as the growth of small industrial undertakings. These changes necessarily modified the occupational composition and the class structure. The intensification of the tempo of industry and the consequent growth of transportation and trade had altered social and economic conditions by the end of the nineteenth century. Although the amazing growth in the urban population during this period had intensified the demand for food products, which was met by increasing agricultural production, still there was a marked decline in the number of individuals supported by agricultural activity. In 1882 about forty per cent of the population were engaged in rural pursuits, while in 1907 only twenty-seven per cent of the population were so employed.

During the Empire the number of people engaged in industry and manufacturing almost doubled, while the number in trade and transportation more than doubled. It is important to note that during this period, when the total population of the Reich was increasing by leaps and bounds, there was another decline in the actual number of persons engaged in agriculture, while over twelve million individuals were added to the working forces of the towns and cities. Manpower needs in industry not only absorbed the population increase, but also drew in over a million farmers and peasants. The growing complexity of German economy was accompanied by a marked increase in national and state administrative controls. This extension of supervision led to a gradual enlargement of the civil service group, which increased from two million in the early days of the Empire to over three million by the first World War.

These occupational changes naturally brought about a new class structure. Although the greater nobility retained its official position, the Junkers of the East and the squires of the West lost much of their old power to the new bourgeoisie (a growth of capitalists that formed less than one-half of one per cent of the entire population) and to the independent owners of smaller industrial and commercial establishments, who formed about eight per cent of the gainfully employed. The old burgher middle class became much changed in composition, for the former small merchants and the craftsmen had become in large measure clerical workers and technicians.

The process of specialization, entailed by the growing complexity of an industrial-urban society, created a new professional class composed of lawyers, doctors, clergymen, professors, writers, and artists. The peasant remained the stable social element in western and central Germany. Social conditions in eastern Germany disintegrated, for many of the dispossessed serfs who had become tenant farmers were paid in terms of poor housing, bad food, and small wages. Many, however, had left the large estates to become seasonal day laborers. While this rural proletariat was forming in East Elbia, the urban proletariat, consisting of the propertyless industrial workers and their families, was rapidly developing.

The period between World War I and World War II was marked by the continuation of the same basic tendencies in occupational composition that had prevailed under the Empire. There was a further decline in the number of persons supported by agriculture, while there were further increases in the numbers supported by manufacturing, commerce, transportation, and government service. In 1933 there were only fourteen million individuals supported by agriculture, whereas twenty-six million derived their living from industry and manufacturing, and eleven million from trade and transportation. The increasing complexity of government and administration, largely resulting from the extension of the functions of the national government, brought an increase of two million individuals supported by the civil service and the professions between 1907 and 1933. It is also interesting to note that there was a steady decline in the number of domestic servants between 1871 and 1939.

The development of the present occupational composition was also affected by the increasing number of occupationless or unemployed individuals. As early as the eighties of the last century, Germany had an average of two million people in this class. Increasing unemployment enlarged the number of individuals without economic support to over three and one-half millions. The economic disturbances following World War I brought a further increase, which was only partly reduced by the brief period of economic revival under the Weimar Republic. The world economic depression of 1929-1933 was marked by a rapid increase of the number of individuals without economic support to over nine millions. The artificial revival of German economy by the Nazis, through establishment of a program for war production, not only eliminated the unemployment problem but created a condition of labor scarcity.

The impact of World War I destroyed the class structure which had been developed during the nineteenth century. Kings, dukes, and princes, together with the emperor, lost their official holdings and retired from public life to become members of the landed gentry. They were differentiated from the latter only by the prestige surviving from their former position. The Junkers and squires, whose economic security was based upon their landed holdings, feared the social and economic philosophy of both the bourgeoisie and the proletariat. They half-heartedly supported the Weimar Republic in return for tariff protection and government subsidies designed to protect their landed holdings. The agrarian crisis of the late twenties and early thirties brought many of these traditionally conservative landowners into the arms of National Socialism. The capitalistic bourgeoisie, composed of the powerful industrial, commercial, and financial groups, was not affected by the fall of the Empire, since it found that the more centralized Republic was a more useful economic tool.

The collapse of economic conditions toward the end of the Republic, together with the fear of a radical political solution of the economic problem, forced the greater part of the bourgeois class into the Nazi movement. The middle class suffered most from World War I, for it lost a large part of its capital during the war and the subsequent period of inflation. After the inflation, a new lower middle class was formed consisting of: pensioned persons, constituting about 6.2 per cent of the total population; members of the civil service and the liberal professions, constituting 8.3 per cent of all gainfully employed; members of the technical and clerical groups, constituting 11 per cent; and small independent owners of industrial and commercial enterprises, constituting 8.8 per cent. Although the middle class suffered from post-war disillusionment, it retained strong nationalistic and patriotic sentiments, to which Nazi propaganda made an effective appeal when the world depression set in after 1929.

The large urban proletariat, composed of industrial and commercial wage earners and domestic servants, formed about forty-one per cent of all gainfully occupied persons in 1933. This class sought higher wages, better working conditions, social security, and above all steady employment. The depression, with its low real wages and widespread unemployment, resulted in a moderate increase of communism among the workers; but there was no strongly developed radical movement except in a few of the highly urbanized centers, such as Hamburg and Berlin, or in the highly industrialized areas such as the Ruhr.

The rural proletariat did not fare well under the Republic. Their scattered distribution made organized effort impossible; hence they formed a class without great political or economic power. Chancellor Brüning attempted to make use of the lands of the East Elbian Junkers to help them. The Nazis also appealed to them by offering the promise of land; but the peasantry continued to hold their conservative and often reactionary political and social philosophy. They had profited from the economic difficulties following the war. Inflation had brought prosperity through reduction of the agrarian debt, which was paid off in cheap marks. The subsequent economic depression of 1929-1933, however, brought the peasant low prices and increasing debts. Finally, he turned to National Socialism with enthusiasm.

The period between the two World Wars was one of increasing mobility in the class structure, which was marked by widespread shifts of individuals and groups from class to class. Although the new middle class took up from the older one the responsibility of holding Germany together, deep fissures were appearing in the social structure. The middle class civil servants, with their ideal of service to the state, formed a gigantic bureaucracy whose influence was felt in every corner of German life. Backed by law and the courts and supported by a maze of regulations, they managed to bridge the gap between the proletariat and the landowners and the bourgeoisie. It is interesting to note that each of the classes, now differentiated on the basis of religion, occupation, and income rather than upon descent and education, sought expression in political movements with fixed principles and programs, until the Nazis brought about the forcible unification of all openly expressed political and class hopes and aspirations.

THE REGIONS OF GERMANY

Modern Germany, with its diverse and complex physical setting, represents the transformation of an agrarian land, studded with market towns once serving as centers for handicrafts, commerce, and politics, into a highly industrialized and urbanized country. The processes of change brought not only a vast redistribution of population densities through the development of urban centers, but a greater differentiation of the occupational and class groups as a result of the specializations required by an industrial society. While these movements brought vast changes in physical composition, occupational composition, and class structure, they also tended to pull the nation together through elimination of particularism and sectionalism—a process which was further aided by the political unification of the Reich, first under the federalized Empire and Republic and finally under the centralized totalitarian Reich of the Nazis.

Nevertheless, Germany remains one of the most culturally diverse lands in Europe. Differences based upon dialect, agricultural practices, house and village forms, customs and folkways, and religious beliefs, continue to divide the rural peoples of Germany. The people of the cities speak much the same language and share a common political outlook, but differences in tradition and economic orientation, coupled with subtle cultural variations, have tended to differentiate the cities and towns of one part of Germany from another.

Modern Germany may still be divided into five distinct cultural regions set apart by clear differences in ways of living.

1. In the east beyond the Elbe, the coastal area with its cold, humid climate is occupied by Mecklenburgers, Pomeranians, and East Prussians, while the drier and warmer interior plains are in the hands of the people of Brandenburg and Silesia. These people, speaking an East Elbian variety of Low Ger-

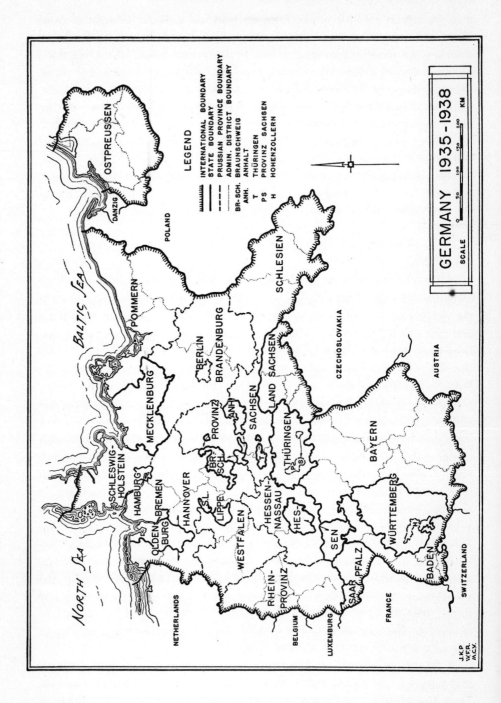

man (except in the case of the Silesians who use a dialect brought in from Middle Germany), dwell in small villages dominated by a brick Lutheran church, or on an estate centering about a Junker manor house. Most of the rural people of this area derive their living from the cultivation of rye and potatoes, although dairying and livestock raising are dominant along the Baltic coast, while a more varied and more productive type of crop cultivation may be found in parts of Silesia. This dominantly agrarian area is served by a limited number of large cities, such as the coastal towns of Rostock, Stettin, and Königsberg, the industrialized towns of Silesia including Görlitz, Breslau, Oppeln, and Beuthen, and the nationally important political, governmental, industrial, and commercial center of Berlin. Most of the population dwells in the small village or on the large estates close to their work on the soil.

2. The life of the damp plains of northwestern Germany contrasts strongly with that of the Prussian East. The northern and central portions of the Low Saxon Northwest is mainly agrarian in its economic organization. The farms of the coastal and river marshes, which are worked by independent peasants dwelling in villages built along elevated dykes, and the medium sized farms of the interior heath lands, containing isolated farm houses constructed of brick and timber, are mainly concerned with dairying and livestock raising. Aside from the scattered market towns there are few centers of urban type, except for the port cities of Bremen and Hamburg on the North Sea, and Lübeck on the Baltic, which have evolved from small Hanseatic cities into thriving ports with a considerable amount of specialized manufacturing. In the southeastern part of Low Saxony on the border, extending from Hanover to Magdeburg, the rich loess soils have made possible the intensive development of agriculture, with cereals and sugar beets as important crops. There is, in addition, some livestock raising. This portion of the Northwest is more heavily settled; and its position astride the major east-west land and canal routes of northern Germany, as well as its resources in local deposits of lignite and salt, made possible the development of Hanover, Brunswick (Braunschweig), and other cities. In the Southwest the Protestant Low Saxons give way to the Catholic Westphalians, who speak a variety of Low German. Although the Westphalians have many affinities with the Low Saxons in terms of folkways, dialect, and customs, the development of the Rhine-Ruhr industrial complex has oriented their economy toward the Rhenish West. This economic orientation is supplemented by strong religious ties with the Rhineland, for both areas are dominantly Catholic.

3. The western portion of the Reich, tied together by cultural, economic, and religious interrelationships, embraces the Rhenish and Westphalian lowlands, the Rhenish and Hessian uplands, and the valley lands along the Mosel,

Rhine, and Lower Main. The lowlands to the north, which are occupied by the Westphalian and Riparian Frankish peasants, dwelling on medium-sized farms, are dominated by the great cities of the Rhine and Ruhr region, including Aix-la-Chapelle, Cologne, Düsseldorf, Essen, and Dortmund. To the south of this highly industrialized and heavily settled area are the Rhenish and Hessian uplands, essentially agrarian in their economic organization. The peasants of this rolling upland area, who speak Mosel and Rhenish varieties of Franconian, and the closely related Hessian dialect, dwell on small to medium-sized farms which are utilized for the cultivation of grain and the raising of livestock. The valley areas along the Mosel, Rhine, and Main, famous for their fruit and wine, have a dense rural population. The economy is dependent chiefly on manufacturing and commercial activities concentrated in the cities of Coblenz, Mainz, Darmstadt, and Frankfort.

4. The Central German area, which is bordered by the Low Saxon Northwest, the East Elbian Northeast, and the Rhenish West, epitomizes the essential characteristics of modern industrialized Germany. This land, which once belonged to the Thuringian peasants and the colonial Upper Saxon settlers, possesses not only a well developed agriculture, but a thriving industrial and manufacturing life which grew out of the traditional craft industries going back to the Middle Ages in Halle, Leipzig, Magdeburg, and Chemnitz. The rapid economic development of this area between World War I and World War II has converted the entire central German region into a vast industrial complex centering about the great commercial centers of Halle and Leipzig.

5. Southern Germany, beyond the line of the river Main, stands apart from the rest of the country owing to the traditional importance of the states of Baden, Württemberg, and Bavaria, which constantly challenged the growing power of the northeastern state of Prussia until their defeat in 1866 and their absorption into the German Empire in 1871. Although the South is held by three distinct cultural groups, the Franconians gravitating toward Nuremberg, the Bavarians centering about Munich, and the Swabians oriented about Stuttgart, the entire region has a distinct atmosphere which sets it off from the rest of Germany. The south is interested mainly in agriculture and rural pursuits. Its manufacturing and commercial life is restricted to a few limited areas, which are dominated by the cities of Mannheim, Stuttgart, Nuremberg, and Munich.

The contrast between rural Germany with its interests in crops, forests, and crafts, and urban Germany with its interests in industry, manufacturing, and commerce, is marked by the sharp transitions from open country to areas of crowded housing, factories and mines, and public buildings. The complex distribution of urban centers and areas resulting from unique combinations of location, topography, and local resources, has its counterpart in rural Germany. The large estates of sparsely populated northeastern Germany contrast strongly with the tiny peasant farms of the western and southwestern parts of the Reich, while these, in turn, contrast with the intensive agrarian undertakings of the Rhine-Ruhr, Rhine-Main, Central German, and Silesian areas, where a combination of good soil and a large demand for foodstuffs from near-by urban populations has resulted in a dense settlement of rural lands.

Physically, there is a marked difference between the rural and urban populations of Germany. While the smaller towns and villages are characterized by large families, a relatively younger population, and a high birth rate, the cities and larger towns have a statistically older population composed of small families and large numbers of unmarried people. While the country people are divided by marked differences in dialect and religion, the more sophisticated urban populations speak the same language and have lost much of the deep religious convictions of the past. The contrast between rural and urban Germany in social organization is great. Life is socially simple in rural areas, where society is composed of the surviving landed nobility, the peasantry, and the rural workers, who are served by merchant and artisan groups of the small towns. The cities, with their small upper class of capitalists, a dwindling middle class, and an unrooted proletariat, are infinitely complex in their social stratifications. The urban areas are further divided from the rural areas by the fact that they have long been the centers not only of artistic, intellectual, and educational activities, but also the foci of political and governmental power.

The unity of Germany will always be conditioned by the tensions and conflicts growing out of the diversity of landscape and population and the complexity of the social and economic interests of its population. Regional variations influence the social, economic, political, and intellectual conflict between rural and urban Germany. The agrarian conditions of the Northeast will always be productive of problems involving labor, capital, and production, which will be in marked contrast with the rural problems of western and southern Germany. The economic interests of the ports of Hamburg, Bremen, and Stettin will always be at variance with the desires of the southern industrial centers, such as Nuremberg and Augsburg. The problems of the Ruhr will turn on questions of producing coal and iron, while the manufacturing towns of the Rhine-Main and the central German area will be more interested in sources of raw material and markets. These economic problems, resulting from the regional variation of interests, will be further complicated by the hopes, aspirations, and motives of the various social classes, each seeking to implement their desires through political action. The influence of the traditional rural areas has waned with the decline in importance of the agrarian activities of the landed gentry and peasantry, while the urban areas have assumed a leading role in the social, economic, and political life of the Reich. The traditional cultural areas, however, based upon the peasantry and the burghers of the small towns, are still living realities. Through their landscape, dialects, customs and folkways, they have a more vivid meaning to the average German than the more modern concept of the Reich as a national all-embracing unit of economic activity and political life.

BIBLIOGRAPHY

Geography

Baring-Gould, S. *Germany* (London, 1883).

Brandt, B. *et al.* "Das Deutsche Reich," in *Handbuch der Geographischen Wissenschaft,* Bd I (Potsdam, 1936).

Braun, G. *Deutschland* (Berlin, 1916).

Dickinson, R. E. *The Regions of Germany* (New York, Oxford University Press, 1945).

Gruber, *Deutsches Wirtschaftsleben auf geographischer Grundlage,* 4th ed. (Leipzig, Berlin, 1919).

Koch, W. *Die Deutschen Gemeindegrenzen und ihr historischer Wert* (Quakenbrück, 1933).

Martonne E. de "Europe centrale," in *Geographie Universelle,* T. IV (Paris, 1931).

Partsch, J. F. W. *Central Europe* (New York, 1903).

Pflug, H. *Deutschland, Landschaft, Volkstum, Kultur* (Leipzig, 1937).

Ratzel, F. *Deutschland, Einführung in die Heimatkunde,* 6th ed. (Berlin, Leipzig, 1932).

Ule, W. *Das Deutsche Reich* (Leipzig, 1925).

Settlement

Burgdörfer, F. *Bevölkerungsentwicklung im Dritten Reich* (Heidelberg-Berlin, 1938).

Childe, V. G. *The Dawn of European Civilization* (London, 1939).

East, G. *An Historical Geography of Europe* (London, 1935).

Frercks, R. *German Population Policy* (Berlin, 1938).

Friedemann, H. *Reichsdeutsches Volk und Land im Werdegang der Zeiten* (Stuttgart, 1906).

Hall, G. S. *Aspects of German Culture* (Boston, 1881).

Hawkes, C. F. C. *The Prehistoric Foundations of Europe* (London, 1940).

International Labor Office, *The Rural Exodus in Germany* (Geneva, 1933).

Kampffmeyer, P. *Geschichte der modernen Gesellschaftsklassen in Deutschland* (Berlin, 1921).

Statistisches Reichsamt, *Die Bewegung der Bevölkerung* (1907-   ).

Taeuber, C. *Migration to and from German Cities* (Roma, 1932).

Language

Bach, A. *Geschichte der deutschen Sprache* (Leipzig, 1938).

Bahaghel, O. *Geschichte der deutschen Sprache,* 5th ed. (Leipzig-Berlin, 1928).

Cornish, V. *Borderlands of Language in Europe* (London, 1937).

Dominian, L. *The Frontiers of Language and Nationality in Europe* (New York, 1937).

Grimm, J. K. L. *Geschichte der deutschen Sprache,* 4th ed. (Leipzig, 1880).

Priebsch & Collinson, *History of the German Language* (London,   ).

Weise, O. *Unsere Mundarten* (Leipzig-Berlin, 1919).

Composition

Chmelar, J. *National Minorities in Central Europe* (Prague, 1937).

Coon, C. *The Races of Europe* (New York, 1939).

Junghann, O. *National Minorities in Europe* (New York, 1932).

Kosok, P. *Modern Germany* (Chicago, 1933).

Morant, G. M. *The Races of Central Europe* (London, 1939).

Chapter 2

GOVERNMENT AND ADMINISTRATION

During the past thousand years German government and administration have been determined by social and economic movements and by the interplay of political forces derived from the regional patterns of social, economic, and cultural life. The rural society of the Middle Ages produced first a feudal monarchy and later an aristocratic federated empire to serve its governmental needs. While France and England were developing strong national states, Germany disintegrated into a heterogeneous collection of ecclesiastical and aristocratic holdings, held together only by the most tenuous ties of national loyalty. The disastrous Thirty Years' War sharpened the internal division of the German area by adding religious disunity to an already impossible political situation. Although the emergence of a united German state was foreshadowed in the eighteenth century by the growth of the strong territorial states of Austria and Prussia, the movement toward unification did not come until after the beginning of the nineteenth century.

Political forces released by the French Revolution brought a political simplification of Germany through consolidation of the multitude of states left behind by the medieval era, and introduced the spirit of nationalism. Although the work of Napoleon constituted an essential step toward unification, drastic social and economic changes were to be more important. The rapid transformation of a rural country into a highly industrialized state with a large urban population having new social and economic aspirations and interests, pointed toward a more centralized form of government and administration.

The trend toward a unified Reich was slow in developing and was complicated by the particularistic governmental legacy of the past. Although unity was achieved with the creation of the Second Empire in 1871 and was given a more solid foundation under the Republic, sectionalism and particularism still survive not only in the contemporary attachment of the people for their provinces and states, but also in the actual everyday governmental and administrative forms. Germany is still a complex land with an amazing diversity of regional and social interests. To understand the character of recent developments, one must evaluate not only Germany's governmental heritage, but also the stages of social and economic development through which it has passed.

THE FRANKISH STATE

The roots of German governmental development are embedded in the Frankish State of the Merovingian and Carolingian kings. The kingdom of the Franks, which first comprised the lands along the Main, Rhine, Mosel, Meuse, and Scheldt, rose on the ruins of the Western Roman Empire along with the tribal kingdoms of the Goths, Burgundians, and Alemannians. Under the leadership of the Merovingian, Clovis (A.D. 481-511), the Franks defeated the Roman governor Syagrius in the battle of Soissons and added to the Frankish realm all of northern France, except Brittany. Victories over the Alemanni (A.D. 496 and 502), the Burgundians (A.D. 532), and the West Goths (A.D. 507), brought the addition of southwestern Germany and southern France to the Frankish State. Establishment of political supremacy over the Bavarians and conquest of the Frisians completed the territorial framework of the Merovingian realm.

Although the Frankish State had become politically the leading state of western Europe, the resultant union of German tribes under the Frankish kings was unstable. The government of the Frankish state was headed by an absolute monarch, vested with executive, legislative, and judicial powers. The officials of the Frankish court included the German Cupbearer, the Lord-High Steward, the Marshal, and the Roman Chamberlain (*Camerarius* or Treasurer), and Director of the Royal Chancery (*Referendarius*). Local administration was under an array of counts and dukes, who had emerged from the old tribal aristocracies. This nobility, which provided local military leadership and justice, was based upon service to the king for which were received grants of land and the right to organize and control local government and administration. Political conditions were weakened still more by the system of royal succession and inheritance. At the death of each Merovingian monarch, the realm was divided among the royal heirs, a process which was productive of numerous family quarrels and feuds, and afforded the nobility an opportunity to enlarge the scope of their local rights and prerogatives.

The decline of the Merovingian dynasty (A.D. 486-752) was marked by the rise of the so-called Mayors of the Palace (*Hausmeier, majores domus*), who gradually became leaders of the feudal retainers. The family of Pepin, afterward known as Carolingians, first rose to power as the palace mayors in Austrasia, the eastern hereditary division of the Merovingian realm. In 687 Pepin of Heristal defeated the major domus of western Neustria and assumed the title of "dux et princeps Francorum" (leader and prince of the Franks). His successor, Charles Martel, the grandfather of Charlemagne, was victorious over the Arabs in the battle of Tours (A.D. 732) and not only saved western Europe from the threat of Islam, but further strengthened the political power of the Pepins. After securing the support of the Papacy in return for aid against the Lombards and the Eastern Empire, Pepin the Short deposed the last Merovingian ruler in 751 and established himself as the King of the Franks. Three years later, Pope Stephen III anointed Pepin as King of the Franks, thereby establishing the concept of divine right; a theory which was to be of fundamental importance throughout the Middle Ages.

Charlemagne, who came to power in 768, inherited a united realm in which the basic pattern of medieval life with its fusion of Germanic, Greco-Roman, and Christian elements was already established. His reign brought a further expansion of the Frankish realm. Wars against the Saxon tribes of northwestern Germany and campaigns against the Bavarians and Avars added vast territories to the Frankish State. Advance of the Carolingian forces was marked by extensive missionary activities, often carried out with the aid of the sword. Monks and priests, following in the wake of the armies, established churches and monasteries in the Northwest which became the nuclei of future towns. The newly conquered lands were secured by forts, placed under Counts of the Palatinate (*Pfalzgrafen*), while border areas in the East along the German-Slav frontier were entrusted to Margraves or Counts of the Marches (*Markgrafen*) who were granted extraordinary powers to deal with matters affecting the security of the empire. Like his forebears, Charlemagne went to the aid of the Papacy in Italy. Defeat of the Lombards brought him the Lombard Crown and control of northern Italy. In the southwest he established the Spanish Mark to protect his realm against the Arabs, the first step toward the Christian recovery of Spain.

In return for his services to the Papacy, Charlemagne was crowned Emperor of the West by Pope Leo III on Christmas Day in the year A.D. 800. This revival of the fiction of the universal Roman State was of great historical importance, for it proved to be one of the theoretical determinants of governmental structure for Germany during the long era of the Holy Roman Empire, which lasted from 800 to 1806 when it was dissolved by Napoleon. The royal government, which traveled with the Emperor or centered at the royal residences at Aix-la-Chapelle Ingelheim, or Nymegen, consisted of a Chancellor, responsible for ecclesiastical affairs; a Palgrave, in charge of lay matters; a Chamberlain, in control of palace and treasury affairs; and a Constable. The

Emperor was also assisted by an annual assembly of ecclesiastical and lay retainers.

The Carolingian era marked the completion of a transition from the primitive tribal organization to the medieval feudal system. The tribal chiefs of the migration period had been replaced by Counts of Districts (*Gaugrafen*) and by Counts of Frontier Districts (*Markgrafen*) who possessed broad executive, fiscal, and military powers. They were aided by local assemblies of freemen, the landowners of the counties. The counts, bound to the Emperor by an oath of fealty, were kept under control by Royal Commissioners (*Sendgrafen*) who were sent out periodically from the royal court to inspect different parts of the realm. This system of local government and administration met the needs of a society which was concentrated in small agrarian villages, where the arable soil was held by freemen subject to military service, and worked by bondsmen and serfs. The rapid drift toward a feudal society in this period is further indicated by the fact that great numbers of freemen, desiring to escape military service, placed themselves under protection of the Counts of Districts and accepted the status of retainers.

The reign of Charlemagne brought a temporary renewal of the fortunes of western Europe. The patronage of the Emperor led to a revival of culture and learning. He encouraged the Church to establish better educational standards for the clergy and endeavored to secure church schools for the education of the upper class. These efforts bore fruit in the Carolingian Renaissance, which produced such scholars as Alcuin and Paulus Diaconus. While the scholars and writers of Charlemagne's day accomplished little in the way of creative work, they did seek to provide for transmission of the Latin heritage. This cultural movement was accompanied by extensive religious activities. New monasteries and churches were erected throughout the land. Economically the religious, cultural, and political life of the Carolingian West was supported by a prosperous peasantry and by improving agricultural conditions.

The death of Charlemagne in 814 was followed by a rapid disintegration of the Frankish state, when the heirs began a long series of wars for possession of the empire. The important division of lands among the grandsons of Charlemagne at Verdun in 843 placed "France" under Charles, the "German" portion lying between the Rhine and Elbe under Ludwig, and the lands situated between the two, comprising the Netherlands, Lorraine, Burgundy, and Italy, under Lothar. In 870 a division of Lothar's kingdom, which was made by the Treaty of Meersen, divided the northern area between Charles and Ludwig and established the North Italian portion as an independent kingdom. This disruption of the Carolingian realm was inevitable, for the successors were not only divided one against another, but were beset by both domestic and foreign

troubles. Internally, they were faced with the growing power of the feudal retainers, while, externally, they were harassed by the inroads of the Vikings in
the north, the Slavs and Magyars in the east, and the Arabs in the southwest.
The Carolingian era ended with a divided Western Europe. From this time on-
wards, France, Germany, and Italy were destined to follow separate paths of
historical and political development.

The First Reich

The foundation of the First Reich came in 911 at Forchheim with the election as Emperor of Konrad of Franconia by the Saxon and Franconian nobility.
He was immediately faced with an almost impossible political situation, for
the revival of the great tribal duchies during the chaotic ninth century had
placed the land, and with it the power, in the hands of local leaders. His attempt
to subjugate the rebellious duchies failed, and his reign came to an unsuccessful
end in 918. The election of Henry I of Saxony (Heinrich I of Sachsen) as Emperor in 919 at Fritzlar on the Eder firmly established the monarchial tradition on a German basis. Where Conrad had failed, Henry succeeded, for with
his power as Duke of Saxony he subjugated the partially independent duchies
of Lorraine (*Lothringen*), Franconia, Thuringia, Swabia, and Bavaria, which
had developed in the old tribal areas during the period of Carolingian decline
to meet needs of security against the attacks of the Norse, Slavs, and Magyars.
Henry's son and successor, Otto the Great, brought to fruition a further development of royal power through the reduction of the power of the dukes and
through the wise use of gifts bestowed upon the Church. His defeat of the
Slavic tribes in the Northeast made possible the first German colonization of
East Elbia, while his victory over the Magyars at Augsburg (A.D. 955) opened
the way for the German settlement of Austria. His campaigns in Italy in support of the Papacy led to a revival of the imperial title through his coronation
by the Pope in 962. He is considered to be the founder of the Holy Roman Empire of the German Nation.

The peak of German monarchial development came under the Franconian
dynasty, which began in 1025. The power of the Emperor, both sovereign and
feudal, was buttressed by consolidation of ducal power in the hands of the
Franconian family. At the height of Franconian power, Henry III, the Holy
Roman Emperor, was also Duke of Bavaria, Swabia, and Franconia. During
this period the western portion of the Reich was held by the dukes of the two
Lorraines, while the Northwest was ruled by the dukes of Saxony and the tribal
leaders of the Frisians. In the North Mecklenburg was conquered and opened
for colonization by the dukes of Saxony, but remained under its Slavic princes
who became vassals of the Emperor in 1170. The lands between the Elbe and
Oder to the south of Mecklenburg were first organized under a single Count

and later divided between the Counts of Nordmark, Meissen, and Mark Lausitz. Bohemia was brought into the Empire when its Slavic rulers were recognized as vassal kings in 1086. Northern Austria was organized under a Count, while the southeastern portion fell to the Duke of Carinthia after its separation from the Duchy of Bavaria in 976. In the West, Burgundy was acquired by the Emperor, while in the East Poland fell under his suzerainty from 1032 to 1079.

The courts of the Saxon and Franconian Emperors followed similar patterns, which had been inherited from the Carolingians. The Emperor was assisted by three Archchancellors, who were responsible for Germany, Italy, and Burgundy respectively. The archchancellorship of Germany gradually became the hereditary right of the Archbishops of Mainz. The Emperor was also assisted by an Archchamberlain, an Archconstable, and an Archsteward. At first, the Archchamberlains were the Kings of Bohemia, but later this office became an hereditary right of the Counts of Brandenburg. The dukes of Saxony acquired control of the office of archconstable, while the Franconian Palgraves gained control of the office of archsteward. The actual work involved in these offices was delegated to deputies. The Emperor was also assisted by irregular meetings of the Reichstag, which was composed of the lay and ecclesiastical nobility.

The local government and administration of the First Reich can be understood only in terms of the feudal and manorial systems. Feudalism, which achieved its initial form during the eighth and ninth centuries, involved the surrender of allodial land for possessory ownership with usufruct and the development of dependent relationships between the feudal lords and their retainers or vassals. The old system of counties under Counts of the District, which had flourished in Carolingian times, broke up under the impact of feudalism. After the death of Charlemagne the tribal dukes assumed control of large areas in the Reich and brought the Counts of the Districts under their control as feudal retainers. The Saxon and Franconian Emperors managed to bring the Stem Duchies under limited imperial control; but the constant demands for military forces, which could not be met from the imperial purse, forced the Emperors not only to grant to the duchies additional tracts of land as royal fiefs, but also to implement the powers of the Greater Nobility with grants of seignorial prerogatives and immunities.

Although the granting of a fief by the Emperor involved an act of homage and an oath of fealty which established a feudal bond entailing certain obligations and responsibilities, military force rather than legal persuasion was used to hold the system together. Weak emperors were constantly faced with rebellious vassals. In times of war the imperial army, which was made up of contingents led by the retainers of the Emperor, was held together by promises of booty and by imperial grants of land acquired by the Emperor either through confiscation of the fiefs of rebellious vassals or through conquest of the lands of foreign rulers. The structural weakness of the system led to almost constant disorder and violence.

By the close of the twelfth century the greater nobles, who had acquired hereditary rights to their fiefs during the tenth and eleventh centuries, included the following Princes of the Realm (*Reichsfürsten*): the King of Bohemia, the dukes of Bavaria, Saxony, Lorraine, Franconia, Austria, Carinthia, and Styria, the counts of Meissen, Lausatia, Brandenburg, Moravia, and Namur, the Palgraves of the Rhine and Saxony, and the Landgraves of Thuringia. The process of infeudation brought not only subordination of the Counts of the District to the greater nobility, but also led to the creation of a large class of landed barons and knights (*Ritter*) as the old system of counties crumbled away. The barons and knights held their large estates in military tenure, that is, on condition of rendering military service. The growth of the petty nobility was also accompanied by the granting of immunities and privileges, giving them considerable freedom in the management of local affairs.

Under the Saxon and Franconian Emperors the majority of the German people dwelt upon manorial estates, which were governed either by deputies of the Emperor, by the greater nobility, or, directly, by the petty nobility. The manorial estate, which comprised the feudal retainers' establishments and fields, the village and fields of the peasants, and the surrounding pasture and woodland, was governed by the lord of the manor, who served as the head of local government, administration, and justice. The populace of this small and isolated local community consisted of the manorial lord and his officers, the local priest, a few craftsmen who enjoyed the status of freemen, and the tenant serfs who were bound to the soil and obliged to render service to the manorial lord. The landed freemen, who had played an important role in local affairs during Merovingian times, had largely disappeared. To escape an impossible economic situation the mass of freemen had renounced their freedom and transferred their lands to the feudal nobility. In the East many of the free peasants received grants of land on condition of military service. Other peasants frequently held small plots of land from the petty knights on condition of proper services and dues.

The affairs of this agrarian society were regulated by bodies of local law consisting of traditional customs and usages. The old codes of the Germanic tribes, which had been in force in Carolingian times, had disappeared, although their influence survived in the three main types of law regulating the society of early medieval Germany. Relations between the Emperor and the nobility were set forth in the feudal laws (*Lehnrechte*), while affairs of the manorial estates were governed by the numerous local manorial laws (*Hof-*

rechte). The varied common laws (*Landrechte*) were gradually reduced to writing.

The development of a feudal nobility between the Emperor and the freemen, who had once served as lawgivers, judges, and soldiers of the local communities in the days of the Counts of the District, had a profound effect upon later German development. The rise of the feudal and manorial system brought decentralization of government and administration; and the imperial grants of immunities and the development of the right of inheritance to fiefs, gave the nobility control of German society. For the people the local feudal lord became the supreme authority. The mass of Germans gradually lost the feeling that there was a still higher authority, the Emperor, who was representative of the whole German people.

The Church had also been gradually drawn into the feudal system through acquisition of large land holdings as gifts from the Emperor and the greater nobility. Bishops and abbots became vassals holding fiefs from lay rulers. The Church gradually lost control of its organization since the holders of the ecclesiastical fiefs were selected by the Emperor and the feudal lords. Church elections of ecclesiastical officials became a farce. Furthermore, the investiture of the church dignitaries, which conferred both temporal and spiritual powers, was in the hands of the feudal lords.

The Western Church was in a particularly weak position. At the local level, its power was decentralized and subject to the control of lay lords, while at the top the situation was complicated by the fact that for a period there were three rival Popes. Internally, there was weakness and corruption resulting from illicit marriages, simony, and graft. Reform of the Church was demanded from every quarter. The Emperor Henry III took action at the Council of Sutri (1046). His reform brought the elimination of the rival Popes; and by the appointment of Clement II as sole Pope, the foundations were laid for the powers of the later Popes. In the latter half of the eleventh century, the powerful Pope Nicholas II solved the problem of papal succession by establishing the College of Cardinals. But schemes for strengthening the power of the Papacy were blocked by the independence of the higher clergy, by national church feeling, by lay control, and by corruption.

The major problem for the revival of papal control centered in the custom of lay investiture. The successors of Pope Nicholas took little action until Pope Gregory VII (1073-1085) demanded the right of the Church to absolute control over its officials and members, and insisted upon the pre-eminence of the Pope over all lay rulers and princes. Opposition of Henry IV in 1076 to the papal demands led to his excommunication and a declaration of open war between the German Emperor and the Pope. The settlement of the investiture issue came under Henry IV's son and successor, Henry V, who signed the Concordat of Worms (1122). This pact provided for the election of ecclesiastical officials in the imperial presence and established the custom of double investiture by Church and State, in this way recognizing the feudal relationship between the Empire and the Papacy. However, the Emperor in reality had lost control of all ecclesiastical fiefs, and the triumph of the Church marked a first step toward the disintegration of the first German Empire.

With the Hohenstaufen dynasty (1138-1254), which began with the rule of Conrad III, Duke of Swabia, came the final phase of German imperial power. Conrad's successor, Frederick I (Friedrich Barbarossa, 1152-1190), managed to keep the Empire united only by military force. The great vassals, the Papacy, and the Lombard cities of northern Italy were at last determined upon the destruction of the Emperor's powers. The revolt against imperial authority began in the Lombard cities, which were backed by the Papacy and a portion of the German nobility. Although Frederick's first expeditions into Italy met with some success, he was finally driven out and forced back into Germany. The Treaty of Venice (1177), a victory for the Papacy and the Lombard Cities failed, however, to bring peace; in fact, it succeeded only in setting the stage for the final struggle between the Hohenstaufen or Imperialists and the Guelphs or Anti-Imperialists: the Papacy, the Lombard Cities, and the Greater German Nobility. The rebellion which followed the peace of Venice was put down by Frederick through an alliance with a few remaining feudal supporters, who were interested in acquiring further increases in their powers at the expense of the Emperor. Although the Empire had won a temporary victory, its cause was lost.

These changes in the fortunes of the Empire were accompanied by important social and economic developments. A gradual revival of commerce came in the tenth century as a result of increases in agrarian production and the demand for luxuries. Market centers grew at strategically placed manors, monasteries, and castles. The old Roman towns along the Rhine and Danube began to take a new lease upon life. Furthermore, the Crusades of the eleventh and twelfth centuries increased the tempo of commercial activity.

The market centers gradually grew into small fortified towns, the control of which was at first vested in the lay and ecclesiastical lords, who had long before received from the Emperor the right to local taxes, market dues, tolls, and coinage. The freemen, who represented the bulk of the population in the early towns, associated themselves in fraternities and guilds for the regulation of commerce and crafts. These associations gradually gained immunities from the control of the local feudal lords, and the cities began to lead a semi-independent existence. City councils, composed of Councilors (*Rathsmänner*) and presided over by Mayors (*Bürgermeister*), first appeared in the twelfth century.

City laws derived from the common law gradually made their appearance. The city codes of Cologne and Frankfort became models for Franconia, while the laws of Soest and Dortmund became popular in Westphalia and spread to the developing Hanseatic towns. Strassburg served as the model for Swabian cities, while the legal customs of Magdeburg were carried into East Elbia by German settlers.

The impact of the growth of towns on German society brought many drastic changes. In the first place, it provided commercial and craft occupations for the increasing population. The development of coinage in the towns gradually led to the displacement of barter and introduced the use of money payments instead of services. These innovations helped to bring about the gradual destruction of the manorial system and serfdom. Many serfs left the estates for the refuge provided by the city, while others were able to better their condition on the land. The payment of rent gradually replaced the rendering of services, giving the serf the status of a tenant. Slowly, the bondsmen, a class going back to the freemen of Carolingian times, bought back their holdings and assumed the position of independent peasants. The whole social structure of medieval Germany was in a state of flux.

The Welf-Hohenstaufen struggle over imperialism continued to plague the ruling family. Frederick II, the last Hohenstaufen Emperor, failed not only in his attempt to bring Italy back under control, but also in his efforts to bring about the political consolidation of Germany. His quarrel with Pope Gregory IX led to his excommunication in 1241. Under strong pressure he was forced to confirm the rights of sovereignty that had been assumed by the lay and ecclesiastical princes. Legally these constitutional laws marked the final collapse of medieval imperial power. In 1245 the ban on Frederick II was renewed by Innocent IV, who summoned the Council of Lyons to call the German princes to a new imperial election. A general revolt against the German Emperor was demanded by the Papacy. Frederick II and his son Conrad fought on in Italy until their deaths in 1250 and 1254. The fall of the Hohenstaufen dynasty left Germany without central authority and at the mercy of the forces of chaos and disorder. Germany was disintegrating into a number of hopelessly divided principalities; the era of the first Imperial Reich was over.

The Aristocratic Confederation

The transition from feudal and monarchial Germany to the aristocratic and oligarchic federation was marked by the Great Interregnum (1254-1273) when Germany was ruled by a number of rival emperors, elected by various portions of the German nobility. Although the reign of Rudolf I, Count of Habsburg and Kyburg, who was elected in 1273, brought restoration of the public peace, the power of the Emperor continued to decline. The emperorship, which had once been based upon sovereign and feudal powers, became more and more dependent upon the dynastic and territorial resources of the ruling emperor. In turn, the remaining imperial prerogatives were used to increase the possessions of the ruling Emperor's dynasty.

Collapse of the central government was accompanied by the disintegration of the old duchies and by the development of a great number of small dynastic and ecclesiastical states. While the Habsburgs were slowly consolidating their territorial holdings in southeastern Central Europe, the old duchies of Bavaria, Swabia, Franconia, Lorraine, and Saxony were falling to pieces. During the period of kings and emperors of various houses,[1] the dukes of Geldern and Pomerania, the counts of Jülich, the landgraves of Hesse, and the princes of Nassau were elevated from the ranks of the petty nobility and made Princes of the Realm. In 1309 the Swiss cantons of Schwyz, Uri, and Nidwalden finally gained their freedom from Habsburg domination and were given an immediate feudal position within the Empire by Henry of Luxemburg.

The Luxemburg Emperors (1347-1437), who rose to power after the imperial elections at Rense (*Kurverein* of Rense), derived their eminence from dynastic holdings in eastern Germany, which included the Kingdom of Bohemia, the Duchy of Silesia, and the Margraviates of Brandenburg, Lausitz, and Moravia. Charles IV, the first Luxemburg Emperor, who is famous today as the scholar and statesman who founded the first German university at Prague (1348), attempted to bring some order into the complex political condition by constitutional reform. The famous Golden Bull of 1356, a fundamental law of the Empire, settled the difficult question of the election of the emperor, which in the past had led to constant strife and disorder between the various rival groups of candidates and their supporters. Under the Golden Bull, the election of the emperor was intrusted to seven electors: the archbishops of Mainz, Treves, and Cologne, the King of Bohemia, the Count Palatine of the Rhine, the Duke of Saxon-Wittenberg, and the Count of Brandenburg. The Golden Bull also established the indivisibility of the Electoral States by establishing the principle of primogeniture for succession. This latter provision was gradually copied by many of the dynastic families; thus it eliminated strife over the division of lands following the death of a ruler. Introduction of this principle was to prove of great importance in the later growth of the territorial states. The Golden Bull further defined the rights and prerogatives of the Princes of the Realm and attempted to provide a pattern for the Imperial Diet. In general it may be said to have provided the aristocratic confederation of lay and ecclesiastical states with a constitutional structure.

---

[1] (1273-1347): (Adolf of Nassau, Albert of Habsburg, Henry of Luxemburg, Ludwig of Bavaria, and Frederick of Habsburg, the latter two being Emperors at the same time—Frederick 1314-1330, Ludwig 1314-1347).

During this era the Germans lived under many rulers. Disintegration of the duchies of Saxony and Franconia left the peoples of northwestern and western Germany under the rule of the archbishops of Cologne, Bremen, Treves, and Mainz, the bishops of Münster, Minden, Paderborn, and Halberstadt, the counts of Nassau, the landgraves of Hesse, and the dukes of Lüneburg-Braunschweig. The latter duchy was to provide the basis for the later development of the Kingdom of Hanover, while the lands of the rulers of Hesse and Nassau, which occupied the junction of the Rhine and Main rivers were to evolve into principalities of the same name. The citizens of the cities of Lübeck, Bremen, Hamburg, Dortmund, Cologne, Aix-la-Chapelle, and Frankfort had been free from the old feudal lords for a considerable time and now these cities were recognized as imperial cities.

In the territory of the old Duchy of Swabia, which had been ruled by the Hohenstaufen family, the land was already under control of the Count Palatine of the Rhine and the Counts of Württemberg. The Habsburgs and the Bishops of Augsburg held wide areas in the southern part of the duchy, while the population of the towns along the Rhine, Neckar, and Danube, such as Strasbourg, Worms, Speyer, Heilbronn, Ulm, and Augsburg, lived in imperial cities. The Bavarian area was in the hands of the dukes of Bavaria, the burgraves of Nuremberg, and the bishops of Würzburg and Bamberg. Central Germany was ruled by the landgraves of Thuringia, the Counts and Electors of Saxony, and the Archbishop of Magdeburg. The eastern portion of the Reich which had been brought under German control through colonization during the tenth to twelfth centuries, was largely in the hands of the imperial Luxemburg family; however, the Teutonic Knights and the Slavic princes of Mecklenburg and Pomerania, who ruled as vassals of the Emperor, held large tracts of land in the north along the Baltic. The southeastern portion of the Empire was firmly held by the Habsburg family.

These numerous lay and ecclesiastical states, which had gained sovereignty after the collapse of the Hohenstaufen dynasty, exercised complete independence in the management of their internal and external affairs. The Emperor was hardly more than the titular head of a loose confederation of independent states. The lay rulers of the developing territorial states were aided by a court composed of a body of knights. They were also assisted by a scribe, the prototype of the chancellor. Justice was entrusted to a Palace Court (*Hofgericht*) composed of trusted knights. The control of affairs within the state was carried out through a system of regional bailiwicks (*Vogteien*) headed by officials, who were responsible to the ruler, these officials were invested with military, judicial, and tax powers.

The disintegration of the feudal structure after the fall of the Hohenstaufens, coupled with the constant family divisions of the once indivisible fiefs, placed the feudal lords in a hopeless financial position. This condition they sought to remedy by granting privileges and immunities to their feudal retainers, who were in this way able to acquire absolute control of local affairs. The development of a system of patrimonial administration in rural areas, coupled with the growing independence of the ecclesiastical rulers within the area of the old fiefs and the emergence of free and imperial cities, destroyed the sovereign power of the lay rulers, except within their immediate family holdings.

The political situation was complicated further by the growth of the imperial and free cities and by the later development of City Leagues, created for the protection of commerce. The long struggle during the tenth to twelfth centuries between the burghers and the dukes and bishops had ended with a victory for the cities. This success made possible the organization of self-government and the administration of internal affairs. Most of the cities were governed by a city council composed of members from local commercial and artisan guilds. The councils, which were headed by from two to four Mayors, dealt with matters relating to trade and industry, justice, public safety, defense, taxes and finance, and welfare and education. The administration of each city was headed by the Mayor, who came largely from the patrician merchant class. City government dealt with the regulation of the markets, the maintenance of public baths, streets and the water supply, and the inspection of buildings and houses. Many of the cities established local postal systems; others maintained fire brigades. Welfare, public health (including hospitals), and education, which had been entirely under the control of the Church, were gradually taken over by the cities.

As indicated above, the autonomous cities secured their freedom within the troubled Empire by associating themselves in leagues designed for protection of their independence and trade. In the North the Hanseatic League, which evolved from an alliance of Hamburg and Lübeck, embraced over ninety coastal and inland cities by the middle of the fourteenth century. Along the Rhine, peace was secured by an alliance of the cities of Worms and Mainz; this association was joined later by numerous lay and ecclesiastical princes, as well as by other towns. The Swabian city league was formed in the southwestern portion of the Empire for the protection of the cities against the Counts of Württemberg.

The power of the temporal and spiritual princes was curbed further by the growth of associations of the petty nobility. The Imperial Knights of Swabia, Franconia, and the Rhineland joined together to protect their insecure position against the cities on the one hand and the Princes of the Realm on the other. While the knights were able to protect their position within the Empire by constant warfare against their enemies, their independent status was being undermined slowly by the disintegration of the manorial system and the advent of the citizen foot soldier. The early medieval social and economic system was breaking up. It was a period of transition and the old medieval ways were slowly giving way to more modern forms. Although the legal and political bonds of feudalism survived for many centuries, the heart of the old system had been destroyed by the economic changes of the twelfth and thirteenth centuries. The lay rulers became more and more dependent upon the prelates, knights, and burghers for financial support and governmental cooperation. As early as the thirteenth century, these groups had brought about the establishment of Territorial Diets (*Landstände*) to handle local governmental affairs. During the fifteenth century, the tendency toward state disorganization gradually came to an end as the stronger dynastic families began to restore their lost rights and privileges through military action. The advent of more prosperous conditions, resulting from the commercial and craft activities of the cities, demanded protection from the violence and disorder left behind by the feudal system.

Even though the government and administration of the land had passed into the hands of the lay and ecclesiastical princes, the petty nobility, and the cities, the Emperor and the Imperial Diet were constantly faced with tasks of defense and internal security. The Luxemburg Emperors turned frequently to the Imperial Diet for a general levy of troops from all parts of the Empire. Military levies were often voted, but it was more difficult to persuade the Imperial Diet to raise taxes on its constituent members. In the field of justice, the Emperor had lost all the old prerogatives of the crown. Under the Luxemburg Emperors, Wenzel, Sigismund, and Albert II, an attempt was made to provide for public peace and internal security by a division of the realm into districts in which the local princes and cities would assume responsibility for public order. Since the administration of justice was now entirely in the hands of the courts of the quarreling territorial states, this attempt failed because of the lack of a strong central power.

The last years of Luxemburg rule were filled with strife. The Habsburgs were in constant conflict with the Swiss, while the Swabian and Rhenish city leagues warred continuously with the Counts of Württemberg and the Count Palatine of the Rhine. The political situation was also complicated by troubles within the Church. In 1414 representatives from all parts of Christian Europe gathered at Constance to consider ways of Church reform and methods for the suppression of heresy. Although the efforts for Church reform failed, action was taken against heresy. John Hus of Bohemia, who was placed under the ban in 1410, was captured after a guarantee of free conduct (1415) and executed, precipitating the Hussite War (1419-1436) in which the imperial army was defeated and driven from Bohemia. Although Sigismund defeated the Hussites at Böhmisch-Brod in 1434, nevertheless the cause of the House of Luxemburg was lost.

In 1438 the emperorship passed to the Habsburg family, who were destined to rule the Holy Roman Empire from that time until its dissolution in 1806. The Habsburg Emperors faced the task of holding together a land divided against itself. The Imperial Realm, which theoretically had once embraced all of Christendom, was divided into over three hundred states, principalities, and cities, held together by only the loosest form of imperial control. Significantly, Habsburg Austria, Hohenzollern Brandenburg, Wettin Saxony, Wittelsbach Bavaria, and Württemberg had already assumed important positions within the German body politic. The Emperor, who was chosen by the seven princely electors, could act only by consent of the Imperial Diet, which was composed of the Chamber of Electors, the Chamber of the Princes of the Realm, and the Chamber of Imperial Cities. The individual states and principalities possessed sovereign powers, reserving to themselves the management of all their external and internal affairs.

The Habsburg Emperor Maximilian I (1493-1519) attempted to find a formula for maintenance of the public peace within the Empire. After long discussions the Diet established the Court of the Imperial Chamber (*Reichskammergericht*). This high court, which was composed of members appointed by the Emperor and the Imperial Diet, worked through ten regional judicial areas. Although it functioned until 1806, it did not solve the political problems of the Empire, since most of the political troubles derived from lack of central authority.

The Emperor's powers were limited to foreign relations, to the appointment of certain imperial councils, to the granting of imperial fiefs and titles, and to the conferring of university degrees. Political power had shifted to the territorial states which were slowly expanding their control by dynastic aggrandizement. Many of the families secured their territorial holdings against further dynastic bickering by establishing the principle of primogeniture for succession. The revival of the power of the territorial state was further strengthened by the establishment of standing armies, which replaced the feudal levies, and by the creation of new court systems administered by state officials. The Empire, which could not escape disunity and weakness in this welter of internal rivalry and bickering, became more and more a venerable tradition, respected by all Europeans, but incapable of direct action in the political troubles of the day.

After the failure of Maximilian's attempt at imperial reform, the Habsburgs turned their energies more and more to dynastic expansion, leaving the affairs of empire to shift for themselves. Under Charles V the Habsburgs fell heir to the kingdoms of Aragon, Naples, and Castile and their American colonies, to the Burgundian lands, which included the Netherlands, and the kingdoms of Bohemia and Hungary, which they added to their traditional holdings in Austria and along the Upper Rhine. This dominion was the inheritance of

Charles V. His reign, however, was marked not only by the consummation of the Habsburg program of dynastic expansion, but also by the beginning of the Protestant Reformation. In 1520 Luther was excommunicated from the Church. Charles V, desirous of maintaining the support of the Catholic Church which was necessary for the maintenance of Habsburg power in Europe, attempted to bring an end to the Lutheran revolt at the Imperial Diet of Worms (1521). Despite his efforts, the Protestant Revolt, which was based upon serious economic issues affecting the welfare of the knights and peasants, as well as upon the universal desire for reform within and without the Church, spread rapidly throughout the land, splitting the people into two sharply divided religious camps.

The first years of the Reformation brought several severe economic changes. In the early years of the Lutheran revolt, the Protestant princes profited at the expense of the Catholic Church by seizing vast areas of ecclesiastical land. Their prosperity was ephemeral for the drastic inflation produced by the flood of gold and silver from the New World destroyed the financial basis of the states. The knights were able to take advantage of the desperate financial condition of the princes, because of their control of local taxation. The knights and the wealthy burghers of the towns were once more able to reassert themselves in government through the agency of the local Diets. As has been noted before, conflicts between the rulers, knights, and peasants led to the Knights' War (1522) and the Peasants' Revolt (1525); these contests were followed by the struggle of the Catholic and the Protestant Leagues. The strife and trouble dragged on until the temporary peace of Augsburg in 1555, which allowed the princes, imperial cities, and imperial knights to choose between the Lutheran faith and the Catholic Church. The failure of the Peace of Augsburg to allow for other Protestant groups, and its impossible arrangements for the settlement of difficulties between the Church and the princes who had seized ecclesiastical lands, prepared the way for further trouble.

Once the Catholic and Protestant Leagues were re-formed during the first decade of the century, the Thirty Years' War (1618-1648) was inevitable. The war opened in Protestant Bohemia, where the Habsburgs broke the arrangements for religious toleration. The next phase was marked by the entry of Danish forces and the third phase of the long war opened with the intervention of Swedish forces under Gustavus Adolphus, who sought to support German Protestantism in order to gain territorial holdings in Baltic Germany. Under the leadership of the Catholic Cardinal, Richelieu, the French entered the war in 1635 on the Protestant side because of their desire to gain control of Habsburg possessions in western Germany and the Low Countries.

This long series of wars, which had been fought almost entirely within the frontiers of the Empire, left Germany seriously depopulated and in a state of general exhaustion. Two-thirds of the German population had been slaughtered and five-sixths of the villages had been plundered and destroyed. Large areas of land had gone out of cultivation, while trade had been taken over by the French and Dutch.

The Treaty of Westphalia, which really consisted of a series of treaties negotiated at Münster and Osnabrück, brought the restoration of peace. These treaties, which were negotiated by representatives of France and Sweden and by delegates of the electors, princes, and imperial cities, marked the end of the political power of the Holy Roman Empire. While the pattern of the struggle had been determined by religious differences, there were other real issues—dynastic, political, and economic. The war had brought to an end the power and prestige of the Habsburg Dynastic Empire, and had destroyed the fiction of the universal supremacy of the Holy Roman Empire. The German states were at last free to assume positions within the emerging European state system. Divided and enfeebled, Germany was open for foreign intervention.

Sweden received the Isle of Rügen and western Pomerania (Vorpommern) as a fief of the Empire, while France obtained scattered territories in Alsace-Lorraine. Both states were awarded votes in the Imperial Diet. The Peace of Westphalia also brought the first serious territorial losses to the Empire, for both Switzerland and the United Netherlands were given their freedom. There were also several important territorial changes within the Empire. Brandenburg, which had lost western Pomerania to Sweden, received as indemnification eastern Pomerania and the secularized bishoprics of Halberstadt, Minden, Cammin, and Magdeburg. The Duke of Brunswick received the secularized bishopric of Osnabrück, while the ruler of Mecklenburg obtained the bishoprics of Schwerin and Ratzeburg.

The settlement of domestic affairs involved a general amnesty and the recognition of the sovereignty of the German states. Furthermore, the treaty permitted the German states to handle their own foreign affairs and to form foreign and domestic alliances as long as these were not directed against the Emperor. In ecclesiastical matters of the Empire, the Catholic and Protestant states were given equality; and the religious toleration granted by the Peace of Augsburg was extended to include the Calvinists. The difficult problem of church lands was solved by recognizing the property changes which had taken place during the war. An interesting feature of the peace was its guaranty by France and Sweden.

The Peace of Westphalia left Germany divided into some three hundred sovereign states and about fifteen hundred small quasi-sovereign principalities and imperial cities. Economic conditions were serious within these numerous states. The merchant aristocracy, which had played a dominant part in European finance and commerce during the sixteenth century, had been destroyed.

The powerful leagues of cities had been abandoned because of financial troubles. Destruction of the rising middle class of the cities was accompanied by impoverishment of the peasantry. Schools and ecclesiastical centers, which had played an important role in the brief German Renaissance of the days of Maximilian and Charles V, were closed. Scholars, scientists, and artists like Erasmus, Helgesen, Dürer, Holbein, Kepler, Paracelsus, and von Gesner, had no immediate successors. The intellectual and artistic man disappeared as the masses turned to religious enthusiasm and superstition.

The Electors continued to vote the imperial crown to the Habsburgs; but their position as emperors became hopeless after all political power had passed to the states. The Imperial Diet, which received its final form at Regensburg in 1663, consisted of the eight Electors (*Kurfürsten*), the sixty-nine ecclesiastical princes, the ninety-six lay princes, and representatives from the imperial cities. Religious matters had passed into the hands of the *Corpus Catholicorum* and the *Corpus Evangelicorum,* the corporate organizations of the Catholic and Protestant churches. Although the Court of the Imperial Chamber was restored and placed under equal numbers of Catholics and Protestants, it had few functions of importance. The decline of the imperial government was marked by the gradually increasing power of the territorial states.

The affairs of Germany quickly passed into the hands of the Hohenzollerns of Brandenburg, the Wettins of Saxony, the Wittelsbachs of Bavaria, and the rulers of Hanover. These rulers, who had profited from seizing wide areas of ecclesiastical lands, were at last free from political interference on the part of the Emperor and the Imperial Diet. Each of the ruling dynasties turned to political intrigue and war for the purpose of territorial aggrandizement.

The Austrian Habsburgs emerged from the Thirty Years' War in control of Austria, Bohemia, Silesia, and Hungary; but their energies were divided between wars with the Turks in the Middle Danubian basin and wars with Louis XIV along the Rhine. In the East the struggle culminated in the acquisition by Austria of extensive tracts of land along the Danube, while the wars with the French came to a temporary pause with the treaty of Utrecht (1713), which awarded to the Habsburgs the Spanish Netherlands, the Duchy of Milan, and the Kingdom of the Two Sicilies.

After the Thirty Years' War the politics of the Empire in the north were dominated by the Hohenzollern Electors of Brandenburg, and under the Great Elector, Frederick William (1640-1688), Brandenburg developed into a strong power. His son and successor, Frederick III, was granted the rank of King *in* Prussia by the Emperor in 1701 (King Frederick I). He continued the internal reforms and military preparations initiated by the Great Elector, and prepared the way for an expansion of Prussia under Frederick the Great (1740-1786) who was the first to call himself King *of* Prussia. Rivalry between Prussia and

Austria, which had been developing gradually in the early eighteenth century, led to the War of the Austrian Succession (1740-1748). This war brought into being the alliance of Prussia, France, and Bavaria against Austria, the Netherlands, and England, and ended with Frederick the Great in possession of Silesia. The next struggle between Prussia and Austria came with the Seven Years' War (1756-1763), which found Prussia and England allied against Austria, France, Russia, Sweden, and Saxony. Frederick the Great completed his territorial program by participating with the rulers of Austria and Russia in the partition of Poland. Prussia had emerged at last as the most powerful of the German states, providing the bastion around which the later German Empire was to develop in the late nineteenth century.

During the period following the Peace of Westphalia each state had rapidly developed its own particular brand of despotism. The formation of the absolute state in Germany came gradually after 1648. Its beginning may be seen in the Privy Council, 1604 (*Geheimer Rat*) of Prussia and in the councils, administrative offices, and chancelleries (*Räte, Regierungen, und Kanzleien*) established in the other German states during the late seventeenth and early eighteenth centuries. Growth in the power of state governments brought about the departmentalization of the central administration to meet the increasing complexity of state business. The strengthening of the power of the central government was accompanied by an extension of control over local affairs. The territorial units were brought under agents of the crown. These steps brought a gradual elimination of the territorial Diets and other institutions of self-government, which had been formed during the late Middle Ages.

The cities, which had enjoyed great independence under the rule of the patrician merchants and guilds, were also brought under state control by subordinating their councils to traveling tax commissioners. The administration of justice was centralized and the powers of the police, which had now been brought under a lose state control, were extended to all aspects of internal administration. Legal reform, which had started in Renaissance times with the modification of local bodies of law through the introduction of principles of Roman law, was carried forward by the princes. After the reign of the Emperor, Charles V, the local common law and city codes were rewritten in terms of Roman law. As a corollary to this change, the period between the Peace of Westphalia and the French Revolution was marked by a systematic codification of law in many of the German states.

The development of the absolute states with a centralized government directly responsible to the rulers was accompanied by numerous paternalistic social and economic reforms initiated by the enlightened despots. Extensive agrarian improvements, road and canal construction, and craft and industrial developments, were made possible by the introduction of advanced techniques from western Europe. In Prussia a common school system was introduced and elementary education was made compulsory. The governmental and administrative reforms and the enlightened patronage of the despots did not, however, bridge the growing gap between the rulers of the states and the mass of the German people. In many ways the reforms had not solved the basic problems of government and administration within the states. The necessary compromises had only created cumbersome central governments and established arbitrary local controls, which excluded the mass of the people from participation in governmental affairs.

GERMANY OF NAPOLEONIC DAYS

The Revolutionary and Napoleonic Wars laid the foundations for modern Germany through the destruction of the old order. Germany was ripe for change. The wide differences in government, customs, and laws among the almost numberless states, coupled with the economic disunity created by the numerous customs barriers which divided the land into a mosaic of independent economic units, impeded commercial advancement. The miserable condition of the peasantry and the increasing demands of the slowly reviving middle class in the towns required fundamental changes. The old Regime had to be brought to an end to prepare the way for modern social and economic institutions.

Within the worn-out Empire the reorganization of life began slowly after the Declaration of Pillnitz in 1791; this document brought with it the threat of Austrian and Prussian intervention in the French Revolution. The French, beset by revolt and by the fear of intervention on the part of Austria, declared war upon the Habsburgs in 1792. They were successful in the first part of the struggle against the Austrian and Prussian Coalition, which had sought to protect the interests of the French Crown. By 1793 the French had occupied Savoy, the lands to the west of the Rhine, and the Austrian Netherlands.

The Napoleonic phase of the wars opened with the Italian campaign, which brought the French occupation of the Austrian Duchy of Milan. During this period the Prussian and Spanish forces deserted the coalition, leaving Austria, England and Sardinia to deal with the French under Napoleon. After the Egyptian campaign (1798-1799) Napoleon, who had meanwhile established himself as the first Consul of France, renewed the war with Austria. The war ended with the French in complete possession of the left bank of the Rhine and resulted in the consequent indemnification of the rulers who had lost territory to France. This exchange was the first of a long series of territorial adjustments which led to the official end of the Holy Roman Empire in 1806. The redistribution of lands was undertaken by the Imperial Committee (*Reichsdeputationshauptausschuss*) at Regensburg. The arrangements negotiated there in 1803 resulted in the abolition of all ecclesiastical states except the archbishopric of Mainz and the dissolution of all the forty-eight imperial cities, except Hamburg, Bremen, Lübeck, Frankfort, Nuremberg, and Augsburg. Prussia gained extensive holdings in Westphalia, Hanover, and Franconia, while the Counts of Baden added bits of land to the northern and southern portions of their holdings along the Rhine. The Electors of Bavaria managed to acquire most of the Franconian lands along the Main which had belonged to the bishops of Bamberg and Würzburg. These territorial arrangements brought the number of German states down to less than one hundred.

The next phase of the Napoleonic Wars (1803-1806) brought about a second reorganization of the German land. After the battle of Austerlitz, Napoleon dissolved the Holy Roman Empire and assumed the role of Protector over wide areas of western Germany. The Confederation of the Rhine, which was established by the French for the management of German affairs, included at its height Bavaria, Württemberg, Baden, Hesse, Nassau, Westphalia, Thuringia, and Saxony. Within this political framework, the leaders of Baden, Bavaria, and Württemberg managed to add large areas to their respective territories.

The Napoleonic War with Prussia and Russia between 1806 and 1807 brought further French successes and still more territorial rearrangements. The victories of the French over the Prussians at Jena (1806) and over the Russians at Friedland (1807) led to important changes. France seized the larger part of northwestern Germany; northwestern Hanover, Oldenburg, Bremen, Hamburg, and Lübeck were annexed to the French Empire; and eastern Westphalia and southern Hanover were organized as the Kingdom of Westphalia. In the East the Duchy of Warsaw was reconstructed out of the partitioned divisions of the old Polish Kingdom. At this juncture, the states of Mecklenburg, Thuringia, and Saxony joined the Confederation of the Rhine. Napoleonic power continued to grow until 1812, despite the effects of the continental blockade imposed by the English Navy and the French reverses sustained in the Peninsular Wars.

The decline of Napoleonic power came with the disastrous campaign against Russia in 1812, which opened the way for German participation in the Wars of Liberation, the foundation for which was slowly being laid between 1806 and 1812. Prussia, which was to take the lead in the struggle to expel the French, undertook a series of important political and economic reforms under the leadership of Freiherr vom Stein and Prince Hardenberg. Self-government was granted to the Prussian cities. Serfdom was abolished and limited amounts of land were granted to the new peasantry. The old restrictions upon the guilds were eliminated, opening the way for modern economic and financial developments. In 1812 the Jews were granted equal political rights. There were even hopes of creating a new Parliament and a further decentralization of the ad-

ministrative system. These reforms, which had been inspired by the same philosophy that lay back of the French Revolution, brought about the internal
regeneration of Prussia, preparing her for leadership of the Germans in the last
phase of the Napoleonic Wars.

The spirit of reform was also making itself felt in other parts of Germany.
In Bavaria, Montgelas undertook the reorganization of the state government.
In 1808, he destroyed the old territorial system and divided the land, for pur-
poses of state administration, into eight districts (*Kreise*), corresponding to the
Prussian administrative divisions. In the areas under French control and influ-
ence, forms of local government and law were copied after French models.
These reforms of government and administration had at last eliminated the
feudal survivals which had plagued the eighteenth century states.

After Napoleon's retreat from Russia, Prussia joined with Austria, Russia,
and England, and the coalition defeated Napoleon in the famous Battle of Leipzig (1813). In 1814 the Allies invaded France and forced the abdication of
Napoleon. In the same year the victorious Allies met at Vienna to undertake
the reconstruction of Europe. The negotiations of the Congress of Vienna were
unfortunately interrupted by the return of Napoleon from Elba. Although
Napoleon was finally defeated at Waterloo, the renewed Napoleonic aggression
had a profound effect upon the negotiations for peace.

The Treaty of Vienna and the Germanic Confederation (Deutscher Bund)

The Congress of Vienna, which met from November 1814 to June 1815, was
dominated by the five great powers—Russia, England, Austria, Prussia, and
France. Their work was frequently opposed by the smaller states, which were
constantly protesting their exclusion from the negotiations; however, the real
change in the character of the negotiations which was to effect the fate of the
Germanies came after Waterloo, when the Prussian delegates abandoned their
position as the champions of liberalism and nationalism. The work of the Congress was based upon the restoration of the Old Order. There was a complete
disregard of the nationalism which had made possible the defeat of Napoleon.
Nevertheless, the legacy of the Napoleonic territorial reorganizations had an
important influence upon the negotiations. The destruction of the Holy Roman
Empire, which had long outlived its usefulness, necessitated the reorganization
of the German government. This task was simplified by reason of the fact that
the difficult political situation of the eighteenth century had been considerably
cleared through elimination of vast numbers of small lay and ecclesiastical
states. However, the Congress of Vienna had not dealt adequately with the
ever increasing demands for constitutional government: a desire for which
was a legacy of the democratic movement of the Napoleonic era.

The governmental and territorial arrangements imposed by the Congress had a profound effect upon all of Central Europe. The territory of Germany, which was defined by the Act of Vienna, was organized into a loose federation, composed of thirty-four sovereign principalities and four free cities, which were at last permitted to develop governmental systems along more modern lines. In the West, Switzerland, whose independence had been recognized by the Peace of Westphalia, was increased in size at the expense of Italy and France. The Alsace-Lorraine area on the left bank of the Rhine was ceded to France. In the Northwest, the Austrian Netherlands (later Belgium) was placed under the Dutch Kingdom, permitting the King of the Netherlands to become a member of the new Germanic Confederation. The King of Denmark occupied a similar position, since he was left in control of the Duchies of Schleswig-Holstein. In the East the Big Five quarreled over the disposition of Poland. The compromise, which was arranged by France between the opposing Russian-Prussian and Austro-English factions, resulted in a repartition of the Polish area. Austria received Galicia, while Prussia obtained control of West Prussia and Posen, and the Russians added central Poland to their Empire.

The internal territorial reorganization of Germany was even more complex. Prussia gained the lion's share of the spoils. Sweden gave up the isle of Rügen and western Pomerania. In the West the old Hohenzollern holdings in Westphalia and the northern Rhineland were enlarged to form Westphalia and the Rhine Province. The northern part of the Kingdom of Saxony, which had aided Napoleon in 1813, was ceded to Prussia. Most of the area was combined with the Altmark region to form the modern Province of Saxony (*Provinz Sachsen*). The remaining Prussian lands were reorganized to form the provinces of *Pomerania, Brandenburg, Silesia, Posen,* and *Prussia.* In the Northwest the Kingdom of Hanover, which was still united with the British Crown, was revived and enlarged through the addition of East Friesland, which had been under Prussian control during the late eighteenth century. The other states of North Germany, which were recognized under the Act of Vienna, included Mecklenburg, Oldenburg, Brunswick, Anhalt, Waldeck, Lippe, and Schaumburg-Lippe and the free cities of Hamburg, Bremen, and Lübeck.

In Central Germany, the numerous Thuringian principalities and duchies gained recognition, while the Grand Duchy of Hesse-Darmstadt, the Duchy of Nassau, the Principality of Hesse-Kassel, and the Free City of Frankfort emerged in Western Germany. In South Germany the Grand Duchy of Baden and the new Kingdom of Württemberg were allowed to retain control of the territories they had acquired during the Napoleonic Wars. Bavaria obtained control of the Ansbach and Bayreuth areas, completing her mastery of the Franconian region along the Main. German Austria was enlarged by the addition of Salzburg and the return of the Tyrol, which had been under Bavarian rule during the Napoleonic era. The territory of the Habsburgs, which formed an integral part of the Germanic Confederation, included Upper Austria (*Oberösterreich*), Lower Austria (*Niederösterreich*), Styria (*Steiermark*), Carinthinia (*Kärnten*), Carniola (*Krain*), Illyria (*Illyrien*), Moravia (*Mähren*), and Bohemia (*Böhmen*). Beyond the frontiers of the Confederation, the Habsburgs ruled Lombardy, Venetia, Croatia, Hungary, and Galicia.

The Confederation was pledged to the maintenance of internal and external security and the independence of the member states. The latter were represented in a Federal Diet (*Bundestag*) consisting of delegates appointed by the local sovereigns and subject to their instructions. The Diet, which met at Frankfort under the presidency of Austria, had a distinct international flavor, since it included representatives of the crowns of England, of the Netherlands, and of Denmark, as well as delegations representing the German states and cities. The Diet was further organized into a narrower assembly (*Engere Versammlung*) in which the eleven largest states possessed one vote, while the twenty-eight smaller states shared six votes. This body handled the ordinary business, but extraordinary measures required a two-thirds vote of the General Assembly (*Plenum*), in which the various states were represented according to their importance. Although the constitution of the Confederation gave the Diet the right to deal with all matters of mutual interest, such as internal and external security and commercial and navigation problems, its competence was actually very limited. The Diet was empowered to deal with questions relating to constitutional liberties and religious toleration, but did nothing in these fields until 1848. The first Act of Confederation was supplemented by the constitutional act of 1820, which defined the powers of the Diet in cases of war and revolution.

The Confederation was destined to failure, for it had not provided Germany with the unifying national government, which was becoming more and more necessary due to the expansion and development of trade and industry. It also failed to satisfy the wide-spread demands for a free national life regulated by constitutional guarantees. The Confederation was essentially a product of Austrian diplomacy under Metternich, which sought to deny both liberty and unity to the Germans in the interests of the Austrian Crown. The two dominant powers within the Confederation, Austria and Prussia, were both discontented with their constitutional positions. Their rivalry for control of German affairs constantly colored the political life of the day.

After the spirit of liberal reform had given way to reactionary oppression, the concerns of the people of Germany remained under the firm rule of the princes of the realm. The Peace of Vienna had not taken into account the major effects of the Revolutionary and Napoleonic Wars. It had ignored the genuine national feeling which had been generated among the peoples of all parts of the Reich during the later years of the struggle against Napoleon. It had ignored completely the movement for national constitutional liberty, although it had provided that each of the thirty-four states should frame and promulgate a state constitution.

During the period between the Congress of Vienna and the Revolution of 1848, there were frequent attempts to initiate movements for national and state constitutions as well as attempts to bring about the establishment of a truly national government. These movements were supported by the faculties and students of the universities, by liberal lawyers and journalists, and by the more enlightened sections of the middle class. They culminated first in the famous Wartburg Festival of 1817, at which the liberals made direct demands for national liberty and unity. The opposition, which was led by Metternich of Austria and Hardenberg of Prussia, produced the famous Carlsbad Resolutions (1819), which provided for the supervision of the universities and the press and laid down the principle that no constitution inconsistent with monarchial rule should be tolerated within the Germanic Confederation. When the German states met at Vienna in 1820, Metternich, the leader of the forces of reaction, faced a liberal opposition led by the rulers of Bavaria, Württemberg, Baden, and Hesse-Darmstadt, who had granted constitutions between 1818 and 1820. These states, with the diplomatic support of Russia and England, defeated Metternich's effort to strengthen the federal Diet in order to make it an instrument of political oppression.

After 1820 the four South German states achieved a liberal form of government. They became constitutional as well as hereditary monarchies, with bicameral legislatures consisting of an aristocratic upper chamber and an almost democratic lower chamber. The delegates to the lower house were elected on the basis of secret and direct (and in some cases universal) male suffrage. Administrative reforms had brought about the establishment of Councils of State, State Ministries, and Supreme Administrative Courts to deal with the business of state government. Reforms in local administration had brought about the reorganization of the state territory into provinces and smaller county units and had granted a certain measure of local self-government.

The revolutionary movement of 1830, which swept France and Western Europe, produced only minor repercussions in Germany. Liberal movements in the Kingdoms of Hanover and Saxony, the Duchy of Brunswick, and the principalities of Hesse and Lippe led to the granting of constitutions. Prussia, Oldenburg, Anhalt, and most of the tiny duchies and principalities of Thuringia managed to resist the constitutional movement until after 1848. Although the political movements for unity and liberty were easily suppressed by the governments of Austria and Prussia, important economic changes were beginning to force political decisions. At the beginning of the nineteenth century,

Germany was still dominated by a medieval economy. Over eighty per cent of the population derived its living from agriculture. The medieval institution of serfdom was still present. In the Northeast it formed the basis of the rural economy. In the western parts of the Reich the open field system still prevailed, while the traditional three-field crop system was common everywhere. In towns the economy was in the hands of artisans and merchants, who were organized in guilds, which had established endless regulations for manufacturing and commerce. While technical improvements introduced in the eighteenth century had brought isolated advances, the economy of Germany was still extremely primitive. Economic conditions were complicated further by the fact that each of the thirty-eight states (34 principalities and 4 free cities) had its own currency, taxes, laws, and tariffs. Agricultural, industrial, and commercial advances were impossible under these conditions.

The first half of the nineteenth century brought a gradual improvement in economic conditions. During the first years of the century Prussia abolished serfdom. While emancipation of the serfs led to the formation of an independent peasantry in Western and Central Germany, it created a dependent tenant class in the Northeast, where the Junker class managed to obtain most of the agricultural land. The freeing of the serfs was followed by the introduction of new agricultural methods, the introduction of a modern form of crop rotation, and the rapid increase of agricultural production. In the towns the abuses of the archaic guild system were slowly being eliminated.

The improvement of commercial conditions, which was prerequisite to any betterment of the general economy, came with the gradual formation of the Customs Union. In 1818 Prussia eliminated all of the internal tariffs and began negotiations with the other German states for the formation of such a union. By 1834 over two-thirds of the German area was included within the Prussian organization. The effect of this movement was profound. It brought not only an extension of the commercial areas, but made possible an advance of both internal and foreign trade. The growth of the Customs Union also coincided with the introduction of the railway, which added impetus to the commercial development resulting from the elimination of internal tariffs. The commercial advances were followed by the beginnings of industrialization, which was to eliminate the artisan and guild system by the end of the century. The Customs Union formed the first important step toward political unification. The rising middle class which was emerging through the development of industry and commerce, became more and more interested in German unity. Prussia's leadership in this movement tended to shift the attention of the Germans from Vienna to Berlin. Germany was at last prepared economically for a political change.

The French revolution of 1848 touched off a series of revolutionary movements which spread throughout Europe. In Austria the liberals forced Metternich from office. Revolutions broke out among the Slavs of Bohemia. Austria, beset by internal upheaval and by nationalistic uprisings in Hungary and northern Italy, did not set a good example for the other German states. The Austrian revolution was followed by disturbances in Berlin which were quickly suppressed by the King of Prussia, although he was forced to grant a measure of constitutional reform. The liberals, taking advantage of all of these difficulties, called for the formation of a national constituent assembly.

The National Assembly, which met at Frankfort in 1848, was composed of delegates elected by direct manhood suffrage. The Assembly was dominated by middle class lawyers, professors, judges, civil servants, and businessmen, for most of the conservative delegates refused to participate in the task of drafting an enlightened constitution. After extended discussions and exhaustive debates, the assembly issued a well formulated constitution for a federal Empire to replace the weak and reactionary Confederation. In the spring of 1848 the liberals had every reason to hope for success, but a gradual renewal of conservative opposition and mistrust of radical elements doomed the plan to failure.

The work of the Assembly was also disturbed by the Schleswig-Holstein incident which had been precipitated by the efforts of the King of Denmark to incorporate Schleswig into his kingdom on the basis of inheritance. The revolt of the duchies against Danish occupation led to Prussian intervention, which was supported by the Frankfort Assembly. The Armistice of Malmö and the Peace of 1850 brought only a temporary solution. Liberal sentiment gave way, and the rulers of the German states gradually regained control of the situation. The forces of reaction and absolutism triumphed and the course of German history was turned into reactionary channels. Prussia, which had supported the work of the Assembly, turned against it when Friedrich Wilhelm declared that he would neither accept the leadership of the proposed federal empire nor the crown from "butchers and bakers." The National Assembly had failed. Prussia's Union Scheme, which was formulated by the Erfurt Parliament (1850) and the Conference of States at Dresden, also failed. The old Germanic Confederation was re-established to handle the affairs of the German states. The failure of the revolutionary movement of 1848 with its hopes for national unity and economic reorganization was followed by the restoration of the Confederation under the leadership of Austria and Prussia.

The Prussian conservatives now concluded that it was Prussia's mission to bring about the unification of Germany. Economic developments involving the improvement of agriculture and the beginnings of the industrialization of Germany, which had brought the land to a transitional position between a rural agrarian and an urban industrial economy, were rapidly preparing the way for political and administrative measures. In 1862 Bismarck became Prime Minister of Prussia. His regime brought a new approach to the problem of unification. He prepared the way within Prussia by discrediting the liberals and their parliamentary institutions through a program of militarization aimed at making Prussia the dominant German power. The liberal parliamentary opposition was crushed when Bismarck ignored the rights of the Prussian Assembly.

Military action was precipitated by Denmark's annexation of Schleswig. Austria and Prussia were determined to prevent the Danish Crown from incorporating the duchy. In 1864 the Austrian and Prussian forces defeated Denmark and occupied the two duchies. Austria desired that they be placed under the Prince of Augustenburg, while Bismarck, who had long been seeking grounds for a war with Austria in order to expel her from the Confederation, seized upon this opportunity to precipitate the military action which would at last make possible the unification of Germany. After carefully isolating Austria through diplomatic arrangements with Italy, France, and Russia, Bismarck proposed a reorganization of the Confederation. Austria countered by bringing the Schleswig-Holstein issue before the Federal Diet; whereupon Prussia denounced the Austrian move. In 1866 the Federal Diet upon the motion of Austria ordered a general mobilization against Prussia. Bismarck's long series of intrigues had at last borne fruit. The brief Seven Weeks' War followed Prussia's withdrawal from the Confederation. Austria was quickly defeated by the well trained Prussian army. The Treaty of Prague, which followed, ordered the dissolution of the old Confederation and the formation of a new Confederation which was to exclude Austria. Schleswig-Holstein, together with the states of Hanover, Nassau, Hesse-Kassel, and the Free City of Frankfort, all of which had sided with Austria, were annexed to Prussia.

North German Confederation (Norddeutscher Bund)

Bismarck's next move brought about the formation of the North German Confederation (*Norddeutscher Bund*), which consisted of the twenty-two states situated to the north of the Main River. The four southern states of Hesse-Darmstadt, Bavaria, Württemberg, and Baden were allowed to remain outside the Confederation, and later they made secret alliances with it. The constitution of the North German Confederation, which was largely written by Bismarck, provided for the establishment of a Federal Council (*Bundesrat*), composed of delegates of the states, and a *Reichstag,* composed of representatives of the people elected by universal manhood suffrage. The King of Prussia was made hereditary President of the Confederation. Prussia was at last entrenched as the leader of a powerful federal state, and Austria had finally been banished from the German body politic. Bismarck was the popular hero of Germany.

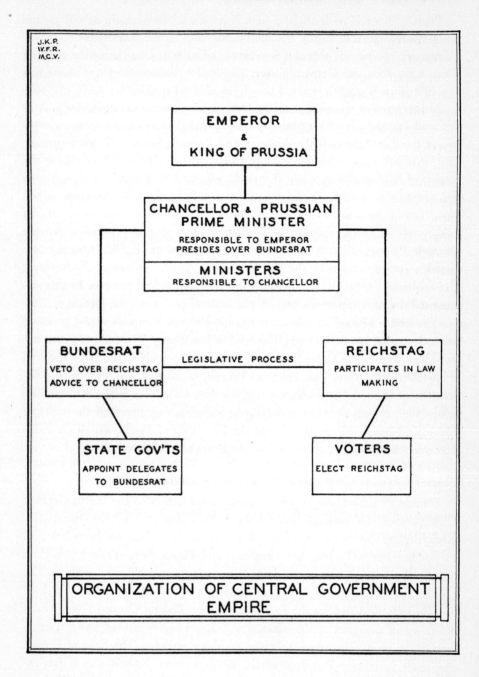

J.K.P.
W.F.R.
A.C.V.

EMPEROR
&
KING OF PRUSSIA

CHANCELLOR & PRUSSIAN
PRIME MINISTER
RESPONSIBLE TO EMPEROR
PRESIDES OVER BUNDESRAT

MINISTERS
RESPONSIBLE TO CHANCELLOR

BUNDESRAT
VETO OVER REICHSTAG
ADVICE TO CHANCELLOR

LEGISLATIVE PROCESS

REICHSTAG
PARTICIPATES IN LAW
MAKING

STATE GOV'TS
APPOINT DELEGATES
TO BUNDESRAT

VOTERS
ELECT REICHSTAG

ORGANIZATION OF CENTRAL GOVERNMENT
EMPIRE

THE SECOND REICH

The Franco-Prussian War (1870-1871), which grew partly out of France's efforts under Napoleon III to block the final unification of Germany and partly out of Bismarck's desire for a foreign war to use as an anvil upon which to forge the spiritual unification of the Reich, led to the formal proclamation of the German Empire at Versailles. The war had accomplished its purpose; for Bavaria, Baden, Württemberg, and Hesse-Darmstadt, after fighting in alliance with Prussia against France, joined the states of the North German Confederation. Although the way toward political unification had been prepared by the consolidation of the German states during the Napoleonic era, by the development of economic unity within the Customs Union, and by the emergence of state governments based upon constitutional laws, the final unification of the Reich was forged through political intrigue and military action. The diplomatic maneuvers and the wars of 1864, 1866, and 1871 had destroyed the Germanic Confederation, eliminated Austria from German politics, and placed the German states under the domination of Prussia.

The Second Reich was a federal empire consisting of Prussia, the seven smaller states of Baden, Bavaria, Württemberg, Saxony, Hesse, Mecklenburg-Schwerin, and Oldenburg, fifteen tiny states, and three free and imperial cities. Alsace-Lorraine had the status of an imperial territory within the Empire. The government of the Second Reich was based upon the Imperial Constitution of 1871, which was a revision of the constitution of the North German Confederation. It contained provisions for the inclusion of the four South German states, and for the elevation of the Prussian King from the rank of President to the dignity of Emperor. Under the Imperial Constitution the federal government of the Empire, which consisted of an Emperor, an Imperial Chancellor, Federal Council (*Bundesrat*), and the *Reichstag,* received certain limited and expressly enumerated powers. The new national government was given control of foreign affairs, military and naval matters, imperial finances, foreign commerce, posts and telegraphs (except in Bavaria and Württemberg), and matters relating to the use of railways for national defense. The laws of the empire took precedence over those of the states in matters affecting citizenship, regulation of banking, patents, copyrights, navigation, and labor, and the control of the press and associations. The national government also possessed prior rights in the fields of industrial, trade, and labor regulation, and social insurance. The administration of federal affairs, except in the case of foreign, naval, and postal matters, was carried out by the state governments under imperial supervision. The rights of the states, which were both enumerated and residual, extended to matters of interior, police, health, economic, fiscal, and cultural administration. Several of the states retained control of their military establishments, while

Saxony, Bavaria, and Württemberg continued to maintain diplomatic missions at Vienna, St. Petersburg, and the Vatican.

As the dominant power within the federal empire, Prussia enjoyed a special position. Constitutionally, the Prussian King was ex officio German Emperor. In the Federal Council Prussians held the presidency and the chairmanships of all standing committees. Within this body they possessed sufficient votes to defeat any constitutional amendment, and had a veto on all proposed changes respecting the army, the navy, and finances. Prussia was also granted the right to combine the important offices of the Prussian and the Imperial Chancellor. Prussia's dominant position within the Federal Council was further reinforced by her position as the largest and strongest of the German states, and was strengthened by her powerful army and efficient civil service.

The sovereignty of the Second Empire was in effect vested in the Federal Council, which was composed of representatives of the state governments. Representation of the states was not equal, for Prussia possessed seventeen of the sixty-one votes and controlled the three votes of Alsace-Lorraine and the one vote of Waldeck, because their administrations were under the Prussian King. Bavaria, the next largest state, had six votes, while Saxony, Württemberg, Baden, Hesse, Mecklenburg-Schwerin, and Brunswick had from two to four votes each in the Council. The seventeen smaller states had one vote each. At the meetings of this body, which were held under the chairmanship of the Chancellor, each state was usually represented by one delegate, who cast the votes as a single block upon the instructions of his government. The Federal Council occupied a central position in the government of the Empire because of its executive, legislative, judicial, and administrative functions and powers. In executive matters it shared the tasks of making treaties, authorizing appointments, and declaring war. It served as an administrative and consultative board, working through its eight standing committees for: army; marine; taxes; commerce and trade; railways, posts, and telegraphs; judicial affairs; accounts; and foreign affairs. In the field of legislation the Federal Council had full authority, determining what bills were to be brought before the *Reichstag* and what resolutions were passed by the same. It also served as the Supreme Constitutional and Administrative Court of the Empire, which rendered interpretations of the constitution and dealt with legal controversies between the states.

The executive function was vested in the Emperor, whose office was but a continuation of the presidency of the North German Confederation, cloaked in imperial dignity and made hereditary in the Hohenzollern family. The power of the Emperor was exercised in the name of the federated states. Constitutionally, the "Prussian" Emperor possessed several important functions. He was the supreme commander of the army and navy and exercised almost complete control over foreign affairs. He also had the right to convoke and prorogue both the Federal Council and the *Reichstag*. His right to appoint the Chancellor and other high governmental officials gave him an important position in the business of government. Although the functions and prerogatives invested the office of Emperor with considerable power, his real strength came from his position as the King of Prussia.

The traditional office of Chancellor (*Reichskanzler*) modified by Bismarck as an institution to suit his own particular talents, occupied a central position in the administration of the Empire. The Chancellor, who headed both the Prussian and the Imperial administrations, was appointed by and was responsible only to the Emperor. Although he required the support and consent of the Federal Council, which he headed and directed, his leadership was seldom curbed by their acts. Furthermore, his power was not limited by the *Reichstag*. Although its approval of legislation was required, and the Chancellor had to keep it informed of his major policies, his administration did not need the confidence of the *Reichstag*. The actual task of administration was carried out by State Secretaries for: Foreign Affairs, Interior, Naval Matters, Justice, Posts, Finance, and Colonies, and by several independent Imperial Authorities. These officials, who were appointed by and made directly responsible to the Chancellor, were never brought together into a cabinet. Their work, which was the direct responsibility of the Chancellor, was coordinated by the Office of the National Chancellor (*Reichskanzlei*). The growing complexity of imperial administration led to the creation of the office of Vice-Chancellor in 1878. This official, who was appointed by the Emperor upon the advice of the Chancellor, substituted for the Chancellor during periods of emergency and assisted in the general administration of the Empire.

The scope of purely federal administration was extremely limited. The major administrative functions carried out solely by the imperial government included foreign affairs, posts, naval affairs, colonial matters, and the administration of conquered Alsace-Lorraine. While there were national offices and agencies for interior, finance, justice, railways, banking, and accounts, their function with few exceptions was to establish national regulations and to exercise supervision and control over the execution of the federal laws in these fields, the states being responsible for the actual administration.

The administration of foreign affairs for both the Empire and Prussia was centralized in the Foreign Office (*Auswärtiges Amt*). Its responsibilities under the Chancellor for the implementation of the policies of the Emperor, and the treaties which had been validated by the Federal Council and *Reichstag,* included control of the legally trained diplomatic corps, which was largely drawn from the wealthy upper classes and the aristocracy, and the administration consular service, which was responsible for the commercial relations of the Empire. It was also responsible for the colonies, which the Empire had acquired in Africa and the Pacific after 1880. These colonial territories, which were organized as Protectorates under Governors responsible for administration, defense, finance, and justice, were placed under a separate Colonial Office in 1907. The government and administration of Alsace-Lorraine were carried out by a Governor (*Statthalter*), who was directly responsible to the Emperor. After 1879, this Imperial Province (*Reichsland*) was ruled under imperial laws, or under laws passed by popular representatives constituting a Provincial Committee (*Landesausschuss*) and approved by the Emperor, the Governor, and the Federal Council.

While the Emperor was the supreme commander of the naval and military forces of the Empire, only the navy was subject to direct imperial administration. The fleet and the major naval bases, which were located at Kiel, Wilhelmshaven, and Helgoland, were under the Imperial Marine Office (*Reichsmarineamt*), which was headed by a State Secretary directly responsible to the Chancellor. The growth of the Imperial Navy, which generally received the support of the *Reichstag,* was justified by the leaders of the Empire on the basis of Germany's expanding commercial, maritime, and colonial activities, as well as in terms of national defense. Military affairs of the Empire were coordinated by the Standing Committee for Army and Fortresses of the Federal Council, although much of the central administration of army affairs was provided by the Prussian Ministry of War and its General Staff. During the late nineteenth century Prussia gradually gained control of all the state military establishments, except those of Bavaria, Württemberg, and Saxony.

In the sphere of interior administration, the imperial government received the right to establish national regulations and controls for a number of social, economic, and commercial activities. Most of the work at the federal level was carried out by the Imperial Office for the Interior (*Reichsamt des Innern*). This office, which was responsible in general for implementing the legislation of the *Reichstag* and the Federal Council, was charged with the administration of national elections, citizenship, and the civilian aspects of military and naval affairs. After the passage of the Imperial Civil Service Code (1873), it received supervisory control of all imperial public servants in the direct service of the Emperor. The Disciplinary Court (*Disziplinarhof*) at Leipzig and the regional Chambers of Discipline (*Disziplinarkammern*), which were established for the control of the actions of civil servants, were placed under the Imperial Office for the Interior. The same office was made responsible for the Imperial supervision of the Trade Law (*Gewerbe-Ordnung*), which had been passed in 1869 to meet the needs of the growing economy and the "demands for protection and paternalism." This law, which sought to establish regulations for industry, trade, and crafts, for the guild organizations of craftsmen and artisans, and for labor and working conditions, was administered under delegated powers, by the pertinent state ministries and their local inspectors.

The need for uniform weights and measures was met by the organization of the national Normal Weight Commission (*Normal-Eichungskommission*) in Berlin. This agency, which was under the Imperial Office for the Interior, supervised the state Offices of Weights and Measures (*Eichungsämter*). The control of patents was centralized in the Patent Office (*Patentamt*), while the stock exchanges were brought under the supervision of the Stock Exchange Committee (*Börsenausschuss*). The system of social insurance—sickness, accident, old age, and invalid insurance—which was carried out through communal bodies, sick-benefit associations, and cooperative associations of occupational groups, was also brought under the general supervision of the Imperial Office for the Interior. Its National Insurance Office (*Reichsversicherungsamt*), which also served as a supreme administrative court for social insurance difficulties, provided for the supervision of the state and local Insurance Offices, (*Versicherungsämter*), which were responsible for the actual task of local supervision of social insurance. The operations of private insurance companies doing business in more than one state were brought under the control of the Supervisory Office for Private Insurance (*Aufsichtsamt für Privatversicherung*).

The imperial laws for compulsory vaccination, regulation of contagious diseases, and the inspection of foods and drugs were administered by the states under the supervision of the Federal Health Office (*Gesundheitsamt*). The Federal Office for Welfare Matters (*Bundesamt für Heimatwesen*) was established to supervise the state offices and the local Town Welfare Unions (*Ortsarmenverbände*) which were responsible for public relief and the maintenance of welfare institutions. The administration of the national statistical controls, however, was placed under the Office for General Statistics (*Statistisches Amt*) and the Commission for Labor Statistics (*Kommission für Arbeiterstatistik*) of the Imperial Office for the Interior. The supervision of imperial legislation, relating to social (social insurance, welfare, and health) and economic (trade and industry, labor, weights and measures, patents, and insurance) affairs, remained under the Imperial Office for the Interior until the fall of the Empire, but the administration of these measures was always delegated to the states.

The administration of transportation and communications was shared by the Imperial government and the state governments. The railroads, which were at first constructed by both private companies and the state governments, grew rapidly during the period between 1840 and 1880. After the turn of the century, Prussia, following the examples of Hanover and the South German states, gradually took over control of the private railway systems. Under the

Empire, the economic need for a systematic interlocking railroad system, operating under uniform rates, was met by the establishment of the Imperial Railroad Office (*Reichseisenbahnamt*), although the actual operation of the railway systems remained in the hands of the state governments.

The importance of natural and artificial waterways for the transportation of coal, iron ore, and grain, which were needed by Germany's expanding industries, was recognized by the state governments. In Prussia, where canal building and waterway improvements had been started in the days of the Great Elector and Frederick the Great, an extensive canal system was already in operation by the middle of the nineteenth century. During the period of the Empire, Prussia and the other states continued to expand and improve their waterway systems. The only canal project which was carried out by the Imperial government was the Kaiser Wilhelm (Kiel) canal, which was needed for purposes of naval defense. The construction and maintenance of this canal were placed under a Canal Office (*Kanalamt*) in the Imperial Office for the Interior.

The Empire also brought about the centralization of the administration of the posts, telephones, and telegraph. Before 1871 the postal system had been partly under the states and free cities and partly under the Counts of Thurn and Taxis, who had served the central German states under a monopoly granted by the Holy Roman Emperor in 1615. Under the Empire the national postal system was administered through a National Post Office (*Reichspostamt*) working through special regional directorates for Posts and for Telephone and Telegraph (*Reichspostdirektionen*). Bavaria and Württemberg, however, maintained separate and independently administered postal organizations.

The increasing scope of governmental administrative activities and services, coupled with the increasing financial demands of the navy, brought as a natural consequence increased national expenditures. In a space of thirty-five years the cost of government increased fourfold. These expenses were met by monies raised through customs duties, excise taxes on beer (the beer tax was not a federal prerogative in south Germany), tobacco, salt, matches, and sugar and stamp taxes. This income was supplemented by contributions from the states. Although the Empire began its career free of debt, its sources of revenue were never able to keep up with the increasing expenditures. Bismarck's high protective tariffs and other financial measures did not solve the problem of the increasing imperial debt, which was placed under the National Debt Commission (*Reichsschuldenkommission*) and the National Debt Administration (*Reichsschuldenverwaltung*). General control of imperial finances was vested in the Imperial Treasury (*Reichsschatzamt*), which was responsible for the preparation of the imperial budget and the supervision of the collection of imperial revenues, directly administered by the states. Further control was imposed by the Court of Accounts (*Rechnungshof*), which was an independent imperial authority responsible for the auditing of all imperial finances. Currency and banking, which had been regulated by the individual states, were brought under imperial control. The issuance of coinage by the states was regulated by the imperial administration. The old paper money of the states was abolished and replaced by a uniform paper currency, issued by the newly established *Reichsbank* (based upon the Old Bank of Prussia) and by the state banks of Bavaria, Württemberg, Baden, and Saxony. The National Debt Administration received the right to issue imperial treasury bonds.

It must always be borne in mind that the bulk of the administrative work of the Empire was carried out through delegation to the state governments and their administrative officials. The work of the imperial civil servants was not extensive except in the fields of foreign affairs, naval matters, and postal affairs. The need for agencies to settle conflicts within the administrative structure and to provide for the protection of the interests of the German citizen as against the administration was limited, for most of these cases were settled by the administrative courts of the states. The few imperial cases, which were settled on the basis of the Constitution and the legislative acts of the Federal Council and the *Reichstag,* were handled either by the former or by such special courts as those of the Railway, Welfare Social Insurance, and the Patent offices.

The unification of the German state under the Empire also brought with it the gradual establishment of uniform legal and judicial systems. The first step toward legal unification grew out of the commercial necessities of the middle nineteenth century. In 1859 the Germanic Confederation adopted the Commercial Code of the Customs Union. In 1869 this code was adopted by the North German Confederation, and it was later carried on by the Empire until the issuance of the Commercial Code (*Handelsgesetzbuch*) in 1897.

At the beginning of the Empire, Germany was divided by several differing systems of civil and criminal law. Prussia was under the General Land Law (*Allgemeines Landrecht*) of 1794, while the German Common Law (*Gemeines Deutsches Recht*)—a blend of German, Roman and ecclesiastical laws—prevailed in northwest, central, and southern Germany. Forms of the French civil code, adapted from the Code Napoleon, prevailed in Baden and the Rhineland. Under the principle of legal unification, established in the Imperial Constitution, codes of criminal law, criminal and civil procedure, and court organization were drawn up during the Empire. The law of 1877 for a uniform court organization established the present judicial system. These legal accomplishments are important landmarks in German development.

The National Supreme Court (*Reichsgericht*) at Leipzig was set up to serve as a court of appeals for cases coming from the state courts. With the exception of the highest court of judicature, the right to establish courts and the exercise of sovereign rights in the administration of justice, was left to the individual states. The numerous local Courts of First Instance (*Amtsgerichte*), which were the lowest of the German courts, handled minor civil and criminal cases and dealt with the registration of land titles, guardianships, probate matters, and the registration of associations, companies, and corporations. The more serious criminal and civil cases and appeals from these lower courts went to the district Courts of First and Second Instance (*Landgerichte*), where civil cases were handled by a bench of three judges, while criminal cases went either to a Chamber for Criminal Cases (*Strafkammer*) or the Jury Court for Criminal Cases (*Schwurgericht*). A Chamber for Commercial Affairs (*Kammer für Handelssachen*) was attached to the district courts for commercial cases. Civil and criminal cases were appealed from the district courts to the State Supreme Courts (*Oberlandesgerichte*). In Prussia and Bavaria, where there was more than one State Supreme Court, higher courts of appeal existed. The last phase in the unification of the German legal and judicial system under the Empire came in 1896 with the issuance of the German Civil Code (*Bürgerliches Gesetzbuch*). Although many subsequent amendments have been made and state, common, or customary law may supplement it, this civil code is still basic.

The people of Germany played only a minor role in the government and administration of the Empire because the instrument of representation, the *Reichstag,* which Bismarck had designed to appease the liberal elements, possessed little real power. It did serve, however, as a kind of national parliament, composed, as it was, of members elected on the basis of almost universal manhood suffrage. Its extremely limited powers did not include control of the Chancellor and his administrative assistants, the State Secretaries. In financial matters its control was small, since it had only restricted powers in budget matters and no control over the mounting national debt. Its legislative activity was curbed by the constitutional provision which gave the Federal Council the right to initiate all legislation. Its requests for information from the Chancellor on administrative policies could be ignored. Finally, it was subject to frequent dissolutions by the Emperor.

Although the *Reichstag* partially represented the people through delegates who spoke and voted as individuals, the affairs of state were actually controlled by the Federal Council, which represented the states and their conservative and frequently reactionary monarchs. At no time during the Empire did the *Reichstag* represent the people of Germany with any effectiveness. After 1871 this body tended to lose even its representative character because of shifts in population accompanying the industrialization of Germany and because of the failure to change the distribution of seats. Control of the *Reichstag* consequently passed to rural Germany. Attempts to reapportion the seats of the *Reichstag,* to give the new urban areas proper representation, were always resisted by the conservatives, who held control of rural elections. The *Reichstag's* position within the framework of government was quite hopeless, the real power of government being held by Prussia through the Federal Council.

The development of a central administration naturally carried with it a parallel decrease in the powers of the several states. Foreign affairs, naval matters, and posts, except in Bavaria and Württemberg, had been taken over by the imperial government. Although the states retained control of the organizations for the administration of justice, finance, railways, health, social, and economic affairs, many aspects of the actual task of administration were under the immediate supervision of the imperial government. The states retained independent control only in the fields of interior, police, education, church, and cultural administration.

The State Governments

The states of Germany were governed by hereditary and constitutional monarchs, princes, or dukes. The three imperial free cities were independent constitutional republics. The sovereign rulers possessed almost absolute power as heads of the state government, the army, and the church. This power was not curbed by the representative assemblies which had been either inspired by the French Revolution or created under the pressure of domestic revolution. Even in the city republics of Hamburg, Bremen, and Lübeck, the governments remained in the hands of conservative interests.

The larger states, Prussia, Saxony, Bavaria, Württemberg, Baden, and Hesse, had bicameral legislatures, with upper houses composed of the aristocracy, and lower houses composed of delegates elected by systems of suffrage, ranging from the limited three-class system in Prussia to systems based upon direct, secret, and universal franchise in South Germany. The smaller states possessed unicameral legislatures whose delegates were elected by a variety of electoral systems. The legislatures of the three city republics—Hamburg, Lübeck, Bremen were composed of two houses, a Senate, consisting of life members responsible for the administration of the cities, and a Citizens' Assembly (*Bürgerschaft*), consisting mostly of representatives of the conservative upper classes. The legislative power of these parliaments was mostly limited to the discussion of laws which were initiated by the rulers or their ministers. Furthermore, the generally conservative delegates seldom opposed the government's policies and actions, which were determined by ministers responsible to the state ruler. The lack of ministerial responsibility to the legislature, coupled with the limited suffrage, rather effectively excluded most citizens of the states from any real participation in government.

The rulers of the states exercised their executive functions through a State Ministry (*Staatsministerium*), consisting of a committee of state ministers who headed the departments of government under the chairmanship of the state Minister President (*Ministerpräsident*). In Prussia and most of the other states, the State Ministry served as a council for the discussion of general policy and as an administrative agency for the control of certain independent administrative authorities, such as the Disciplinary Court and the Supreme Administrative Court (*Oberverwaltungsgericht*). In Prussia and Bavaria, the King was also assisted by a Council of State (*Staatsrat*), while in Württemberg, the King was aided by a Privy Council (*Geheimer Rat*). These councils, which were survivals from the days of state absolutism, met irregularly and had only limited functions. The actual work of government was carried out by the ministers, who were directly responsible to the King.

Most of the larger states had ministries for Foreign Affairs, Interior, Finance, Education, Economics, Justice, and War to meet the increasingly complex needs of the state during the middle nineteenth century. The smaller states had ministries for Foreign Affairs, Interior, Finance, and Justice; or a single state ministry whose subordinate sections handled the varied administrative functions of the state. Most of the states had State Weights and Measures Offices (*Landeseichungsämter*), State Insurance Offices (*Landesversicherungsämter*), State Welfare Offices (*Landesarmendirektionen*), and State Offices for Customs Duties and Excise Taxes (*Landeszolldirektionen*) for the administration of tasks usually delegated by the imperial government. These offices were subordinated to the pertinent ministry. The state supervision of the trade law was generally placed under the state minister or official responsible for trade and industrial affairs.

Local Government

The organization of local government and administration varied considerably from state to state. In general, local affairs were in the hands of highly trained civil servants who were under the direct control of the state, but who were also held in check by local advisory bodies. In Prussia, the fourteen provinces of imperial days were headed by Chief Presidents (*Oberpräsidenten*) who were directly responsible to the state Minister of the Interior. The Chief Presidents served as the heads of state administration in the provinces. In turn, the provinces were divided into governmental administrative districts (*Regierungsbezirke*), which were areas of state administration without local autonomy. These districts were headed by District Presidents (*Regierungspräsidenten*), who were responsible for the administration of interior, church and school, tax, and forest affairs. The Prussian governmental administrative district had its territorial equivalents in Bavaria, Saxony, and Württemberg, where there existed units of state administration under the immediate supervision of the state minister of the interior. The Bavarian governmental administrative district and the district of Württemberg, however, served more as areas of self-government and decentralized state administration. The Saxon administrative district (*Kreishauptmannschaft*) was only an area of state administration, while the Baden county or district (*Kreis* different from the "Kreis" of Prussia) formed a state area of supervision to which was attached a resident deputy of the state ministry of the interior.

The county or *Kreis,* regulated by codes which differed from state to state (and within Prussia from province to province), generally served both as an area for state administration and local self-government. The Prussian counties, which existed in the form of rural *Landkreise* and urban *Stadtkreise,* the Baden and Hesse *Kreise,* the Bavarian *Distrikt,* the Württemberg *Oberamt,* and the Saxon *Amtshauptmannschaft,* as well as the counties which constituted the sole territorial division of the smaller states, were headed by officials bearing a variety of titles; these officials were ultimately responsible to the District Presidents in the larger states and to the Ministers of the Interior in the smaller states. In general they were assisted in their capacities as heads of decentralized state administration by county committees, which had certain functions with respect to interior, police, tax, welfare, and other state activities. In the sphere of local self-government, the county official worked with the County Assembly (*Kreistag*), which was composed of delegates from rural communes. It is important to note that in Prussia the county assembly elected the delegates who composed the provincial assembly. The backward Mecklenburgs did not make use of the district or county systems for administration, since the land was still administered in terms of landownership; that is, by the towns, convent estates, knights' estates, and the ducal estates.

The rural villages (*Landgemeinden*) and the urban towns (*Stadtgemeinden*) which were under the administrative jurisdiction of the counties, displayed several patterns of local government. The rural villages generally had a General Assembly or "town meeting" (*Gemeindeversammlung*) composed of all qualified inhabitants or an elected Representative Assembly (*Gemeindevertretung*), which in turn elected the local mayor. In Württemberg and the Prussian Rhine Province, the village governments frequently joined together in Communal Unions (*Amtsverbände*) to carry out enterprises which required greater financial support than could be provided by any single village.

The urban towns had one or another of three general types of government. The Magisterial Plan (*Magistratsverfassung*), which went back to the Stein reform, consisted of an elected city council which in turn elected the Administrative Board (*Magistrat*) and its chairman, the mayor. This form of city government obtained in all of Prussia, except in the Rhine Province, Hesse-

Nassau, Hanover, and western Pomerania. In the last two areas, an older form of city government, based on medieval charters, survived until the World War. In the Rhine Province, the Bavarian Palatinate, Hesse, Waldeck, and a few of the states of Thuringia, the Mayor Plan (*Bürgermeisterverfassung*), consisting of an elected chamber presided over by a mayor, was inspired by French influence. The City Council Plan (*Stadtratsverfassung*) consisting of a council composed of elected lay and professional administrative officials, presided over by a mayor, was common in Bavaria, Württemberg, Baden, and Hesse-Nassau. The form of city government varied considerably from town to town in the Mecklenburgs and in some parts of the state of Thuringia.

The larger cities were called *Stadtkreise* or city counties, and unlike the small villages and cities were not under county supervision. Generally speaking, local government, under the Empire, although subjected to a considerable amount of state supervision, actually enjoyed a good measure of local autonomy. This sphere of government was the only one in which the citizens had the benefits of democratic rule.

Administration of the affairs of the states was carried on by professional civil servants whose appointment, duties and responsibilities, maintenance, and status were regulated by state civil service codes. They were permitted to issue administrative orders to implement the legislation of the state within their respective administrative organizations. In the execution of administrative tasks they could promulgate police ordinances and compel action, desistance, or payment on the part of the citizens. Further controls were provided by the right to issue licenses and permits for activities regulated by law. The citizen was protected by his right to lodge formal protests or to bring legal action in either the administrative courts or the ordinary courts of the state.

Development of Germany under the Empire

The first two decades of the German Empire were dominated by Bismarck, who directed both foreign and domestic affairs. Although he possessed great powers, the task of government was not easy because of difficulties between civil and military authorities and conflicts between the imperial, Prussian, and other state governments. During the reigns of Wilhelm I (1861-1888) and Friedrich III (1888), Bismarck always enjoyed the imperial and royal confidence, and was, therefore, able to weather many of the serious governmental crises. Nevertheless, Bismarck's work was complicated by rapidly changing economic and social situations.

After 1870 Germany underwent an unparalleled industrial development which transformed almost every aspect of German life. Although the way for industrialization had been prepared by the Customs Union, the introduction of the factory system, and the agrarian reforms, national and state policies played an ever increasing role in the final industrialization of the Reich. After 1870, the states, particularly Prussia, undertook extensive programs of railroad, canal, and road construction in the interests of the national economy. Bismarck's regime brought an ever-increasing supervision of trade, industry, and commerce by the government. The trade law, coupled with programs of protectionism and paternalism, gave the imperial government the essential controls in the field of economic activity. Bismarck encouraged the formation of large scale enterprises through the establishment of policies favorable to cartels and combines. In the field of industrial finance, the government encouraged the formation of large banks. Protective tariffs were established to maintain home markets for agrarian Junkers and to strengthen the position of export industries. The amazing economic development of the Empire, made possible by political unification coupled with a planned utilization of natural resources, brought a period of great internal prosperity and harmony.

The growth of the chief industries clearly reveals the extent of the transformation. Coal production in 1913 was eight times that of 1870. Iron and steel production increased sevenfold between 1880 and 1910. In 1913 Germany was producing more than one-third of the world's electrical goods. The German chemical industry became one of the greatest in the world. These domestic economic developments were followed by the rapid expansion of Germany's foreign trade and investments. Thanks to government subsidies, the merchant fleet grew from 640,000 tons in 1870 to over five million tons in 1914. Hamburg became the largest port of continental Europe. The impact of these economic changes had wiped out the old artisan, merchant, peasant economy and social structure that had prevailed in Germany until 1860. The rise of large urban industrial centers was accompanied by the formation of a new working class. Bismarck placated the working class through social insurance and pension laws, but kept a firm control over labor unions, which had been illegal in most of Germany until 1869. All radical movements were kept in check, although they never constituted a serious threat to the established state and imperial authorities. The working class under the Empire formed a well disciplined, obedient, and industrious group which accepted leadership from the top.

Bismarck's foreign policy, which was supported by the rapidly developing German economy, was based upon a system of foreign alliances, with the major objective of isolating France. In 1872 he secured Germany's diplomatic position temporarily by negotiation of the informal Three Emperors' League (*Dreikaiserbund*) between Germany, Austria, and Russia. This pact, which was formalized in 1881, remained in force until 1887. In 1879 Bismarck's moderate policy toward Austria bore fruit in a definite military alliance, designed to guarantee the security of the Central Powers. After Russia's withdrawal from the agreements of 1872 and 1881, Bismarck cultivated the Italians. In 1882 the Triple

Alliance of Austria, Germany, and Italy was formed. Germany's position in relation to Russia was secured by the Reinsurance Treaty which lasted from 1887 to 1890. Internally Germany undertook to preserve her status by the establishment of a large military and naval establishment. The diplomatic, military, and economic measures of Bismarck had set the stage for the reign of Emperor Wilhelm II.

Upon assuming power, this ruler immediately began to take an active part in the formulation and direction of both domestic and foreign policy. After the fall of Bismarck in 1890, the succeeding prewar Chancellors—Caprivi, Hohenlohe, and Bülow—and the prewar and war Chancellor Bethmann-Hollweg (1909-1917) were relegated to subordinate positions in the direction of the Empire's affairs. Wilhelm's adventurous foreign policy began with his support of the Boers. His extensive naval construction program added further fuel to the fire. England, Germany's major commercial rival, attempted to secure her position by negotiating the Triple Entente between Britain, France, and Russia. World War I found Germany militarily prepared, but diplomatically in trouble, for the Triple Alliance was already weakened by Italian discontent. The war, which had largely resulted from Germany's unlimited support of Austria's anti-Serbian and anti-Russian policies, received enthusiastic support at home. All parties, including the growing Social Democratic party, joined with the Emperor and military leaders. Governmental authority passed to the army. Even the Kaiser and his chancellors—Bethmann-Hollweg, Michaelis, Hertling, and Maximilian of Baden—were subordinated to the military. In administration, there was an increasing tendency toward centralized control over every aspect of German life. The economic life of wartime Germany was placed under the Imperial Economic Office, which was established when things became more difficult in 1917. The movement for constitutional reform, aimed at the establishment of a parliamentary system with ministerial responsibility, did not grow until the military reverses of 1918. Modifications in the Imperial Constitution, which were hurriedly passed in October 1918, came too late to save the imperial regime. The final military defeat in November 1918, which brought about the dissolution of the Empire by the abdication of the Kaiser and the kings, dukes, and princes of the German states, left Germany in the hands of a coalition of the liberal parties in the *Reichstag*.

THE WEIMAR REPUBLIC

The German revolution of 1918 was precipitated by the military collapse of the imperial armies. It followed but did not precede the defeat of the army. The hungry German people were tired of war and yearning for peace, while the military, faced with the imminent collapse of Austria and the breakdown of Turkey and Bulgaria, feared another winter of war. After the failure of the

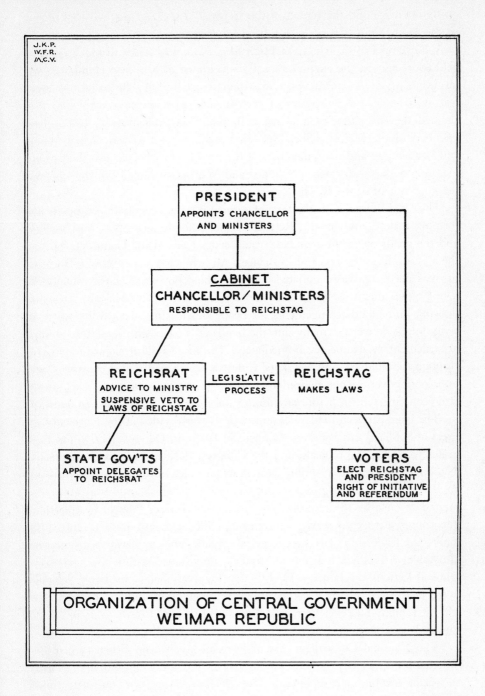

J.K.P.
W.F.R.
M.C.V.

PRESIDENT
APPOINTS CHANCELLOR
AND MINISTERS

CABINET
CHANCELLOR / MINISTERS
RESPONSIBLE TO REICHSTAG

REICHSRAT
ADVICE TO MINISTRY
SUSPENSIVE VETO TO
LAWS OF REICHSTAG

LEGISLATIVE
PROCESS

REICHSTAG
MAKES LAWS

STATE GOV'TS
APPOINT DELEGATES
TO REICHSRAT

VOTERS
ELECT REICHSTAG
AND PRESIDENT
RIGHT OF INITIATIVE
AND REFERENDUM

ORGANIZATION OF CENTRAL GOVERNMENT
WEIMAR REPUBLIC

spring offensive and the retreat of the German armies, strikes had broken out on the home front, while small mutinies began to take place in the army. In early November 1918, when the High Seas Fleet was about to make one last bold effort against the enemy, the sailors mutinied at Kiel and Hamburg, and revolutionary disturbances swept to Munich and Berlin. The socialist leaders, fearing a successful revolution of the Russian type, seized control and proclaimed the formation of a German Republic on November 9, 1918. Three members of the Majority Socialists (Social Democrats)—Ebert, Scheidemann, and Landsberg—and three members of the Independent Socialists—Haase, Dittmann, and Barth—formed a Soldiers' and Workers' Council which took over the government of the Reich.

They were faced with the task of restoring order, negotiating a peace, and forming a new government. Refusal of the generals to support the Emperor and the heads of the numerous German states enabled the Council to prevent the spread of revolutionary disturbances. An armistice, which now was an immediate necessity, was negotiated with the Allied Powers. The task of forming a new government, however, was more complicated. The Majority Socialists, desiring immediate arrangements for peace and fearing that revolutionary activity might deliver Germany into the hands of bolshevism, wanted to establish a parliamentary democracy immediately. The more radical elements, working through the Soldiers' and Workers' Councils which had seized control of state and local governments, desired to undertake an extensive program of social and economic reform before attempting the formation of a stable government.

The issue between moderates and radicals was decided at the National Congress of Soldiers' and Workers' Councils in Berlin in December 1918. The moderates won over the radicals, and the Congress decided to hold elections for a National Constituent Assembly as soon as possible. Revolutionary disturbances in Berlin and Hamburg and in the Saxon and Rhenish industrial areas were started at once by the radicals. The moderates retained control by support of the conservative civil service and through the action of military formations under the leadership of former imperial officers. The conservative groups were thus able to retain a position of strategic importance within the Socialist regime. Elections on January 19, 1919 for the National Constituent Assembly were held on the basis of proportional representation and the broadest franchise Germany had ever known. All men and women twenty years of age and upward were permitted to vote. There were no disturbances.

The National Constituent Assembly was convened on February 6, 1919 at Weimar, a small city famous for liberalism and idealism, and safe from the threat of revolutionary upheavals. The elections had given control to the old majority parties of the *Reichstag*—the Social Democrats, the Catholic Center, and the Progressive Liberals, the last named party having changed its name to the German Democratic party. A provisional government, which consisted of a committee of the states serving as an upper house, and an assembly serving as a lower house, was dominated by the moderate Social Democrats, who gained control of the provisional presidency, the chancellorship, and six cabinet posts. This provisional government, established by the act passed by the Constituent Assembly on February 10, 1919, assumed complete control of Germany's affairs. The laws of both the Empire and the Soldiers' and Workers' Council remained in force, except where they were amended by the provisional constitution. The National Constituent Assembly was then free to accept the Treaty of Versailles and to proceed with the drafting of a new constitution.

The long and detailed Weimar Constitution was drawn up on the basis of the abortive Constitution of 1848, the Constitution of the German Empire (1866-1871), and the Erfurt Program of the Social Democrats (1891); and these German constitutional sources were further modified by ideas borrowed from French, American, and British experience. Although it was primarily a product of the moderate socialists who desired to create a strong national government, the final draft of the constitution embodied a series of compromises with the forces of federalism and states' rights.

The first draft of the actual constitution was prepared by the democrat Hugo Preuss, a Prussian professor of constitutional law, well in advance of the meetings at Weimar. It was submitted to a conference of state representatives in January 1919. At Weimar the draft constitution of Preuss went first to a Committee of States and then to a Committee of the Assembly on the Constitution, which added further modifications and finally issued a fifth draft. Extensive discussions in the Assembly led to the preparation of the sixth draft, which on third reading was adopted by a vote of 262 to 75. On August 11, 1919, it was promulgated as the law of the land. It replaced the Imperial Constitution of 1871 and the Provisional Constitution of 1919, and established in law a liberal, federal, and parliamentary form of government. Its elaborate bill of rights for the individual and the community, for religion and education, and its involved economic provisions, were great improvements over the previous German Constitution. It was a long, detailed, and complicated document full of liberal, democratic provisions.

National Government

The structure of the Republic's government represented a completion of trends which had been pointing toward a parliamentary democracy for over one hundred years. It confirmed the constitutional changes of the last Imperial *Reichstag,* which made the Chancellor responsible to that body. The word *Reich* (realm or commonwealth) was used instead of Empire. The National President (*Reichspräsident*) chosen by direct popular election, replaced the

Prussian Emperor. The old Federal Council became the Senate (*Reichsrat*) and continued the task of representing the states. The National Economic Council (*Reichswirtschaftsrat*), which was designed to represent the interests of labor and management, was never fully successful under the Republic.

At first the Weimar Assembly had desired to create a strong central government. Originally, there were plans for the division of Prussia into a number of small states to keep it from dominating national affairs, but as it turned out, eighteen states were constituted, and Prussia remained intact. The new constitution provided that each state should have a Cabinet responsible to a Parliament composed of members elected by universal suffrage under the principles of proportional representation. The main changes in the relations between the states and the central government came through the extension of the Reich's functions. The powers of the Reich government were increased in a number of fields. In the fields of poor relief, civil rights, industry and trade, labor, mining, and finance, national legislation took precedence over state law. The railroads were nationalized, and financial control and administration fell more and more into the hands of the central government. The power of the Reich over the states extended even to education and religious associations, which had nominally been left under state control, for the national government received the right to establish fundamental principles of policy in these fields.

The national government exercised its control over the states through constitutional provisions providing for the superiority of national law over state law. This was backed by judicial controls, regulating administrative differences through the National Constitutional Tribunal (*Staatsgerichthof*), and financial differences through the National Finance Court (*Reichfinanzhof*). Control over the administration of national laws by the states was achieved through the national ministers. The National President (*Reichspräsident*) possessed executive powers which allowed him the right to require a state to carry out its national duties, if necessary by armed force.

Difficulties between the national and state governments, growing out of the illogical territorial organization of the states, complicated by the existence of small states and large numbers of enclaves and exclaves, were not solved by the Republic. The situation was further complicated by the impoverished financial condition of most of the states, resulting in their inability to carry out certain national administrative tasks. The course of national-state relations under the Republic was, therefore, not always smooth. Although the Constitution provided for a federal system of government, the states were stripped of many rights and powers which they previously held, and the national government was able to intervene effectively in state government and administration. The states retained most of their powers over interior, police, health, justice, religious, educational, and agrarian matters. However, while the form and appearance of federalism were preserved, much governmental power had shifted to Berlin, leaving the once important state capitals to become secondary governmental centers.

The democratic basis of the Weimar Republic was provided by elections to the *Reichstag,* by the presidential election, and by provisions for the initiative, referendum, and recall. Each citizen, male or female, over twenty years of age, was entitled to vote under the constitution. The *Reichstag* was the center of the democratic framework of government under the Republic. It was composed of members elected according to proportional representation from thirty-five electoral districts for a term of four years. Although the electoral system had the advantage of distributing representation proportionally among parties through the use of national, district, and union lists of party candidates, it had several disadvantages which hampered the workings of the *Reichstag.* The electoral system gave too much power to the political parties, so that the voters really voted for a particular party and not for a qualified candidate. Rigid party control of members in the *Reichstag* prevented real discussion of important issues, and forced members to vote along party lines. Internally, the *Reichstag* was organized under a President of the Chamber (*Reichstagspräsident*) and a Council of Elders chosen by the members. The seventeen standing committees, appointed by the Council of Elders, paralleled the ministerial administrative organization. Select Committees (*Untersuchungsausschüsse*) were appointed from time to time for investigations. When the *Reichstag* was not in session, its affairs were handled by its President and his bureau, and its rights were to be safeguarded under Article 35 by an Interim Committee (*Überwachungsausschuss*).

Legislation was introduced by the Cabinet, the Senate, the National Economic Council (*Reichswirtschaftsrat*), or by members working through a cabinet minister or acting with the endorsement of fifteen members. The Constitution also provided that legislation could be introduced by popular initiative (*Volksbegehren*) through petitions signed by one-tenth of the voters. The actual work on legislative measures took place in committee meetings with the aid of expert civil servants. Most legislation was restricted largely to policy, leaving the details of administration to supplementary decrees issued by the executive. A bill passed by the National Assembly went to the Senate and then to the National President for signature. If the bill was rejected by the Senate, it could still become law if by a two-thirds vote the *Reichstag* overruled the Senate. The National President could refer any law to the public for referendum (*Volksentscheid*). If one-third of the *Reichstag* demanded the postponement of the publication of a law, a petition of one-twentieth of the voters could cause any such law to be submitted to the public for referendum. Also a referendum could be held if one-tenth of the qualified voters petitioned for the introduction of a bill in the *Reichstag* which was not passed without change by that chamber.

The legislative work was constantly influenced by the cabinet minister, who in the name of the cabinet could introduce legislation, plan budgets, and formulate the detailed regulations necessary to carry out provisions of legislative acts. Cabinet ministers could also attend sessions of the *Reichstag* and its committees, and speak at such sessions. Although the *Reichstag* failed to develop real control over foreign affairs and finance, it did have the right to demand information from the cabinet. All cabinet ministers could be questioned by the *Reichstag*. Control over the government and administration was based on the principle of ministerial responsibility and the power of impeachment. When a fundamental disagreement existed between the government and the *Reichstag*, the National President could on the advice of the Chancellor dissolve the *Reichstag* and call for new elections.

The failure of parliamentary government under the Weimar system grew out of a combination of difficulties. The multiple party system, coupled with rigid control of party members, made parliamentary procedures difficult. The situation was complicated by the fact that the parties were not always willing to assume governmental responsibility; as a result, governments fell because of troubles encountered in forming party coalitions and not because of votes of no confidence. Although the *Reichstag* was hampered by the strong position of the National President and hindered by multiple party politics, it was nevertheless the constitutional and political pivot of the Weimar system.

The Senate assumed a position of considerable importance in the Weimar Republic, although it possessed extremely limited constitutional powers in comparison with the Federal Council (Imperial *Bundesrat*). This council of the German states was composed of members of the state cabinets, except in the case of Prussia, where half of the delegation consisted of cabinet members and the other half of members of the provincial administration. The representation of the states was apportioned, as far as possible, according to population, but no state could have more than two-fifths of the total votes in the upper house. This last provision was meant to prevent domination by Prussia.

Internally, the Senate was organized under a President and eleven standing committees. Its powers included the right to have its proposed legislation introduced by the cabinet into the *Reichstag*, to exercise a suspensory veto over *Reichstag* acts, and to question cabinet ministers on matters of policy and administration. It served as a consultative body in ordinance making and played a part in the issuance of executive orders and decrees relating to matters concerning the states, transportation, or communication. The Senate also possessed partial or complete right to nominations and appointments of officials of over twenty-four public agencies dealing with judicial, economic, insurance, health, banking, and patent matters. It played an important part in the coordination of legislation affecting the states. Although it lacked the powers of the Federal Council, it continued to play an important role in the affairs of the Republic through its influence on the work of the cabinet, through its check on the work of the *Reichstag,* and through its efforts to coordinate state and national affairs.

The National Economic Council was established under the Weimar Constitution to provide advisory assistance on economic legislation. It had the right to review such legislation before it was submitted to the *Reichstag* by the cabinet, and also the right to cause the cabinet to initiate economic legislation in the *Reichstag.* The original Weimar plan envisaged an elaborate scheme of economic representation. The National Economic Council was to be composed of representatives from the National Workers' Council, the National Employers' Council, and the consumer organizations. The National Workers' Council was to represent the District Workers' Councils and its local factory councils. The National Employer's Council comprised several District Employers' Associations, which consisted of individual employers. Although these organizations were formed throughout Germany, they had little real power. The activities of the factory councils were restricted largely to labor welfare matters. The provisional National Economic Council, which was set up in 1920 with 326 members representing ten different economic interests, was never permitted to exercise its full constitutional rights. Its actual prerogatives were limited to advisory and consultative functions without even the power of a suspensory veto.

The Weimar Constitutional Assembly intentionally gave the National President a strong position, which was fortified by the fact that he was the popularly elected head of the state. The President, who served for a term of seven years, was to be elected by majority vote. If no candidate received a majority in the first election, a second election followed with merely a plurality required. The President was subject to impeachment by the *Reichstag* and trial by the National Constitutional Tribunal. There was also a provision for recall by popular vote upon proposal by a two-thirds majority of the *Reichstag.* The President, serving as the executive head of state, had the right to represent the Reich in international relations, although treaties and declarations of war required the consent of the *Reichstag.* The promulgation of laws by publication in the National Law Gazette (*Reichsgesetzblatt*) was a function of the National President, subject to certain limitations. In the field of administration, the President had the right to appoint and dismiss the Chancellor and the Ministers (both of whom, however, had to have the confidence of the *Reichstag*) and the right to organize the administrative departments of the government. His power was strengthened by his command of all military and naval forces.

The constitution also conferred upon the President the right of federal execution, which enabled him to oblige the states to carry out their constitutional obligations.

The famous Article 48 of the Constitution gave the President extraordinary powers in the case of a national emergency. If the public order and safety were seriously endangered, the National President could take all necessary measures with the counter-signature of the Chancellor. These measures had to fall within the framework of the Constitution, and they could be revoked by the *Reichstag.* While the use of dictatorial powers granted by Article 48 was frequently necessary in the unstable years of the early Republic, their extravagant use after 1930 helped to bring about the destruction of the Republic. The President also possessed extensive ordinance powers. The legal and administrative ordinances issued by the president to national public authorities were subject to control by the Chancellor, the Cabinet, the *Reichstag,* and the courts. The relations of the President with the Cabinet and the *Reichstag* are extremely important. While the Cabinet Ministers and the Chancellors were appointed by the President, they were responsible to the *Reichstag,* so that appointments had to be made in terms of the political situation within that body. Furthermore, the *Reichstag* had a certain control over the President, since all his official acts had to be countersigned by the Chancellor or the appropriate national minister, who thereby assumed responsibility for the acts in question. This provision meant that the broad executive powers of the President, which were subject to the limitations of the Constitution and the laws of the land, were exercised in cooperation with the Cabinet, which, in turn, was responsible to the people's representatives. The actual work of the President was carried on by the Office of the National President (*Büro des Reichspräsidenten*). In practice the National President possessed greater powers and influence than the Constitution anticipated, owing to the political conditions which existed under the Republic. The multiple party system always made it difficult to form coalition cabinets; as a result, a large measure of power normally possessed by the parties was allowed to fall into the hands of the President. The situation was made more difficult by disagreements among the President, the Chancellor, the Ministers, and the *Reichstag.*

The chancellorship had lost most of its old Imperial powers. The Republican Chancellor (*Reichskanzler*) was appointed by the National President but was responsible to the *Reichstag* for national policy. In practice he divided this responsibility with the other members of the Cabinet. The exigencies of party politics and the requirements of national administration forced the Chancellor to compromise divergent political programs and to delegate the formulation of policy, and even its presentation to the *Reichstag,* to individual ministers. It was difficult for him to exercise strong leadership either in the Cabinet or in the *Reichstag*.

During the Republic the National Cabinet (*Reichsregierung*) consisted of the ministers for Foreign Affairs, Interior, Finance, Economics, Labor, Justice, War, Posts, Transportation, Agriculture, and Occupied Areas. Each ministry was headed by a National Minister (*Reichsminister*) who was assisted by one or more under secretaries. Each ministry was divided into departments (*Abteilungen*) headed by Ministerial Directors. The work of the ministers was carried out by ministerial councillors and other civil servants. The ministers, who were chosen by the Chancellor after extensive party discussions, aided in the formulation of national policy, countersigned acts of the National President, and issued administrative orders and decrees within their own departments. Although they were constitutionally responsible only for their own ministries, cabinet solidarity was required constitutionally and generally prevailed.

In the Weimar period numerous changes occurred in the field of national administration. The central government, which had been completely responsible only for foreign, naval, and postal affairs under the Empire, took over the administration of defense, railways, finance, and certain aspects of social insurance, which, formerly, had been partly carried out by the states upon delegation from the imperial government. The development of special administrative structures, involving numerous regional and local offices under direct national officials responsible to the appropriate national minister, foreshadowed the amazing development of special administration under the Nazis. From the ministries in Berlin, lines of control extended to systems of regional offices for naval and military affairs, finance, posts, railways, labor and welfare. The acute problems of unemployment were met by the regional and local offices of the National Employment and Unemployment Insurance Office, which was responsible to the National Chancellor. The extension of national administration under the Republic cut deeply into the spheres of state activity and interest. Although the states had managed to retain control over interior (police and health), economic, church, and educational administration, the work of the state ministries was subjected to increasing national supervision.

The Foreign Office, which had been one of the main strongholds of the aristocracy under the Empire, continued as a bulwark of conservatism under the Republic. In addition to the usual control of the diplomatic and consular services, the Foreign Office also handled relations with the International River Commissions and the International Court of Mixed Claims, agencies which had been set up after the end of World War I. Within Germany the Foreign Office maintained information centers in the major cities to keep in touch with local interests in connection with foreign trade.

For national defense, the Republic established a unified military command. State armies were abolished and replaced by a small and highly efficient national army under the National Defense Ministry (*Reichswehrministerium*), which was also given control of the naval forces of the Republic. Army administration was carried out through eight corps areas (*Wehrkreise*) while naval affairs centered in the bases at Kiel and Wilhelmshaven and a number of smaller service stations. Under the Republic, the small army of 100,000 was largely used for the maintenance of public order, while the naval forces, which were also limited by the Treaty of Versailles, were employed to assist commercial navigation.

Under the Republic many services formerly belonging to the National Office of the Interior (*Reichsamt des Innern*) were transferred to the new Republican ministries for Economics, Labor, and Agriculture. The newly designated National Minister for the Interior (*Reichsministerium des Innern*) remained responsible for matters pertaining to constitutional, administrative, and election problems, and continued to serve as the top-agency for the enlarged national civil service. The National Disciplinary Court (*Reichsdisziplinarhof*) at Leipzig and the 32 regional chambers continued to handle disciplinary cases within the national civil service. The old national offices for health (*Reichsgesundheitsamt*) and welfare (*Bundesamt für Heimatwesen*) were retained, while the new offices for emigration (*Reichsstelle für Auswanderungswesen*), archives (*Reichsarchiv*), at Potsdam, and topography (*Reichsamt für Landesaufnahme*) and its fourteen regional survey offices, were added to the Ministry of the Interior. This ministry, as the main constitutional and administrative agency of the Republic, continued to gain in importance during the Weimar era, although most of its activities were still carried out through state authorities.

The trend toward a state controlled and nationally planned economy continued under the Republic. The Republican Ministries for Agriculture, Economics, and Labor, which had been preceded by imperial offices created to meet the pressing economic problems of the last years of World War I, held most of the governmental responsibility for the control and coordination of economic life under the Republic. The National Ministry for Food and Agriculture (*Reichsministerium für Ernährung und Landwirtschaft*), which was responsible for food production, food prices, agrarian labor, forestry, fisheries, and customs and trade arrangements, worked through the appropriate state ministries and agencies. A number of boards, commissions, and research institutes, interested in the promotion of rural economic life, were attached to this ministry. The German Council for Agriculture (*Deutscher Landwirschaftsrat*) and its affiliated organizations: the State Agricultural Chambers and the Prussian Provincial Chambers, as well as a number of agricultural cooperatives, were subject to the supervision of the National Ministry of Food and Agriculture.

The promotion of trade and industry at the national level was in the hands of the National Economics Ministry (*Reichswirtschaftsministerium*). The agencies for the collection of statistics (*Statistisches Reichsamt*), supervision of state controlled stock exchange (*Börsenausschuss*), control of private insurance organizations (*Reichsaufsichtsamt für Privatversicherung*), and inspection of shipping were taken over from the old National Office for the Interior. New agencies were established for handling economic problems arising from the Versailles Treaty: for misuse of economic power, the National Economic Council (*Reichswirtschaftsgericht*); for manipulations of the cartels, the Cartel Court (*Kartellgericht*); and for the desperate coal situation, the National Coal Council (*Reichskohlenrat*). The National Rationalization Board (*Reichskuratorium für Wirtschaftlichkeit*) was established to promote industrial and commercial efficiency.

The Ministry for Economics also provided for the national supervision of the German business and industrial associations. Private enterprises belonged to top Employer's Associations (*Spitzenverbände*) for industry, wholesale trade, retail trade, banks, and insurance. These associations, which were largely reorganized in 1919, consisted of trade associations (*Fachverbände*) with regional divisions for the administration of local commodity problems. The national Employer's Associations, which played an important role in the formation of labor policies, were members of the Diet for German Industry and Commerce (*Deutscher Industrie- und Handelstag*). This national organization for trade and industry embraced a great number of territorial Chambers of Industry and Commerce (*Industrie- und Handelskammern*) which were supervised by the state ministries for economics. The national organizations, including the Central Committee of Employer's Associations (*Zentralausschuss der Unternehmerverbände*), were subject to the supervision of the National Ministry of Economics. The national organization for crafts and handicrafts, the *Handwerks- und Gewerbetag,* which was also under the supervision of the National Minister of Economics, worked through the *Reichsverband des Deutschen Handwerks,* which was composed of local guilds and handicraft organizations. Although these national organizations were subject to public control and supervision at the federal and state levels, they were allowed considerable freedom in the control of the commodity, labor, and political policies of German trade and industry.

The Republican National Labor Ministry (*Reichsarbeitsministerium*) received responsibility for the enforcement of labor legislation, labor arbitration, social insurance, unemployment, labor welfare, and housing and settlement. Labor problems and conditions of work were under the National Labor Administration (*Reichsarbeitsverwaltung*) which worked through the state labor authorities. Its work was supplemented by a system of labor courts, which handled dis-

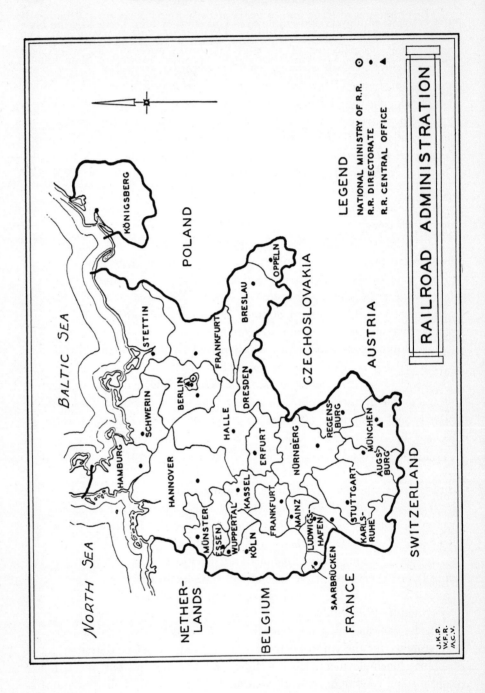

RAILROAD ADMINISTRATION

LEGEND

NATIONAL MINISTRY OF R.R.
R.R. DIRECTORATE
R.R. CENTRAL OFFICE

J.K.P.
W.F.R.
A.C.N.

putes between employers and employees. This court system, headed by the National Labor Court (*Reichsarbeitsgericht*), which was attached to the National Supreme Court (*Reichsgericht*) at Leipzig, consisted further of State Labor Courts (*Landesarbeitsgerichte*) and Local Labor Courts (*Arbeitsgerichte*) which were attached to the ordinary state court systems.

The unemployment problems of the Republic were met partly by the establishment, in 1927, of the National Institute for Employment and Unemployment Insurance (*Reichsanstalt für Arbeitsvermittlung und Arbeitslosenversicherung*). This agency, which functioned under the general supervision of the Minister of Labor, worked through its own regional and local organization, consisting of thirteen State Labor Offices (*Landesarbeitsämter*) and numerous local labor offices (*Arbeitsämter*), which cooperated with local health insurance bodies for the collection of contributions and with local welfare authorities for purposes of certification.

The social insurance system, involving old-age, accident, and health insurance, was under a variety of agencies, which were supervised partly by the National Insurance Office (*Reichsversicherungsamt*) and partly by the state and local insurance offices. Old-age and invalid insurance for workers in agriculture and industry was handled by the various national Occupational Associations of Workers (*Berufsgenossenschaften*) cooperating with other agencies of local government, such as the local police, who handled insurance forms, and the local post offices, which issued insurance stamps and paid benefits. There were separate national funds for railway, mine, marine, and salaried employees. Industrial accident insurance was organized under three separate funds: one for public servants, one for agricultural workers, and one for industrial workers. Its funds, which were entirely financed by the employers, operated on a national basis. Health insurance funds were organized territorially by city-counties (*Stadtkreise*), counties (*Landkreise*), and miner's associations (*Reichsknappschaften*); and functionally by nation-wide guilds, institutes, and associations. The county funds were administered by the local Workmen's Sick-funds, *Krankenkassen*, which were subject to state insurance offices, while the other health insurance funds were under national supervision. The Ministry of Labor also played a part in the administration of welfare and public assistance.

The national Public Assistance Act of 1924, which provided for the care of persons who were not covered adequately by the social insurance systems, brought the consolidation of the local *Armenverbände* into County and City-County Welfare Unions (*Fürsorgeverbände*) which worked through county Welfare Offices (*Wohlfahrtsämter*). The unions were supervised by Provincial and State Welfare Offices (*Landesfürsorgestellen*), which were generally supervised in turn by the National Ministry of Labor. Disputes over welfare matters were settled by the state and provincial Welfare Courts (*Versorgungsgerichte*) or by the National Supreme Welfare Court (*Reichsversorgungsgericht*) of the Ministry of Labor. Cerain welfare problems affecting labor at the local level were handled directly by the Ministry of Labor through its eleven regional Main Welfare Offices (*Hauptversorgungsämter*) and their numerous local agencies. Housing and settlement problems also fell under the jurisdiction of this ministry. In 1919 it was given supervision over the state and provincial authorities, which had been established during the first World War to meet the acute housing shortage. The work of the local welfare organizations was supplemented by that of the private agencies, operated by the Lutheran Church, the Catholic Church, the Humanitarians, the Socialists, and the Jews. These groups maintained nation-wide organizations with agencies at the federal, state, provincial, county, and community levels.

The Ministry of Labor also had prime responsibility for the administration of national labor legislation, regulating labor conditions, and wage fixing. In this sphere it worked with the national employer's associations and the trade unions, which emerged as powerful working class organizations during the Weimar era. The trade unions, which were generally organized along craft lines, included the Free Trade Unions affiliated with the Social Democratic party, the National Christian Trade Unions associated with the Center party, and the Hirsch-Duncker Trade Unions, which included chiefly salaried workers associated with the German Democratic party. In addition to these major groups of unions, there were a number of company unions, Communist federations of revolutionary workers, and a few National Socialist Factory Cell units, which were affiliated with the Nazi party. The three major union groups, which were recognized as competent to undertake collective bargaining, were generally subdivided into unions for manual workers, for salaried workers, and for civil servants. The fraternal and political work of the unions was supplementary to their activity as collective bargaining agencies, which dealt either with the individual employer or an association representing his interests. Labor disputes arising over wages and working conditions were settled by voluntary òr government mediation boards. The latter were subject to the supervision and control of the regional mediation boards of the National Ministry of Labor. Conflicts over legal provisions or contract obligations were settled within the state labor courts or appealed to the National Labor Court (*Reichsarbeitsgericht*) at Leipzig. Minor disputes over shop rules and grievances within a factory were handled by the local Factory Councils (*Betriebsräte*), which had been established by the Factory Council Act of 1920.

The Republican National Transportation Ministry (*Reichsverkehrsministerium*), established in 1919, was made responsible for the supervision of railway and automobile traffic, major rivers and canals, and aviation. In 1920 the state railways, which were left with run-down operating equipment and serious financial problems after the war, were taken over by the federal government and placed under the National Transportation Ministry. While the states had in that way lost one of their major sources of revenue, the national government gained a source of income needed for the payment of reparations. The railway budget became a part of the national budget and was openly discussed in the *Reichstag*. The impact of the inflation led to serious financial troubles, which were finally solved by transforming the railway administration into a mixed state-private enterprise, known as the German Railway Corporation (*Deutsche Reichsbahn-Gesellschaft*). This change was made to meet the terms of the Dawes Plan, which stipulated that the railways should be used to meet approximately one-third of the reparations payments.

The German Railway Corporation, which was under the supervision of the Ministry of Transportation, consisted of a General Board (*Verwaltungsrat*) of official and lay members, which elected the General Director, who in turn appointed the members of the General Administration (*Hauptverwaltung*) of the railways. The railway system was placed under twenty-seven regional National Railroad Directorates (*Reichsbahndirektionen*), which worked through the regional Construction Offices (*Bauämter*), Operating Offices (*Betriebsämter*), Traffic Offices (*Verkehrsämter*), and the Machine Offices (*Maschinenämter*). Local administration and operations were carried out by the Railway Stations (*Bahnhöfe*) or by the Local Agencies for Passenger and Freight Traffic (*Selbstständige Abfertigungsstellen*). In addition to the regional administration for operations, there were five Central Offices (*Zentralämter*) one in Munich and four in Berlin, which handled technical problems directly under the General Administration. A Central Accounting Office (*Hauptprüfungsamt*) and seven district accounting offices (*Prüfungsämter*) were set up for accounting and financial control.

In 1921 the national government assumed responsibility for supervising the construction, maintenance, operation, and policing of the major waterways of the Reich. It carried out these functions through the state and provincial waterways authorities. The administration of the extensive waterways network was complicated by the fact that the Rhine, Elbe, Oder, Memel, and Danube were under International Commissions. The coordination of waterways affairs was accomplished by the establishment of a National Waterways Council and eight District Waterways Associations, which were composed of representatives of interested transportation and economic groups. The Kiel canal, which had been built by the imperial government, continued under the Canal Office, which was transferred to the Ministry of Transportation. This ministry also assumed responsibility for the National Sea Office (*Reichsoberseeamt*) and the local sea offices (*Seeämter*), which handled disasters at sea. It is important to note that the coastal and river ports and their facilities remained under the municipal governments and local corporations.

The roads and highways of Germany remained under the state or provincial, county, and local authorities, although the national Ministry of Transportation established uniform regulations for motor vehicle traffic and promoted motor transportation. The control of air traffic (registration of aircraft, licensing of pilots, and the authorization of airports) was under the general supervision of the National Transportation Ministry and its National Aviation Council, although the actual administration was carried out by state authorities. Air transportation was furnished by the *Deutsche Lufthansa,* a private corporation which was formed through the merger of a number of private airlines in 1926.

Postal and communication affairs continued under the National Ministry of Posts (*Reichspostministerium*), which took over the functions of the Imperial Post Office (*Reichspostamt*). This ministry assumed prime responsibility for posts, telephone, telegraph, and radio. The administration of the postal service was carried out through a National Postal Central Office (*Reichspostzentralamt*), and thirty-eight Main Postal Directorates (*Oberpostdirektionen*), which supervised the local post offices, railway post offices, money order offices, telegraph and telephone offices, telegraph construction offices, and radio stations. The old Postal Administrations of Bavaria and Württemberg were absorbed into the national organization. Public control of the postal administration was provided by the Administrative Board of the German National Post (*Verwaltungsrat der Deutschen Reichspost*), which was composed of members recruited from the *Reichstag,* the National Ministry of Finance, the National Ministry of Posts, and from business firms interested in communications.

The rapid growth of government services and functions, coupled with serious financial conditions, made the work of the National Ministry of Finance extremely difficult during the Weimar period. This office handled the salaries, pensions, and finances of the national civil service, prepared the national and departmental budgets, and administered the financial and tax systems. It assumed jurisdiction over disputes in its particular field through its system of financial courts. It was also charged with the administration of national buildings and construction, and also with carrying out the economic provisions of the Versailles Treaty.

The Weimar Constitution and the financial legislation of 1919 completely reversed the old imperial financial system, which had been based upon indirect taxes and contributions from the states. The so-called Eizberger financial reforms of 1919 gave the national government exclusive rights to tax legislation. Subsequent legislation regulated the character of state and local taxes, the distribution of taxes among the Reich, the states, and the local units, and the national supervision of budgets and finances. The organization for the collection and administration of taxes was headed by the national Minister of Finance, who worked through the Finance Presidents (*Finanzpräsidenten*) who headed the twenty-three regional State Finance Offices (*Landesfinanzämter*). These offices were responsible for the collection, custody, and distribution of national funds at the regional level. They coordinated the revenues and expenditures and managed the local credit operations of the Reich. The Section for Property Taxes and Traffic Taxes—Income and Commercial (*Abteilung für Besitz und Verkehrsteuren*) of the County Finance Office (*Landesfinanzamt*) controlled the local finance offices situated in the counties and city counties, while the Section for Customs and Excise Taxes (*Abteilung für Zölle und Verbrauchsabgaben*) worked through the local Main Customs Offices (*Hauptzollämter*). Tax disputes were handled by the local finance office. Appeals on local tax decisions could be taken to the Finance Court attached to the County Finance Office and ultimately to the National Finance Court (*Reichsfinanzhof*) at Munich. The administration of national buildings at the regional level was handled by National Construction Offices (*Reichsbauämter*) attached to the regional County Finance Office.

The establishment of this centralized system for tax and financial administration eliminated the once independent financial controls of the states. During the Republic, the states and lower units of government participated in the tax administration through a system of committees, working with the officials of the County Finance Offices and the local finance offices. But the superior financial position of the Reich gave it not only uniform financial control, but also extensive indirect administrative powers over the state governments. The financial and tax system was subject to the control of the *Reichstag* through legislative action. Auditing was done by the independent German National Court of Audit (*Rechnungshof des Deutschen Reichs*), which was directly responsible to the Chancellor.

The German banking and monetary system was regulated and administered by a number of national agencies. The National Minister of Finance, acting with the consent of the Senate, exercised prime responsibility for coinage and the regulation of the gold value of the German mark (*Reichsmark*). The actual monetary needs of the German economy, however, were met by the *Reichsbank*, the central bank of issue, which was established in 1924 as an independent public corporation under the Chancellor. It shared the right of issue to a limited extent with the state banks of Bavaria, Württemberg, Baden, and Saxony. The *Reichsbank* also maintained an extensive system of branch banks, which carried out discount operations and the usual governmental services. Other national banks included the German Gold Discount Bank (*Deutsche Golddiskontbank*), which was organized in 1924 to meet the banking needs of the export business: the Bank for German Industrial Obligations (*Bank für*

Deutsche Industrieobligationen), which was established in 1924 to serve the needs of economic groups burdened by the effects of the reparations; and the German Agricultural Credit Bank (*Deutsche Rentenbank-Kreditanstalt*), which was established to handle the liquidation of the inflation.

The work of the public banks was supplemented by that of the great commercial banks of Berlin, Munich, and Dresden. The commercial banks in Bavaria and Saxony developed out of older state banks. Private banks were limited both in size and number; the most important ones were in Cologne, Munich, and Berlin. The savings banks (*Sparkassen*), which were largely operated by the municipalities, were associated in regional and national associations called German Central Deposit Banks (*Deutsche Giro-Zentrale*), which acted as reserve banks and clearing centers. Mortgage banks were largely operated by public authorities. The rural *Landschaften* and the urban *Stadtschaften* handled most of the long term mortgages on town real estate and agricultural property. Credit was also supplied by cooperative credit organizations, which were associated in the German Central Cooperative Bank (*Deutsche Zentral-Genossenschaftskasse*). There were special credit institutions for financing industry, shipping, rural settlement, and agriculture. The work of the banks was further supplemented by that of the Post Offices, which handled money orders and travellers' checks.

The operation of the German banking system under the Republic was disturbed first by the inflation and secondly by the payment of reparations, which delivered control of banking and credit into the hands of the *Reichsbank*. The chaotic financial conditions of the first years of the Republic wiped out most of the private mortgage banks. This field of banking was taken over by public credit institutions. The Republican period also witnessed the final development of the great commercial banks with their extensive systems of branch banks, which worked closely with local credit cooperatives and public mortgage banks and savings banks. Public control of the banking system was exercised by the National Ministry of Economics and the state ministries and agencies for the regulation of banking and credit. But behind this façade of public control, most of the financial movements were determined by the manipulations of the *Reichsbank*.

There were few changes in the legal and judicial system during the Republican period. There was a wider use of judicial review, but no complete centralization of the whole court system was attempted. A desirable unification of judicial administration had already been achieved, and the thorough training of judges and lawyers continued to be an outstanding feature of the German court system.

Under the Republic, the National Ministry of Justice (*Reichsjustizministerium*), like the Imperial *Reichsjustizamt,* was concerned largely with judicial administration. The Weimar Republic retained the old National Supreme Court (*Reichsgericht*) at Leipzig and added the new National Constitutional Tribunal (*Staatsgerichthof*) to handle the somewhat similar judicial functions of the old Imperial Federal Council. The latter court was responsible for impeachment cases and had jurisdiction over disputes between states and between the national government and the state governments. The judicial function of the national government in administrative cases, which had belonged to the Federal Council, disappeared under the Republic, although the administrative court systems survived within the states. The combination of a highly uniform system of national laws and a uniform court system administered largely by the individual states, subject to guiding principles laid down by the Reich, survived until the middle thirties.

Under the Republic the states were responsible for the execution of federal laws for certain aspects of interior (health, welfare, and education), economics (agriculture, trade and industry, labor arbitration, social insurance), transportation (waterways, highway and air traffic), and banking. The state governments, whose administration of national laws was under the direct supervision of the competent national ministry or authority, delegated in turn certain national functions to lower units of state administration. While the Weimar period brought a rapid extension of delegated tasks to be carried out by the states, it was also marked by further development of the special administrative services of the national government. Foreign and naval affairs continued as direct national functions, while military matters, which had been under the states, were brought under uniform national control. In the field of economic affairs, the new national ministries of Agriculture, Labor, and Economics were empowered to work with the national organizations for agriculture, trade and industry, and the labor unions. The Ministry of Labor was made responsible for certain aspects of welfare. For administrative purposes, its National Welfare Office (*Reichsversorgungsamt*) carried out welfare functions through a regional administrative organization operating independently of the state governments. In the fields of communications, the Ministry of Posts established a special administrative organization for the posts, which operated independently of the states. It should be noted, also, that after 1924 the railway administration was placed under an independent authority, directly responsible to the Chancellor.

The Weimar period also brought a centralized and uniform system of direct national administration of taxes and finances. While most of the administrative activities of the Weimar period were carried out under one of the national ministries, either by delegation to the states or through special administrative arrangements, a limited number of governmental activities were under the Supreme Administrative Authorities (*Oberste Reichsbehörden*), which were responsible to the Chancellor. They included the *Rechnungshof, Reichsschulden-ausschuss, Reichsanstalt für Arbeitsvermittlung und Arbeitslosenversicherung,* the *Reichsbank,* and the *Deutsche Reichsbahn-Gesellschaft,* whose functions in the fields of audit control, debt administration, employment and unemployment insurance, banking, and railways have already been indicated.

The administration of national affairs was carried out by authorities endowed with powers equal to the tasks imposed by legislative action. The heads of the ministries and agencies had the function of drafting legislation and cooperating with the *Reichstag* in the formulation of laws, and possessed broad power to issue ordinances, rules, and regulations needed for the administration of national affairs. Each administrative authority was the organizing agency for all subordinate administration; it was, therefore, free to plan its own machinery and to develop as much flexibility or rigidity in administration as it liked. The administrative machine of the national government was hierarchial in organization so that every agency and authority was subject to the supervision and control of the next higher authority. In a few cases, however, there was a lack of logical grouping of functions among and within the departments. During the later years of the Republic, administrative reforms eliminated some of these duplications of services.

The work of the administration was subjected to a variety of controls. Constitutional provisions established the spheres of administration and regulated the broad interrelationships between major authorities. Popular control could be exercised through the procedures of referendum, recall, and initiative and through the representatives of the people, the members of the *Reichstag.* The national administration always worked within the broad limitations of the laws enacted by the *Reichstag* and the ministers responsible for the administration of national affairs required its confidence.

The legislative branch of the Weimar Republic exercised further control of administration through its powers of investigation, budget control, and impeachment. The constitutional, popular, and legislative controls were supplemented by controls within the administrative machine. The centralized organization of the administration, coupled with the disciplinary courts for civil servants and the administrative courts for conflicts within the administration and for cases involving the administration and a private citizen, kept the administrative structure in reasonable balance. The frequent use of Advisory Councillors, technical experts and lay members (*Beiräte*), not only provided the administrative authorities with technical information, but enabled the officials to keep in close touch with the people.

The task of national administration was carried on by a national civil service, composed of well-trained officials, who had passed a first state examination, served several probationary years, and then passed a second examination, which led to life tenure. Although many restrictions and duties were imposed upon the civil servants, they were guaranteed freedom of political opinion and association, and were even permitted to hold elective office. Their work was governed by a civil service code and was subject to disciplinary action by the appropriate officials of the Ministry of the Interior, whose decisions were reviewed by a set of disciplinary courts. Financial control of the civil service was vested in the national Minister of Finance. The actual recruitment and supervision of civil servants were left to the heads of the various departments.

The integrity of the service was sound, for the monetary advantages of graft and corruption were counterbalanced by the risk of disgrace and the destruction of a life career. The work of the national civil service involved only matters pertaining to direct national administration. Tasks delegated to the states were carried out by state civil servants, who worked under regulations established by the states. Friction between the state and national civil services led to widespread demands for a uniform civil service code, demands which were not satisfied until the advent of the Nazi regime. The conservative traditions of the Empire continued into the Republic. The civil servants, many of whom were hold-overs from imperial days, adhered to the law, but feared that the left-wing political groups would destroy the traditional aristocratic basis of the civil service by introducing democratic or patronage elements.

State and Local Government Under Weimar

The eighteen states and free and Hanseatic cities, which survived the war, experienced minor revolutions which swept away their old dynastic sovereigns. Between 1918 and 1923 the states gradually adopted new constitutions which established moderate republican governments. The sovereign powers of the states were thus shifted from the hereditary rulers to the people. All the states except Prussia established unicameral legislatures, composed of deputies elected by equal, direct, secret, and universal suffrage, under the principle of proportional representation as prescribed by the Weimar Constitution. The State Diets (*Landtage*), invested with legislative powers, served as the supervising authority for the state cabinets which headed the state administrative organizations. The representatives of the people controlled the acts of the state executive through direct or indirect selection of all top officials and through ministerial responsibility. These powers were supplemented by the rights of interpellation, investigation, and impeachment and also by initiative and referendum. In Prussia, the work of the State Diet was supplemented by that of the State Council (*Staatsrat*), which was composed of delegates from the provincial diets. The latter chamber could introduce legislation into the State Diet and was empowered to exercise a suspensive veto over legislation. The so-called Committee of Three (*Dreierausschuss*) possessed the power to dissolve the State Diet. Dissolution could also take place by virtue of a vote of the chamber itself or as the result of an initiative petition.

The state executive and administrative authority, generally called the State Ministry (*Staatsministerium*), was headed by a Minister President who was selected by the State Diet. In most of the states, this official served only as the chairman of the administration, which consisted of from five to eight ministers, who were also selected by the state diets. In Prussia, Württemberg, Saxony, and Hesse, the ministers were selected by the Minister-President and approved by the State Diet. The ministers, who headed the administrative departments (typically: Interior, Justice, Finance, Economics, Agriculture, and Education), were individually responsible to the State Diet. The State Ministry served both as the top state authority and as the delegated authority of the Reich for the administration of national laws.

The great variations and differences in the forms of local government and administration, which had prevailed under the Empire, continued during the Weimar era. Local government and administration remained the primary concern of the states, although the national government took an increasing interest in local affairs. The form of local government, which was broadly guaranteed in the Weimar Constitution, was delineated by the state constitutions and by state codes and ordinances. The basis of the German system involved the local administration of state functions by state appointed or approved officials, and local self-government with respect to affairs of local interest by popularly elected officials. Within the complex maze of local government and administration, the National Government sought to establish norms of administrative action, such as principles underlying elections, laws governing public bodies, and broad provisions for education, welfare, health, labor, commerce, and public enterprises.

There were only limited changes in the pattern and structure of local government and administration. The Prussian province continued as an area of decentralized state administration and as an area for provincial self-government. The major change at the provincial level involved the introduction of greater freedom in the sphere of self-government. The intermediary Prussian and Saxon districts continued as areas of decentralized state administration, while the districts of Bavaria and Württemberg served both state and local purposes. The county, which continued as the major area of rural government and administration, was regulated by new or modified codes which continued to vary from state to state. There were few changes in county structure and functions.

The numerous varieties of village, town, and city governments, developed under the Empire, continued in force. The only basic change introduced by the Republic was universal suffrage and proportional representation in city elections. There was a great increase in partisan politics at the local level. The basic forms of local government and administration established under the Empire were continued by the states. The state administrations also continued to exercise administrative supervision over self-government functions, and administrative control over delegated state functions carried out at the county and city levels. State administrative supervision took the form of advice, observation, inspection, approval, or disapproval. The local units were subjected to complete financial control, for the national government had assumed complete responsibiliy for the collection and distribution of taxes. Although German local government and administration was essentially sound in structure, it was handicapped by its extreme diversity and by the impact of the financial crisis. Demands for reform, which included plans for uniform national, municipal and county codes, met with little success.

The administration of the affairs of the states at the provincial, district, county, and city-county levels continued under a highly trained and professionalized civil service, whose work was regulated by widely differing state codes. The citizens of the states continued to enjoy the protection of the ordinary and administrative courts of the states.

A Review of the Problems and Accomplishments of the Weimar Republic

The Weimar Constitution gave Germany a federal and parliamentary democracy with an adequately strong central government. The rule of law was firmly established and the individual was protected in the enjoyment of all civil liberties. The bill of rights was, unfortunately, as confusing as the social and economic conditions within the Reich, and was the typical result of a compromise of the different parties. Its diverse statements regarding the rights of the individual, the community, the church, and the school, in effect, declared that many ways of life were admissible under the Constitution. While the Constitution opened the way to socialization and provided for the organization of labor, it granted the forces of conservatism the guarantee of private property and security. The impact of party politics, together with the continuing influence of the civil service and the army and the numerous conflicts between the state and national governments, never allowed the German people to utilize fully the democratic forms provided for them by the Constitution. A brief review of the principal events during the twelve-year Weimar period makes these and other points clear.

First of all, when the Congress of Versailles submitted the peace treaty to the German delegation, the work of the Weimar Assembly was interrupted in May 1919. There was immediate indignation throughout Germany. The provisional government declared the treaty unacceptable and considered the possibility of further military resistance. After consultation with the German army, the Scheidemann government resigned, and a coalition of the Catholic Center party and the Social Democrats formed a new government on June 21, 1919 to make preparations for the acceptance of the Versailles Treaty. The final ratification of the treaty by the Weimar Assembly came on June 27, 1919. Under the treaty Germany lost Alsace-Lorraine to France, Eupen and Malmedy to Belgium, Posen and West Prussia to Poland, and all of her overseas colonies and special economic rights. Parts of Upper Silesia later went to Poland and Czechoslovakia under treaty plebiscites. Another plebiscite brought the cession of northern Schleswig to Denmark. Danzig was organized as a free city under the League of Nations; and to compensate France, the Saar was placed under international control for fifteen years. The German General Staff was supposedly eliminated and the army and navy were reduced to insignificance. Germany was also required to pay reparations for the losses and damages suffered by the Allies. The execution of the treaty was guaranteed by the Allied military occupation of the left bank of the Rhine together with certain bridgeheads. Germany had been reduced to the status of a second rate power. In an atmosphere of defeat and popular indignation over the treaty, the Weimar Constitution was accepted as the law of the land on August 11, 1919. The Weimar National Constituent Assembly became the first *Reichstag* of the Republic on September 30, 1919. It met in Berlin during the remainder of that year and until May 21, 1920. On June 6, 1920, a new *Reichstag* was elected by the people. It took up the difficult task of government on June 24, 1920.

The new Republican government was immediately faced with difficult political and economic problems. The war left Germany economically exhausted. The general disruption of economic life, characterized by shortages of food and fuel, by the breakdown of transportation, and by low agrarian and industrial production, was complicated further by reparations, mounting taxes, and a depreciating currency. The leaders of the Republic, faced with the inflationary situation left behind by imperial war financing with war bonds and paper money, met the currency situation by resorting to further inflation. This policy enabled the agricultural and industrial groups to liquidate their domestic debts. It also provided a way for the government to facilitate demobilization and to prevent unemployment during 1920 and 1921. The cheap mark was used to improve the export position and to build up needed foreign credits, although there were drastic shortages within the Reich. The government, recognizing that the task of economic reconstruction could not be carried out by private interests, immediately began to establish a planned government controlled economy. The result was the rapid formation of numerous large financial and industrial combines, which strengthened the traditionally anti-democratic capitalistic groups. The once strong middle class disintegrated and became a potential revolutionary group. Although the Weimar Constitution and the Versailles Treaty had been signed and accepted by the German government, the disintegrating economic situation resulted in several serious political disturbances.

Reactionary army groups, under the leadership of Wolfgang Kapp, supported by General Ludendorff, attempted a *coup d'état* in March 1920. It was suppressed through a general strike of the German workers. The government, which had majority support in its action against Kapp, feared further military revolts and did not take advantage of this opportunity to reorganize the armed forces, which were still needed to watch the widespread radical movements in the industrial areas. The counter-revolutionary movements that were supported by the reactionary army and the conservative civil service continued to disturb the political situation. In the summer of 1922 the moderate Minister of Foreign Affairs, Rathenau, was assassinated by the reactionaries. Meanwhile, the reactionary opposition had shifted from the army to the federal states. Although Prussia remained in line with the democratic developments within the Reich, Bavaria fell into the hands of the conservatives after an ephemeral Communist regime. Saxony and Thuringia went Communist. Conflicts between the central government and the states and difficulties over reparations and foreign policy enabled the reactionary and conservative groups to seize power toward the end of 1922.

A right-wing coalition, headed by Cuno, decided to try a strong foreign policy, based upon the assumption that the political tension between England and France would prevent counter-measures. The Cuno government began by delaying delivery of reparation payments. Although England did not act, Belgium and France immediately occupied the Ruhr. The German government retaliated by following a policy of passive resistance; a policy subsidized by printing paper money. While the reparations and the loss of Upper Silesia had intensified the inflationary situation, the new policy released a runaway inflation. The mark declined rapidly in value. In 1920 it had been devaluated to 8.5 to the dollar; by November 1922, to 8000 to the dollar; and by November 1923, to 6.6 trillion to the dollar. The situation within the Reich went from bad to worse until leaders of the rightist German Peoples' party were forced to take action to end the policy of passive resistance. Stresemann, leading a coalition of the Catholic Center, the Social Democrats, the Democrats, and the German Peoples' party, faced the tasks of liquidating the passive resistance, fulfilling the terms of the Versailles Treaty, and stabilizing the mark. Opposed by a conservative Bavarian government and Communist regimes in Saxony and Thuringia, he declared a state of national emergency and turned to the army. His policy led to the fall of the opposing left-wing governments in central Germany, but the Bavarian situation did not improve. Adolf Hitler, leader of one of the nationalistic Bavarian parties, attempted a "putsch" against the Bavarian government. Upon orders from Berlin the army quickly assumed control in Munich. By the end of November 1923, order had been restored within the Reich.

The Schacht-Luther stabilization decrees of October 15, 1923, provided for a limited new currency backed by a national mortgage. With the solution of the political and economic problems came an easing of the difficult diplomatic situation. The French were ready to negotiate the problems of reparations and the question of the occupation of the Ruhr. The Weimar Republic was then in a position to begin the consolidation of the foreign and domestic situation.

The period between 1924 and 1929 was marked by rapid recovery of the social, economic, and political situation within Germany. Under the leadership of the Bürgerbloc, consisting of the Catholic Center, Democrats, and the German Peoples' party, aided from time to time either by the Social Democrats or the German Nationalist party, Germany enjoyed a moderate government, administered by the conservative civil service. The reactionary army and the judiciary, refraining from open or direct intervention in German politics, resorted to subterfuge.

The power of the rightists was strengthened by the election of Hindenburg in 1925. A falling-off in the support of the liberal parties which had created the Weimar Republic, coupled with the realignment of domestic forces, made reform and any change in the German social and economic structure impossible. The political disturbances between 1918 and 1923 had ended with a partial neutralization of the extremists of the right and left. Germany was left in the hands of moderates who did not dare to take action against either the Junkers of the agrarian Northeast or the capitalists of the densely settled industrial areas.

The revival of the German economy and the stabilization of the Reich during the last half of the twenties were made possible by the Dawes Plan, which came into effect in 1924. It set up a reasonable schedule of reparations payments and opened the way for the financial reorganization of the Reich. It opened the way also for foreign loans, which were used by German government and industry for modernization and rationalization. German industry, which had been freed of its debts and its small competitors during the inflation, rapidly made good the losses inflicted by the war and the inflation period. By 1928 the volume of physical production greatly exceeded that of 1913.

The government continued to play an important role in the industrial economy through both control and financial participation. In the late twenties from twelve to fifteen per cent of the entire economic activity was in the hands of the government. In 1920 the state railroads, which were in a bad physical and financial condition, were taken over by the Reich. Five years later the unified German railroad system was the best equipped and the most efficient in Europe. The improvement of economic conditions favorably affected the laboring class. After the brief period of unrest and unemployment during the inflation, wages rose rapidly, and a more comprehensive system of social insurance was set up than had prevailed under the Empire. Also much improved was the economic status of the working class. During the late twenties Germany developed the best living standard it had ever known. This revival of German social and economic conditions was accompanied by a remarkable cultural renaissance. A new flowering of the German genius produced such men as Reinhardt, Hauptmann, the Mann brothers, Ludwig, and Feuchtwanger. Germany again took a leading place in pure and applied science. Rapid advances were made in the fields of architecture, literature, and the fine arts.

The period of consolidation also brought a great effort to mitigate the penalties of defeat and to restore Germany to its place among the Great Powers. Throughout the Weimar era, the Germans continued to rationalize the humiliation of defeat by attacking the provisions of the Treaty of Versailles as an unjust peace. While Versailles was mild indeed when compared with the treaty of Brest-Litovsk, there were many who sought to mitigate its penalties.

The actual foreign policy of the Republic resulted from a number of domestic political forces. The nationalists and militarists still advocated open defiance, while the conservatives backed a policy of obstructionism and opportunism. The liberals supported policies aimed at the fulfillment of the treaty terms, while the radicals openly desired an alliance with Russia and a revolutionary approach to the problem of relations with western Europe. Under Stresemann, who dominated German foreign policy from 1923 to 1928, the German government sought to reduce its obligations through negotiations. The realistic and nationalistic policy of Stresemann brought into being the Dawes Plan (1924), the Treaty of Locarno (1925), and finally admission to the League of Nations (1926). By 1929 his policies had resulted in the removal of the Allied Control Commissions, in the partial evacuation of the Rhineland, and in the Young Plan, which had replaced the Dawes Plan; the new financial arrangements allowed Germany to regain complete control over the *Reichsbank* and the railroads. Germany had regained her freedom of action in foreign affairs.

The End of the Weimar Republic

The weaknesses of the Weimar Republic, however, came to the front with the world economic depression of 1929. The financial collapse of Germany revived at once the reparations issue. The Young Plan of 1930, which provided for the reduction of the reparations debt and the establishment of German financial autonomy, was not well received in Germany. It did not solve Germany's precarious financial situation, which was going from bad to worse because of the recall of large amounts of short-term loans. Conditions in Germany steadily worsened and the World Economic Conference brought no relief. In the midst of this difficult financial situation, on March 27, 1930, Dr. Heinrich Brüning of the Catholic Center party became Chancellor of Germany. In attempting to solve the economic problems, he used Article 48 of the Constitution as a basis for issuing emergency financial decrees. Meeting with strong opposition in the *Reichstag,* Brüning persuaded Hindenburg to dissolve that body and to call for new elections on September 14, 1930. This election brought a great increase in the strength of the National Socialist party and significant gains in the strength of the Communist party.

The political situation was once more in a state of flux. The reactionaries began preparations for a counter-revolution. They could count on the conservative Junkers, the capitalistic industrialists, and the dispossessed middle classes. While the liberal groups had been trying to build a new and progressive Germany despite the legacy of defeat, the reactionaries and conservatives had steadily maintained their opposition to the Republic. In the late twenties, particularly after the beginning of the depression, reactionary parties, like the German National People's party under Hugenberg and the National Socialist party under Hitler, intensified their work aimed at the destruction of parliamentary government.

Chancellor Brüning, faced with opposition from both the right-wing and the left-wing parties, proceeded to operate the government by the extensive use of emergency decrees. The failure of the Republican forces during the prosperous twenties to liquidate the disloyal civil servants of the old imperial regime and their failure to take action against the extremists, coupled with the inefficacy of the *Reichstag,* doomed the parliamentary system. Meeting fewer and fewer times, the *Reichstag* allowed the powers of government to be exercised more and more by the Cabinet. The next crisis came with the Presidential elections of 1932. In the first ballot, Hindenburg, who was running against Hitler, Thälmann, Winter, and Duesterberg, failed to poll a majority. But the second ballot brought the re-election of the old Marshal. Brüning had worked hard for the re-election of Hindenburg, but although he was successful in this endeavor, he was rapidly losing his political control. He had succeeded in gaining agreement on the cancellation of reparations at Geneva, which would have strengthened his political position at home, but political intrigues, centering around the old President and led by General von Schleicher and Herr von Papen—until this time a very conservative member of Brüning's party—brought his downfall in June, 1932.

The von Papen regime secured the dissolution of the *Reichstag* by Hindenburg and a new election. In the midst of the election campaign, von Papen seized the government of Prussia, despite the protests of the Senate. Although this meant that the last stronghold of the republicans had fallen, they took no action in defense of the Constitution. The new *Reichstag,* which was elected July 31, 1932, was composed largely of members belonging to parties opposed to von Papen and his "Cabinet of the Barons." Von Papen failed to obtain the support of the National Socialists, who had gained two hundred and thirty seats out of a total of six hundred and eight. When this *Reichstag* returned a vote of no confidence shortly after it assembled in September, it was dissolved by the President. The second *Reichstag* election of 1932, held November 6, did not improve the situation for von Papen and weakened the strength of the Nazis. Hindenburg accepted his resignation on November 17th and appointed General von Schleicher, Chancellor of Germany.

The new Chancellor attempted to bring order out of chaos with the support of the labor groups and the army. The *Reichstag,* which met in December 1932, supported his regime. Although popular government had been discredited by frequent elections, it seemed that moderation had won the day. Von Schleicher's revival of Brüning's plan for land reform in East Prussia met the immediate opposition of the Junkers, who turned to Hindenburg for aid. An intrigue formed by Hitler, von Papen, and Hugenberg resulted in the forced resignation of von Schleicher's cabinet on January 28, 1933. Hitler, who a few months before had been rejected by Hindenburg, was asked to form a coalition cabinet composed of Nationalists and National Socialists. Republican Germany had come to its official end.

THE THIRD REICH

Hitler took immediate steps to bring about the establishment of a new type of government which he called the Third Reich. On February 1 Hindenburg dissolved the *Reichstag* at the request of the new Chancellor. The emergency decree of February 6 placed severe restrictions upon freedom of assembly and press in order to prepare the way for the election of March 5, 1933. The *Reichstag* fire on February 27, attributed by the Nazis to the Socialists and Communists, gave the new Nazi government an excuse to take drastic action against the radical elements. The emergency decree of February 28, 1933, "for the protection of the people and the state," swept away the civil liberties of the German people. Despite these measures of suppression, the National Socialist German Workers party polled only forty-three per cent of the total vote in the election of March 5, 1933. The opposition parties, the Social Democratic party, the Center party, the Bavarian People's party, and the Communists had obtained sufficient seats in the *Reichstag* to prevent any regular constitutional change. However, on March 29 Hitler was able to obtain the passage by the assembly of the Enabling Act (*Ermächtigungsgesetz*). This act, which was passed by a coalition of the National Socialists and Nationalists in a *Reichstag* session from which the Communists and many Socialists had been excluded by force, provided the constitutional basis for the Third Reich. It was in fact a revolu-

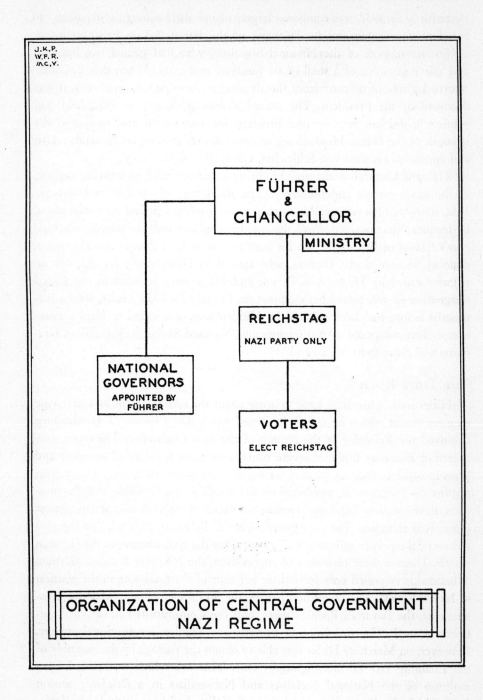

J.K.P.
W.F.R.
MC.V.

FÜHRER
&
CHANCELLOR

MINISTRY

REICHSTAG

NAZI PARTY ONLY

NATIONAL
GOVERNORS

APPOINTED BY
FÜHRER

VOTERS

ELECT REICHSTAG

ORGANIZATION OF CENTRAL GOVERNMENT
NAZI REGIME

tionary instrument aimed at the subversion of the constitutional regime. The right of law-making was bestowed by it upon the Cabinet without reference to the *Reichstag,* the Constitution, or the people. The Nazi legal transformation of the Republic into a centralized totalitarian state was effected by a series of laws and decrees based upon the Enabling Act. The Weimar Constitution, which had been the hope of republican Germany, was never completely abrogated. But so many parts were later on amended by Cabinet decrees, by Nazi plebiscites, or by actions of the Nazi *Reichstag,* that very few of the institutions and practices established by it were allowed to continue.

The political consolidation of the Third Reich was accomplished through elimination of all party opposition. After the stormy *Reichstag* meetings of March 1933, most of the opposition political parties "voluntarily" disbanded. On July 14, 1933, the Law concerning the Formation of Political Parties (*Gesetz über die Neubildung politischer Parteien*) abolished all parties, except the National Socialist party. Six months later, in December 1933, the Law Uniting Party and State (*Einheitsgesetz von Partei und Staat*) was issued, making the Nazi party a branch of the government. This law made possible a gradual intertwining of party and state bureaucracy for purposes of totalitarian control. These two laws provided an ostensibly legal basis for the one-party Nazi state.

The Nazis also purged the public services of all elements that were deemed unreliable. Control of the political situation was strengthened by seizure of the police organizations, whose activities were supplemented by Party security organizations. The position of the Nazi regime was further secured by a campaign to coordinate all kinds of organizations under the leadership of the Party. Business and commercial, industrial and transportation, educational and cultural, and religious organizations were rapidly nazified after April 1933.

In the summer of 1934, the budding Storm Troop revolution provided Hitler with an opportuniy to purge the Party of its radical and left-wing elements. Later in the year, Hitler took action against his erstwhile allies, the German Nationalist People's party. The *Stahlhelm* of the Nationalists was finally disbanded in November 1935. The carefully managed Nazi plebiscite of November 12, 1933, had given "popular" approval to Hitler's policies. His assumption of the powers of the presidency after the death of Hindenburg on August 2, 1934, was approved by the people in the Nazi plebiscite of August 13, 1934. This brought to completion the consolidation of National Socialist power.

National Government

The power of the Nazi state was concentrated in the hands of Hitler, who, as Führer and National Chancellor, exercised supreme power. Technically, Hitler derived personal power from his position as head of the Party, the State, and the Army. After August 1934, the Führer possessed not only the combined powers of the presidency and the chancellorship, but also supreme legislative and judicial powers. These powers, together with his position as the head of the German government and administrative machine which operated on the basis of the "leadership principle," made him by far the most powerful executive in Europe.

He was assisted in his work as head of the Folk Leader State (*Völkischer Führerstaat*) by four chancelleries. The old Presidential Chancellery (*Präsidialkanzlei*), which had been managed by Otto Meissner under Ebert, Hindenburg, and finally Hitler, lost many of its old powers and functions. Under the Nazis it was concerned with matters of ceremony, diplomatic receptions, and the bestowal of orders, titles, and pardons. Although it continued to make all governmental appointments, its functions in this respect were purely formal, since all government personnel was actually cleared by the Party Chancellery (*Parteikanzlei*). This chancellery, first under Hess, the one-time deputy of the Führer, and later under Martin Bormann, was responsible for party affairs and played a part in the appointment and dismissal of all civil servants.

The National Chancellery, which had long been attached to the office of the Chancellor, was placed under Lammers, an old civil servant of the Republic. Its functions included the preparation of material for decisions by the Führer, the coordination of the work of the Ministries, and the prevention of conflicts in the administration of national affairs. This chancellery also handled the political aspects of major civil service appointments and dealt with matters related to the budget and personnel. The Supreme Administrative authorities (*Oberste Reichsbehörden*) were administratively subordinated to this chancellery. The Chancellery of the Leader of the National Socialist German Workers' party (*Kanzlei des Führer der NSDAP*) handled only the private affairs of the Führer. It is interesting to note that while the main offices of these chancelleries were concentrated in Berlin, branch offices were also maintained at Berchtesgaden near Hitler's country villa. Taken together, these four chancelleries provided the top governmental and administrative machinery of the Third Reich.

The elimination of the principle of ministerial responsibility brought about a complete reversal in the position of the National Cabinet. The ministers were reduced to the status of advisers, responsible only to the Führer. They lost even their positions as heads of administration within their respective departments. Under the Nazis, the Cabinet advised only in the matter of law making, for all legislation was in the hands of the Führer. The flow of Cabinet business took place in the National Chancellery, which either kept the Führer informed or arranged for the rare Cabinet meetings at which the Führer decided. Minor affairs required only approval by the Minister of the Interior and the Minister of Finance, if the Deputy Leader and the head of the National Chancellery did not object. Statutes, which under the Republic were passed by the *Reichstag,* were now issued under the authority of the Führer after approval of the Deputy Leader and the head of the National Chancellery and after signature by the various ministers. The Nazis retained the old ministries for Foreign Affairs, Interior, Finance, Justice, Defense, Economics, Agriculture, Labor, Transport, and Posts and added the new Ministries of Propaganda, Air, Education, and Church Affairs, which were required to meet the needs of the new totalitarian state. The Cabinet was supplemented also by several ministers without portfolio. Although members of the Cabinet had lost much of their old power and responsibility, they enjoyed considerable discretion in the task of administering the affairs of their respective departments.

Most of the old Supreme Administrative Authorities, which came under the supervision of the National Chancellery, continued to function under the Nazis. The old Court of Accounts of the Reich, the National Debt Administration, and the *Reichsbank* were retained as Supreme Administrative Authorities. The German Railways, however, were transferred to the Ministry of Transportation in 1937. During the period before World War II, the Nazi government appointed National Commissioners, Inspectors, or Authorities for the administration of a number of activities essential for war. In 1936 Hermann Göring was made the General Deputy for the Four-Year Plan (*Generalbeauftragter für den Vierjahresplan*), and took over the task of reorganizing Germany's economy for war. The following years brought about the creation of an increasing number of new agencies to handle the domestic and war problems.

The administration of Nazi Germany was headed by Hitler, who as Führer and National Chancellor led all public services, the armed forces, and the Nazi party. These administrative tasks were carried out by the chancelleries, the fourteen ministries—with the Ministry of the Interior occupying a pivotal position as the constitutional, administrative, civil service, and police agency—the Supreme Administrative Authorities, and the Nazi Estates for Agriculture, Trade and Industry, and Cultural Activities. The first years of the Nazi regime brought the establishment of a centralized system of internal administration through the subordination of the states to the central government. The two laws of 1933, the Law for the New Structure of the Reich of 1934 (*Neuaufbaugesetz*) and the Law Relating to National Governors of 1935 (*Reichsstatthaltergesetz*) resulted in: the imposition on the states of National Governors (*Reichsstatthalter*) responsible to the Ministry of the Interior, the transfer of the sovereign rights of the states to the Reich, and the subordination of the state administrations to the will of the national Cabinet.

In Prussia, the state government continued with Hitler as National Governor (*Reichsstatthalter*) and Göring as Minister President after the absorption of the Prussian ministries into the national government. The Prussian provinces meanwhile received a new status, for their Chief Presidents were subordinated to the national Minister of the Interior. The National Governors and the Chief Presidents thus became intermediate national authorities with powers of general supervision. In many of the states the National Governor was aided by the old state ministries, which became intermediate national authorities. Under the National Governors of the States and the Chief Presidents of the Prussian provinces came the intermediate (District Presidents) and local (County Managers of the Counties and the Chief Mayors of the City Counties) administrative officials, who thus became national officials.

The work of the general administrative officials at the national, state and provincial, and local levels was supplemented by that carried on by the agencies of special and technical administration—the so-called *Sonderverwaltungen* or special administrations. These services, which operated independently of the general administration, were under the control either of the National Ministries or the Supreme Administrative Authorities in Berlin. The services—finance, railways, post, labor, welfare, and propaganda—were administered through special regional agencies with their own territorial divisions. The officers of general administration did not have control of the regional and local offices of the special administrative services, although they did have the right to information and the power to coordinate the work of all officials within their areas of jurisdiction: state, province, county, and city-county. During the latter years of the Third Reich the delegation of administrative tasks from the national level led to the attachment of offices for forest control, economics, rationing, and price control at the provincial, district, and local levels. The services and functions carried out by the General and Special Administrative systems were further supplemented by the extensive network of corporate administrations, which provided for further regimentation and control over the population. National Socialist controls, which intertwined with and supplemented German administration at all levels, were provided for through another elaborate national and territorial party administrative organization.

The administration of foreign affairs and military and naval matters continued as national administrative functions, but as in all aspects of German administrative activity, the impact of National Socialism was strong. In the field of foreign affairs, all political decisions and policies were made by the Führer. Although there were few changes of importance in the personnel of the Foreign Office in the early years of the Third Reich, the drastic reorganization of the Foreign Office in 1938 brought about the nazification of the foreign service. Between 1933 and 1938 the work of the Foreign Office was overshadowed by that of the unofficial Nazi party Office for Foreign Affairs and the infamous *Bureau Ribbentrop,* which were gradually laying the foundations for peaceful penetration and easy military conquest through the establishment of fifth columns throughout Europe. Although the reorganization of 1938 brought much of this activity within the jurisdiction of the Foreign Office, the Nazi party Overseas Organization (*Auslandsorganisation*) engaged in the task of organizing German nationals in foreign lands. In economic matters the Nazi Foreign Office worked through the National Foreign Trade Office (*Reichsstelle für Aussenhandel*) which it managed in cooperation with the Ministry of Economics. Foreign propaganda programs were developed in conjunction with the new Nazi Ministry for Propaganda.

The first Nazi reorganization of military and naval affairs came in 1934, when the Ministry of National Defense was replaced by the Ministry of War, which conducted the first phase of military preparation for World War II. The defense acts of 1935 revived military conscription and started Germany on a vast program of military expansion. In 1938 Hitler, fearing opposition from the conservative military and naval leaders, undertook an even more drastic reorganization of the armed forces. After removing several military leaders, who were considered as politically dangerous, Hitler established the High Command of the Armed Forces (*Oberkommando der Wehrmacht*). The Chief of the High Command was made subject to Hitler, who had assumed the position of Supreme Commander of the Armed Forces as early as 1935. Army affairs were placed under the High Command of the Army (*Oberkommando des Heeres*); naval affairs fell to the High Command of the Navy (*Oberkommando der Kriegsmarine*); and the air force, which had been developed by the Nazi National Air Ministry (*Reichsluftfahrtministerium*), was brought under the High Command by making the Air Minister Chief of the High Command of the Air Forces. The administration of army affairs was carried out through a central command and an elaborate territorial organization based upon sixteen corps areas (*Wehrkreise*). The program of naval expansion included the refitting of the old naval bases at Kiel and Wilhelmshaven and of the smaller stations scattered along the North Sea and Baltic Sea coasts. Military aviation under the National Ministry of Aviation, which was also responsible for civil aviation affairs, was administered through fourteen regional Aviation Offices (*Luftämter*). The *Deutsche Lufthansa,* the National Socialist Flying Corps, 1933 (*Nationalsozialistisches Fliegerkorps*), the German Air Raid Protection League, 1933 (*Reichsluftschutzbund*) and a number of aviation research agencies and institutes established by the Nazis were brought under the supervision of the National Air Ministry.

The functions of the National Ministry of the Interior were greatly increased under the Nazis through the nationalization of all internal administration and through the centralization of control over police and health. This ministry carried on all the functions of the old Republican ministry, except those pertaining to educational and cultural activities, which were transferred to the new Nazi ministries for Education and Propaganda. In 1934 it absorbed the Prussian Ministry of the Interior and the National Labor Service (*Reichsarbeitsdienst*) which had been a voluntary labor service organization under the Republic. The significant Nazi additions to the sphere of the Ministry of the Interior included the National Office for Ancestry Research (*Reichssippenamt*) the National Sport Office (*Reichssportamt*), and the Nazi National Chambers for Physicians, Veterinarians, Pharmacists, and Dentists, which replaced the old professional organizations. The organizations for towns, counties, and villages of the Republic were absorbed into the Nazi German Municipal League (*Deutscher Gemeindetag*), which was established in 1933 and placed under the Ministry of the Interior. Altogether, the work of the Ministry of the Interior in the fields of interior, police, welfare, and health administration was of extreme importance, for it provided direct administrative control of the Reich in respect to many functions of primary importance at all levels of authority.

Control of interior affairs under the Minister of the Interior was achieved through the Chief Presidents and the National Governors, who were appointed by and subject to dismissal by Hitler, but were made administratively responsible to the Minister of the Interior. In the States (*Länder*), the National Governors who were the deputies of the Reich as well as the heads of State administration and government, were assisted by a Deputy for Local Government (*Gauhauptmann*), an Advisory Board of *Gauräte,* and by Advisory Councillors for Special Purposes (*Beiräte*). The actual work was carried out by the state Minister Presidents and the state cabinets, acting under the direction of the National Governors. In the provinces of Prussia, the Chief Presidents, who were appointed by Hitler at the suggestion of the Minister of the Interior, had a status equivalent to that of the National Governor. In keeping with Nazi principles, the provincial diets and the state legislatures, which had provided for popular government under the Republic were eliminated along with the Senate, which had become obsolete with the elimination of the federal organization of the Reich. Political control by the Nazi party was easily guaranteed in most of the provinces and states, for the Chief Presidents and the National Governors were usually Nazi party Regional Party Leaders (*Gauleiter*). The Governmental Administrative Districts, which survived in Prussia and Bavaria, formed the next lower echelon of administration.

State and Local Administration

The county (*Landkreis*) and the city county (*Stadtkreis*) constituted the basic areas for administration and self-government in the provinces and states.

The city county constituted a built up urban area with a population of more than 20,000, while the county was a rural area with varying population, containing small towns (*Stadtgemeinden*) and rural villages (*Landgemeinden*). The Chief Mayors *Oberbürgermeister* of the city county and the County Managers (*Landräte*) of the county were responsible to the Regional President (*Regierungspräsidenten*) in Prussia and Bavaria and to the National Governors (*Reichsstatthalter*) in the other states. Within the counties, the Mayors of the small towns and the village chairmen (*Amtsvorsteher*) of the rural villages were under the supervision of the County Managers.

The Nazi effort to provide Germany with a uniform system of local administration met with only partial success. Originally, the Nazis had envisaged uniform administrative systems for the provinces and states and their component counties, city counties, and communes (*Gemeinden*). The German Municipal Code (*Deutsche Gemeindeordnung*) of January 1935, which provided for uniform municipal administration, was the major Nazi reform in the field of local government. The Nazis drastically modified the character and organization of local government and administration by establishing the right of the Reich government to control both local self-government and the local administration of tasks delegated from the top. They eliminated all local representative bodies and strengthened the position of the local executives. In 1938 they discarded the conflicting terminology and designations for local areas and officials, by applying Prussian titles and names to officials and areas throughout the Reich.

In the sphere of county government and administration, the County Manager (*Landrat*), who was appointed by Hitler on the recommendation of the Minister of the Interior, was responsible for central administration and county self-government. He served as the police authority and had complete responsibility for the supervision of the government and administration of the villages and towns of the county. He was assisted by a County Secretary (*Kreissekretär*), an appointed County Advisory Committee (*Kreisausschuss*), and, occasionally, in the larger counties by Governmental Administrative Councilors (*Regierungsräte*). He also worked in close cooperation with the local Party Agent, whom he had to keep informed of all important administrative acts. The Nazis eliminated the republican County Assembly (*Kreistag*) and transferred some of its functions to the appointed County Advisory Committee which was finally eliminated in 1939 when the Nazis sought to strengthen further the position of the County Manager. Within the office of the latter official, there were divisions for county personnel, supervision of towns and villages, local taxes, labor and land settlement, agricultural cooperation, public works, welfare, and finances. The County Manager, in his capacity as the head of local self-government, provided for the administration of the county hospitals, savings banks, utilities, and other enterprises, which were still organized under the Leagues of County Municipalities (*Kreisverbände*). In addition to these duties he cooperated with the numerous local officials responsible for national, provincial, and state special and technical services, the officials of the Nazi Estates, and the local leaders and officials of the Nazi party.

In the government and administration of the larger cities or city counties, the Chief Mayor (*Oberbürgermeister*), who was appointed by the Minister of the Interior in the case of the larger cities and by the National Governor or the Chief President in the case of cities between 20,000 and 100,000, was a professionally-trained individual. He was assisted by a number of professional Administrative Department heads (*Beigeordnete*), including a first *Beigeordneter* or deputy Chief Mayor, and by a number of Advisory Councilors, consisting usually of technical experts, who worked with the various departments of the city government. The departmental organization, which varied from city to city, generally included a central administration for police, economic matters, and finance, with sections for taxes, accounts, and surveying, education, welfare, housing and land settlement, building and construction, and public works and utilities. Under the Nazis the Chief Mayor was assisted by an appointed body of Councilors (*Ratsherren*) which replaced the old elected city councils of the Republic. The importance of the Councilors was gradually reduced, but during the war, as matters grew difficult, they came to be consulted more frequently by the Mayor. The old administrative boards, which were subject to the control of the city councils in Republican times, had been replaced by the Administrative Department heads. Under the Nazis the Mayor was also assisted by a Nazi Party Agent (*Parteibeauftragter*) who was present to guarantee the political reliability of the city administration.

The abolition of the democratic and representative features of the old system of city government, the strengthening of the position of the Chief Mayor, and the introduction of Nazi party controls, constituted the basic Nazi changes in municipal government introduced under the German Municipal Code. This Code did not disturb the scope of local powers, but it did eliminate all local popular control of the Mayor and gave him all necessary legislative and administrative powers. And while it established the principles of municipal government, the actual administration of each large city was regulated in detail by its own city charter (*Hauptsatzung*) and by ordinances issued by the Mayor with the approval of the higher supervisory authority of the Reich. The services and functions of the cities were supplemented by those of the national government, the state government, the Nazi Estates, and the Nazi party, which were carried out by local officials subject to regional offices outside the jurisdiction of the general state or city administration.

In the sphere of local government and administration, the small towns and the rural villages were headed by Mayors who were assisted by two or three Administrative Department heads—usually in honorary service—an appointed town or village council, and a Nazi party agent. The elected town and village councils were abolished by the Nazis. Although village and town self-government was once important, with the advent of the Nazis the management of rural life was placed under the effective control of higher county, district, provincial, or state authorities.

Organization for Special Administration

Great changes occurred in the sphere of special administration. Here the Nazis were less confined by traditional patterns and were able to devise and adapt administrative forms to the requirements of a highly centralized system. The special needs of crisis government were easily met without the necessity of conforming to older German ideas of local autonomy and judicial review. A consideration of a number of special administrative functions will make those points clear.

Police.—The administration of public safety was also nationalized by the Nazi regime. The old state police systems were transferred from the states to the Reich and placed under the National Chief of German Police, whose office was attached to the national Ministry of the Interior. The German Police under the Nazis, who were subjected to uniform national standards and training, were divided into two main branches: the Order Police (*Ordnungspolizei*) and the Security Police (*Sicherheitspolizei*). The Order Police, who were under the Main Office of the Order Police (*Hauptamt Ordnungspolizei*), had numerous functional and territorial groupings. Administrative control was provided at these levels by the state and district Police Authorities (*Landespolizeibehörden*) who were the District Presidents of Prussia and Bavaria and the National Governors in the other states; by the county and city county police authorities (*Kreispolizeibehörden*), who were the County Managers of the counties or the chief Mayors of the city counties and by the local police authorities (*Ortspolizeibehörden*) who were the Mayors of the communes. In the larger cities there were National Police Administrations headed by Police Presidents (*Polizeipräsidenten*).

The functional groups of the Order Police included the Protection Police of the city counties and municipalities (*Schutzpolizei*), the Rural Police of the counties (*Gendarmerie*), and the Administrative Police (*Verwaltungspolizei*). The Administrative Police of the city counties, counties, and communes performed the administrative functions of record keeping, licensing, registering, and enforcing local regulations, through special detachments: the Buildings Police (*Baupolizei*), Factory and Shops Police (*Gewerbepolizei*), School Police (*Schulpolizei*), Market Police (*Marktpolizei*), Health Police (*Gesundheitspolizei*), and Housing Police (*Wohnungspolizei*). Police control of the population of the Reich was aided by a long established system of registration which was maintained by the Administrative Police. Based upon the new decrees of 1938 and 1939, there were four different registers: the Register of Persons (*Melderegister* or *Personenregister*) which permitted the easy tracing of the whereabouts of everyone; the Index of Buildings (*Hausregister*) which showed how many persons lived in each house and who they were; the People's Index (*Volkskartei*) which listed individuals from five to seventy-four years of age for purposes of military, labor, and medical recruiting; and the Aliens' Register (*Ausländerkartei*) which was used for the control of foreigners. Most of these registers were not restricted to police use, for they were available to the army for military recruiting, the air raid protection service, and the labor service. They were also used by the Nazi party for control purposes. Copies of the Register of Persons went to the local finance offices and were ultimately sent to the statistical services of the Reich. The operational supervision of the Protection Police, the Rural Police, and the Administrative Police was provided by Inspectors attached to the State and District Police authorities (*Landespolizeibehörden*), who were responsible to the Main Office of the Order Police.

Preparations for war involved the establishment of additional Order Police Formations. The Fire Protection Police (*Feuerschutzpolizei*), a branch of the Order Police established for ninety of the larger cities in 1938, were organized under the Office for Fire Protection Agencies (*Amt Feuerwehren*), and an Inspector-General of Fire Protection Police (*Generalinspekteur der Feuerschutzpolizei*), both attached to the Main Office of the Order Police in Berlin. Regional administration was carried out by the police authorities of the Reich. In the larger cities the work of the Fire Protection Police was supplemented by that of auxiliary fire fighting units. The smaller cities and towns depended upon small professionally trained units and auxiliary fire fighting units, which were established to meet war needs. Operational control of the fire fighting service was carried out under the County Leader (*Kreisführer*) in the counties and city counties by the District Leader (*Bezirksführer*) in governmental administrative district (*Regierungsbezirke*) and by the Sectional Inspector (*Abschnittsinspekteur*) in the corps areas who was responsible to the Inspector General of Fire Protection Police in Berlin.

The work of the police was also supplemented by the Technical Emergency Service (*Technische Nothilfe*), which was an auxiliary police force composed of engineers and skilled workmen used to restore essential public utilities damaged by warfare or internal disturbances. This service, which was established on a voluntary basis in 1919 to repair damages left behind by World War I, was taken over by the Nazis in 1933 and attached to the national Ministry of the Interior. It was finally integrated into the Order Police organization in late 1939. These forces were further strengthened by the addition of the Auxiliary

Police (*Hilfspolizei*), which was composed of civilian volunteers organized in rural guard (*Landwacht*) units which aided the Rural Police, and city guard (*Stadtwacht*) units which worked with the Protection Police.

The Nazi Security Police and its branches: the Criminal Police (*Kriminalpolizei*), the Secret State Police (*Geheime Staatspolizei*), and the Security Service (*Sicherheitsdienst*) were subject to the Main Office for the Security of the Reich (*Reichssicherheitshauptamt*) and were under the command of the Chief of the Security Police (*Chef der Sicherheitspolizei*) and the Security Service of the Elite Guard (*Schutzstaffel*). The Security Service which was a party organization attached to the Elite Guard (*SS-Schutzstaffel*), served as an intelligence organization. Action against subversive political activity was taken by the Gestapo (*Geheime Staatspolizei*), which worked through regional offices under a central directorate in Berlin. The Border Police (*Grenzpolizei*) formed a separate Gestapo police formation. Action against ordinary crimes was taken by the Criminal Police, which worked through criminal police offices attached to the National Police Administrations of the larger cities. Control was provided by regional offices and a central directorate in Berlin. The work of the Security Police was carried out by a highly trained force of criminologists, political agents, and party agents who worked in separate organizations with specialized functions. Coordination of security efforts was made possible by a joint command and by liaison between the field offices of the three organizations.

The work of the Order Police and the Security Police in the field of public safety and national security was further supplemented by several specialized police organizations, which were administered by the various national administrative authorities. The Railway Police (*Eisenbahnpolizei*) and the Harbor Police (*Hafenpolizei*) were under the Ministry of Transport; while the Post Office Guards (*Postschutzwächter*) were under the Ministry of Posts. The Mine Police (*Bergpolizei*) operated from the Mining Offices (*Bergämter*) of the Ministry of Economics. The Forest Police (*Forstschutzpolizei*) and the Agricultural Police (*Flurschutzpolizei*) were supervised by the Ministry of Agriculture.

The German concept of the police function goes back to the days of the paternalistic and absolute state, when the functions of the police included the whole range of internal administration. The differentiation of administrative functions in the late eighteenth century, and the gradual emergence of the personal rights of citizens, tended to limit the power of the police to protective activities. The introduction of constitutional provisions for the protection of the individual during the nineteenth century further limited the powers of the police by establishing legal limitations for police action. Nevertheless, the powers of the German police remained broad and elastic, and much wider in scope than those granted to the police under the Anglo-American legal systems. The German police have always had the task of aiding other branches of administration in the enforcement of rules and regulations, as well as protecting the public and the individual from dangers threatening public order and security.

But the Nazi regime revived and extended older concepts of police power and consequently there was an enormous expansion of police functions and activities. This was carried out through the establishment of special police organizations such as the Gestapo, and through the interlocking of police and party organizations. Even more important was the nationalization of police administration and the standardization of police methods, procedures, and training. These changes were accompanied by the progressive withdrawal of all significant police activity from the legal controls established during the nineteenth and early twentieth centuries and by the gradual nazification of all police personnel. The police became the guardians of the Nazi State.

Public Health.—The Nazi regime also established national control over public health. Authority over public health activities was vested in the national Ministry of the Interior, which was made responsible for health legislation, racial and hereditary policies, disease control, and medical and scientific training. It worked in close cooperation with the national Ministry of Propaganda in matters related to health and medical propaganda, and was advised by a number of national organizations and committees interested in such matters as hospitals, tuberculosis, venereal disease, and racial problems. Technical and scientific aid was provided by the National Health Office (*Reichsgesundheitsamt*), which provided for the coordination of scientific work in the fields of medicine, genetics, hygiene, pharmacology, and chemistry.

Regional and local health and administration was carried out under a uniform national code. The office of the Prussian Chief President included a Governmental Medical Council (*Regierungs- und Medizinalrat*) in charge of a Medical Department head (*Medizinal Dezernent*) who was responsible for the administration of the provincial insitutions for the deaf, blind, and feeble-minded, the supervision of the licensing of pharmacies and professional organizations in the province, and the control of lower public health authorities. In the states, public health functions were carried out under the National Governor by a local health ministry or agency. The Governmental Medical Council, attached to the offices of the Prussian and Bavarian District Presidents, was responsible for the collection of vital and health statistics, for the supervision of health laws and regulations, and for the control of the local health offices.

Public health work at the city, county, and village levels was carried out through the Health Offices (*Gesundheitsämter*) which were under local health officers (*Amtsärzte*) directly responsible to higher health authorities— the Governmental Medical Councils of the Prussian and Bavarian Districts, or

the Health Offices or Ministries of the States. A few of the larger German cities
were permitted to retain their old health offices and organizations under the
city administrations. The local health offices had numerous responsibilities.
They supervised the local physicians, dentists, veterinaries, and pharmacists,
and their local professional organizations. The Health Police (*Gesundheitspolizei*) who were subject to the control of the local police authorities, carried out
the inspection of health conditions of plants, dwellings, public buildings, and
institutions, supervised water purification and sewage and garbage disposal,
and enforced the pure food and drug regulations under the supervision of the
Health Officer. The Health Office also provided for the control of communica-
ble disease and epidemics, the collection of vital statistics, and administration
of the Nazi marriage and hereditary laws. The Health Officer had prime
responsibility for the enforcement of all health laws formulated by the Reich
and issued through the District President in Prussia and Bavaria and through
the health offices of the states. The local Health Office also cooperated with the
offices of the voluntary organizations of the Nazi party, the Red Cross, and the
Church. The Nazi party provided for public health activities, which were
mainly directed toward education of backward communities, through its central Public Health Office at Munich and the District Offices for Public Health
(*Gauämter für Volksgesundheit*), one of which was attached to the office of
each Nazi regional party leader. Locally public health work was carried forward by the National Socialist League of German Doctors (NSD-*Ärztebund*),
the German Labor Front (*Deutsche Arbeitsfront*), and other Nazi party organizations.

*Economic Organization.—The Nazi regime brought about a rapid change
from a comparatively free and competitive economy to a planned and carefully
controlled economy suited to the needs of a nation preparing for war.* The economic life of the Reich was subjected to a complex system of national control,
which was vested in the national ministries for agriculture, economics,
finance, and labor, in the central authorities for banking, forestry, and other
economic activities, and in the Nazi corporate estates. The Nazi economic
preparations for war were derived from memories of World War I and the effects of the blockade, and were based upon totalitarian principles calling for an
economic order involving dictatorial planning, absolute political control, and
economic self-sufficiency. The whole economic structure, which was an elaboration of the socialist concepts of a labor-capitalistic state imbedded in a nationalistic ideology, was directed toward the demands of war and conditioned by
efforts to overcome shortages of material and labor.

Economic planning, an essential of the Nazi war economy (*Wehrwirtschaft*), was placed under a National Office for Regional Planning (*Reichsstelle
für Raumordnung*), which was given the task of determining the proper uti-

lization of land and resources needed for war. Regional State and Provincial Planning Associations (*Landesplanungsgemeinschaften*) were set up under the District Presidents and the National Governors for planning at the regional level. These associations, like the national one, represented every aspect of life within the land: social, economic, political, administrative, and academic. The complicated economic organization described in the following pages was created by the Nazi regime between 1933 and the outbreak of war in 1939.

The agricultural activities of the Third Reich were organized under the National Food Estate (*Reichsnährstand*) attached to the National Minister for Food and Agriculture (*Reichsministerium für Ernährung und Landwirtschaft*), which carried forward the work of the old Republican ministry. The National Food Estate which absorbed the Republican Agricultural Council (*Deutscher Landwirtschaftsrat*) and its affiliated state and provincial organizations, included within its structure individuals and organizations interested in agriculture, forestry, horticulture, viniculture, fisheries, hunting, agricultural cooperatives, wholesale and retail agricultural and food trade, and the food proccessing industries. It sought to increase the production of food and to prepare Germany for war by reducing her dependence on imports. This was to be accomplished through detailed planning for production and the wholesale introduction of scientific methods. The administration of the Nazi food program was carried out under the National Peasants' Leader (*Reichsbauernführer*) who headed both the National Food Estate and the National Ministry of Food and Agriculture.

Production control was provided through the State or Provincial Peasants' Associations (*Landesbauernschaften*), the County Peasants' Associations (*Kreisbauernschaften*), and the Local Peasants' Associations (*Ortsbauernschaften*), each of which was under a Peasant or Farm Leader (*Bauernführer*) who was usually a Nazi official. The State or Provincial Peasants' Associations maintained general controls, while the County Peasants' Associations had supervisory control over the local associations. The activities of the latter bureau were reflected in the names of their offices: The Man—propaganda, welfare, and labor (*Der Mensch*), The Farm—production, education, and farm records (*Der Hof*), and The Market—distribution and marketing (*Der Markt*). The Local Peasants' Association maintained the system of Homestead Cards (*Hofkarte*) for the control of production and delivery obligations, and established the production quotas of the farmers. All sales were regulated by a system of certificates and licenses. Market control was also provided by the National Food Estate. Its Central Market Associations (*Hauptvereinigungen* or *Marktverbände*), which maintained controls for eight major commodity groups, determined the quantities of each product which were required by the Reich for civilian and military purposes. These National Market Associations were used by the National Food Estate to determine regional crop production quotas which were allotted to the State or Provincial Peasants' Associations. The regional Economic Unions (*Wirtschaftsverbände*), which were subordinated to the Central Marketing Associations, handled the local problems of distribution and consumption in conjunction with the State or Provincial Peasants' Associations. The National Food Estate which determined the policies of the peasant associations and the Central Market Associations and the Economic Unions, also worked with the National Boards of the Four-Year Plan (*Reichsstellen*), which had a monopoly control over all imports and exports of foodstuffs as well as the right to purchase and store food obtained on the domestic market. These boards had the function of adjusting the importation of agricultural products to domestic needs.

The fisheries of the Reich were also under the National Food Estate, and its National Association of Fisheries maintained branch offices at the fishing ports of Wesermünde, Cuxhaven, and Hamburg, and liaison officers at the State or Provincial Peasants' Associations of the coastal provinces. Although the private forest interests of the Reich were organized under the National Food Estate, administrative control was provided by the National Forest Office (*Reichsforstamt*), which had taken over supervision of forestry and game from the forestry agencies, that had been under the states in the days of the Republic. Regional Forest Offices (*Landesforstämter*) were attached to the district and state governments. These offices, which were headed by a State Forester (*Landforstmeister*) supervised the work of the county Chief Forester (*Oberförster*) and the local forester (*Förster*). These officials were responsible for the administration of the state forests and the supervision of the forestry affairs of the counties, towns, and private interests. Market control over forest products was provided by the regional Forest and Wood Market Control Offices (*Forst- und Holzwirtschaftsämter*) of the National Forest Office in Berlin.

The control of trade and industry in general was maintained through the Ministries of Economics and Finance, through the Estate for Trade and Industry, and through the various business cartels and syndicates. Before the outbreak of war, national policies for war preparedness in the economic sphere were determined in the Office for the Four-Year Plan, which was responsible for the allocation of raw materials, manpower, prices, and foreign exchange. Administrative control of German trade and industry was exercised through the Organization of Trade and Industrial Economy (*Organisation der gewerblichen Wirtschaft*). This organization, established by the Nazis as a self-governing agency for trade and industry, absorbed the republican business and industrial organizations. It was attached to the National Ministry of Economics and centered in the National Economic Chamber (*Reichswirtschaftskammer*). This National Chamber was composed of representatives of the regional

Economic Chambers (*Wirtschaftskammern*) in the several provinces and states, of the five National Associations for Trade, Industry, Banking, Power, and Insurance (*Reichsgruppen*) and of the National Chamber of Handicrafts (*Reichshandwerkskammer*). The regional Economic Chambers were in turn composed of delegates from the local chambers of Trade and Industry (*Industrie- und Handelskammern*), the regional groups of the *Reichsgruppen,* and the local chambers of Handcraftsmen (*Handwerkskammern*). The German business and industrial enterprises were members of the Chamber of Trade and Industry and were subject to coordination by the local offices of the various *Reichsgruppen*. The latter organizations and their regional groups served as clearing houses for technical and economic education, production efficiency (shop management and cost accounting), taxation, cartel questions, transportation problems, research, and the training of workers for specific groups of trade enterprises and industrial undertakings. The regional Economic Chambers also served as coordinating agencies for all funcional and territorial economic organizations and as clearing houses for regional economic problems. The craftsmen belonged to local guilds which were represented in the Chamber of Handcraftsmen. This elaborate territorial and functional organization for industry, trade, and crafts was supplemented by the involved organizational arrangements which had been made by the cartels and the nationally controlled industries set up under the Four-Year Plan.

The mineral and fuel resources of the Reich were placed under still further controls in 1935. The national Ministry of Economics took over from the states the supervision of safety and health in the mines. The Reich was divided into regional Regional Mining Districts (*Oberbergamtsbezirke*) which were further subdivided under Mining Offices (*Bergämter*). The control of production and the coordination of mining activities remained under the Four-Year Plan and the Estate for Trade and Industry.

Effective national economic control was also provided for through the system of price regulation. At first, the maintenance of price levels in Germany was not easy or effective. All prices tended to move upward after 1934, and the various legislative and administrative acts of the Reich government until 1936 had little real effect. The Price Stop Decree of 1936, which established the office of the National Commissioner for Price Formation (*Reichskommissar für Preisbildung*) in the Four-Year Plan, established firm control over all prices, including rents and the costs of services, except wages, security prices, interest rates, and certain transportation costs. The determination of food prices, however, was delegated to the Ministry for Agriculture and the National Food Estate. This change amounted to the elimination of market prices determined by supply and demand, for after that date prices were based upon costs plus a reasonable profit to the producer. Some prices were even forcibly reduced by the

new organization. Prices were fixed and stabilized through the office of the
National Commissioner for Price Formation who was assisted by the Minister of Economics and the Organization of Trade and Industrial Economy (*Organisation der gewerblichen Wirtschaft*), the Minister of Agriculture and the
National Food Estate and by the cartels and syndicates, which sought to establish guiding prices. All these agencies cooperated to standardize commodities
and to eliminate unjustified price differentials. Regional price control was
carried out through Offices for Price Formation (*Preisbildungsstellen*) attached to the offices of the National Governors and the Chief Presidents. These
offices were empowered to fix prices of regional significance and to supervise
the Price Supervisory Offices (*Preisüberwachungsstellen*) which were attached
to the offices of the District Presidents and the Price Offices (*Preisstellen*).
These Price Offices were attached to the office of the Chief Mayor of the city
counties or the County Manager of the counties. These local offices were mainly
charged with the enforcement of price regulations.

A loose system of rationing control was maintained prior to the outbreak
of World War II. The market rationing of food was handled by the Minister of
Agriculture working through the Central Market Associations of the National
Food Estate, while nonagrarian products were rationed to the wholesalers and
distributors through the Ministry of Economics and its Organization of Trade
and Industrial Economy. These agencies worked in close cooperation with the
offices for price control in efforts to guide consumption.

The control of the flow of commerce was also subject to special National
Trade Control Boards (*Reichsstellen*) which were established under the Four-
Year Plan to handle the import-export trade of German industry. They were
responsible for clearing agreements, exchange control, and export subsidies,
which were directed toward the importation of raw materials and foodstuffs
needed for the Nazi war effort. Foreign trade was subject to still further controls. The Ministry of Economics operated through the National Office for Foreign Trade (*Reichsstelle für Aussenhandel*), which was also under the Foreign
Office for coordinaion of export activities, while the *Reichsbank* controlled all
exchange and clearing payments. The National Trade Central Boards, which
guided the flow of trade within specific commodity groups in cooperation
with the Organization of Trade and Industrial Economy, were thus subject to
higher political and economic authorities. The industries of Germany had become agents of the government, for production quotas, distribution, and prices
were wholly dictated by government agencies.

The monetary and financial systems were brought under tighter national
control by the National Socialist regime. The Ministers of Economics and
Finance continued to exercise prime control, and their power was greatly
increased by a series of sweeping financial decrees. The *Reichsbank* continued

as the central bank of issue, although it lost its independent status in 1939, when it was placed under the Minister of Economics. The system of control for all transactions in foreign exchange, first established in 1931, was under the *Reichsbank,* which was given complete authority over all dealing in foreign exchange. Responsibility for coinage and the regulation of the money value of the German mark remained under the National Finance Ministry. The German banking system was organized under the National Organization of Banks of the Organization of Trade and Industrial Economy, and was brought under the highly centralized control and supervision of the Credit Supervisory Board (*Aufsichtsamt für das Kreditwesen*) of the Ministry of Economics, which was given the power to amalgamate and close banks, to permit or refuse the establishment of new banks, and to give instructions as to the investment of deposits. Control over the banking structure was also shared by the *Reichsbank,* which was given broad powers over investment policies. The stock and commodity exchanges and the private insurance organizations were subjected to similar types of stringent financial control. The whole German monetary and financial system was directed toward the complete mobilization of liquid resources in the interest of war preparations.

Transportation and Communications.—Government controls for transportation were rapidly extended by the Nazis. The National Transportation Ministry, which had the major responsibility for the administration of railways, docks, ports, and shipping, inland waterways, and road transportation, was given greater powers of supervision and control. All of the transportation services and enterprises were organized in the National Transportation Groups (*Reichsverkehrsgruppen*) which were subordinated to the national Minister of Transportation. Regional groups, which included representatives of transportation, provincial or state governments, and the Nazi party and Nazi Economic Estates, were established for the regional coordination of transportation activities. These National Transportation Groups maintained representatives in the regional Economic Chambers and were subdivided into functional groups for rail, sea, inland waterways, and road transportation, each embracing the local transportation enterprises, which were allowed to retain their membership in the local chamber of Trade and Industry. The administration of the German Railroad Company (*Deutsche Reichsbahn Gesellschaft*) underwent few changes under the Nazis, except that it lost its position as a public corporation when it was placed directly under the National Minister of Transportation. It remained outside the National Transportation Organization (*Reichsverkehrsgruppe*). The National Waterways Council, however, was absorbed into the new organization for transportation.

The greatest series of administrative changes came in the field of road transportation. The major roads remained under the state and provincial

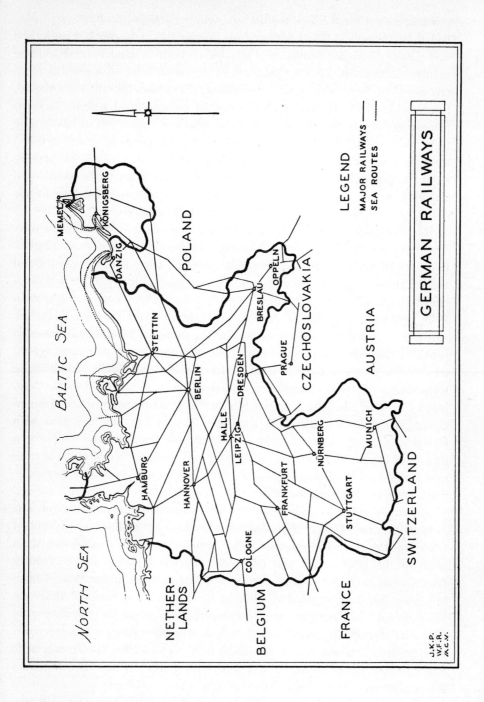

governments, while the local roads of the counties and city counties were maintained by the county Road Master (*Strassenmeister*), who worked under the
supervision of higher provincial and state authorities. Under the Nazis the
regular road system was supplemented by the construction of a series of modern superhighways called *Reichsautobahnen,* which were placed under the administration of the General Inspector for the German road system (*Generalinspekteur für das deusche Strassenwesen*) who was responsible to Hitler. The
General Inspector headed the Super-highway Corporation which worked
through several regional construction offices and local field offices. He also assumed responsibility for the improvement of certain main roads which were
classified as national roads. These improvements, which were financed by the
Reich, were carried out by the state and provincial governments.

There were few changes in the administration of the communication services of the Reich. The National Ministry of Posts continued to have jurisdiction over all public telephone, telegraph, cable and teletype services, posts, and
the postal cheque and transfer system. The National Ministry of Posts also operated an extensive motor transport system for mails and some passengers. In
1938, after the annexation of Austria, the Austrian Postal Savings Bank System was extended throughout the Reich. The National Ministry of Posts also
provided the technical personnel and maintenance for the broadcasting system, although the programs were under the National Radio Broadcasting
Corporation (*Reichsrundfunkgesellschaft*), which was supervised by the Ministry of Propaganda. The National Ministry of Posts maintained a number of
commercial radio telephone and telegraph stations for communication with
foreign stations. It cooperated with the Ministry of Transport and the Navy in
matters of communication with ships at sea and with the Air Ministry in communications with aircraft. Elaborate communications networks were also
maintained by the army, the police, and the railroads.

Labor.—The labor supply of the Reich was under firm national control. The
National Labor Ministry (*Reichsarbeitsministerium*) retained its control of
labor legislation, social insurance, labor welfare, and labor problems. Much
work of the labor courts was taken over by the National Labor Trustees
(*Reichstreuhänder der Arbeit*), who were given supreme authority in regulating labor disputes, wages, and working conditions. The National Office for
Employment and Unemployment Insurance (*Reichsanstalt für Arbeitsvermittlung und Arbeitslosenversicherung*), which was now given a full monopoly
over employment, was placed within the Ministry of Labor. Its regional State
Labor Offices (*Landesarbeitsämter*) and local Labor Offices (*Arbeitsämter*)
maintained records of wages, hours of work, and conditions of employment
for all workers through a system of labor books (*Arbeitsbücher*) which contained a full vocational record for each worker. The State Labor Offices

served as regional agencies for the wholesale planning of the utilization of the German labor supply. They carried out the administration of the labor laws relating to apprenticeships, compulsory service, and labor conscription. The work of the Head Welfare Office (*Hauptversorgungsamt*) continued without interruption, as did the elaborate social insurance system which had been built up by the Empire and Republic under the Ministry of Labor.

Public Welfare.—There were, however, vast changes in the character of public welfare. While the old public welfare structure remained (except for the introduction of the "leadership principle" into the numerous welfare organizations), the Nazi party undertook a large welfare program of its own to prepare for the emergency conditions that would come with war. The party welfare agencies, the Nazi People's Welfare Organization (*NS Volkswohlfahrt*), the Nazi Women's Organization (*NS Frauenschaft*), the Nazi War Victims Organization (*NS Kriegsopferversorgung*), the Winter Help (*Winterhilfe*), the Hitler Youth (*Hitler Jugend*), and the Strength through Joy (*Kraft durch Freude*) of the German Labor Front (*Deutsche Arbeitsfront*), took over much of the work of private and public agencies. Under the Nazis, welfare work was characterized by widespread discrimination on the basis of race, and by the use of welfare for the purposes of party control to finance the party officials, and to subsidize specially favored groups. The centralization of welfare work under the party agencies tended to limit the operations of public and private programs. In practice all private welfare agencies, except the Domestic Mission (*Innere Mission*) of the Lutheran Church, the welfare agency of the Catholic Church, and the German Red Cross, were eliminated.

The administrative controls of the Ministry of Labor were supplemented by the establishment of the German Labor Front (*Deutsche Arbeitsfront*), which was founded as an affiliated organization of the Nazi party to replace the trade unions of the Republic. It took over the assets and membership of the dissolved labor unions. The German Labor Front, which embraced not only all town and city workers but also all employers, maintained in each Labor District (*Gau*) a Labor Chamber (*Arbeitskammer*) of Employees and Employer's representatives, a District Administration (*Gauwaltung*) and a District Office for Legal Advice (*Gaurechtsberatungsstelle*). The District Administration supervised the work of the county and local offices of the German Labor Front, which were composed of factory organizations of employees and employers. The German Labor Front, with a membership of about thirty millions, was used largely as an instrument of control to enforce the labor policies of the Nazi regime. Rural agrarian labor fell under the exclusive jurisdiction of the National Food Estate.

Education and Church.—The Nazi regime brought about the nationalization of education, which had long been in the hands of the states. The first state school organizations had emerged in Thuringia in the seventeenth century and in Prussia in the eighteenth century. During the nineteenth century the liberal and the conservative educational forces were in conflict, the outcome of which was the organization of systematic school systems controlled by the state governments. The lower classes attended the state elementary schools (*Volksschulen*) for eight years and then went on to the middle schools (*Mittelschulen*) or the trade and vocational schools (*Fach-und Berufsschulen*) to complete their education. The upper classes had a more complicated educational system. Elementary education was provided by a four year primary school (*Vorschule*), while secondary education involved nine years of work in the classical secondary school (*Gymnasium*), the scientific semi-classical secondary school (*Realgymnasium*), or work in the more modern non-classical secondary school (*Realschule*) or higher non-classical secondary schools (*Oberrealschule*). These secondary schools led to work in the universities or higher technical schools. The state administered schools of the Empire were used to meet the needs of German industry for trained technicians and professional people and to foster the growth of nationalism.

During the period of the Weimar Republic several basic reforms were introduced, many of which were aimed at the elimination of the class system of education. The republican Foundation School (*Grundschule*) was set up to serve as a common elementary school for all children, while the secondary school system was modified through the establishment of the high school and the *Aufbauschule* to bridge the gap between the elementary and secondary education of the upper and lower classes, so that the gifted children of the masses could have access to higher education. Modifications of curriculum and method were introduced, and efforts were made to democratize the spirit and administration of education through stress upon ethical principles and through the establishment of self-governing organizations of teachers, parents, and students. The programs of elementary schools were considerably liberalized; but the secondary school, representing a more conservative viewpoint, for the most part, rather successfully resisted change.

The National Socialist regime reversed educational trends which had been developing for over a hundred years. All German education was centralized under the National Ministry for Science, Education, and Popular Culture (*Reichsministerium für Wissenschaft, Erziehung, und Volksbildung*). The Nazis brought about an immediate reduction of the length of secondary and university education. The number of classical Gymnasiums was drastically reduced, while the more technical high school became the predominant secondary school. Three new types of secondary schools were set up: the National Political Educational Institutes (*Nationalpolitische Erziehungsanstalten*); the *Adolf-Hitler-Schools* (*Schulen*), which were planned to educate especially selected students destined for party leadership; and the German Home Schools (*Deutsche Heimschulen*), established for the children of parents who were living abroad or who were war victims. The Nazis "purged" the schools of students and teachers with questionable political views, emphasized physical fitness rather than intellectual activity, and stressed National Socialist ideology. The administration of the school system was dominated by the new Nazi Ministry of Education, which exercised legislative control over all of Germany and executive power within Prussia. The remaining states retained their old educational ministries, subject to the new controls. The elementary and intermediate schools were controlled by the National Minister of Education through the educational ministries of the states, and the District Presidents. Locally these schools were administered by School Superintendents (*Schulräte*) under the Chief Mayors and the County Manager. The secondary schools were administered under the Chief Mayors who were directly responsible to either a state ministry of education or to a Chief President. Vocational school administration was handled in a similar fashion, except that agricultural schools were handled by the National Food Estate. The universities of Prussia were directly under the national Ministry of Education, while those of each state were supervised by the appropriate state ministry. All democratic methods were eliminated under the Nazis. Only the Advisory School Council (*Schulbeirat*) survived at the local level.

Nazi control was further strengthened by the activities of party organizations for the leadership of youth. The free youth organizations of the Republic were abolished and replaced by the German Young People from 10 to 14 years of age (*Deutsches Jungvolk*), the Hitler Youth for lads from 14 to 18 years old (*Hitler Jugend*), the Young Girls (*Jungmädel*) from 10 to 14 years old, and the League of German Girls (*Bund Deutscher Mädel*). German students and teachers were organized under the Nazi Main Office for Teachers (*Hauptamt für Erzieher*) at Munich and the National Socialist Teachers' League (NS *Lehrerbund*), the National Socialist Lecturers' Association (*NSD-Dozentenbund*), the National Socialist German Students' League (*NSD-Studentenbund*), and the German Students' Association (*Deutsche Studentenschaft*). All German sport activities were placed under the National Sport Office which was in the national Ministry of the Interior. Its regional offices worked in cooperation with the local offices of the National Physical Training League (*Reichsbund für Leibesübungen*) and the German Association to Promote Sports (*Deutsche Sporthilfe*). The Nazified school system, coupled with the student, youth, and sport organizations, gave the Nazi regime almost complete control of the youth of the German nation.

Religion.—The Nazification of the educational system was accompanied by the extension of Nazi control to the churches of Germany. The Catholic

Church had six archdioceses, dioceses, deaconries, and twelve thousand parishes when the Nazis came into power. The Protestant German (Lutheran) Evangelical Church, which was headed by a national bishop, was organized into state and provincial Regional Churches (*Landeskirche*) each headed by a bishop and a synod. Locally the Evangelical Church was divided into deaconries, prelatures, district congregations, and parishes. Smaller religious groups included the Methodists, Baptists, Mormons, and a variety of Lutheran sects. The German Jews were organized under orthodox, conservative, and reformed synagogues. Under the Empire and the Republic, there were close relationships between the churches and the German states. Before World War I many of the states had exercised close control over church affairs. In Prussia the state government played an important role in the selection of clergymen of the Protestant churches. The Weimar Republic continued to enforce the collection of church taxes from all citizens registered as Catholics, Protestants, or Jews. The income from church taxes was further supplemented by state subsidies.

The National Socialist regime completely revised the attitude of the state toward the churches of Germany. Although the Nazis sought to establish a "folk religion" based upon "blood, race, and soil," Hitler was cautious in his church policies. But the doctrines and actions of the Nazis resulted in bitter conflicts with both the Catholic and the Protestant churches. The Concordat with the Vatican, which was signed in 1933, forced the Catholic priests to desist from political activity. The Nazis violated the terms of the Concordat by gradually restricting the activities of the Catholic Church in the fields of charity, education, sports, and youth work. Although the encroachments of the Nazis were denounced by papal bulls and episcopal pastoral letters, many of the Catholic leaders supported the Nazis in what was described as a war against bolshevism.

The Protestant churches suffered more severely than the Catholic, for they lacked the support of a world organization. The Nazi religious propaganda divided their forces. Germans with neo-pagan beliefs based upon the old Germanic worship of Wotan gradually gained control of the Lutheran Churches, with the aid of the Nazi party and through the use of terroristic methods. The conflict within the Lutheran church was partially resolved by the creation of the National Ministry for Church Affairs (*Reichsministerium für die kirchlichen Angelegenheiten*), which was established to restore orderly conditions within the German Evangelical Church. The new minister took over control of Protestant church appointments and finances. The Lutheran clergy were forced to take an oath of loyalty to the Führer. The Protestant opposition to the Nazis, which was led by Niemöller, gradually gave way; when war came most of the clergy had taken the oath of loyalty.

Propaganda.—The integration of the social, economic, and political life of Germany was strengthened by extensive propaganda and educational controls for the intellectual, political, and artistic activities of the nation. National Socialist control of public attitudes and opinions was carried out through Party, Government, and Corporate organizations. Within the Nazi party, propaganda activities were carried out by the National Propaganda Chief (*Reichspropagandaleiter*) of the Nazi party through the district, county and local party propaganda leaders. Their work was supplemented by that of the party offices for the press, literature, and intellectual training. The Hitler Youth, the German Labor Front, the Elite Guard, and other Nazi party organizations carried on extensive propaganda programs for their members. Governmental propaganda activities were carried out by the National Ministry for Public Enlightenment and Propaganda (*Reichsministerium für Volksaufklärung und Propaganda*) established in 1933, which was responsible for the control, organization, and distribution of propaganda. All activities for the molding of public opinion —press, radio, motion pictures, theater, literature, and fine arts—were placed under the Propaganda Ministry. Within the Reich, this ministry carried out its work through a regional organization, which followed the district pattern of the Nazi party. The National Propaganda Offices (*Reichspropagandaämter*) of the Ministry used the Nazi party propaganda organization for work at the local level.

The work of the Propaganda Ministry was supplemented by that of the National Chamber of Culture (*Reichskulturkammer*), which was a public corporation organized to control the cultural life of the German nation and to provide for the organization of professional people engaged in creative work. It consisted of National Chambers for Music, for Painting and Plastic Arts, for Literature, Press, Radio, Theater, and Films. The National Chamber of Culture also provided for the supervision of the National Radio Broadcasting Corporation (*Reichsrundfunkgesellschaft*) and the UFA film industry. Regional control was accomplished by the Regional Cultural Administrators (*Landeskulturwalter*) of the National Chamber of Culture which followed the party district pattern, and by the professional organizations and cultural societies which were organized under the various chambers. The party, governmental, and corporate organizations gave the National Socialist regime absolute control of all radio, press, theater, film, and music activities within the Reich. The Nazis exercised complete and rigid supervision over every medium for propaganda.

*Finance and Taxation.—*The extension of administrative controls over interior, economic, and cultural affairs placed a heavy burden on the financial structure of the Reich. The rapid expansion of military preparations for World War II added an almost crushing financial burden. These problems were met in part by the centralized financial administration which the Nazis had inherited from the Republic. *The major Nazi changes in the sphere of public finance involved new and heavier tax levies to meet the needs of war, and the assumption of complete financial sovereignty by the Reich.* The states lost control over their budgets and accounting systems, which they had retained after the Weimar financial reforms. Under the Nazis the entire financial system was brought under the national Minister of Finance. The budgets, which were prepared by the departments and agencies of the Reich—the states, provinces, city counties, and counties—were ultimately approved by the national Minister of Finance and promulgated without the consent of the cabinet or the *Reichstag.* The Minister of Finance was also vested with the power of administering the budget. Further controls were provided by the National Court of Audit, which absorbed the auditing powers of the states when they lost their budgetary rights in 1936. The National Court of Audit continued to occupy an independent position in the German administrative machine for it was directly under the Führer.

There were few changes in the structure of the tax organization, which functioned under the Ministry of Finance. The knotty problems of distributing the taxes between the national and state governments, which had plagued the Republic, were solved by eliminating the surviving tax rights of the states. The tax changes of the middle thirties gave Germany a completely unified and integrated system of taxation. The political problem of tax division vanished, for within the unitary state it was only a question of dividing revenues between the national government and its administrative units. The all-inclusive budget system and the integrated accounting system, coupled with a centralized system of taxation, provided the Nazis with an excellent means of collecting, preserving, and distributing public moneys, of coordinating revenues and expenditures, and of managing the credit operations of the Reich, all of which were essential to the vast program of military preparations. Estimates of the German finances before World War II indicate that the rearmament program was met by limiting expenditures on administration, housing, education, and economic improvements, by reducing the costs of unemployment and welfare relief, and by increasing the tax yield through the extension of old taxes and the imposition of new ones. German war costs were met by current income and long term loans. The difficult problems of public finance were aided by the economic boom which accompanied Germany's preparations for war.

Justice.—The Nazi regime brought about the subordination of the judicial system to political control as well as the Nazification of law; in the process, statutory and judicial safeguards against executive, legislative, and administrative excesses or abuses were omitted. The codified legal system of Germany with its civil, commercial, and criminal codes, was thoroughly overhauled by the Nazis. The judges were given the power to punish without a specific legal provision, where such action was demanded by the "sound instinct of the people." The Gestapo was given the right to act outside the courts; the "rule of law" was abolished and the legal system turned into a weapon for Nazi domination. Hitler became the Chief Judge of the Reich.

The administration of the judicial system was transferred from the states to the Reich and placed under the National Ministry of Justice. Aside from a few minor changes in internal court organization, the old system of ordinary courts —National Supreme Court, the State Supreme Courts (*Oberlandesgerichte*), the Collegiate Courts of First and Second Instance (*Landgerichte*) and the Court of First Instance (*Amtsgerichte*)—continued, but under national administration. Likewise, the system of administrative courts continued, although it lost most of its former importance and power. During the war the administrative courts were reorganized through the elimination of those at the county level and the establishment of a National Administrative Court (*Reichsverwaltungsgericht*) in the Ministry of the Interior.

The special systems of labor courts, finance courts, and welfare courts continued under the jurisdiction of the ministries of labor, finance, and interior. The Nazis established several special courts to deal with political and other activities of particular interest to the Nazi regime. The People's Court (*Volksgerichtshof*) was established in Berlin to handle cases against the state and the Nazi party. Locally, cases of this type went to the special courts (*Sondergerichte*) attached to the lower ordinary courts. Special Honor Courts (*Ehrengerichte*) were organized to control activities of the various corporate bodies which had been set up for the organization of the social, economic, and cultural life of Germany. These controls over the legal and judicial systems were supplemented by offices for the examination of all judges, lawyers, and notaries and by the National Legal League (*Reichswahrerbund*) which provided for the organization of all officials concerned with the administration of justice.

Summary: The Nazi State and Administration

The consolidation of National Socialist power had been accomplished through the totalitarian coordination (*Gleichschaltung*) of every aspect of German Life. *The liberal Republic had been transformed into a unitary, highly centralized, and monocratic state, controlled by the Nazi party.* The consolidation of power was accompanied by the elimination of all legal, constitutional, and popular controls over the government and administration. The *Reichstag* was turned into an instrument for dictatorship, a sounding board for the official declarations of the Führer. All legislative power had been transferred to the Führer, and the *Reichstag* was retained only as a ratifying assembly which met to hear the speeches of Hitler or other high Nazi leaders. The well-managed Nazi plebiscites gave the voter no choice but to vote for the policies supported by the Nazi government. National Socialist theory was based on a myth to the effect that the Führer represented the will of the *"Volk,"* a mystical entity embracing the total German Aryan population. The elections, which always went in favor of the Nazis, were represented as manifestations of the homogeneity of the will of the German *"Volk."*

Administration under the Nazis was highly centralized, with all ultimate controls in Berlin. The central administration was the organizing authority for all subordinate administration; it was, therefore, free to plan its own machinery and to develop as much flexibility or rigidity in administration as it liked. The unified national administrative machine created by the Nazis operated under the "leadership principle." Although much power was concentrated at the top of the administrative pyramid under the Führer, the Chancelleries, the Ministries, and the Supreme Authorities, yet the administrative authorities at the regional level were given powers equal to the tasks imposed upon them from above. The German administrative machine was hierarchical in organization, so that every agency and authority was subject to the supervision and control of the next higher authority. With the exception of those agencies which were directly under the Führer, there were no boards, commissions, or agencies with independent status. Every organization was subordinate to or supervised by some appropriate department of government. There was also, on the whole, a logical grouping of functions by departments and within departments. The elimination of the sovereignty of the states, which gave the national government control over all public authorities within the Reich gave Hitler a powerful and effective organization for carrying out the purposes of National Socialism. So, also, did the extension of special and technical administrative services; the formation of corporate structures for the control of social, economic, and cultural activities; and the interpenetrating control of the Nazi party.

The structure of unified and centralized administration was further fortified by a national civil service, which combined Reich and state services into one uniform system. Under the Nazis there were only Reich officials. Even those who were directly in the service of some municipality or public corporation were, nevertheless, indirectly national officials. Entrance into the service of the Nazi state was conditioned by requirements of "blood," training, and attitudes toward the state. If a citizen could meet these basic requirements, he or she could begin a period of probationary service by passing a first state examination. After several years of probationary service and the passing of another examination, the official was appointed for life. The work of the civil servant was governed by a civil service code and a civil service disciplinary code. Financial control of the civil service was vested in the national Minister of Finance. The actual recruitment and supervision was left to the departments. Although the civil service was not completely taken over by the Nazi party, its plans for the organization and indoctrination of public officials and for party control over entrance into the service had a decisive effect. The nazification of German government and administration and of the officials of the Reich and the states, coupled with the work of the Estates and the Nazi party, gave the Nazis by 1935 a firm control over every aspect of German life. The task of consolidation was completed and the National Socialist regime turned its attention to the more direct preparations for war.

Preparation for War

The Nazi government began active preparations for World War II after the establishment of stable conditions within the Reich.[2] The diplomatic preparations began with Germany's withdrawal from the League of Nations as well as from the work of the Disarmament Conference on October 14, 1933. These moves met ready acceptance in Germany, for the Nazis had prepared the way with propaganda promising revision of the Versailles Treaty and revenge for defeat in World War I. The improvement, both in economic conditions and the unemployment situation which resulted originally from Brüning's measures and later from the war preparations, strengthened the Nazi position on the home front. Between 1933 and 1935 the Nazi government, which had isolated itself diplomatically from the rest of Europe, followed a moderate foreign policy. After stabilizing domestic conditions the Nazis slowly began to rearm. The Air Ministry, established in 1934, marked the first step toward rearmament. In 1935 the Saar plebiscite went in favor of Germany. Strengthened by this success, the Nazi authorities began large-scale rearmament on land and sea and in the air. Conscription was reintroduced on March 16, 1935. In the following year, the Nazi government denounced the Locarno Pact, into which it had voluntarily entered, and began the remilitarization of the Rhineland in direct violation of the Versailles Treaty. The Four-Year Plan, which was instituted in 1936, laid the foundations for a complete war economy. This program, which was placed under Göring, brought extensive controls over manpower, raw materials, and production. The civilian economy rapidly disintegrated under the impact of war needs.

Toward the end of 1936, the Nazi government adopted a more active foreign policy following upon the formation of the Rome-Berlin Axis, which had grown out of Italy's difficulties with the League of Nations over her Ethiopian adventure. The Axis served as a counterblast to the Franco-Soviet Pact and as a base for diplomatic operations. In November 1936, Italy and Germany recognized the Franco government in Spain and proceeded to send it military assist-

[2] No attempt is made here to review the total impact of World War II on German life and government. This will be treated in the second volume.

ance. The National Socialist opposition to Russia and bolshevism, which had long been a major principle of the party, led to the formation of the Japanese-Italo-German Anti-Comintern Pact on November 24, 1936. The days of diplomatic isolation were over, and the German position was strengthened by the alliances with Italy and Japan. With these diplomatic assurances, the Nazi leaders were ready to embark on a program of power politics aimed at the incorporation of large so-called German areas in Central Europe and at the political domination of the world.

The Nazi diplomats moved rapidly to hasten the impending collapse of the security system represented by the League of Nations. European disunity was an essential for their purposes. An active propaganda campaign, coupled with extensive fifth column activity, was used to weaken neighboring states. Germany had temporarily secured her eastern frontier by the German-Polish Non-Aggression Pact of 1934. In 1937 Germany moved to secure the western frontier. This was accomplished by "guarantees" of the integrity of Belgian territory. Belgium, in turn, obtained releases from Britain and France from her obligations under the Treaty of Locarno. Germany was at last prepared for the first steps in the conquest of Central Europe, the seizure of Austria and Czechoslovakia.

The seizure of Austria in 1938 was preceded by one final reorganization on the home front. The army, which had retained considerable independence during the first years of the Nazi regime, despite the fact that Hitler exercised the powers of Commander-in-Chief, had long been in opposition to many of the Nazi party plans. Hitler solved this problem through a purge of the armed forces. On February 4, 1938, he assumed direct control over all air, naval, and land forces of the Reich. Germany was at last prepared for her first foreign adventure in Austria. Although the Austrian Union (*Anschluss*) problem had been an important issue since the early days of the Republic, German intervention came as a result of growing troubles between the Austrian government and the Austrian National Socialist party. The plebiscite on the union which had been ordered by Schuschnigg, the Austrian Chancellor, was not held under the auspices of Austria, for German troops accompanied by Hitler invaded Austria on March 11, 1938, and Austria was absorbed thereby into the German Reich as *Ostmark*.

Czechoslovakia had, by that method, been outflanked. The Nazi government began an immediate propaganda campaign aimed at the acquisition of this vital Central European area. The German minorities in the bordering Sudetenland, under the leadership of Henlein and encouraged by Berlin, made a number of direct demands upon the Czech government, including their right to full German nationality and political aspirations. The tension between Prague and Berlin was intensified by the movement of German troops along the Czech frontier. Extensive German military maneuvers raised the threat of a general European war. France mobilized her reserves and began to man the Maginot Line. At this tense moment, Germany demanded self-determination for the Sudeten Germans. In an effort to ease the situation Prime Minister Chamberlain began the negotiations which led to the Munich Pact of September 30, 1938, under which Czechoslovakia ceded large areas to Germany, Poland, and Hungary. The final destruction of Czechoslovakia came in the following year. On March 15, 1939, the German army occupied the western portions of Czechoslovakia, declaring the formation of the Protectorate of Bohemia and Moravia. The Slovakian Republic, which had precipitated the final dissolution of Czechoslovakia, enjoyed one day of independence before it was placed under the "protection" of the Reich. Poland was now outflanked.

German preparations for World War II were greatly intensified during 1938 and 1939. The trend toward war could not be stopped, for the whole Nazi effort had been based upon economic and psychological preparations for war. These were strongly influenced by vivid memories of the economic troubles which had accompanied World War I. The drastically changed social conditions, which had partly resulted from the inflation, made possible a new ideological approach to the economic task. Elimination of the largest portion of the middle class led in due time to the development of a state controlled economy which utilized fully the potentials of labor and capital. The Nazi war economy (*Wehrwirtschaft*) brought a rapid change from free and competitive to state planned and politically controlled economic conditions. The whole economic structure was directed toward war needs. National economic planning, an essential of the Nazi regime, was placed under a national planning agency and its regional planning units.

The first year of the Nazi regime, as has been indicated above, brought about the compulsory organization of industry, commerce, and transportation in the Organization of Trade and Industrial Economy. In 1936 the Four-Year Plan for the organization of the war economy was superimposed upon the economic structure and given the task of handling the allocation of raw materials, manpower, prices, and foreign exchange. The work of the Four-Year Plan was supplemented by that of the Trade Control Boards, which were given control of imports and exports. Government financing was used to encourage the development of essential war industries necessary for the purposes of economic self-sufficiency. *Legislation, issued as decrees, encouraged the formation of cartels and combines in order to place the task of rearmament in the hands of the more efficient larger corporations.* The task of coordinating the industrial and transportation activities fell to the Ministries of Transport and Economics within the Four-Year Plan. The industrial preparation for war was accompanied by an all-embracing agricultural program, which was carried out by the

National Food Estate under the general supervision of the Ministry of Agriculture. It was responsible not only for agrarian production and the direction of consumption, but also for the ideological supervision of the German peasants. These prewar Nazi economic controls were further supplemented by an extensive price control and rationing apparatus, which was administered under the Four-Year Plan by the Ministries of Agriculture and Economics.

The monetary and financial structure of the Reich was also prepared for war. The law for the regulation of credit subjected all banks to complete state control through the National Association for Trade, Industry, Banking, Power, and Insurance and the National Office for the Supervision of Credit (*Aufsichtsamt für das Kreditwesen*), which fell ultimately under the jurisdiction of the Ministry of Economics. In 1939 the New Financial Plan brought the mobilization of all liquid resources in the interest of public financial needs. These economic moves were backed by forced savings, forced bond buying, forced insurance contributions, and increased taxation.

The organization of the labor force of the Reich, another essential for the Nazi war effort, fell to the German Labor Front which provided for the social and psychological control of the thirty million German workers in industry, commerce, and transportation. Agrarian workers were organized under the National Food Estate. The control of labor fell to the National Labor Trustees who were empowered to regulate labor problems, settle labor disputes, and to fix wages and working conditions. The old Republican National Office for Employment and Unemployment Insurance was given a complete monopoly over employment. The summer of 1938 brought the Compulsory Labor Decrees, while the winter of 1939 was marked by the establishment of the ten-hour day.

Supported by these careful economic preparations which had been under way since 1933, Germany began the diplomatic offensive which led to the precipitation of World War II. On April 28, 1939, the German government denounced the German-Polish Non-Aggression Pact of 1934 and began a propaganda campaign against the Polish state. On May 5, 1939, the Polish Government rejected German demands for a reorganization of the German-Polish frontier. Germany followed with diplomatic arrangements aimed at the isolation of Poland. During the month of May 1939, the Italo-German Military Treaty was signed. It was followed by the negotiation of Non-Aggression Pacts with Estonia and Latvia. The final isolation of Poland was accomplished through the negotiation of the Russo-German Non-Aggression Pact of August 23, 1939. With political and strategic security in the east and with hopes for the temporary neutrality of France and Great Britain, Germany presented Poland with a new series of demands. Without awaiting a Polish reply, the German forces invaded Poland on September 1, 1939, a move which precipitated World War II.

By September 3, 1939, Germany found herself in a general European war. Britain and France mobilized and declared war, while Italy, Germany's only ally, declared her neutrality. Few changes were necessary on the home front under the totalitarian system of controls.

There was an immediate effort to make the German administrative machine ready for war. Shortly after the opening of hostilities, a Ministerial Council for Defense of the Reich was established in order to free Hitler from domestic responsibilities. This council, which met under the chairmanship of Field Marshal Göring, consisted of Hess (Deputy Leader, later succeeded by Bormann, head of the Party Chancellery), Lammers (head of the National Chancellery), Himmler (later Minister of the Interior), Funk (Minister of Economics), and Keitel (Chief of the High Command). Each of these officials had under his jurisdiction a great number of vital administrative agencies. Hermann Göring was the Minister of Aviation, the National Forester, and head of the Four-Year Plan. Frick and his successor Himmler, as the General Plenipotentiary for Administration, received control over the Ministries of the Interior, Justice, Education, and Church Affairs, and Funk, as the General Plenipotentiary for Economics, received control over the Ministries of Economics, Labor, Agriculture, Finance, the *Reichsbank,* and the National Accounting Office. Keitel represented the interests of civil defense and the military, while Bormann and Lammers had key positions as heads of the two most important chancelleries responsible for the coordination of the administration. The Council provided for regional control through an elaborate system of defense districts and subdistricts, where local officials provided for the coordination of administrative, police, economic, labor, and party activities. This super-national organization, designed to coordinate every aspect of German activity, ran the government of the Reich through the first years of the war.

The German *Blitzkrieg* brought rapid successes. Poland was completely subjugated by early October. Under an agreement between the Russians and Germans, Eastern Poland and the Baltic states were occupied by Russian forces, while western Poland fell to Germany. The western provinces of Poland were incorporated into the Reich as the Danzig-West Prussian (Danzig-Westpreussen), Warthe, and Upper Silesian (Oberschlesien) National Districts (*Reichsgaue*). The central Polish area was placed under the German Government-General at Cracow. The last months of 1939 witnessed a return of thousands of Baltic Germans, who were now settled in the new territories acquired from Poland.

After a quiet winter of military preparations, the German army turned its attention to the West. On April 9, 1940, the Germans invaded Denmark and Norway. One month later German forces invaded Belgium and the Netherlands under the pretext of securing their neutrality. France was the next victim.

By the end of May, all of northern France was in German hands. The complete conquest of the French Republic was accomplished shortly after the Italians under Mussolini had stabbed France in the back. France accepted a German armistice, on June 22. On the same day the governments of Denmark, Norway, Belgium, and the Netherlands were placed under Military Commissioners, while France was controlled by a German Military Commission. Germany had completed her conquest of western Continental Europe. Only Great Britain stood in the way of the complete domination of Atlantic Europe. Germany's attempt to bring the British to their knees ended with the German defeat in the Battle of Britain which was fought in the air between August and October 1940.

Germany and Italy, flushed with their victories in the West, began negotiations with Japan for an extension of the German-Italian Axis Pact. The Tripartite Pact between Germany, Italy, and Japan was finally signed in Berlin on September 27, 1940. These powers pledged themselves to the establishment of a New World Order. Germany apparently hoped that this pact would give her security from both Russia and the United States, while she undertook the liquidation of southeastern Europe.

The German conquest of the Balkans opened with the occupation of Rumania on October 13, 1940; and the first phase of the military penetration of the Balkans was accomplished when Slovakia, Hungary, and Rumania signed the Tripartite Pact in early November 1940. The German position was temporarily secured by the frontier and trade pact which was signed with Russia on January 10, 1941. The next phase of the Balkan campaign led to the military occupation of Bulgaria, which permitted Germany to outflank Jugoslavia. The conquest of the Balkans was completed with the invasion of Jugoslavia and Greece, where Italy was slowly fighting a losing battle. Germany was, at last, in position for the attack upon Russia.

The first years of the war brought few changes within Germany except for a tightening of controls over food, labor, and propaganda. The war production administration was overhauled in 1940 when many functions were transferred to the newly created Ministry for Armament and War Production. This ministry, which soon established an elaborate regional organization, was given wide controls over every branch of German war economy. The German economic situation improved as new lands were brought under the control of the Reich. Special boards were set up in the conquered territories to administer economic activities. They were given the task of conscripting labor, confiscating property and securities, and coordinating industry and communications. These financial and industrial measures were accompanied by an extensive agricultural program. The Nazis also established large agricultural trusts which forcefully acquired millions of acres of farm land in western as well as eastern Europe. The industrial plants of the occupied areas were geared into the Nazi industrial machine through the radical production system, compulsory cartelization, and production control. The labor of the occupied territories was placed under a labor employment service similar to the German organization. All foreign trade unions were abolished.

Naturally, Germany served as the European trader and banker. As the central market, Germany fixed the prices of all goods and regulated the allocation of supplies. The citizens of the occupied lands were paid in worthless German certificates of obligation. All banks were placed under German commissioners and organized as branches of the German *Reichsbank*. Monetary matters were handled by a Central Clearing Office in Berlin, which was operated as a branch of the *Reichsbank*. It had the function of relating all transactions to the German mark. The insurance organizations of Europe were subordinated to the German Reinsurance Combine at Munich. Germany's control of Europe's economic life was complete and all-embracing.

The attack upon Russia came without warning on June 22, 1941. The German advance to the outskirts of Moscow, Leningrad, Stalingrad, and the Caucasus was accomplished by the end of the year.

The decline of Germany's military power came after America's entry into World War II on December 7, 1941. The following year brought the first major reverses. The Russians defeated the Germans at Stalingrad and began their offensive to the west, while the British began to recover their positions in North Africa. A combined American-British North African offensive of November 1942, drove the Germans and Italians out of that area.

The impact of these military reverses on the German war effort produced several drastic governmental changes. In 1942 the Nazi government made a definite effort to simplify the complicated economic organization of the Reich. This reorganization was followed by a strengthening of the party position in the administration of Reich affairs. The districts of the Ministerial Council for the Defense of the Reich were abolished and their functions were transferred to the party districts, which were established as civil defense districts. The Trade and Industry Chambers lost their functions to party offices, while the offices of the Labor Trustees and the National Office for Employment and Unemployment Insurance (*Reichsanstalt für Arbeitsvermittlung und Arbeitslosenversicherung*) were abolished and their functions transferred to a *Gau* Labor Office (*Gauarbeitsamt*). Wherever possible the other regional units for economic administration were made to conform to the party district. These changes greatly strengthened the power of the Nazi party in government and administration, although many sound rules of administration were sacrificed in putting these innovations into effect.

The next year brought further reverses. During 1943 the Russians continued their offensive to the west, while British and American forces invaded Italy. These reverses in the field were accompanied by a rapid development of the Allied air offensive, which was slowly destroying the vital centers of the German war effort. Germany's military decline increased in tempo throughout 1944. In the summer of that year, the Allies landed in Normandy and liberated France and most of Belgium. The attempted military revolt within the German Army later in the summer led to a further tightening of party controls within Germany.

An attempt upon Hitler's life led to the issuance of a decree which made several changes in the top governmental organization. Göring was invested with supreme authority as the President of the Ministerial Council for the Defense of the Reich, and Goebbels became Reich Plenipotentiary for the total war effort. He was given power to demand information from and to issue instructions to all Reich agencies, although he could not issue administrative rules and regulations, because he had no administrative machinery of his own. Himmler, as the Minister of the Interior and the head of the SS, was given responsibility for the training of officers and the arming and equipment of the German National Guard (*Volkssturm*), which went into active service under his orders. This was Germany's last effort at total mobilization.

The Ardennes offensive in January, 1945, was the last German military attempt to delay the end of the war. Spring offensives of the Allies in Italy, western and eastern Germany completed the destruction of the Reich and its military forces. In May 1945, the Allies announced that all effective resistance had come to an end. The government of the Reich passed from the Nazi party into the hands of the victorious Allies.

BIBLIOGRAPHY

General History

Barraclough, G. *The Origins of Modern Germany,* 2nd rev. ed. (Oxford, 1947).

Diesel, E. *Germany and the Germans* (Transl. by W. D. Robson-Scott) (New York, 1931).

Ellis, E. S., ed. *History of the German People from the First Authentic Annals to the Present Time* (New York, 1918).

Lowie, R. H. *The German People,* A Social Portrait to 1914. (New York, Toronto, 1945).

Pinner, H. *History of Germany,* rev. ed. (London, 1929).

Valentin, V. *The German People* (New York, 1946).

The Frankish State

Kaufmann, G. H. *Deutsche Geschichte bis auf Karl den Grossen,* 2 vols. (Leipzig, 1880-1881).

Previté-Orton, C. W. *Outlines of Medieval History* (Cambridge, 1929).

Thompson, J. K. *An Introduction to Medieval Europe* (New York, 1937).
Stephenson, C. *Medieval History* (New York, 1935).

The First Reich

Bryce, J. *The Holy Roman Empire* (New York, 1912).
Balzani, U. *The Popes and the Hohenstaufen* (London, 1901).
Haller, J. *Das Altdeutsche Kaisertum* (Stuttgart, 1944).
Hampe, K. *Deutsche Kaisergeschichte in der Zeit der Salier und Staufer* (Leipzig, 1912).
Henderson, E. F. *A Short History of Germany* (New York, 1928).
Lindner, T. *Deutsche Geschichte unter den Habsburgern und Luxemburgern* (1273-1437) (Stuttgart, 1890-1893).

The Aristocratic Confederation

Atkinson, C. T. *History of Germany, 1715-1815* (New York, 1908).
Egelhaaf, G. *Deutsche Geschichte im Zeitalter der Reformation,* 2nd ed. (Berlin, 1885).
Erdmannsdörfer, B. *Deutsche Geschichte vom Westfälischen Frieden bis zum Regierungsantritt Friedrichs des Grossen,* 2 vols. (Berlin, 1892-1893).
Heigel, K. T. von. *Deutsche Geschichte vom Tode Friedrichs des Grossen bis zur Auflösung des alten Reiches,* 2 vols. (Stuttgart, 1899-1911).
Janssen, J. *History of the German People at the Close of the Middle Ages,* 16 vols. (London, 1900-1912).
Marriott, J. A. R. and Robertson, C. G. *Evolution of Prussia* (Oxford, 1915).
Ranke, L. von. *Die Deutschen Mächte und der Fürstenbund,* 2 vols. (Leipzig, 1871-1872).
Ranke, L. von. *Deutsche Geschichte im Zeitalter der Reformation,* 6 vols. (Munich, 1925-1926).
Reddaway, W. F. *Frederick the Great and the Rise of Prussia* (New York, 1904).
Tuttle, H. *History of Prussia,* 4 vols. (New York, 1884-1896).
Wedgwood, C. V. *The Thirty Years War* (New Haven, Yale University Press, 1939).

Napoleonic Germany

Ford, G. S. *Stein and the Era of Reform in Prussia* (Princeton, 1922).
Gooch, C. P. *Germany and the French Revolution* (London, 1920).
Rambaud, A. N. *L'Allemagne sous Napoleon I,* 4th ed. (Paris, 1897).

The Germanic Confederation

Kaufmann, G. *Politische Geschichte Deutschlands im Neunzehnten Jahrhundert* (Berlin, 1900).
Treitschke, H. von. *History of Germany in the Nineteenth Century,* 7 vols. (New York, 1915-1919).
Valentin, V. *Geschichte der deutschen Revolution von 1848-1849,* 2 vols. (Berlin, 1930-1931).

Verhandlungen der Deutschen Verfassungsgebenden Reichsversammlung zu Frankfurt am Main, 6 vols. (Frankfurt, 1848-1849).

Ward, A. W. *Germany, 1815-1890,* 3 vols. (Cambridge, 1916-1918).

Webster, C. K. *Congress of Vienna* (London, 1919).

The Second Reich

Bismarck, O. von. *Gedanken und Erinnerungen,* 2 vols. (New York and Stuttgart, 1898).

Bornhak, C. *Grundriss des deutschen Staatsrechts* (Leipzig, 1907).

Bornhak, C. *Grundriss des Verwaltungsrechts* (Leipzig, 1906).

Brandenburg, E. *From Bismarck to the World War* (London, 1927).

Hartung, F. *Deutsche Verfassungsgeschichte vom 15 Jahrhundert bis zur Gegenwart* (Berlin, 1938).

Hue de Grais. *Handbuch der Verfassung und Verwaltung in Preussen und dem Deutschen Reiche* (Berlin, 1908).

Krüger, F. K. *Government and Politics of the German Empire* (New York, 1915).

Kürschner, J. *Staats-, Hof- und Kommunal Handbuch* (Leipzig, 1901).

Lichtenberger, H. *Germany and Its Evolution in Modern Times* (New York, 1913).

Lowell, A. L. *Greater European Governments* (Cambridge, 1918).

Oncken, W. *Das Zeitalter des Kaisers Wilhelm,* 2 vols. (Berlin, 1890-1892).

Schnabel, F. *Deutsche Geschichte im Neunzehnten Jahrhundert* (Freiburg, 1929-1936).

Zeydel, E. *Constitutions of the German Empire and German States* (Washington, 1919).

Weimar Republic

Anschütz, G. *Die Verfassung des Deutschen Reichs,* 4th ed. (Berlin, 1932).

Anschütz, G. und Thoma, R. *Handbuch des Deutschen Staatsrechts,* 2 vols. (Tübingen, 1930-1932).

Blachly, F. F. and Oatman, M. E. *The Government and Administration of Germany* (Baltimore, 1928).

Brecht, A. *Prelude to Silence:* The End of the German Republic (New York, 1944).

Brunet, R. *The New German Constitution* (Transl. from the French) (New York, 1922).

Clark, R. T. *The Fall of the German Republic* (London, 1935).

Fisk, O. H. *Germany's Constitutions of 1871 and 1919* (Cincinnati, 1924).

Handbuch für das Deutsche Reich (Berlin, 1929).

Harms, B. *Recht und Staat im Neuen Deutschland.* 2 vols. (Berlin, 1929).

Hue de Grais, *Handbuch der Verfassung und Verwaltung in Preussen und dem Deutschen Reiche* (Berlin, 1930).

Kraus, K. *The Crisis of German Democracy* (Princeton, 1932).

Lutz, R. H. *Fall of the German Empire,* 1914-1918 (Stanford, 1932).

Mattern, J. *Principles of Constitutional Jurisprudence of the German National Republic* (Baltimore, 1928).

Nipperdey, H. C. *Die Grundrechte und Grundpflichten der Reichsverfassung,* 3 vols. (Berlin, 1929-1930).

Pollock, James K. *German Election Administration* (New York, 1934).

Stier-Somlo, F. *Die Verfassung des Deutschen Reichs vom 11 August 1919,* 3d ed. (Bonn, 1925).

Sutton, E., ed. *Gustav Stresemann,* 2 vols. (New York, 1935-1938).

Watkins, F. M. *The Failure of Constitutional Emergency Powers under the German Republic* (Harvard University Press, 1939).

Ziegler, W. *Die Deutsche Nationalversammlung 1919-1920 und ihr Verfassungswerk* (Berlin, 1932).

The Nazi State

Bouhler, Philipp. *Adolf Hitler, Das Werden einer Volksbewegung,* 25th ed. (Lübeck, 1943).

Brady, R. A. *The Spirit and Structure of German Fascism* (New York, 1937).

Ebenstein, William. *The Nazi State* (New York, Toronto, 1943).

Ermarth, Fritz. *The New Germany,* National Socialist Government in Theory and Practice (Washington, 1936).

Florinsky, M. *Fascism and National Socialism* (New York, 1936).

Frank, H. *Nationalsozialistisches Handbuch für Recht und Gesetz.* 2d ed. (München, 1935).

Göring, Hermann. *Aufbau einer Nation* (Berlin, 1934).

Hitler, Adolf. *Mein Kampf* (Munich, 1927).

Hoover, C. B. *Germany Enters the Third Reich* (New York, 1933).

Koellreutter, O. *Deutsches Verfassungsrecht* (Berlin, 1938).

Koellreutter, O. *Deutsches Verwaltungsrecht* (Berlin, 1936).

Kosok, P. *Modern Germany* (Chicago, 1933).

Köttgen, A. *Deutsche Verwaltung,* 2d ed. (Berlin, 1937).

Kussmann, Herbert. *Verfassungsleben des Deutschen* (Berlin, 1937).

Lichtenberger, H. *The Third Reich* (New York, 1937).

Marx, F. M. *Government in the Third Reich* (New York, 1936).

Mason, John Brown. *Hitler's First Foes: A Study in Religion and Politics* (Minneapolis, 1936).

Maunz, T. *Verwaltung,* 2d ed. (Hamburg, 1937).

Medicus, Franz Albrecht. "Der Neuaufbau des Reichs," in *Archiv des öffentlichen Rechts,* Vol. 25, No. 1, 1934, pp. 64 ff.

Meissner, O. und Kaisenberg, G. *Staats- und Verwaltungsrecht im Dritten Reich* (Berlin, 1935).

Micklem, Nathaniel I. *National Socialism and the Roman Catholic Church* (Oxford University Press, 1939).

Moeller, van den Bruck. *Das Dritte Reich,* 3d ed. (Hamburg, 1931).

Mowrer, E. A. *Germany Puts the Clock Back* (New York, 1933).

Neumann, Franz. *Behemoth. The Structure and Practice of National Socialism* (Oxford University Press, 1942).

Olden, Rudolf. *Hitler* (New York, 1936).

Pfundtner, Hans. *Vom Bismarckreich zum Dritten Reich* (Berlin, 1934).

Pollock, J. K. *The Government of Greater Germany* (New York, 1940).

Pollock, J. K. and Heneman, H. J. *The Hitler Decrees* (Ann Arbor, 1934).

Rauschning, Hermann. *The Revolution of Nihilism* (New York, 1939).

Roberts, Stephen H. *The House that Hitler Built,* 5th ed. (London, 1938).

Rosenberg, Alfred. *Der Mythus des XX Jahrhunderts,* 4th ed. (Munich, 1932).

Schuman, F. L. *The Nazi Dictatorship* (New York, 1936).

Shotwell, J. T. *What Germany Forgot* (New York, 1942).

Steed, Wickham. *Hitler, Whence and Whither?* 3d ed. (New York, 1934).

Valtin, Jan. *Out of the Night* (New York, 1941).

Villard, O. G. *The German Phoenix* (New York, 1933).

Wertheimer, Mildred S. *Germany under Hitler* (World Affairs Pamphlets No. 8, 1935).

Special Works

Brecht, Arnold and Glaser, Comstock. *The Art and Technique of Administration in German Ministries* (Harvard, 1940).

Brecht, Arnold. *Federalism and Regionalism in Germany* (New York, 1945).

Cole, Taylor. "The Evolution of the German Labor Front," in *Political Science Quarterly,* Vol. LII, No. 4, December, 1937, pp. 532 ff.

Constantin-Stein, eds. *Die deutschen Landkreise,* Vols. 1 and 2 (Berlin: Friedman, 1926).

Ensor, C. K. *Courts and Judges in France, Germany and England* (London, 1933).

Goldberg, Otto. *Die politischen Beamten im deutschen Rechts, insbesondere im Reiche, im Preussen and Sachsen* (Dresden, 1932).

Handbuch für das Deutsche Reich (Berlin, 1936).

Heneman, Harlow J. *The Growth of the Executive Power in Germany* (Minneapolis, 1934).

Kaisenberg, Georg. *Die Wahl des Reichspräsidenten,* 3d ed. (Berlin, 1932).

Kaisenberg, Georg. "Gleichschaltung der Länder mit dem Reich," in *Das Recht der national Revolution,* Heft 2 (Berlin, 1933).

Kaisenberg, Georg. *Volksentscheid und Volksbegehren* (Berlin, 1926).

Kunz, Guba, Theissig. *Die Deutsche Gemeindeordnung,* 2d ed. 2 vols. (Berlin, 1939).

Macmahon, Arthur W. and Dittmer, W. R. "Autonomous Public Enterprise—the German Railways," *Political Science Quarterly,* Vol. LIV, No. 4, December, 1939, pp. 481 ff; Vol. LV, No. 1, March, 1940, pp. 25 ff; Vol. LV, No. 2, June, 1940, pp. 177 ff.

Medicus, Franz Albert. "Programm der Reichsregierung und Ermächtigungsgesetz," in *Das Recht der national Revolution,* Heft 1 (Berlin, 1933).

Münz, L. *Führer durch die Behörden und Organisationen* (Berlin, 1939).

Papers Concerning the Treatment of German Nationals in Germany 1938-1939.

Presented by the Secretary of State for Foreign Affairs to Parliament by command of His Majesty, Cmd. 6120 (London, 1939).

Pfundtner-Neubert. *Das neue Deutsche Reichsrecht* (Law Collection) (Berlin).

Pollock, James K. and Boerner, Alfred V., Jr. *The German Civil Service Act* (Civil Service Assembly of the United States and Canada, 1938).

Rappard, William E. and others. *Source Book on European Governments* (New York, 1937).

Schmitt, Carl. "Volksentscheid und Volksbegehren," in *Beitrage zum ausländischen öffentlichen Recht und Völkerrecht,* Heft 2 (Berlin, Leipzig, 1927).

Statistisches Jahrbuch für das Deutsche Reich.

Statistisches Jahrbuch Deutscher Städte (Jena).

Taschenbuch für Verwaltungsbeamte (Berlin, 1943).

Wells, Roger H. *German Cities,* A Study of Contemporary Politics and Administration (Princeton, 1932).

Zeitler, R., Biller, W., and v. Dreschau, B. *Deutsche Gemeindeordnung vom 30 Januar 1935* (Berlin, 1935).

Chapter 3

POLITICAL MOVEMENTS
AND POLITICS

Introduction

The experience of the German people as a whole with self-government has been very limited. The government and administration of the nation and most of its component states had long been dominated by a small ruling class intent upon maintaining its authority and power over the German people. An hereditary nobility, which was later joined by economically privileged classes created by Germany's more recent industrial and commercial expansion, excluded the mass of Germans from effective participation in the affairs of government through control of the machinery of administration. Political activity on the part of the German people, aimed at the control of government personnel and policy, was delayed for a considerable period at the state level by the rule of despotic sovereigns and at the national level by the absence of political unity within the German nation. Even limited representative control of the affairs of state by the people, which began at the state level only with the granting of constitutional governments and limited suffrage in the early nineteenth century, did not begin at the national level until the creation of the Second Empire in 1871. The political parties, which emerged within the states and the Empire, were not built upon genuine public issues of general character, but upon factional interests of a regional, religious, social, and economic nature. Party politics lacked a real foundation in public opinion. Not only did the multiparty system fail to give the people a means of exercising direct control over the ruling class, but the constitutional prerogatives of the imperial executive and the class systems of voting within some of the states, plus a failure to reapportion representatives as the population increased and shifted, provided further limitations upon popular control. Under the Empire, German political parties served as a restraining rather than a directing force. Therefore, it can be said that, although many Germans went through the forms of political organization and

172

participation, they did not exhibit, either in or out of government, the kind of
political understanding or action which can properly be defined as the political
experience one associates with genuine political democracy. At best one can say
only that the Germans, especially at the local level, became acquainted with the
forms of political action, but never quite understood their democratic spirit
and content.

*Although the Weimar Constitution placed the government of the Reich in
the hands of the representatives of the people, who were elected through the
instrumentality of the political parties, the German people were not too well
prepared to exercise their political rights.* The government was actually run by
the executive without too much attention to or control by the people, while the
administration was carried on by a conservative civil service little changed from
Empire days. Multiparty politics with their consequent coalition governments
tended to interfere with the development of responsible cabinet government
and to weaken party unity. Lacking a sound political experience, the German
people were hindered in the exercise of real control over the *Reichstag* and the
legislatures of the states. The weaknesses of the republican party system led not
only to the exercise of more power by the bureaucracy, but to the undermining
of the democratic institutions established by the Weimar Constitution. *The
struggle between the parties in the early thirties, coupled with economic dis-
tress, foreign pressure, and political intrigue, which eventually made a farce
out of popular government, delivered the politically inexperienced Germans
into the hands of the Nazis. The republican and democratic elements lacked
courage, experience, and determination. Their forces crumbled without a fight
before the fanatical strength of the determined National Socialist movement.*

The roots of the political inexperience and troubles of the German people
with national politics are embedded in their historical past. The political life of
the Germans during the first nine centuries of their development was centered
entirely in a small ruling class. Under the medieval First Reich, the affairs of
state were managed by the Emperors, the feudal lords, and the manorial nobility with no recourse whatever to the popular will. Political activity consisted
of struggles and intrigues within the structure of the feudal system; there was
almost constant disorder and strife marked by the growth of the political power
of the lay and ecclesiastical nobility as a result of the Emperor's grants of immunities, privileges, and hereditary rights. The contention for power among
the nobility was complicated further by the efforts of the Church to establish
independent rights within the Empire and by the gradual emergence of the
towns, which sought independence from the political control of the nobility.
The conflict of political forces within the medieval Empire culminated in the
struggle of the Welf-Hohenstaufen factions. In this contest, the lay and ecclesiastical princes, backed by the Papacy and the Lombard cities, not only de-

stroyed the power of the medieval Emperor, but also secured sovereign rights for their immediate territories, resulting in the establishment of dynastic and territorial states.

Under the aristocratic Confederation, imperial political power within the Reich was dependent upon the dynastic and territorial resources of the Habsburg and Luxemburg emperors. The people of Germany, who were bound to the soil, had nothing to say of affairs within the numerous lay and ecclesiastical states. These states had gained complete independence in the management of their internal and external affairs after the collapse of Hohenstaufen power. Political conditions were constantly disturbed by the struggles within the old dynastic families for the rights of inheritance and by the conflict between the rapidly growing free or imperial cities and the lay and ecclesiastical nobility. Further disturbances resulted from the efforts of the Imperial Knights to secure their position within the Empire against the cities and the greater nobility. The gradual consolidation of political conditions by the rulers of the larger states during the fourteenth and fifteenth centuries was marked by several important changes within the Reich. Locally, territorial diets were established that gave the petty nobility, the cities, and the church a voice in the management of local affairs. The same pattern of representation was reflected in the Chambers of Electors (*Kurfürsten*), (*Reichsfürsten*), and the cities of the Imperial *Reichstag*. Drastic social and economic changes, which were undermining the foundations of the manorial and feudal system, were opening the way for the establishment of strong territorial states; the rivalries and antagonisms of these states, however, only added to the disunity and weakness of the Empire.

The development of the absolute states of the Hohenzollerns, Habsburgs, Wettins, Wittelsbachs, and Hanovarians was delayed by further political troubles, by the medieval revolts of the peasants and the knights who were seeking a more secure economic position within the Empire, and by the so-called religious wars of the Protestants and the Catholics. It is interesting to note that before the onset of the Thirty Years' War, which plunged Germany into utter chaos, the bourgeoisie of the towns had begun to take part in the governments of the emerging absolute states which were then in the process of laying the foundations for permanent administrative machinery. Their services were sought in an effort to counterbalance the political power of the petty nobility, that had carried on the administrative affairs of the land in earlier times. During the troubled era of the religious wars and the Thirty Years' War, the aristocracy, always seeking to curb the centralizing tendencies of the absolute states, took advantage of the economic decline of the bourgeoisie and forced, in many instances, the rulers of the larger states to appoint members of the nobility to the important administrative posts.

With the early eighteenth century came a gradual recovery of economic and political conditions within the three hundred sovereign German states. The rulers turned once more to the bourgeoisie in order to strengthen their power over the aristocracy. The development of centralized administrative machinery for the control of internal, police, financial, and legal affairs, and the formation of state civil service systems composed of officials drawn from the army and from the bourgeoisie, gave the upper classes a quasi-representative control over the affairs of government. The impact of the French Revolution and the Napoleonic Wars further strengthened the power of the bourgeoisie in the governments of the states. The reforms of Stein and Hardenberg in Prussia and Montgelas in Bavaria, which centralized and enlarged the administrative bureaucracy, worked in the same direction. Reforms of local government in many of the states eliminated direct state control over city government and introduced the plan of electing local officials on the basis of a limited suffrage, thereby preparing the way for some modern democratic control of affairs on the local level. This basis of representative control was gradually expanding antecedent to the great nationalistic and constitutional movements of the nineteenth century.

The Napoleonic Wars and the Peace of Vienna had resulted in the territorial consolidation and governmental reorganization within the Reich, but the demands for national unity and for parliamentary government within the states and the Reich were not satisfied. Although liberal elements demanded national liberty and unity as early as 1817, genuine nation-wide political movements were impossible in the atmosphere of political and economic disunity which prevailed in early nineteenth century Germany. Some political progress was made, however, in many of the German states. There the bourgeoisie continued to strengthen its control over the rapidly developing administrative machinery, subject only to the general supervision of the ruler.

Within the states, parliamentary governments became more and more subject to constitutions that were either granted by liberal rulers or forced from reactionary rulers by revolutionary activity. Such efforts frequently led to the establishment of state Diets, composed of delegates of the people who were elected by almost universal male suffrage in the more liberal states or by restricted systems of class suffrage in the reactionary states. These developments led to the formation of political parties at the state level. Unfortunately, the parties developed on the basis of many specific and factional state, religious, social, and economic interests under the leadership of dynastic, bourgeois, and, occasionally, popular leaders; in this way, the foundations were laid for the multiparty system which was to plague Germany under the Empire and the Republic.

Some political party life on a national level began in the atmosphere of the abortive revolution of 1848. The representatives of the states consisted of delegates who had had experience in the local Diets, where parties had developed into three basic groups—the Right or Aristocratic Conservatives, the Liberal Center, and the Left or Democratic Progressives. Most of the delegates, who met at Frankfort in 1848 for the purpose of forming a constitution for a united Germany, were idealists primarily representing the Democratic Progressive parties of the states. The Frankfort Assembly split over the issue of Hohenzollern and Habsburg rivalry and divided into pro-Austrian and pro-Prussian factions.

The Berlin Assembly, which had been set up under revolutionary pressure to form a constitution for Prussia, was much more significant for the development of German political parties. The Royalists, the Center, and the Democratic blocks of this Assembly passed into the Prussian Diet of 1850 and gradually developed into the parties which were to dominate the politics of the German Empire. At first, however, differences in politics were manifested in the formation by political cliques under the leadership of influential politicians. The Prussian delegates were not elected by a faction to support a particular policy or platform, but as individuals. In the early sixties the idea that the delegates elected by the people should represent the people and should exercise a positive influence upon governmental and administrative policies gradually became popular throughout Germany and led to the formation of political parties.

The first Prussian Chamber of Deputies belonged to the Conservatives, who largely represented the landed aristocracy. They believed in absolute monarchy, ordained by God, and were therefore fundamentally opposed to all forms of genuine popular government. They supported the state church and believed that all educational and cultural activities should enjoy the protection and supervision of the religious authorities. They dominated the affairs of Prussia until the reign of Wilhelm I (1858), when the Liberals entered the Chamber of Deputies with the expectation of bringing about more moderate governmental policies. They turned against the government when Bismarck sought funds for the reorganization of the army.

The Liberal campaign against Bismarck brought the first real organization of a political party with the aim of carrying votes at the elections. The Liberal party, supporting the cause of German unity, obtained a majority in the Prussian Chamber of Deputies over the Conservatives who believed that it was Prussia's mission to unify Germany by force through the exclusion of Austria from German national politics. Despite the existence of an opposing majority, Bismarck ignored the Liberal party and proceeded with his design for Prussian leadership. The success of Bismarck's policy in the Schleswig-Holstein affair, the Seven Weeks' War, and in the establishment of the North German Confederation wrecked the Liberal party. It was replaced by the National-Liberal party, which was supported by the large commercial and industrial interests. This new party was formed through a coalition of liberals who believed in Prussian leadership, with the National Club (*Nationalverein*), an organization founded in 1859 to promote the unification of the Reich on a Prussian basis. It dominated the *Reichstag* in its management of the affairs of the North German Confederation and was aided and abetted in its work by the Free-Conservative party, a creation of the large industrialists who needed a more liberal conservative bloc to thwart all radical, socialist, or reactionary movements.

The Free-Conservative party, which assumed the name of Imperial party (*Reichspartei*) in 1867, supported German nationalism and backed the policies of Bismarck. The only opposition to the Conservatives consisted of minor parties formed by the disgruntled Poles, Hannovarians, and Danes, and of the remnants of the Liberal party. The establishment of the *Reichstag* of the North German Confederation, which was composed of delegates elected on the basis of universal male suffrage, opened the way for the real development of party politics within Germany which, however, were never effective as a means of opposition to the acts of the executive.

IMPERIAL POLITICAL PARTIES

The Imperial period (1871-1918) permitted the gradual development of well organized political parties based upon regional, religious, social, and economic differences within the Reich. The Imperial party and the National-Liberals, who had seized power under the North German Confederation, dominated the political life of the first years of the Second Empire. The National-Liberals sought to support German nationalism in terms of the general welfare of the German people. They favored Bismarck's policies of imperialism and centralization and supported economic policies favorable to the large commercial and industrial interests. This coalition of the liberal and conservative parties was supported by the Economic Union, an agrarian party advocating social legislation for the middle class, and by the old German conservative party.

The major political issue of the first years of the Empire revolved around the issue of the *Kulturkampf,* the struggle between the Catholic Church and the German government primarily over the control of education. The Catholic Center party or Clerical party was organized in 1870 after Bismarck refused to recognize the temporal power of the Pope. It attacked the national laws of the Bismarck government forbidding the religious orders to engage in educational activities, and the Prussian laws providing for the state supervision of education, the state appointment of clergymen, compulsory civil marriage, and the suppression of religious orders. The clergy of the Catholic Church with the support of the Pope openly defied the Prussian laws, and Bismarck retaliated with punitive measures. The struggle split the Catholic Church into pro-Papal and pro-German factions and ended in 1877 only when the Clerical party won the support of the *Reichstag*. Bismarck was forced to come to terms with the Papacy, and the government gradually abandoned the laws which had been directed against the Catholic Church.

The Clerical party was based upon support of the cause of the Catholic Church and continued as an important political bloc within the *Reichstag*. Politically, its members occupied a strategic central position for they combined democratic concepts with a moderate conservatism. They stood for social reform, anti-trust legislation, and laws directed against the concentration of wealth. Had they not sought to place the interests of the Catholic Church above those of the state, they would have gained the support of many non-Catholic voters. The Clerical party continued to serve a useful function under the Empire for it always sought to protect the rights of the *Reichstag* and constantly worked for economy in government. Its anti-nationalistic and anti-imperialistic principles gave support to attacks upon the excessive expenditures of the government for the military and naval establishments.

The next basic change in the German political scene came between 1874 and 1881 and was marked by the rapid decline of the National-Liberal party. The change in the fortunes of this party were largely due to the manipulations of Bismarck who feared the presence of any strong party within the *Reichstag*. The struggle between Bismarck and the National-Liberal party broke out over imperial finances. The constitution provided that imperial taxes voted by the *Reichstag* could only be repealed by a constitutional amendment, which Prussia could always veto. The National-Liberals naturally objected to this and demanded that the Imperial Secretary of State for Finance should be made responsible to the *Reichstag*. They also objected to Bismarck's plans for national ownership of the railroads and for a national tobacco monopoly. Bismarck turned to the Free Conservatives, the Conservatives, and the Clericals for support and managed to defeat the National-Liberals in the *Reichstag* elections of 1878. The real power of the National-Liberal party had ended.

During the era of the political power of Bismarck, the Social Democratic party was slowly assuming a position of importance. It grew out of the unions and the clubs of workingmen, who had supported the principles of the Marx-Engels Communist Manifesto which had been issued during the Revolution of 1848; and it also attracted the more moderate labor movement centering in the German Workingmen's Union led by Lassalle. Although the communists' unions and the workingmen's clubs had been dissolved in the fifties, the socialist labor movement under the leadership of Lassalle continued an organized fight for the socialist cause. It gained two seats in the *Reichstag* of 1871 and nineteen in 1874. The merger of the more moderate and nationalistic socialist group with the international workers' groups in 1875 resulted in the formation of the Social Democratic party.

Fearing revolutionary activity, Bismarck took immediate action. Although his proposed laws for the suppression of the Social Democratic party were at first defeated by the National-Liberals, who were afraid to grant the government extensive emergency powers, a second attempt on the life of the Kaiser gave Bismarck a pretext for dissolving the *Reichstag*. He now formally abandoned the National-Liberals and turned to the clerical and conservative parties, which supported the laws directed against the Social Democrats (*Socialistengesetze*). This gave Bismarck the opportunity of finally ridding himself of the National-Liberal opposition. The Social Democrats continued to demand the socialization of the means of production. They advocated universal male and female suffrage and proportional representation, freedom of speech and worship, free state schools and universities, free medical and legal aid, and a taxation system aimed at the destruction of the bourgeoisie. In principle they were absolutely opposed to the monarchy, and with it, to nationalism, imperialism, and militarism. The radical elements within the party advocated revolutionary methods of change, while the more moderate wing, which was supported by individuals desiring to protest against social, economic, and political systems supported by the imperial government, desired to achieve their ends through reform legislation. In 1890 the party changed its name to the Social Democratic party of Germany (*Sozialdemokratische Partei Deutschlands* [S.P.D.]).

The tariff issue produced the next realignment of political forces within the Empire. The Bismarck government backed a program for high protective tariffs on the basis of aid to Germany's growing industry and commerce and as a source of additional and much-needed state revenues. The Conservatives, Free Conservatives, and the Economic Union group supported the government for they believed tariffs were essential for the protection of their agricultural, industrial, and craft products. Bismarck secured also the support of the Clericals through further concessions to the Catholic Church. The National-Liberal party split over the tariff issue. A small bloc of delegates who supported Bismarck withdrew to form the Liberal party. This action started a general breakdown within the liberal movement. The Liberal Union group, which supported the principles of free trade, seceded from the National-Liberal party in 1880. In general the liberal parties were based upon concepts of personal and individual liberty. The fact that their leadership was made up of intellectuals may partially explain the frequent conflicts and troubles within the liberal movement. Although they believed in the old laissez-faire doctrine of social and economic policy and represented the business interests of Germany, they worked for social reforms based upon the ideal of the equality of classes within the German economic system.

The break-up of the National-Liberal party had deprived Bismarck of

needed support in the *Reichstag*. The Clerical party, despite the concessions of
the Bismarck government, joined with the dissatisfied Liberal groups and the
revolutionary Social Democrats in opposition to the proposals for financial
reform, military preparations, and colonial expansion. But the *Reichstag* elections of 1887, which were held in a tense atmosphere created by the French demands for the revenge of Alsace-Lorraine and by French military preparations,
returned Conservative and National-Liberal delegates who were willing to support Bismarck's policies.

Bismarck immediately embarked upon a new policy directed toward the
solution of the Social Democratic problem. His social insurance scheme only
partially met the demands of the opposition. He was forced to continue his re-
pressive policy toward the Social Democratic party. Official threats and action,
which took the form of imprisonment of Social Democratic leaders and the
suppression of Social Democratic newspapers and meetings, resulted in a
steady growth of the now well organized Social Democratic party. Bismarck's
anti-socialist policy continued despite the mild opposition of the National-Liberal party, the Clerical party, and the liberal groups.

The elections of 1890 brought another drastic change in the German political scene. The Conservative-National Liberal coalition was turned out and
the Clerical party once more regained its tactically favorable position of
dominance within the *Reichstag*. At this juncture of affairs, Bismarck, who
was opposed by the new *Reichstag,* lost the confidence of the new Emperor,
Wilhelm II, who came to the throne in 1888. The new Chancellor, Caprivi,
turned to the Conservatives and Clericals for support against the National-Liberal and Free Conservative opposition. His liberal economic policy was based
upon a series of commercial treaties favoring industry, which were passed by
the *Reichstag*. But Caprivi's attempt to force through a bill for the improvement of Germany's military establishment brought about the dissolution of
the *Reichstag* and the formation of the Conservative-Clerical bloc, which was
to support the government until 1907. During the period between 1893 and
1907 the Clerical party constantly used its position within the *Reichstag* to
force concessions from the Government for the Catholic Church. The issue
came to a head in 1907 when the Clericals and the Social Democrats combined
to defeat the government in the matter of colonial policy in German Southwest
Africa.

The bitter elections of 1907 found all parties united against the Clerical
party and the Social Democratic party over the issue of imperialism and nationalism. The patriotic parties won the day and the new *Reichstag* fell into the
hands of the Conservative party and the liberal groups. Kaiser Wilhelm II had
received the popular support which he believed necessary for his adventurous
foreign policy. Although the Clerical party had lost in the elections, it still

retained a position of importance both in and outside of the *Reichstag*. The Social Democratic party, however, had lost heavily, thanks to the well managed campaigns of the conservative and liberal groups. The coalition of conservatives and liberals, however, did not last long for these groups soon split over financial issues involving the introduction of new taxes to support the naval preparations of the Empire. The old Conservative-Clerical bloc was revived once more to meet the needs of the government. The financial policy of the new government shifted the burden of taxation to industry and commerce, and to the middle and lower classes. There was immediate opposition throughout the land. The elections of 1912 brought sweeping victories for the Social Democratic party and losses to all of the old majority parties, including the Clerical party, which now called itself *Deutsche Centrums partei*. The balance of power in the new *Reichstag* fell to the National-Liberals, but they refused to work with the Social Democrats for the revision of the financial measures of 1908 and for the control of German imperialism.

It must be remembered that under the Empire, the *Reichstag* played only a limited role in government. Although its delegates were elected by universal male suffrage, it failed to represent the German people satisfactorily owing to the discriminatory apportionment provisions which resulted in the under-representation of the urban areas. The lack of ministerial responsibility prevented real popular control over the government, which was dominated by the upper classes and the army. With the outbreak of World War I, all civil power was shifted into the hands of the military. All of the political parties, even the Clericals and the Social Democrats, who had earlier declared themselves against war, rallied to the cause of the Fatherland. The Social Democrats, who had once been considered a menace to the Empire, had become one of its strong supports. During the war they backed the imperial government in its suppression of strikes carried out by the revolutionary *Spartacus Bund* founded in 1917 by Karl Liebknecht and Rosa Luxemburg, and the pacifistic Independent Social Democratic groups under Kautsky and Haase. Strong support for the war came likewise from the nationalistic Conservative party and the National-Liberals, who hoped that a victory would bring further expansion to German industry and commerce. The only vocal opposition to the war came from the Catholic Center party (supported by some members from the Progressives and Social Democrats); it issued its famous peace resolution in 1917, but only when defeat seemed inevitable.

Political activity within the *Reichstag* during the war was limited until the dark year of 1917, when reverses in the field brought political demands for constitutional changes. Finally in October 1918, party action resulted in the adoption of the principle of ministerial responsibility and the establishment of parliamentary government; but it was too late to save the old regime. Noteworthy is the fact that on the eve of the Revolution of 1918 the Social Democratic party refused to come out for a Republic, and it was only after the abdication of the Kaiser and under the threat of the Workers and Soldiers' Councils that the once revolutionary German party declared itself for the formation of a Republic.

THE REPUBLICAN PARTIES

The Revolution of 1918 swept away the old regime. The Emperor, kings, dukes, and princes were swept away, leaving Germany open to control by the people. The Social Democrats, under the leadership of Ebert and Scheidemann, assumed power as the only organized political force within the Reich. The Social Democrats—often called Majority Socialists—were joined for a time by the Independent Socialists, the radical wing of which later formed the Communist party. The troubles which were attendant upon the formation of the National Constituent Assembly have been discussed earlier, although it might be pointed out here once more that the work at Weimar was dominated by the Social Democrats (*Majority Socialists*), the Clericals, who had become known as the Catholic Center party (*Zentrum*), and the *Fortschrittliche* Progressive Liberals (*Volkspartei*), who organized themselves as the Democratic party (*Deutsche Demokratische Partei*). Politically, the work of the National Constituent Assembly represented a compromise between the forces of moderate socialism and the forces of liberalism and sectionalism—a compromise which was made under the threat of red revolution. The Assembly gave Germany a federal, parliamentary, and liberal government and re-established the rule of law.

The German parliamentary system was handicapped by the fact that the Constitution, which had been a product of the Social Democrats, the Catholic Center, and the Democrats, was never really accepted by all the parties. It was regarded by many as a temporary measure. It was an experiment opposed by all nationalistic and conservative groups, and it was handicapped by difficult internal conditions and by hostile foreign pressures. The operations of the Weimar government were also hindered by the strong position of the elected President and by the usual troubles of Cabinet government under a multi-party system.

Although the first President, Ebert, was reasonably successful during the difficult inflation period, his successor, Hindenburg, who derived his support from his fame as a war leader and his position as a faithful public servant, was not able to give purposeful direction to the constantly changing governments. Perhaps the chief weakness of the young Republic lay in the traditional multiplicity of political parties which were constantly jockeying for power, with a resulting turnover in leadership. During the Weimar era, Germany had nineteen governments, which had an average life span of eight months. The shifting coalition governments made it difficult to form consistent governmental policies and to get at the real troubles of the Republic. Governmental and administrative power consequently fell into the hands of the old bureaucracy, which had not been effectively dislodged by the revolution of 1918. These old officials exercised decisive power.

The political parties, which continued to function along lines of regional, social, economic, and religious cleavage rather than in terms of genuine differences of political opinion over basic national issues, did not become the controlling factors in government. Conflicts between parties made it difficult to form coalitions and impossible for the *Reichstag* to exercise adequate control over governmental policies. As a result, the civil servant was often required to make the necessary decisions. Party warfare constantly gave the officials the freedom they desired in the formulation of policy.

The political parties prepared themselves for the long period of party strife under the Republic by establishing strong party organizations capable of maintaining the party discipline necessary for the struggles within the *Reichstag* and at the elections. Most of the German political parties were organized under a national chairman, executive committee, and advisory council which worked through the annual national meetings of party members. Regionally and locally, they established congresses and committees for each of the states, provinces, districts, counties, city counties, and towns, in this way providing the national leadership of the party with controls over the rank and file membership. This type of party machinery enabled the parties to develop elaborate propaganda campaigns for the bitterly contested elections. The efficiently organized and centrally controlled party organizations were well financed, sometimes by small contributions and the payment of party dues, as in the case of the S.P.D., sometimes by large corporate and individual contributions, as in the case of the Nationalists.

The political troubles were further aggravated by the particular list system of proportional representation, which gave the political parties almost absolute control over the nomination of candidates. The election system established in 1919 provided that political parties should receive seats in the *Reichstag* in proportion to the votes cast for them, in the ratio of one seat for each sixty thousand votes. The country was divided into thirty-five electoral districts within which the party could elect as many delegates as was possible in terms of multiples of sixty thousand. The left-over votes within the districts were either combined in unions of districts or carried over to a national list. Although this system was mathematically accurate, it permitted several abuses. First, any block of sixty thousand voters could band together into a small "splinter" party and send a delegate to the *Reichstag* to represent its particular interests. This led to the formation of numerous small parties, which only fur-

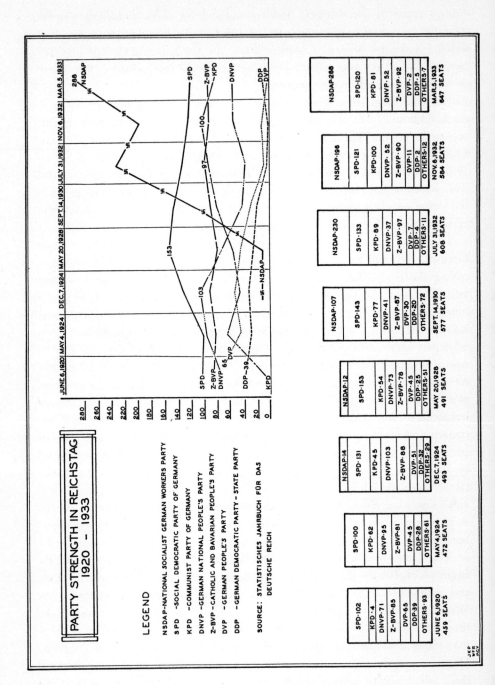

PARTY STRENGTH IN REICHSTAG
1920 – 1933

LEGEND

NSDAP – NATIONAL SOCIALIST GERMAN WORKERS PARTY

SPD – SOCIAL DEMOCRATIC PARTY OF GERMANY

KPD – COMMUNIST PARTY OF GERMANY

DNVP – GERMAN NATIONAL PEOPLE'S PARTY

Z-BVP – CATHOLIC AND BAVARIAN PEOPLE'S PARTY

DVP – GERMAN PEOPLE'S PARTY

DDP – GERMAN DEMOCRATIC PARTY – STATE PARTY

SOURCE: STATISTISCHES JAHRBUCH FÜR DAS
DEUTSCHE REICH

ther complicated the situation within the *Reichstag*. The election system also gave the party managers very strong control over the nomination of party candidates submitted in strictly binding lists. The German citizen voted for parties, not for individuals qualified to represent the interests of the nation. Party control over the nominating process and the election lists gave it direct control over the delegates in the *Reichstag*.

The Social Democratic party, which had led the Weimar Coalition and had accepted the responsibility for signing the Versailles Treaty along with the Center, was the chief support of the Weimar regime. The impact of World War I had brought a complete reorientation of Social Democratic principles. The Russian Bolshevik threat had turned the once international leaders of the party into strong nationalistic supporters of the war. The danger of red revolution in 1918 converted the Social Democrats to the cause of liberal democracy and moderate social reform. They assumed the championship of the German state and the German bourgeois society, which they claimed was in transition to a more socialized form in order to escape the turmoil of revolution. They participated in the government during the first years of the Weimar regime with the hope that Germany would be gradually transformed into a socialist state by peaceful parliamentary means. After the first difficult years, when the Conservatives under the leadership of Wirth, Cuno, and Stresemann gained more influence, the Social Democrats continued to support the government, but without the forcefulness of earlier days, for political power had drifted into the hands of the Conservatives. The effectiveness of the party was lessened not only by giving lip service to some principles of Marxian traditions and revolutionary slogans, which were no longer of significance, but also by the after-effects of the war and the Versailles Treaty, which the reactionaries blamed upon the Social Democrats. Although the party opposed the revolutionary activities of both the radicals (Communists) and the nationalists (Nazis), it was unable to prevent the Republic from being undermined. As late as 1928 it won 153 seats in the *Reichstag* and formed a Cabinet. It always retained a strong position in Prussia.

The German Democratic party, which was the Weimar successor of the Imperial Progressive Liberal party, genuinely adhered to the principle of a liberal parliamentary and federal republic. It sought to support the cause of the Weimar Republic with the aid of the liberal elements of the bourgeoisie and the middle classes, against both the reactionaries and the socialists. At Weimar this party, although it had polled only half as many votes as the Social Democrats in the elections of 1919, bridged the gap between the socialists and the Catholics. Hugo Preuss, a member of the Democratic party, was mainly responsible for the drafting of the Weimar Constitution. During the first years of the Republic, the Democrats continued their cooperation with the Social

Democratic party and the Catholic Center party, although this cost them much of their middle class support. Their support of socialist policies in the early twenties cost the Democrats the support of the reactionary elements which had suported them in 1919. The gradual shift of wide segments of the bourgeoisie and middle class to the more nationalistic and conservative parties brought the steady decline of the fortunes of the Democratic party at the polls; in 1919, they won seventy-four seats; in 1928, twenty-five seats. The attempt of the party to reorganize along nationalistic lines in 1930 failed to bring a revival of party fortunes. In the last election before the Nazi regime, the Democratic party—now calling itself the *Staatspartei*—was able to obtain only two seats in the *Reichstag;* it had once formed one of the bulwarks of the Republic. The decline of this party clearly reflects the decline of liberal, democratic and nonsocialist principles in Germany.

The Catholic Center party, which sought to protect the interests of the Catholics in Germany, was an effectively organized political party with close organizational ties with the Catholic Church. It drew support from the Catholic areas of western, southern, and southeastern Germany. It was supported by the Catholic middle class of the small towns, by the independent Catholic peasantry of the country, and by Catholic workers, organized in the Christian Trade Unions (*Christliche Gewerkschaften*). Although it was based upon religious and economic interests, the Catholic Center party always sought to support the cause of liberal democracy. It joined the Weimar Coalition with the Social Democrats and the Democrats to aid in the formation of a constitutional republic, and took part of the responsibility for the Versailles Treaty. The conservative Bavarian elements, which were strongly particularistic in their political outlook, split off from the Center party at Weimar over the issue of federalism and formed the Bavarian People's party (*Bayrische Volkspartei*). The Center party, which was usually supported by the Bavarian People's party on religious issues, occupied a strategic position in the government. It gave Germany several important chancellors during the Weimar era: Fehrenbach, Wirth, Marx, and Brüning. Although its continuous participation in the government during the growing economic crisis cost it great numbers of supporters, the Center party was always able to bridge the gap between the leftist Social Democrats and the conservative nationalists, thus playing an important role in the formation of the policies of the Republic.

The so-called Weimar Coalition, consisting of the Social Democrats, who leaned to the left, the liberal Democratic party, and the Catholic Center which leaned to the right, were always faced with the opposition of the small but well organized and well financed conservative parties. Under the leadership of Gustav Stresemann, the German People's party (*Deutsche Volkspartei*), which succeeded the Imperial National Liberal party, continued to enjoy the support of the big industrial and commercial interests. It should be remembered that this party was constituted out of the wreckage of the old National-Liberal party after the more liberal elements withdrew to form the Democratic party. The remnants, who were liberal nationalists with strong leanings to the right, opposed the Weimar Coalition. Public discontent over governmental policies added strength to the German People's party during the early twenties. The party continued to oppose the governmental coalitions until after the failure of the Cuno government over the Ruhr issue and the inflation. In August 1923, it entered into the Great Coalition (*Grosse Koalition*) with the Social Democrats, Centrists, and Democrats, which solved the problem of inflation and negotiated the French evacuation of the Ruhr. Under the leadership of Stresemann, a member of the German People's party who served as Chancellor in 1923 and as Foreign Minister from 1923 to 1929, Germany instituted a new foreign policy based upon the revision of the Versailles Treaty through diplomatic negotiations, which greatly improved the political and economic status of the Republic.

The conservative and reactionary forces supported the German Nationalists People's party (*Deutschnationale Volkspartei*) which developed out of the earlier Imperial Conservative party. After the war this party, largely made up of landowners and aristocrats, came out for the monarchy and Empire, although it participated in the Weimar Assembly because of its fear of communism. The revival of the German Nationalists People's party was based primarily upon dissatisfaction with governmental policies during the difficult inflation period. In 1924 the combined vote of the conservative parties and the reactionary Agricultural League (*Landbund*) amounted to over twenty-two per cent of the popular vote. Economic pressure and the necessity for higher tariffs forced the Conservatives into the Great Coalition. After 1925 their strength declined and was largely restricted to small reactionary groups in northeastern Germany. Their influence, however, was out of all proportion to their numbers.

Politically, the Weimar Republic was dominated by coalitions of the leftist Social Democrats, the liberal Democratic and Center parties, and the rightist German People's party. Political troubles, resulting from the friction between parties and the inability of any party to take full responsibility for the foreign and domestic affairs of Germany, were apparent from the time of the Weimar Assembly. The Coalition of Social Democrats, Democrats, and Centrists in 1919 (the Weimar Coalition), which drafted the Weimar Constitution, broke up when the Democratic party refused to participate in the acceptance of the Versailles Treaty. The Scheidemann cabinet gave way to the Bauer cabinet, supported by a coalition of the Social Democrats and Centrists. After the election of the first *Reichstag* in June 1920, a coalition of the Democratic, Center, and German People's parties faced the difficult task of solving Germany's postwar domestic and foreign problems, which were now becoming further intensified by the growing inflation.

In the face of the increasing political and economic troubles of 1921 and 1922, the old Weimar Coalition was re-established under the leadership of Wirth. This government was forced to weather a series of violent political disturbances instigated by the Communists and reactionaries. The governments of Bavaria, Saxony, and Thuringia were seized by communist regimes, while the reactionaries under the leadership of Kapp and Ludendorff tried to overthrow the national government in Berlin (Kapp Putsch, March 1920). The political situation was not, however, ripe for radical action. The Social Democrats, whose membership was scattered throughout the Reich, had particularly strong followings in industrial portions of Silesia, Central Germany, Westphalia, the northern Rhineland, Hesse-Nassau, Franconia, Southwest Germany, Hamburg, and Berlin, where the working class was large enough to play an important political role. The Center party had large followings in the Catholic areas of Silesia and western and southern Germany. The liberal Democratic party was strong in the cities of Brandenburg, Hesse-Nassau, Westphalia, Franconia, and Southwest Germany, while the moderate German People's party had strong followings in East Prussia, Westphalia, Schleswig-Holstein, Central Germany, and Hesse-Nassau. The conservatives dominated the northeastern portion of the Reich and had strong holdings in rural areas of northern Central Germany, Schleswig-Holstein, Westphalia, Franconia, and eastern Saxony. These parties, which supported the constitutional regime, were strong enough during the early twenties to stem the tide of revolutionary activity which grew out of the troubles of the inflation.

The Communist party of Germany (*Kommunistische Partei Deutschlands*) developed after the war through the separation of the left-wing elements from the old Social Democratic party under the leadership of Rosa Luxemburg and Karl Liebknecht. It evolved out of the *Spartacus* group that had offered overt opposition to the imperial war effort. The party was hastily and poorly organized in December 1918, and in cooperation with revolutionary groups in Russia and other lands, it made several unsuccessful attempts to seize control through revolts in Berlin, Bremen, Munich, the Ruhr, and Brunswick. Although its initial efforts had failed, the deteriorating economic conditions of the early twenties resulted in its steady growth. In particular, late in the inflation period, this party was strong enough to attempt to seize control of the governments of Saxony and Thuringia in preparation for a general German revolution.

After the restoration of economic stability in 1924 and the revival of German industrial and commercial life in the middle twenties, the strength of the Communist party declined throughout the Reich. The party organization,

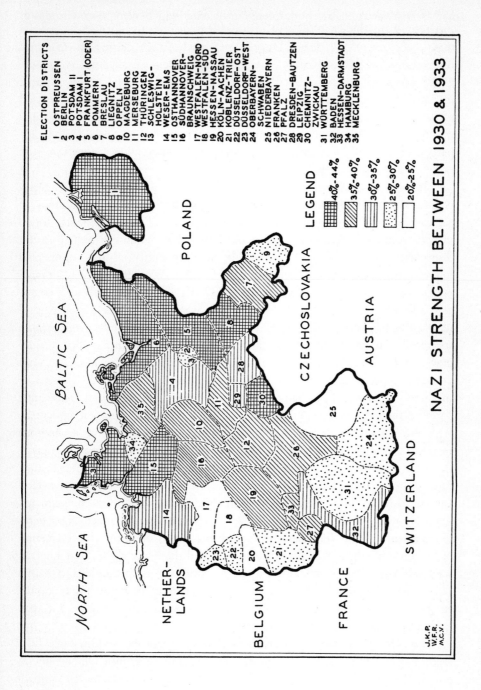

ELECTION DISTRICTS
1 OSTPREUSSEN
2 BERLIN
3 POTSDAM II
4 POTSDAM I
5 FRANKFURT (ODER)
6 POMMERN
7 BRESLAU
8 LIEGNITZ
9 OPPELN
10 MAGDEBURG
11 MERSEBURG
12 THÜRINGEN
13 SCHLESWIG-HOLSTEIN
14 WESER-EMS
15 OSTHANNOVER
16 SÜDHANNOVER-BRAUNSCHWEIG
17 WESTFALEN-NORD
18 WESTFALEN-SÜD
19 HESSEN-NASSAU
20 KÖLN-AACHEN
21 KOBLENZ-TRIER
22 DÜSSELDORF-OST
23 DÜSSELDORF-WEST
24 OBERBAYERN-SCHWABEN
25 NIEDERBAYERN
26 FRANKEN
27 PFALZ
28 DRESDEN-BAUTZEN
29 LEIPZIG
30 CHEMNITZ-ZWICKAU
31 WÜRTTEMBERG
32 BADEN
33 HESSEN-DARMSTADT
34 HAMBURG
35 MECKLENBURG

LEGEND
40%-44%
35%-40%
30%-35%
25%-30%
20%-25%

NAZI STRENGTH BETWEEN 1930 & 1933

J.K.P.
W.F.R.
M.C.V.

however, continued to press its program for the destruction of bourgeois society and for the establishment of a proletarian state to be ruled by a dictatorship of the working classes. During the period of their decline, the Communists created an efficiently organized party and developed an attractive propaganda campaign that continued to draw the support of the workers in large industrial plants and in the mines. They made special efforts to enlist the aid of the rural workers of the northeast and the bankrupt elements of the lower middle class. Politically, the Communists fought against the Social Democratic party and especially against the reactionary and conservative groups that supported the bourgeois regime.

The aggressive elements of the bourgeoisie acted through the Social Democratic, Center, and conservative parties to stem the tide of revolution in the early days of the Republic. Certain reactionary and racial elements, drawn in part from the officer group of the old imperial army, and in part from the disgruntled lower middle class, aided by wealthy industrial and commercial interests, organized the National Socialist German Worker's party (*Nationalsozialistische Deutsche Arbeiterpartei*—NSDAP) during the difficult postwar and inflation years. This party, which later was to obtain dictatorial control of the Reich, grew partly out of postwar disillusionment, but perhaps more specifically out of the failure of the middle classes to maintain their former power and control of Germany by legal and constitutional means. The once powerful upper classes, although they were still in control of the administrative machinery of government, had to share their power with the Social Democratic party in the necessary coalitions. The difficult economic situation under the Republic, coupled with the chaotic social and political condition bearing the threat of a possible victory for the Left, led many of the bourgeoisie to support the cause of a protective dictatorship. During the twenties, they began to turn to the Nazis. The National Socialist party, after its defeat in the Beer Hall Putsch at Munich in 1923, had seemed dead. But when the depression fell upon Germany in 1929, the policies of a revived and reorganized Nazi party made a wide appeal. The party's program was based upon the transformation of the anti-capitalistic feelings of the middle and the lower classes into a hatred for foreign and Jewish capitalism, upon the national socialization of Germany's economy, and upon the destruction of parliamentary government. It gained support from many German capitalists, a considerable segment of the German middle class, and part of the lower classes.

The Nazi party had very humble beginnings, for it evolved, in early 1919, from the meetings of a group of six obscure and disgruntled men, among whom was Adolf Hitler. By early 1920, it had expanded its membership to sixty-four and taken the name of National Socialist German Worker's party. Gradually, the party, thanks to Hitler's ability as an orator, began to attract widespread attention throughout Bavaria. In 1921 Hitler had at last established himself as Leader within the new party, and Göring was beginning to organize the party's Storm Troops (*Sturmabteilung-SA*), which were recruited from the German underworld and from German unemployed of all classes. Beginning to operate more aggressively the party, in 1922, was outlawed in seven of the German states, including Prussia. The first struggle for power came in 1923 with the French occupation of the Ruhr. Hitler, trusting that the discontent and dissatisfaction current throughout Germany would lend support to a revolutionary move, undertook the Putsch of 1923. The attempted revolt, which was restricted to Munich, was quickly put down by the army. Hitler was captured, convicted, and sentenced to imprisonment for five years at Landsberg for his leadership in the Putsch. The first phase in the development of the National Socialist party had ended.

The improvement of social, economic, and political conditions within Germany after the stabilization of 1924 brought an end to the first successes of the Communists and National Socialists. The Stresemann government, with the aid of the Great Coalition consisting of the Social Democrats, Democrats, Centrists, and the German People's party, restored order within the Reich. The revival of German economic life from 1924 to 1929 neutralized the work of the political extremists of the Right and the Left. The government fell to the moderates of the Democratic, Centrist, and German People's parties and the conservatives of the German Nationalist People's party, who would not take decisive action against either the National Socialists or the Communists. In 1928 the Social Democrats formed a cabinet under Herman Müller, following their victory in the elections of that year.

During this passing phase of relative political stability, the Nazi party was engaged in building up a more effective organization. In early 1925 Hitler was released from Landsberg, where he had been busy writing *Mein Kampf*. He immediately began preparations for the coming struggle for power. The political activity of the party was limited, for it was still under ban in Prussia and six other German states. The gradual removal of these bans slowly opened the way for more intensive campaigns. In 1928, after all of the prohibitions had been removed, the Nazi party entered its first significant *Reichstag* campaign. Although it did not poll many votes, it did gain followings in Thuringia, Schleswig-Holstein, Hanover, Brunswick, Hesse-Nassau, Franconia, Southern Bavaria, and southeastern Saxony.

The revival of the troubled German political situation came with the World economic depression of 1929. In the midst of the difficult financial and economic situation, Brüning of the Catholic Center party was called to the Chancellorship in 1930 and attempted to bring order out of chaos. When his measures were rejected by the *Reichstag,* Brüning requested that the body be dissolved and that the President call for new elections. The *Reichstag* election of September 1930 brought an amazing increase in the strength of the Nazi party, making it the second strongest party with 107 seats. Significant increases in the strength of the Communists were also registered. The Brüning coalition of Center, Democratic, German People's, and Bavarian People's parties, supported also by the Social Democrats, was faced with danger from both the Right and the Left.

The Nazis began an all out effort, based upon oratory and riotous demonstrations, to gain the support of the suffering middle class of the towns and the disgruntled peasantry of the country, two groups who desired an easy way back to their former prosperity. These groups fell an easy prey for they preferred a rightist solution, and all their traditions mitigated against the acceptance of the revolutionary solution offered by the Communists. The Nazis promised a revival of old social and economic conditions and the solution of all foreign and domestic problems, through the simple expedient of abolishing parliamentary government and substituting for it the effective action of a dictatorial regime. They promised revenge for the war and its after effects through the creation of a strong national state, and a revival of the mythical power of Germany's great medieval Empire. The Nazis promised anything to any class that would gain votes.

Despite growing opposition, the Brüning government carried on by the extensive use of emergency decrees. Political power shifted rapidly from the *Reichstag* to the President and the Chancellor. The cumulative effects of economic and financial crises, coupled with the weakness of parliamentary government and the aggressiveness of the National Socialist and Communist parties, shook the Republic to its foundations. The bitterly fought presidential election campaign of 1932 further widened the breaches in the structure of the Weimar regime. Hindenburg's re-election as President, achieved largely through Brüning's efforts, was followed by the ouster of the Brüning government by the old President and his clique just at the moment when the economic situation was beginning to improve, and while Brüning still retained majority support in the *Reichstag*.

Franz von Papen, who had been an inconspicuous member of the conservative wing of the Catholic party, was called to the chancellorship. Hindenburg immediately called for a new *Reichstag* election, the fourth electoral campaign in four months. In the midst of the campaign, the von Papen cabinet seized control of the government of Prussia and began the consolidation of all power in the hands of the executive. The leaders of the opposition parties, which had long supported the republican system, took no effective counter-action. The elections of July 1932, brought further victories for both the Nazis and the Communists. The National Socialist party secured two hundred and thirty of the total of six hundred and eight *Reichstag* seats, making it the largest party. The von Papen government, unable to gain the support of the *Reichstag,* had the President dissolve it before a vote of confidence was completed. Popular government was disintegrating, and the people were growing weary and disillusioned because of the political maneuvers of the parties and their leaders.

No real effort was made by the Republican forces to meet the critical situation. Nevertheless, the *Reichstag* elections of November 1932, left von Papen without either popular or *Reichstag* support. Reluctantly, the old President accepted von Papen's resignation and appointed to the chancellorship General von Schleicher, who had the support of the army and contacts with some of the labor groups. One striking result of the election was that the Nazis lost ground, while the Communist party made considerable gains. Despite an auspicious start in December 1932, the von Schleicher regime was rapidly undermined by the intrigues of von Papen and the Junker nationalists. On January 28, 1933, Hindenburg's refusal to dissolve the *Reichstag* as requested by the Schleicher cabinet, forced the cabinet to resign. Three days later a coalition of the Nationalists under Hugenberg and the National Socialists assumed control of Germany with Hitler as Chancellor, von Papen as Vice Chancellor, and Hugenberg as Minister for Economics and Agriculture. Although he had abruptly refused to offer the chancellorship to Hitler a few months before, Hindenburg now handed over the reins of office to the Nazi leader, with the apparent belief that von Papen, Hugenberg and the Nationalists could control the Nazis and still remain in the saddle. Events proved otherwise, and in a few weeks Hitler was in unchallenged control.

The fall of the Weimar Republic and the establishment of the Third Reich can be explained on the basis of the failure of the republican forces to liquidate the mistakes of the imperial regime, the intrigues which surrounded the office of the President, and the lack of courage and determination on the part of the republican forces to put an end to the arbitrary rule of the von Papen and von Schleicher regimes. The political inexperience of the German people, coupled with the sharp cleavages between the parties over special interests, stand out among the other fundamental causes for the failure of the liberal Weimar Republic. Naturally, the economic crisis and the liquidation of a lost war were also of the greatest importance.

The German people, nevertheless, must bear the principal responsibility for the Nazi regime, because it was their votes which permitted Hitler to acquire control of the Reich. Although Hitler was able to seize power on the basis of a revival of German nationalism and imperialism, he did not receive the full support of the German people. Studies of the numerous elections between 1930 and 1933 reveal that he came into power through the efforts of a strong minority group which was able to triumph over the disillusioned and divided major-

ity. Hitler did receive strong support in eastern Germany in Pomerania, East
Prussia, eastern Brandenburg, and northern Silesia where he appealed to both
the Junkers and the peasants. He also obtained sizable votes in northern Hanover, Schleswig-Holstein, and southwestern Saxony. The middle class of the
towns and the peasantry of the country gave him a moderate following in the
old Franconian and Low Saxon areas lying between the Rhine and Elbe.

The chief opposition to Hitler was found in western and southern Germany,
Silesia, and the big cities, where the Catholics and the laboring classes refused
to give their support to the Nazi cause. The Nazi movement, which appealed to German prejudices against Jew, intellectual, and Communist, offered
hope to the ruined middle classes. The unemployed were offered jobs within
the numerous party organizations, and the hope of abundant opportunity in
an expanding German economy. The upper classes and the business interests,
who actively financed the party, and the German military caste, backed the
Nazis in order to counter "potential" revolutionary activity from the Left. The
working classes, too, believing in Hitler's denunciation of capitalism, flocked
to the support of the Nazis in great numbers. However, Hitler's rise cannot be
entirely explained in terms of social, economic, and political issues. Nazi uniforms, ceremony, and mysticism, backed by an elaborate propaganda campaign, appealed to the masses. Hitler offered the Germans power and dominance in the world, and an escape from the "evils" of the Republic. *Although
Germany did not give the Nazis majority support, Hitler and the Nazis were
able to persuade a sufficient number of German citizens of the validity of their
cause to permit the establishment of the Third Reich.* Thereafter, Hitler succeeded in winning over the overwhelming majority of the German people.

The National Socialist Party

Although the National Socialists never clearly defined their ideological program in specific terms, the party had a definite political philosophy. The basic
Nazi concepts rested upon anti-democratic, anti-intellectual, anti-Semitic, anti-
Marxian, and anti-international principles. The Nazis held that the state
should be under the guidance of a "Leader" and a small élite, with authority
extending down from the Führer to the people. They replaced reason and rational thinking with emotion and hatred. The racial program became of prime
political importance. The so-called Aryan Germans were invested with the
leadership of the Reich. All creativeness was said to be a product of Aryan
minds which were destined to rule the world. The Jews were attacked as the
source of all corruption, and, consequently, were the objects of numerous anti-
racial laws which deprived them of most of their civil and political rights; they
became the victims of boycotts and persecutions. The anti-Marxian position of
the Nazis led to the development of a variation of economic nationalism, un-

der which the capitalists continued to profit under a system of state control, while the workers were deprived of their traditional rights and subjugated to regimented state control.

The concept of racial nationalism, which was basic to the National Socialist movement, contended that the German soil and the German blood produced an invincible community of supermen under the leadership of a Führer, Adolf Hitler, who was responsible only to the mythical nation. The roots of racial hatred and compensatory dreams of national power, which exist after a losing war, were used in Germany. The ideological sources for these debased principles are deeply rooted in German nationalist philosophy and in anti-Semitic doctrines. The Nazis simply utilized them to create a practical political psychology which would dazzle the German citizen and draw his support to the cause of National Socialism.

The organization of the National Socialist party, which controlled every aspect of German life from 1933 to 1945, was highly complicated in structure, although the control and coordination of the party activities under the leadership of the Führer were relatively simple and clear cut. The party was headed by Adolf Hitler, who was aided by a Party Chancellery and a private chancellery. While the fundamental policies of the party were determined by Hitler, much of the actual administration was under the Deputy Leader (Rudolf Hess until 1941), who was also responsible for routine relations between the party and the German government. The Führer was also assisted by a Party Cabinet, consisting of twenty national leaders (*Reichsleiter*) who were responsible for such spheres of the party's activities as: Organization, Propaganda, Press, Party Justice, Colonial Affairs, Party Finance, Youth, Labor, Foreign Affairs, Agriculture, Special Guards, Storm Troops, *Reichstag* Affairs, and Municipal Affairs. The members of the Party Cabinet, working under the direction of the Deputy Leader, directed and coordinated the activities of the party. The illogical structure of the Party Cabinet was a natural result of the highly personal character of the party organization. Duplications of function and conflicts of authority, which were regulated in cases of open trouble by the Führer or the Deputy Leader, did not disturb the Nazis. The work of the offices of the Party Cabinet members was supplemented by that of the subordinate Main Offices for Civil Servants, War Victims, Public Health, Technical Affairs, Teachers, and Welfare which were under the National Party Organizer, a member of the Party Cabinet and the National Party Treasurer, who was also a member of the Party Cabinet, but directly responsible to the Führer. This comprehensive and elaborate national party organization had its headquarters in the Brown House at Munich.

Regional and local party control was carried out through an extensive territorial organization consisting of thirty-two Nazi party districts headed by

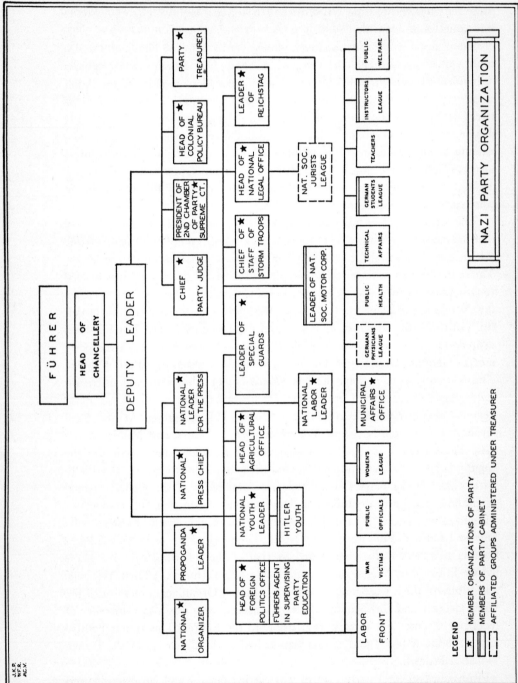

FÜHRER

HEAD OF CHANCELLERY

DEPUTY LEADER

NATIONAL ORGANIZER ★

PROPOGANDA LEADER ★

NATIONAL PRESS CHIEF ★

NATIONAL LEADER FOR THE PRESS ★

CHIEF PARTY JUDGE ★

PRESIDENT OF 2ND CHAMBER OF PARTY SUPREME CT. ★

HEAD OF COLONIAL POLICY BUREAU ★

PARTY TREASURER ★

HEAD OF FOREIGN POLITICS OFFICE ★

NATIONAL YOUTH LEADER ★

HEAD OF AGRICULTURAL OFFICE ★

LEADER OF SPECIAL GUARDS ★

CHIEF OF STAFF OF STORM TROOPS ★

HEAD OF NATIONAL LEGAL OFFICE ★

LEADER OF REICHSTAG ★

FÜHRER'S AGENT IN SUPERVISING PARTY EDUCATION

HITLER YOUTH

NATIONAL LABOR LEADER ★

LEADER OF NAT. SOC. MOTOR CORP.

NAT. SOC. JURISTS LEAGUE

LABOR FRONT

WAR VICTIMS

PUBLIC OFFICIALS

WOMEN'S LEAGUE

MUNICIPAL AFFAIRS OFFICE ★

GERMAN PHYSICIANS LEAGUE

PUBLIC HEALTH

TECHNICAL AFFAIRS

GERMAN STUDENTS LEAGUE

TEACHERS

INSTRUCTORS LEAGUE

PUBLIC WELFARE

NAZI PARTY ORGANIZATION

LEGEND

★ MEMBER ORGANIZATIONS OF PARTY

☐ MEMBERS OF PARTY CABINET

┆ AFFILIATED GROUPS ADMINISTERED UNDER TREASURER

J.K.P.
W.F.R.
W.C.V.

District Leaders who were appointed by Hitler and responsible to him for all party activities within their respective districts. The party districts were divided into counties under County Leaders (*Kreisleiter*) whose administrative offices possessed divisions similar to those of the district and national offices. The county unit was divided into local town and village groups (*Ortsgruppen*), cells (*Zellen*), and blocks (*Blöcke*), which consisted of a small group of persons living in the same neighborhood or block of houses. Control within this territorial organization was rigid, with each leader subject to the absolute jurisdiction of his immediate superior. Nevertheless, there was a considerable amount of fluctuation in the local organization of the party as the membership increased, and as old leaders were changed for ones considered politically more reliable. At its peak the party had approximately eight million members who were controlled through some fifteen thousand local groups.

The work of the national, district, and local party organizations was further supplemented by that of the member organizations of the party (*Gliederungen der Partei*) and the affiliated organizations (*Angeschlossene Verbände*). The organizations directly responsible to Hitler included the SA-Storm Troops (*Sturmabteilung der NSDAP*), the SS-Elite Guard (*Schutzstaffel der NSDAP*), the National Socialist Motor Corps (*Nationalsozialistisches Kraftfahrkorps*), the Hitler Youth, National Socialist German Students' League (*NSD Studentenbund*), the National Socialist Women's Organization (*NS Frauenschaft*), and the National Socialist Instructors' League (*NS Dozentenbund*). The work of the member organizations, generally carried out through territorial organizations based upon regional patterns differing from that of the general party pattern, provided additional controls for the party. The Storm Troops, the first of the numerous party organizations, played only a minor role after the Röhm revolt of 1934. In the latter years of the Third Reich, its three quarters of a million members were largely used as a demonstration force on party occasions. The Elite Guard, however, formed the most powerful weapon of the Nazi regime. Its leader, Heinrich Himmler, was a member of the Party Cabinet, the Chief of the German Police, and, during the war, Minister of the Interior. This force of approximately two hundred thousand men protected the regime against the threat of conspiracy and treason. The Hitler Youth, to which Hitler gave his special attention because he believed it was the hope for the future of the Nazi party, included all German youth. All of these member party organizations, which were composed of members of the party and the youth of the nation who were preparing for membership in the party, constituted the major bulwark of the Nazi regime.

The affiliated organizations had a separate legal status and were composed of individuals who were not necessarily members of the party. They were organized under the central offices of the party and were subject to the financial control of the party Treasurer. The Labor Front, which provided for the organization and control of employers and their associations as well as control of all German workers, was directly under the National Party Organizer. This organization, which was the most important of the affiliated groups, possessed a vast territorial structure which reached down into every German factory and shop, playing a significant part in the control of the German labor force. The other affiliated groups included organizations for the control of physicians, jurists, teachers, civil servants, technicians, nurses, students, lecturers, lawyers, veterans, and hunters. No aspect of German life was left without some degree of Nazi control. Additional affiliated organizations were established for welfare, health, and war relief activities. The work of these party organizations was further supplemented by that of the Estates for Trade and Industry, Handicrafts, and Cultural Activities, which worked under the supervision of a pertinent government ministry. The pattern of National Socialist control over the life of Germany was complete. Opposition was all but impossible, for every group and every activity had its requisite party control.

Discipline within the national, territorial, and local organizations was maintained by a system of party courts directly under Hitler. The system of party justice consisted of the High Party Court at Munich, the District Courts, and the County Courts, which settled disputes between party members, protected the party's "honor," and handled jurisdictional disputes between the agencies of the party. The work of the courts was tied into the party secret service, which was also under the Chief Party Judge in Munich. Every party member was constantly being checked for his loyalty to the Führer.

The National Socialist party became the only political force within the German state and exercised a profound influence on all governmental and administrative activity. The laws that dissolved the political opposition recognized the unity of the Nazi party and the German State, and established the political monopoly of the party. All German officials were required to render assistance to the party officials and special protection was provided for the party, its leaders, its uniforms, and its property.

The party, with its huge bureaucratic machine permeating every aspect of German life, achieved control of the German government in a number of ways. Important party and state offices were linked together, although the organizations remained distinct. Hitler served as leader of the party and as the head of the German state. The Nazi officials for the party offices for security, agriculture, and propaganda were made heads of the German Police, and of the Ministries for Agriculture and Propaganda. All important governmental and administrative posts at the national, regional, and local levels passed into the hands of Nazi officials. A personal union between party and state offices was established for the offices of the National Governors or Chief Presidents and

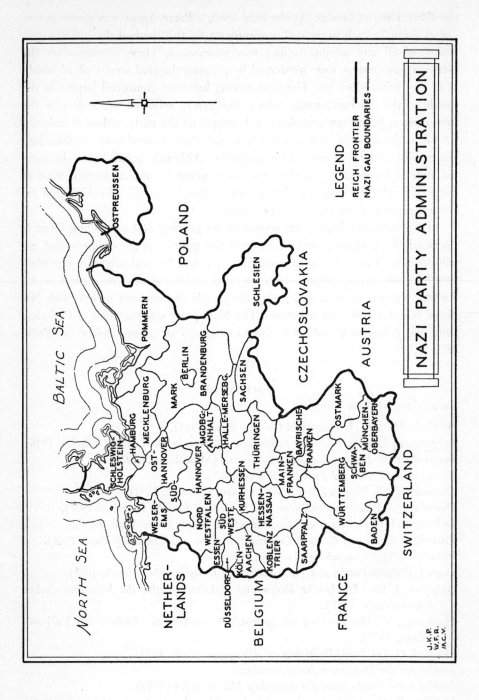

the Party District Leader. At the local level, a Party Agent was given an official position in each municipal government; by this method the political reliability of all city administrations was guaranteed. These controls over the German government were reinforced by purging the civil service of all republican and leftist elements. The civil service, however, continued largely in the hands of the old bureaucrats, who complacently followed the orders of the new master. It was not completely submerged by the party, although indoctrination of the mass of civil servants went far. Party control over entrance into the service ultimately ruined its neutrality. Although collaboration between the state and the party was close, there was never a complete identification of party and state activities, so that a large sphere of public administration remained separate from the party apparatus.

In Germany the Nazi party served as the guiding and controlling force. It provided the leadership and determined the policies of government and administration. It served as a state within a state, as a "second sovereign organization." Its vast organization, which operated under the absolute control of the Führer, had the mission of keeping the people of Germany in line with National Socialist aims and objectives. The Nazi party was the ruler of Germany until the Allies took over, following Germany's shattering defeat in World War II.

BIBLIOGRAPHY

Empire and Weimar Republic

Bebel, A. *My Life* (University of Chicago Press, 1913).
Bergsträsser, L. *Geschichte der politischen Parteien in Deutschland* (Berlin, 1936).
Bergsträsser, L. *Der politische Katholizismus* (Munich, 1921-1923).
Bernstein, E. *Ferdinand Lassalle* (Berlin, 1919).
Dawson, W. H. *Bismarck and State Socialism* (London, 1890).
Dawson, W. H. *German Socialism and Ferdinand Lassalle* (London, 1891).
Delbrück, H. *Government and the Will of the People* (New York, 1923).
Fischer, R. *Stalin and German Communism* (Harvard University Press, 1948).
Frölich, P. *Rosa Luxemburg* (London, 1940).
Gore, J. *Political Parties and Party Policies in Germany* (New York, 1903).
Gumperz, J. *Karl Liebknecht, Reden* und *Aufsätze* (Verlag der Kommunistischen Internationale, 1921).
Hankamer, W. *Das Zentrum die politische Vertretung des katholischen Volksteils* (Essen, 1927).
Hesnard, O. *Les Partis Politiques en Allemagne* (Paris, 1923).
Jahrbücher der Deutschen Sozialdemokratie.
Jahrbuch der Reichspartei des deutschen Mittelstandes (1929).
Mehring, F. *Geschichte der Deutschen Sozialdemokratie,* 4 vols. (Stuttgart, 1909).
Neumann, S. *Die Deutschen Parteien* (Berlin, 1932).

Organisationshandbuch der Deutschen Demokratischen Partei (Berlin, 1926).

Organisations-Handbuch für Zentrumswähler, 2nd ed. (Hildesheim, 1925).

Pollock, J. K. "The German Party System," in *The American Political Science Review,* Vol. XXIII, No. 4, November, 1929, pp. 859 ff.

Pollock, J. K. "The German Reichstag Elections of 1930," in *The American Political Science Review,* Vol. XXIV, No. 4, November, 1930.

Salomon, F., ed. *Die Deutschen Parteiprogramme,* 3 vols. (Leipzig-Berlin, 1912-1920).

Sass, J. *Die 27 deutschen Parteien und ihre Ziele* (Hamburg, 1931).

Schaaff, J. *Die Deutschen Katholiken und die Zentrumspartei* (Köln, 1928).

Schreiber, G., ed. *Politisches Jahrbuch* (München-Gladbach).

Schreiber, G. *Brüning, Hitler, Schleicher, Das Zentrum in der Opposition* (Köln, 1932).

Sulzbach, W. *Die Grundlagen der politischen Parteibildung* (Tübingen, 1921).

National Socialism

Boerner, A. V. "The Position of the NSDAP in the German Constitutional Order," in *The American Political Science Review,* Vol. XXXII, No. 6, December, 1938, pp. 1059 ff.

Fabricius, H. *Geschichte der Nationalsozialistischen Bewegung* (Berlin, 1937).

Feder, G. *The Programme of the NSDAP* (Munich, 1932).

Heiden, K. *A History of National Socialism* (London, 1934).

Heiden, K. *Adolf Hitler,* 2 vols. (Zurich, 1936-1937).

Huber, E. *Das ist Nationalsozialismus,* 5th ed. (Stuttgart, Berlin, Leipzig, 1934).

Killinger, M. von. *Die S.A. in Wort und Bild* (Leipzig, 1934).

Koch, E. *Die N.S.D.A.P. Idee, Führer und Partei* (Berlin, 1934).

Lüddecke, T. *Nationalsozialistische Menschenführung in den Betrieben* (Hamburg, 1934).

Murphy, R. E. *et al. National Socialism,* Department of State Publication #1864 (Washington, D. C., 1943).

Nationalsozialismus in Staat, Gemeinde und Wirtschaft (Essen, 1934).

Neesse, G. *Die Nationalsozialistische Deutsche Arbeiterpartei* (Stuttgart, 1935).

Starke, G. *N.S.B.O. und Deutsche Arbeitsfront* (Berlin, 1934).

General Information

Kaisenberg, *Die Wahl zum Reichstag,* 4th ed. (Berlin, 1930).

Pollock, J. K. *German Election Administration* (New York, 1934).

Pollock, J. K. "An Areal Study of the German Electorate," in *The American Political Science Review,* Vol XXXVIII, No. 1, February, 1944, pp. 89 ff.

Part II

REGIONAL COMPOSITION OF GERMANY

Chapter 4

INTRODUCTION TO EAST ELBIA

Eastern Germany, that part of the Reich lying to the east of the Elbe River, and hence sometimes referred to as East Elbia, embraced the Prussian provinces of Brandenburg, Pomerania, Silesia, and East Prussia, the Prussian politically independent city of Berlin, Danzig, and the state of Mecklenburg. The several parts of this region are characterized by a traditional feeling of unity and mutual interdependence. Integrated by common landscape features, the region is also bound together in close political, economic, social, and cultural interrelationships.

The land forms a part of the great lowland plain of Europe, which extends from the Paris Basin to the Ural Mountains. Within Eastern Germany, however, the plain subdivides into several more or less distinctive zones that have given rise to certain ecological variations in the pattern of the life of the people. In the north, the coastal provinces of East Prussia and Pomerania and the state of Mecklenburg constitute the Baltic zone, which divides into five basic areas: the Mecklenburg lake plateau, the lower Oder Valley, the Pomeranian lake plateau, the lower Vistula Valley, and the East Prussian lake plateau. The Baltic Sea washes the northern boundary of this zone, forming sandy beaches and dune covered coastal areas in eastern Pomerania and East Prussia and cutting deep *Förden* or Fjords (*Bodden*) into the coast line of western Pomerania and Mecklenburg. The seaward slopes, traversed by numerous streams flowing northward to the Baltic, consist of clay soils which support a dairy and livestock industry. The southern margins of the plateaus, although higher, are characterized by poor drainage, which has given rise to numerous marshes and lakes. Life within the coastal zone is focused upon the port towns of Stettin and Königsberg.

To the south of the sparsely settled Baltic zone lies the zone of the Ancient River Valleys (*Urstromtäler*) which embraces most of the Province of Brandenburg. With the exception of the dominating city of Berlin and the smaller cities of Brandenburg and Frankfort-on-the-Oder, life within Brandenburg is dependent on agrarian activities and centers in the small villages and small towns of the region. The valley zone, which forms the core of East Elbia, is bordered on the south by the low hills of Fläming and Nieder Lausitz, which divide Brandenburg from Central Germany, and by the Katzen Gebirge, which divides the upper Oder Valley portion of the Province of Silesia from the northern part of the province.

The lowland Bay of Silesia lying along the upper Oder Valley, constitutes a third zone of East Elbia. This area, which is hemmed in by the Sudeten uplands and the southwest Polish plateaus, is important because of its industries and manufacturing establishments which are based upon the mineral wealth of the upper Oder Valley. Although Silesia with its areas of intensive agriculture, upland dairying, and heavy industry is oriented internally toward Breslau and the industrial cities of Upper Silesia, it is drawn into the life of East Elbia because of its dependence upon the markets of Berlin and the port facilities of Stettin. Yet, there is a certain unity to East Elbian Germany, despite the three geographical zones just described. The dairy and livestock industries of the Baltic, the rye and potato agriculture of the central Brandenburg valley zone, and the agrarian and industrial resources of Silesia, all contribute to the economic well-being of the total area. This land, lying between the Elbe River to the west and the lands of the Poles to the east, and between the Baltic on the north and the central highlands of Middle Europe on the south, is tied together by a network of road, rail, and water transportation arteries all oriented toward the city of Berlin—the political, economic, and cultural capital of the area.

The people of Eastern Germany are a blend of many racial and cultural groups. The earliest known occupants were the peoples of Palaeolithic and Mesolithic times, whose hunting and collecting activities are inferred from stone implements found in numerous East Elbian sites. During the Neolithic, Bronze, and Iron Ages, East Elbia was occupied by agrarian peoples, who may have been akin to the Illyrian peoples of ancient times. Toward the middle of the first millennium A.D., pastoral Slavic tribes pushing westward from the basin of the Vistula and the upper Dnieper occupied most of the land. The beginning of German settlement dates from the time of the military conquest of Eastern Germany, which began in the tenth century and which was carried out under the leadership of the Saxon, the Franconian, and the Hohenstaufen Emperors. Low Saxon settlers from Northwest Germany pushed into Mecklenburg and Brandenburg, while Frankish and Thuringian peoples, who had taken possession of the lands along the Elbe and Saale, moved into Silesia and southeastern Brandenburg. During the twelfth and thirteenth centuries, the Germans penetrated into eastern Brandenburg and Pomerania.

East Prussia was occupied by seaborne groups of German settlers, whose incursions were spearheaded by the Teutonic Knights. The Knights occupied a unique place in the early history of the region. The Order of Teutonic Knights of St. Mary's Hospital at Jerusalem was founded in 1190 during the Crusades. Half a century later the efforts of the Order were shifted from the Moslems to the pagans of the Baltic area. Its method of Christianization was strictly military and the Knights' subjugation of East Prussia was completed by 1238. By military campaigns in Lithuania, Latvia, and Estonia the power of the Order was extended northwards; it lasted until their defeat by the Lithuanians and Poles at Tannenberg in 1410. Thereafter, the Order declined slowly until it was finally abolished by Napoleon in 1809.

The main colonial movements of the Germans into East Elbia were completed by the middle of the thirteenth century. After that time, their efforts were directed chiefly toward the consolidation of their new-won holdings through the subjugation and Germanization of the old Slavic population. The Germanization of Mecklenburg, Brandenburg, Pomerania, and Silesia was successful, but in East Prussia the Germans were successful only in the northern part of the province. The southern lake district has remained permanently in the hands of the Slavic Masurians, while the lands along the Memel River are still held by the Baltic Lithuanians. These movements of peoples explain the heterogeneous racial composition of Eastern Germany.

There are also marked variations in the language of the people. Although standard German is spoken in the cities and larger towns, traditional dialects are still common among the rural peoples of Mecklenburg, Pomerania, Brandenburg, and East Prussia. These dialects have developed from Low Saxon, whereas the dialects of Silesia, southeast Brandenburg, and southwest East Prussia, go back to the Middle German Language brought into Eastern Germany by the Franks and Thuringians. The Spreewald near Berlin is a Slavic enclave. Although there are many sharp differences between the peoples of Eastern Germany, as reflected in their physique, dialect, customs, and folklore, they have been bound together by a common Protestant faith since 1525, by common economic interests, and by a common Prussian political past.

The political history of Eastern Germany goes back to the days of the German conquest of East Elbia. In the tenth century, political development begins with the establishment of the frontier districts of Nordmark (central and northwest Brandenburg) and Ostmark (the state of Saxony and southern Brandenburg). The state of Mecklenburg and its Slavic princes were brought into the Holy Roman Empire through the efforts of the powerful dukes of Saxony, while the Pomeranian lands along the Baltic entered the Holy Roman Empire when the Slavic rulers of this Baltic area were recognized as Princes of the Realm (*Reichsfürsten*) by the Hohenstaufen Emperors who ruled Germany between 1138 and 1254. Silesia became an integral part of the Reich in

1201 as the result of a partition of Polish Crown lands. It was during this era of eastern colonization, when the territories of the East Elbian plain were being brought under German control, that East Prussia was conquered by the Teutonic Knights. There was no single political entity based upon dynastic and territorial holdings strong enough to dominate Eastern Germany.

After the fall of the Hohenstaufen Emperors, conditions within East Elbia bordered on anarchy, for the petty nobility had gained full control of local affairs. Meanwhile the power of the Wittelsbach family of Bavaria was being extended and its rulers were given the status of Electors within the Empire. In 1324, after the extinction of the line of Albrecht of Saxony, which had ruled the central portion of the East Elbian plain from the time of its conquest in the tenth century, the Wittelsbachs obtained control of the territories of Brandenburg. Later, in 1373, the electorship and the territories of Brandenburg passed to the Luxemburg emperors who had also gained an ephemeral control over Bohemia, Moravia, and Silesia. During this period the Slavic princes of Mecklenburg and Pomerania and the Teutonic Knights of East Prussia continued to dominate the lands along the Baltic.

The first change in the political fortunes of East Germany came with the fall of Luxemburg power in East Elbia. In 1411 the Hohenzollern nobleman, Friedrich, Burgraf of Nuremberg, was granted the electorship of Brandenburg. During the fifteenth and sixteenth centuries, the Hohenzollerns were too weak to expand their holdings beyond the central plains lying between the Elbe and Oder. Silesia, Pomerania, Mecklenburg, and East Prussia continued as distinct political entities, each following its own pattern of development. Silesia, which had been ruled by the dukes of Upper and Lower Silesia after its separation from Poland in the eleventh century, had disintegrated into a number of rival feudal entities, which were brought under the control of the Luxemburgers of Bohemia and finally, in 1526, under the Austrian Habsburgs. Mecklenburg had attained a certain amount of territorial stability under its traditional Slavic princes; Pomerania, on the other hand, was subjected to constant divisions resulting from the internal struggles of its Slavic rulers. In the East, the Teutonic Knights continued to rule East Prussia until their defeat by the Poles. In Brandenburg, Freidrich Wilhelm I (IV), the first Hohenzollern Elector, established order by force of arms. The towns and petty nobility were brought under the control of the Hohenzollern court, which was moved from Brandenburg to the city of Berlin.

The first important territorial expansion of Hohenzollern Brandenburg came with the acquisition of the Duchy of Prussia in 1618. It was inherited by Johann Sigismund, Elector and Margrave of Brandenburg under a marriage arrangement with the consent of Poland. His weak successor, the Protestant Elector Georg Wilhelm (1619-1640) maintained a feeble neutrality during the

Thirty Years' War, with the result that the lands of the Hohenzollerns were ravaged by both sides. His attempt to drive the Swedes under Gustavus Adolphus from Brandenburg ended in defeat and his flight to Königsberg and the safety of the Duchy of Prussia. His successor, Friedrich Wilhelm, "The Great Elector" (1640-1688), found Brandenburg occupied by a Swedish army; the land was in a deplorable economic and political condition. He immediately arranged for the evacuation of Swedish troops and began a series of sweeping internal reforms designed to prevent a recurrence of the evil days of the Thirty Years' War when the Hohenzollern lands had not been able to defend themselves. Brandenburg withdrew from the long and costly wars and prepared for an advantageous position in the peace negotiations.

The Treaty of Westphalia (1648) added eastern Pomerania and the secularized bishoprics of Halberstadt, Minden, and Kammin to the territory of Brandenburg and some lands along the lower Rhine to the holdings of the Hohenzollern family. The Great Elector made Brandenburg into one of the more important European states through his wise domestic and foreign policies. His measures in the field of foreign affairs had brought the territorial enlargement of the electorate, the overthrow of Swedish power in the Baltic, and the curbing of the powers of France under Louis XIV. Internally, he strengthened the power of the central administration and laid the foundations for the development of the absolute monarchy of the later Hohenzollern rulers. His reign, which had placed the Hohenzollern lands on a firm financial and economic basis, had brought about a marked recovery from the ravages of the Thirty Years' War and prepared the Hohenzollerns for a larger role in European affairs.

Friedrich II, the successor of the Great Elector, transformed his duchy into a kingdom. He was crowned at Königsberg as Friedrich I, King *in* Prussia, on January 18, 1701. Poland, weakened by her long wars with the Turks, was not able to take action against the Hohenzollerns. The second King of Prussia, Friedrich Wilhelm I (1713-1740) found the state deeply involved in debt and in considerable disorder. Although the efforts of the Great Elector had resulted in considerable improvement, the people were still impoverished, vast areas of agricultural land were out of cultivation, and the industries of the cities were at a low ebb.

To meet this situation, a number of reforms of the central government and administration were instituted. The power of the Privy Council (*Geheimer Rat*) which had been established in 1604 was strengthened, and collegial bodies were established for Interior and Finance (1723), for Foreign Affairs (1728), and for Justice, Schools, and Church Affairs (1739). Control over local affairs was accomplished through the establishment of a General Commissioner for War (*Generalkriegskommissar*), whose regional and local agents gradually gained control over the traditional territorial diets and local assemblies of knights and landowners. Collegial bodies, which were headed by executives responsible to the Prussian King, assumed control of the internal and financial administration of the territories of the Prussian Crown. County Managers (*Landräte*), who were representatives of the landed interests as well as appointees of the ruler, took over the police and finance functions of the local assemblies. These changes in administration were accompanied by tax reforms designed to raise money for the expanding administrative services and the growing army. Taxation, which was administered by the state and its territorial and local agents, was extended to the petty nobility and the cities, which had formerly enjoyed a traditional exemption from all state taxes. Church affairs and education were removed from the territorial governments and placed under central control.

The domestic reforms of Friedrich Wilhelm I freed Prussia of its heavy public debts and brought an amazing revival of agriculture and industry. He left his heir, Friedrich II (1740-1786), later known as Frederick the Great, a treasury surplus and a well disciplined army of 70,000 men. Military action against the Austrian Habsburgs, who were beset by succession difficulties, brought the addition of Silesia in 1742. The next struggle between Austria and Prussia came with the Seven Years' War, in which Friedrich was able to save his realm from the Austrians, Russians, and French only with the aid of the English (1756-1763). Frederick the Great completed his territorial program by participating in the first partition of Poland of 1772. The Polish territories of West Prussia and Ermeland were added to the Hohenzollern holdings, thus joining isolated East Prussia to the main territorial holdings of Prussia. Although the older lands of the Hohenzollerns were weakened to provide resources for these aggressions, the evils of the wars were partly mitigated by the wise administration of internal affairs.

During the Napoleonic era, Prussia was ruled by Friedrich Wilhelm III (1797-1840). At the beginning of the French Revolution, Prussia had joined with Austria in an effort to save the French Crown. However, their efforts ended in the victory of the armies of the French Republic. Napoleon's campaigns in Germany, which have been briefly described in the introduction, brought the total defeat of Prussia at Jena in 1806. This defeat was followed by a series of drastic internal reforms aimed at the regeneration of the state. Freiherr vom Stein undertook the reorganization of local government. His City Government Act of 1808 freed the cities from the old system of guild control and established city councils elected on the basis of a limited property suffrage. Although Stein's reform deprived the cities of control over justice and police, it did establish the principle of local self-government within the framework of Prussia's bureaucratic and absolute monarchy. This reform was followed by a drastic reorganization of the Prussian government. Ministries for Interior, Foreign Affairs, War, and Justice were established and placed under a chancellor, responsible to the Prussian King. The attempts under Hardenberg to reform the tax system and to create a system of centralized local administration, based upon the French model, were largely unsuccessful, owing to universal opposition on the part of local authorities. These reforms in government and administration, coupled with the abolition of serfdom and the destruction of the guild system, prepared the way for modern social and economic development.

Prussia emerged from the Napoleonic Wars as one of the victorious Allies, and consequently the territorial arrangements at Vienna (1815) brought a substantial enlargement of the Prussian state. The Hohenzollern lands lying to the east of the Elbe achieved their final form through the addition of Saxon Nieder Lausitz to Brandenburg, Swedish Western Pomerania to Prussian Pomerania, and Polish Posen and West Prussia to eastern Brandenburg and Pomerania. The Province of Saxony was established in Central Germany through the consolidation of a group of older Hohenzollern territories with the lands acquired from the State of Saxony at Vienna. The western holdings of Prussia were also enlarged and were established as the Province of Westphalia and the Rhine Province.

Although the citizens of Prussia participated in the movements for national unity and constitutional liberty, the initiative for the administrative reforms designed to strengthen the unity of the state came from the government and not from the people. Friedrich Wilhelm III had promised a constitutional government built around a state parliament and provincial assemblies, but the forces of reaction won out and the program for constitutional reform was postponed.

The early nineteenth century Prussian state retained its basic eighteenth century form as an absolute monarchy. The Prussian King, who was vested with both legislative and executive powers, was aided by a Minister President and four ministers. In 1817 a reorganization of the central government brought the establishment of a Council of State. This body, which was composed of royal princes, ministers, and high officials appointed by the King, reviewed all legislation and served as a quasi-administrative court. A "parliament of officials" carried through the administrative reforms required for unification and the centralization of power in the Prussian state.

After 1815 there was a drastic reorganization of local government and administration. The Hohenzollern lands were divided into ten provinces. In East Elbia, the Provinces of Brandenburg, Pomerania, Silesia, West Prussia, Posen and East Prussia emerged at this time. Each province was placed under a Chief President, whose duties were defined in the Royal Ordinance of 1825. He was the representative of the state administration, the supervisory agent for subordinate state authorities, and the personal representative of the King and his Ministers in the province. The provinces were also given a limited degree of self-government through the establishment of Provincial Assemblies (*Landtage*). The delegates to this body, who were elected by the landed gentry and by the cities and towns on the basis of a limited property suffrage, had little power for they lacked the right to tax. Although provincial and state legislative measures were submitted to the assembly, the delegates could voice only an advisory opinion.

The provinces, in turn, were divided into governmental administrative districts whose administrative machinery had evolved from the War and Lands Chamber (*Kriegs- und Domänenkammer*), which had originally been established through the consolidation of the County Chambers (*Amtskammern*) and the War Commissariats (*Kriegskommissariate*) in 1723. Each governmental district was headed by a District President (*Regierungspräsident*) whose powers, duties, and functions were regulated by the Royal Ordinances of 1815, 1817, and 1825. The office of the District President included departments for Interior and Police Administration; Finance, Domains, and Forests; and Church and Educational Institutions. The directors of each department supervised the work of the local offices situated in the counties and city counties.

The administrative districts consisted of counties which were headed by County Managers (an official who goes back to the early sixteenth century in Brandenburg), and of city counties which were headed by Chief Mayors. The County Manager of the rural county, who was a controlling and coordinating rather than an active administrative official, was aided by a County Assembly whose delegates were elected on the basis of a narrow class system. County administration in East Elbia was regulated by the separate provincial County Charters (*Kreisordnungen*) issued between 1825 and 1828. The city-counties and the towns and villages of the counties of East Elbia were organized on the basis of the Stein Municipal Government Act of 1808. Most of the cities and towns had a Magisterial Charter (*Magistratsverfassung*), which provided for an elected city council which in turn elected the Magistrate (*Magistrat*) and its chairman, the Mayor. The only exception was western Pomerania, where old medieval forms of city government survived until World War I.

A number of administrative reforms were undertaken by the King's Ministers at the state level. In September 1814, universal military service was introduced with the establishment of the State Army (*Landwehr*). Five military areas were created for purposes of the defense of Prussia. The efforts of the Minister of Finance brought the establishment of a more uniform system of taxation. The fields of education, church affairs, and public health were transferred in 1817 from the Ministry of the Interior to the new Ministry for Religious, Educational, and Health Affairs (*Ministerium der Geistlichen, Unterrichts- und*

Medizinal-Angelegenheiten). It assumed the direct administration of the Prussian universities, technical schools, institutes, and various state examining boards.

The impact of the Revolution of 1848 had a profound effect upon the structure of the Prussian government. Revolutionary uprisings swept across Germany to Berlin. In the midst of the political crisis, Friedrich Wilhelm IV promised a constitution, and turned the revolutionary situation over to the Prussian army, which quickly restored order. In April 1849, the Prussian King promulgated the famous Electoral Law, which divided the parliamentary electors into three classes elected on the basis of property and status. This made possible the election of conservatives, who willingly accepted the limited constitution which was proclaimed on January 31, 1850. The Prussian Constitution of 1850, which was to remain in effect until the end of World War I, established a hereditary constitutional monarchy in which the king served as the head of the state, the army, and the church, and shared the legislative power with a two-chamber parliament. Although his acts required the counter-signature of his ministers, his constitutional position was strengthened by traditional rights and prerogatives.

The Prussian Assembly consisted of two chambers which met annually to consider legislation proposed by the King or the delegates of either chamber. The powers of both chambers were limited by the fact that the Ministers of the Crown were not responsible to the delegates of the people but to the King. The House of Lords (*Herrenhaus*) consisted of hereditary royal princes, imperial nobles, and territorial nobles, and nonhereditary representatives either chosen by the King from the upper classes or appointed by the King upon proposal of provinces, city counties, and universities. The Chamber of Deputies (*Abgeordnetenhaus*), which consisted of representatives elected for five years on the basis of a limited three-class system of suffrage provided by the Electoral Law of 1849, was dominated by the Junkers and bourgeoisie, who were bound to support the reactionary Hohenzollern government.

The King exercised his executive functions through a Council of Ministers which met to discuss general policy, and through the individual ministers, who were responsible to the King for their actions within their respective departments. When the Council of Ministers met under the chairmanship of the King, it was known as the Crown Council (*Kronrat*). The Council of State lost most of its functions under the constitutional arrangements of 1850, while the Privy Council, which was reorganized as a Royal Secretariat with divisions for civil, military, and naval affairs, gained in power. It is important to note that these changes in governmental structure were not accompanied by needed reforms in the fields of state, provincial, and local administration.

In 1861 Wilhelm became King of Prussia, having served three years as regent for his insane brother, Friedrich Wilhelm IV. Bismarck, who became Minister President in 1862, shared Wilhelm's view that the rights of the Prussian Crown were not to be sacrificed to constitutional principles. They believed that the problem of German unity could only be solved through the expulsion of Austria from the Confederation and through the assumption of national leadership by Prussia. The policies of Bismarck culminated in the Seven Weeks' War and the defeat of Austria and her German allies in 1866. The Prussian victory brought the acquisition of Hanover, the Electorate of Hesse, the Duchy of Nassau, and the free city of Frankfort. After 1866, Prussia's political history tends to merge with that of the German Reich. Under the North German Confederation (1866-1871) and the Empire (1871-1918), Prussia played the leading role. Her king became the Emperor and her Minister President was the Chancellor of the Empire. Prussia's position was further secured by her control of the Imperial Council.

PRUSSIA UNDER THE EMPIRE

After 1871, Prussia was faced with a number of pressing governmental and administrative problems. The industrial revolution was rapidly drawing workers from farms to the growing industrial centers, creating a new laboring class. The new lands, acquired in 1866, had to be assimilated; and the administration of the traditional Hohenzollern lands demanded reform and reorganization. The administration of these problems fell to the King, who was vested with supreme administrative authority. He acted in his administrative capacity through his ministers. The limited functions of the Ministry for Foreign Affairs (*Ministerium der Auswärtigen Angelegenheiten*) the important position of the War Ministry (*Kriegsministerium*) within the Empire, and the character of the Justice Ministry (*Justizministerium*) which administered the State Supreme Courts, Courts of First and Second Instance, and Courts of First Instance of Prussia, have been indicated in previous chapters.

The Prussian Ministry of the Interior which was established in 1810, had prime responsibility for all internal administration and the supervision of the police. The finances of Prussia were administered by the Finance Ministry which had jurisdiction over budget and treasury affairs, collection of taxes, management of revenues, and the administration of debts. The provincial, district, and local collections of taxes were carried out by tax offices under the general state administration. The Ministry for Religious, Educational, and Health Affairs (*Ministerium der Geistlichen, Unterrichts- und Medizinal-Angelegenheiten*) was responsible for relations with the Catholic and the Protestant Churches, for the supervision of the elementary and secondary educational system, and for the administration of universities, technical schools, institutes, medical boards, and sanitary commissions. Trade and industrial affairs were placed under the Ministry for Trade and Industry which was established in 1878. It supervised the provincial Mining Authorities (*Bergbehörden*) and the provincial Weight and Measures Inspection Services (*Eichungsinspektionen*) which worked through local offices scattered through the provinces. It was also responsible for the administration of national industry and trade regulations.

The Ministry for Agriculture, Domains, and Forests (*Ministerium für Landwirtschaft, Domänen, und Forsten*), which was established in 1878, administered the public domains and forest reserves, supervised institutes and educational authorities interested in agriculture and forestry, and promoted the development of agriculture. The Ministry of Public Works (*Ministerium der öffentlichen Arbeiten*), which was also established in 1878, supervised the construction and maintenance of provincial public highways and buildings, administered the construction and maintenance of state buildings and works, and the Prussian railroad system.

The heads of these nine ministries, together with ministers without portfolio and three or four Imperial Secretaries of State, constituted the Prussian State Ministry, which was responsible for the formation of the major policies of the Prussian kingdom. This body met under the chairmanship of a Minister President, who also usually held the posts of Minister for Foreign Affairs and Imperial Chancellor. The Ministry of State possessed a few limited executive and administrative functions. It had the right to nominate the Chief President, the Regional President, and other top administrative officials. The Disciplinary Court for Prussian Civil Servants (*Disziplinarhof*) the Jurisdictional Court of Prussia (*Kompetenzgerichtshof*) with the function of determining conflicts of jurisdiction between administrative and judicial courts, and the Supreme Administrative Court (*Oberverwaltungsgericht*) were subordinated to the Ministry of State. The Supreme Chamber of Accounts (*Oberrechnungskammer*) which was first established in 1714, remained directly under the king.

The first important changes in provincial and local administration since the days of Stein and Hardenberg came in the seventies. It had become necessary to introduce a wider measure of self-government into the system of provincial and local government. Except in the cities there was too much state administrative control. In 1872, the County Ordinance for the Eastern Provinces (*Kreisordnung für die östlichen Provinzen*)—Brandenburg, Pomerania, Silesia, Saxony, and West and East Prussia, established the county as an area of state administration and local self-government. In 1875 further administrative legislation granted the provinces of the East the right of self-government and a system of administrative courts. During the eighties these laws were extensively revised and modified and were extended to the western Prussian provinces. These legislative measures for the reform of the system of provincial and local government and administration put an end to the old, traditional ways and provided Prussia with a uniform system of control. The consolidation of the lands acquired in 1815, 1864, and 1866 had at last been completed.

The Prussian province, which was headed by a Chief President responsible to the Prussian Minister of the Interior, served as an area of state administration and provincial self-government. In his capacity as the head of state administration, the Chief President was in charge of the supervision of subordinate state authorities and acted as the personal representative of the King and his ministers in the province. His office usually consisted of a general section (*Allgemeine Abteilung*), a section for Higher "Secondary" Education (*Abteilung für höheres Schulwesen*), and a section for Provincial Land Affairs (*Landeskulturabteilung*). The work of these offices was carried out under a Chief Councilor to the Chief President (*Oberpräsidialrat*).

The Chief President headed all provincial boards and committees which were concerned with state administrative matters, maintained working relations with the churches, cooperated with the military authorities, and issued provincial police regulations and ordinances. As the personal representative of the King, he opened and closed the meetings of the Provincial Assembly (*Provinzial-Landtag*) and served as the representative of the state in cases of war and emergency.

In 1883 the Provincial Council (*Provinzialrat*) was added to the provincial administration. It consisted of the Chief President as chairman, a high administrative official, and five lay members. The Provincial Council served as an advisory body to the Chief President and acted as an administrative court rendering decisions on administrative cases appealed from the district.

Special fields of administration, such as taxes, secondary schools, and health affairs were handled by special provincial boards. The Chief President served as the chairman of the Provincial School Board (*Provinzialschulkollegium*) and the Board of Health (*Medizinalkollegium*). The Provincial Board for Indirect Taxes (*Oberzolldirektion*), the Provincial Tax Administration (*Provinzialsteuerverwaltung*), and the Provincial Land Board (*Generalkommission*) operated under the appropriate state ministries and were subject only to coordination by the Chief President. He maintained working relations with the state Mining Authority, Weight Inspection, Railway Directorate (*Eisenbahn-Direktoren*), and Judicial Authority (*Justizbehörde*), and with the regional offices of the imperial postal office. He was also responsible for the administration of a variety of tasks delegated to the Prussian state by the imperial government.

Under the Provincial Ordinances of 1875 and 1881, the provinces were allowed to incorporate as self-governing bodies for certain specific purposes. The affairs of the Provincial Corporation (*Provinzialverband*), subject to the general control of the Chief President, were carried out by a Provincial Assembly

(*Provinziallandtag*), a Provincial Committee (*Provinzialausschuss*), and a Provincial Director (*Landesdirektor* or *Landeshauptmann*). The Provincial Assembly, which was composed of elected representatives from the city-county and county governments, was convoked and prorogued by the Chief President in the name of the King. The Assembly was empowered to legislate in matters pertaining to provincial institutions, properties, taxes, finance, and budgets. It elected the Provincial Committee, which was responsible for the preparation and execution of the measures of the Assembly.

The Provincial Director, who was an ex-officio member of the Provincial Committee, was elected by the Assembly upon approval of the King. He served as the executive for the Provincial Corporation. The Provincial Director was assisted by several Councilors (*Landesräte*), who were appointed by the Provincial Assembly. The activities of the Provincial Corporation were at first extremely limited; but after the granting of state financial subventions to the provincial corporations in 1872 and 1875, many functions which had been carried out by the state were transferred to this organization. The increase of obligatory functions, which came with state subventions, gradually placed under the Provincial Corporation the maintenance of roads, health, welfare, and charitable institutions, and the support of scientific and artistic associations. The state subventions were always inadequate and the tax power of the provincial corporation was limited, with the result that the province had to rely increasingly upon income from the numerous provincially owned enterprises. These included agricultural and forestry establishments, utilities, narrow-gauge railroads, mines, provincial banks, and insurance companies. The activities of the Provincial Corporation increased steadily during the late nineteenth and early twentieth centuries, until they had the prime responsibility for welfare activities, health and welfare institutions, and major roads within the provinces. The operations of the Provincial Corporations were under the close supervision of the Chief President and the state ministers. Conflicts between the corporations and the state administrative authorities were settled by the Supreme Administrative Court in Berlin.

The governmental administrative districts of the provinces were organized under district governments consisting of a District President and a District Committee (*Bezirksausschuss*). The district government, which was a collegial body under the chairmanship of the District President, consisted of Chief District Councilors, Department Heads (*Oberregierungsräte*), District Councilors, District Technical Advisors and Assistants (*Regierungsassessoren*), and the District State Forest Master (*Landesforstmeister*). The District President headed the Department for General Internal Administration (*Innere Verwaltung*), which was responsible for the supervision of the police, public health, public welfare, public corporations, and local affairs. He was directly responsible for the supervision of the government and administration of the counties and city counties of the district. He was the supervisory authority for the County Medical Officers (*Kreisärzte*), County Veterinarians (*Kreistierärzte*), County Land Registration Offices (*Katasterämter*), County Treasuries (*Kreiskassen*), County Industrial Inspection Offices (*Gewerbeaufsichtsämter*), the County Construction Offices (*Hochbauämter*), and the County Police Offices (*Polizeidirektionen*), whose activities were coordinated locally by the Councilors.

The District President was aided by two special departments. The Department for Direct Taxes, Domains, and Forest Preserves (*Abteilung für Direkte Steuern, Domänen, und Forsten*) was under a Chief District Councilor (*Oberregierungsrat*), who had the right to act independently on all routine matters. Questions of general policy, however, required action by the District Governments and the District Presidents. The *Landesforstmeister,* who was attached to this department, supervised the local county Forest Offices, which were under Chief Foresters (*Oberförster*). The Department for Church and School Affairs (*Abteilung für Kirchen und Schulsachen*) supervised the administration of the elementary schools, which was carried out by School Councilors attached to the counties or city counties.

A Chief Insurance Office (*Oberversicherungsamt*) was attached to the district governments for the supervision of social insurance operations. It was charged with responsibility for the County Insurance Office. The governments of the district were also assisted by a District Committee, which was established in 1883 through the fusion of the District Council (established in 1875) and the District Administrative Court. It consisted of the District President, who served as presiding officer, two professional officials, and four lay members. The District Committee served as an administrative agency (aiding the District President in supervision of local administration and in the application of health, welfare, highway, industry and trade, and police regulations) and as an administrative court, which received appeals from the county administrative courts and had jurisdiction over conflicts within the governmental administrative district. The District President and the District Committee were subject to the supervision of the Chief President and the state Ministry of the Interior.

The Prussian governmental administrative districts were composed of rural counties and city counties, which served as areas of state administration as well as local self-government after the passage of the County Code of 1872. The state administration of the county was headed by a County Manager who was responsible for internal administration, police, and the supervision of the government and administrations of the villages and towns of the county. He coordinated the work of the County Chief Forester, the County Medical Officer, the County Veterinarian, the County Treasury, the County Industrial Inspection

Office, the County Construction Offices (*Kulturbauamt*), the Soil Conservation Office, the Insurance Office (*Versicherungsamt*), and the School Council, which were subject to district authorities. He maintained working relations with local offices of the state Mining Authority, Weights and Measures Inspectors (*Eichungs-Inspektionen*), Railway Directors (*Eisenbahn-Direktoren*), Judicial Authorities, and the local offices and stations of the national postal administration.

After 1872 the County Manager was assisted by a County Committee which was originally a limited body only responsible for the few self-governing functions granted by the earlier county codes. The committee, which was composed of the County Manager serving as presiding officer, and six lay members, served as an advisory body and an administrative court of first instance. It was associated with the County Manager in the enforcement of regulations for roads, welfare, drainage, health, and police, and in the supervision of the municipalities within the county.

The extension of self-government brought the establishment of a County Assembly, which was composed of delegates elected on the basis of an indirect and limited three-class system of suffrage. It received the right to legislate in a general way on all county matters: land settlement problems, local agrarian matters, county welfare, health, charitable institutions, and county-owned utilities and enterprises. The County Manager and the Committee served as the executive for the county corporation or *Kreisverband*. State control and supervision of the county were provided by the District President, the Chief President, and the Royal Ministers.

The county of East Elbia was composed of rural villages or towns, urban municipalities (*Stadtgemeinden*), and manorial estates (*Gutsbezirke*). The towns, which were regulated under the Town Constitution for the Eastern Provinces of 1891, were headed by a Municipal Chairman (*Gemeindevorsteher*), usually in honorary service, who served as the agent of state administration as well as of local self-government. He was elected by the Municipal Council (*Gemeindevertretung*), which was composed of from three to twenty-four Assemblymen elected on the basis of the limited three-class system of suffrage. The Municipal Chairman and his assistants, who were members of the Municipal Council, administered the affairs of the rural municipality, which included the maintenance of roads, drainage, relief, fire protection, education, and a few public enterprises, such as a town market, a forest, or a small utility plant. The government and administration of rural areas was also based upon the manorial estate, headed by a Manorial Director (*Gutsvorsteher*) who was responsible to the County Manager.

The situation was further complicated by the system of precinct administration. Under the County Constitution of 1872, the administration of rural police, which had been under Royal Commissioners, was transferred to Precinct Directors (*Amtsvorsteher*) who were appointed by the State Minister of the Interior, in collaboration with the County Committee and the County Assembly. Each precinct (*Amtsbezirk*) included several manorial estates and villages and towns. Their directors, who were assisted by a Precinct Committee (*Amtsausschuss*), which was made up of delegates from the local units within the precinct, were responsible for police administration, welfare, public health, roads, and fire protection within the precinct. The Precinct Directors were subject to the supervision of the County Manager and the County Committee.

The larger urban communities of the counties were governed by the Town Constitution of 1853. The government of the Prussian towns consisted of a Town Council (*Stadtverordnetenversammlung*) composed of members elected on the basis of the usual limited suffrage, and a Magistry of the Town Council. The latter, which was composed of the Mayor, serving as chairman, several paid professional experts (*Beigeordnete*), and honorary Aldermen (*Ratsherren*), all appointed by the Town Council upon approval of higher authorities, was responsible for the execution of administrative orders, laws, and ordinances. The Mayor was responsible for the direction of the municipal administration.

The services and functions and their departmental structure varied from city to city, but the normal city administration included the following typical departments: Administrative Office (*Verwaltungsamt*), Finance and Tax Office (*Finanz- und Steueramt*), Treasurer's and Controller's Office (*Kassen- und Rechnungsprüfungsamt*), Order Police Office (*Ordnungspolizeiamt*), School Office (*Schulamt*), Welfare Office (*Wohlfahrtsamt*), Health Office (*Gesundheitsamt*), City Construction Office (*Stadtbauamt*), and a Public Works Office (*Betriebsamt*) for management of city enterprises. In the larger cities the Mayor maintained working relations with the local offices of state and national special administrative agencies. It is important to note that the rural villages and towns and the larger urban communities (*Stadtgemeinden*) could join with one another or with other public corporations in voluntary unions to carry out special undertakings, such as educational, highway, welfare, and utility programs. These Special Unions (*Zweckverbände*) constituted public corporations, each headed by a Union Director (*Verbandsvorsteher*) and a Union Committee (*Verbandsausschuss*).

Under the administrative acts of 1815 and 1872, the larger urban communities could petition the Minister of the Interior (or in exceptional cases appeal to the King) for the right to establish themselves as independent city-county units or city counties. The city county of Prussia exercised the rights of self-government and carried out the functions of state administration. A City Committee (*Stadtausschuss*), which was composed of the Chief Mayor and members of the Magistry, carried out the functions of state administration. The scope of its activities was narrower than that of the County Committee, because most of the activities which were state functions in the rural areas were handled by the agencies of the city government. It is important to recall that while the manorial estates and rural villages or towns, with populations of less than 10,000, were under the administrative supervision of the County Manager and the County Committee, the larger towns which had been granted the status of city counties were under Chief Mayors and City Committees for purposes of state administration and under a Magistry for purposes of self-government. The intermediate towns, with populations of 10,000 to 25,000, occupied a mixed position in terms of state administration. Although they were under the supervision of the County Manager (*Landrät*), their Magistry took over the functions of the County Committee. The towns also had the right to appeal certain matters directly to the district (*Regierung*).

During the period of the Second Empire, the Prussian government consolidated the structure of local government and administration. The nineteenth century was marked by the gradual extension of the rights of local self-government, which had been granted in a limited fashion to the cities in 1808 and the provinces in 1823. Under the Empire the base of provincial self-government was broadened after 1875. In 1872 the counties received the rights and privileges of corporate life. These laws and regulations, together with the city ordinance of 1853 and the Rural Town Ordinance of 1891, were not extended to all Prussian territories. These codes gave Eastern Germany a uniform pattern of local government and administration in which a large measure of regional and local autonomy was coupled with state supervision. The administration of special affairs as such remained in the hands of a highly professionalized class of officials. The class system of suffrage kept all the representative controls of provincial, county, and municipal government in the hands of the upper classes.

Prussia Under the Weimar Republic

The Revolution of 1918 swept the old regime from power. The government of Prussia passed into the hands of a provisional government, which ruled for a time without popular controls. The Prussian Constituent Assembly, which was elected in January 1919, drafted a new Constitution which was issued on November 30, 1920. It established Prussia as a federal republic within the German Reich. The sovereignty of the state passed to the people, who were given the right of exercising their will by referendum or indirectly through their constitutionally elected representatives. The State Assembly, which received the right to all legislative powers, consisted of delegates elected by the people on the basis of general, equal, secret, and direct suffrage. It was, however, subject to the people's right of direct popular initiative. The old House of Lords, the Council of State, the Privy Council, and other royal institutions were abolished. The new Council of State which was established under the Republican Constitution consisted of representatives elected by the Provincial Diets. It had the power to approve or object to the legislative acts of the Assembly.

The top administration of the Prussian state was carried out by the State Ministry, which served as the collegial executive of Prussia. It consisted of a Minister President, who was elected by the State Assembly, and seven ministers, who were nominated by the Minister President, and were subject to approval by the State Assembly. The State Ministry acted on matters of general policy, while the individual departments, whose ministers were individually responsible to the Assembly, carried on the administration of affairs within their respective fields.

The impact of the war and the formation of the new German Republic brought several changes in the state administration. The Reich assumed all responsibilities for foreign affairs and military matters, making it necessary for Prussia to abolish her traditional Ministries for Foreign Affairs and War. The Prussian Ministries for Interior, Justice, Finance, Trade and Industry, and Agriculture, Domains, and Forests continued; although, on the one hand, they lost several of their old functions to the Reich, and, on the other hand, they were required to carry out various national functions which were delegated to the states for administration. The old Prussian Ministry for Religious, Educational, and Health Affairs became the new Ministry for Public Welfare (*Ministerium für Volkswohlfahrt*) which assumed responsibility for relief, public health, and public health matters. The reorganized Ministry for Science, Art, and Education (*Ministerium für Wissenschaft, Kunst, und Volksbildung*) carried on the religious and educational work of the old Royal Ministry. The nationalization of the railroads and the advent of national supervision over waterways led to the dissolution of the old Ministry of Public Works, its functions being transferred to the National Transportation Ministry, the German Railroad Company, and the Prussian Ministry of Finance. The old Supreme Administrative Authorities, such as the Supreme Administrative Court and the Supreme Court of Accounts, continued under the State Ministry.

The revolutionary changes in the government of Prussia were not accompanied by drastic modifications in the organization of local government and administration. The old structure was retained, but the spirit of provincial and local administration contrasted sharply with that of the kingdom. While leaving local government primarily to the states, the Weimar Constitution established special guarantees for the perpetuation of local self-government and introduced the principle of universal suffrage. The state administration continued to have primary responsibility for interior, police, education, health, forest, trade and industry, and construction, which were administered at the provincial level by the Chief President and the Provincial Council, at the district level by the District President and the District Committee, and at the county and city-county levels by the County Manager and the County Committee or by the Chief Mayor and the Town Committee. Provincial and local self-government, which continued to concern itself with roads, welfare, charitable and health institutions, utilities, and public enterprises, continued in the hands of the Provincial Corporations and their Provincial Director, Provincial Committee and Provincial Assembly, the counties and their County Manager, County Committees, and County Assemblies, and the city counties and their Chief Mayor, Magistry, and City or Town Council.

The most important changes were in the methods of election to the representative bodies responsible for self-government at the provincial, county, and city-county levels. The people were given the means of democratic control.

There were few changes in the methods of state supervision. Even the offices remained much the same. In the province the Medical College was replaced by a Medical Legal Committee. There were only a few minor changes in titles and terms for officials and offices at the district and county levels. The Chief President continued to exercise a general supervisory control, while the District President exercised direct supervisory control over the city counties and cities. The County Manager continued as the responsible official for the supervision of the rural towns or villages. It is important to note that the manorial estate was gradually liquidated under the Republic.

Administrative supervision, which involved forms of advice, observation and inspection, approval and objection, compulsion, and even the dissolution of the municipal or county organization, took the form of administrative supervision of self-government functions (*Staatsaufsicht*) and administrative control over delegated state functions: police, vital statistics, welfare, etc. (*Dienstaufsicht*).

National legislation in fields such as welfare, housing, and health exercised an increasing influence on local self-government, despite the absence of direct legal controls. County and City-County Housing and Land Settlement Offices (*Wohnungs- und Siedlungsämter*), Welfare Offices (*Wohlfahrtämter*), and Youth Offices (*Jugendämter*) were set up to carry out national laws. National control over the public finances of the Reich deprived the municipalities of their traditional financial autonomy.

The officials at the provincial, district, and county levels continued to cooperate with the regional and local offices of the state Mining Authorities, Regional Agricultural Authorities (*Landeskulturbehörden*) and Judicial Authorities. They also maintained working relationships with the regional and local offices of the National Ministry of Finance, the Provincial Finance Offices, the local finance offices, the main customs offices, and the National Construction Offices, the German Railroad Company (the Railroad Directorate and local stations), the National Ministry of Posts (National Post Directorate and local stations), the National Association for Employment and Unemployment Insurance (State Labor Offices and local Labor Offices), and the National Ministry of Labor (Main Welfare Offices and local Welfare Offices).

Within each Prussian province during the republican era, there was a dense web of administrative organizations. The core of the administrative structure was provided by the interwoven systems of state administration and self-government, which cared for general interior affairs, police, education, public health, trade and industrial supervision, roads, forests and parks, institutions, public utilities and enterprises. This administrative apparatus was supplemented first by the special and technical services of the Prussian state for mining, weights and measures, and justice, and secondly by the growing national special and technical services for finance, railways, post, employment, and insurance. The republican phase in the development of Prussia had brought a change in controls, but it did not affect the basic bureaucratic structure of administration.

Prussia Under the Nazi Regime

The Nazi regime produced a series of drastic alterations in the government and administration of Prussia. Hitler became the National Governor for Prussia, while Hermann Göring was appointed Minister President. Unlike other state executives, he was responsible only to the Führer. Göring, as Minister President and as the personal representative of the Führer, headed the Prussian state administration. All of the Prussian ministries, except finance, were combined with the appropriate national ministry. The process of centralization continued until 1944 when the Prussian Ministry of Finance was abolished and absorbed into the national Ministry of Finance. The State Ministry, which was composed of Göring, the national ministers for Interior, Agriculture, Economics, Transport, Labor, Church, and Education, and the Prussian Minister of Finance, continued to meet during the Nazi period. The Minister President was also advised by a Leader Council (*Führerrat*), which replaced the old Council of State and the State Assembly. It was composed of the Minister President and ministers of state, who served as ex officio members, and of representatives chosen from the Nazi party, church, business, labor, science, and art fields. The members of the Leader Council, who were also members of the provincial councils in the areas of their residence, had little real power.

The nationalization of the state government of Prussia led to a complete reorganization of the controls for provincial and local government and administration. The Prussian Province became for all practical purposes a territorial unit of national administration. The structure of administration was not fundamentally changed, although it was greatly enlarged through the addition of new functions and services at all levels. The Nazi regime brought many changes in the position of the Chief President. This official, who was appointed by the Führer upon proposal of the Prussian Minister President, was vested with broader political power and supervisory control of administrative activities. The Provincial Assembly and the Provincial Council of the imperial and republican periods were replaced by a Provincial Advisory Council (*Provinzialrat*). The Chief President was made the representative of the national government in the province and was charged with the general supervision of provincial officials and the execution of orders from national ministries and authorities. His position in most provinces was strengthened by the fact that he was also the District Leader. In the eastern provinces, the Nazi party district coincided with the provincial area. There were few changes in the basic tasks of the Chief President. The collegial bodies for education, public health, and land disappeared after 1933. The Provincial Corporation lost most of its powers as a result of the merger of provincial self-government with the state administration of the province. The controlling Provincial Assembly was eliminated and the Provincial Director was made a deputy of the Chief President.

The Nazis expanded the functions of the provincial administration through the delegation of major tasks to the Chief President. He served, for instance, as the general provincial authority for the Order Police. In this capacity he was aided by an Inspector of the Order Police and by a Chief of SS and Order Police (*Höherer SS- und Polizeiführer*). He was also head of the Regional Planning Association, which was administered upon delegation by the Provincial Corporation. The Chief Presidents were entrusted with numerous defense and war administration functions. The Price Fixing Offices (*Preisbildungsstellen*), the Provincial Economic Offices (*Landeswirtschaftsämter*), the Provincial Food Office (*Provinzialernährungsämter*), the Forest and Wood Economy Control Offices (*Forst- und Holzwirtschaftsämter*), and the Waterway Control Office (*Wasserstrassendirektionen*) were attached to the office of the Chief President. He also became the Regional Delegate for Local Transportation. (*Bevollmächtigter für den Nahverkehr*). He maintained working relations with the regional offices of the numerous national administrative services, such as the State Finance Offices, the State Supreme Court, the State Labor Courts, the Main Welfare Offices, the Chief Mining Offices (*Oberbergämter*), the National Post Directors, the National Bank Directors, the Propaganda Offices, the Air Offices, and the various military and munitions authorities and agencies. Various wartime administrative changes, which involved the transfer of certain economic offices to the party district, however, brought a slight decline in the status of the Chief President after 1941. The administrative situation was further complicated by the regional activities of the Nazi party, the Estates (*Stände*), and the National Defense Organization.

The District Presidents were the direct administrative authorities of the Reich, acting immediately under the national Minister of the Interior. They were subject only to the most general supervision of the Chief President. The District Presidents, who were appointed by the national Minister of the Interior, upon delegation from Hitler, had prime responsibility for the supervision of local government and for police administration within their districts. The Nazi regime introduced few changes in their functions or departmental organization. Interestingly enough, the Nazis did not utilize the administrative district as an area of administration for war economy or defense, leaving these functions to the provinces and the counties.

Although the government and administration of the counties did not undergo an all-out Nazi reorganization, there were significant changes in the political controls. The County Manager, who became the key rural administrative official, was appointed by the Chief President. He was assisted by an appointed County Committee, which replaced the old County Assembly and its County Committee. During the first years of the Nazi regime, the County Manager was assisted by a Nazi Party Agent (*Parteibeauftragter*) who was generally the local Nazi Party County Leader.

With the beginning of World War II, the position of the County Manager was steadily strengthened. The Party Agent lost his controlling position, while the County Committee was abolished. The County Manager, who was a national official under the Nazis, represented the central government in the county. He had complete responsibility for county administration and for the supervision of the government and administration of the villages and towns of the county. He was the administrative authority for the county Order Police and served as the head of the local defense of the Reich, handling matters of recruiting and war damages. After the beginning of the war, the County Manager assumed full control of the functions of self-government. He was made the head of the County Corporation, after the elimination of the County Assembly and the subordination of the County Committee. It is important to note that the distinction between county administration and county self-government disappeared in practice, with consolidation of the staffs and offices of the two spheres. The County Manager, like the Chief President, was entrusted with numerous war and defense functions. The county food offices, economic offices, and price fixing offices were attached to his office. In addition to these duties and tasks he had to be prepared to cooperate with the numerous local offices of the national special and technical services (the local finance offices,

Courts of First Instance, labor offices, welfare offices, mining offices, post offices, railroad stations, and local military authorities), the Nazi party, the Nazi estates, and other corporations of public law.

The rural villages and towns, the larger towns (*Stadtgemeinde*), and the cities which were large enough to have the status of city counties, were subjected to a drastic reorganization. The German Municipal Code of 1935 laid down a new national pattern for all municipal government and administration. The Chief Mayors of the city counties and the Mayors of the larger towns and the rural villages and towns became the most important municipal officials. The Chief Mayor, who was appointed by the Minister of the Interior in cities over 100,000 and by the Chief President in towns under 100,000, was required to be a salaried and professionally trained individual in towns with populations of over 10,000. Under the code, the Chief Mayor of the city county was assisted by a number of professional administrative department heads and a number of advisory councils of technical experts who assisted the administrative departments. The organs of representative government, the City or Town Council and the Magistry, were abolished and replaced by an appointed Advisory Council who had little real power, although under the code the Mayor was bound to consult with them on important issues before taking action. The political reliability of the city administration was guaranteed by the Nazi Party Agent who was associated with the Mayor in the administration of the city. There were, however, few changes in the basic services and functions of the cities. The services and functions of the city-county administration were supplemented by those of the offices and agencies under direct national control. The food offices, economic offices, and the price fixing offices, which were under national supervision, were attached to the city administration and operated by city officials. Each city also had a national finance office, a Court of First Instance, and a labor office, which were administered directly by national officials. Some of the larger cities had offices of the Nazi Estates. The railway and postal facilities of each city county were also administered by direct national officials. Each large city was, therefore, a complex municipal and national office.

The smaller towns and the rural villages and towns of the county, which were governed by a Mayor, two or three city experts usually in honorary service, an appointed Town Council and a Nazi Party Agent, were less complex in their governmental and administrative organization.

The basic changes in municipal government under the Nazis did not disturb the scope of local powers, although the Nazi reform did eliminate local control over the Mayor and gave him all necessary legislative and administrative powers. The German municipalities continued to handle, subject to national and regional budget controls, housing, public works, health, municipal enterprises, libraries, theatres, and other cultural activities. The abolition of democratic and representative controls, the strengthening of the position of the Mayor, the appointment of a Party Agent, and the extension of services delegated from the Reich, constituted the basic Nazi changes in municipal government and administration.

Chapter 5

GREATER BERLIN

The city of Berlin, which was the capital of the German Reich from 1871 to the end of World War II, was Germany's administrative, commercial, and manufacturing center and continental Europe's greatest city. Situated at the heart of the East Elbian plains, its immediate hinterland is the Prussian Province of Brandenburg. It lies in the midst of a flat sandy plain bordering the river Spree. This stream, which rises in the Sudeten uplands (*Lausitzer Gebirge*), flows northward until it reaches the Ancient River Valley extending from Warsaw to Hamburg. The Spree then flows northwestward beyond the heart of Berlin to join the Havel River, which originates in the lakeland of southeastern Mecklenburg. The Havel, cutting through the western margins of Greater Berlin, ultimately empties into the Elbe. The original landscape of the Berlin area was typical of the zone of river lowlands which occupy the greater part of Northeast Germany. It consisted of a broad swampy valley flanked by sandy plains. Until the time of modern water control through canalization, it was subject to frequent floods. The plains, which are composed of sands and gravels left behind by the last glaciation, were heavily forested. With the growth of the city, the swampy river valleys have been drained and canalized, while the plains have been given over to urban construction and parkland.

The heart of Berlin consists of the old city and Altkölln, which developed on the Spree in medieval times. This area, with that portion of the city which lies immediately to the west, developed into the main business district. Together these three areas embraced most of eighteenth-century Berlin. The rapid development of Berlin as a governmental, administrative, commercial, manufacturing, and transportation center in the nineteenth century produced an amazing expansion of the urban area. The western and southwestern sections, which include the Spandau, the Charlottenburg, the Wilmersdorf, and the Zehlendorf districts, as well as the Grunewald forest and the Havel lakes areas, are essentially residential. The northwestern portion of Greater Berlin, the Rei-

229

nickendorf section, includes the Spandauer Stadtwald and became the seat of a variety of academic, scientific, and military institutions. The northern, eastern, and southeastern portions, which were given over to factories and poor, low-cost housing, include the Pankow, Weissensee, Lichtenberg, and Köpenick districts. The southern area, which includes the Treptow, Neukölln, Tempelhof, and Steglitz areas, is situated on the Spree River and the Teltow canal, and constitutes the main area of transportation facilities for the city. The old city, together with the new sections, which form Greater Berlin, measures about 50 kilometers from east to west and about 30 kilometers from north to south, and has an area of 883 sq. km.

The people of modern Berlin are extremely mixed from the point of view of race, language, and culture. The Slavs occupied the Berlin area along with the rest of East Elbian Germany during the first 500 years of our era. The German colonization of the lands east of the Elbe brought the city area under German domination in the Middle Ages. The first Germans to settle on the Spree were Low Saxons from northwestern Germany. They mixed and blended with the Slavs to form the basic population of the city, to which the succeeding centuries have added people from every part of the Reich and Central Europe. Although there is a Berlin variety of the German language, which is a Low Saxon or East Elbian (*Plattdeutsch*) dialect heavily colored by Slavic, standard German is the present day language of the city. Berlin is a cosmopolitan and European city. Although it is predominantly Protestant, like the rest of Northeast Germany, there is a large Catholic minority. The Jewish population was the largest for any city, province, or state in the Reich. In 1933, out of a total population of 4,242,000, there were 3,014,000 Protestants, 441,000 Catholics, and 160,000 Jews.

In 1933 the city of Berlin ranked fourth among the Prussian territories, despite its relatively small area of 883 sq. km. Its population density was 4,800 per sq. km., making Berlin the most densely settled area within the Reich. This population was largely concentrated in the central Berlin area along the Spree. Other areas of dense population included Charlottenburg, Spandau, and Wilmersdorf in the west, Schöneberg and Neukölln in the south, and Lichtenberg in the east. While sixty-three per cent of the Berlin area was built up, the remaining portion was given over to parks, forests, farm land, and lakes; these latter areas were only sparsely settled.

In the late Middle Ages the population of the city numbered less than 15,-000. Although it increased gradually during the seventeenth and eighteenth centuries under the impetus of prosperity made possible by the good fortunes of the Hohenzollerns, Berlin was a city of only 172,000 at the beginning of the nineteenth century. The growing strength and power of Prussia in the early nineteenth century was marked in the capital city by a rapid increase in population, for by 1870 Berlin had 768,800 inhabitants. The victory over France in 1871 marks the beginning of the growth of present-day Berlin. The successful conclusion of the Franco-Prussian war found Germany under Prussian domination and established Berlin as the capital of the Reich as well as of Prussia. In 1913 the population stood at 2,820,000. Although the difficult war years resulted in a decrease of 334,000 in the population by 1918, recovery was extremely rapid, and by 1922 Berlin had a population of 3,925,000. The twenties and thirties brought almost another million and one-half residents to the city. This population increase is to be accounted for largely in terms of migration from rural parts of Germany to the capital city.

The origins of Berlin are extremely obscure. The island site of the old city was occupied by Slavic fisher folk during the first half of the first millennium of our era. The German settlement of the site came in the eleventh century, when a group of colonists led by the Dukes of Saxony established a village community on the island in the Spree. By the middle of the eleventh century two towns, Berlin and Kölln, had developed on the Spree. In 1230 Berlin had already achieved the status of a town, for in that year it received its official charter from the Counts of Brandenburg. The administration of the two towns was especially influenced by the Magdeburg City Charter (*Magdeburger Stadtrecht*). The municipal government involved the supervision of local affairs by a Count, who was also responsible for protection and legal affairs. He was assisted by a city council which elected a smaller administrative council. The two towns gradually grew in size under the impetus of the developing trade and settlement in East Elbian Germany. The attempt to unify the administration of the two towns in 1307 failed because of their commercial rivalry.

In 1411 Friedrich of Hohenzollern, the Burgrave of Nuremberg, was invested with the Mark Brandenburg and given an electoral vote in the Empire. The administrative and governmental status of Berlin gradually began to change under the Hohenzollerns, for they ignored the charter rights of the cities and sought to increase their powers. The Electors won, and local self-government all but disappeared in the ensuing centuries. Toward the middle of the thirteenth century, the city of Kölln was made the residence city (*Residenzstadt*) of Brandenburg. Although the two cities attempted to join forces against the Electors in 1442 by forming a common government, this attempt failed, for Friedrich II of Brandenburg dissolved the common council and established a fortification at Kölln. The latter city became the capital of Brandenburg, and all official acts were dated from Kölln until 1713. The Elector Johann Cicero (1486-1499) was the first Hohenzollern to establish a permanent court on the sandy banks of the Spree.

During the Reformation, Berlin and Mark Brandenburg turned to Protestantism. The Thirty Years' War brought ruin and destruction, and the population of the two cities declined from 14,000 in 1600 to 8,000 by the end of the war in 1648, even though the Hohenzollern family had never played an important role in the long struggle. The reign of the Great Elector, Friedrich Wilhelm, was a period of reconstruction and prosperity. A city wall was built about Kölln and Berlin, and although the two towns had learned to work together, they continued under separate administrations. During this period the small towns of Friedrichswerder, Dorotheenstadt, and Friedrichstadt grew up beyond the new city walls.

The Elector of Brandenburg became the King in Prussia in 1701. Eight years later, King Friedrich I of Prussia unified the government and administration of the five towns and established the city of Berlin. Although official acts were dated from Kölln for four more years, Berlin was at last the capital of Prussia.

The reign of Friedrich Wilhelm I (1713-1740) was marked in Berlin by the construction of streets and public buildings to make the city a fitting place for royalty. During the early years of the reign of Frederick the Great (1740-1786) the city walls were removed, prematurely, as it later transpired, for in 1757 during the Seven Years' War, the Austrians penetrated the city, while the Russians occupied Berlin for a short time in 1760. The later eighteenth century marked the beginnings of modern commercial and manufacturing activities. In 1765 the Royal Prussian Bank was established, and in 1800 the Berlin government founded a city postal system.

During the Napoleonic wars, from 1806-1808, Berlin was occupied by the French army. After the evacuation of the French, Berlin again turned to reconstruction. Under the influence of the reforms of Baron vom Stein, who traced Prussia's collapse before the Napoleonic forces to domestic troubles, a new City Constitution was granted in 1809. It provided for wide powers of local self-government, subject to a "reasonable" amount of state supervision. This government, which was to last until 1920, consisted of a Chief Mayor, a Mayor, and a City Council which formed the Civil Authority. The first two officials and the members of the Council of State were elected by the City Assembly, which consisted of three members from each city ward chosen by limited manhood suffrage. The Civil Authority and the City Council met together on matters of general policy, and appointed committees for special purposes which worked under various members of the Civil Authority. This municipal organization was responsible for streets, utilities, welfare, public health, and education. The Chief Mayor was responsible to the Chief President of the Province of Brandenburg, who provided for the administrative supervision of health, police, trade and industry, and education through the District President of the administrative district of Mittelmark.

Although the French temporarily reoccupied the city in 1810, the victory of the Allies over Napoleon at Leipzig and Waterloo brought an end to the long struggle. After 1815, Berlin grew rapidly, the population increasing from 193,-000 to over 400,000 by 1848. The early nineteenth century was marked by an extensive building and construction program, partly inspired by the great architect, Schinkel. The first railway, which linked Berlin to Potsdam, was built in 1838. Berlin was growing up. After the short March revolution of 1848, the city established its first public utilities, built canals, and laid the foundations for the late nineteenth century commercial and industrial development. The first modern industries and manufacturing establishments were beginning to develop on the margins of Berlin. The city was slowly expanding territorially through the gradual incorporation of suburban communities. Living conditions in Berlin were still primitive. The street and sewer systems were antiquated and consisted of cobblestone roads and alleys, open sewers, and street pumps. Housing conditions were extremely bad.

The unification of Germany in 1871 under the leadership of Prussia made Berlin the capital of the Reich. Although it was already the capital of Germany's largest and most powerful state, it was not prepared for its new role as one of the important cities and capitals of the world. The great influx of civil servants and military personnel and the rapid increase of the working class overtaxed the housing and living facilities of the city. Berlin met the problem with many effective measures. In the space of a few years streets were paved and lighted, a sewer and water system was established, and better housing replaced the primitive structures of an earlier day. By the end of the nineteenth century, it was one of the cleanest capitals of Europe. Although the reconstruction of Berlin was inspired and made possible by the government of Prussia, the actual task was carried out by local municipal and private interests.

This improvement did not, however, solve the problem of the Greater Berlin area, for population and industrial establishments had overflowed the administrative limits of the old city and established themselves in a number of developing suburban towns. Attempts to expand the limits of Berlin through the incorporation of suburban towns and areas failed, largely because the city of Berlin, while willing to include the rich areas to the west, was unwilling to accept responsibility for the worker and factory districts to the east and southeast. By 1881, Greater Berlin was a city of 1,138,000, which was rapidly expanding into its Brandenburg hinterland.

The Prussian government attempted to solve the problem of the metropolitan area, after the failure of negotiations with municipal authorities, through the separation of the Berlin area from the regional district of Mittelmark. The rapid growth of suburban Berlin into a conglomeration of municipalities, whose political boundaries did not permit adequate administration of the social, economic, and political problems, made the problem of the Greater Berlin area more and more serious. The administrative conflicts and difficulties had to be solved, and cooperation seemed to provide a way.

In 1905 negotiations began which eventuated in the Public Service Law for Greater Berlin of 1911 (*Zweckverbandgesetz für Gross-Berlin*). The cities of Berlin, Charlottenburg, Schöneberg, Neukölln, Wilmersdorf, Lichtenberg, and Köpenick, the counties of Teltow and Niederbarnim, and seven smaller towns were compelled to join the Greater Berlin Corporation (*Verband Gross-Berlin*). This Special Union, which was organized under a joint director, joint executive, and a joint assembly in which the city of Berlin received an unjustifiably small representation, had the following limited tasks: city planning, construction, and zoning; development and maintenance of parks and forests; and, finally, local transportation. The work of the association was limited and hardly a success. World War I brought further difficulties and troubles which were intensified by the great influx of officials and war workers. New unions to supplement the work of the Special Union were set up to handle problems like food, housing, employment, and fuel. In retrospect the Special Union can be considered only as a transitional step toward the formation of Greater Berlin.

Under the Empire, Berlin had become one of the great cities of Europe. It was not only the capital of imperial Germany, but thanks to its position on the main east-west waterway of North Germany, it had developed into one of the major commercial and manufacturing cities of the Reich. Its position as the capital of an increasingly nationalistic Germany made possible its development as the main center of German culture and learning.

The German defeat in World War I was a great blow. From November 1918 to the Communist outbreak in 1923, the streets of the city were the scene of sporadic fighting. Although the city was occasionally in a state of siege, the revolutionary disturbances were not extreme. The failure of the Special Union and the troubles which had accompanied and followed the war made it plain that a more complete union, embracing all of metropolitan and suburban Berlin, was needed. In 1920 the Special Union of Greater-Berlin was abolished and the law concerning the formation of a Municipality of Berlin (*Gesetz über die Bildung einer Stadtgemeinde Berlin*) was enacted and put into operation. No less than ninety-five local authorities formerly included in the Berlin Special Union were abolished and absorbed into the new Greater-Berlin: eight cities (Berlin, Charlottenburg, Köpenick, Lichtenberg, Neukölln, Schöneberg, Spandau, and Wilmersdorf), fifty-nine rural villages and towns, and twenty-seven manorial estates. This new metropolitan area was detached from the Province of Brandenburg and given a status equivalent to that of a province, although limited rights of state supervision were still vested in the Chief President of Brandenburg. The central government of Berlin under the new arrangement followed the Magisterial Charter (*Magistratsverfassung*) form, with a Chief

Mayor, a Mayor (*Bürgermeister*), a Civil Authority (*Magistrat*), and a Municipal Council composed of representatives elected from the fifteen electoral districts of the city. This central administration was responsible for finance and taxation, utilities, transport, parks and forests, savings banks, and other activities affecting the city as a whole.

The charter also provided for a certain amount of decentralization through the division of Greater Berlin into twenty administrative districts, each with a self-government of the magisterial charter type, including a district Mayor and a District Administrative Board of seven members. The officials, who formed the district Civil Authority were elected by the District Council, which was in turn elected by the voters of the district. It should be pointed out that the fifteen electoral districts indicated above corresponded to the administrative districts, except in a few cases where suburban districts were combined to form one electoral district. The suburban districts were further subdivided into precincts (*Ortsbezirke*), each headed by a Precinct Chairman (*Ortsbezirksvorsteher*), chosen by the district government. The power of the districts was limited and was subject to the general supervision of the central city administration. The district governments were responsible for the supervision and operation of local establishments and institutions, welfare and relief, health and sanitation, streets, and local enterprises, which they administered under general city regulations and directives. Education was the most decentralized function, but it was subject to state supervision. In matters of finance, the districts could make suggestions in regard to the local situation. Although the District Administrative Board appointed the officials of the district, the general regulation of the city civil service was a function of the central city government.

The operation of the new government and administration of Berlin between 1920 and 1931 was beset with several difficulties. The Municipal Council, consisting of 225 members, was large and divided by partisan strife, while the Chief Mayor did not possess sufficient power to dominate the Civil Authority. The district governments had even greater troubles. They lacked cohesion, and there was not sufficient integration between central and district affairs. The impact of the depression of 1929-32, with the consequent relief and welfare loads and their depressing effect upon city finances, as well as certain political scandals, revealed the need for further governmental reform. The amendments to the charter in 1931, which were the result of political compromise, resulted in the creation of the Municipal Affairs Committee (*Stadtgemeindeausschuss*), consisting of forty-five members under the chairmanship of the Chief Mayor. This committee, which was elected by the Municipal Council, received power to handle all matters except those placed specifically under the city council. The Civil Authority, which was reduced in size, then included the Chief Mayor, two Mayors (assistants with rank of Mayor), nine professional City

Councilors, and six nonprofessional City Councilors, all elected by the Municipal Council. The powers of the Chief Mayor were greatly increased, making him a real executive with control over officials, employees, and committees. The District Mayors and the members of the District Administrative Boards were made responsible to the Chief Mayor. Although the character of the government of the administrative district was changed, the position of the District Mayor in the District Administrative Office was strengthened. Coordination of central and district government was secured by joint meetings of the Chief Mayors, the central Civil Authority, and the District Mayors. The government of the city of Berlin on the eve of the Nazi coup was neither of the magisterial charter nor the mayoral form, but a type of its own with a Chief Mayor, a Civil Authority, a Municipal Committee, and a Municipal Council and twenty administrative district governments, each with a Mayor, a District Administrative Office, and a District Council. It is perhaps best described as a unitary plan with extensive provision for decentralization of administrative powers.

The advent of the Nazi regime brought further changes in the government and administration of Berlin. The first change came in May 1933, with the appointment of a Commissar for the National Capital (*Reichshauptstadt*). In 1934 he was given the powers of state supervision, which had been vested in the Chief President of the Province of Brandenburg. When the German Municipal Code was passed in 1935, Berlin was exempted from its provisions. The Law concerning the Constitution and Administration of the National Capital, Berlin (*Gesetz über die Verfassung und Verwaltung der Reichshauptstadt Berlin*) of December 1936, while allowing for certain necessary exceptions required by the character of the Berlin area, made the German Municipal Code generally applicable to Greater Berlin. Under this new arrangement, Berlin was a city-county with the perquisites of a Prussian Province.

The Chief Mayor was also made the City President (*Stadtpräsident*), receiving the powers of higher supervision which had been vested in the Chief President of Brandenburg and later in the *Commissar* for Berlin. As a result, there was a personal union of national and municipal authority in one person, who as Chief Mayor acted as the head of city self-government and as City President served as the highest state supervisory official of Berlin. In his latter capacity, he was directly responsible to the national Minister of the Interior. The Chief Mayor was assisted by a deputy with the rank of Mayor, by ten professional administrative department heads, and by a number of advisory councilors with technical knowledge who assisted the administrative department heads.

The Chief Mayor was assisted, in addition, by an appointed Advisory Council of forty-five councilors, which replaced the Municipal Affairs Committee of 1931. The democratic and representative Municipal Council was dissolved because it was considered by the Nazis an unnecessary source of trouble. The Chief Mayor was also assisted by a Nazi Party Agent, who was present to guarantee the political reliability of the city administration. This office, as well as that of District Leader for the district of Berlin was filled by Dr. Goebbels, the national Minister of Propaganda. This gave the National Socialist party one of the key positions in the Berlin government, for the Party Agent worked with the Chief Mayor on matters of city planning, transportation, culture, press affairs, and personnel appointments and regulations.

The twenty administrative districts which had been established in 1920 were retained, except for a slight modification of the boundaries of several districts in March 1938. The districts were under District Mayors, who were responsible to the Chief Mayor of Greater Berlin. Each district mayor was assisted by four or five administrative department heads, by advisory district councilors and by a Nazi Party Agent (*Parteibeauftragter*). The democratic and representative district council was destroyed by the Nazis. The abolition of democratic and representative controls, the strengthening of the position of the Chief Mayors and the District Mayors, and the appointment of Party Agents constituted the basic Nazi changes in the municipal government of Berlin.

While the German Municipal Code and the Berlin Act of 1936 did not disturb the scope of local powers, the latter eliminated local control over the Chief Mayor and gave him all executive, legislative, and administrative powers. The professionally trained Chief Mayor, who was nominated by the national Minister of the Interior and appointed directly by Hitler, worked in his capacity of City President under the national Minister of the Interior. In that capacity, he was responsible for higher education, church taxes, public assistance, city planning, and the supervision of public foundations. He had the same functions as the Chief President of a Prussian province and the District President of a Prussian governmental district.

The administration of the national capital, Berlin, under the Nazis occupied a special place in the state administration of Prussia, for it was an area both of state administration and of local self-government, headed by one individual who was both the City President and the Chief Mayor. There was a separate staff supporting the office of City President which was distinct from the staff of the municipal government. The City President served as educational authority for the city (although the University of Berlin and the Technical School were directly under the national Ministry of Education), while elementary, secondary, and some higher schools were administered by the municipal government. He was also head of the Regional Planning Association (*Landesplanungsgemeinschaft*). The cultural and archival affairs of the city were also under the office of the City President. In the field of price control, rationing, and economics, the Price Fixing Office, the Regional Food Office, the Forest and Wood Economy Control Office, and the Regional Economics Office were also attached to this office. In insurance affairs, the State Employment Insurance Association (*Landesversicherungsanstalt*), was likewise under the City President. The police administration of the city, however, was handled separately. Berlin had a Police President who served as the authority and administrator for all police matters. The Chief Mayor as head of local self-government, had his own organization and staff. The administrative departments of the city were headed by ten professional experts, who were assisted by a number of advisory councilors dealing with a variety of technical problems. The following departments, each under one of the ten administrative experts handled the services and functions of city administration in the thirties.

General Administration (*Allgemeine Verwaltung*): Internal administrative relations, the city civil service, city personnel matters, and the general economic activities of Berlin.

Finance (*Finanzen*): City taxation, finances, and the financial aspects of the city enterprises and economic activities. There was a main finance office, a main tax office (*Hauptsteueramt*)—which formulated general tax regulations—and a city treasury and controller's office (*Kassen- und Rechnungsprüfungsamt*), the city bank, and the city savings banks.

Education and Cultural Activities (*Schule und Kultur*): Educational administration, City School Council and physical education.

Transportation (*Verkehrswesen*): The transportation facilities of Greater Berlin were administered by a City Councilor who was responsible for the city transit lines, railways, bus lines, airport, and travel facilities. He was also responsible for the city harbor and canals. The air raid protection service of Berlin was administered by this department.

Construction (*Tiefbauwesen*): The road, canal, and waterways construction office was under a City Building Councilor (*Stadtbaurat*). He was also responsible for the city water system and the surveyor's office (*Vermessungsamt*). The Chief Construction Office (*Haupttiefbauamt*) was responsible for the care of facilities which served the city as a whole, and supervised the local construction activities within the administrative district.

Public Building (*Hochbauwesen*): This department, which was headed by a City Councilor, included the settlement and housing office (*Siedlungs- und Wohnungsamt*), and the main building inspection office (*Haupthochbauamt*). It was also responsible for the supervision of the city cemeteries, parks, and lands.

Fire Protection (*Feuerlöschwesen*): The department for fire protection was headed by a City Councilor. It was responsible for fire protection measures and fire fighting. It was also in charge of certain aspects of fire and building inspection.

Health (*Gesundheitswesen*): The city health department, which was headed by a City Medical Board (*Stadtmedizinalrat*), was subject to the national Health Office. It was responsible for the city hospitals and handled general matters

relating to public health and medicine. It also supervised the Administrative
District Health Office.

Welfare (*Volkswohlfahrt*): The welfare and relief services of the city were under
one City Councilor. He administered the regional welfare office (*Landes-
wohlfahrtsamt*) and the city youth office (*Landesjugendamt*).

Market Administration (*Marktverwaltung*): The administration of the main city
markets and the supervision of the local markets and slaughterhouses, as well
as the administration of public foundations, was under one City Councilor.

The work of these departments and their offices, except in the case of finances,
taxation, utilities, transportation, parks and forests, and banks, which affected
the city as a whole, was actually carried out at the district level. The offices of
central administration served as agencies for planning, policy, direction, and
supervision.

Each of the twenty administrative districts was under a District Mayor, four
or five district experts assisted by a number of councilors, and a Party Agent.
Although each administrative district had the same general type of administrative organization, they varied somewhat in the departmental structure of
their local services and functions in order to meet differing local conditions.
There was a main bureau (*Hauptbüro*) for general local administration and
personnel, which worked under regulations established by the central administration. The local finances and taxes were handled by a finance bureau (*Finanz-
büro*) a district treasury (*Bezirkskasse*), and a district tax office (*Bezirkssteuer-
amt*). These offices, which worked under the Berlin Treasurer (*Kämmerer*)
handled the local budget and finances and made the local tax assessments and
collections. The District Health Office administered the local tuberculosis, welfare, medical and dental services for schools, local health institutions (first aid
stations, hospitals, and baths), and public health activities. It was subject to the
regulations of the central Health Office. Welfare and relief came under the District Welfare Office and the District Youth Office (*Bezirksjugendamt*); while
housing and land settlement were administered by the District Housing and
Land Settlement Office (*Bezirkswohnungs- und Siedlungsamt*). The district
construction offices sometimes consisted of a single building inspection office
(*Bauamt*) with buildings (*Hochbau*) and roads and canals (*Tiefbau*) sections,
while in many districts there were separate building offices and road and canal
offices. The school administration and local cultural activities were under the
District School Office. The economic enterprises of the administrative district
were limited to those which have only local significance, such as local markets,
small slaughterhouses, baths, parks, and cemeteries. The transportation facilities, utilities, and savings banks of Greater Berlin were managed by the central
administration.

The suburban administrative districts were further divided into precincts, each of which was headed by a Precinct Chairman chosen by the district government.

Under the Nazis a number of direct national authorities for specific administrative functions (Finance, Labor, Justice, Post, Railway, etc.) operated independently of the general administration provided by the City President and Chief Mayor of Berlin. Their numerous offices in Berlin were under regional agencies, which were directly responsible to national authorities, national ministers, and Supreme Authorities (*Oberste Reichsbehörden*) also located in Berlin. The City President-Chief Mayor, as an official of general administration, did not have control of the regional and local offices of these special national administrative authorities; for he had only the right to information and the power to coordinate the work of the officials within his jurisdiction when the need arose.

Under the Empire and the Republic, the development of the special and technical administrative services of the city of Berlin was gradual. During the imperial period, only the state administered courts, railways, and mining offices, and the postal system were nationally operated. Justice, which was administered under the Prussian Ministry of Justice until the Nazis came into power, was handled by the Berlin Superior Court of Appeals (*Kammergericht*) and the Courts of First and Second Instance of Berlin and several local Courts of First Instance (*Amtsgerichte*). After 1934 these courts fell under the jurisdiction of the National Minister of Justice.

The postal system, which was nationalized in imperial times, was operated in the Capital under the Chief Postal Directorate of Berlin. During the Republic and the Third Reich, the postal, telephone, and telegraph systems of Berlin continued under the National Postal Directorate of Berlin, which was subject to the National Ministry of Post. It must be recalled that national regulation of trade and industry, weights and measures, social insurance and welfare, public health and the collection of imperial revenues was delegated to the state of Prussia, which carried out these tasks through its apparatus for general administration.

The republican period brought the extension of direct national administration to finance, railways, unemployment insurance and employment, and labor welfare. National control of public finances by the National Ministry of Finance was carried out in the Greater Berlin Area through the State Finance Office of Berlin and its local finance offices and main customs offices. The maintenance of the numerous national buildings in Berlin was under the National Construction Office in Berlin, which was attached to the State Finance Office. The nationalized railways, which were operated by the German Railroad Company, were handled in the Berlin area through the National Railroad Director-ate of Berlin. Labor and labor welfare problems, which were extremely acute during the years following World War II, were under direct national control. The National Office for Employment and Unemployment, which was made responsible for employment and unemployment insurance, operated in the Cap-ital through the State Labor Office of Brandenburg (Berlin). Labor welfare matters of the Berlin area were handled through the local welfare offices of the main welfare office in Brandenburg-Pomerania (Berlin). Although there had been a great extension of nationally administered services under the Republic, the states continued to administer welfare (*Landesfürsorgestellen*), social in-surance (*Landesversicherungsämter*), labor disputes (*Landesarbeitsgerichte*), and health (*Landesgesundheitsbehörden*), upon delegation and under the su-pervision of the pertinent national authority. Many aspects of the economic life of Berlin, which were organized under the German Industry and Trade Diets, the Diet of Craft and Industry, the National Union of the German Handicrafts, the German Agricultural Council, and the Trade Unions, were subject only to the loose supervision of the national and state ministries or authorities for economics, agriculture, and labor.

Berlin, a city of civil servants, middle class business and commercial people, and workers, has long manifested its cosmopolitan spirit in political move-ments which have tended toward the left. Although Berlin was the political center of Prussian Junkerdom, the people of the city have followed a more lib-eral variety of politics. In 1848 the stand of the Berliners against the absolute monarchy of the Hohenzollerns resulted in the establishment of a constitu-tional monarchy. The political reaction, which came during the fifties, was dependent for its political support on the conservatives of Berlin's hinterland. During the imperial period, the elections to the Reichstag revealed that the political sympathies of the Berliners were largely with the Social Democrats and the Progressives. The city government of republican times was largely con-trolled by the Social Democrats.

The critical national elections between 1930 and 1933 clearly pictured the political feelings of the citizens of Berlin on the eve of the Third Reich. Gener-ally speaking, the northern, eastern, and southern voting districts were strongly Communist and Socialist. The same was true for the center of the city, except for the aristocratic Tiergarten section. The districts of Kreuzberg, Lichten-berg, Neukölln, Treptow, and Wedding gave the two proletarian parties regu-lar majorities ranging from three-fifths to two-thirds in every election—national, state, and local. The western and more wealthy residential areas like Charlottenburg, Spandau, and Wilmersdorf always had a sizable Nationalist, German People's, and Democratic party vote. But with the rise of Hitlerism these districts went over into the National Socialist column. In the vote for National President in 1932, however, Hitler carried only one of the districts in the city, namely Steglitz.

As the Nazis grew stronger in the summer of 1932, the Communists likewise acquired strength and supplanted the Socialists as the most numerous party in the northern, southern, and central districts. By the time of the November 1932 election, the Nazi strength in Berlin had subsided, and only eight of the city's twenty voting districts gave Hitler the leading position. Before 1933 the National Socialists were unable to secure more than one-third of the total vote of Greater Berlin.

The politics of the city during the republican era were clearly dominated by the Social Democrats and the Communists. In the wealthier residential areas the elected District Councils were in the hands of the bourgeois parties; but in the other districts, as well as in the council of Greater Berlin, Socialist and Communist members controlled the government. Berlin was Germany's strongest Communist area, the vote for this party usually amounting to about one-third of the total vote in the city during the early thirties. Actually, the Social Democrats, who had been more powerful during the twenties before the depression, were more influential than the Communists in the city's government because their strength was more evenly distributed over the whole metropolitan area, while the Communist strength was concentrated in a few working-class districts, where most of the unemployed workers lived.

The National Socialist victory, which was made possible by the vote of a large minority of the German population coupled with astute political moves and intrigue, drastically changed political conditions within Greater Berlin. The National Socialist organization rapidly provided for the control of almost every aspect of Berlin life. The general administration of party affairs was under the notorious Minister of Propaganda, Dr. Goebbels, District Leader for the district of Berlin.

The nationalization and centralization of government under the Nazis brought an amazing extension of the agencies for special and technical administration. Direct national administration continued for finance, posts, labor and labor welfare, and railways, and was extended to justice, air matters, propaganda, and labor relations.

Berlin lost many of its traditional privileges and rights, as the Nazis brought police, health, welfare, education, and certain aspects of social insurance under tighter national control.

The services and functions of the general and special administrative systems operating in Greater Berlin were supplemented by an extensive network of corporate administration which provided further regimentation of the activities of the German people. These changes were ephemeral, for with the fall of

Berlin to the Allies all of the special, corporate, and party apparatus for administration were swept away leaving only the basic Berlin city administration.

For the past seventy years Berlin has been an important governmental and
administrative center. It has served as the national capital as well as the center
of the government of Prussia and the administration of the Province of Brandenburg. While it is the traditional center of political power in eastern Germany, its position within the Reich was dependent in part on the strength of
the Prussian state. Since the Prussian victory over Austria in 1866, when the
national capital was moved from Frankfort, Berlin has been the political and
administrative center of Germany.

ECONOMIC AND SOCIAL ASPECTS

Until its destruction in World War II, Berlin was the greatest city of continental Europe. It was also Germany's major governmental and administrative
capital and its most important commercial and manufacturing center. The importance of Berlin as a center of trade goes back to late medieval times, when it
was already a market town playing its part in the colonization and settlement
of northeastern Germany. The early development of Berlin was largely due to
its position as the residence city (*Residenzstadt*) of the Hohenzollerns and its
location at the junction of trade routes connecting Leipzig, Stettin, Frankfort,
Warsaw, Danzig, and Lübeck. The small medieval towns of Berlin and Kölln
grew rapidly with the increasing power of the Hohenzollerns, who became the
Electors of Brandenburg (1415), the Kings of Prussia (1701) and the Emperors
of Germany (1871). The rapid expansion of Prussian power in the early nineteenth century was marked in Berlin by a rapid expansion of population from
172,100 in 1800 to almost 800,000 by 1871. Much of this increase came after 1840,
during the period of railroad and canal construction. The improvement of
transportation facilities made it possible for Berlin to reach out beyond impoverished Brandenburg to the more productive areas of the Reich for the natural
resources required by modern industry.

After 1871, Berlin's development as the governmental and administrative
center of the German Empire, coupled with the improvement of transportation
facilities and the impetus of the German industrial revolution, encouraged the
growth of commercial and industrial enterprises. The rapid development of
Berlin was indicated by the fact that by 1913 the population numbered 2,820,-
000. Although the loss of World War I impoverished Berlin's economy, the
Republican period, with its further centralization of governmental and administrative activities at Berlin, stimulated the further growth of the city. By 1933,
it had a population of 4,242,000. By 1939, Berlin had become a massive urban
agglomeration situated astride the Elbe-Oder waterways and located at the center of the German railway system. A city of boundless energy, where life was

lived at a rapid tempo. Even at the height of its development it lacked unity, owing to the admixture of governmental, economic, and cultural interests, no one of which predominated.

The city of Berlin formed a distinct socio-economic area, since it was an isolated urban mass in the plains of Northeast Germany. It did not form a part of an urbanized zone like the Ruhr, but existed within itself, surrounded by the rural hinterland of Brandenburg. This sharp division of urban and rural life was fully recognized by the Nazis when they placed the city of Berlin under a separate Regional Planning Association (*Landesplanungsgemeinschaft*).

The diversified manufacturing establishments have tended to specialize in clothing, machinery, electrical goods, and scientific instruments. The industrial areas of Berlin were concentrated in the north, east, and southeast districts of Pankow, Weissensee, Lichtenberg, and Köpenick. No basic or heavy industries were originally developed in Berlin because of the lack of raw materials in the immediate vicinity. The first industry to take root in Berlin was the wool industry. In the eighteenth century Berlin became one of the leading clothing manufacturing centers on the continent; until relatively recent times it was important for silk. The first sugar refineries were established in 1747. The beginnings of the iron industry go back to the establishment of the Royal Iron Foundry in 1804, while the first machine plant was erected in 1815. The machine industry grew rapidly during the early nineteenth century, while the late nineteenth century brought the development of the electrical goods, chemical, and food industries. These industries evolved through the use of materials brought in from other parts of the Reich by rail and canal, for Berlin's immediate environs had little in the way of raw materials.

In point of number of firms and capitalization, the major industries of the city during the Nazi era ranked as follows: electrical goods, chemicals, machinery, and food products. The electrical industry, and particularly the plants of the Siemens Corporation, were concentrated in an area between Charlottenburg and Spandau. Much of the machine industry and the A.E.G. was concentrated in the southeast. In addition to the major industries and manufacturing establishments, great numbers of smaller plants produced leather goods, furniture, paper, wood products, and clothing.

Many of the industries of Berlin owed their remarkable development to the introduction of electrical power, which was derived from the extensive lignite fields of Brandenburg and Central Germany. The real development came in the twentieth century, particularly after World War I, with the improvements in methods of transmitting electricity, and as the demands for power by industry became pressing. After the loss of the coal in the Silesian area to Poland as a result of the plebiscite of 1921, there was a more extensive exploitation of the local lignite for electrical power.

The electrical system which supplied Greater Berlin began with the establishment of the first electrical power station in 1884. Electrical power for the
Greater Berlin area was supplied by the Berlin Power and Light Company
(*Berliner Kraft- und Licht AG*), which was owned by the city of Berlin, the
state of Prussia, and the Reich government. Its major plants were located in
west Berlin, Klingenberg, Charlottenburg, Rummelsburg, Moabit, Wilmersdorf, Schöneberg, and Spandau. There were also four other small power stations. For supplementary power supplies, Berlin drew upon the power network
of the Markisches Electrical Works (*Märkisches Elektrizitätswerke*), which
had plants throughout northeastern Germany, although its major works were
located in the lignite fields of southern Brandenburg and the east part of the
Province of Saxony. Berlin also received some power from the network of the
Electrical Works, which had its major station in southeastern Brandenburg.

Gas for industrial and domestic use was furnished by the joint stock corporation of the gas industry (*Gasbetriebsgesellschaft AG*) serving southern
Greater Berlin and the Berlin City Gas Works (*Berliner Städtische Gaswerke
AG*) serving central and northern Berlin. There were eight gas-producing
plants and one distributing works.

The water system, which was established in 1878, was highly centralized.
The water supply, based upon wells, lakes, and the Spree and Havel rivers, was
handled by the public Berlin City Water Works (*Berliner Städtische-Wasser-
werke*) and its eighty-five pumping stations.

The rural industries of the Greater Berlin area were extremely limited, for
only 19 per cent of the land area is given over to agriculture and husbandry.
Most of the agricultural land, which is located in the northern, eastern, and
southern suburban margins, is largely devoted to small gardens, although there
are a number of farms interested in the cultivation of grain, root crops, and
vegetables for the Berlin markets. The area under pasture, which is given over
to dairying, constitutes only about 4 per cent of the Berlin area. It should
be noted that the Berlin City Property Corporation (*Berliner Stadtgüter
GmbH*) operated several large city-owned agricultural estates. The city also
owned several large forests, which were administered by the Forest Administration of the City of Berlin (*Forstverwaltung der Stadt* Berlin). Most of the
forest land, which was used for both recreation and wood production, is
situated in the districts of Spandau, Wilmersdorf, Köpenick, and Reinicken-
dorf. The city, which owned most of the forest land of the Berlin area, also had
extensive forest holdings in the adjacent counties of the Province of Brandenburg. The forest area constituted about 18 per cent of the total Berlin land area.

Owing to its central position in the Northeast German Plain, Berlin plays an
important role in the national transportation system. The movement of mer-
chandise in Berlin was vital to its commercial and industrial life. Its position

at the center of an extensive rail network and its location on the Elbe-Oder canal gave the city easy access to the basic industries of western and southeastern Germany. The city of Berlin has been a key road junction since its foundation. Today roads radiate from the old bridge across the Spree to Magdeburg, Halle, Leipzig, Dresden, Cottbus, Posen, Stettin, Stralsund, Lübeck, and Hamburg. These major national roads have been supplemented by the Nazi national highways.

The road and street system of Greater Berlin centers around the Unter den Linden, which extends westward from the island in the Spree to the Brandenburg Gate (*Brandenburger Tor*). It is crossed by several important streets, such as Friedrichstrasse and Leipziger Strasse. The street system of central Berlin consists of a number of central squares from which streets radiate to various parts of the outer city. Major streets lead from central Berlin via Steglitz and Zehlendorf to Potsdam, via Treptow to Köpenick, and via Wedding to the suburbs of the northwest. The city of Berlin owned and operated the local transportation system. The city bus lines, which had their beginnings in 1846, were operated by the General Berlin Bus Company (*Allgemeine Berliner Omnibus AG*), while the electrical street car system, which was started in 1881, was managed by the Berlin Street Railways Company (*Berliner Strassenbahn Betriebs GmbH*). The elevated and underground railway system, which was constructed during the latter part of the nineteenth and the early twentieth centuries, connects central and suburban Berlin. The Loop Railway (*Ringbahn*), which circles the heart of the city, is an essential feature of this system, providing a way for the easy movement of traffic within Greater Berlin. The City Railway (*Stadtbahn*) connects all city stations with the principal railway depots. It was operated by the Association for the Electrical Elevated and Underground Railways (*Gesellschaft für elektrische Hoch- und Untergrundbahnen AG*). These three transportation companies are branches of the *Berliner Verkehrs AG,* which was under the City Councilor for Transportation of the central administration.

Berlin is situated at the center of the northeastern German railway network. The major rail lines follow almost the same basic pattern as the road system, for major railroad lines radiate from Berlin to Hanover, Halle, Leipzig, Dresden, Breslau, Frankfort-on-the-Oder, Danzig, Stettin, Stralsund, Lübeck, and Hamburg. The east-west traffic goes through the heart of the city, stopping at the Zoological Gardens (Zoologischer Garten), Friedrichstrasse, Alexanderplatz, and Schlesischer stations. The Lehrter station serves Bremen and Hamburg, while the Stettiner station serves Stettin and Danzig. Rail traffic from the South terminates at the Potsdamer, Anhalter, and Görlitzer stations. The railroads were under the national Railway Director of Berlin.

River and canal transportation is extremely important for the economic life of Berlin. Berlin has an excellent position on the waterways of the North German Plains. The Spree and Havel rivers serve as the basis of a canal system, which consists of the Landwehr, Teltow, Hohenzollern, Havel, and Oder-Spree canals. The Landwehr canal, which was originally constructed in 1850, was built to relieve the congested river traffic on the Spree. In 1906 the Teltow canal, which leaves the Spree at Köpenick and crosses through the factory district of southern Berlin to enter the Havel at Teltow, superseded the Landwehr canal. The Hohenzollern canal serves northeast central Berlin. The Havel canal and river system extends northwestward to connect with the port of Wismar in Mecklenburg and with the Oder River, while the Oder-Spree canal connects Berlin with the Oder and the Province of Silesia. Traffic flows west on the Havel River to the Elbe and thence to the port of Hamburg.

The dock and harbor facilities, including basins and arrangements for loading and unloading were vastly improved during the latter part of the twenties. Berlin was one of the vital points in the waterways system of Germany. It was also Germany's most important center for air traffic. The airlines of the Reich, which were operated by the German Airways Corporation (*Deutsche Lufthansa AG*), used the airports operated by the city-owned Berlin Airport (*Berliner Flughafen GmbH*). The major airport is at Tempelhof.

Berlin was not only the major financial and commercial city of the Reich, but also the headquarters of the national economic administration. Although it was significant as the center of economic life in northeastern Germany, it was far more important as a national and international business center. The commercial function is difficult to separate from the industrial life of the city. From the point of view of commerce it was important for the production of electrical goods, machinery and precision instruments, and clothing. To sustain this industrial and manufacturing activity, Berlin must import from other parts of the Reich such things as coal, lignite, iron and steel, and textiles. In terms of the movement of freight traffic, Berlin obtained most of its raw materials from the Ruhr and the Province of Silesia. After the loss of the Silesian coal fields, Berlin was dependent upon supplies from the Ruhr. In peace times even English coal reached the Berlin market. Lignite was supplied by the fields of southern Brandenburg. Berlin also carried on an extensive trade in machine tools with the Saxony and Hanover areas. Cloth manufactured in Silesia was sent to Berlin, where it was manufactured into clothing for distribution via wholesalers to northeastern Germany. Most of the overseas trade of Berlin went out by rail or river via Stettin, although there was some trade with foreign lands via Hamburg.

The food supply for the city of Berlin came largely from Brandenburg and Central Germany, although the meat supply was drawn from such distant areas as Württemberg and a portion of the supply even came from Holland and Sweden. The milk supply, which was organized under the Berlin Milk Association (*Berliner Milchversorgungverband*), came largely from adjacent Brandenburg. The government of Berlin took an active part in the commercial life of the city through its ownership in the Berlin Harbor and Warehouse Company (*Berliner Hafen- und Lagerhausgesellschaft*) and its operation of the larger city markets and slaughterhouses. The supplies needed by the city administration were purchased by a municipal central purchasing agency, the *Berliner Anschaffungsgesellschaft GmbH*.

Most of the major financial and banking institutions of Germany had their headquarters in Berlin. The great commercial banks, which were mainly interested in industrial investment, included the *Deutsche Bank*, the *Dresdner Bank*, the *Commerzbank*, the *Darmstadter- und Nationalbank*, the *Bank der deutschen Arbeit*, the *Reichs-Kredit-Gesellschaft*, and the *Berliner-Handels-Gesellschaft*. The headquarters of the *Reichsbank* and its subsidiaries, the *Deutsche Girozentrale—Deutsche Kommunalbank*, and the *Deutscher Sparkassen- und Giroverband;* several credit cooperatives; mortgage banking institutions; and agricultural credit organizations were located in Berlin. It was also the center for the Prussian State Bank (*Preussische Staatsbank*), the Prussian Central City Association (*Preussische Zentralstadtschaft*), and several other financial institutions of the state of Prussia. The banks which were owned and operated by municipalities included the *Berliner Stadtbank*, the *Neuköllner Stadtbank*, the *Sparkasse der Stadt Berlin*, the *Berliner Stadtschaft*, and the *Berliner Hypothekenbankverein*. These institutions were supervised by the City Treasurer. Several large national insurance organizations, such as the *Allianz und Stuttgarter Versicherungs AG*, the *Nordstern Allgemeine Versicherungs AG*, the *Victoria Feuerversicherungs AG*, and the *Victoria Rückversicherungs AG*, had their headquarters in Berlin.

The Berlin stock exchange dominated the industrial and commercial finances of the Reich. The financial and commercial enterprises centered in Berlin, plus the national, Prussian, and municipal financial institutions and the extensive manufacturing establishments of the suburban area, made this city one of the great economic centers of the world. Each year it had fairs, conventions, and business meetings which attracted people from all parts of the Reich and Europe. Berlin was particularly important for its annual exhibitions of leather goods, automobiles, machinery, paper products, and photographic equipment. In the middle thirties it was host to between forty and fifty conventions and congresses each year.

As of 1939 the population of Greater Berlin was mainly engaged in industry and crafts, for over 1,680,000 individuals or 39 per cent of the population were supported by the factories and shops of the city. Of this group the electrical goods industries employed about 239,000 in 1939, while the machinery industry engaged 186,000. The foundries and metal goods plants employed about 90,000, the chemical industry 38,000, and the optical industry about 23,000. It is estimated that the war industries of Greater Berlin in 1939 employed about 576,000 workers. The trade and transportation enterprises engaged about 1,175,-000 or 27 per cent of the population. The rural industries, agriculture and forestry, supported only about 50,000 persons, or a little over 1 per cent of the population. The resultant class structure presents several interesting features. The working class of Berlin, which is still concentrated in the northern, southern, and eastern districts of the city, constituted about 42 per cent of the population, while the white collar class, the largest in Germany in comparison with those of the provinces and states of the Reich, accounted for about 20 per cent of the population. The upper class and civil servant group, still living in the western part of Berlin, were relatively small, accounting for only 18 per cent of the population. The civil servant group alone constituted only 7.2 per cent of the Berlin population.

Berlin had grown rapidly since 1871, thanks to its position as the capital of the German Empire, the Republic, and the Third Reich. Although it was the major governmental, manufacturing, commercial, and cultural center of the Reich, it was not a natural center since it had no deep historical, cultural, and geographical roots. From the point of view of Germany as a whole, Berlin is located on the frontier. It is, however, the natural center of the Prussian Northeast. Since the late Middle Ages, this city has been the Hohenzollern capital, while towns like Aix-la-Chapelle (Aachen) and Frankfort-on-the-Main served as the successive capitals of the old German Empire. The governmental structure of Greater Berlin reflects its slow development under the Prussian kings and its rapid progress as the capital of the Reich. The old city of Berlin, which flourished on the banks of the Spree during the later medieval and early modern periods under the governments of the towns of Berlin, Kölln, Dorotheenstadt, Friedrichswerder, and Friedrichstadt, survives today in the administrative district of Mitte. This section, which is traversed by the famous Unter den Linden, was given its final form by the Great Elector and King Friedrich I. It became the official and financial portion of the city.

On the Wilhelmstrasse were built the chief government buildings, including the National President's Palace (*Reichspräsidentenpalais*), the National Chancellery (*Reichskanzlei*), and several ministries. Near-by Behrenstrasse has long been the center of finance, Leipziger Strasse grew to be a fashionable shopping district, and Friedrichstrasse, which intersects the Unter den Linden, a street of restaurants and shops. The famous Unter den Linden was the scene of the military triumphs of the Empire and the diplomatic and military victories of the Third Reich. This mile-long promenade, which was lined by trees, was the center of official life. The opera house, university, state library, and the

embassies of several foreign lands once lined this processional way. The ancient
city east of the isle in the Spree contains the City Hall (*Rathaus*), the old *Ma-
rienkirche,* and the stock exchange (*Börse*). The *Reichstag,* the home of Germany's parliamentary institution, was outside the old city, beyond the Brandenburg Gate on the edge of the Tiergarten, which was famous for its zoo and
planetarium. Central Berlin also contained a number of hotels including the
Adlon, Bristol, Esplanada, and Kaiserhof, while Haus Vaterland on Pots-
damer-Platz and Haus Europa on Anhalter-Platz became the larger centers
of Berlin night life. The new shopping and amusement area developed along
the Kurfürstendamm in the west end. The architecture of central Berlin was
frequently done in the florid, heavy Berlin Renaissance style, although a few
buildings of classical revival type date from an earlier part of the nineteenth
century. The Nazis added several buildings constructed in the new and approved functional-classical style, such as the Air Ministry on the Leipziger
Strasse and the Propaganda Ministry and the new Chancellery on the Wilhelmstrasse.

During the nineteenth century, the old central Berlin overflowed into the
districts of Wedding, Prenzlauer-Berg, Friedrichshain and Kreuzberg, while
the Tiergarten area was set aside as a park. Eastward beyond the old town with
its official architecture, the city became an endless sea of working class residences, characterized by depressing dullness broken only occasionally by new
modernistic structures of the functional type. In the west, in the districts of
Spandau, Charlottenburg, Wilmersdorf, and Zehlendorf, conditions improved,
for this is the area of middle and upper class homes, while to the north, east,
and south, the urban landscape was increasingly dominated by factories and
workshops set among dreary slums. Here the railroad and its marshalling
yards and shops, and the canals with their docking and warehouse facilities cut
through the smoky landscape. The outer margins of the residential western and
the industrialized northern and eastern sections give way to dense pine forests.
The northwestern and northern portions of the town are dominated by the
Spandauer Stadtforst, Tegeler Forst, and the Jungfernheide, while the western
residential area has the Spandauer Forst and the Grunewald, which are bordered on the west by the beautiful chain of Havel lakes.

The character of the people of Greater Berlin is difficult to grasp. Basically,
the population is a fusion of Germans and Slavs, to which has been added Germans from every part of the Reich. The people are almost cosmopolitan, without any real interest in Prussia and not sharing the particularism of the provincial areas. The city is hardly Prussian in spirit and it certainly does not share in
the military enthusiasms of the Northeast. Berlin became a practical, efficient,
and materialistic metropolis, rejecting the ways of its hinterland. Although the
German immigrants to the heart of the Reich brought the ways and traditions

of their home, these were soon lost, and the satisfactions of the transplanted people were lost in the industrial congestion, the bourgeois complacency or metropolitan sophistication.

The cultural beginnings are found in the early part of the eighteenth century, when Leibnitz founded the Academy of Science (*Akademie der Wissenschaft*). The eighteenth century city was famous for the French and rationalistic court culture of Frederick the Great at Potsdam, while in the early nineteenth century Berlin was the center of German romanticism under the leadership of Tieck, Arnim, Fichte, and Müller. The University of Berlin, which was founded in 1810, became the academic home of many of Germany's most famous scholars during the nineteenth and twentieth centuries: Humboldt, Niebuhr, Hegel, Schelling, Virchow, von Ranke, Helmholtz, Koch, Mommsen, Treitschke, Sybel, and Harnack. After 1933 most of the cultural facilities of Berlin, including over eleven institutions of higher learning and thirty-five museums as well as a great number of national scientific and cultural institutes, were under the Nazi Ministry of Education. Berlin was also famous for music and the theater. The State Opera was opened in the eighteenth century, while the nineteenth century was marked by the establishment of numerous private playhouses. Although Berlin, until very recently, was able to attract the best of European talent, the departure of numerous artists, writers, and musicians with the advent of the Third Reich brought a period of cultural depression.

For the past seventy-five years the life of Berlin has been supported by governmental activity and developing industry and trade. Although Hitler attempted to make it the truly nationalistic capital of a militaristic Reich, Germany's defeat in World War II left the capital in indescribable ruins. Its future is not now clearly discernible.

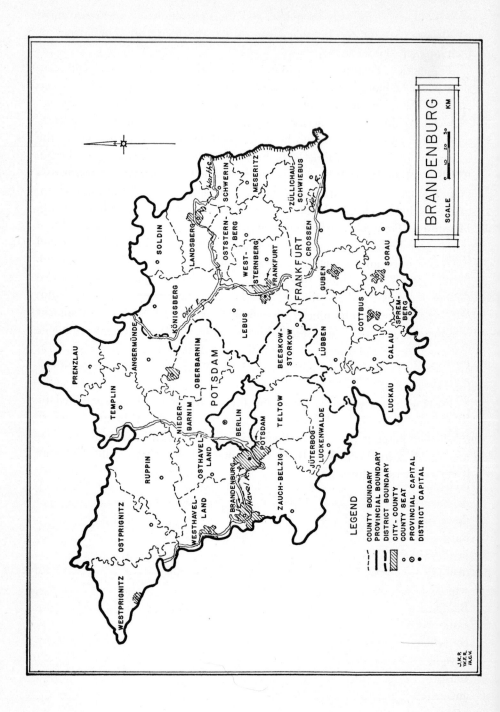

Chapter 6

THE PROVINCE OF BRANDENBURG

The Prussian Province of Brandenburg lies in the Elbe-Oder river lowland country of northeastern Germany. It is bounded on the north by Mecklenburg and Pomerania. To the east its frontiers adjoin those of Poland in the swampy Warthe region, while on the south and west it is bounded by Silesia and Saxony. It is crossed by the Oder and by the Ancient River Valleys which divide the higher sandy areas into a number of minor regions. The three major valleys, which originated in the glacial era when they drained away the water of the melting glaciers as they retreated northward, cut across northern, central, and southern Brandenburg. Once swampy, with dense thickets in the damper areas and heath in the drier sandy marginal areas, these ancient valleys have been largely transformed into cultivated fields and meadows, thanks to two centuries of drainage and reclamation.

The present river system is formed by the development of valleys at right angles to the Ancient River Valleys. The Elbe, which rises in Czechoslovakia and flows north through the state and the Province of Saxony, borders Brandenburg on the northwest, while the Oder, which originates in Moravia and flows north through the Province of Silesia, runs through eastern Brandenburg and central Pomerania to the Baltic. The Spree River, whose source lies in the Sudeten Mountains, flows northward until it reaches the central Brandenburg Ancient Valley, where it turns westward to join the lower Havel which flows north and westward ultimately to join the Elbe. Northeastern Brandenburg is drained by the Warthe, tributary of the Oder, while the southeastern part of the province is drained by other tributaries of the Oder. These rivers have only a slight gradient and their valleys are subject to floods which have left behind extensive alluvial deposits. The land between the river valleys consists of extensive areas of ground moraine with moderately fertile loam soils and a few infertile sandy districts. The northern and central portions of the province are dotted with numerous small lakes, while the southern area is dominated by the eroded hills of Fläming and Nieder Lausitz, whose dry sandy soils support an extensive forest cover. These hills, which mark the southern-most advance of the last glaciation, should be regarded as terminal moraines. They seem high only in contrast with the surrounding lowland, for in no case do they exceed an elevation of 760 feet.

The north and central portions of the province lying north of the Fläming and Nieder Lausitz hills are divided by the rivers and Ancient River Valleys into a number of traditionally distinct regions. The famous Spreewald, which is the home of the Slavic Wends, is situated on the upper Spree just north of the Nieder Lausitz. This forested valley area is famous for its labyrinth of canals. The region of Mittelmark and the districts of Zauche and Teltow are located to the south of the central Havel-Spree Ancient Valley, while the districts of Havelland and Barnim are situated between the central and northern ancient valleys. Northern Brandenburg is divided into the districts of Prignitz and Ukermark, while the lands to the east of the Oder are known as Neumark.

Berlin, the capital of the province, is, however, a separate administrative unit, independent of the Province of Brandenburg. The cities of Branden-burg, Potsdam, and Frankfort-on-the-Oder lie on higher sandy areas which jut into the central ancient valley. Landsberg in northeast Brandenburg, and Cottbus, Forst, and Guben in the southeast are valley towns on important rail and water routes. Eberswalde on the Finow canal, Rathenow on the lower Havel, and Wittenberge on the Elbe are on important waterways in northern and northwestern Brandenburg. Outside of Berlin, Brandenburg is essentially rural with its broad valleys, sandy plains, fertile fields and stretches of forested land. Each of its several rural districts is dominated by one or two towns of moderate size along the trade routes that have long threaded their way through the maze of river valleys of northeastern Germany.

The people of Brandenburg are more heterogeneous in their composition than the people of most German states and provinces. Although northeastern Germany was occupied by East Germanic peoples during the first centuries of our era, they deserted the lands east of the Elbe during the Migration Era of the fourth to eighth centuries. Slavic peoples, whose homeland is presumed to have been in the basin of the upper Dnieper, pushed westward across the Vis-tula to the Elbe, occupying Brandenburg and all of East Elbian Germany dur-ing the fifth century. The Slavs avoided the swampy valley land and dwelt upon the dry sandy plains which they used to pasture their flocks of sheep. Many place names ending in "ow" (Teltow, Beeskow, etc.) testify to the early slavic occupation. After the Carolingian period (751-911), Low Saxon peo-ples from west of the Elbe pushed eastward to colonize and settle the lands along the Spree and Havel. The names of the districts of Altmark, Mittelmark, and Neumark indicate the stages of the eastward advance of the Low Saxons, since it will be recalled that "mark" means boundary. Until the fifteenth century German settlers occupied only the high, dry areas, but after that time they turned to the task of draining and reclaiming the swampy valley land. During early modern times the Prussian nobles imported serfs and impoverished peasants from almost every part of Germany to work the land. Many came to Brandenburg as refugees during and after the Thirty Years' War.

During the late seventeenth century, the Electors of Brandenburg encouraged the settlement of Flemings and French Protestants. The original Slavic population of the province dwindled rapidly under the pressure of German settlement. Although many were absorbed by intermarriage, a few Slavs, who are known as Wends or Sorbs, still survive in the Spreewald.

The dialect of modern Brandenburg is *Märkisch,* a variety of East Elbian, which developed from Low Saxon conditioned by the Slavic tongue of the original inhabitants. The Upper Saxony dialect is spoken in the southwest, while East Middle German is common in the southeast. Pure Low Saxon is still spoken in certain areas of western Brandenburg. Standard German, however, is spoken in most towns and cities and is becoming increasingly common in the rural areas.

The province is predominantly Protestant, for out of a total population of 2,692,000 (without Berlin) in 1933 almost 90 per cent of the population, or 2,407,000 individuals, were Lutherans. The Catholic minority was small, numbering 168,000. The Jewish population, which was also very small, numbered 7,400 before 1933.

Although in area it is the third largest Prussian province, it is relatively sparsely settled. The population density of the province as a whole was seventy per sq. km., ranging from sixty to eighty in the Spree and Havel valley to twenty to forty in the north (Ukermark). During the last century and a half, there has been a marked increase in the population of eastern Brandenburg and the area along the Spree between Potsdam and Frankfort, while in the western portion of the province there has been no corresponding increase. In the early nineteenth century, the province had a total population of about 1,500,-000. The greatest period of expansion came between 1871 and 1910; it was due to the rapid industrialization of many of the smaller towns. Since 1910, there has been an increase of about 293,000. Population movement in terms of emigration to other lands is hardly a factor in Brandenburg. In contrast with southern or northwestern Germany, very few individuals left the province for lands outside the Reich. On the other hand, because its economic opportunities are limited, there has been only a slight movement of peoples into the province from other parts of the Reich.

Brandenburg as a margraviate, electorate, and province has played major roles in the development of Prussia and modern Germany. Although the region was brought under temporary German control by Charlemagne, the history of the province begins with the German defeat of the Slavic Havelli and the capture of their capital at Brandenburg (Brennabor). The German conquest of Brandenburg began in A.D. 929 under the leadership of Count Bernhard. In the late tenth century, it was divided into Nordmark (central and northwest Brandenburg) and Ostmark (state of Saxony and southern Brandenburg). Although the Slavs managed to regain some control in East Elbian Brandenburg, the twelfth century was marked by the revival of German power under the leadership of Albrecht of Anhalt, a vassal of the Emperor Lothar of Saxony. The reign of Count (Margrave) Albrecht marks the beginnings of the history of Brandenburg. German colonization and settlement were rapidly expanding at the expense of the Slavs. The successors of Albrecht managed to add the districts of Prignitz, Zauche, Havelland and Teltow to the margraviate. Western Neumark was added in 1257. The middle of the thirteenth century found Brandenburg divided into three territories, Altmark west of the Elbe, Mittelmark between the Elbe and Oder, and Neumark, beyond the Oder, the latter under the Order of the Teutonic Knights. The wars of the fourteenth century left Brandenburg in a deplorable state. The extinction of the family of Albrecht in 1320 plunged the Margraviate of Brandenburg into further turmoil. In 1324 the Wittelsbach family of Bavaria gained control of Brandenburg, and in 1356 they were recognized as Electors of the Holy Roman Empire. After a brief war over succession, the Luxemburg family secured control of the Electorate in 1373 and acquired Neumark from the Order of the Teutonic Knights. However, their rule was characterized by political anarchy and economic depression.

Through a split within the Luxemburg family at the imperial elections of 1410, the Hohenzollern Friedrich Wilhelm VI, Burgrave of Nuremberg, gained control of Brandenburg, and in 1411, as has been noted, he became Friedrich Wilhelm I, Elector of Brandenburg, receiving a limited territory consisting of Altmark, Mittelmark, Prignitz, Ukermark, and Sternberg. Although Brandenburg continued to serve as the basis for Hohenzollern power during the fifteenth to eighteenth centuries, its history gradually merged with that of Prussia. The first important holding of the Hohenzollerns was administered through its traditional subdivisions: Mittelmark, Altmark, Prignitz, Ukermark, and Neumark.

The actual organization of Prussia into provinces did not take place until after the Treaty of Vienna in 1815, when the province was given its present form with the joining together of the old districts of Mittelmark, Prignitz, Ukermark, and Neumark. Altmark was lost to the newly formed Province of Saxony, while Nieder Lausitz was acquired from the state of Saxony. During the nineteenth century, Brandenburg was administered from Berlin by a Chief President, and was divided for the purposes of administration into two administrative districts, Potsdam and Frankfort; but, although it retained its political identity, it tended to be more and more submerged in the general flow of Prussian history. Provincial self-government, which was originally introduced in 1823, was broadened by the Provincial Constitution of 1875-1881.

When, in November 1918, the state of Prussia became a constituent republic of Weimar Germany, Brandenburg continued as one of the twelve Prussian provinces. The reorganization of the City of Berlin affected the province very little. The office of the Chief President and the Provincial Council, Provincial Committee, and Provincial Assembly, although changed in character, were retained along with the two administrative districts.

The work of the general administration of the province, which was provided by the Chief President, the two District Presidents, the County Managers and Chief Mayors, was supplemented by special and technical administrative services under direct national control. The development of the special and technical administrative services was gradual under the Empire and the Republic. During the imperial period, the state administered only the courts, railways, and mining offices, while the nationally operated postal system lay outside the jurisdiction of the general administration of the Province of Brandenburg. Justice, as in Berlin, was administered by the Prussian Ministry of Justice until the Nazi reorganization; the Superior Court of Appeals of Berlin (*Kammergericht*) and the Courts of First and Second Instance of Berlin, Cottbus, Frankfort, Guben, Landsberg, Neuruppin, Potsdam, and Prenzlau, and numerous local Courts of First Instance heard the cases. Brandenburg's postal system had also been nationalized in imperial times; it was operated at that time by the imperial Chief Postal Directorates and later by the republican National Postal Directorates of Potsdam and Frankfort. National regulations for trade and industry, weights and measures, social insurance and welfare, public health, and the collection of imperial revenues were administered upon delegation from the Reich.

Again, as in Berlin, the republican period brought the further extension of direct national administration to finance, railways, unemployment insurance and employment service, and labor welfare. National control of public finances within Brandenburg was effected through the same offices as were those of Berlin. National Construction Offices were located at Potsdam and Frankfort. The nationalized railways were operated by the National Railway Directors of Berlin, and Frankfort-on-the-Oder. Labor and employment problems were met by the State Labor Office of Brandenburg (Berlin) and its labor offices and by the main Welfare Office of Brandenburg-Pomerania (both in Berlin). Just as in Berlin, services subject to national legislation, were administered upon delegation by the general administration of the province. The economic life of the province, like that of Berlin, was, also, subject to limited provincial control; it was organized under the local branches of the German Industrial and Trade Assembly, the Diet of Craft and Industry, the National Corporation of the German Handicrafts, the German Agricultural Council, and the Trade Unions.

POLITICAL ASPECT

Politically, the Province of Brandenburg has long been dominated by the Social Democratic party. During the Empire, when the National Assembly elections gave the only trustworthy picture of political feelings because of the three class system of limited suffrage used in state, provincial, and local elections in Prussia, the Social Democratic party was the most powerful element in the imperial politics of the province. The strongest socialist areas were located in the western and southern portions of the province, where the peasants dwelling on the small farms of Nieder Lausitz and Fläming and the moderate sized farms of the Spree and Havel valleys supported liberal political policies. The Conservatives had their largest followings in the north and northeast, where political life was subject to the Junker class. Under the Republic, the Social Democratic party SPD (*Sozialdemokratische Partei*) grew in strength, particularly in the western part of the province. On the other hand, the nationalistic German National People's party (*Deutschnationale Volkspartei*) retained a considerable following throughout the province. The middle parties—Catholic Center (*Zentrumspartei*), German People's party (*Deutsche-Volkspartei*), and the Democratic party (*Deutsche Demokratische Partei*) did not have significant followings in Brandenburg. During the critical elections between 1930 and 1933, the two million qualified voters of Brandenburg gave their support at first to the Social Democratic party and the German National People's party. The Social Democrats, who drew their support from the middle and working classes of the small towns, and the Nationalists, who derived their following from the rural areas, were not able to withstand the impact of National Socialism.

With the growth of Hitler's strength in 1930, thousands of Nationalist voters among others flocked to the Nazi banner, and together with numerous new voters and nonvoters made the Nazi party the second largest in the province—the Social Democrats retaining first place against desperate odds. In the 1932 elections, nearly every voting district gave the Nazis first place, and the Nazi percentage of the total vote averaged about forty-five per cent. Hindenburg barely carried the province against Hitler in the presidential election, losing to him in many rural areas and also in the cities of Frankfort and Schneidemühl. An average of all the *Reichstag* elections during the critical period after 1930 for the entire province of Brandenburg shows the Nazis received over 40 per cent of the votes cast. The eastern frontier areas were overwhelmingly Nazi. It was in this province therefore that Hitler secured some of the strongest support he received anywhere in Germany. Only a few of the urban areas, like Brandenburg and Rathenow, held to the Social Democratic party. Quite uniformly throughout the province, the National Socialists outdistanced all other parties, except the National German People's party, which was able to retain something of a following in the Potsdam area. It is not without interest that the Junker-ridden eastern portion of the province, where the large estate dominates the scene, gave the Nazis approximately 45 per cent of the total vote in the 1930-1933 elections, while the traditionally liberal west, where the independent peasants and shopkeepers play a more important role, only gave the Nazis 35 per cent of their total vote.

The National Socialist victory brought about the rapid organization of the province by the party. The general administration of party affairs was placed under the District Leader for the district of Brandenburg.

The Nazi regime, however, made several changes in the province. Although there were few basic changes in the structure of the administration, the Chief President received broadened powers, as did the two Regional Presidents of the regional districts Potsdam and Frankfort. The province was organized as the district Kurmark for the purposes of Nazi party administration. The only territorial change was the addition of the counties of Schwerin, Meseritz, and a portion of the county of Bomst, which were added to the regional district of Frankfort as the result of the liquidation of the old province of *Grenzmark,* Posen-West Prussia; the latter had been formed at the conclusion of World War I, when the Imperial Provinces of Posen and West Prussia were ceded to Poland.

The centralization of government under the Nazis brought an amazing extension of administrative controls. Direct national administration, which continued for finance, posts, labor and labor welfare, and railways, was extended to justice, air matters, propaganda, and labor relations. Many of the traditional fields of state administration—police, health, welfare, education, and certain aspects of social insurance—were brought under tight national control. The services and functions of general administration were supplemented by an extensive system of corporate administrations which provided for further regimentation of life within the province.

In all likelihood, the government and administration of the Province of Brandenburg will continue to center about the cities of Berlin, Potsdam, and Frankfort. Although Berlin is of prime importance as the capital city, the other two provincial centers contain clusters of offices of basic and essential services necessary to the life of the province.

RURAL ASPECT

The sandy uplands of Nieder Lausitz and Fläming, and the elevated areas between the Ancient River Valleys and the valleys of the Havel, Spree, Oder, and Warthe, were not exploited by the peasant cultivator on an intensive basis until the German colonization of Brandenburg. Before that time the Slavic shepherds used the grass of the dry sandy plains for their flocks of sheep. Agriculture in the sense of crop production did not begin until the early Middle Ages, for the German peasant had to contend not only with extensive forests, but also with the swampy valleys and Ancient River Valleys. After the fifteenth century the scattered clearings which the earlier Slavic settlers had used for crops were expanded through the clearing of the forests, and the dry sandy open spaces between the woodlands were put under cultivation. Many of the swampy valleys were cleared and drained. Villages grew up on sandy dry areas adjacent to the river valleys or to the lakes which dot the interior of the province. Today, like the rest of East Elbian Germany, the Province of Brandenburg is mainly a rural and agrarian region. Although there is a large amount of manufacturing in the larger towns, about 757,000 individuals are supported by agriculture and forestry. Taking the Province of Brandenburg as a whole, outside of Berlin an unusually large proportion of the population still dwells in small villages close to the soil. In 1933 about 50 per cent of the population lived in villages of less than 2,000 while another 30 per cent dwelt in small towns ranging in size from 2,000 to 20,000. The remaining 20 per cent of the population was concentrated in the larger towns and cities, such as Frankfort, Potsdam, and Brandenburg. The economic support of the villages and small towns comes largely from agriculture, except in the south, where deposits of salt, lignite, limestone, gypsum, alum, and potter's earth, which have been exploited on an expanding scale since the middle of the nineteenth century, have given village and small town economic life a new orientation. Although the soils are poor and the mineral resources limited, the Province of Brandenburg has a more stable rural life and economy than the other areas of Eastern Germany.

Under the Nazis, rural Brandenburg was administered through thirty-one county administrations, each consisting of a County Manager, assisted by a county committee and a county assembly, who headed both state administration and county self-government. The state administration was regulated by the County Constitutions of 1825, 1872, 1881, and the Nazi Ordinances of 1933; while the county administrative structure, which was abolished by the Nazis, was regulated by the County Constitution of 1872 and 1881 and the liberalizing ordinances of the Republic. The villages of the Province of Brandenburg, which were once administered under the Rural Village and Town Constitution of 1872, followed the German Municipal Code after 1935.

Although the area of the province is small, there is some significant variation in its surface features. It may be divided into two main agrarian regions, the northern lowlands and the southern uplands. First, the river lowland area between the Elbe and the Oder, which embraces most of central and northern Brandenburg, is crossed by the broad and formerly marshy Ancient River Valleys which are now drained and converted into fields and meadowland; the province consists, also, of higher areas of ground moraine covered with relatively fertile sandy or loamy soils. The valleys divide the Elbe-Oder lowlands into several minor landscape areas, which can be grouped into three zones separated by the broad Ancient River Valleys. North of the ancient valley now traversed by the Rhin and Finow canals, and to the west of the lower Oder Valley is the Prignitz zone with its open rolling country that gives way eastward to the marshland of the Havel Valley separating it from the Ukermark zone. The latter district is relatively well forested and is dotted with lakes and moors. Central Brandenburg embraces the Havelland-Barnim districts lying between the Rhin-Finow Ancient River Valley and the Havel-Spree Ancient River Valley. Away from the broad valleys, the land is open and rolling. East of the Oder the lands of Brandenburg are divided into the northern Neumark and southern Sternberg areas, which are separated by the broad valleys of the Warthe and Netze. These districts, which were the last to be colonized by the Germans, are relatively high in comparison with central Brandenburg. Northern Neumark is open and rolling, much like Pomerania, while Sternberg, which is more hilly than Neumark, is heavily forested. Southward from central Brandenburg between the Spree-Havel Ancient River Valley and the southernmost Ancient River Valley of Brandenburg lie the moderately forested districts of Zauche, Teltow, and the Spreewald. Although these districts have a similar landscape, which owes its character to the Pleistocene glaciation, there are small variations in the pattern of lakeland, forests, and open cultivated plain; these differences, coupled with traditional factors, set them apart from one another.

The western part of the river lowlands, which is drained by the Elbe, enjoys from 255 to 275 days of open weather without frost, while the eastern lowlands of the Oder, which have a much more severe winter, have only from 235 to 255 days of such weather. All of northern and central Brandenburg falls within the sub-Sarmatian climatic zone, which is characterized by a drier and warmer climate than is found in northwestern or southern Germany. The average summer temperature (May to September) ranges between 15 and 16 degrees C. throughout Brandenburg, while average temperature for January in western Brandenburg is about −1 degree C. and −2 degrees C. in eastern Brandenburg. There is considerable variation in the amount of rainfall. The districts of Havelland, Barnim, Zauche, and the Spreewald have about 500-600 mm. of rainfall, while the northwest and north central districts of Prignitz and

Ukermark are more moist, with from 600 to 800 mm. of moisture each year. The region along the lower Oder and the Warthe rivers is extremely dry, with from 400 to 500 mm. of annual rainfall.

These variations of relief, soil, and climate have resulted in a regional variation of crops. Although rye and potatoes are grown throughout Brandenburg, rye is the dominant crop in eastern Prignitz and along the Oder and upper Spree. Wheat is grown particularly in the north central district of Ukermark, along with sugar beets and potatoes. This district has some of the best agricultural land in the province. The Prignitz, Havelland, Barnim, Neumark, and Sternberg districts have moderately good agricultural land. Again rye and potatoes are the major crops, but there are significant variations in crop production. The growth of Berlin as a market for agricultural products has led to the extensive development of dairying and market gardening in its immediate vicinity. These activities are concentrated particularly in the Havel-Spree Ancient River Valley whose reclaimed lands support fertile crop and good meadow.

The Oder Valley is used for growing sugar beets, while much of the upland of Sternberg is devoted to hops. The poor soils of the southern Zauche and Teltow are used largely for rye and potatoes. There is little crop specialization except in those parts adjacent to Berlin. The Spreewald, however, is important for its market gardens and dairy products. The Province of Brandenburg produces some tobacco along the lower Oder and in Ukermark, while grapes are grown for wine on the southern slopes of the hills bordering the Oder near the Silesian border. The climate of Brandenburg is not moist enough for forage crops and pasture, hence cattle raising and dairying are much less important than crop cultivation. The farms of this part of Brandenburg tend to be large, averaging over 100 hectares in size. This is true particularly in the north and northeast. The medium sized farm with 20 to 100 hectares becomes more common in western and central Brandenburg. Large estates, once manors (*Gutshöfe*), are widely scattered throughout the province. The larger farms are almost universally mechanized. The numbers of day laborers required at harvest time constitute the important rural labor problem.

The second main agrarian region lies to the south of the river lowlands of central Brandenburg where the land rises into the hills of Fläming and Nieder Lausitz, which separate the Brandenburg lowlands from the rich agricultural lands of Central Germany. These hills, which constitute a vast terminal moraine left behind by the last glaciation of the North German Plain, are covered with dry, unproductive, and infertile sandy soils which support a cover of heath and forest. The few fertile areas are used for the cultivation of rye and potatoes; and the wide stretches of heath and rough pasture are used for sheep grazing. The wool of Nieder Lausitz has long supported an extensive home textile industry. By working in the forests, the farmers of this area further supplement their meager incomes; the average farm is small, ranging between five and twenty hectares.

About 53 per cent of the land area of Brandenburg is devoted to cultivated fields and pasture. Although the major emphasis is placed upon cereals and root crops, fruit and vegetables are raised in surprising amounts and there are considerable quantities of hemp, flax, hops, and tobacco raised each year. Brandenburg has surplusses of rye and potatoes for export to Berlin and other parts of the Reich. There are deficits, however, in wheat, barley, oats, and corn. The Province of Brandenburg is also dependent upon other areas of the Reich for cattle and pigs, although there is considerable surplus production of sheep and wool for export. The following figures for land utilization given below (in hectares) indicate the amount and types of land available for agriculture in the province.

LAND UTILIZATION (HECTARES)

Cultivated Land		1,499,100
Grain	932,000	
Legumes	45,700	
Root Crops	406,200	
Green Vegetables	12,700	
Industrial Crops	11,800	
Fodder Crops	91,700	
Small Gardens		49,200
Meadow		363,700
Pasture		97,000
Orchards		8,300
Vineyards		30
Forests		1,342,800
Waste Land		114,900
Houses and Barns		58,300
Roads and Parks		256,300

Of the 53 per cent of the land of the Province of Brandenburg devoted to agrarian activity, 40 per cent is devoted to crop cultivation and 13 per cent to pastoral activities. The remaining land is divided between forests (36 per cent) and waste land (11 per cent).

The forests occupy a considerable proportion of the province. The central and southern portions of Brandenburg are largely covered by pine which grows on the poorer sandy soils. The alder is common in the swampy river valleys, as are stands of oak in the western part of the province. The northern part of Brandenburg also has extensive and continuous stands of pine, but the beech, hornbeam, and oak are also found. The forest land is owned by a variety of interests. The state owns about 471,800 hectares, or about 35 per cent of the total forest area. This land is administered through 78 state forest reserves. Over one-half of the remaining forest land is held by private forest interests, while the remaining areas are owned by county and municipal governments.

The people of rural Brandenburg may be divided into the East Elbian *Märkische* group of central, northern, and eastern Brandenburg, the Upper Saxon group of the southwest, the East Middle German group of the southeast, and the Lower Saxon group of the west. To these groups one must add the Slavic Wends on the Upper Spree. The present pattern of rural distribution of peoples came about largely as a result of the accidents of migration, though the immigration of serfs from many parts of the Reich and refugees from the Netherlands and France during and after the Reformation and Thirty Years' War introduced many inharmonious elements into the pattern of colonization.

The round (*Rundling*) type of village of the earlier Slavic occupation of Brandenburg is found in the northwestern part of the province, where it was taken over by the German settlers. In central and eastern Brandenburg the more common form is the colonial *Strassendorf,* consisting of houses and public buildings situated on a long street. Some houses are of the Lower Saxon style, characterized by a single building of brick and timber sheltering a barn and living quarters, while others are of the Middle German style, consisting of a separate dwelling with two or three barns located on a farmyard square. Both kinds of villages are found in the southern hills of Fläming and Nieder Lausitz.

The villages of Brandenburg are small with a population ranging in size from 200 to 1,600. The estates, which were widely distributed throughout the province and particularly common in north and northeast Brandenburg, consisted of a manor house and a group of near-by barns and row houses for workers.

The area is hard to characterize from the point of view of folk culture because of the mixed background of the people. There is, however, a considerable peasant insistence upon traditional rights and ancient privileges, which go back to the early Middle Ages. The repression of the peasantry in early modern times has overlaid the earlier independent spirit with a feeling of subservience. The folk arts of the area are somewhat better developed than in adjacent Mecklenburg and Pomerania because Brandenburg, fortunately, has a more substantial peasantry. The greater proportion of the modern rural population, however, has given up its old local and particularistic ways for what might be called the German way.

Urban Aspect

The cities of Brandenburg are small in size and population in comparison with those of the western Prussian provinces. The three largest cities, except for Berlin—Brandenburg, Potsdam, and Frankfort—are situated on the main east-west land and water routes. The city of Brandenburg, which with Potsdam was among the first cities to be established in the province, has been an important market center serving the Havelland area since the days when it was the capital of the Margraviate of Brandenburg. Potsdam remained unimportant until the seventeenth century when the Great Elector made it one of the residences of the Hohenzollern family. Under the Empire it bulked very large in social and political importance, although it was soon overshadowed by its great neighbor, Berlin. Frankfort, established by Franconian merchants in the thirteenth century, is the major center of east central Brandenburg.

The seven remaining cities of the province, which were for the most part established in the course of the twelfth and thirteenth centuries, have been important market centers since the Middle Ages. These cities remained small in size until the late nineteenth century, when the German industrial revolution brought an influx of population through the development of small manufacturing establishments. Today, they have an important economic function as regional centers for trade and industry. While Brandenburg and Frankfort serve west central and east central Brandenburg respectively, Landsberg is the market town for the northeastern district of Neumark. The northern districts of Ukermark and Prignitz are served by the cities of Eberswalde, Rathenow, and Wittenberge. The small commercial and manufacturing towns of Cottbus on the Spree, and Guben and Forst on the Neisse, tributary of the Oder, serve the hilly districts of Fläming and Nieder Lausitz. The economic life of these regional centers and their hinterland is oriented toward Greater Berlin which is situated in the center of the province. About 20 per cent of the population of Brandenburg was concentrated in these towns and cities.

The ten larger cities of the Province of Brandenburg were organized as city counties. Under the Nazis, municipal government and administration followed the national pattern laid down by the German Municipal Code of 1935. There was a chief mayor, who was responsible to the Regional President, for each of the city counties. The democratic features of city government and administration, which were provided by the Stein Constitution of 1808, the City Constitutions of 1831 and 1853, and the liberal measures of the Weimar period, were swept away by the Nazis.

The Province of Brandenburg and Berlin constitute a distinct economic area which is linked together by intimate economic ties and interrelationships. In addition to the cultivation of rye and potatoes, the economic life of Brandenburg is based upon the exploitation of lignite and upon the trade and manufacturing enterprises of the larger towns and cities of the province. While its economy is oriented toward, and dominated by, the great city of Berlin, industries and manufacturing establishments of cities like Brandenburg, Frankfort, and Cottbus have played their part in the economic life of the province—a part made possible by the expansion of transportation facilities during the late nineteenth century. Without this expansion, the impetus of the industrial revolution would have had little effect, and the towns and cities of Brandenburg would have remained small market towns dependent upon a limited rural hinterland. In order to understand the economic life of urban Brandenburg, one must examine the resources, industries, commerce, and transportation facilities of the province.

Although the city of Berlin and the Province of Brandenburg have many closely coordinated economic ties and affiliations, the vast difference between the essentially urban problems faced by Greater Berlin and the rural problems of the province was fully realized by the Nazis when they placed the province of Brandenburg under a separate provincial planning association. The counties of Hoyerswerda and Rathenburg of the western Province of Silesia were also placed under this association, because their lignite fields are utilized in the production of electrical power destined for Brandenburg. The importance of Berlin in relation to Brandenburg was recognized, for the Economic Chamber for Brandenburg, serving as a coordinating agency for all functional and territorial economic organizations, was centered in Berlin.

Many of the industries of the Brandenburg area owe their remarkable development to the introduction of the briquetting press in the middle of the last century which made possible the extensive use of lignite. The lignite deposits of Brandenburg, which are covered by a thin mantle of glacial material and are easily mined by surface stripping, are widely distributed throughout the province. The major lignite deposits are situated in the southeastern portion of the Province of Brandenburg and extend northward along both sides of the Oder and eastward on both sides of the Warthe. A few minor deposits are located in the northwest district of Prignitz. The Brandenburg lignite has a high bitumen content, making it especially useful to the chemical industry which uses it for the production of oil, tar, gas, and wax. It is also used as a substitute for coal. The real development of lignite came in the twentieth century, particularly after World War I, when the loss of the coal in the Upper Silesian area to Poland, brought about a more extensive exploitation of the lignite fields for the production of electrical power.

Important lignite electrical power stations, vital to the industries of the towns of Brandenburg and Berlin, were located at Finkenheerd, Lauta, and Trattendorf, whose high tension lines connected them with the cities of the eastern State of Saxony and Greater Berlin, where there were several major power plants. Other high tension lines reached out to connect with the smaller hydroelectrical power stations at Deichow (the largest such plant north of the Danube), Steinbusch, Guben, and Forst in the southeast, and the small coal or diesel plants of north Brandenburg. The electrical power system of the Province of Brandenburg was dominated by the *Märkisches Elektrizitätswerk AG* (Berlin), the largest German utility company. It was owned jointly by the Province of Brandenburg, the Province of Pomerania, and the state of Mecklenburg. It had full control of the production and distribution of electrical power down to the smallest consumer in the Province of Brandenburg, except for a few county and municipally owned and operated power systems. The only other important natural resources are salt and clay. Salt was mined near Sperenberg in the foothills of Nieder Lausitz, while excellent potter's clay was obtained near Berlin.

In the field of light manufacturing the province was important for textiles and machinery. The textile industry was concentrated in the southeastern part of Brandenburg in Cottbus, Guben, and Forst, where it developed as a craft and home industry during the late Middle Ages on the basis of wool grown in the rolling Nieder Lausitz area. The textile industry had been industrialized and wool gave way to cotton imported from overseas. Smaller textile plants were located at Wittenberge, Neuruppin, and Perleberg in northwest Brandenburg and at Landsberg in the northeast. There were several textile mills in the vicinity of the city of Brandenburg. Despite the absence of hard coal and iron resources, the Province of Brandenburg had an important metallurgical and machine industry. The cities of Brandenburg, Wittenberge, Eberswalde, Landsberg, Frankfort, and Guben had important machinery plants. The Opelwerke and the Brennaborwerke, which manufacture automobiles, had plants at Brandenburg; Wittenberge was important for sewing machines; and Eberswalde, for iron foundries. The city of Guben in the heart of the textile manufacturing area was noted for textile machinery. The chemical industry of Brandenburg was limited to the few small plants at Frankfort and Potsdam. The leather industry was widely distributed in the small towns of Nieder Lausitz, while the wood and food products industries had a province-wide distribution. There were also a number of specialized industries with limited distribution. Chocolate was manufactured at Cottbus; Frankfort and Brandenburg had important ceramic works. Rathenow was a small but important center for optical goods. This brief survey of the industries of Brandenburg, emphasizing the importance of textiles and machinery, to which might be added the wood industry, indicates that, although the province was handicapped by the lack of raw material and resources, lighter industries dependent in part on raw material shipped in from other parts of the Reich have developed on a moderate scale.

The Province of Brandenburg has a key position on the major land and water routes serving northeastern Germany. The backbone of the road transportation system is a circular road connecting Frankfort, Eberswalde, Rathenow, Brandenburg, Cottbus, Guben, and Frankfort. This road is intersected by major north-south roads running from Halle, Dresden, and Breslau in the south via Berlin to Stettin, Stralsund, and Hamburg in the north. A major east-west road crosses the province running from Frankfort via Berlin and Potsdam to Brandenburg, from where it continues westward to Magdeburg and Bruns-wick. In addition to these major national arteries, there is an extensive network of local roads within the province. The major provincial roads were main-tained by the Provincial Corporation and the local county roads were under the county Road Master. Under the Nazi regime, the normal road system was sup-plemented by the national super-highways.

The major rail lines of Brandenburg radiate from Greater Berlin, whence lines run to Potsdam, Brandenburg, and Magdeburg, to Wittenberg and Ham-burg, to Eberswalde and Stettin, to Frankfort and Posen, and to Guben and Breslau. The railroads, which were owned and operated by the national gov-ernment, were under the national Ministry of Transportation. In the Province of Brandenburg, they were operated by the National Railway Directorates of Berlin and Frankfort.

The river and canal system of Brandenburg links the major cities of the province with the Rhine-Ruhr and the Silesian heavy industrial regions. The important east-west Mittelland canal system crosses the Province of Branden-burg by means of the Planer canal, Havel and Spree rivers, Friedrich-Wilhelm canal, and the Oder and Warthe rivers. This section of the Mittelland canal links the Elbe and Oder rivers, giving Brandenburg access to the ports of Stet-tin and Hamburg and the industrial areas of central Germany, the Ruhr, and Silesia. The Finow canal runs from the Havel via Eberswalde to the Oder River, while the Havel-Elde canal links western Brandenburg with Mecklen-burg and the port of Wismar. The province does not have an adequate air serv-ice; there are no major national or international airports outside Berlin.

The Province of Brandenburg was commercially and financially oriented toward Berlin. The two small market and banking centers of Brandenburg and Frankfort were relatively unimportant in the commercial and financial activi-ties of the province in comparison with Greater Berlin's activities. These two cities, like Cottbus in the southeast, Landsberg in the northeast, and Ebers-walde in the north, are regional commercial centers doing business with an agrarian hinterland. In terms of rail freight traffic, lignite, stone and clay, and agricultural products were the main industrial resources produced and shipped from the province to other parts of the Reich, whereas coal and metal to sup-port the local metallurgical and machine industry were the main products brought in from adjacent areas. The lignite of the Province of Brandenburg was shipped to adjacent Lower Silesia and Pomerania; coal was brought in from the Ruhr and Silesia. There was also a limited trade in machinery and machine tools. Western Brandenburg was oriented toward Brunswick and Hanover, while southeast Brandenburg traded with the machine shops of Central Germany. There was a lively trade in textiles between the state of Saxony, the Province of Silesia and the Province of Brandenburg, but this was strongly conditioned by the influence of the Berlin textile and clothing markets. The overseas trade of the province went by rail or river and canal to Stettin. Only a limited amount of the commerce went out via the port of Hamburg.

The banking and credit institutions of the Province of Brandenburg ranged from branches of the great commercial banks of Berlin, which were mainly interested in investments of the industrial type, to the local county and municipal mortgage and savings banks. The provincially owned banks and financial institutions were concentrated in Berlin. They included the *Brandenburgische Provinzialbank und Girozentrale,* the *Brandenburgischer Sparkassen und Giroverband,* the *Stadtschaft der Provinz Brandenburg,* the *Märkische Landschaft,* and the *Landschaftliche Bank für Brandenburg.* The operations of these banks were supplemented by those of the main branches of the *Reichsbank* at Brandenburg and Frankfort. There were a great number of small offices of the National Bank scattered throughout the province. The provincial government operated a life insurance and a fire insurance organization. The province was served by the Berlin Stock Exchange.

In 1933, 33 per cent of the urban population or 910,000 individuals were in the industries, manufacturing establishments, and craft fields, while only 14 per cent or 387,000 individuals were occupied in trade and transportation activities. Another 7 per cent of the population were engaged in professional work or public service. The resultant class structure has several interesting features. The working class was the largest proportionally in northeast Germany, constituting about 44 per cent of the population. The white collar class, 7.5 per cent, and the civil servant group, 5.3 per cent, were quite small in comparison with those of other states and provinces. The upper class, which accounted for 16 per cent of the population, was small in comparison with that of other Northeast German provinces.

While the province as a whole is overshadowed by the great urban agglomeration of Berlin, it is nevertheless a land of small regional centers. To the west, it looks toward the large city of Brandenburg and the smaller market towns of Wittenberge and Rathenow and the residence and garrison city of Potsdam. The city of Brandenburg, which was founded by Germans moving eastward from Magdeburg in the course of the tenth century, was originally a small Slavic settlement. The Altstadt on the right bank of the Havel and Neustadt which has developed on the left bank, embrace a third district, an island in the Havel, the most distinguishing feature of which is the Brandenburger *Domkirche.* This church dates back to the days when Brandenburg was the center for the first bishop of the German frontier. Brandenburg is also historically important, for it was the first capital of the Brandenburg Mark. It became a thriving commercial town with a busy textile and machinery industry.

Potsdam, which is located to the east of Brandenburg, also on the Havel, was originally a Slavic fishing village named Poztupimi. Although Potsdam remained a village community until early modern times, it grew rapidly during the seventeenth and eighteenth centuries, owing to the patronage of the Great Elector and Frederick the Great. Until World War I, it was one of the principal residences of the Kings of Prussia. The rulers have left behind a legacy of palaces (Sansouci and Friedrichskron), parks and pleasure grounds (Lustgarten, Wilhelmsplatz, and Plantage), and churches (*Nikolaikirche, Garnisonkirche, Friedenskirche*). Potsdam may properly be called the German Versailles. The nineteenth century brought the addition of some industrial and commercial establishments. It is the seat of the regional district of Potsdam and the center for a number of national administrative and military agencies. Potsdam under the Republic and the Third Reich remained a garrison and governmental city, although the kings and emperors have departed.

Eastern Brandenburg and the small market towns of Cottbus, Guben, Forst, and Landsberg are oriented toward Frankfort, the district seat of the regional district of Frankfort. These towns, which were settled by later German colonists pushing eastward during the thirteenth century, have been important market centers ever since. Frankfort, which was founded by Franconian merchants from the Rhineland, has long played an important role in the life of the German frontier. During the Middle Ages it was a member of the Hanseatic League and the home of the University of Frankfort, an important center of learning for eastern Germany until 1811, when it was transferred to Breslau. Although the city of Frankfort suffered severely during the Thirty Years' War and the wars of Frederick the Great, the nineteenth century brought a revival and expansion of its commercial prosperity.

Chapter 7

THE PROVINCE OF POMERANIA*

The Prussian Province of Pomerania is situated along the Baltic Sea in northeastern Germany just to the north of Brandenburg, between the so-called Polish Corridor and Mecklenburg. It is divided into three major areas from west to east, western Pomerania, the Lower Oder Valley, and eastern Pomerania. Western Pomerania, west of the Oder Valley, forms a part of the Mecklenburg lake plateau, a ground moraine zone, cut by the low marshy valleys of the Peene, Ücker, and Randow rivers, which flow into the Baltic Sea. The coast line is very irregular, and off shore lie the sandy islands of Usedom and Wollin, which block the shallow and funnel-shaped estuary of the Oder River. The larger island of Rügen is separated from the coast of western Pomerania by a narrow channel known as the Strela Sund. Western Pomerania is separated from eastern or Hinterpommern by the broad valley of the lower Oder River, which empties into a large bay separated from the Pomeranian Bay (*Pommersche Bucht*) by the islands of Usedom and Wollin.

Eastern Pomerania consists of ground moraine country which gives way in the southern part to higher end-moraines rising to several hundred feet. The eastern part of the province, which is sometimes designated as the Pomeranian Sea Plain (*Pommersche Seenplatte*), is characterized by a poor drainage system which has given rise to numerous swamps, marshes, and inland lakes. The coast of East Pomerania, east of the estuary of the Oder, is smooth in outline and is bordered by extensive sand dunes. Several small, non-navigable streams —the Rega, the Persante, the Wipper, the Stolpe, the Lupow, and the Leba—rise in the southern terminal moraines and flow northwestward across East Pomerania to the Baltic Sea. Most of these rivers end in small coastal lakes, which are separated from the Baltic by narrow strips of land. The southern part of East Pomerania is drained by small streams which flow into the Netze River, a tributary of the Warthe.

The Province of Pomerania is essentially an impoverished agrarian region

* German spelling—Pommern.

271

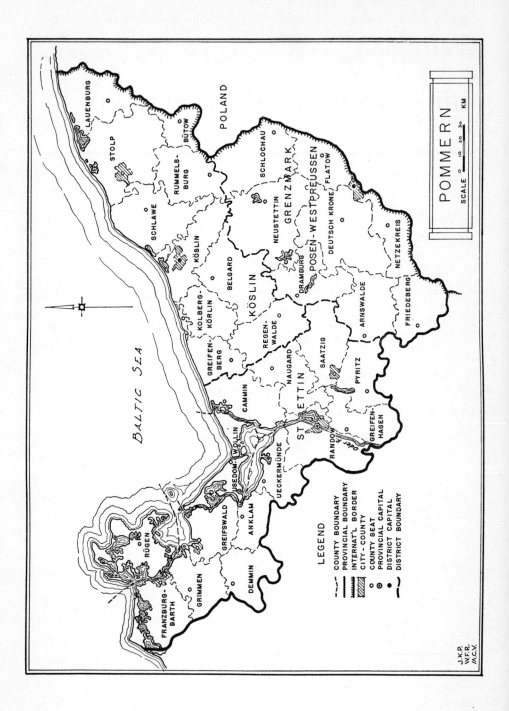

with a sparse population consisting of peasants who work for a small landowning class. The towns are small and few in number. Only the port city of Stettin on the lower Oder River is important, and it owes its significance not to Pomerania, but to its commercial hinterland which extends to Berlin and Upper Silesia. The small port towns of Greifswald, Stralsund, and Kolberg, which are located in the western and central portion of the province, are relatively unimportant, while the inland market towns of Köslin, Stolp, and Schneidemühl serve the rural areas of eastern Pomerania.

At the beginning of our era the population of the Province of Pomerania was German of the East German type, consisting of Gothic peoples who were already migrating southeastward to the Balkans. After the East Germans moved out of Pomerania, Slavic peoples from the basin of the Vistula and upper Dnieper drove westward across the Oder to the Elbe, leaving Pomerania in the hands of the Slavic Wilzi and Pomerani tribes. By the time of Charlemagne (A.D. 800), the term *Pomore* or Pommern ("On the Sea") was being applied to the coastal region between the lower Oder and the lower Vistula. Slavic Pomerania was ruled by native princes, who were dependent upon the Kingdom of Poland during the tenth and eleventh centuries. Toward the end of the twelfth century, the princes were admitted to the Holy Roman Empire and granted the rank of duke. With the advent of German political control came the rapid Germanization of this Slavic area. Germans from west of the Elbe poured eastward to take over the land of the Slavs for agrarian settlements. In spite of the extensive settlement of Germans in Pomerania since the twelfth century, the basic Slavic stock survived, which, although now Germanized, still constitutes the underlying population group. The Pomeranian dialect of the modern province is of the East Elbian type, but in many ways it differs from East Elbian (*Plattdeutsch*) Low German because of the survival of elements of the earlier Slavic language. The dialect difference between East Pomerania where the Slavic background is apparent, and West Pomerania, where a purer form of East Elbian is spoken, can be accounted for in terms of the more intensive settlement of the west by German peoples. Today, however, standard German is spoken in most towns and cities and is becoming increasingly common in the rural areas owing to the influence of public education and the radio. The province is predominantly Protestant. In 1933 there were 2,081,000 Protestants and only 146,000 Catholics. The Jewish population, which was extremely small, numbering about 9,000, was concentrated in the larger towns and cities of the province.

In 1933 the Province of Pomerania had a population of 2,268,000 and a population density of fifty-nine individuals per sq. km. Although Pomerania was the second largest of the Prussian provinces, it was very sparsely settled, having the lowest population density of any German administrative area except Mecklenburg. Its population was concentrated in the valley of the lower Oder and along the coast of West Pomerania between Stralsund and Greifswald, where the average density ranged between sixty and eighty per sq. km. The interior of West Pomerania and the coastal portions of East Pomerania had a population density ranging between forty and sixty individuals per sq. km., while the sparsely populated interior of West Pomerania had an average density ranging between twenty and forty.

Historically, the terms West Pomerania and East Pomerania are much more significant than the present administrative designations, for in the twelfth century these areas were ruled by two Slavic princes, who were admitted to the Holy Roman Empire and raised to the dignity of dukes by the emperor Friedrich I, thus marking the beginning of German history in the Province of Pomerania. The medieval development was characterized by endless internal struggles resulting in numerous and frequent subdivisions of the land. The fortunes of the dynasts of Pomerania were made more difficult by the fact that the Electors of Brandenburg claimed to be their feudal superiors. Parts of West Pomerania were held from time to time by the Danes, while the large island of Rügen, which became a part of Pomerania in 1325, had been under the rule of the Princes of Rügen. Although the two duchies were united for a short time during the fourteenth century, thereafter until the early seventeenth century Pomerania was divided between the duchies of West Pomerania and East Pomerania. In 1625 they were united under the rule of Boleslav XIV. Upon his death in 1637 without issue, the Electors of Brandenburg claimed the entire holdings of the old Slavic family by virtue of a family agreement dating back to 1571. The Thirty Years' War interfered with the settlement, during which most of Pomerania was occupied by the Swedes. At the Peace of Westphalia (1648) both the Swedes and Brandenburgers claimed all of Pomerania. Sweden received West Pomerania and Brandenburg got East Pomerania. At the Peace of Stockholm in 1720, Sweden ceded the eastern part of West Pomerania to Prussia; while the general settlement at Vienna following the Napoleonic Wars in 1815 brought the cession of the rest of West Pomerania to the former Electors of Brandenburg, the then Kings of Prussia. Shortly after 1815 the Prussian government established the Province of Pomerania and subdivided it into the regional districts of Stettin, Stralsund, and Köslin.

In 1938, under the Nazis, there were major territorial and administrative reorganizations, the old administrative districts of Stralsund and Stettin being combined to form the administrative district of Stettin. The district of Grenzmark Posen-West Prussia, which was added to the Province of Pomerania at this time, was originally a part of the holdings of the Slavic princes and dukes of Pomerania. During the later Middle Ages, it was held by the Order of the Teutonic Knights and by the Kings of Poland. During the period of great

Polish power in early modern times, all of the district was under Polish rule. In the partition of Poland in 1772, it was annexed by Prussia. This area remained largely under Prussian control despite the temporary revival of the Duchy of Warsaw in Napoleonic times (1807).

After the Treaty of Vienna (1815), the Prussian government organized the northeastern corner of its realm into the provinces of Posen, West Prussia, and East Prussia, with the Grenzmark Posen-West Prussia area falling between the latter two provinces. In 1824 the provinces of West and East Prussia were joined together only to be separated again in 1878. This arrangement lasted until the Treaty of Versailles (1919) when the provinces of Posen and West Prussia were detached from the Reich and given to Poland to provide a corridor to the Baltic Sea. There were two exceptions: first, the territory of the city of Danzig was detached and placed under international control; and secondly, the solidly German portions of western Posen and West Prussia were left within the Reich, where they were organized in 1922 as the Province of Grenzmark Posen-West Prussia.

In 1938, there was also a territorial reorganization which affected changes in the administrative areas of eastern Pomerania and eastern Brandenburg. The former skeleton province of Grenzmark Posen-West Prussia was liquidated. The counties of Schlochau, Flatow, Deutsch-Krone, and Netzekreis, and the city county of Schneidemühl were added to the city counties of Dramburg and Neustettin, formerly belonging to the governmental district of Köslin, and to the counties of Answalde and Friedeberg, formerly belonging to the district of Frankfort of the Province of Brandenburg, to form the new Pomeranian administrative district (*Regierungsbezirk*) of Grenzmark Posen-West Prussia. At the same time the counties of Greifenberg and Regenwalde were taken from the regional district of Stettin and added to the regional districts of Köslin. Other parts of the same reorganization affected the provinces of Brandenburg and Silesia. In Pomerania, however, this administrative reorganization had resulted in the creation of three substantially new administrative districts: Stettin, Köslin, and Grenzmark Posen-West Prussia with its seat at Schneidemühl.

The administration of the Province of Pomerania continued to follow the regular pattern of Prussian administration and was headed by a Chief President who resided at Stettin. The provincial administration and self-government were regulated by the Provincial Constitution of 1823, 1871, 1881, and the minor republican and major Nazi laws. Much of the administration was carried out by the District Presidents of the administrative districts of Stettin, Köslin, and Grenzmark Posen-West Prussia.

The work of the general administration was supplemented by special and technical services under direct national control. During the imperial period only the state administered courts, railways, and mining offices and the nationally operated postal system lay outside the scope of the general administration of the province. As in the other Prussian provinces, justice was administered by the Prussian Ministry of Justice until the advent of the Nazis. Civilian trials were handled by the State Supreme Court of Stettin, the Collegiate Courts of First and Second Instance of Greifswald, Köslin, Stargard, Stettin, and Stolp, and the numerous local Courts of First Instance. The national postal system in the province was under the Chief Postal Directorate (under the Empire) or National Postal Directorates (under the Republic and the Third Reich) of Stettin and Köslin. National regulations for trade and industry, weights and measures, social insurance and welfare, public health, and the collection of imperial revenues were, as usual, administered upon delegation from the Reich.

Under the Republic there was a further extension of direct national administration to finance, railways, unemployment insurance and employment, and labor welfare. Financial control was carried out through the State Finance Office at Stettin, and its local finance offices and main customs offices. National Construction Offices were located at Schneidemühl, Stettin, and Stolp. The national railways in the province were operated under the National Railway Director of Stettin and Frankfort-on-the-Oder. The State Labor Court of Pomerania at Stettin and the main Welfare Office at Brandenburg-Pomerania (Berlin) handled the labor problems. Certain aspects of welfare, social insurance, health, trade and industry, and labor, which were subject to national legislation, were administered upon delegation by the province. The economic life of the province, which was subject to limited provincial control, was organized under local branches of the German Diet of Industry and Trade, the Diet of Crafts and Industry, the National Corporation of the German Handicrafts, the German Agricultural Council, and the Trade Unions.

The Province of Pomerania has long been a stronghold of conservative and even reactionary forces. During the Empire, when the *Reichstag* gave a fair picture of political feelings, the province went conservative, except in the area about Stettin. During the Republic, it was a stronghold of the German National People's party. No other district in Germany cast so many Nationalist votes, and no other province gave such a large percentage of its total vote to this party of Junkers and Industrialists. The Social Democrats were a poor second, and, regionally, they drew most of their strength from the urban area about Stettin. Beginning with the election of 1930, the whole province went over to Hitler, and by 1932 not even Hindenburg could carry it against Hitler for President. The Pomeranians plumped for *Der Führer* with a 52.6 per cent vote; only the cities of Stettin, Köslin, and Kolberg remained faithful to the hero of Tannenberg. In the two *Reichstag* elections of 1932, the Nazis received 48 and 43 per cent of the total vote respectively. In this Nazi wave, the Nationalist vote dropped below the Social Democratic vote, but it was not submerged until after Hitler came into power, and it remained an important factor in local politics. Adding the Nationalist to the Nazi vote, there was an overwhelming majority in the province opposed to the Republic. In the city of Stettin and in the county of Randow, there was substantial Socialist and Communist strength, but elsewhere reactionary politics prevailed and made possible the Hitler victory. Excepting only the Province of Schleswig-Holstein, Pomerania was Hitler's strongest and most consistent supporter. In this predominantly rural and frontier area, Germany's most extreme form of politics found fertile soil for development.

The Province of Pomerania was constituted as the district of Pomerania for purposes of party administration. The district headquarters, located at Stettin, were organized along functional lines as in other provinces.

National Administrative Controls and Organization

The Nazi regime extended national administrative controls. Justice, air matters, propaganda, and labor relations were placed under national control.

An extensive system of corporate administration provided for the total regimentation of life within the province. Stettin has always been the major center of general and special administration in the Province of Pomerania. It was the seat of the provincial government and the administration of the district of Stettin, where the regional offices for most of the special and technical services were also concentrated. The district centers of Schneidemühl and Köslin ranked next in administrative importance.

Rural Aspect

The pattern of settlement and rural life of the Province of Pomerania goes back to the Middle Ages and must be regarded as a product of the German colonization of the twelfth to fourteenth centuries. During the period of Slavic occupation, the land had been used largely for pastoral activities with agriculture playing only a secondary role. The German colonist from beyond the Elbe introduced large-scale agriculture and village life, with the result that the large estates developed during the later Middle Ages and the early modern period at the expense of the once independent peasantry. In recent years, almost 40 per cent of the population of the Province of Pomerania was engaged in agriculture and forestry. Taking the province as a whole, a surprisingly large number of individuals dwelt in small agrarian villages close to the soil. In 1933 about 50 per cent of the population lived in small villages of less than 2,000, while another 7 per cent dwelt in small towns with populations ranging between 2,000 and 5,000.

The general administration of the Province of Pomerania centered in the city of Stettin, the provincial capital, and in the other two district capitals of

Köslin and Schneidemühl. The day-to-day administration of rural Pomerania was carried on in the thirty-two counties into which the administrative districts were divided. These counties were headed by County Managers (*Landräte*) who served as agents both of the central government and of local self-government. The state administration was regulated by the County Constitutions of 1825, 1872/1881, and the Nazi laws of 1933, while the county corporate structure, which was abolished by the Nazis, was regulated by the ordinances of 1872/1881 and the liberal laws of the Republic. The villages, which were once governed by the Constitution for Rural Villages and Towns of 1872, followed the German Municipal Code after 1935.

The Province of Pomerania may be divided into three distinct agricultural areas. The humid-cool coastal zone is important for pastoral activities, while the interior portions of East Pomerania, with its drier, warmer climate, are more favorable for crop cultivation. The lower Oder, which has the best soils, constitutes the most important agrarian area. The moist coastal zone has 60 to 80 cm. of rainfall each year, while the interior portions of the province generally receive 50 to 60 cm. of moisture. Although the average January temperature for the whole area ranges between 0 and −2 degrees C., growing colder as one moves eastward, there is a definite difference in summer temperatures between the northern and southern portions. The coastal area enjoys a cool summer with the temperatures ranging between 16 and 18 degrees C., while the interior areas have an average July temperature ranging between 18 and 20 degrees C.

The soils of Pomerania are of the clayey loam type, with sandy and gravelly areas becoming more common in the southern parts of the province. Most of the soils of the province might be classified as brown forest type, though the lower Oder Valley has several patches of black and brown steppe soils, which are extremely fertile. Areas of damp moor soil are widely scattered throughout the coastal zone, which, with its rolling landscape dotted with numerous lakes, is given over to pasture and fodder crops that are favored by the moist cool climate and the clayey loam soils.

The agrarian activities were cattle and horse raising and dairying. Butter and cheese were the chief dairy products because of the distance from urban markets. The rye and wheat crops of the coastal area were unimportant, although coastal Pomerania once exported a considerable quantity of soft wheat to the British Isles. The rolling country of the interior portions of East Pomerania had an agrarian economy typical of most of East Elbian Germany. This area, which was characterized by the succession of low pine-clad terminal moraines, level cultivated land, pasture, lakes, and swamps, was important for the production of rye and potatoes. Occasional loam areas were used for wheat. Although there was some livestock raising, the dry-warm climate favors crop cultivation. Transportation difficulties and unfavorable market conditions led the small farmers of the area to the production of hogs, and turned the attention of the large estates to the distilling of alcohol; many of the small rural towns, however, had starch and potato-meal factories. The Oder Valley area, with its rich meadowland and its patches of fertile steppe soils, raised wheat, barley, sugar beets, and some livestock.

With the exception of the rich farming area located along the lower Oder, most of the Province of Pomerania is moderately good for agriculture. This statement would not have been true a hundred years ago; but since the middle of the nineteenth century, the reclamation of the moors and swamps has increased the area for crop cultivation, and the introduction of deep plowing and scientific fertilizing has brought wide areas of poor soil under cultivation. Taking the province as a whole, it produced surpluses of rye, potatoes, wheat, barley, and oats. There were also surpluses of cattle and pigs; the only agricultural deficit was wheat. The figures for land utilization (given below in hectares) indicate the amounts and types of land available for agriculture in 1933.

Cultivated Land		1,799,100
Grain	1,096,000	
Legumes	64,000	
Root Crops	469,000	
Green Vegetables	2,600	
Industrial Crops	6,500	
Fodder Crops	161,000	
Small Gardens		30,500
Pasture and Meadow		490,000
Orchards		1,900
Forests		1,016,000
Waste Land		138,000
Houses and Barns		48,200
Roads and Parks		236,000

About 62 per cent of the land of the Province of Pomerania was devoted to agrarian activity, with 49 per cent devoted to crop cultivation and 13 per cent to pastures and livestock. The remaining land was divided between forests (26 per cent) and waste land (12 per cent).

The province has a moderate forest cover, beech in western West Pomerania, with some pine and occasional oak in the east. Alder is common in the swampy areas, while birch grows in the drier parts of the moraine country. The forest land was owned by a variety of interests. The state of Prussia owned about 267,-000 hectares, about 26 per cent of the total forest area, which was administered through forty-eight state forest reserves under the ultimate jurisdiction of the

National Forest Office in Berlin. About 40 per cent of the forest land was held by private interests, while the remaining areas are owned by county and municipal governments.

The rural Pomeranians, with their East Elbian dialect and their orthodox Lutheran Protestant religion, constituted a dependent peasant group living for the most part on large estates. The Pomeranian manorial estate, which generally embraced from 600 to 1,000 hectares, centered about the home of the landowner, frequently located in a forest. The barns and the long row houses of the permanent farm workers and the barracks for the seasonal workers were located near-by, while the fields and pasture surrounded the entire establishment. The laborer (*Inste*), living in a rented house on the large estates received a small plot of land for a garden and most of his wages in kind. Mechanized agriculture was practiced in this part of the Reich, because of the large scale of operations made possible by the large capitalization of the estates. Although large estates predominated, there were many moderate-sized farms of 20 to 100 hectares, and a number of smaller farms in the Oder Valley and Stolp areas.

The independent peasants of the villages dwelt in brick and timber houses of the Low Saxon type, with a barn with stables and dwelling quarters covered by one roof. In West Pomerania these houses were situated in small villages (70 to 200 inhabitants) of the single row (*Strassendörfer*) type, while in East Pomerania, where the villages were somewhat larger with a population ranging between 200 and 600 inhabitants, the settlements were of two types. The *Marschhufendorf,* which was common along the Pomeranian coast, was built along an elevated strip of land traversed by a single road. The single row type which was common in West Pomerania, was also typical in southern East Pomerania. The interior portion of eastern Pomerania also had a number of isolated homesteads belonging to independent peasant cultivators. The rural people of the province were politically and socially conservative. Their life was stolid and routinized, and they found enjoyment in heavy eating and drinking.

URBAN ASPECT

Most of the modern towns and cities of the Province of Pomerania were established by German colonists during the twelfth and thirteenth centuries on the ruins of earlier Slavic settlements. The coastal towns of Stettin, Stralsund, Greifswald, and Kolberg, which are located on the major east-west coastal road running from Hamburg via Lübeck and Rostock to Danzig, developed rapidly on the basis of Baltic trade during the days of the Hanseatic League. Stettin, which is located near the mouth of the Lower Oder, a vital river artery in the commercial life of eastern Germany, was the dominant city of the Pomeranian area. Its central location on the Oder astride the major east-west and north-south routes cutting across the Province of Pomerania, coupled with its position as the most important Baltic Sea port of the German Reich, made it the logical political as well as the economic center of the life of the province. The western or *Vorpommern* portion of the province was served by Greifswald and Stralsund; while the small town of Stargard, on the eastern margins of the broad valley of the lower Oder, served southern Pomerania. Stolp, the second largest Pomeranian town, was the economic center of the northeastern portion of the province, although Köslin, which is more centrally located, was the administrative center for East Pomerania. The Grenzmark Posen-West Prussia area, in southeastern Pomerania on the edge of the Polish Corridor, looked toward the old frontier town of Schneidemühl, an important administrative, manufacturing, commercial, and transportation center. The eight larger cities of Pomerania contained about 25 per cent of the total population of the province.

These cities were organized as city counties. Under the Nazis, municipal government and administration followed the national pattern laid down by the German Municipal Code of 1935. The democratic features of city government and administration, which were provided by the Stein Constitution of 1808, the Constitution for Cities of 1831 and 1853 and the liberal measures of the Weimar period, were swept away by the Nazis.

The Province of Pomerania constituted a distinct economic area tied together by intimate economic interrelations; it was oriented toward the port city of Stettin. This city had wide economic relations which extended to every corner of northeastern Germany, in contrast with most of the other cities of Pomerania (with the possible exception of the small port cities), which had a limited agrarian hinterland and were economically important only as provincial market towns. That the province forms a distinct economic area was recognized by the Nazis when they placed it under one Regional Planning Association and one Economic Office.

The industries were not of the heavy or extractive type. Mineral resources were limited to a few lignite deposits in the Oder Valley. The forests, plus the local flax and wool, supported a number of local manufacturing enterprises. Wood products, including furniture and paper, were produced at Stettin, Köslin, Stolp, and Schneidemühl, while wool and flax textiles were produced at Stargard and Stolp. The cattle raising in coastal Pomerania supported the leather industry at Stargard. It was natural that many of the cities in this agricultural province should have brewing and food processing plants.

The development of the machinery industries resulted from the local demand for agricultural machinery and the modern development of the port towns. These industries were dependent upon supplies of raw material shipped in from Sweden or Upper Silesia. Stettin gradually became one of the important ship-building centers of Germany; automobiles, machinery, and

other metal products were also manufactured there. Other ship-building establishments were located at Greifswald. Stargard, Kolberg, and Stolp had small
machine plants which produced agricultural machinery for the local market.
These industries were supported by a well developed electrical power industry,
which had coal electrical power stations at Stettin, Swinemünde, and Belgard
and water power plants at Stolp and Glambocksee. The power stations at
Stettin and Swinemünde were connected by high tension lines serving all of
western Pomerania, while the latter three stations were producing units within
the power network serving East Pomerania. In brief, most of the industries of
the Province of Pomerania were developed on the basis of local raw materials,
such as, wood, paper, textiles, and leather; or were introduced, as in the case of
agricultural machinery, to meet the needs of the economic life of the province.
The ship-building industry of the port cities had evolved as a result of Baltic
and Oder river trade.

The backbone of the road transportation system is formed by roads radiating from Stettin, which penetrate to every corner of the province. In the east,
roads run from Stettin along the coast to Köslin, Stolp, and Danzig and
through the southern part of East Pomerania to Stargard, Stolp, and Schneidemühl. Roads extend southward from Stettin to Frankfort-on-the-Oder and
Berlin, while others go westward and northwestward to Hamburg, Lübeck,
Rostock, and Stralsund. Aside from these major national roads, there is an extensive network of roads within the province. The major provincial roads were
maintained by the Provincial Corporation, while the local county roads were
under the supervision of the county Road Master. Under the Nazi regime, the
normal road system has been supplemented by the national super-highways.

The major rail lines follow almost the same basic patterns as the road systems. The railroads, which were owned by the national government, were
operated by the German Railroad Company, an integral part of the national
Ministry of Transport. In the Province of Pomerania they were under the
National Railway Directorates of Frankfort-on-the-Oder and Stettin.

The ports of Stettin, Greifswald, Stralsund, and Kolberg have played an
important part in the life of the Province of Pomerania since the late Middle Ages. The port of Stettin consisted of a free harbor and two other harbor
basins, equipped with warehouses, grain elevators, and a number of ship-repair-
ing yards. In the thirties, it handled approximately 6,000,000 metric tons of sea
freight traffic and about 3,500,000 metric tons of river freight traffic each year;
it had excellent connections with other Baltic ports as well as access to the inland waterways of Northeast Germany. The Oder River gave Stettin an excellent connection with the heavy industrial areas of Upper Silesia, while the
Havel-Spree canal provided for connections with Berlin and Central Germany. East Pomerania was served by the small port of Kolberg, while West

Pomerania was served by the old port towns of Greifswald and Stralsund. During the icy winter months these ports were kept open with ice-breakers. Stettin was the major center for air transportation in the Province of Pomerania, although there were minor airports on the islands of Rügen and Usedom.

The commercial and financial life of the province centered in the port city of Stettin, which had developed on the basis of its Oder Valley commercial hinterland as well as the local agrarian and forestry activities of the province. Cities like Stralsund and Greifswald in West Pomerania, Köslin, Kolberg, and Stolp in East Pomerania, and Schneidemühl in southeastern Pomerania must be regarded as regional market towns supported by a limited agricultural hinterland. Agricultural products, lumber, wood products, paper, and textiles were the major commodities produced and shipped from the Province of Pomerania, while coal, stone, and certain agricultural products were brought in from adjacent areas. The limited machinery industry of Pomerania depended upon Berlin, Sweden, and Upper Silesia for raw materials, while in exchange Pomerania gave its dairy and meat supply.

The banking and credit institutions of the province ranged from branches of the great commercial banks of Berlin, which were mainly interested in investments of the industrial type, to the local county and municipal mortgage and savings banks. The operations of these banks were supplemented by those of the branches of the *Reichsbank* at Köslin, Stettin, Stolp, Stralsund, and Schneidemühl. The provincial government operated a life insurance and a fire insurance organization. These enterprises, like the provincially operated banks, were under the Provincial Corporation.

The urban population of the Province of Pomerania was of moderate size in comparison with that of other Prussian provinces. Twenty-three per cent of the population or 536,000 individuals were engaged in industry and crafts, in 1933; while only 14 per cent were employed in transportation and commercial enterprises. Another 7 per cent were engaged in professional work or public service. The resultant class structure had several interesting features. The working class, constituting 43 per cent of the population, was relatively large considering the economic characteristics of this area, while the upper class, forming about 18 per cent of the population, was large for northeastern Germany, although only moderately sized in comparison with the states of southern Germany. The white collar and civil servant groups were small in comparison with those of other Prussian provinces.

Stettin, which was the traditional capital of the province as well as the modern administrative, economic, and cultural center, was established in the Middle Ages by German colonists; the site was, however, occupied earlier by Slavic settlers. During the later Middle Ages, it was not only the residence city of the Pomeranian dukes, but was, also, a member of the Hanseatic League.

Historically it was also interesting as the birthplace of a princess of Anhalt-Zerbst, who became Empress Catherine II of Russia. With its excellent position on the Baltic Sea at the mouth of the commercially important Oder River, it will always be an important Northeast German center. The small port towns of Greifswald and Stralsund in West Pomerania were essentially provincial places, although the former was traditionally important for its university which is the oldest institution of this type in Prussia. Stralsund, which was next to Lübeck in commercial importance during the later Middle Ages, has lost its position in Baltic trade to Stettin. Köslin and Kolberg in East Pomerania were simply provincial towns. Stolp in the northeastern corner of the province was an important center for the agricultural trade. It ranks as the second largest city of Pomerania. Schneidemühl in the southeast was important because of its status as a frontier railroad town on the edge of Polish territory.

Chapter 8

THE PROVINCE OF SILESIA*

Under the Weimar Republic and the Nazis, Silesia was Germany's frontier province. It was a diagonal strip of land with Polish territory on its northeast side and Czech territory on its southwest side. On the northwest, it borders the Province of Brandenburg and the state of Saxony. This area is traversed throughout its entire length by the upper Oder River, which rises in the east Bohemian uplands and flows northwestward through the province to divide it into two approximately equal portions. The broad valley of the Oder, an extension of the North German Plain, is bordered on the southwest by the ranges of the Sudeten Mountains forming the frontier between southeastern Germany and Czechoslovakia. On the northeast the Oder Basin merges into the south Polish Plateau lands. The northern portion of the Silesian lowlands has a typical Northeast German landscape—sandy areas covered with forest and open heath, except for the low Katzen Gebirge (260 meters) on the east side of the Oder. South of this range of hills lie the rich agricultural lands of central Silesia, which raise bumper crops of rye, wheat, sugar beets, and potatoes. The fertile soils continue southeastward into Upper Silesia on the west side of the Oder, while the land to the east of the Oder, where the south Polish Plateau juts far into the Oder Basin, is extremely hilly with extensive coal fields and deposits of iron, zinc, and lead. The Tarnowitzer Höhen, on the southeastern German-Polish border, constitute the most impressive extension of the Polish Plateau country. West of the Oder is a loess zone beyond which lie the southeastern Sudeten Mountains, with the Altvater Gebirge and the Reichensteiner Gebirge in the Upper Silesian area. Northwestward from these ranges of the Sudeten chain lies the so-called Glatz triangle, which juts into Czech territory and is formed by the valley of the upper Glatzer River, surrounded by the Reichsensteiner, Habelschwerdter, Heuscheuer, and Eulen ranges. Northwestward, these ranges give way to the Riesen Gebirge in the central Sudeten mountain zone. Numerous streams, including the Spree, Bober, Katzbach,

* German spelling—Schlesien.

285

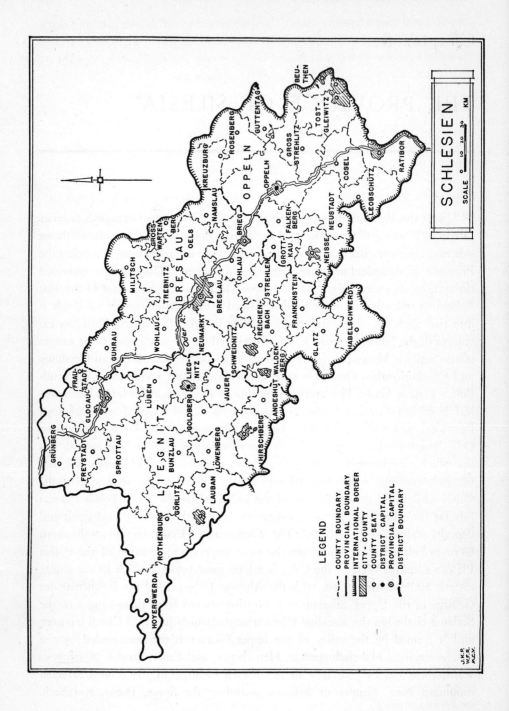

Glatzer, and Hotzenplotz, rise in these mountains and flow north and north-eastward through the Silesian lowlands to join the Oder River. The eastern tributaries of the Oder, which rise in the south Polish Plateau, include the Bartsch, Weide, Stober, Malapane, and Klodnitz rivers.

Silesia, therefore, has a well diversified economy. Its northern region is given over to dairying and livestock with the cities of Görlitz and Liegnitz serving as centers. Its central portion is devoted primarily to agriculture, with Breslau as the center and is tied in commercially with the north and also with the mining and industrial region to the south.

Silesia has been settled by agrarian people since the Neolithic period. During the Bronze and Iron Ages, it was probably settled by the Illyrians, who left eastern Germany for the Balkans during the first centuries before our era, when East Germans from the Baltic on their way to southeastern Europe pushed into the valley of the upper Oder River. Later, in the first centuries of our era, it was occupied by pastoral Slavic tribes, who later came under the protection of the Kings of Poland, and managed to hold their own against the eastward expanding Germans until the beginning of the thirteenth century, when Silesia fell under German rule. It was at this time that the new German rulers embarked on a policy of settling the area with German colonists. As a result, the following century witnessed extensive emigration from the west which brought almost all of Silesia under German settlement. Towns were established and the land was assigned on a feudal basis. By the beginning of the fourteenth century, almost all of Silesia was German land except for the eastern portion of Upper Silesia, where numerous Polish settlements have managed to survive to the present day.

The German spoken in the Province of Silesia, an East Middle German variety of High German, is a distinctive dialect strongly colored by Polish. Standard German, however, is spoken in the larger cities and is becoming increasingly common in the smaller towns and rural areas. The people of the province were about equally divided between Protestantism and Catholicism, for there were 2,320,000 Lutheran Protestants and 2,250,000 Roman Catholics. The Catholic population is concentrated largely in the southern Upper Silesian area, while the Protestants dominate the central and northern portions of the province. Areas of mixed religious faith exist along the Oder near Breslau and Brieg. The Jewish population of the province, which was to a great extent concentrated in the urban areas, was quite large, numbering 34,400 in 1933.

In 1933 the Province of Silesia ranked fifth in size and third in population among the provinces of Prussia. Its population numbered 4,710,000 with a population density of 128 individuals per sq. km., making it one of the more densely settled territories of the Reich. This population did not have a uniform spatial distribution. The northern and eastern portion of the province, where agri-

culture is the dominant activity, had a moderate population density with 60 to
80 individuals per sq. km., while in the heavily industrialized areas it was as
great as 200 per sq. km. In the past century and a half, the population steadily
increased; the greatest period of population expansion came between 1870 and
1910; it was due to the rapid industrialization of this part of the Reich in the
late nineteenth century.

The Silesian area became a part of the German Reich in 1138 through the
partition of the Polish crown lands, although it did not become an integral part
of the Reich until 1201. When Silesia was added to the Reich, it was placed under an independent dynasty, which divided the land in 1163, establishing the
duchies of Lower Silesia and Upper Silesia. During this period the western portions of Silesia were held by the Kings of Bohemia and the Margraves of Lausitz. The German occupation of Silesia resulted in a rapid transformation of
the area, for the forests and swamps were cleared for settlement, while villages
grew into towns interested in commerce, mining, and textiles. The early dukes
of Silesia served Germany well. In 1241 they defeated the Mongols in the battle of Liegnitz, blocking the Mongol invasion of Central Europe. However,
the early medieval prosperity of Silesia declined rapidly after the thirteenth
century, for the process of internal partition upon each succession divided the
land against itself.

By the beginning of the fifteenth century, Silesia was divided into over
eighteen principalities. Faced with growing anarchy and disorder, the princes
turned to the Luxemburg Kings of Bohemia for protection. The Bohemian
overlords liquidated a number of the principalities and established an orderly
administration. During the fifteenth century, the Silesians supported the Bohemian King in the Hussite wars, with the result that the Bohemian rebels, who
were largely Slavs, overran Upper Silesia and brought several areas back under Slavic control. In 1469 Matthias Corvinus, the Hungarian King who had
seized the crown of Bohemia, became the overlord of Silesia. His rule brought
the establishment of a Diet of Silesian princes, a move which did much to unify
the area. Although the Silesians had profited by the rule of Matthias, they re-
sented the financial control imposed by Bohemia. Under his successor they
managed to gain practical autonomy. Shortly after the Reformation, during
which the Silesians had taken the Protestant side, Silesia fell more and more
under foreign rule.

Meanwhile, the Bohemian throne was occupied by the Habsburgs in 1526,
and Silesia became a Habsburg territory. The old rights and privileges of the
Silesian princes were limited or abolished, and the land was given a highly centralized administration. Although the political history of the sixteenth and
seventeenth centuries in Silesia was uneventful, the area suffered severely during the religious wars of the Reformation and particularly during the Thirty

Years' War, when the Silesians joined with the Bohemian rebels in revolt against the Habsburgs. It is estimated that over three-quarters of the population lost their lives during this war.

The next major event in the history of Silesia came in 1740 when Frederick the Great of Prussia occupied Lower Silesia, which was ceded by the Habsburgs to Prussia in 1741. Upper Silesia fell to Prussia in 1742. Although Maria Theresa of Austria attempted to regain Silesia in 1744 and again during the Seven Years' War (1756-1763), Prussia managed to retain the entire area. The annexation of Silesia by Prussia brought the complete administrative reorganization of the area. The powers of the numerous local princes were abolished and the area was made a Prussian province. A special minister for Silesia was appointed and under his regime numerous political and administrative reforms were undertaken. Prussian subsidies brought a revival and expansion of the mining and textile industries. Feudalism was routed out and strict religious toleration was enforced. The history of Silesia was merged with that of Prussia. During the Napoleonic Wars the area was occupied by French troops from 1806-1813. After the Treaty of Vienna (1815), the Silesian area was enlarged through the addition of a part of Ober Lausitz, which had been acquired by Prussia from the state of Saxony at the conclusion of the Napoleonic Wars. The nineteenth century history of the Province of Silesia is one of rapid industrial development and prosperity.

After World War I, under Article 88 of the Versailles Treaty, Upper Silesia, except for the counties of Falkenberg, Grottkau, Neisse, and portions of Neustadt and Hultschin, which are purely German, was subjected to a plebiscite to determine whether the area should be assigned to Poland or Germany. The area, except for a small portion of the county of Ratibor, which was ceded to Czechoslovakia, was placed under an International Commission, composed of representatives from Great Britain, France, and Italy. After many disturbances the plebiscite was held on March 20, 1921. Over 40 per cent of the population voted to join with Poland, but this vote was concentrated in the southern and eastern counties of Upper Silesia. The majority of the population, however, voted to remain within the Reich. The decision as to the actual allocation of the counties was delayed by several difficulties. Shortly after the plebiscite, a Polish insurrection led by Korfanty broke out, putting an end to negotiations. Meanwhile, the commission was divided on the issue of how to partition the area between Germany and Poland. The situation was further complicaed by a German defense force led by General Höfer. The area was finally pacified in June 1922 by reinforced French and British military forces.

In October 1921, the new League of Nations took over the Silesian affair and appointed another commission. This body awarded the richer industrial portion, which contained about 75 per cent of the material wealth of Upper

Silesia, to Poland. Germany received the poorer although larger portion of the territory. Owing to the intensive economic interrelationships which made all of Upper Silesia a single economic area, the League recommended that the entire territory be placed under a special regime to handle common economic problems and to work for the protection of minority groups (October 12, 1922). This was done following the German-Polish conference of November 1921, which led to the Polish-German Convention of May 1922. This second convention established the Upper Silesian Mixed Commission for the control of industrial, transportation, and labor problems throughout German and Polish Upper Silesia. Therefore, although the League of Nations had established an arbitrary frontier giving Germany the larger part of the territory and its population, and Poland the smaller area with the mines and heavy industries, the arrangements for Upper Silesia under the convention, which was to remain effective until 1936, overcame many of the economic disadvantages by ignoring the new frontier. This arrangement led the Prussian government under Hitler to divide the Silesian area into the provinces of Lower Silesia and Upper Silesia to simplify the administrative problems of southern Silesia. Aside from a few minor charges and counter-charges, things went as well as could be expected in view of the difficult background of the Upper Silesian problem.

In 1936 the Nazi government allowed the Upper Silesian convention to lapse and in 1938 consolidated the provinces of Lower Silesia and Upper Silesia, dividing them into three administrative districts: Liegnitz, Breslau, and Oppeln. Other territorial changes came at the same time with the liquidation of the former Province of Grenzmark Posen-West Prussia. Its southernmost county, Fraustadt, and ten towns of the adjacent county of Bomst, which was given to the Silesian county of Grünberg, were absorbed into the administrative district of Liegnitz of the Province of Silesia. The rest of the skeleton province of Grenzmark Posen-West Prussia was assigned to the provinces of Brandenburg and Pomerania.

The next change in the territorial status of the Silesian area came with the Munich Pact, which among other things brought the cession of the southern part of the county of Ratibor to Germany. This small area had been ceded to Czechoslovakia after World War I. After the conquest of Poland in 1939, the Silesian area was reorganized once more with the re-establishment of the two provinces of Lower Silesia and Upper Silesia. Although there was no change in the status of the Lower Silesia area (the districts of Liegnitz and Breslau), Upper Silesia was not only enlarged to its pre-World War I size, but was further expanded through the addition of Polish and Czech territory. The Teschen area, which had been acquired by Poland during the Munich crisis of 1938 was added to upper Silesia; so, also, was a strip of Polish territory (consisting of the Nazi counties of Blachstädt, Warthenau, Lobben, Bendsburg, Ilkenau, Krenau, and the city county of Sosnowitz, and the formerly German portion of Upper Silesia) that had been ceded to Poland after the plebiscite of 1921. The wartime province of Upper Silesia consisted of the new district of Oppeln (old Oppeln with the counties of Blachstädt and Warthenau and without the county of Gleiwitz and the city county of Gleiwitz, Beuthen, and Hindenburg) and the new district of Kattowitz (Polish Upper Silesia and Teschen, the counties of Lobben, Bendsburg, Ilkenau, Krenau, the city county of Sosnowitz, and a portion of the old district of Oppeln). In this study, the Silesian area will be treated in terms of its status immediately after 1938, when it was made into one province.

Its administration followed the regular pattern of Prussian administration and was headed by a chief president who resided at Breslau. The provincial administration and self-government came under Nazi laws which modified the Provincial Constitutions of 1823, 1871/1881 and the liberal republican laws. Much of the actual administration was carried out by the District Presidents of the administrative districts of Liegnitz, Oppeln, and Breslau.

The work of the general administration was supplemented by special and technical services under direct national control. During the imperial period only the state administered courts, railways, and mining offices and the nationally operated postal system were outside the sphere of the general administration of the Province of Silesia. In this province, too, justice was administered by the Prussian Ministry of Justice; it was handled by the Superior State Court at Breslau, Collegiate Courts of First and Second Instance of Beuthen, Breslau, Brieg, Glatz, Gleiwitz, Glogau, Görlitz, Hirschberg, Liegnitz, Neisse, Oels, Oppeln, Ratibor and Schweidnitz, and numerous local Courts of First Instance. The national postal system was under the Chief Postal Directorates of Breslau, Liegnitz, and Oppeln—the National Postal Directorates of the Republic and the Third Reich. As usual, national regulations for trade and industry, weights and measures, social insurance, welfare, public health, and the collection of imperial revenues were administered upon delegation from the Reich.

Under the Republic there was a further extension of direct national administration to finance, railways, unemployment insurance and employment, and labor welfare. National control of finances within Silesia was carried out through the State Finance Office of Silesia (Breslau) and its local finance offices and main customs offices. National Construction Offices were located at Breslau, Gleiwitz, Neisse, and Liegnitz. The national railways of the province were operated under the National Postal Directorates of Breslau, Oppeln, and Frankfort. Labor and unemployment problems were met by the State Labor Office of Silesia (Breslau) and the Main Welfare Office of Silesia (Breslau).

Certain aspects of welfare, social insurance, health, trade and industry, and labor, which were subject to national legislation, were still administered upon delegation by the provincial administration. Subject to limited provincial supervision, the economic life of the province was placed under local branches of the German Diet of Industry and Trade, the Diet of Crafts and Industry, the National Corporation of the German Handicrafts, the German Agricultural Council, and the Trade Unions.

The Province of Silesia has long been a heterogeneous political area. During the Empire, the strongly Catholic Upper Silesian area followed the Catholic Center party, although the industrial areas around Beuthen and Gleiwitz, where there was a large Polish working class, generally voted for the Polish minority party which had its major stronghold in the old provinces of Posen and West Prussia. The Breslau region was largely Social Democratic, while the Liegnitz district followed the National Liberal party. It should be noted that the Conservative party had a large following in the agrarian areas of northern Silesia.

During the republican period, Catholic Upper Silesia continued to adhere to the Catholic Center. In the 1928 elections, for instance, every city and county in the administrative district of Oppeln, with the exception of one which went Nationalist and one which went Communist, gave large pluralities to the Catholic Center party.

As Nazi strength grew throughout Germany, it remained relatively weak in Upper Silesia except in the one formerly Nationalist county of Kreuzberg which went over to the Nazis in the *Reichstag* elections of 1932 and also supported Hitler against Hindenburg for President. In the whole Upper Silesian area the Nationalists and Communists were stronger than the Social Democrats. The county of Beuthen and the city of Beuthen were major Communist strongholds. In Lower Silesia, on the other hand, the Social Democrats dominated the political picture during the Republican era. The National German People's party was the second strongest party in the Republican era but in the elections of the thirties, their vote dropped significantly and the Nazis captured most of it and also made inroads into the formerly Socialist cities like Breslau and Waldenburg. In the Liegnitz district, the Nationalists were relatively stronger than in the other Silesian districts, and when the Nazis became the most powerful party in the district, their vote was larger than elsewhere (48 per cent in 1932). Formerly strong Socialist cities like Görlitz, Liegnitz, and Hirschberg went over to the Hitler column and strong Nationalist areas like the county and city of Glogau did likewise. In both the 1932 elections for the *Reichstag,* the Nazis carried every city and city county in the Liegnitz district. The Catholic vote in the Breslau district was responsible for keeping that area just a shade less for Hitler than the Liegnitz area.

The Province of Silesia was constituted by the Nazis as the district of Silesia for purposes of party administration. The district headquarters at Breslau included offices similar to those in other districts, which exercised control over the provincial government and administration. The member and affiliated organizations of the party maintained offices at Breslau for control within the Silesian area. This dense network of party organization guaranteed the political stability of Silesia.

With the Nazi regime came an extension of national administrative controls. Direct national administration, which continued for finance, posts, labor and labor welfare, and railways, was extended to justice, air matters, propaganda, and labor affairs. Many of the traditional fields of state administration—police, health, welfare, education, and certain aspects of social insurance—were brought under tight national control.

The services and functions of the general and special administrative systems were supplemented by an extensive system of corporate administration which provided for the total regimentation of life within the province. Breslau, the traditional capital of the province and the administrative seat of the regional district of Breslau, has always been the major center for general and special administration. It is worthy of note that Oppeln, the administrative seat of the governmental administrative district of Oppeln, had numerous branch offices of agencies for special administration because of its position within the heavy industrial area of Upper Silesia. It was much more important than the administrative seat of Liegnitz which is situated in the agrarian north.

Rural Aspect

The southeastern Prussian Province of Silesia has a predominantly rural landscape of forests and fields, except in the rather small though economically important industrial area in Upper Silesia. The foothills and uplands of the Sudeten ranges which border the province on the southwest are still heavily forested. This area remained the domain of the hunter and shepherd until the thirteenth and fourteenth centuries of our era, when German peasants cleared various parts of the uplands for pasture and crops by cutting and burning the forest. Owing to the long development of mining, this region was relatively heavily settled by people who made their living from industries and crafts. On the other hand, the rural population, which was largely dependent upon dairying, was limited. Northern and eastern Silesia is much like the North German Plains. Its poor soils are good only for rye and potato cultivation. It was essentially a region of large estates and tenant farmers.

In the Province of Silesia as a whole, a large proportion of the population made its living from agriculture and forestry. In 1933 over 25 per cent of the population was engaged in these rural occupations. An even larger proportion of the population lived in the small villages, whose main economic interest was in agriculture and forestry. Approximately 43 per cent of the population dwelt in the 7,800 villages which had a population of less than 2,000. Another 8 per cent of the population lived in the 135 small rural market towns with a population of between 2,000 and 5,000 inhabitants, while approximately another 14 per cent was concentrated in the 65 small provincial towns with populations ranging between 5,000 and 20,000.

The general administration of the province of Silesia has centered in the city of Breslau, the provincial capital, and in the three district capitals of Breslau, Liegnitz, and Oppeln. The day-to-day administration of rural Silesia was carried on in the forty-nine counties into which the administrative districts were divided. These counties were headed by County Managers who served as agents both of the central government and of local self-government. The state administration was regulated by the County Constitutions of 1825, 1872/1881 and the Nazi laws of 1933, while the county corporate structure was governed by the Ordinances of 1872/1881 and the liberal laws of the Republic. The villages of Silesia, which were once governed by the Constitutions for Rural Villages and Towns of 1872, followed the German Municipal Code after 1935.

There is considerable regional variation in rural conditions and agriculture throughout Silesia. Broadly it may be divided into three agrarian zones. The best agricultural area in Silesia occupies the broad strip of territory lying on the west side of the Oder and extending into the foothills of the Sudeten Mountains. This area enjoys a dry-warm climate of sub-Sarmatian type, which is characterized by an average yearly temperature of 8-9 degrees C. (average July temperature: 18-19 degrees C. and average January temperature: −1 to −2 degrees C.), and by an average annual rainfall of 500 mm. in Lower Silesia, increasing to 800 mm. in Upper Silesia. The soils of this foothill-valley region extending from Ratibor to Breslau and Liegnitz are among the most fertile of Germany. They are of the brown and black steppe type, consisting mostly of loess which was laid down after the last glacial period. In this zone, which formed a part of the real tillage area of the Reich, from 70 to 80 per cent of the surface was under cultivation. Wheat, barley, sugar beets, and some industrial crops are grown on the largest mechanized farms of this part of Silesia. The cattle industry, which was built up on the basis of the utilization of beet waste, was important, but crop cultivation was the mainstay of the farm system.

The forested uplands in the southwestern border of the province form the second important agrarian zone. This hilly and even mountainous area has a cool moist climate with an average annual rainfall much greater than that of the Oder Valley area. In the lower uplands, the average precipitation each year ranges between 800 and 1000 mm., while in the higher portions of the Sudeten ranges, there is frequently as much as 1600 mm. of rainfall each year. The summers are cool (average July temperature 14 to 15 degrees C.), while the winters are cold (average January temperature -2 to -7 degrees C.). The infertile mountain soils are covered by forests and pastures. In this part of Silesia, dairying forms the core of the agricultural system, for the uplands and rough mountain slopes can be used only for sheep and cattle raising. Crop cultivation was unimportant and was only undertaken for home consumption. The local crops, raised on small stony fields, include the usual oats, rye and potatoes. Relatively unimportant from the point of view of agricultural production are the dry sandy northern and eastern portions of Silesia. The summers are warm (average July temperature 18-19 degrees C.) and the winters cold (average January temperature -2 degrees C.), with an average yearly rainfall of about 500 to 600 mm. Here, too, the poor soils are used for the cultivation of rye and potatoes, although some wheat is grown on the scattered patches of better soil.

The numerous industrial and manufacturing towns of Silesia provide an excellent market for the agricultural products of the province. The dairy products of the upland areas found their way to the many small mining and manufacturing towns of the Sudeten area or were shipped to the industrial section in Upper Silesia. Although the province possesses one of the best agricultural sections of the Reich, the local demand for cereals outstrips the locally produced supply, with the result that Silesia had deficits of wheat, rye, barley, and oats, which was made good by imports from other parts of the Reich and from overseas. The only surplus foodstuff was potatoes. In livestock production, Silesia had a surplus of cattle, but a deficit in swine. The figures for land utilization given below (in hectares) indicate the amount and type of land available for agriculture.

Cultivated Land		1,792,000
Grain	1,109,000	
Legumes	38,000	
Root Crops	475,000	
Green Vegetables	7,000	
Industrial Crops	26,000	
Fodder Crops	137,000	
Small Gardens		42,600
Meadow and Pasture		400,000
Orchards		5,600
Forests		1,033,000
Waste Land		67,900
Houses and Barns		72,600
Roads and Parks		186,000

About 50 per cent of the land was devoted to crop cultivation and 12 per cent to pastoral activities. The remaining land was divided between forests (30 per cent) and waste land (8 per cent).

The forests of Silesia occupy a goodly portion of the territory of the province. A mixed forest of spruce, fir, and beech covers the southwestern uplands. The higher parts of the Sudeten ranges are covered by a typical alpine spruce forest. Along the Oder, the rich agricultural region is very sparsely wooded, although there are a few scattered patches of deciduous woodland. The moderately dense forests of Upper Silesia are composed of stands of pine, spruce, and fir, with the typical north German pine predominating in eastern and northern Lower Silesia. The forest land is owned by a variety of interests, the state owning about 224,000 hectares or 22 per cent of the total forest area. This land was administered through twenty-six state forests reserves. Over 60 per cent of the remaining forest land was held by private interests, while the remaining areas were owned by county and municipal governments.

Conditions of rural life in Silesia were extremely varied. The excellent agricultural area lying to the west of the Oder and extending into the foothills of the Sudeten uplands was occupied by Silesian Germans dwelling in large villages which centered about a church. These villages, which had populations ranging between 600 and 1600, consisted of a number of houses of Middle German type with a dwelling house and barns arranged about a farmyard. They were carefully planned, clean, and orderly places well known for their neatness. These traits applied only to the German villages, for the Polish settlements in the southeast, although frequently similar in construction and arrangement, have the look of eastern Europe. The farms adjoining the villages tend to be large, averaging over 100 hectares in size.

In the poorer north and eastern portions of the province, the manorial estates with a landlord's dwelling, neatly kept barns, and the impoverished huts of the tenants were more common. The villages of this area tend to be small, with populations ranging between 100 and 600. The uplands which border the province on the southwest were occupied by small forest villages (*Waldhufendörfer*) and isolated farmsteads. The farms are small averaging, on the whole, less than five hectares in size. Although the peasantry of the uplands were an economically independent group, always insistent upon their ways and rights, they had to supplement their meager farm incomes, which were derived from dairying, by working in the numerous small industrialized towns of the Sudeten area. In Silesia as a whole, the rural people, although about equally divided between Lutheranism and Catholicism, were frequently believers in weird superstitions. Their folklore was filled with tales of ghosts and vampires. Many Germans regarded the Silesians as a soft and untrustworthy people.

Urban Aspect

Almost all of the cities of the Province of Silesia were established by the Germans on the site of Slavic settlements during the thirteenth and fourteenth centuries. During the medieval period, Breslau, Glogau, Görlitz, and Liegnitz in Lower Silesia grew to importance as residences of the local nobility or as trading centers doing business with eastern Europe. Breslau became the metropolitan center of provincial life. Görlitz, located in the western part of Lower Silesia, Glogau, which serves northern Silesia, and Liegnitz, located in the heart of rural Lower Silesia, were provincial centers serving a more limited rural hinterland. The old towns of Hirschberg, Schweidnitz, and Waldenburg, which are located in the foothills of the Sudeten uplands, developed during the Middle Ages as the result of gold and silver mining and became industrialized towns functioning on the basis of local resources. They had little significance as commercial centers. In Upper Silesia, Beuthen, Gleiwitz, Oppeln, Hindenburg, and Ratibor, were relatively unimportant until the late nineteenth century, which brought the rapid development of the mineral resources of this part of Silesia. Although they prospered as trading towns during the early Middle Ages, the shift of trade which came with the discovery of America and the effects of the Thirty Years' War, left them without resources or contacts for a revival of their earlier commercial prosperity. The industrial revolution turned the attention of all Upper Silesia to the rich coal, lead, zinc, and iron deposits, which were exploited by German capital utilizing Polish labor. Germany's loss of the greater part of the Upper Silesian heavy industrial area in 1922 was partly made good through the more intensive working of the mines and industries of Gleiwitz, Hindenburg, and Beuthen. The larger towns and cities of the Province of Silesia contain about 35 per cent of the total population of the province.

The fourteen larger cities and towns of the province were organized as city-counties. Under the Nazis municipal government and administration followed the national pattern laid down by the German Municipal Code of 1935. The democratic features of city government and administration, which were provided by the Stein Constitution of 1808, the Constitutions for Cities of 1831 and 1853, and the liberal measures of the Republic, were swept away by the Nazis.

The Province of Silesia was one of the most distinctive and stable areas within the Reich. This stability resulted from its position on the frontier, where it was surrounded on three sides by Czechoslovakia and Poland, and from the unifying influence of the Oder River. Urban Silesia had three principal areas of settlement. The important Breslau metropolitan area is situated on the Oder in the center of the province, while the Upper Silesian heavy industrial region is located in the southernmost corner of the area on the 1922-1939 Polish-German frontier. The third urban area, which consists of a great number of small industrialized towns, occupies the foothills of the Sudeten Mountains. The entire province was linked together by intimate economic ties and inter-relationships.

The cultural and economic unity of the Silesian area was recognized by the Nazis when they placed all of the province, except the region of Ober Lausitz (the counties of Hoyerswerda and Rothenburg) under one Regional Planning Association. These counties were the two that were placed under the planning association of Brandenburg, because their local lignite resources were utilized for electrical power used in the Kurmark area (Berlin and Brandenburg).

The rich mineral resources of Upper Silesia, which were the basis of the modern industrial development of the southern part of the province, have been worked on a limited scale since the early Middle Ages. Lead and iron were the first minerals to be mined. Zinc, which now comes mostly from a mine astride the 1922-1939 boundary, was exploited in the early modern period. Coal mining became important only in recent times. The first coal mined in Upper Silesia was used for fuel to run the water pumps of the lead mines. Later it was used in the smelting of iron and zinc. The late nineteenth century industrial revolution brought the rapid development of the extensive Upper Silesian coal measures. During the period between World War I and World War II, when Poland held over 77 per cent of the coal resources of the area, Germany was left with the mines near Hindenburg, Gleiwitz, and Beuthen, which produce a high-grade bituminous coal, excellent for steam and domestic use.

After 1922 the mines in the German portion of Upper Silesia were intensively exploited to free eastern Germany from the necessity of importing coal from the more extensive coal fields of Polish Upper Silesia. Large deposits of coal are located in the western part of Silesia near Waldenburg, but they are, unfortunately, far from the cheap water transportation facilities provided by the Oder River. The Province of Silesia also has a number of lignite deposits, which are mostly situated in the northwestern part of the province near Glogau, Görlitz, and Sagan. Other smaller deposits of lignite are found along the Oder in the vicinity of Brieg. The major iron ore deposits are located strategically near the coal fields of Upper Silesia and the Waldenburg area. Most of the lead has been mined, and little of the former copper remains. Zinc, however, is still mined in quantity.

Electrical power, which was of vital importance for the industries of Silesia, was produced from lignite and coal and by means of water power. The small German Upper Silesian industrial area was largely dependent upon the large electrical plant at Zaborze near Hindenburg, whereas central Silesia was furnished with power by the coal electrical power stations at Waldenburg, Mölke, and Mittelsteine in the Sudeten uplands, and by the stations at Breslau and Tschechnitz on the Oder, which used coal shipped downstream from the coal mines of Upper Silesia. These stations were linked together by high tension lines, which connected with the water power electrical plants at Marklissa, Havnau, and Mauer in the Sudeten uplands. The only major lignite electrical power plant serving the Silesian area was at Kohlfurt in northwest Silesia. The other lignite power stations in the Northwest were oriented toward Brandenburg.

Aside from mining, the heavy industries of Upper Silesia were limited to iron and zinc smelting. The limited Hindenburg, Gleiwitz, and Beuthen area was a sea of iron and steel mills, zinc foundries, blast furnaces, metal fabricating plants, and machine shops. Lighter industries did not develop in this area because of the lack of earlier craft traditions, the distance from good markets, and the isolated position on the frontier. Economically, the heavy industries of the German portion of Upper Silesia were on the decline, since the local iron ores are giving out and the local coal is poor for coke. The area, however, had enjoyed a considerable period of prosperity because of the subsidies during the republican period and the war orders during the Nazi regime.

The other major Silesian industrial area, which was situated in the Sudeten uplands, had a far more varied industrial structure. This area, consisting of numerous small industrialized towns, extended in a narrow belt from Görlitz in the northwest to Ratibor in the southeast. The heavy and extractive industries were concentrated in the Waldenburg-Glatz area, which occupies the foothills of the Riesen Gebirge and Eulen Gebirge. Although coal and iron have been extracted recently, copper and silver mining, which has been carried on since the early Middle Ages, formed the traditional basis for the industry. Machinery plants were located at Görlitz, Schweidnitz, Hirschberg, Waldenburg, Neisse, and Ratibor. The textile industry has been important in this part of Silesia since the fourteenth century, Waldenburg having long been the capital of the Silesian linen industry. Textiles and clothing constituted important industries at Schweidnitz, Hirschberg, and Görlitz. The isolated industrial towns of Ratibor and Oppeln in Upper Silesia were important for the production of iron and steel, machinery, and wood products. Ratibor was particularly noted for its river boats and railway cars.

There were several isolated industrial and manufacturing areas; the large manufacturing center of Breslau, important for the production of machinery, clothing, and food products; the smaller centers of Brieg for leather, clothing, and sugar; Liegnitz for machinery, wood, and food products; and Glogau for machinery, furniture, sugar, and food products. These regions were largely dependent upon their surrounding agrarian hinterland to furnish the needed raw materials, although metal, coal, and other materials were brought in from the Upper Silesian and Western Sudeten heavy industrial areas.

The backbone of the road transportation system is formed by the Frankfort-(Oder)-Breslau-Oppeln-Beuthen road, which runs along the eastern side of the Oder Valley. Within the Province of Silesia, roads radiate from Oppeln to the southern part of the province, from Breslau to the central part, from Liegnitz to the northeastern area, and from Görlitz, which is linked with Breslau by roads running via Liegnitz and Waldenburg, to the northwestern portion of Silesia. These key road junctions have been important transportation points since the German colonization of southeastern Germany. Aside from the major national roads, there is an extensive network of secondary roads within the province, which were maintained by the Provincial Corporation at Breslau. The local county roads were under the supervision of the county Road Master. Under the Nazi regime, the normal road system was supplemented by the national super-highways.

The major rail lines follow almost the same basic pattern as the road system. The railroads, which were owned by the Reich, were operated by the German Railroad Company, an integral part of the national Ministry of Transport. In the Province of Silesia the railroads were under the National Railway Directorates of Breslau, Oppeln, and Frankfort-on-the-Oder.

The Oder River has long played a vital role in the life of this province. This river, which flows through the province, makes cheap water transportation accessible to almost every part of Silesia. Navigation begins at Ratibor in the southernmost part of the province. At a short distance from Ratibor, the port of Kosel is connected with the German part of the Upper Silesian industrial area by the Klodnitz canal. Kosel, which is the most important river port in the province, handled a yearly goods traffic of nearly 2,550,000 metric tons in 1933. The river harbors at Oppeln, Breslau, and Glogau are less important. The Oder River not only provided cheap water transportation to the Baltic Sea port of Stettin, but also connected the industries of Silesia with the large Berlin markets via the Oder-Spree canal. River shipping in the Province of Silesia was organized in the Ship Operation Corporation for the Oder (*Schifferbetriebsverband für die Oder*), which had its headquarters in Breslau. The latter city, the key road, rail, and waterway transportation center of the province, was also the major point for international air transportation. The airports at Hirschberg and Gleiwitz were small.

Breslau, the capital of the province, was the center of most of the economic life of the area. It was the major commercial and financial city of the Silesian area. Many of the larger towns and cities were primarily provincial centers serving an agrarian hinterland. Glogau, Liegnitz, Oppeln, and Brieg were of this type. The large industrial towns of the South, such as Gleiwitz, Hindenburg, and Beuthen, looked toward Breslau, although they have adequate local financial and commercial facilities. The hill towns of Neisse, Waldenburg, Schweidnitz, and Görlitz were supported by industry and light manufacturing. In terms of rail freight traffic, coal and metal products were the main commodities produced and shipped from the province, while scrap iron, some ores, timber, grain and other food products were brought in from adjacent areas within the Reich. Most of the coal used in eastern and northeastern Germany originated in the fields of Upper Silesia. In the field of machinery and machine tools a lively trade was carried on between the Breslau industries and the heavy industries of Upper Silesia. The machine plants of the Sudeten industrial area, however, looked toward the state of Saxony for trade, as did the textile industry; while the clothing factories, which utilized yarn and cloth produced in the cotton mills of South and West Germany, looked to Berlin for their markets. The overseas trade of the province went largely by river to the port of Stettin.

The banking and credit institutions of the province ranged from branches of the great commercial banks of Berlin, which were mainly interested in investments of the industrial type, to the local county and municipal mortgage and savings banks. The provincially owned banks and financial institutions were located at Breslau. The operations of these banks were supplemented by those of the branches of the *Reichsbank*. The provincial government operated a life insurance and a fire insurance organization. These, like the provincially operated banks, were under the Provincial Corporation. The province had a stock exchange at Breslau.

The urban population of the Province of Silesia was largely engaged in industries and crafts. In 1933, 36 per cent of the population or 1,696,000 individuals were employed by the industries and manufacturing establishments of the province. Only 14 per cent of the population or 681,000 individuals were engaged in trade and transportation activities and 7 per cent in professional work or public service. The resultant class structure has several interesting features. The working class, which constituted about 44 per cent of the population, became one of the largest in the Reich. The upper class, the professional group, and the civil service groups were small in comparison with those of other states and provinces of the Reich. The white collar group was about average in comparison with that of other Prussian provinces.

The cities of the rich agrarian zone, along the west side of the Oder Valley, included Breslau, Brieg, Oppeln, and Liegnitz. Breslau, already mentioned as a commercial center, was the largest city of the province; it was also its main political, administrative, and financial center. Traditionally the town is important as the birthplace of the politician von Gentz, the poet Kopisch, and the painter von Menzel. The smaller city of Liegnitz is important today as an agricultural market town. It is the garden and residential city of Silesia. Brieg and

Oppeln, which are located to the south of Breslau on the Oder River, were also market towns catering to rural customers. Oppeln was one of the important grain markets of Germany, while Liegnitz had one of the largest vegetable markets of the Reich.

The poorer north Silesian agricultural area was served by the town of Glogau, previously mentioned for its important role in the affairs of Lower Silesia since the Middle Ages. The small industrial towns of the Sudeten uplands constituted another group remaining from earlier times; the group includes the towns of Görlitz, Hirschberg, Schweidnitz, Waldenburg, and Neisse.

The urban and industrial area of Upper Silesia is set off sharply from the surrounding fields and forests of the region, which covered almost the entire area a hundred and fifty years ago. Within the industrialized portion of Upper Silesia, the landscape was given over to factories, mines, steel mills, railroad facilities, and blocks of workers' houses and flats, but unlike many of the German industrial areas, this region was disorderly and without plan.

Chapter 9

PROVINCE OF EAST PRUSSIA*

The Prussian Province of East Prussia on the Baltic Sea (Ostsee) was Germany's northeastern frontier, an exclave bordering on Polish and Lithuanian territory. Although it was connected geographically with the German Reich by the Province of West Prussia from 1772 to 1920, after 1920 it was separated from the Reich by the Polish Corridor, which was created at Versailles to give Poland free access to the sea. During the period between World War I and World War II, it was bordered on the south and east for a distance of 608 kilometers by Polish territory, on the east and north for a distance of 232 kilometers by Lithuanian territory, and on the west for a short distance by the territory of the Free City of Danzig.

East Prussia forms a part of the Baltic coastal zone, a product of the last glaciation. The northern portions of the province consist of ground moraines composed of boulder clays deposited by the glaciers, and the southern area is dominated by terminal moraines, rising into moderately high east-west ranges of hills composed of clays, sands, gravels, and boulders. The terminal moraine area, which is known as the Masurian Lake region, is marshy and abounds in lakes, owing to its poor drainage. The northern portion of East Prussia, with better drainage, has a good deal of moderately useful agricultural land. The two glacial areas are hemmed in between the broad low valley of the Vistula to the west, which flows northwestward to Bromberg (*Bydgoszez*) and thence north-northeast to the Danzig Bay (*Danziger Bucht*), and the valley of the less important Pregel River, which rises in the eastern part of the terminal moraine area and flows westward through northern East Prussia to enter the Baltic through the *Frisches* (*Haff*) lagoon just west of the port city of Königsberg. The northern Masurian region is drained by the Alle and Angerapp rivers, which are tributaries of the Pregel, and by the Passarge River, which flows into the Baltic, while the southern slopes of the moraines are drained by the Pissa, Orshiz, and Wkra streams, which are tributaries of the Vistula. Between the

* German spelling—Ostpreussen.

LEGEND
County Boundary
District Boundary
Provincial & Internat'l Boundary
City-County
County Seat
District Capital
Provincial Capital

BALTIC SEA

LITHUANIA

Memel R.

ELCHNIEDERUNG
HEINRICHS-WALDE
TILSIT-RAGNIT
SCHLOSSBERG

SAMLAND
LABIAU
GUMBINEN
INSTERBURG
EBEN-RODE

KÖNIGSBERG
Pregel R.
WEHLAU
GUMBINNEN

HEILIGENBEIL
BARTEN-STEIN
GERDAUEN
ANGERAPP
GOLDAP

PREUSSISCH EYLAU

DANZIG

BRAUNSBERG
ANGER-BURG
ELBING
RASTENBURG
HEILSBERG
TREUBURG

MARIEN-BURG
PREUSSISCH HOLLAND
RÖSSEL
LÖTZEN
STUHM
BISCHOFS-BURG
WEST
MOHRUNGEN
LYCK
PREUSSEN
ALLENSTEIN
SENSBURG
MARIEN-WERDER
ROSENBERG
ALLENSTEIN
OSTERODE
JOHANNISBURG
ORTELSBURG
POLAND

NEIDENBURG

OSTPREUSSEN
SCALE 0 10 20 30 KM

J.K.P.
W.F.R.
M.C.V.

mouths of the Pregel River and the Memel River, which later formed the frontier between German and Lithuanian territory from 1920 to 1939, lies a narrow strip of ground moraine country that juts out into the Baltic Sea to form the Samland Peninsula. The rest of the coast of East Prussia is barred from the Baltic Sea by two long narrow sand spits. The *Frische* (*Nehrung*) sand spit, which extends from the Danzig area to the southwestern corner of Samland, encloses the *Frisches* lagoon, while the *Kurische* sand spit, which extends from Samland to near Memel, enclosing the *Kurisches* lagoon, bars the northern part of East Prussia from direct access to the Baltic Sea.

The first known inhabitants of East Prussia were the Borussi (Prussians), who are classified linguistically as Balts and whose closest surviving kindred are the Lithuanians. The Borussi managed to hold most of East Prussia under their control with the exception of the Masurian lake country, which was occupied by Slavs. In the thirteenth century, the Teutonic Knights pushed into East Prussia and began the Germanization of the area through the enforced use of the German language and the importation of German settlers from the Reich, who were attracted by free land. The local population was dispossessed and reduced to serfdom. Owing to the inadequate number of German settlers, Polish settlers were allowed to occupy the infertile lake country of southern East Prussia. Thus the effort of the Teutonic Knights to convert all East Prussia into a thoroughly German area failed, for only the northern and southwestern portions of the modern province were Germanized.

Although most of the East Prussians came originally from northern Germany and spoke an East Elbian variety of *Plattdeutsch,* the southwestern (Marienburg) area was occupied by German settlers from Central Germany, whose descendants spoke a Middle German dialect. In the southern part of East Prussia, the Polish Masurians were dominant, while in the west along the Polish Corridor, other Poles lived within the frontiers of the province. South of the Memel River Lithuanian peasants occupied extensive tracts of land. Although some of these Polish and Lithuanian peoples have been settled in East Prussia since the time of the Teutonic Knights, many of them came in as agricultural laborers during the nineteenth and early twentieth centuries. It is difficult to estimate the actual number of Poles and Lithuanians once dwelling in East Prussia, because the German government has long doctored its published statistics. Polish figures for the number of Polish settlers in East Prussia held that there were 340,000 Poles in the southern district of Allenstein and 100,000 in the rest of the province. There are no accurate statistics for the number of Lithuanians living in northeast East Prussia. These Polish and Lithuanian groups, which have been regarded as German, must be distinguished from temporary foreign residents. Although German (Low and Middle), Masurian, and

Lithuanian were spoken in the rural areas and small towns, standard German was common in most of the larger towns and cities.

The province was strongly Protestant, for in 1933 almost 83 per cent of the population or 1,941,000 individuals were Lutherans. The Catholic minority was small, numbering only 364,000, and was largely concentrated in the region of Ermland, centering on Allenstein, which was held by the Kingdom of Poland during the early modern period. Most of the Catholics of East Prussia, however, were German, and the Masurian Polish and Lithuanian groups were Protestant, which was one of the important factors conditioning their decision to remain within the German Reich in the East Prussian plebiscites of 1920. The Jewish population, which was restricted to small urban groups, numbered only 8,800 in 1933.

In 1933 the Province of East Prussia had a population of 2,333,000 individuals. Although it was territorially the fourth largest Prussian province, it ranked ninth in population and, with its average of sixty-three individuals per sq. km., eleventh in population density. The most densely settled areas were located along the Baltic coast and the lower Memel River, where the density was sixty to eighty per sq. km. For the level ground moraine lands of northern East Prussia, the figures ran between forty and sixty, while in the sparsely settled Masurian lake country they were between twenty and forty. During the last century and a half, the population of East Prussia had grown very slowly. Since 1871 when it stood at 1,822,000, there was an increase of only 511,000 during the next sixty years, which is very small in comparison with the industrialized provinces of Western and Central Germany. Although the birth rate followed the national pattern, it was constantly higher than the average for the Reich. Hence the slow growth of the provincial population can best be accounted for by the emigration of many who sought better economic opportunities in other parts of the Reich and overseas. This situation, which was recognized before World War I, is the direct cause of the small population of the province and its low population density, which has long plagued the German militarists, politicians, and economists. German attempts to stem the tide of westward emigration have always failed; the economic instability of the area resulting from its distance from German markets, the artificial isolation from Polish markets, and the economic problems created by the great estates were the reasons.

During the first millennium of our era, when East Prussia was under the rule of the Borussi, the land was controlled by a number of tribal groups led by a small warrior class. Prior to the appearance of the Teutonic Knights, these tribes were subjected to Viking raids, and sporadic Polish attempts at conquest, as well as to Polish missionary efforts. The decline of Norse power and the disintegration of political conditions within Poland during the twelfth century left the still pagan Borussi with a considerable measure of freedom. During the thirteenth century, however, the Poles, not foreseeing the threat to their supremacy, invited the Teutonic Knights to subdue and Christianize the Borussi. The Knights, under the Grand Master, Hermann von Salza (1210-59), attacked and conquered the territory of East Prussia between 1231 and 1287. Well fortified towns were established, large estates were granted to retainers, and the slow processes of Christianization and Germanization were begun. The German language was forced upon the Borussi. German peasants were imported from the Reich. During the fourteenth century the Teutonic Knights extended their conquests northward into Lithuania and westward into Pommerellen, later the Polish Corridor, linking East Prussia with the Reich and cutting Poland off from the Baltic Sea. The coalition of Polish-Lithuanian forces in the fifteenth century under the Jagello dynasty, coupled with the ebbing of the German colonial movement and the oppressive domestic rule of the Knights, brought about the decline of their internal strength. In 1410 the armies of Poland and Lithuania defeated them at Tannenberg, destroying the military power of the Order. After this battle the internal affairs of the Teutonic Knights went from bad to worse. In 1466 Poland regained Pommerellen and Chelmnoland, and added the territory of Ermland in the heart of southwestern East Prussia, while the Teutonic Knights, as previously noted, retained the remainder of East Prussia, although as vassals of the Polish Kings. In 1519 the Knights broke this agreement and attacked the Polish forces. Although Poland won the military campaign, the Knights won the peace, for by the treaty of 1525 the Teutonic Order was dissolved, but the Master of the Teutonic Knights became the Duke of Prussia and vassal of the Polish King.

The secularization of East Prussia was followed by its conversion to the Protestant cause. The political change did not at the time affect Polish interests or culture in East Prussia, for Poles were allowed to settle and colonize throughout the province. The University at Königsberg became a center of Polish learning and of Protestantism. This was the age of great Polish power, and Polish culture was expanding throughout eastern Central Europe. During this period East Prussia as a Polish dependency became more and more Polish in culture and feeling. In 1618, however, the King of Poland granted the right of succession in the duchy to the Hohenzollerns, despite the objections of the East Prussian Diet. The Polish-Swedish war of 1655 gave the Hohenzollerns their long awaited opportunity. The Great Elector joined with Sweden against Poland and received as a Swedish vassal the rights to Pommerellen and East Prussia. Between 1655 and 1677, when Brandenburg actually gained direct control over this area, Poland, aided by a large pro-Polish faction in East Prussia, managed to oppose the aims of the Hohenzollerns. Finally, Poland, weakened by her long wars with the Turks, was forced to abandon East Prussia to the Hohenzollerns.

Since East Prussia was the only sovereign territory held by the Hohenzollerns, Friedrich I was crowned King in Prussia at Königsberg in 1701. Although the effort of the Teutonic Knights to Germanize East Prussia had failed, the rule of the Hohenzollern dynasty during the eighteenth and nineteenth centuries was eminently successful. The desire of the Hohenzollerns to join East Prussia to the rest of their holdings was satisfied by the partition of Poland in 1772, which gave them the Polish Corridor area of West Prussia. Under the Kings of Prussia, East Prussia was systematically Germanized. The Polish landowners were dispossessed and Polish immigration was forbidden. German colonists were brought in great numbers and settled on formerly Polish-owned land. In 1834 the Polish and Lithuanian languages were eliminated from the schools, churches, and governmental offices.

By the end of the nineteenth century, East Prussia, thanks to the thorough methods of the Hohenzollerns and Bismarck, was effectively Germanized. For a period during the middle of the nineteenth century (1824-1878), the provinces of East Prussia and West Prussia, which had been separate administrative units during the eighteenth and early nineteenth centuries, were joined together. This administrative arrangement did not work well, and finally in 1878 the two were separated and re-established as separate administrative units.

After World War I, Poland received from Germany the provinces of Posen and West Prussia, while the city of Danzig and a small hinterland was established as a Free City under the administrative control of the League of Nations. Difficulty arose when Poland claimed all of the administrative district of Allenstein of the old Province of East Prussia, while Germany desired to retain at least the eastern portion of the Province of West Prussia. Following the plebiscites in 1920, the county and city-county of Elbing, which was a part of the old administrative district of Danzig, and the counties of Marienburg, Stuhm, Marienwerder, and Rosenberg of the old administrative district of Marienwerder, were constituted as the administrative district of West Prussia and added to the Province of East Prussia.

In the northern part of the Province of East Prussia, the Memel area was surrendered to the Allies. Opinion was divided as to whether to cede it to Lithuania, or to Poland, or to establish it as a Free City like Danzig. In 1923 Lithuanian forces occupied the area. The League decision of 1924 provided that Lithuania should have full control over the territory, and that the port of Memel should be under an International Harbor Commission.

Under the pressure of Nazi propaganda the German population of Memel clamored for the return of the area to East Prussia. By 1935 the local Nazi party in the Memel area had won political control. In 1939 the Nazi government took the Memel area and re-annexed the counties of Memel, Pogegen, and Heydekrug, and the city county of Memel to the administrative district of Gumbinnen.

The victory over Poland at the beginning of World War II brought the Polish Corridor and Danzig back under German control. The Province of West Prussia was re-established and the counties of Elbing, Marienburg, Stuhm, Marienwerder, and Rosenberg, and the city county of Elbing were detached from East Prussia. This latter province, however, was expanded through the addition of the administrative district of Zichenau, nine counties carved out of Polish territory, in the south, and by the addition of the county of Sudauen (Suwalki territory taken from Poland) to the administrative district of Gumbinnen. The Province of East Prussia will be treated in this study in terms of its 1939 status before the seizure of Memel and the various portions of Polish territory.

The administration of the province followed the regular pattern of Prussian administration and was headed by a Chief President who resided at Königsberg. The provincial administration and self-government were placed under Nazi laws which modified the Provincial Constitutions of 1823, 1871/1881 and liberal republican laws. Much of the actual administration was carried out by the District Presidents of the administrative districts of Königsberg, Gumbinnen, Allenstein, and West Prussia.

The work of the provincial administration was supplemented by a number of special and technical services under direct national control. During the imperial period only the state administered courts, railways and mining offices and the nationally operated postal system were outside the sphere of general administration. Justice, within the province, was administered by the Prussian Ministry of Justice, and was directed by the Superior State Court of Königsberg, the Collegiate Courts of First and Second Instance (*Landgerichte*) of Allenstein, Bartenstein, Braunsberg, Insterburg, Königsberg, Lyck, and Tilsit and the Superior State Court of Marienwerder and the Collegiate Court of First and Second Instance at Elbing and their local Court of First Instance. The national postal system was under the Imperial Chief Postal Directorate at Gumbinnen and Königsberg—the national Postal Directorates of the Republic and Third Reich. Following the usual pattern, national regulations for trade and industry, weights and measures, social insurance, welfare, public health, and the collection of imperial revenues were administered upon delegation from the Reich.

Under the Republic there was a further extension of direct national administration to finance, railways, unemployment insurance and employment, and labor welfare. National control of finances within East Prussia was carried out through the State Finance Office at Königsberg and its local finance offices and main customs offices. National Construction offices were located in Allenstein, Lötzen, Insterburg and Königsberg. The national railways of the province were operated under the National Railroad Directorates at Königsberg. The State Labor Office and the main Welfare Office of East Prussia (Königsberg) cared for the problems of labor. Still administered upon delegation by the provincial administration were the particular aspects of welfare, social insurance, health, trade and industry, and labor, which were subject to national legislation. The economic life of the province, which was subject to limited provincial supervision, was organized under the local branches of the German Diet of Industry and Commerce, and the Diet of Crafts and Industry, the National Corporation of the German Handicrafts, the German Agricultural Councils, and the Trade Unions.

Under the Empire, the Province of East Prussia was dominated by the conservative parties, although it must be noted that urban Königsberg went Social Democratic, while there were a few Catholic Center areas in the southwest portion of the province. The National Liberals and the Progressives had limited followings in the northern districts. During most of the Weimar era, it followed the conservative way, serving as one of the strongholds of the German National People's party. In the 1928 elections for the *Reichstag,* this party received 31.4 per cent of the total popular vote while the Social Democrats were second with 26.8 per cent. In elections to the Prussian state legislature the Socialists were stronger, but in the local elections, outside the cities, the Nationalists were the leading party. Nearly 300,000 voters gave support to the Nationalists in parliamentary elections up to the rise of Hitlerism. In 1930 the National Socialists supplanted the Nationalists as the strongest party in the province, increasing their popular support phenomenally by 230,000 votes, the Nationalists at the same time losing 108,000 votes. The Socialist vote meanwhile dropped a little but remained quite constant during this critical period, while the Communist vote increased somewhat.

When the July 1932 elections rolled around, the Nazis swept the province with a voting percentage of 47.1 per cent—an increase of 300,000 votes over the previous election. The Nationalists dropped another 100,000 votes, indicating a trend from this party to the Nazis. Although the province remained faithful to Hindenburg when he ran for President, several of the voting districts, such as the counties of Goldap, Gumbinnen, Marienwerder, and Rosenberg strongly supported Hitler for the highest office. In the March 1933 *Reichstag* election, the Nazis received a clear and undoubted majority of all the votes cast, namely 56.5 per cent. Every district in the province went for Hitler except the county of Rössel, where the Catholic voters held their ground against the Nazis, and kept their voting record consistently straight for the Catholic party. In Königsberg, Insterburg, Tilsit, and Elbing there was always a sizable Socialist and Communist vote, and in the city of Allenstein the Catholic party remained strong. In the end, however, all of the cities went into the Hitler column, only Allenstein remaining close with a large Catholic vote. East Prussia, therefore, ranks with Schleswig-Holstein and Pomerania as one of the strongest centers of Nazi strength in the whole of Germany.

The Province of East Prussia was constituted as the Nazi party district of East Prussia for purposes of party administration. The party district headquarters at Königsberg included the usual offices which exercised control over the provincial government and administration. The member and affiliated party organizations maintained offices for the party district of East Prussia at Königsberg. This dense network of party organizations guaranteed the political reliability of the area.

With the Nazi regime came an extension of national administrative controls. Direct national administration, which continued for Finance, Posts, Labor and Labor Welfare, and Railways, was extended to Justice, air matters and labor affairs. Many of the traditional fields of state administration—police, health, welfare, education, and certain aspects of social insurance—were brought under tight national control.

Total regimentation of life within the province was the order of the day with corporate administrations supplementing the general and special administrative systems.

Rural Aspect

The Province of East Prussia was primarily an agricultural region and had a basic rural economy similar to that of Pomerania and Mecklenburg. The northern portion of the province, which contains the better agrarian land, has been exploited on an intensive basis only since the arrival of the German peasant cultivator and landlord during the thirteenth and fourteenth centuries, for the earlier Borussi were more interested in pastoral activities. The southern part of East Prussia with its hills, lakes, and forests was not brought under cultivation until the modern period. Although the people of the other provinces and states of Germany turned to industry and manufacturing during the late nineteenth and early twentieth centuries, the East Prussians clung to their old rural economy. About 42 per cent of the population was supported by agriculture and forestry, while by contrast even in the agrarian provinces of northeast Germany the percentage engaged in agriculture and forestry seldom exceeds 35 per cent, and the percentage for the Reich as a whole is 20.8. During the thirties of this century, about 62 per cent of the population lived in villages of less than 2,000, while another 6 per cent lived in small rural market towns with populations ranging between 2,000 and 5,000. Although the province had over

136,000 farms, a large proportion of the rural population was dependent upon the four thousand large Junker estates which hold approximately 46 per cent of the agricultural land. During the Republic efforts were made, particularly by Chancellor Brüning, to divide up these estates, but without success. Most of the remaining land was largely held by independent farmers with moderate-sized holdings. About 20 per cent of the fields of East Prussia were divided into small peasant holdings of less than 20 hectares. The large estates had control of the better agrarian areas in the northern and southeastern portions of the province, while the small peasant holdings, which were largely in the hands of the Masurians, were located among the hills and lakes of southern East Prussia.

The general administration of the Province of East Prussia centered in the city of Königsberg, the provincial capital, and in the four district capitals of Königsberg, Gumbinnen, Allenstein, and Marienwerder. The day-to-day administration of the rural area was carried on in the thirty-seven counties, headed by County Managers who served both as agents of the central government and of local self-government. Before the Nazis, the state aspect of county administration was regulated by the County Constitutions of 1825, 1872/1881, while the county corporate structure was governed by the Ordinances of 1872/1881 and the liberal laws of the Republic. The villages and small towns, which were once governed by the Constitution for Rural Villages and Towns of 1872, followed the German Municipal Code after 1935.

There is considerable regional variation in the character of agriculture and rural conditions throughout the province, but it may, for general purposes, be divided into two basic agrarian regions. The northern part of East Prussia enjoys a humid-moist climate. It is characterized by relatively severe winters with an average January temperature of —2 degrees to —4 degrees C. and cool summers with an average July temperature ranging between 16 and 17 degrees C. Most of the area has a moderate rainfall which ranges between 600 and 800 mm. per year. The landscape of northern East Prussia is marked by numerous moors and scattered forests. The fields were largely devoted to forage crops and pasture which did well on the clay and loam in this climatic region. The large estates tended to specialize in cattle and horse raising. Dairying was important, and butter and cheese were also important, owing to the great distance from markets. The crops were limited to rye, potatoes, and some wheat; the latter of which was largely grown on the large estates.

The rolling terminal moraine country in southern East Prussia with its sandy soils has extensive areas of woodland and lakeland. The summers in the south are somewhat warmer than those farther north with the average July temperature averaging from 18 degrees to 19 degrees C. The winters are cold and the temperature range is much the same as that in the north.

The southern part of East Prussia is, however, much drier than the northern; the average yearly rainfall ranges between 500 and 600 mm. While the northern part of the province was largely devoted to dairying and cattle raising, the southern area derived most of its agricultural income from the cultivation of rye and potatoes. In East Prussia, these crops are not shipped directly to market, because of the cost of transportation. On the small farms the potatoes were fed to swine, and on the large estates they were used in the production of alcohol and starch. The best agricultural area in East Prussia is located in the southeast and consists of a small area of rich soil enjoying a dry-warm climate. It was utilized for the cultivation of wheat, sugar beets, and barley, and the raising of livestock. The large estates, which dominated the province, were first class economic enterprises, making use of agricultural machinery and large numbers of day laborers, who were brought in from Poland and Lithuania. The few small farms were occupied by unprogressive, backward, and impoverished peasants.

There were large surpluses of rye and potatoes and smaller amounts of wheat, barley, oats, and maize for exportation to other parts of Germany. In terms of surpluses of cattle, East Prussia ranked fifth in Germany, while in pig raising the province ranked third. The figures for land utilization (given below in hectares) indicate the amount and types of land available for agriculture in 1933.

Cultivated Land		1,584,400
Grain	913,000	
Legumes	104,000	
Root Crops	260,000	
Green Vegetables	1,900	
Industrial Crops	2,500	
Fodder Crops	303,000	
Small Gardens		30,000
Meadow and Pasture		740,000
Orchards		5,500
Forest and Woodland		715,000
Waste Land		129,000
Houses, Buildings, and Barns		58,200
Roads and Parks		276,000

This province devoted about 68 per cent of its land to agrarian activity; 48 per cent to crop cultivation, and 13 per cent to pastoral activities. The remaining land was divided between forests and woodland (20 per cent) and waste land (12 per cent).

The forests are widely scattered throughout the province, occupying only a moderate proportion of the total area. The northern section of East Prussia is partly covered by forests of spruce, mixed with oak, ash, aspen, and linden; these forests extend northward into Lithuania. The central portion of the province also has several areas of spruce forest, but here the subsidiary stands include beech and hornbeam. In the Masurian lake country of southern East Prussia, there are mixed forests of pine and spruce, which give way to pine forests in the southwestern portion of the province adjacent to the Polish Corridor. The forest land was owned by a variety of interests. The state owned about 80 per cent of the total forest area, which it administered through 78 forest reserves. The remaining forest areas were owned by county, municipal, and private interests.

The people of East Prussia, who should be regarded basically as Germanized Balts or Borussians, include also German, Slavic Masurian, and Lithuanian settlers, who have occupied the area since the early Middle Ages. Although the settlements of East Prussia were largely of the *Strassendörfer* type, consisting of houses and buildings situated along a single road, the agglomerated *Marschhufendorf* was common in the Masurian lake country. The former type of settlement was certainly introduced by the German settlers in the days of the Teutonic Order, while the latter type dates from the later Middle Ages when the Germans penetrated the lake country. The older Baltic (Borussian) and Slavic patterns of settlement have largely disappeared under the impact of Germanization. The houses of the villages varied considerably throughout the province, but in general the old Baltic house type, which was characterized by a house and farm yard with scattered farm buildings, could be found in the northeastern part of the province, while the Middle German type of house, with a separate dwelling and two or three barns located on a farm yard square, was common in the southern and central part of the province. The Slavic block house, constructed of logs, was still found in the Masurian lake area, where it was introduced by Polish settlers.

The villages of most of East Prussia tended to be small, with populations averaging between 100 and 600. In the northeast, however, the small hamlet with a population of 20 to 100 individuals was more common, while the large village with a population of 600 to 1600 occurred in southwestern East Prussia. It must be noted that in addition to the village form of settlement, there were two other varieties of settlement: the manorial estate and the farmstead (*Einzelsiedlung*). The manorial estates, which were located largely in the southwestern and northern portions of the province, consisted of a manor house and a group of barns and row houses for workers. There was usually a barracks for seasonal laborers. The isolated farmsteads were uniformly distributed in small numbers throughout the province.

The peasants of East Prussia were industrious and persevering. Their long struggle for the Germanization of the east has left a tradition of strong patriotism. Their capacity for hard work was derived in large measure from their efforts to make a living from the poor soils of the province. The regiments raised in East Prussia were noted for their fanatical devotion to duty. The officer class, which was provided by the Junker landlords and their families, had long played an important role in the German armies. Economically, rural East Prussia had long been in a serious state of crisis. This was intensified by its organic separation from the Reich after World War I. Distance from markets and high transportation costs, as well as the artificial isolation of East Prussia from Polish markets resulted in a further impoverishment of the Junker class. The various programs for Eastern Relief (*Osthilfe*) initiated by the Republic, which involved conversion of mounting agricultural debt, colonization, and public works plus high artificial prices were continued and expanded by the Nazis. These efforts failed to give agricultural East Prussia a sound economic structure.

The Nazi colonization movement and the Nazi attempt to parcel out the large estates, like previous efforts, have failed. Only the elaborate public works program brought temporary relief during the thirties.

Urban Aspect

The province of East Prussia had only one large city, Königsberg, and four large towns, Insterburg, Tilsit, Allenstein, and Elbing, with populations ranging between 40,000 and 75,000. Taken together these five urban centers contained over 22 per cent of the total population of the province. Another 10 per cent of the population dwelt in the twenty-nine smaller agrarian towns which were widely scattered throughout the province. Most of the important towns of the province were established during the thirteenth and fourteenth centuries by the Order of the Teutonic Knights. Today their old churches, fortresses, and city walls survive in many cases as testimony of the days when they were isolated German strong points embedded in a foreign land. The towns increased in size during the fourteenth century as a consequence of trade with western Europe, which was facilitated by their connections with the Hanseatic League. It must be recalled, however, that from the fifteenth through the seventeenth centuries the cities of East Prussia fell under the spell of Polish culture and civilization, for the entire area was a fief of the Polish crown during this period. The revival of German power under the Hohenzollerns brought the revival of the movement for Germanization. By the beginning of the nineteenth century, most of the towns of the province had been thoroughly Prussianized.

The towns of East Prussia have been important market towns dependent upon an agrarian hinterland since the Middle Ages. Except for Königsberg and Elbing, the nineteenth century industrial revolution brought little change in their economic status; each sustained only a minor increase in population and added a few industries based upon the utilization of local agrarian resources. Today, they are regional commercial and trade centers catering to the agricultural population. Economically, they are oriented toward the large city of Königsberg, the political, governmental, administrative, economic, financial, and cultural capital of East Prussia.

The five larger cities of the province were organized as city counties. Municipal government and administration followed the national pattern laid down by the German Municipal Code of 1935. The democratic features of city government and administration, which were provided by the Stein Constitution of 1808, the City Constitutions of 1831, and 1853, and the liberal measures of the Republic, were swept away by the Nazis.

The East Prussian area, which was characterized by a sparse population, large estates, and the production of rye, potatoes, and dairy products, constitutes a distinct economic area dominated by agriculture and forestry. Aside from Königsberg, the main center of East Prussian economic life, the cities and towns of the area, with the possible exception of the port town of Elbing, were small market towns dependent upon their rather limited rural hinterlands. Economically, urban East Prussia was handicapped by its distance from German markets and industries, by its isolation from Polish resources, markets, and industries, and by its lack of a prosperous agricultural hinterland. Nazi efforts to relieve the situation by awarding numerous war contracts to East Prussian factories brought only temporary relief. In order to understand the economic life of this province, which was isolated from the main body of the Reich by the Polish Corridor between the two World Wars, one must examine its industries, commerce, and transportation facilities with a constant view to the impoverished agricultural and forestry activities of the area. Recognizing the distinct economic character of the East Prussian area, the Nazis placed the province under a separate planning association.

Aside from agricultural products—cereals, potatoes, butter, cheese, and meat —and forestry products, the province had little in the way of natural resources, except amber for ornaments and jewelry. Cattle raising had long supported a well developed leather industry, which continued to flourish in the towns of Elbing, Königsberg, and Tilsit. The textile industry, which had utilized the flax raised in western East Prussia since the late Middle Ages, was still important at Elbing. The modern woolen mills of Königsberg did not develop until recent times; and the only other important textile center was located at Insterburg. Small plants at Königsberg, Elbing, Tilsit, Insterburg, and Allenstein met the metal ware and machinery needs of the agricultural population. The major centers of the wood products industry were located at Königsberg, Tilsit, Allenstein, and Elbing. At Königsberg, and Elbing, the industries and manufacturing establishments were on a somewhat larger scale than in the other cities, for these two towns had port facilities giving them easy access to the industrial resources of the Reich. At Königsberg, in addition to textiles, leather, wood, and food products, shipbuilding and machinery became important economic activities. The smaller town of Elbing was an even more important manufacturing center; it was famous for its cigars, which were made from tobacco raised in the lower Vistula Valley.

The power needs of the manufacturing centers of the province were met by an electrical power station in Königsberg, operated by means of coal shipped by sea and river from the Upper Silesian coal fields. It was connected by high tension line with a small water power plant at Friedland in central East Prussia, while other high tension lines connected these power plants with Elbing, Insterburg, and Rastenburg.

The backbone of the road transportation system is formed by a circular road from Königsberg, through Insterburg, Gumbinnen, Lyck, Allenstein, Elbing, and back to Königsberg. Other main highways radiate from Königsberg, Insterburg, and Allenstein, the major road junctions, to all parts of the province. In addition to these main arteries, there is an extensive network of local roads. The major provincial highways were maintained by the Provincial Corporation, while the local county roads were under the county Road Master. After 1933, the super-highways augmented the normal road system.

Although the railroad system serving East Prussia follows the road pattern, the major rail lines run from Danzig via Elbing, Königsberg, and Insterburg to Gumbinnen and points in Russia, or from Frankfort via Posen, Thorn, Allenstein, Insterburg, and Tilsit to Memel in Lithuania. The railroads, which were owned and operated by the national government, were under the national Ministry of Transportation and operated by the National Railroad Directorate of Königsberg.

The province is served by a few excellent though small ports and canals. The ports of Königsberg and Elbing, which must be kept open in the winter with ice breakers, were used for the importation of coal, coke, building materials, fertilizer, and oil, and the export of cereals, wood pulp, timber, and food products produced in the province. Elbing, the smaller of the two ports, handling about 160,000 metric tons of freight each year, was connected with the interior of southwestern East Prussia by the small Upper State Canal (*Oberländischer Kanal*). Königsberg, which ranked fifth among the German ports, handled over 2,860,000 metric tons of ocean freight and 920,000 metric tons of river freight each year. The outport of Pillau served as the passenger port for Königsberg. The real development of the port of Königsberg came in the nineties of the last century after the Russian-German Commercial Treaty of 1896, which diverted a considerable proportion of Russia's overseas trade to the port of Königsberg. Naturally, this trade was lost after World War I. The navigable Pregel River gives Königsberg access not only to Insterburg and eastern East Prussia, but also to Tilsit via a small canal, and to southeastern East Prussia via the Masurian Canal (*Masurischer Kanal*), which connects the Pregel River with the Masurian lakes. The province had two major airports, Tilsit and Königsberg. Although the air transportation service was operated by the German Airways Corporation (*Deutsche Lufthansa*), which was under the national Ministry of Aviation, the local airports were owned and operated by the municipalities of Tilsit and Königsberg.

The Province of East Prussia was commercially and financially oriented toward the city of Königsberg. Elbing in the southwest, Allenstein in the south, and Insterburg and Tilsit in the north cannot be regarded as anything more than well developed regional commercial and manufacturing centers serving the agricultural and forestry interests of the province. The surpluses of cereals, potatoes, meat, and dairy products raised in the province were shipped via rail or sea through the ports of Elbing and Königsberg to the Berlin and central German industrial area. The coal, coke, and metal products required by the limited industries of East Prussia came from Upper Silesia and central Germany. Fertilizer, which was vital for the agriculture of East Prussia, was imported from the central German area. The pulp and wood products of the province found a ready market within the Reich.

The banking and credit institutions of the province ranged from branches of the great commercial banks of Berlin, which were mainly interested in investments of the industrial type, to the local county and municipal mortgage and savings banks. The provincially owned banks and financial institutions were concentrated in Königsberg. The operations of these banks were supplemented by those of the branches of the *Reichsbank*. The provincial governments operated a life and fire insurance organization. Königsberg was the center for a Stock Exchange.

The urban population of East Prussia was largely engaged in industry and crafts. Of the total population in 1933, 21 per cent or 503,000 individuals were engaged in industry, manufacturing, or crafts, while only 12 per cent or 288,000 individuals were employed in commercial and transportation enterprises. Another 7 per cent of the population were engaged in professional work or public service. An unusual class pattern is the result. The working class, including both the industrial and agricultural workers, was large, accounting for about 41 per cent of the population. The white collar class, 6 per cent, and the civil servant group, 5.6 per cent, were quite small in comparison with those of the provinces and states of western and central Germany. The upper class, which accounted for 19 per cent of the population, was about normal for northeastern Germany

Königsberg was East Prussia's only important urban center. Its location on the Pregel River near the Baltic Sea, which has long been a factor in its commercial development, plus its status as the capital of the province, contributed to its position as the major center of life in the area. Historically, Königsberg will always be important as the city where the first Prussian kings were crowned. Culturally, it is significant as the home of the great philosopher Kant (1724-1804) and as the seat of the oldest German university in eastern Germany. The port city of Elbing in southwestern East Prussia was the second city of the province and a one-time commercial rival of Danzig in the days of the Hanseatic League. Famous for its Old City (*Altstadt*), rich in ancient gabled houses, it became an important center for machinery, food products, and agricultural trade. The small town of Marienwerder, the seat of the administration for the governmental administrative district of West Prussia, was founded by the Teutonic Knights in 1233. Its old castle was used by the Eastern Leadership School (*Ostland Führerschule*) of the Hitler Youth. Allenstein, an agricultural market town in the Masurian lake country, was built around an old castle established by the Teutonic Knights in 1348. The bishop's palace was used as a residence by the famous Polish astronomer Copernicus. Not far from Allenstein is the battlefield of Tannenberg, marked by a large memorial where Hindenburg is buried. Insterburg in northern East Prussia was a market and manufacturing town, particularly important for its famous horse market. Tilsit, the largest town in the northern part of the province, was another market center. Gumbinnen in eastern East Prussia was a small garrison and residence town, the seat of the administration for the governmental district of Gumbinnen. East Prussia has long been the symbol of Germany's struggle with the Slav and the spiritual emblem of Prussian militarism.

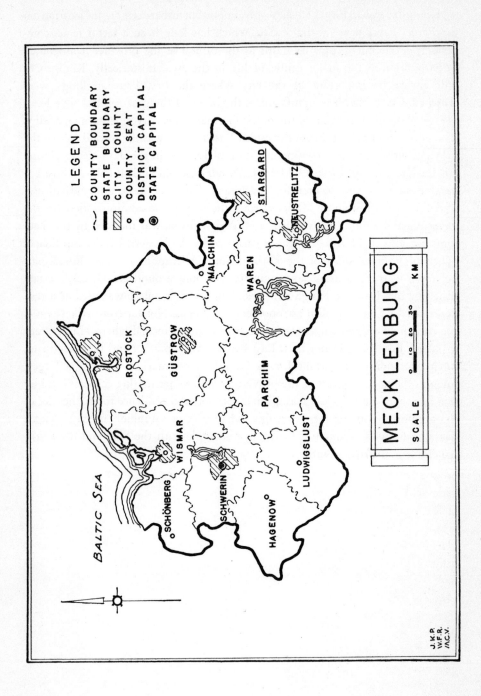

LEGEND

COUNTY BOUNDARY
STATE BOUNDARY
CITY - COUNTY
COUNTY SEAT
DISTRICT CAPITAL
STATE CAPITAL

MECKLENBURG

SCALE
0 10 20 30
KM

BALTIC SEA

ROSTOCK

GÜSTROW

MALCHIN

WAREN

STARGARD

NEUSTRELITZ

PARCHIM

WISMAR

SCHÖNBERG

SCHWERIN

HAGENOW

LUDWIGSLUST

J.K.P.
W.F.R.
IAC.V.

Chapter 10

THE STATE OF MECKLENBURG

___

   The state of Mecklenburg, which is a union of the old duchies of Mecklenburg-Schwerin and Mecklenburg-Strelitz, lies along the Baltic Sea and is bordered by the Prussian Province of Schleswig-Holstein on the west, by the provinces of Hanover and Brandenburg on the south, and on the east by the Province of Pomerania. It lies within the area of the North German Plains, a part of the Baltic coastal lands, which consist of a series of lake-plateaus extending from the Elbe River to the Vistula. The low Mecklenburg Plateau, like the plateaus of Pomerania and East Prussia, is crossed by east-west terminal moraines, composed of the clay, sand, gravel, and boulders of the last glacial period, and characterized by moderately fertile northern slopes with boulder clay soils, and infertile southern slopes whose sandy soils support woodland and pasture. The inadequate drainage of this glaciated area has given rise to extensive marshes and moors, as well as a great number of small lakes of which there are about 400 in Mecklenburg. The land surface is drained by the Warnow, Recknitz, and Peene rivers, which empty into the Baltic Sea, and by the Elde River in southwestern Mecklenburg, which flows into the Elbe. The coast of Mecklenburg has an unusually large number of ports for the German Baltic area. The inlets or *Bodden* of Wismar and Rostock, formed through the postglacial depression of the coast and the consequent flooding of river valleys, are quite shallow, restricting the development of port facilities. The ports which have developed along the larger estuaries and inlets of the flat, sandy, and occasionally dune-covered coast of Mecklenburg are frequently blocked by the formation of winter ice. Although the state enjoys a summer climate of North Atlantic type much like that of Northwest Germany, the winters are more severe. With its moraines, sandy coast, marshes, and numerous lakes it is an area geographically transitional between western and eastern Elbian Germany.

   Mecklenburg has been occupied by Indo-European speaking peoples since the Neolithic period. Although the Germanic peoples, who differentiated from the general Indo-European group in the second millennium B.C., occupied

321

northern Germany and Mecklenburg during the Bronze and Iron Ages, during the Migration Age (A.D. 400-800) they deserted Mecklenburg and eastern Germany for lands to the west of the Elbe or to the southeast. Their place was taken by Slavic tribes who held most of Mecklenburg from the sixth to the early twelfth century, despite the attempts of the Germans to conquer Mecklenburg under the leadership of Charlemagne and the Saxon Emperors. After the early twelfth century, Low Saxon Germans from west of the Elbe and from southern Schleswig-Holstein pushed eastward to colonize Mecklenburg. Today, the Slav has vanished and Mecklenburg is occupied by a distinct Mecklenburger group speaking a separate northern East Elbian dialect. Standard German is spoken in most towns and cities. The people of Mecklenburg are almost entirely Protestant; in 1933 there were 764,400 Protestants, 31,800 Catholics, and only about 1,000 Jews.

Mecklenburg, one of the most isolated and provincial regions of Germany, was very sparsely settled. In 1933 the state had a population of 804,900 individuals occupying an area of 15,720 sq. km. The population density was 51 per sq. km., the smallest for any German state or province, and ranged from 40 to 60 in the north and west, where the larger towns of Güstrow, Rostock, Wismar, and Schwerin are located, to less than 20 in the southeastern area. In contrast with Central and Western Germany, the population has not increased rapidly. It is significant that, although in some parts of Germany the population increased as much as 75 per cent between 1875 and 1925, the increase in Mecklenburg did not exceed 20 per cent.

From the sixth to the early twelfth century, Mecklenburg was ruled by the Slavic Obotrite tribe whose chief center was located at Michilenburg, hence the name Mecklenburg for the modern state. Charlemagne partly subdued this land during the later eighth century; but, with the disintegration of the Carolingian Empire, the Slavs regained their freedom. The first Saxon Emperors of Germany conquered the Slavs of Mecklenburg and introduced Christianity during the tenth century. The next century brought a period of Slavic freedom which gave way in the early twelfth century with the final conquest of Mecklenburg by the Germans under the leadership of the Dukes of Saxony. In the latter part of the twelfth century Pribislaus, the last Obotrite prince, submitted to Henry the Lion (Heinrich der Löwe), Duke of Saxony. He married his daughter to a son of the Duke and was permitted to retain his holdings in Mecklenburg. Pribislaus, who became a prince of the German Empire, thus established the only Slavic dynasty in Germany which survived until modern times. Following this settlement, German colonists poured into Mecklenburg, and the German language gradually began to replace the Slavic.

The lands of Mecklenburg remained intact until the death of the successor of Pribislaus, when they were divided between the lines of Mecklenburg, Rostock, Parchim, and Werle. All of the lines became extinct during the thirteenth and fourteenth centuries, except the line of Mecklenburg which had been elevated to ducal dignity in 1348 by the Emperor Charles IV. In 1471, by reasons of inheritance, all of Mecklenburg fell under the rule of the Duke of Mecklenburg. Although the principle of primogeniture was established in the late sixteenth century by Duke Johann Albert, a new division of lands came in 1611, when the grandsons of Johann Albert divided Mecklenburg to establish the lines of Mecklenburg-Schwerin and Mecklenburg-Güstrow.

During the Reformation, Mecklenburg supported Protestantism, and in the Thirty Years' War both duchies were on the Protestant side. Mecklenburg was severely ravaged and was for a time under the rule of the Catholic General Wallenstein. However, through the efforts of Gustavus Adolphus of Sweden, the dukes were restored to power. Although the Treaty of Westphalia in 1648 gave the Swedes the city of Wismar and other parts of Mecklenburg, the dukes received the secularized bishoprics of Schwerin and Ratzeburg. As a result of this war, many peasants were reduced to serfdom, and whole villages vanished. The eighteenth century opened with still another dispute over inheritance following the extinction of the line of Mecklenburg-Güstrow.

The Treaty of Hamburg in 1701, involving the rulers of Mecklenburg, Brandenburg, and Sweden, established the lines of Mecklenburg-Schwerin and Mecklenburg-Strelitz, which survived until 1918. During the eighteenth century, Mecklenburg-Schwerin was beset by constitutional troubles and wars with Prussia. The smaller duchy of Mecklenburg-Strelitz avoided the struggle over constitutional affairs by adopting the constitution of her sister duchy in 1755.

During the French Revolution, both duchies joined the Confederation of the Rhine; and both later joined the alliance against Napoleon. In 1815 they became members of the Germanic Confederation and the dukes assumed the title of Grand Duke. Serfdom was abolished in Mecklenburg-Schwerin in 1819, but the government and administration of the Grand Duchy remained reactionary and conservative. Although a few reforms were granted under the pressure of the revolutionary movement of 1848, the subsequent reaction brought their retraction and further restrictive measures. In 1866 both duchies sided with Prussia against Austria. They joined the North German Confederation and, in 1871, became states of the German Empire.

Throughout the nineteenth and early twentieth centuries the governments of the two duchies retained their feudal character. They had a common Diet whose seats belonged to the proprietors of knights' estates (*Ritterschaft*) and the mayors of the towns of the two duchies (*Landschaft*). After 1871 the people had some representation through their delegates elected to the National Assembly. Most of the legislative and all of the executive power was invested in the Grand Dukes. In Mecklenburg-Schwerin, state affairs were administered by a Ministry of State and three ministries: Interior, Labor, Economics, Weights and Measures (*Inneres*); Finances, Domains and Forests (*Finanzen*); and Justice, Church, Education, and Health (*Justiz*). Military matters were handled by a special department.

State affairs in Mecklenburg-Strelitz were handled by a Ministry of State and its state government. The Ministry of State and ministers of both states were appointed by and responsible to their respective Grand Dukes. The administration of local affairs followed the pattern of land ownership: Grand Ducal domains, knights' manorial estates (*Rittergüter*), convent manorial holdings (*Klostergüter*), and town corporations. The last ruler of Mecklenburg was Grand Duke Friedrich Franz IV of Mecklenburg-Schwerin. In February 1918, upon the extinction of the line of Strelitz, all of Mecklenburg fell under his control; his power lasted, however, only until November 1918, when the German Revolution swept away the old feudal government.

The two duchies were declared republics. The constitution of the Free State (*Freistaat*) of Mecklenburg-Schwerin, which is dated May 1920, provided for a collegial Ministry of State headed by a Minister President and consisting of two ministers and five Expert Ministers (*Fachminister*) elected by and responsible to an elected assembly. The five Expert Ministers headed the ministries of Interior; Finance; Agriculture, Public Lands, Forests (*Ministerium für Landwirtschaft, Domänen und Forsten*); Justice; and the Ministry for Education, Art, Religions and Medical Affairs (*Ministerium für Unterricht, Kunst, Geistliche und Medizinalangelegenheiten*). Other supreme administrative agencies, which were subordinated to the Ministry of State, included the State Administrative Council (*Landesverwaltungsrat*), the State Administrative Court (*Landesverwaltungsgericht*), the State Auditing Office (*Rechnungsprüfungsbehörde*), and the main State Treasury (*Hauptstaatskasse*).

The Constitution of the Free State of Mecklenburg-Strelitz, which is dated May 1923, provided for a Ministry of State consisting of five ministers who were named by and responsible to an elected assembly. They headed the Ministry of State and its four Ministerial Departments for Interior, Education and Art, Justice, and Finance. The two states had their own personnel and budget systems and their own forms of local government. The state legislatures of the two states were elected by universal suffrage and, according to the principles of proportional representation and although their sessions were brief and infrequent, they controlled the state ministries. There was a complete modernization of local government and administration in both states. Naturally the newly formed states became constituent republics of Weimar Germany and had direct representation in the national *Reichstag* and the Senate.

With the Republic came the further extension of direct national administration to finance, railways, unemployment insurance and employment, and labor welfare. National control of finances within the two Mecklenburgs was at first under the State Finance Office of Mecklenburg-Lübeck (Schwerin). Under the Nazis, the Mecklenburg and Schleswig-Holstein areas were combined for financial administration and placed under the State Finance Office of Nordmark at Kiel. A construction office was located at Schwerin. The national railways of the state were operated under the National Railroad Directorates at Schwerin and Stettin. The affairs of labor were handled by the State Labor Office of Nordmark (Hamburg), which served the Hansa City of Hamburg, the Province of Schleswig-Holstein, the northern Province of Hanover, and the state of Mecklenburg, and by the Main Welfare Office at Hanover, which had local offices scattered throughout northwestern Germany. As in the other areas considered, some aspects of welfare, social insurance, health, trade and industry, and labor, which were subject to national legislation, were still administered upon delegation by the state authorities of the two Mecklenburgs. The economic life of these two Baltic states, which was subject to only limited national and state supervision under the Empire and the Republic, was organized in national associations for industry, trade, crafts, and agriculture.

During the imperial period the only indexes of political life within the two Mecklenburgs were provided by the *Reichstag* elections. The areas of large estates voted consistently for the Conservative party, while the people on the poorer agrarian lands in the southern part of the states voted for the liberal Progressives. Rostock and Schwerin, the two major urban centers of the two states, voted for the Social Democrats. In both Mecklenburg-Schwerin and Mecklenburg-Strelitz in republican days, the Social Democratic party was the strongest, with the Nationalists second, and the German People's party third. In all of the political subdivisions of these two states, with the exception of the precinct of Stargard, the Socialists were the leading party. In the latter area the Nationalists came first.

By 1930, however, the Nazis had displaced the Nationalists as the second strongest party, increasing their vote from 7,000 to 72,000 in Mecklenburg-Schwerin, and from 500 to 13,000 in Mecklenburg-Strelitz. The city of Neubrandenburg gave the Nazis first place in this election. In the presidential elections of 1932, both Mecklenburgs voted for Hindenburg against Hitler by close margins, although Hitler carried several of the rural counties such as Hagenow, Parchim, and Ludwigslust. In the critical July 1932 *Reichstag* election, the Nazis became the strongest party in both of these states, the Social Democrats trailing far behind in second place. The cities of Güstrow, Neustrelitz, Rostock, and Schwerin went into the Hitler column, following the earlier lead of Neubrandenburg, and all of the rural counties followed suit. The November 1932 election registered a significant drop in the Nazi vote in Mecklenburg, but

Hitler's party held its lead. The Socialists and Communists together, however, received more votes than the Nazis in this election. The cities, with the exception of Neubrandenburg and Neustrelitz in Mecklenburg-Strelitz, slipped back into the Socialist fold by small pluralities, but the rural areas remained predominantly Nazi. The Nationalist vote remained significant. In the 1933 election, the Nazis were able to garner 48 per cent of the votes, just short of a clear majority. Comparatively speaking, therefore, the two Mecklenburgs are to be listed with the areas which gave strong support to Hitler and thus helped his rise to power.

The advent of the Nazi regime brought drastic changes in the government and administration of the two Mecklenburgs. In 1933 the two states were combined and placed under a National Governor with headquarters at Schwerin, the state capital of former Mecklenburg-Schwerin. Like the other German states, the two Mecklenburgs lost their status as federal republics, and their rights were transferred to the Reich. The National Governor, who was in charge of the government and administration of the state, was directly responsible to the national Minister of the Interior, but was also subject to directives from other national ministers. The Governor for Mecklenburg was also the Nazi party District Leader for the party district of Mecklenburg.

The work of the state administration was supplemented by a number of special and technical services under direct national control. During the imperial period the Prussian administered railways and the imperially operated postal system lay outside the sphere of general state administration. Justice, which was handled separately from local government and administration under the duchies, was carried out by the Superior State Court at Rostock, the Collegiate Courts of First and Second Instance at Güstrow, Neustrelitz, Rostock, and Schwerin, and the numerous local Courts of First Instance. The national imperial postal system was under the Chief Postal Directorates at Schwerin—the National Postal Directorates of the Republic and the Third Reich. National regulations for trade and industry, weights and measures, social insurance, public health, and the collection of imperial revenues were administered upon delegation from the Reich through special offices attached to the state ministries or departments.

The Nazi regime brought an extension of national administrative controls to justice, air matters, propaganda, and labor affairs. In addition, the services and functions of the general and special administrative systems were augmented by a comprehensive system of corporate administration; the result was total regimentation. The vital centers of control within Mecklenburg included Schwerin and Rostock. Schwerin, the capital of Mecklenburg, is important as the center for general administration and the regional seat for many aspects of special administration (Economic, Defense, Police, Party, Propaganda, Railways, and Post). Rostock, on the other hand, had considerable importance because of its position as the regional center for economic, labor, and justice administration.

RURAL ASPECT

Rural and agrarian activities are of major importance in the state of Mecklenburg. Until the period of German colonization, the Slavic peoples used the land for grazing, although there was a limited amount of crop cultivation near their round villages. German settlement brought the extension of agrarian activity. In 1933 over 38 per cent of the population was engaged in agrarian and forestry activities. Considering the state as a whole, a surprisingly large proportion of the people live close to the soil: about 46 per cent of the population in villages of less than 2,000, and 29 per cent in towns ranging in size from 2,000 to 20,000.

Modern local administration in Mecklenburg dates from World War I, because until 1918 the administration followed the medieval pattern of landownership. Under the Empire, Mecklenburg-Schwerin was divided into grand ducal domains, knights' manorial estates, convent manorial holdings, and town estates, while Mecklenburg-Strelitz was divided into grand ducal domains, lands of titled and untitled nobles, and lands of town corporations. After World War I there was a complete modernization and reorganization of local administration in both states. Under the Laws of 1920, Mecklenburg-Schwerin was divided into ten counties (*Ämter*) and four city counties (*Selbständige Stadtbezirke*). The state supervision of the county was provided by a County Leader (*Amtshauptmann*), while local self-government was under a county committee (*Amtsausschuss*) and a county assembly (*Amtsversammlung*). In Mecklenburg-Strelitz the land was divided into three counties and eleven free cities. The state supervision of the county was provided by a County Manager, while local self-government was under a county committee (*Amtsausschuss*) and a county assembly (*Amtstag*). County government was regulated by the County Constitutions (*Amtsordnungen*) of 1920 and 1926.

The unification of Mecklenburg in 1933 brought about a further reorganization of local administration. Under the Nazis the county (*Landkreis*)—new designation for *Amt*—was headed by a County Manager who was responsible for both county administration and local self-government. He was responsible to the head of the Department of the Interior at Schwerin, who was ultimately subject to the national Minister of the Interior. The County Manager was assisted by an appointed and advisory county committee which replaced the old *Amtsausschuss*. The County Assembly and County Diet were abolished, for they were democratic and representative institutions. The County Manager was also assisted by a Nazi Party Agent who was present to guarantee the political reliability of the county administration. The County Manager had the supervision of the government and administration of the towns and villages of the county. He was the administrative authority for all county Order Police. He had control over all officials of the Registration Offices for Vital Statistics (*Standesamtbeamte*) and maintained close working relationships with the County Health Office (*Kreisgesundheitsamt*) and the local Town Health Offices. He worked with the County School Office (*Kreisschulamt*) and the local school officials. In construction affairs he was aided by the state Road and Waterways Construction Office (*Strassen- und Wasserbauverwaltung*) and the local Road and Waterway Office. He also worked with the officials of the Youth Office (*Kreisjugendamt*), Welfare Office (*Kreiswohlfahrtsamt*), and the Insurance Office (*Kreisversicherungsamt*). In commercial and industrial affairs he was assisted by officials of the Office for the Supervision of Trade and Industry (*Gewerbeaufsichtsamt*). The County Manager maintained working relations with the county Forest Office, which was under the state Afforestation Office (*Forsteinrichtungsanstalt*) at Schwerin, and the Surveyor's Office (*Katasteramt*) which was under the State Weights and Measure Office (*Landesvermessungsamt*) at Schwerin. He, also, administered the county roads, welfare and relief, and other activities which were once under the county self-government. Unlike most German counties, those of Mecklenburg owned and operated few if any county enterprises.

The system of town and village government and administration which prevailed until the adoption of the uniform German Municipal Code of 1935 was much the same in both states. The Constitution for Rural Villages and Towns of 1919 for Mecklenburg-Schwerin and the Constitutions for Rural Villages and Towns of 1920/1922 of Mecklenburg-Strelitz provided for the magisterial form of government, consisting of a town council (*Gemeindevorstand*) and a town assembly (*Gemeindeversammlung*) which shared the legislative power. The latter, which was an elected and representative body, chose the members of the town council, which served as an administrative board or commission and elected its head, the Mayor. Under the Nazis, municipal government and administration of the towns and villages follow the pattern laid down in the new German Municipal Code of 1935. Under this code the management and control of municipal activities were under the effective supervision of an appointed Mayor, usually in honorary service, who was assisted by two or three administrative department heads and an appointed advisory council, which had replaced the old town council and town assembly. A Nazi Party Agent was associated with the Mayor to guarantee the political reliability of the city administration. The towns and villages of Mecklenburg continued, however, to handle public works, welfare, and a few enterprises—town forest, market, and an occasional utility plant—on a local basis. Most local activities were under the effective supervision of national or state authorities.

The low Mecklenburg Plateau is moderately fertile. The podzol soils of northern Mecklenburg are good for crop cultivation, while the poorer southern soils are largely given over to pasture and woodland. However, the best soils from the point of view of agriculture are those of the marshy river valleys. North Mecklenburg forms a part of the cool humid Baltic coastal agrarian zone, while southern Mecklenburg falls within the dry warm lowlands of the Elbe. The northern part of the state has an average January temperature ranging between 0 and —1 degrees C., while the southeastern part has an average January temperature ranging between —1 and —2 degrees C. In midsummer the northern and coastal area is cooler than the southern part of the state, for the average July temperature in the north ranges between 16 and 17 degrees C., while the average for the south ranges between 17 and 18 degrees C. The average yearly rainfall for the state averages 500 to 600 mm., with a greater amount of rainfall in the northern and coastal portions of Mecklenburg. In the cool, humid northern portion of the state, the chief crops which are grown upon the glacial clays and loam include rye, oats, and forage crops. Most of the farm income in this area comes from cattle and horse-raising. The chief dairy products are butter and cheese, for there are no markets for milk. The drier, warmer southern section with its infertile sandy soils is largely used for woodland and pasture. In the better agrarian areas rye and potatoes are the main crops, while the extensive pasture areas are utilized for cattle raising and horse breeding. Mecklenburg is particularly famous for its fine sturdy horses. The rich alluvial soils of the low river valleys, where the swampy and marshy land has been drained, are used for cereals, sugar beets, and pasture. Buckwheat, wheat, rape seed, flax, hemp, and tobacco are grown in limited areas of rich loam soil.

Rural life in Mecklenburg is based mainly upon cattle and horse raising. Much of the crop land goes to the production of feed to support the livestock industry. The cultivation of crops for cash income is relatively unimportant. The figures for land utilization (given below in hectares) indicate the amount and types of land available for agriculture.

Cultivated Land		742,000
Grain	473,000	
Legumes	25,500	
Root Crops	153,000	
Green Vegetables	1,300	
Industrial Crops	9,300	
Fodder Crops	79,900	

Small Gardens	16,100
Meadow	121,400
Pasture	122,600
Orchards	470
Vineyards	
Forests	329,800
Waste Land	43,600
Houses and Barns	16,000
Roads and Parks	114,000

Approximately 67 per cent of the land area of the state of Mecklenburg is devoted to agrarian activity, 50 per cent to crop cultivation, 17 per cent for pasture and meadow. The remainder of the area is divided between forests (21 per cent) and waste land (12 per cent).

The flora of Mecklenburg is transitional between the North Atlantic flora of northwestern Germany, the South Baltic flora of northeastern Germany, and the sub-Sarmatian flora of the Elbe-Oder-Vistula river lowlands. The North Atlantic oak is typical in north and western Mecklenburg, with mixed forests of beech and pine of South Baltic type extending into the eastern portions. The poorer sandy soils of the south support extensive stands of north German pine as well as beech, oak, and birch. All of Mecklenburg, particularly the southern portion, is well forested in comparison with northeastern Germany. The state owns about 50 per cent of the forests, or 180,700 hectares, which is administered through 45 state forest reserves, under the State Forest Administration at Schwerin. Another 30 per cent of the forests, or 97,000 hectares, was held by the muncipal governments, while the remaining land was owned by private interests. There were no county forest holdings in Mecklenburg. The work of the State Forest Administration at Schwerin was not restricted to state-owned forest areas, for its county Forest Offices supervised the forestry affairs of muncipal and private interests.

Mecklenburg is a rural state of large manorial estates, small villages, and tiny hamlets. The many large estates, frequently over 400 hectares, center about a manor house complex, consisting of the home of the landowner, his barns, and the houses of the farm workers, who receive for their labor a small plot of land and most of their wages in kind. These estates may also have barracks for seasonal workers, but the housing and living conditions are poor. The small villages, situated among lakes and pine-clad ridges, range in population from 70 to 200. They are most frequently of the round type, betraying their Slavic origin, and consist of simple houses of Low Saxon type. The dwellings of the farmers whose holdings range in size from 20 to 100 hectares, contrast strongly with the impoverished row-houses of the hired agricultural workers. Although the village green, the pond, and the adjacent Lutheran church lend a certain distinctiveness to the villages of Mecklenburg, there is everywhere dull uniformity. The large estates and farms with their considerable capital investment make extensive use of machinery and farm labor.

Politically and socially, the people of Mecklenburg are extremely conservative. They tend to cling to old ways and traditions. This tendency may well be an outgrowth of their long struggle with the Slavs, which ended in the fusion of the German colonists and the Slavic inhabitants. While the speech of the peasantry of Mecklenburg still retains traces of the old Slavic language, the rural landowning class remains almost wholly German and Low Saxon. Living conditions among the peasants and farm workers are poor. There is no illiteracy, but folk arts and music have not developed, although coarse folk tales of the Fritz Reuter type are common. The diet of the workers on the land consists chiefly of heavy rye bread and pork, supplemented by beer. Heavy drinking is common. Family life is patriarchal, and the women and children share in the heavy work of the farm. The poverty of the land, the character of land tenure, and the absence of real social and economic reform have conspired to make Mecklenburg one of the most backward areas of the Reich.

Urban Aspect

The six larger towns of the state of Mecklenburg have extremely varied interests and backgrounds. Rostock and Wismar are mainly port towns, which date back to the time of the Hanseatic League but which later developed important industries to support their economic life. Schwerin and Neustrelitz, which served as the capitals of the two Mecklenburgs until 1933, are, on the other hand, primarily administrative and cultural centers. Güstrow, located in the interior of old Mecklenburg-Schwerin, and Neubrandenburg, in the northern part of old Mecklenburg-Strelitz, are market towns serving an agricultural hinterland. Rostock and Schwerin, the two largest urban centers, have a population of only 93,500 and 55,600 respectively. The others range in size from 20,-000 to 30,000 population. Together the population of the six larger towns of Mecklenburg accounts for about 25 per cent of the total population of the state.

The five larger towns of Mecklenburg were established as city counties under the German Municipal Code of 1935. Prior to that time there were four independent city areas in Mecklenburg-Schwerin: Schwerin, Güstrow, Wismar, and Rostock. Their government under the City Constitution of 1919 was of the magisterial form with an administrative council and an elected city assembly. The latter elected the administrative council and its chairman, the Chief Mayor. In Mecklenburg-Strelitz there were eleven free cities with governments consisting of a mayor, an administrative council, and a city assembly (*Stadtverordnetenversammlung*). They were governed under the City Constitutions of 1919/1923. When Mecklenburg was unified, the number of free cities was reduced to two: Neubrandenburg and Neustrelitz. After 1935 the government and administration of the larger towns followed the pattern laid down in the German Municipal Code. All of the six larger towns except Neubrandenburg were recognized as city counties under the terms of the Code. Although Neubrandenburg was not recognized nationally as a city county, it had this status in Mecklenburg.

Under the Nazis the government and administration of each of the cities was headed by a Chief Mayor, who was directly responsible to the Department of the Interior at Schwerin. He was assisted by a number of professional administrative department heads and a number of lay advisory councilors with technical knowledge who were assisted by the administrative council. The functions of the Chief Mayor, who was professionally trained, frequently extended beyond matters of general administration, for in many cases he was in charge of some specialized service or services, delegated by state or national authorities. The services and their departmental structure varied from city to city. Most cities had an Organization and Personnel Office (*Organisations- und Personalamt*), an Agricultural and Economic Office (*Landwirtschafts- und Wirtschaftsamt*), and an Order Police Office (*Ordnungspolizeiamt*) to handle general administration, police affairs, and agricultural and industrial problems of the city. City finances were generally handled by a finance office, a Tax Office (*Steueramt*), and a Treasurer's and Controller's Office (*Kassen- und Rechnungsprüfungsamt*). Schools of the elementary and secondary type were administered under national supervision by a School Office, while city cultural affairs were under a special office subject to the ultimate jurisdiction of the national Ministry of Propaganda and the national Cultural Chamber. The city Welfare Office, Youth Office, Housing and Settlement Office and the Health Office were all subject to national supervision. City buildings and road maintenance and construction were under a City Construction Office. Most cities own and operate a number of economic enterprises (utilities, harbors, airports, baths, cemeteries, banks, markets, etc.). Sometimes all the various enterprises of the city were managed by one Public Service Office (*Betriebsamt*), while in other cases the management of the various enterprises were placed under different administrative department heads. Under the Nazis, democratic control was replaced by party political control. The Chief Mayor was assisted by a Nazi Party Agent who was present to guarantee the political reliability of the city administration. Thus while the German Municipal Code did not disturb the scope of local powers, it did eliminate all local control of the Chief Mayor and gave him full legislative, executive, and administrative powers.

Mecklenburg along with the Baltic provinces of Pomerania and East Prussia forms a distinct agrarian zone characterized by large estates, a sparse, backward peasant population, and a landowning upper class. The economic life of the state of Mecklenburg is oriented toward the capital city, Schwerin, and the port city of Rostock. The other large towns are significant mainly as market towns serving an agricultural hinterland. Although there is some industrial activity, it is overshadowed by the commercial interests of the towns. The distinct social-economic character of the state of Mecklenburg as a real unit of human activity was recognized by the Nazis when they made this area into a separate Regional Planning Association. They also recognized the predominance of agriculture and the secondary importance of industry and commerce. They placed the state under a separate State Peasant Association for agricultural organization, while in the fields of industrial and commercial organization they made Mecklenburg a part of the Nordmark area including the Hanseatic City of Hamburg and the Province of Schleswig-Holstein.

The natural resources of Mecklenburg are extremely limited, being restricted to a few salt deposits near Rostock. The power needs of the limited industries of Mecklenburg are met by coal shipped in from the Ruhr and lignite obtained from the mines of Brandenburg. The electrical power for the industries is supplied by numerous local plants, which are frequently owned and operated by the municipalities. Aside from a small electrical transmission line connecting Lübeck and Wismar, Mecklenburg is isolated from the power network which links much of the Reich. Rostock and Wismar are the only important industrial centers. The former is important for the manufacturing of bricks and tile, chemicals, beer, and some machinery. The latter industry in Rostock is largely connected with the Heinkel airplane works and local shipbuilding yards. Wismar also has a machinery industry; it is connected with the local Dornier airplane works and ship repairing and refitting plants. The other industries at Wismar include the manufacturing of wagons, sugar, and food products. Both cities are important as fishing centers. Güstrow is the only other manufacturing center of importance. It has a small machinery industry and plants interested in wood products and furniture. Schwerin, Neustrelitz, and Neubrandenburg are primarily market towns; still each has a few plants producing food and wood products. In comparison with the manufacturing areas of Central and Western Germany, Mecklenburg has little importance in the total framework of German industrial activity.

The state of Mecklenburg does not play an important role in the national transportation system, because its roads and rail lines are not directly on any of the main north-south or east-west transportation routes. The basic road transportation system consists of an east-west road running from Hamburg via Lübeck, Wismar, and Rostock to Stralsund and Stettin in Pomerania and two short north-south roads running through Schwerin and Neustrelitz to connect with the main Berlin-Hamburg road which crosses the southwestern corner of Mecklenburg. The construction and maintenance of the main state roads were handled by the Department of the Interior at Schwerin, while local roads were under the county administrations.

The major rail lines are oriented toward Berlin. One rail line runs from Berlin to Neustrelitz, where it connects with lines running to Stralsund and Rostock. The latter town is the rail port for Sweden. The coastal rail line running from Lübeck via Wismar and Rostock to Stralsund and the two interior lines crossing central and southern Mecklenburg are of minor importance. The railroads were owned and operated by the German Railroad Company, which administered local railroad operations through the National Railroad Directorates at Schwerin and Stettin.

Water transportation is important in Mecklenburg, which includes the two ports of Rostock and Wismar. The former port, which is situated on the Warnow River, has been important since the days of the Hanseatic League. In the thirties, the port of Rostock and the down-stream port of Warnemünde handled about 400,000 tons of traffic each year. Ships with a draft of 18 feet can reach the excellent port facilities at Rostock. During the winter months the Warnow has to be kept open with ice-breakers. The smaller port of Wismar, which is situated at the head of a deep inlet, handled about 200,000 tons of traffic each year. It is connected with the Elbe River by a canal which runs via Schwerin to connect with the Elde River, a tributary of the Elbe. Another canal runs eastward from the Elde to give Wismar connections with Berlin and the Oder River. Both ports have excellent docks, warehouse facilities, and coal bunkering services. The Reich government maintained a Sea Office (*Seeamt*) at Rostock, which handled claims and legal matters growing out of accidents at sea. There were no major airports or air services for Mecklenburg.

Schwerin and Rostock constitute the major commercial and financial centers of the state of Mecklenburg. These two towns, like the smaller port town of Wismar and the market towns of Güstrow, Neustrelitz, and Neubrandenburg, are important centers for local commerce and finance. The commercial interests of Mecklenburg reflect its agricultural, forestry, and quarrying activities. In terms of freight traffic carried by rail, food products, wood and timber, and brick and tile were the important commodities produced and shipped from Mecklenburg, while coal and fertilizer were shipped in from adjacent areas. The coal, which is needed for domestic and industrial uses, came from the Ruhr. Much of the metal used by the industries came from Sweden via the ports of Wismar and Rostock. Fertilizer from central Germany is essential for the poor clay soils of Mecklenburg. Trade in agricultural products, livestock, and dairy products is vital to the economy of Mecklenburg. Most of the agrarian surpluses of this state went to the Berlin markets.

The banking and credit institutions of Mecklenburg ranged from branches of the great commercial banks in Berlin, which were mainly interested in investments of the industrial type, to the local municipal savings banks. Schwerin and Rostock were the major banking and finance centers. Although there were no state banks, the national government-supervised *Reichsbank* maintained branches at Rostock (branches at Güstrow, Neubrandenburg, and Neustralitz), and at Schwerin (branch at Wismar). The state of Mecklenburg operated an insurance organization: the *Mecklenburgische Landesbrandkasse* at Rostock.

The population of Mecklenburg is largely engaged in agricultural and forestry activities. The limited urban population living in towns over 20,000, which constitutes about 20 per cent of the total population, was occupationally divided as follows in terms of the total population: industries and crafts 22 per cent, trade and transportation 14 per cent, professions and civil service 8 per cent, household servants 3 per cent. The upper class, which formed about 17.8 per cent of the population of the state, was about average for the Reich, although it was relatively small when it is compared with the upper classes of states like Bavaria and Württemberg. On the other hand, it was about the same size as that of the average East Elbian Prussian province. The civil servant group which constituted 5.6 per cent of the population was about average for the East Elbian area. The smallness of the white collar class, which accounted for 7.2 per cent of the population, is to be expected in an agrarian area. Mecklenburg also had a large working class, 43.4 per cent of the population. This class was as large as those of the Province of Saxony and the Rhine Province, where great numbers of people were employed in industrial and manufacturing enterprises, although here most of the workers were employed on the large estates as agricultural workers.

The six larger towns of rural and agrarian Mecklenburg have diverse origins. Although all of the large towns may well have had a Slavic village origin, only Schwerin and Rostock were of any importance before the German colonization and settlement of Mecklenburg. The Germanization of the towns began in the twelfth century. Schwerin, the present capital of Mecklenburg, was conquered in 1611 by the Low Saxons. Its Germanization came in the late twelfth and thirteenth centuries. This city has developed as a governmental administrative center during the ensuing centuries, for it has never had strong commercial or industrial interests. The port towns of Rostock and Wismar, which were likewise Germanized in the twelfth and thirteenth centuries, grew rapidly during the medieval period on the thriving Baltic trade. Both towns became members of the Hanseatic League, whose commercial interests were oriented toward continental and eastern Europe. The splendid Gothic structures of these towns reveal their early wealth. In 1419 a university, the first in northern Germany, was established at Rostock. The discovery of America and the consequent increasing use of the North Sea and North Atlantic trade routes brought the decline of the Baltic ports of Mecklenburg, which became of only minor importance in comparison with the North Sea ports of Germany. Rostock was the birthplace of the Prussian General von Blücher and the nineteenth century poet Brinckman, while Wismar must look back for its eminence to the sixteenth and seventeenth centuries when it was the residence of one line of Mecklenburg princes. Güstrow was also once the residence of Mecklenburg nobility; today, it is a thriving agrarian and market center. Neustrelitz developed because of its former importance as the capital of the old Grand Duchy and State of Mecklenburg-Strelitz, while Neubrandenburg is important as the home of the writer Fritz Reuter, who has immortalized the spirit of Mecklenburg.

BIBLIOGRAPHY

Adler, F. *Pommern* (München, 1930).

Ambrassat, A. *Die Provinz Ostpreussen* (Königsberg, 1912).

Anon. *Looking East: Germany beyond the Vistula* (Berlin, 1933).

Arendt, M. (ed.) *Geschichte der Stadt Berlin* (Berlin, 1937).

Brandt, B. *Der Nordesten, Landeskunde von Deutschland,* Bd. II (Leipzig, 1931).

Brosien, H. *Geschichte der Mark Brandenburg im Mittelalter* (Leipzig, 1887).

Deecke, W. *Landeskunde von Pommern* (Leipzig, 1912).

Emmerich, W. *Der Deutsche Osten* (Leipzig, 1935).

Evers, E. *Brandenburg-Preussische Geschichte bis auf die neueste Zeit,* 2d ed. (Berlin, 1912).

Fay, S. B. *The Rise of Brandenburg-Prussia to 1786* (New York, 1937).

Ford, G. *Stein and the Era of Reform in Prussia* (Princeton, 1922).

Geisler, W. (ed.) *Wirtschafts- und verkehrsgeographischer Atlas von Schlesien* (Breslau, 1932).

Great Britain, Foreign Office *Upper Silesia* (Peace Handbook, Vol. XII, No. 40, London, 1920).

Hartung, F. *Preussen und das Deutsche Reich seit 1871* (Berlin 1932).

Hegemann, W. *Das steinerne Berlin* (Berlin, 1930).

Heinze, H. *Die Provinz Brandenburg* (Berlin, 1901).

Hergesheimer, J. *Berlin* (New York, 1932).

James, H. G. *Principles of Prussian Administration* (New York, 1913).

Jeserich, K. *Die Preussischen Provinzen* (Berlin, 1931).

Kaeckenbeeck, G.S.F.C. *The International Experiment of Upper Silesia* (London, New York, 1942).

Kallweit, E. *Die wirtschaftsgeographische Entwicklung Ostpreussen* (Stallupönen, 1933).

Kern, R. *Preussische Geschichte* (Leipzig, 1913).

Loos, W. *Die Bezichungen zwischen dem Deutsch-Ordenstaat und Pommern* (Doctoral Dissertation, Königsberg, 1937, University of Königsberg).

Machray, R. *East Prussia* (London, 1943).

Martens, O. *Wegweiser durch die Urgeschichte Schlesiens* (Breslau, 1906).

Meier, E. *Die Reform der Verwaltungsorganisation unter Stein und Hardenberg* (Leipzig, 1888).

Mielert, F. *Ostpreussen* (Bielefeld & Leipzig, 1926).

Olbricht, K. *Schlesien* (Breslau, 1933).

Osborne, T. *Landownership and Population in Pommeraine* (Tornú, Poland, 1933).

Partsch, J. *Landeskunde der provinz Schlesien* (Breslau, 1918).

Reddaway, W. *Friedrich the Great and the Rise of Prussia* (New York, 1904).

Ringleb, A. *Die Stellung Preussens im Dritten Reich* (Zeulenroda, 1937).

Schaffner, J. *Die Landschaft Brandenburg* (Berlin, 1938).

Schlesischer Verkehrsverband, *Schlesien* (Berlin, 1925).

Schulz, B. *Die Deutsche Ostsee* (Bielefeld & Leipzig, 1931).

Sommer, O. *Die Provinz Pommern* (Berlin, 1913).

Srokowski, S. *East Prussia* (Tornú, Poland, 1934).

Statistisches Handbuch für den Preussischen Staat, 4 vol. (Berlin, 1888-1903).

Thalheim, K. C., and Hillen, A. (ed.) *Der Deutsche Osten, seine Geschichte, sein Wesen und seine Aufgabe* (Berlin, 1936).

Ule, W. *Mecklenburg* (Bielefeld & Leipzig, 1930).

Volz, W. *Schlesien im Rahmen der wirtschaftsgeographischen Lage Deutschlands* (Breslau, 1925).

Wegener, G. *Deutsche Ostsseküste* (Bielefeld & Leipzig, 1900).

Wulle, F. *Die Provinz Schlesien* (Berlin, 1901).

Ziesemer, J. *Die Provinzen Ost- und Westpreussen* (Berlin, 1901).

Zobeltitz, F. von *Berlin und die Mark Brandenburg* (Bielefeld & Leipzig, 1902).

Chapter 11

INTRODUCTION TO NORTHWESTERN GERMANY

Northwestern Germany, long known as *Niedersachsen* or Lower Saxony, includes the Prussian provinces of Schleswig-Holstein and Hanover, the states of Oldenburg and Brunswick, and the Hansa or Free cities of Hamburg and Bremen. It is part of the north German lowland plain extending from the Baltic Sea and the North Sea southward to the mountains of Central Germany. The region lies between the Ems and Elbe rivers. Because of their organic governmental and administrative ties with the rest of the Low Saxon region, the uplands of southern Hanover and Brunswick are included in this area. Internally, the lowlands of Northwest Germany may be divided into several distinctive regions. The coastal portions of Hanover, Oldenburg, and Schleswig-Holstein, which lie along the North Sea, are characterized by low lying coastal marshes, separated by broad tidal mud flats from the Frisian Isles fringing the coast. These marshes or polders, which are now protected from the sea by dykes, extend down the valley of the Weser and Elbe beyond Bremen and Hamburg respectively.

Inland, the marshes give way to the infertile geest of central Schleswig-Holstein, the Lüneburger Heide, between the Aller and Elbe, and western Hanover, the Aller-Ems area. Both the coastal polders and the sandy and frequently boggy geest constitute a natural meadowland for cattle raising. On the southeast, the geest is replaced by a narrow strip of fertile loess soils, extending from Hanover to Magdeburg on the Elbe. The northwestern plain is separated from Central Germany by the low Weser uplands and by the Harz Mountains which dominate the southern part of Hanover and the southern portion of Brunswick. The southernmost section of Hanover is characterized by hilly country situated between the Harz Mountains and the Weser River.

The people of northwestern Germany are largely of Low Saxon stock, which has been settled in northern Germany since the time of their differentia-

338

tion from the West Germanic group in the late Iron Age. By the time of the Roman Empire, most of northwestern Germany was in the hands of the Low Saxons. Later, however, during the fifth century, Frisian tribes spread eastward from their homeland in northern Holland to occupy the coastal marshes and islands of the North Sea. During the Middle Ages, the Frisians were driven from the mainland marshes, so that today they are found principally in the East Frisian Islands. The Low Saxons also pushed northward from the Lower Elbe into Schleswig-Holstein, where they were opposed by other Germanic tribes and by Slavic tribes, which had occupied the eastern portion of this area during the Migration Age. The consolidation of settlement in northwest Germany during the Middle Ages gave the Low Saxons almost complete control of the western plains of northern Germany. Today the peasants of Hanover and Oldenburg speak the same Low Saxon dialect, while those of Schleswig-Holstein use a closely related dialect known as *Holsteinisch*. The Frisian language is restricted to a few islands and the marshes, while the Slavic tongue has completely vanished from this part of Germany.

The physical composition of the population can be explained only in terms of settlement. Basically, the population is Nordic, containing a few ancient racial elements surviving from the Neolithic period, as well as a few Alpine racial types which pushed into Northwest Germany during the Neolithic and Bronze periods. A few types betray a slight East Baltic strain which may date from the period of the westward expansion of the Slavs.

Historically, Northwest Germany begins with the formation of the tribal kingdom of the Low Saxon tribes. Until Carolingian times, this kingdom ruled all of the lands of the Northwest, except the marshes to the west of the Weser, which were held by the Frisians, and the geest to the north of the Eider, which was held by the Danes. Charlemagne, the Emperor of the Franks, brought this portion of the Reich under his control through the bloody campaigns of A.D. 777, 785, and 797. With the break-up of Carolingian power, the dukes of Saxony, who were to become the first Emperors of Germany's medieval empire, regained control of the old tribal realm of the Low Saxons. The Duchy of Saxony played an important role in the development of early Germany, contributing many leaders and colonists to the great East Elbian colonial movement. In 1180 the dukes of Saxony were deposed as a result of their long quarrel and struggle for power within the First Reich. Their enemies, the Hohenstaufens, put an end to the territorial unity of the northwest and transferred the name of Saxony to the Margraviate of Meissen.

During the era of the Aristocratic Confederation, Northwest Germany disintegrated into a large number of ecclesiastical and lay states. The descendants of the last Saxon Duke were able to entrench themselves in the Duchy of Braunschweig-Lüneburg, which occupied the eastern portion of modern Hanover. The western area fell into the hands of the Archbishop of Bremen, the bishops of Münster, Hildesheim and Minden, and the counts of Oldenburg, Hoya, and Tecklenburg. In the north the duchies of Holstein and Schleswig were held by Danish rulers. Only Holstein was held as a fief from the Holy Roman Emperor. During this period the growing commercial cities of Hamburg, Bremen, and Lübeck emerged as free and imperial Hansa towns.

After the wars of the Reformation and the Thirty Years' War, the dukes of Lüneburg, who were made the Electors of Hanover in 1692 and who became kings of England after 1714, began an aggressive policy of aggrandizement. The formerly ecclesiastical states of Bremen and Verden and the territories of Clausthal and Hameln were added to the Electorate of Hanover during the eighteenth century. During the same period the Hohenzollerns had acquired control of the principality of Ostfriesland and the territories of Minden and Tecklenburg, laying the foundations of the nineteenth century rivalry between Hanover and Prussia. The remainder of the Low Saxon area was ruled by the dukes of Oldenburg, Holstein, and Schleswig, and the free and imperial cities of Hamburg, Bremen, and Lübeck.

Following the Treaty of Vienna (1815), Hanover became the dominant power of the Northwest. Its rulers acquired the dignity of kings. They received the territory of Ostfriesland, the northern part of the old bishopric of Münster, and the secularized bishopric of Hildesheim. Hanover had, at last, achieved its modern territorial status. The territorial configurations of Oldenburg, Brunswick, Hamburg, Bremen, and Lübeck, which were to last until the advent of the Nazi regime, were fixed at this time. Only the duchies of Holstein and Schleswig, which had retained their medieval status, awaited final settlement. This came in 1864, when the Prussian intrigues which had been under way since 1830 culminated in the joint occupation of Schleswig-Holstein by Austria and Prussia after a short war with Denmark. In 1866 after the Seven Weeks' War, Prussia occupied both of the duchies and converted them into a province of the Prussian kingdom. At this time the tiny Duchy of Lauenburg was absorbed into the new province, while Oldenburg continued to hold two tiny exclaves within the territory of the province. The Seven Weeks' War also brought the liquidation of the Kingdom of Hanover. The King of Hanover, fearing Prussian expansion, had sided with Austria. The latter's defeat was accompanied by the occupation of Hanover by Prussian forces and by its conversion into a Prussian province.

The territorial division of northwestern Germany into the Prussian provinces of Schleswig-Holstein and Hanover, the states of Oldenburg and Brunswick, and the free cities of Hamburg, Lübeck, and Bremen resulted from the political maneuvering of the nineteenth century. The legacy of enclaves and exclaves, which characterized the holdings of Bremen, Hamburg, Oldenburg, and Brunswick harked back to the medieval era. Under the Empire, these political divisions acquired a certain traditional validity, but underneath there was and still is to a certain extent a fundamental cultural unity among the Low Saxons of the Northwest. This unity was altered to some extent by both political and economic factors. Northern Schleswig-Holstein with its traditional connections with Denmark was economically oriented toward the great port city of Hamburg, which dominated the whole of the lower Elbe region, while Hamburg still retained much of its traditional independence of spirit, a feeling which had its roots in the medieval past when it was a free and imperial city. The greater part of Lower Saxony was dominated by the Province of Hanover, and its life was oriented toward the capital city. The economic and political unity of the northwest plains was, however, interrupted by the lower Weser area, which included the states of Oldenburg and Bremen. In the southwest, the Osnabrück area was transitional to western Germany, while the southern Göttingen region was economically and culturally close to Central Germany. The small state of Brunswick, though exercising a certain political independence, was closely tied to the Low Saxon area by intimate economic and cultural ties.

The periods of the Second Empire and the Weimar Republic brought few changes in the territorial status of the Northwest, except for the loss of northern Schleswig to Denmark after the plebiscite which followed World War I. The Nazi government, however, undertook several important territorial reforms. In 1937 the Hamburg area was reorganized through an exchange of territory with the adjacent Prussian provinces of Schleswig-Holstein and Hanover. This reform eliminated the numerous Hamburg exclaves and gave it an enlarged and consolidated territory. The National Socialist government also liquidated the Oldenburg holdings in Schleswig-Holstein, into which was incorporated the traditionally independent city of Lübeck. In 1939, the port of Bremen, Bremerhaven, was transferred to the Province of Hanover and given the name of Wesermünde. While these reforms put an end to these medieval survivals in the Northwest, they did not resolve the conflict between the early nineteenth century governmental areas and the new economic regions which have emerged since the industrial revolution.

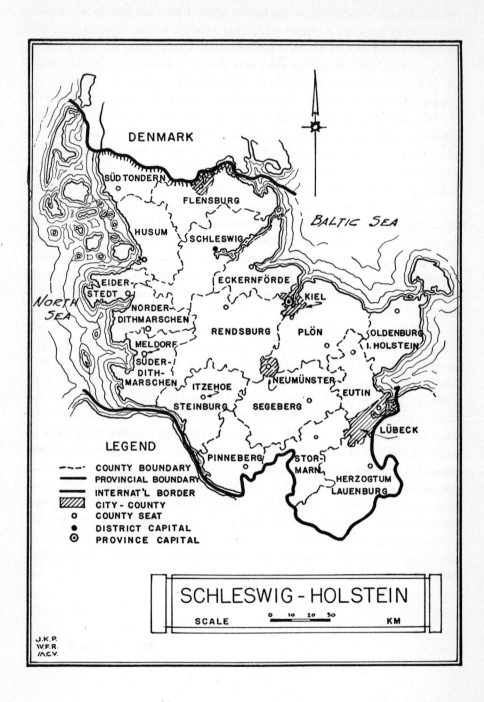

DENMARK

SÜD TONDERN

FLENSBURG

BALTIC SEA

HUSUM

SCHLESWIG

EIDER-
STEDT

ECKERNFÖRDE

NORTH
SEA

NORDER-
DITHMARSCHEN

KIEL

MELDORF

RENDSBURG

PLÖN

OLDENBURG
I. HOLSTEIN

SÜDER-
DITH-
MARSCHEN

NEUMÜNSTER

ITZEHOE

EUTIN

STEINBURG

SEGEBERG

LÜBECK

LEGEND

PINNEBERG

STOR-
MARN

- - - - COUNTY BOUNDARY
───── PROVINCIAL BOUNDARY
━━━━ INTERNAT'L BORDER
▨▨▨ CITY - COUNTY
○ COUNTY SEAT
● DISTRICT CAPITAL
◉ PROVINCE CAPITAL

HERZOGTUM
LAUENBURG

SCHLESWIG - HOLSTEIN

SCALE   0 10 20 30   KM

J.K.P.
W.F.R.
M.C.V.

Chapter 12

THE PROVINCE OF
SCHLESWIG-HOLSTEIN

Schleswig-Holstein forms the base of the Danish peninsula adjoining Denmark on the north. Its eastern coast opens on the Baltic Sea, and its western shore on the North Sea. It borders Mecklenburg on the southeast and is separated from Hanover on the south by the Elbe River.

The land surface is characterized by three types of landscape: coastal and river marshes, geest and moorland, and moraine lands. The western coastal marshes, here and there reclaimed from the sea by means of canals and dykes, are much the same as those extending along the coasts of Hanover and the Netherlands. The marshes of Nord-Friesland, Eiderstedt, and Süder- and Norder-Dithmarschen are divided from the North Frisian Islands of Sylt, Amrum, Föhr, Pellworm, Nord-Sand, and Busch-Sand by extensive *Watten* or tidal flats. All but the last, which stands in the Elbe estuary, are located off Nord-Friesland and the Halligen tidal flats. The coastal marsh is continued by the lower Elbe River marshes. Central Schleswig-Holstein is geest and moorland, with extensive dry areas spotted with moors, marshes, peat bogs, and pools of stagnant water. Eastward the geest gives way to the elevated Baltic Plateau country, a region of moraines, dotted with great numbers of small lakes, which drops abruptly into the Baltic Sea. Most of Schleswig-Holstein is drained by the Scholmerau, Eider, Stör, and a number of smaller streams rising in the eastern plateau land, flowing across the geest to the marshland along the coast, through which they cut their way to the North Sea. The almost riverless east coast is cut by a number of inlets from the Baltic Sea. Schleswig-Holstein is an agrarian province oriented toward northwestern rather than eastern Germany. Its major cities, Kiel and Lübeck, located on the eastern Baltic coast, are closely tied to Hamburg and the lower Elbe.

The population of the province is of only very moderate density for its 1,420,000 individuals occupied an area of 15,681 sq. km. of territory, or an average of about 90 per sq. km. The density ranged from below 80 in the agrarian areas to from 80 to 130 in the regions adjacent to Hamburg, Lübeck, and Kiel.

After A.D. 1000, the West Germanic Saxons pushed north from the Eider into Schleswig and drove the Slavs from the southeast. Today most of the people speak a standard German, though the dialect of the area is a *Holsteinisch* variety of Low Saxon. Frisian (*Friesisch*) is still spoken in the islands and the Nord-Friesland marshes. The Province of Schleswig-Holstein is almost entirely Lutheran. In 1933 there were only 35,000 Catholics in the whole area. The Jewish population, which was the smallest in any Prussian province, numbered about 1,424 individuals.

There has been a steady increase in the population of the province, but with regional variation. For the period between 1875 and 1925 the increase for the area adjacent to Hamburg and near Kiel was well over 150 per cent, while that of the Schleswig area was only 5 to 25 per cent. The old city of Lübeck and a few other isolated areas actually declined in population. Only a slight increase was registered in the provincial population since 1918.

Like the rest of northwestern Germany the area of Holstein fell under Carolingian rule after the final defeat of the Saxon tribes in A.D. 797, while Schleswig was made a part of the new Kingdom of Denmark. After the division of the Kingdom of Charlemagne (843) German rulers held the land as far north as the Eider River. By Hohenstaufen times, the Slavs had been driven from southeastern Holstein, and South Schleswig-Holstein was constituted one of the duchies under Saxon control, but the area north of the Eider River forming the Duchy of Schleswig continued under Danish rule. However, in 1460, the duchies of Schleswig and Holstein fell to the Danish-Oldenburg family and thus begins the complicated history of this long disputed area.

Owing to involved dynastic relations, complications multiplied after the end of the Middle Ages. Holstein, consisting of the counties of Holstein, Stomarn, Dithmarschen, Wagrien, and Pinneberg, sustained a number of family divisions after 1460 during the rule of the Danish vassals, although it remained within the German Empire. The Duchy of Schleswig, a constituent part of the Danish Kingdom, fell upon evil days owing to its control by vassal rulers who were also responsible for the destinies of Holstein. In 1773, the duchies of Schleswig and Holstein fell vacant and were restored to the King of Denmark, both being placed under the same provincial administration. However, these duchies did not control the entire area of the modern province. The Duchy of Lauenburg, which now forms a part of southeastern Schleswig-Holstein, was first ruled by the Saxon Dukes, later by the earls of Anhalt (1180-1369), the dukes of Brunswick (1369-1689), and the princes of Hanover (1689-1814).

Another part of the province was held by the city of Lübeck which managed to retain its independent status until Nazi times (1937) despite three hundred years of economic and commercial decline. Founded by the Saxons in 1143, Lübeck was granted the status of an imperial free city in 1226 and during the later Middle Ages played a prominent role in the Hanseatic League (1241-1630). The Bishop of Lübeck held a bit of territory north of the city near Eutin. During the Napoleonic period, the French extended their control as far as Lübeck and into the southeast part of Schleswig-Holstein. The Treaty of Vienna (1815) divided the provincial territory into the duchies of Holstein (an independent state in the Reich), Schleswig (a constituent part of Denmark), the Free City of Lübeck, the Duchy of Lauenburg, and the territory of Eutin, which belonged to Oldenburg. Until 1830, there was no Schleswig-Holstein Question. In fact, there was little trouble until 1848, when Prussia slowly began to spread her net. Intermittent wars, based upon the pretext of hereditary disputes, lasted until 1865, when Schleswig was placed under Austrian rule, and Holstein under Prussian rule. After the Seven Weeks' War, Prussia took over both duchies (1866). Although the Treaty of Prague, which followed this war, stipulated that North Schleswig might be re-united to Denmark if it was desired by the people, this was not accomplished until the plebiscite of 1919.

Aside from the cession of Northern Schleswig to Denmark after World War I, there were few changes in the territory of the province. The advent of the Third Reich brought the state reforms of the Nazis involving drastic changes of internal administrative boundaries. The Nazis set about to consolidate state and provincial territories. Lübeck was abolished as an independent administrative unit and added to Schleswig-Holstein. The creation of Greater Hamburg brought several changes. Schleswig-Holstein exchanged the city-counties of Altona and Wandsbek for a tiny bit of Hamburg territory in the county of Stomarn and the city of Geesthacht, which had long been surrounded by the county of Herzogtum Lauenburg. The Duchy of Lauenburg had passed to Prussia in 1865 and attached to Schleswig-Holstein in 1867. The territory of Eutin was detached from Oldenburg and incorporated in Schleswig-Holstein.

The government of the province of Schleswig-Holstein was headed by a Chief President at Kiel. Like other Prussian Chief Presidents, he was vested with broad political and supervisory control over administrative, economic, social, and cultural activities. Much of the actual administration was carried out by the District President at Schleswig. The provincial administration and self-government were regulated by the Provincial Constitution of 1888, and later by minor republican orders and drastic Nazi decrees.

The Chief President, vested with supervisory and political powers, was aided under the Nazis by a Provincial Advisory Council which replaced the old elected Provincial Legislature and Provincial Committee. It is important to note that in Nazi times, the Chief President of Schleswig-Holstein was also the Nazi district leader of the party district of Schleswig-Holstein.

The work of the general provincial administration was supplemented by special and technical services under direct national control. During the imperial period, the state administered only the courts, railways, and mining offices while the nationally operated postal system lay outside the scope of the general administration of the province. Following the usual Prussian pattern, justice was administered by the Prussian Ministry of Justice prior to the Nazis and was in the care of the Superior State Court at Kiel, the Collegiate Courts of First and Second Instance at Flensburg, Itzehoe, Kiel, and Lübeck, and the numerous local Courts of First Instance. The national postal system within the province was under the Chief Postal Directorate (under the Empire) or the National Postal Directorate (under the Republic and the Third Reich) of Kiel. Trade and industry, weights and measures, social insurance and welfare, public health, and the collection of imperial revenues were administered upon delegation from the Reich, in so far as national decrees were concerned.

Under the Republic there was a further extension of direct national administration to finance, railways, unemployment insurance and employment, and labor welfare. National control of finances within Schleswig-Holstein was carried out through the State Finance Office of Nordmark (Kiel) and its local finance offices and main customs offices. National Construction Offices were located at Flensburg and Kiel. Operation of the nationalized railways of Schleswig-Holstein was conducted by the National Railroad Directorate of Hamburg (Altona). Labor and unemployment problems were considered by the State Labor Office of Nordmark (Hamburg) and the Main Welfare Office at Hanover. Specified areas of welfare, social insurance, health, trade and industry, and labor, subject to national legislation, were administered by the province upon delegation. The economic life of the province, which was subject to limited provincial control, was organized under various national industrial, trade, agricultural, and labor organizations.

The Province of Schleswig-Holstein was a Social Democratic stronghold under the Empire and the Republic. In Imperial times, the urban centers of Lübeck (then a Free City), Kiel, and Rendsburg voted for the Social Democratic party in all national elections. The rural people did not follow the conservative parties, but gave their vote to the liberal Progressive party. Under the Republic the Social Democratic party maintained the lead in national and provincial elections with the liberal German People's party obtaining a considerable following in the rural areas. The German National People's party, however, was able to obtain a considerable following in the conservative southeastern area. With the critical elections between 1930 and 1933, Schleswig-Holstein turned to National Socialism. In the four *Reichstag* elections of this period, its citizens gave the Nazis 44 per cent of the total vote. In the presidential election of

1932, Hitler received 42 per cent of the vote in the first election and 48 per cent in the second. Schleswig-Holstein became one of the strongholds of the National Socialists.

Under the Nazis the Province of Schleswig-Holstein was constituted as the party district of Schleswig-Holstein for the purposes of party administration. The party district headquarters, which were located at Kiel, included the usual functional offices, which exercised control over the appropriate local offices of provincial government and administration.

During the Nazi regime direct national administration was extended to justice, propaganda, labor relations, and air matters. Several traditional fields of state administration—police, health, welfare, education, and certain aspects of social insurance—were placed under national control. The general and special administrative systems were supplemented by a comprehensive arrangement of corporate administration, providing for the absolute regimentation of life within the province. Kiel, the provincial capital, and Schleswig, the district capital, were the major centers for general administration, while the special administrative services had their centers at Hamburg and Kiel. Hamburg was especially important under the Nazis as a center for economic controls.

Rural Aspect

The marshes, moors, and geest of Schleswig-Holstein support about 997,659 individuals or about 31 per cent of the total provincial population. From 40 to 50 per cent of the people of Schleswig-Holstein dwell in villages and small towns close to the soil. The province and district of Schleswig-Holstein was divided into four city counties and seventeen counties by the Prussians. The counties, which are rural in character, were headed by County Managers who served both as the representatives of the state government in the counties as well as the local self-governing authorities. The county administration and self-government were regulated by the County Constitution of 1888, which was modified by the liberal laws of the Republic and later by the authoritarian Nazi Laws.

The villages, which were once governed under the Constitution for Rural Villages and Towns of 1892, followed the German Municipal Code after 1935. Each village and town administration thereafter consisted of a Mayor, a Party Agent, two or three administrative assistants, and a town council. A number of small hamlets could form *ad hoc* districts called Parish Communities (*Kirchspiellandgemeinden*) for the administration of common affairs. Each parish was headed by a Chairman (*Vorsteher*) who was associated in office with a Party Agent, generally the Precinct Group Leader (*Ortsgruppenleiter*). There were generally one or two administrative assistants and an advisory council. The small parish communities were situated only in the densely settled marsh countries along the North Sea. The counties which have a large number of towns are found principally in southeastern Schleswig-Holstein.

Schleswig-Holstein is better than the average German state or province as an agrarian region. Approximately 78 per cent of the land is devoted to agriculture, with over 44 per cent of the land under cultivation. The character of the agriculture varies widely in the marshes, on the geest, and in the moraine country. Although the entire province has a North Atlantic climate, the marshes and geest have a milder climate than the eastern moraine area. While the average monthly summer temperature in the west is about 18 degrees C., it is only 17 C. in the east. The average annual rainfall for the coastal marshes and the geest is about 730 mm., while it is 750 mm. for the slightly higher land to the east. The coastal marshes and geest have about 85 to 90 days of frost and ice, while the eastern area has about 97 to 100.

The *Marschen* or polders are largely occupied by meadowland which is protected from the North Sea by dykes and drainage canals. The age-long peasant effort to reclaim the marshes from the sea was aided by the German government during the periods of the Empire and the Republic. Although much of this work was abandoned during the depression of the thirties, it was revived by the Third Reich which put the Labor Service (*Arbeitsdienst*) to work at the task. About one-half of the land is arable and is given over to oats, wheat, horse beans, and barley, with smaller areas of sugar beets and vegetables. Market gardens are particularly common in the river marshland near Hamburg, although cattle raising is the most important activity in these lowlands, where lean beef cattle are fattened for the fall market. There is little dairying except in the vicinity of the larger towns and Hamburg.

The slightly elevated geest shares the cool and humid climate of the marshlands, but supports only a scant population, since the land is far from fertile and living is difficult. The best land is to be found in the alluvial river valleys. The extensive moorland, the curse of northwestern Germany, has been partly reclaimed for agrarian activity by means of the "Dutch System," involving drainage and enrichment of the moor soils, and on them new agrarian settlements have been developed known as Finn Colonies (*Fehnkolonien*), which are supported by the cultivation of potatoes, vegetables, and some cereals. The greater portion of the geest is pasture devoted to cattle raising and dairying.

The rolling elevated moraine lands of eastern Schleswig-Holstein have a moist, but colder, climate. Fields of oats and clover mingled with pasture land resting on a glacial soil of loam and clay are found in valleys and plains surrounded by forested hills and dotted with lakes. The chief rural industries are cattle and horse raising, especially in the east-central area, with dairying near the larger cities of Hamburg, Kiel, and Lübeck. Rye is grown in the Baltic region, while wheat and some barley are found in the southeast. However, Schleswig-Holstein ranks low among the Prussian provinces in cereal production, though it is probably the most important province or state in the Reich for cattle production.

The following figures for land utilization for the year 1933 indicate the amount and types of land available for agriculture.

Cultivated Land (in hectares)		566,000
Grain	382,000	
Legumes	18,000	
Root Crops	91,000	
Green Vegetables	7,000	
Industrial Crops	8,000	
Fodder Crops	60,000	
Small Gardens		31,500
Pasture and Meadow		493,000
Orchards		1,000
Forests		125,000
Waste Land		71,000
Houses and Barns		25,000
Roads and Parks		124,000

Nearly 77 per cent of the province is devoted to agrarian activity, with 44 per cent in crop production and 31 per cent in pasture. The remaining land is divided between forests (8 per cent) and waste land, including home sites, roads, etc. (14 per cent).

Particularly striking is the fact that forest and woodland account for only 8 per cent of the area of Schleswig-Holstein. There are only occasional trees in the marshlands and on the geestlands, while in the eastern moraine lands the West Baltic beech is most common in the woodland which covers from 5 to 13 per cent of the area. This limited forest land is owned by state, municipal, and private interests. The state forests were administered through nine forest reserves in 1933.

The contrast between the marsh, geest, and moraine lands holds true for the character of settlement. The *Marschhufendorf* with houses scattered along a narrow road is characteristic of the polder area, where the culture falls into two distinct types: the Frisian of the north and the Low Saxon of the south. The seafaring Frisians of the Nord-Friesland isles and marshes, although mainly interested in fishing and small-scale trade, do a bit of farming on the adjacent marshlands. They are an independent lot, slow moving, stolid, and rational. The well-to-do Low Saxon peasants of the southern coastal and river marshes are more interested in agriculture. They live in similar villages, but their houses tend to vary in type from marsh to marsh. There are a few houses of Low Saxon type—long rectangular structures housing a barn and living quarters—to be found on protective mounds. The houses and villages of the marshlands are designed to be economical in the use of land. The poorer peasants of the infertile geest dwell in the *Haufendorf*—an agglomerated type of village consisting of houses of Low Saxon type built on a series of interlocking streets. To the north, the Low Saxon type of settlement gives way to a Danish type. Southeast Schleswig-Holstein is dominated by the landed nobility dwelling upon large estates. The typical Round Village (*Runddorf*) of the area betrays the earlier Slavic occupation of this part of Germany; the houses are of the Low Saxon type. Contrasts between Nord-Friesland, the Southern Marshes, the Geest, and the Southeast will be found in most aspects of peasant life. Local rural self-government was once important. Cooperatives, inspired from Denmark, were common. After 1933, the management and control of rural life came under the Nazi agencies, though the county and its villages and towns continued to handle local welfare and public works. The smaller towns and a few villages may own a forest, operate a small market, and occasionally own their utilities.

Urban Aspect

Schleswig-Holstein is primarily a rural province, with 24 per cent of the population living in Kiel and Lübeck. Most of the urban centers are small. The most important city counties are Flensburg (66,580), Kiel (218,335), Lübeck (133,021), and Neumünster (46,907), the government and administration of which followed the national pattern laid down by the German Municipal Code of 1935. The democratic features of city government and administration, which were provided by the law concerning the Constitution and Administration for the Cities and Lands in the Province of Schleswig-Holstein (*Gesetz betreffend die Verfassung und Verwaltung der Städte und Flecken in der Provinz Schleswig-Holstein*) of 1869, and the liberal measures of the Weimar era, were swept away by the Nazis.

Although Schleswig-Holstein has intimate economic and cultural connections with both Mecklenburg and Northwest Germany west of the Elbe, its trade is closely tied to Hamburg, chiefly through commercial relations with the coastal towns of Kiel and Lübeck, a relationship which is supported by canals linking the Elbe to the Baltic. The other cities of the province are of minor economic importance.

The land has little mineral wealth, hence aside from salt mining and rock quarrying there is little in the way of extractive industry. Most of the coal comes by barge from Saxony, some by the Dortmund-Ems and the coast (*Küsten*) canals from the Ruhr. The few iron and steel plants used Swedish ores. There are numerous manufacturing industries at Flensburg, Kiel, Lübeck, and Neu-münster, but the industries of Hamburg far outshadow them in importance. Chemical industries, machinery and metal goods were important at Kiel, Lü-beck, and Neumünster; leather goods, textiles, and clothing at Kiel and Neu-münster. Lübeck was also important for food products and a thriving tobacco industry, while Flensburg had important glass and paper products plants. There were no important electrical power plants in the province. Hamburg had the only near-by plant with a capacity of more than 50 million Kwh. Most of the towns and cities of the province had their own utilities systems, but even so, there were over 100 companies engaged in the production and distribution of gas, electricity, and water.

The transportation network of Schleswig-Holstein is based on two major north-south arteries. In the western part of the province, one road runs along the edge of the marshlands from Hamburg to Heide and thence northward via Husum to Tönder in Denmark. Another links the Baltic coastal towns of Flens-burg, Schleswig, Kiel, and Lübeck. Other major roads link Hamburg with Kiel and Lübeck; the only section of the famous natural super-highway to be com-pleted in Schleswig-Holstein links Hamburg and Lübeck. Another was planned to run northward from Hamburg to Flensburg with a branch road to Kiel. The railroads of Schleswig-Holstein were operated by the German Railroad Com-pany through the National Railroad Directorate of Hamburg (formerly Al-tona). The railroad lines of Schleswig-Holstein do not begin to carry the traffic that is borne by such lines as those along the Rhine or those running between Cologne and Berlin. There are two main north-south rail lines: one following the route of the western coastal road, the other running from Flensburg to Neumünster to Bad Oldesloe which is a junction for lines to Hamburg, Lü-beck, and Wittenberg. The heaviest traffic is borne by lines running from Ham-burg to Neumünster and Lübeck. Railroad centers of economic importance include Niebüll, Husum, Tönning, St. Michaelisdeonn, Flensburg, Rendsburg. The only heavy traffic center is Lübeck.

The Elbe River with the port of Hamburg, the Kaiser Wilhelm or Kiel canal, and the Elbe-Trave canal constitute the important waterways of this part of Germany. The Kaiser Wilhelm canal links the North Sea and the Baltic, pro-viding a way to avoid the dangerous passage around Denmark. The canal, which has a set of double locks at each end, begins at Brunsbüttelkoog on the lower Elbe and enters the Baltic at Kiel-Holtenau. There were National Canal Offices at Kiel and Brunsbüttelkoog. The Elbe-Trave canal, which can take boats of 1200 metric tons, links Lübeck to the Elbe (Lauenburg). There is an-other small canal, which can carry vessels of less than 400 metric tons extending from Hamburg to Lübeck. Aside from the canal port of Brunsbüttelkoog, the

North Sea coast and the Elbe side of Schleswig-Holstein are without ports of any importance. Hamburg provides for the sea transportation of most of western and southern Schleswig-Holstein.

The Baltic coast is favored with the ports of Flensburg, Kiel, and Lübeck. The port of Kiel, located at the eastern end of the Kaiser Wilhelm canal, is free from tide and ice. It consisted of the old town harbor, formerly equipped with 7,750 feet of quay, electric cranes, floating cranes, two 150-ton cranes, eleven floating docks, and six dry docks, and the north harbor with 1,560 feet of quay, small electric cranes, sheds and warehouses (82,000 sq. ft.) and grain elevators (12,000 tons). There was a railway connected with the docks. Kiel was important for the export of grain, flour, timber, salt, and machinery and for the importation of coal, oil, timber and grain. Only a very few harbor facilities were available at the small harbor of Kiel-Holtenau and at Kiel-Wik located inside the canal. The Marine Station of the Baltic Sea of the German Navy was at Kiel. The port of Flensburg is an open harbor taking ships with a draft of 26 feet, and an inner harbor which will accommodate only smaller ships. Flensburg harbor was equipped with grain loading and discharging facilities, a floating dock, and coal and oil supplies. The port imported coal, coke, iron, timber, grain, rice, oil, cattle, copper, and coffee; it exported brick, drain pipes, newsprint, machinery, glass, drugs, and dyes. The harbor of Lübeck was equipped with good fixed quays, electric cranes of the 1.5 to 40 ton type, warehouses, and railroad connections, floating steam cranes, floating docks, and bunker coal and oil. Coal, iron, timber, fish, cattle, and grain were imported; and iron, machinery, stone, cement, and potash salts were exported.

The commercial life of Schleswig-Holstein is oriented toward the great port city of Hamburg. The port cities of Kiel and Lübeck are closely tied to the great city on the Elbe by the Kiel canal. They played an important role, however, in Germany's Baltic trade, serving as ports of entry for iron ore, timber, and grain coming in from Scandinavia and the East Baltic. While Kiel, Lübeck, Flensburg, and Neumünster are small though important commercial centers, the economic life of the province is based upon dairying and livestock raising. The meat and dairy products of this northern province were shipped to the Ruhr, Central Germany, and Berlin.

The banking and credit institutions of Schleswig-Holstein ranged from branches of the great commercial banks of Berlin, which were interested mainly in investments of the industrial type, to local municipal savings banks. While there were important financial institutions at Kiel, Hamburg was the major center. The provincial government operated a life insurance organization and a provincial bank.

The population of Schleswig-Holstein was about equally engaged in agriculture (25 per cent) and industry and crafts (29 per cent). Commerce and transportation occupied approximately 18 per cent of the population, while the professions and civil service accounted for another 9 per cent. There was a relatively large independent upper class due to the great number of small commercial and manufacturing enterprises. The working class was relatively small in comparison with the Reich as a whole. The white collar group and the civil servant-professional class were about average for the Reich.

The people of Schleswig-Holstein must be studied in two groups, the Schleswig-Holsteiner majority of the mainland and the Frisian minority, which is settled on the marshes and isles of Nord-Friesland. The latter is a land of villages and small towns, few of which have origins before A.D. 1100. The few large cities are of modern origin, and except for the ancient city of Lübeck lack the traditional character of the cities of the more ancient Rhineland. The Frisians are a coastal and island people, living in small towns and villages. The Schleswig-Holsteiners are sober rural people. Crime and illegitimacy are low. With an independent spirit the upper class was strongly militaristic. There is a local patriotism colored by a recollection of the Schleswig-Holstein question and at times there is a certain anti-Danish feeling.

Chapter 13

THE HANSEATIC CITY
OF HAMBURG

The Hanseatic City of Hamburg, which is one of the more important ports of the world, is situated for the most part on the north bank of the Elbe, about seventy-five miles from the North Sea. Territorially, it is boxed in by the Prussian provinces of Hanover and Schleswig-Holstein. Located at the mouth of the small river Alster, developed on a spit of geest extending into the Elbe marshland, the city proper is built on both sides of the Inner Alster (Binnen Alster) and the Outer Alster (Aussen Alster), small lakes which have been formed by the damming up of this stream. The oldest portion of the city (*Altstadt*) is located between the Inner Alster and the Elbe. Owing to the fire of 1842 little remains of medieval construction. The old city is cut by canals (*Fleeten*) lined by old warehouses and poor dwellings which are sometimes endangered by high tides on the Elbe. The canals have given Hamburg the name of Northern Venice. The New City (*Neustadt*), which was incorporated in 1678, lies to the west. The old suburb of St. Pauli lies farther to the west. The modern city of Hamburg has grown up along the shores of the Outer Alster, and embraces the Rotherbahn, Harvestehude, Uhlenhorst, Hohenfelde, and St. Georg sections which are linked together by a number of small steamers plying the Outer Alster. It lies at the center of a large metropolitan complex forming the State, or Hanseatic City of Hamburg as it is still called. To the west is the city of Altona, eastward the city of Wandsbek, and southward the formerly Prussian city of Harburg-Wilhelmsburg—all were included under the Nazi territorial reform. In addition to metropolitan Hamburg, the old city state embraced four Rural Domains (*Landherrnschaften*): the Geestlande adjoining the city on the north and east, the Marschlande along the Elbe to the south of the city, and the Vierlande extending to the southeast along the Elbe. The city of Bergedorf is located in the southeastern portion of the Vierlande. The Nazi reorganization in 1935 brought about the annexation of rural areas adjacent to Schleswig-

354

Holstein and Hanover, as well as the loss to Schleswig-Holstein of the isolated bits of territory in the county of Stomarn and the county of Herzogtum Lauenburg, and the loss of the Cuxhaven area to Hanover.

Hamburg falls within the North Atlantic climatic zone. The winters are mild in general, although the temperature drops to as low as —11 degrees C. in late January. The average for January, the coldest winter month, is —1.5 degrees C. In the summer the temperature sometimes reaches 34 degrees C. in June though the average summer temperature for the months of June, July, and August is about 17 degrees C. The average yearly rainfall is heavy, about 712 mm., with the heaviest rainfall coming in the spring months. There is only about a month of snow. Autumn begins in middle October, while spring arrives in the middle of May. The soil is not of importance for agrarian reasons, but it does have significance for the pattern of urban settlement. The urban parts of the great city of Hamburg and the smaller towns like Altona, Wandsbek, and Bergedorf are located on the infertile geest. The moors and heath of the geest are occupied by small villages and farms to the north and east of built-up Hamburg. The Elbe River marshes are dominated by the wharves of the port of Hamburg and the city of Harburg-Wilhelmsburg. Down stream the urban area gives way to pastures, meadowland, and market gardens.

Greater Hamburg is one of the most densely settled areas in the world. In 1938 a population of 1,675,703 dwelt in an area of 746 sq. km. The population density is about 2,246 individuals per sq. km. The bulk of the population— 1,130,608—dwells within the city of Hamburg. Another 425,000 people live in the larger satellite cities. Less than 100,000 occupy the rural area. The language of Hamburg is a variety of Low Saxon, although most of the people speak a standard German. Their religion is Lutheran. The Catholic minority was small—93,000. The Jewish population was relatively large; in 1933, they numbered 20,000, only Berlin and the Rhine Province had a greater number. Hamburg, like most of the urban centers of Germany, has sustained a great increase in population since the industrial revolution. Since 1875, the population of the Hamburg area has increased more than 150 per cent. In 1864, the population numbered 176,000. After a slight decline during World War I, the population tended to increase rapidly after 1925. During the Hitler regime considerable numbers left the oppressive Nazi Reich through the port of Hamburg. Over 1,000 individuals left the Hanseatic City of Hamburg each year during the thirties.

The city of Hamburg was founded in 808 by Charlemagne. Its first church, which was established in 811, played a major role in the Christianization of northern Europe. Commercial Hamburg dates from the tenth century when the city was ruled by the counts of Schauenburg. In 1189, the city gained partial independence through a contribution to the crusade of Frederick I. The middle eleventh century brought a defensive alliance with Lübeck which laid the foundations of the Hanseatic League. The tradition of these days survives in the name of the present city—*Hansestadt*. The later medieval history of the city was dominated by the struggle of the merchants and the craft guilds which eventuated in the partial victory of the latter, under the nominal suzerainty of Denmark. In 1510 Hamburg was made a free and imperial city. Hamburg became Protestant during the Reformation; as a Lutheran city it became a refuge for Protestants escaping from the Low Countries as well as for Jews from Spain and Portugal. Although the city received little injury from the Thirty Years' War, it suffered commercially from the consequent decline of German prosperity. After a long struggle with Denmark, Hamburg finally established its independence and was admitted to the Diet of the Empire in 1770. After the depressing effect of the Napoleonic wars, it grew rapidly during the nineteenth century, prospering from trade with the New World. The great fire of 1842 interrupted its commerce only temporarily.

The city entered the North German Confederation in 1866 and the German Empire in 1871. It did not join the Customs Union until after the completion of its free harbor in 1888.

Under the Empire, Hamburg was a City Republic. It was governed under the Constitution of 1861, which was modified in 1879 and 1906. The government of the city was under a *Senat,* consisting of eighteen members who were elected for life by the House of Burgesses (*Bürgerschaft*). The latter body consisted of 160 members, elected in part by all tax paying citizens, by owners of property, and some by members of the House of Burgesses itself. The *Senat* served as the executive body, while the House of Burgesses was responsible for all legislation. The administration of the city of Hamburg was carried out under a First and Second Mayor. The administrative services and offices were headed by appointed members of the *Senat.* These officials were responsible for the administration of both Hamburg State and City as well as the supervisory administration of the cities of Cuxhaven, Geesthacht, and Bergedorf, which were within the territory of Hamburg. The rural areas of the Hanseatic City of Hamburg, the *Landherrenschaften* Marschlande, Geestlande, and Vierlande were under the supervision of a provincial ruler (*Landherr*) with the rank of Senator.

During World War I, Hamburg suffered severely from the blockade. After the war, it became one of the seventeen states of republican Germany. The Republic caused few basic changes in Hamburg administration. The Republican Constitution of 1921 vested supreme power in the House of Burgesses which was elected on a democratic basis. It continued to elect the *Senat,* which served as the executive branch of the government. In the twenties there was a notable recovery in its trade and commerce.

Hamburg had long been a strong Social Democratic center. Even in imperial times the workers of the city always carried the national elections for the Social Democratic party. They were prevented from seizing control of the city government by the system of limited suffrage used in city elections which permitted the conservative upper class to rule the affairs of the city. Under the Republic the democratic system of suffrage in city elections quickly revealed the true political aspirations of the citizens, for the Social Democrats rapidly gained control of the machinery of local government. The convervative National German People's party was never able to regain its old position which had been based upon constitutional prerogatives from imperial days. The impoverished elements of the working class sought the easy solutions of communism for their problems. The Communist party, even in the prosperous period of the late twenties, was the second strongest in national and city elections. During the critical elections between September 1930 and March 1933, Hamburg remained a republican stronghold, although its hinterland gave strong support to the National Socialists. The well organized proletarian population continued to vote for the Social Democrats and the Communists. Hitler was never able to obtain over 25 per cent of the city's vote. Like Berlin and the Catholic areas of western and southern Germany, Hamburg held out against National Socialism until it was forced upon the city by the rest of the Reich.

• The Republic brought the further extension of direct national administration to finance, railways, unemployment insurance and employment, and labor welfare. National control of finances within Hamburg was carried out through the State Finance Office of Hamburg and its local finance offices and main customs offices. There were two National Construction Offices in Hamburg. The nationalized railways of Hamburg were operated by the National Railroad Directorate of Altona (Hamburg). Labor and unemployment problems were met by the State Labor Office of Nordmark (Hamburg) and the main Welfare Office of Hanover. Those features of welfare, social insurance, health, trade and industry, and labor, subject to national legislation, were administered upon delegation by the city of Hamburg. The economic life of the city was organized under various national industrial, trade, commercial, agricultural, and labor organizations, which maintained local branch offices for the Hamburg area.

After the advent of the Nazis, the city of Hamburg was constituted as the party district of Hamburg for the purposes of party administration. The district headquarters included the usual party offices which exercised control over the subordinate offices of government and administration.

Under the Nazis, Hamburg was a metropolitan area with the status of a state (*Land*). This came about under the Reich Law of January 1937, which made possible the formation of the enlarged and consolidated territory of Greater Hamburg. In December 1937, there was a complete reorganization of the government and administration of the Hanseatic City of Hamburg under a new charter. The government and administration was headed by a National Governor after 1934, who was responsible to the national Minister of the Interior, but was also subject to the supervision of other national ministers. The Governor had long been the party district leader for the party district of Hamburg. In his capacity of Governor, he served as head of both the state government and the so-called self-governing municipality.

As head of the state government he assumed responsibility in the territory of Hamburg for certain general administrative affairs, police, higher schools, and certain aspects of economy and transportation. He was assisted by a deputy, known as a President, who headed the following seven departments of government: General Administration; Consular Relations; Police; Higher Schools; Economics, Agrarian and Social Affairs; Construction; and Port Control.

The Governor in his capacity as head of the city administration was represented by a deputy, known as Mayor who directed a separate set of municipal authorities and agencies. His position corresponded to that of *Erster Beigeordneter* or Deputy under the German Municipal Code. The various administrative services were headed by eleven other principal Administrative Department heads called *Senatoren* (if appointed for life), and two honorary administrative department heads. They included a Main Administrative Office (*Hauptverwaltungsamt*), a Controller's Office (*Rechnungsprüfungsamt*), a Statistical Office (*Statistisches Amt*), a Housing and Settlement Office (*Wohnwirtschafts- und Siedlungsamt*), a Treasury (*Kämmerei*), an Office for Administration of Lower Schools (*Schulverwaltung*), a Health Administration (*Gesundheitsverwaltung*), an Administration for Trade, Shipping, and Industry (*Verwaltung für Handel, Schiffahrt und Gewerbe*), a Construction Office (*Bauverwaltungsamt*), and a number of other agencies for cultural, welfare, youth, and sport affairs. There was also a department for the administration of the city-owned utilities and other economic enterprises. The administrative department heads were assisted by a number of Advisory Counselors, citizens with technical knowledge.

For purposes of internal administration, Hamburg was divided into an urban area (*Stadtbezirk*) and a rural area (*Landbezirk*) which constituted administrative districts (*Verwaltungsbezirke*). The administration of the urban area fell directly under the departments and agencies listed above, while the rural area was placed under a separate administrative department head, who carried the title of Rural Area Mayor (*Landbezirksbürgermeister*). His office consisted of sections for general administration, construction, and welfare. He was assisted by a group of special advisors. It should be noted that in most matters the rural area was served by the same offices of general administration as the urban area. Owing to the disjointed character of the distribution of the rural area, seven Main Administrative Offices (*Hauptdienststellen*) and twenty-five Administrative Offices (*Dienststellen*) were set up in the rural areas to handle local affairs. In 1938 the old divisions of the Hanseatic City of Hamburg were replaced by ten principal subdivisions which in turn were subdivided into several districts. The more heavily populated districts were further subdivided into wards (*Ortsteile*). The subdivisions corresponded to the counties of the NSDAP, the wards to the precinct groups.

In the general city administration, the Governor in his capacity as head of the city administration was assisted by an appointed advisory council of 45 City Councilors. He was also the Nazi Party Agent for the Hanseatic City of Hamburg, guaranteeing the political reliability of the city administration. This drastic governmental and administrative reorganization eliminated the old traditional governments of the Prussian city county and rural areas which were attached to the Hanseatic City in the course of the formation of Greater Hamburg. It also abolished the traditional forms of government and administration in Hamburg itself.

The work of the general Hamburg government and administration was supplemented by a number of direct special and technical services under direct national control. During the imperial period only the nationally operated postal system lay outside the scope of the general administration of the city. Justice was administered by the Hanseatic City of Hamburg in the Hanseatic Superior State Court of Hamburg, which served the Collegiate Courts of First and Second Instance of the three Hanseatic cities of Hamburg, Bremen, and Lübeck. The national postal system within the city was under the Chief Postal Directorate (under the Empire) or the National Post Directorate (under the Republic and the Third Reich) of Hamburg, which served the Hanseatic City of Hamburg, southeastern Schleswig-Holstein, and northeastern Hanover. National regulations for trade and industry, weights and measures, social insurance and welfare, public health, and the collection of imperial revenues were administered upon delegation from the Reich.

During the Nazi regime, direct national administration was extended to many additional functions. Also many of the traditional fields of city administration—policy, health, welfare, education, and certain aspects of social insurance—were brought under tight national control.

ECONOMIC AND SOCIAL ASPECTS

Hamburg, as the great commercial center of Northwest Germany, had intimate connection with the whole of the lower Elbe area. Roads, rail lines, and particularly rivers and canals have led to close economic relationships with the old Hanse cities of Bremen and Lübeck and with relatively modern Kiel, as well as with northern Hanover and all of Schleswig-Holstein. The economic significance of this city did not stop here, for the hinterland embraced the whole basin of the Elbe extending as far as Bohemia, and the canals of the German lowlands linked the port of Hamburg to the area drained by the Oder, Weser, and Rhine. The real importance of Germany's second city was based upon its ideal geographical location and its old traditional status as a transport and commercial center. The modern port lies to the south of the city where it has been excavated in the alluvial marshes of the Elbe. Sea-going vessels could use the port without the aid of locks, thanks to the seven-foot differential between high and low tide. The port area totaled 18,199 acres of water and land area, with 6,054 acres of water surface, of which 3,876 acres can be used by sea-going vessels. The length of quay totaled twenty-four miles; and the warehouse accommodations were more than adequate. The port had in normal times over 2,500 cranes of which over 1,100 were attached to warehouses; many of these cranes had a 250-ton capacity. The port was equipped with floating docks, dry docks, slips, and repairing workshops. There were adequate facilities for coal and storage facilities for 650,000 tons of oil; and many of the tanks could handle gasoline. The trade of the port normally involved the importation of coffee, tea, rice, spices, seeds, flour, and other agricultural products; in addition, some metal ore was unloaded at the port. Its export trade normally consisted of machinery, electrical goods, chemicals, metal, paper, china, and glass.

The port of Hamburg is located seventy-five miles from the mouth of the Elbe where the outport of Cuxhaven was developed to handle the Hamburg passenger traffic. Historically, the port developed on the basis of river transportation, for before the advent of the railroad and good roads the Elbe provided the connecting link between Hamburg and the Reich. This river carried over half of the port traffic. Goods shipped by river came from as far upstream as the Bohemian part of Czechoslovakia which once possessed a free section within the port. The inland waterways of north central Germany give the Elbe access to the Rhine area via the famous Mittelland canal linking the Elbe to the Weser, Ems, and Rhine, and access to Berlin and the East via the Spree-Havel canal.

The port was adequately served by railroad facilities, for rail lines from Cologne, Bremen, Hanover, Frankfort-on-Main, and Berlin converged at Hamburg. Most of them passed through Harburg-Wilhelmsburg from which spur lines served the extensive dock area. The national railway system was supplemented within the city area by a metropolitan system linking the various stations. The national railways of the area were operated by the National Railroad Directorate at Hamburg (formerly at Altona). The city was a vital traffic center of the Reich rail system. The heaviest goods traffic was handled by the Hamburg-Bremen, Hamburg-Hanover, and Hamburg-Berlin rail lines.

Hamburg is also a focal point in the road system of Northwest Germany. Major roads radiate from Hamburg to Kiel and Lübeck on the north, to Bremen, Hanover, Brunswick on the south, and to Berlin to the east. The section of the famous national super-highway extending from Hamburg to Flensburg with a branch road to Kiel was not completed before the invasion of Denmark. The section to Lübeck is finished. Hamburg was a major center for civil air transport, for air lines radiated from this city to all parts of the Reich and overseas to Great Britain and Scandinavia.

The real beginnings of manufacturing at Hamburg go back to 1888 when the city joined the German Customs Union permitting her products to find an effective market within the Reich. The types of industries have been strongly conditioned by the character of the trade of the port. Although the variety of industries is great, shipbuilding is the most important. The most important shipbuilding company at Hamburg was the *Blohm* and *Voss* works. In all there were over sixty shipbuilding establishments of importance, including a variety of companies interested in repairing and refitting. The building of passenger ships at Hamburg encouraged the development of a number of firms interested in the manufacture of household furnishings. The important food industries of the city developed as the result of the importation of foodstuffs from overseas. There were a number of flour and spice mills, coffee roasting plants, cocoa and chocolate factories, and other establishments. The tobacco manufacturing had its center in the free harbor to avoid the internal excise taxes. Hamburg had over one hundred important firms dealing in food products which employed well over fifteen thousand workers. The shipbuilding industry encouraged the growth of a number of iron and steel works and the development of a machinery industry which normally employed well over forty thousand workers. Other industries normally produced electrical goods (70 companies), chemicals (50 companies), textiles (20 companies), wood products (100 companies), and clothing (100 companies). These industries were serviced by a well developed utilities system. There were over twenty companies interested in electricity, gas, and water. The great electrical plant was the *Hamburger Elektricitäts-Werke AG* which has a yearly capacity of 200 million kwh. It was not linked with the other great plants of the Reich; it served the whole Hamburg area. There were also important municipal plants at Altona and Harburg-Wilhelmsburg.

About eight large firms and companies in Greater Hamburg formerly engaged in trade and commerce of various types. The rapid commercial development was largely based upon an increasingly flourishing transit trade, with Hamburg serving as an overseas export and import center not only for the Reich, but for a large part of Central Europe. It was the home port for a number of great shipping companies: *Hamburg-Amerika Linie* (*HAPAG*), *Deutsch-Ostafrika Linie,* and the *Woermann-Linie*. Before the war almost 14,-000 ships docked and unloaded cargo and left Hamburg with freight every year.

This did not include the trade coming by river which accounts for half the traffic of the port. Hamburg was also an important banking and finance center. Its stock exchange served most of Northwest Germany. A number of insurance companies also had their headquarters in Hamburg.

The Hanseatic City of Hamburg was an urban agglomeration. Its population made its living by working in the industries, commercial establishments, and the transportation enterprises. Only 2 per cent of the population were concerned with agriculture, while about 33 per cent were engaged in industry and crafts and 38 per cent in commerce and transportation. The city had a large working class (43 per cent) and a small independent upper class (13 per cent). The civil servant-white collar group, however, was quite large, accounting for about 25 per cent of the population. This was possible in view of Hamburg's numerous commercial firms.

The Hansa city of Hamburg possessed strong traditions of independence going back into the Middle Ages. Although its territory was small, it had all the Reich as a field for trade. Its seafaring citizens, traders and businessmen, and politicians were known for their honesty and independence of spirit which developed during the long period of politically independent life. Although Hamburg, along with the other Hansa cities, had been all but absorbed by the Reich, it preserved many of its own special social, economic, political, and cultural interests which were different, setting it off from the rest of Germany. These differences were reflected in its typical architecture and characteristic folkways. Although modern Hamburg had been transformed by the growth of industry which led to the erection of great factory areas in a belt about its warehouses and docks and by the creation of a large proletariat, the city was still dominated by its trade and commerce. The native of Hamburg remained a steady dignified person with bourgeois hopes, with much pride and independence of spirit. Hamburg's cultural life was strongly influenced by the practical interests of the businessman and the religious interests of the Lutheran. The aesthetic aspect of life was provided for by the State Opera, Philharmonic, and State Theatre. The lighter side found its outlets in the Reeperbahn and St. Pauli. The Zoological Institute, Museum for Art and Industry, Museum for Prehistory and Ethnology, Institute for Tropical Diseases, Institute for Foreign Politics, and the Institute for Naval Architecture reflected the interest of the city in trade, industry, and life overseas.

Chapter 14

OLDENBURG-BREMEN

The state of Oldenburg occupies a strip of land bordered by the Province of Hanover, the North Sea, the river Ems, and the Hanseatic City of Bremen. The northern part of Oldenburg, embracing the regions of Jeverland and Butjadingen, is largely coastal marshland and extensive *Watten* or tidal flats that are cut by the channels of the Jade and Weser rivers, which extend into the North Sea. The lowland has gradually been reclaimed from the sea by means of dykes and canals. In northeastern Oldenburg, the marshland extends along the Lower Weser upstream to the city of Bremen, which is built on sandy geest, slightly higher than the surrounding marshland. The geestland extends through central and southern Oldenburg in the form of sandy plains and heaths and moors, and rises gradually in the south to the Dammer upland with an elevation of 150 m. An ancient river valley, which extends west from Bremen across Oldenburg, is occupied by the tributaries of the Leda and extensive moorland.

Such a land surface might be expected to support only a very moderate population density. However, in 1933, the population of Oldenburg was 495,119, occupying an area of 5,396 sq. km., or about 91 individuals per sq. km., which is comparable with that of the provinces of Hanover and Schleswig-Holstein, and is typical for northwestern Germany. The greatest density was to be found in the marshland where it ranges from between 75 and 100 per sq. km., diminishing in the geestland, to between 25 and 75 per sq. km.

Bremen presented quite another situation, for it was an urban complex occupying a very small territory. In 1933, the population was 371,558 in its 257 sq. km.—a density of 1,441 individuals per sq. km., which is comparable with, though considerably less than, Hamburg's 2,246.

Although a Germanic people may have settled the region as early as 600 B.C., the present population of the region are descendants of the Saxons of the Roman period with a slight admixture of Frisians. During the fifth century the Frisians pushed eastward to occupy all of northern Oldenburg. Though most of the people now speak a variety of Low Saxon, standard German is

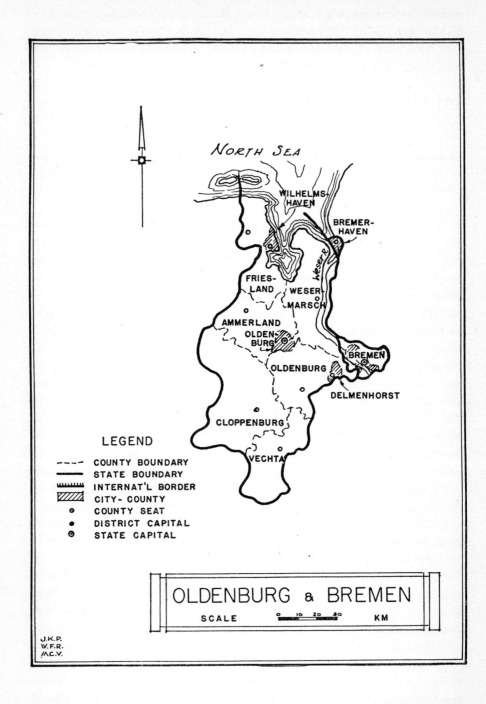

LEGEND

- - - COUNTY BOUNDARY
——— STATE BOUNDARY
▨▨▨ INTERNAT'L BORDER
▨▨▨ CITY- COUNTY
○ COUNTY SEAT
● DISTRICT CAPITAL
◉ STATE CAPITAL

OLDENBURG & BREMEN
SCALE   0 10 20 30   KM

spoken in the cities of the area. The people are almost entirely Lutheran. In 1933 Bremen had 317,000 Protestants and only 24,000 Catholics, while in Oldenburg there were 360,000 Lutherans and 123,000 Catholics. There were only 2,300 Jews in both states.

Both Bremen and Oldenburg have experienced a steady increase in population during the present century. Naturally, urban Bremen grew much more rapidly than Oldenburg. The population of Bremen stood at 299,000 in 1910, and increased to 371,000 by 1933. The increase of population in Oldenburg was subject to regional variation. The greatest increase between 1875 and 1925 was in the marsh area of Jeverland. There was a substantial increase in central Oldenburg, while the population increase in southern Oldenburg was only moderate. Unlike the other river marsh areas, there was an actual loss of population in the Weser river marsh area of Oldenburg. In contrast to the rest of the Reich, considerable numbers of Germans left Bremen and Oldenburg during the twenties and early thirties, between 2000 and 3000 leaving each year for overseas. During the Nazi period emigration decreased markedly, because of the war boom and the restrictions on emigration.

The historical origins of the states of Bremen and Oldenburg go back to Carolingian times. Bremen was established as a bishopric in 787 and elevated to an archbishopric after the Norse raid on Hamburg in 848. Although the city was ruled by the archbishop during the early Middle Ages, the citizens slowly established their rights. The first rulers of Oldenburg seem to have been Saxon Dukes, opponents of Charlemagne. Later, the rulers appear as vassals of the powerful Dukes of Saxony, who occupied themselves with raids upon the city of Bremen. Toward the end of the thirteenth century Bremen was admitted to the Hanseatic League.

The early modern political history of Oldenburg is an involved tale of dynastic disorders with the earldom frequently under the control of Danish rulers. Near the end of the eighteenth century, it achieved the rank of a duchy under a German ruler. During the Reformation, Protestantism was introduced into Oldenburg without great difficulty; Bremen, however, went Protestant only after a long struggle lasting from 1522 to 1618. The city of Bremen was first recognized as an imperial free city in 1646. Sweden, with claims to the archbishopric, protested and resorted to arms. Final recognition of the city's claims came in 1720. During the Napoleonic period, both states were occupied by the French and finally annexed to the French Empire (1810-11). The Treaty of Vienna (1815) restored the independence of Bremen and added the principality of Birkenfeld (in the Rhineland) to the Duchy of Oldenburg. The principality of Lübeck had been acquired by Oldenburg in 1803. During the nineteenth century, the dukes made an attempt to lay claim to the duchies of Schleswig and Holstein, but abandoned their effort in favor of Prussia.

In 1866, both states joined the North German Confederation; and in 1871, they joined the German Empire. During the imperial era, Oldenburg was governed under the Constitution of 1849 which was modified by the enactments of 1852 and 1908. Legislative power was vested in a State Assembly, consisting of members elected by all tax paying citizens, while the executive power was exercised by a responsible State Ministry, consisting of three ministers working under the Grand Duke. The three areas of the Grand Duchy—Oldenburg, Lübeck, and Birkenfeld were administered under separate authorities. The outlying principalities of Birkenfeld and Lübeck also had separate provincial councils.

The Free Hanseatic City of Bremen was governed by the Constitution of 1849, which was revised by the laws of 1879. Legislative power was vested in a House of Burgesses, which consisted of members elected on the basis of a class system of suffrage. The *Senat,* which was elected by the House of Burgesses, chose two Mayors who directed the affairs of the city through twelve departments, each headed by a Senator.

After World War I, Bremen and Oldenburg became federal states of the Weimar Republic. Oldenburg received a new Constitution in November 1918. Under it a democratically elected State Assembly chose the Minister President and two ministers, who headed the Ministry of Foreign Affairs, of Justice, of Church and School (*Ministerium der auswärtigen Angelegenheiten, der Justiz, der Kirchen und Schulen*); the Ministry of the Interior, of Commerce and of Trade (*Ministerium des Innern, des Handels und des Verkehrs*); and the Ministry of Finance, of Social Welfare (*Ministerium der Finanzen, der sozialen Fürsorge*) respectively. The administration of the main portion of Oldenburg was carried out by the Ministry of the Interior, while Lübeck and Birkenfeld were under District Presidents. Bremen adopted a new Constitution in 1920, which provided for a democratically elected House of Burgesses. This council elected the *Senat,* which was composed of fourteen Senators, who in turn chose two mayors from among their number to direct the administration.

In 1934, the Nazis liquidated the federal status of Bremen and Oldenburg, transferring their rights to the Reich. One National Governor was placed in charge of the government and administration of both states. He was under the direct responsibility of the Minister of the Interior, but was also subject to the control and supervision of the other national ministers. The Governor for Bremen-Oldenburg, who maintained his headquarters at Oldenburg, was also the Nazi party district leader of the district of Weser-Ems. Despite the fact that there was a joint national political control for both states, the internal administration of each was quite separate and distinct.

The imposition of the control of the Governor upon the government and administration of Oldenburg did not produce any vital change in the structure of the Oldenburg State Government (*Oldenburgische Landesregierung*), which was still headed by a Minister President, who was the head of the State Ministry. He was assisted by another Minister of State, who also was Minister of Finance and Minister of Churches and Schools. The Minister President also held the important post of Minister of the Interior.

Bremen and Oldenburg have long been liberal strongholds. During the Empire, the city of Bremen voted consistently for the Social Democratic party, while agrarian Oldenburg followed the Progressive Liberal party. The Catholics of southern Oldenburg supported the Catholic Center party. During the era of the Weimar Republic the citizens of both states supported the government. Bremen continued to be a strong center for the Social Democratic party. Oldenburg underwent several political changes. Although the Catholic Center party retained its holdings in the South, the liberal elements turned to the Social Democratic party with the decline of the German Democratic party, the successor of the Progressive Liberals. The conservative German National German People's party was only able to gain a small following in the marshlands, while the radical Communist party obtained a few supporters among the proletarian elements of Bremen. During the critical elections between September 1930 and March 1933, the Social Democrats and Catholics opposed the Nazis. The conservative and disgruntled elements turned to National Socialism, but they were never able to gain sufficient votes. At the height of Nazi electoral strength, the National Socialist party was able to obtain only about 35 per cent of the total vote of Bremen-Oldenburg.

The republican period brought the further extension of direct national administration to finance, railways, unemployment insurance and employment, and labor welfare. In these provinces, national control of finances was carried out through the State Finance Office of Weser-Ems (Bremen) and its local finance offices and main customs offices. The National Construction Office of this area was located at Wilhelmshaven. The nationalized railways were operated by the National Railroad Directorate of Hanover. All problems pertaining to labor and unemployment were met by the State Labor Office of Lower Saxony (Hanover) and the main Welfare Office of Hanover. Administered upon delegation by the states were certain areas of welfare, social insurance, trade and industry, health, and labor which were subject to national legislation. The economic enterprises of the two states, which were subject to only limited state supervision, were organized under various agricultural, industrial, commercial, and labor organizations and associations.

During the Nazi era, the area embracing Bremen, Oldenburg, and Northwest Hanover was constituted as the party district of Weser-Ems. The advent of Nazi rule in Bremen brought little in the way of governmental change except for the imposition of the control of the Governor. The government of Bremen was the *Senat* which was composed of a Governing Mayor (*Regierender Bürgermeister*) and five Senators. The Governing Mayor was responsible, in general, for the over-all supervision of the administration and, in particular, for the operation of the Bremen State Office (*Bremisches Staatsamt*), State Personnel Office (*Staatliches Personalamt*), and the Accounting Office (*Rechnungsamt*). One Senator, who was in charge of the Bremen economic office, had charge of shipping, transportation, trade, and industrial affairs. The finance office, which was headed by another Senator, managed the collection and distribution of public funds and had charge of the Land Registration Office (*Katasteramt*). A third Senator had charge of education, art, learning, and church affairs. The Interior Administration (*Innere Verwaltung*) which was under a fourth Senator was charged with the supervision of police, air defense, and health affairs. He also had charge of local government. The remaining Senator was charged with responsibility for labor, welfare and relief, and insurance. The general administration and the office for finance had their headquarters at the House of Councilors (*Rathaus*), while the offices for Economics (*Wirtschaft*), Education (*Bildungswesen*), and for Labor, Technique, and Welfare (*Arbeit, Technik,* and *Wohlfahrt*), had separate administrative centers. The Interior administration had its headquarters at the Police Station.

The work of the governments of Bremen and Oldenburg was supplemented by a number of special and technical services under direct national control. During the Imperial period only the nationally operated postal system lay outside the scope of the general administrations. Justice in Bremen was handled by a Collegiate Court of First and Second Instance from which appeals went to the Hanseatic Superior Court in Hamburg. In Oldenburg there were the state administered Superior State Court, the Collegiate Courts of First and Second Instance, and the Courts of First Instance. The national postal service within the two states was under the Chief Postal Directorate (Empire) or National Postal Directorate (Republic and Third Reich) of Hanover. National regulations for trade and industry, weights and measures, social insurance, welfare, public health, and the collection of imperial revenues were administered upon delegation from the Reich.

The Nazi regime brought the usual extension of national administrative controls; corporate administrations were developed with the result that total control of life within the two states was under the supervision of the party.

Rural Aspect

The coastal and river marshes and the geest of Bremen and Oldenburg supported about 175,000 individuals or about 33 per cent of the total population of the dominantly rural Oldenburg area and about 2.5 per cent of the Bremen area. Only about 10,000 people in the Bremen area were supported by the soil.

The problems of rural administration were naturally much more important in the state of Oldenburg than in the Hanseatic City of Bremen, where they were limited to one relatively small county.

The state of Oldenburg was subdivided into three city counties and six counties (*Ämter*) or village associations (*Amtsverbände*) which were unions of local areas; and the latter finally into local Communes (*Gemeinden*). During the imperial era, local government and administration in Oldenburg were operated under the Commune Constitution (*Gemeindeordnung*) of 1873 which provided for a wide measure of local independence. The three portions of the state of Oldenburg were governed by separate constitutions in republican times. The Oldenburg portion, which was subject to the Ministry of the Interior, was governed by the Commune Constitution (*Gemeindeordnung*) of 1921, while the Lübeck and Birkenfeld portions, which were under District Presidents, were governed under the two Constitutions of 1922. State administration within the six counties of the Oldenburg portion was carried out by a County Leader, while local self-government was organized under the Administrative Boards, which were governed by a Legislative Assembly and an Administrative Board under the chairmanship of the County Leader. The Communes were governed by a Town Board and a Town Council. The Nazis introduced numerous changes. The Prussian terms *Landrat* and *Landkreis* replaced the Oldenburg ones for *Amtshauptmann* and *Amt*. The democratic Legislative Assembly (*Amtsrat*) disappeared, while the powers of the Nazi County Managers, who were assisted by an advisory County Committee—County Board (*Kreisausschuss-Amtsvorstand*) were enlarged. After 1935 all communes followed the pattern laid down by the Nazi Municipal Code.

The one county of the Hanseatic City of Bremen, which surrounded the urban area, was small and possessed a total population of 17,997. Its local administrator was a Rural Administrator (*Landherr*) with the rank of Senator. Under the Nazis the County Manager was assisted by a Party Agent, who was also the local county leader, and by an Advisory Committee consisting of eleven local citizens. This county and its few villages were subject to the supervision of the Interior Administration of the Hanseatic City of Bremen.

Close to 74 per cent of the land surface of Oldenburg was devoted to agriculture and animal husbandry, but it should be noted that the amount of land under actual cultivation, 24 per cent, is relatively small in comparison with other rural areas. The marsh and geest have an ideal climate for cattle raising. The two areas fall within the north Atlantic zone. The climate is mild and humid. There are numerous storms whose violence is more marked because of the almost complete absence of forest cover. The marshlands are frequently covered by fog. The average January temperature is about —.6 degrees C., while the average July temperature is about 17 degrees C. Yearly rainfall averages about

690 mm. The last frost comes in late April, while the first strikes late in October. The humid, cool marshlands, which are protected from the sea by dykes and drainage canals, are largely occupied by pasture and meadowland.

Although much of this lowland polder area is devoted to cattle and horse raising, the drained marshlands do produce good crops of wheat, oats, rye, barley, and horse beans. Near the larger cities, extensive market gardens have been developed in the marshlands. Livestock raising, however, remains the important activity. Lean beef cattle (feeders) raised on the interior geest are sent here for fattening for the autumn market. Dairying is unimportant except near the larger towns. The slightly elevated geest shares the cool and humid climate of the marshlands, and supports only a scant population owing to its extensive infertile heaths and moorlands. The geest is largely made up of infertile podzol soils. Poor drainage has given rise to numerous moors, the curse of agriculture in northwestern Germany. They are slowly being reclaimed by means of a Dutch reclamation method, involving drainage, removal of peat, and the enrichment of the underlying sands. Hundreds of formerly boggy areas have been brought under cultivation by the Finn Colonies (*Fehnkolonien*), which support themselves by raising potatoes, green vegetables, and cereals. The peat of the bogs is used locally for fuel. A greater portion of the geestland is, however, given over to cattle raising and dairying. In geest areas sheep raising and bee-keeping play an important role in rural life.

In comparison with other parts of the Reich, Oldenburg must be placed at the bottom of the list as far as cultivated crops are concerned. Statistics in land utilization, in hectares, are as follows (for the year 1933):

Cultivated Land	142,560
Grain 92,010	
Legumes 4,455	
Root Crops 40,165	
Green Vegetables 661	
Industrial Crops 586	
Fodder Crops 4,683	
Small Gardens	12,903
Meadow	82,596
Pasture	160,042
Orchards	201
Forests and Woods	38,810
Houses and Barns	12,300
Moorland	34,394
Waste Land	28,425
Roads and Parks	25,621
Total Land Area	539,627

In terms of percentages one has the following land-use picture: agricultural land 70 per cent (cultivated land 26 per cent, pasture 44 per cent), woods and forests 7 per cent, waste land 18 per cent, other land 5 per cent.

The small villages of the marshlands, stretching along roads on the higher ground consist of houses of the Frisian type in the northwest (indicating the survival of ancient Frisian traditions) and of house types of the Low Saxon variety along the Lower Weser. These villages and peasant houses contrast strongly with the pattern of settlement on the geest where one finds separate farm establishments whose life frequently centers in old houses of the Low Saxon type. The small independent farmers of the geest are conservative and patriarchal. Their isolated way of life outside of villages has strengthened their strong spirit of independence. Although the peasant of the marshland is a villager, he shares with the farmer of the geest this same spirit of conservatism and independence.

Urban Aspect

Bremen is an urban complex, in contrast to Oldenburg which is predominantly rural. Aside from the cities of Oldenburg, Delmenhorst, and Wilhelmshaven, described below, there are only two towns, Nordenham and Friesische Wehde, with populations exceeding 10,000. While the people of the Hanseatic City of Bremen are almost entirely dependent upon industry, trade, and transportation for a living, the population of Oldenburg makes a greater proportion of its living from agrarian pursuits. The three larger cities of Oldenburg constitute city counties. City government and administration in Oldenburg, which was regulated by the Municipal Constitutions of 1873 and 1921, was based on the Bicameral Constitution (*Zweikollegienverfassung*). Legislative power was vested in a City Council, while the administration of city affairs was carried out by a Magistry. After 1935 city administration followed the pattern laid down by the German Municipal Code. Under the Nazis, the city counties were headed by Chief Mayors directly responsible to the Minister of the Interior of Oldenburg. The Chief Mayor was assisted by an Advisory Council aided by Administrative Department heads who, in turn, were assisted by Advisory Councilors. The Party Agent was associated with the Chief Mayor.

Economically, the lower Weser area was dominated by Bremen. This somewhat isolated urban agglomeration with its specialized interests was dependent upon its Weser hinterland and trade with the Reich and the world. Its growth had long been hampered by the shallowness of the Weser and the more restricted character of the potential commercial area which it served. While an older port than Hamburg, Bremen, its rival, was the second largest German port. It has always made its living off a more specialized trade in which cotton and tobacco play an important role. Although Oldenburg has a typical northwestern German economy, its basic orientation is toward Bremen and the Lower Weser.

The economic life of the Bremen-Oldenburg area is closely tied to the extensive water transportation facilities of the lower Weser area. The Weser, with the ports of Wilhelmshaven, Bremerhaven, Brake, and Bremen, together with the canals linking Bremen and the Weser to the Lower Elbe on the east and to the Dortmund-Ems canal on the west, constitute the important water transportation facilities of the Weser-Ems area. Another canal connects Wilhelmshaven with Emden. It should be noted that the Weser River is crossed by the Mittelland canal of Central Germany which links the Ruhr with East Germany, thus tying it to the extensive water transportation system of the Reich.

The quays of Bremen are located thirty-four nautical miles downstream from the port of Bremerhaven and sixty-seven nautical miles from the North Sea. Ships with a draft of thirty-eight feet can reach them during a normal tide. During the winter icebreakers must be employed to keep the port open. The port consists of six basins, two of which are in the Free Harbor: European Harbor (*Europahafen*) and the Upper Sea Harbor (*Überseehafen*). The former specialized in handling fruit ships, while the larger *Überseehafen* catered to a more general trade. The Grain Harbor (*Getreidehafen*), which is within the customs area, had extensive facilities for the transhipment of grain, while the Wood and Manufactory Harbor (*Holz- und Fabrikenhafen*) specialized in the lumber trade. The smaller High Gate Harbor (*Hohentorhafen*) was for general trade. The fourth basin of the customs area was the Industry and Commerce Harbor (*Industrie- und Handelshafen*), which consisted of six separate small basins. It was a dock harbor, specializing in the transshipment of potash. The trade of the port normally involved the importation of mineral oils, cotton, wool, paper, wood, ore, coffee, hides, skins, fruit, tobacco, and a number of other products. The normal exports of Bremen consisted of metal wares, coal, coke, cement, textiles, machinery, potash, chemicals, leather, flour, glass, cellulose, and toys.

Bremerhaven is located on the east bank of the Weser about thirty-two nautical miles from the open sea. It has long served as the ocean-going port of Bremen. Although Wesermünde and Bremerhaven, which practically form one town, were united in 1939 and placed under the jurisdiction of Hanover, the port facilities of Bremerhaven remained under the control of Bremen. Many ships which could not reach the port of the city of Bremen lightened or discharged at the numerous quays of Bremerhaven. There were eight wet docks where vessels loaded and unloaded without bothering about locks. The dry docks protected by locks were much more extensive. Bunkering and coal facilities were available at all berths.

Wilhelmshaven had a tidal harbor served by six dry docks equipped with locks. The commercial harbor occupied the southern part of the port area, while the northern portion was taken up by the extensive works of the Command of the North Sea Naval Station (*Kommando der Marinestation der Nordsee*). In normal times, Wilhelmshaven exported brick, oil, and molasses and imported coal, timber, flour, sugar, and a number of other products. It was at best a minor commercial German port. During the periods when Germany had a navy, however, its importance grew.

All these ports were served by the national railway system. Bremen could almost be called a railroad port. It is situated on the Ruhr-Hamburg rail line. Other railroad lines connect Bremen with Hanover, Bremerhaven, and Oldenburg. Smaller lines run from Oldenburg to Wilhelmshaven and Emden. The heavy traffic is borne by the Ruhr-Bremen-Hamburg line. The railways of this area, which were entirely under the National German Railroad, were under the National Railroad Directorate at Hanover.

Bremen is also the hub for roads coming in from Hamburg, Hanover, Osnabrück, and Emden. Oldenburg is traversed by a north-south road extending from Wilhelmshaven to the southern part of Oldenburg. Bremen is on the main highway route running from the Ruhr to Hamburg and Lübeck. A branch road links Bremen with the Hamburg-Hanover national super-highway. The main roads of Bremen and Oldenburg were maintained by the respective state governments. The airports of Bremen and Wilhelmshaven were integral parts of the German air transport system, which was operated by the German Airways Corporation (*Deutsche Lufthansa AC*).

Industrially, as well as economically, the Lower Weser area is dominated by Bremen. The beginnings of manufacturing go back to the late nineteenth century when the city joined the German Customs Union permitting her products to find an effective market within the Reich. The character of the industries of Bremen and Oldenburg has been conditioned by the trade of their ports and the raw materials of the immediate neighborhood. Shipbuilding was not so important here as in Hamburg; about six important yards employed over 10,000 workers at Bremen. The shipyards at Wilhelmshaven have been important for the production of naval craft. The important shipbuilding firms at Bremen included the *Deschimag Deutsche Schiff- und Maschinenbau AG,* and the *Vulkan* works. The Bremen iron and steel industry involves about eight important firms. Over 100 companies were interested in the iron, steel, and metal ware industry, and about another 90 were interested in the machine industry. It was an important center for the manufacture of automobiles: *Hansa-Lloyd-Goliath-Werke.* The production of aircraft has been significant in recent years. It was the center of the *Focke-Wulf Flugzeugbau* and the *Weser Flugzeugbau.* The chemical industry, which involved about 19 companies employing 800 workers in normal times, has developed on the basis of the salt deposits of northern Oldenburg.

The important food industries of Bremen reflect the port's extensive interest in the importation of foodstuffs in normal times. Over 250 factories were engaged in the conversion of raw foodstuffs: flour mills, coffee roasting plants (the city was the center of the *Kaffee-Hag* works), spice mills and other establishments. Tobacco manufacturing establishments had grown up in the free harbor area where they could best escape the internal excise taxes. The fishing industry, which has its main port of operation at Wesermünde, had a number of processing plants at Bremen. Textile and paper industries also played their part in the economy of this city. The limited industries of Oldenburg were largely to be found in the northern part of the state in the cities of Oldenburg, notable for their small metal ware industry, small textile mills, few tobacco manufacturing establishments, and printing; in Delmenhorst, the main center of the German linoleum industry, and home of tobacco, textile, and small metal ware plants; and in Wilhelmshaven where naval shipbuilding and metal industries predominated. These industries were serviced by a well developed utilities system and power industry. An important water power plant is located near Bremen. It was linked to another water power plant at Dörverden, which lies up the Weser in Hanover. From here, lines extended to the important Ahlem coal plant near Hanover and, then, southward to connect with the water power plants of Central Germany. Wilhelmshaven was supplied by a moderate-sized coal power plant at Weismoor in northwestern Hanover. Smaller municipal electrical plants were located at Wilhelmshaven, Delmenhorst, the town of Hasbergen in Oldenburg, and Bremen. Only a few of the larger towns of Oldenburg owned and operated their own gas and water plants.

Bremen is the major commercial center for the Weser-Ems area. Its modern commercial history began in 1827 with the purchase of the port site of Bremerhaven from Hanover. After the middle of the nineteenth century, trade overseas and particularly with America played an increasing role in the commercial life of Bremen. It was particularly famous as the home port of the *Norddeutscher Lloyd* Line. Although the trade of the port of Bremen and Bremerhaven was not as great as that of Hamburg, it did occupy first place within the Reich for trade in cotton, tobacco, and grain. In 1935, 7,112 ships unloaded 5,867,000 metric tons of cargo, while 7,242 ships left the port carrying over 5,900,000 metric tons of cargo. Bremen was also the important money and banking center for the Weser-Ems area. Its stock exchange, which was housed in a modern Gothic structure near the main square of the Old City (*Altstadt*), served both Bremen and Oldenburg. The banking system of Oldenburg was headed by the *Oldenburg Credit Bank*. The *Reichsbank* maintained a number of offices in Bremen and Oldenburg. These banks were supplemented by branches of the great Berlin commercial banks and by local county and city-county mortgage and savings banks.

In 1933, the population of urban Bremen was largely engaged in industrial, commercial, and transport activities. Thirty-three per cent worked in industry and crafts, while 38 per cent were engaged in commerce and transportation. Another 10 per cent was employed in civil service occupations. Only 2.5 per cent was interested in agriculture.

In rural Oldenburg 34 per cent of the population was engaged in agriculture, while 26 per cent was employed in industry and crafts and 15 per cent in trade and transportation. The state has a relatively large upper class, a large working class, and small white collar, civil service, and professional groups.

Both the Hanseatic City of Bremen and the state of Oldenburg possess strong traditions of independence going back into the Middle Ages. While life in Bremen has been based for centuries on shipping and trade, the state of Oldenburg has for a long period of time been largely in the hands of small conservative farmers. Oldenburg, a relatively small city of 70,000, is the major urban center of the state. It consists of an old inner town and a new city of villas and gardens which has grown up beyond the old city walls. Oldenburg is famous for its city hall, ducal palaces, and state museum, all built in a Renaissance style of architecture. Delmenhorst and Wilhelmshaven are small and relatively unimportant. Bremen is a romantic old city with winding streets and lanes and an old moat and walls. Three relatively new business and residential quarters have grown up since the foundation of the Empire in 1871. The traders and businessmen of Bremen and the farmers of Oldenburg have in the past been characterized by their honesty and independence of spirit. They are a sober unemotional lot. Though both of these states form integral parts of the Reich, they still retain their own special social, economic, political, and cultural interests which set them off not only from each other but also from the land about them.

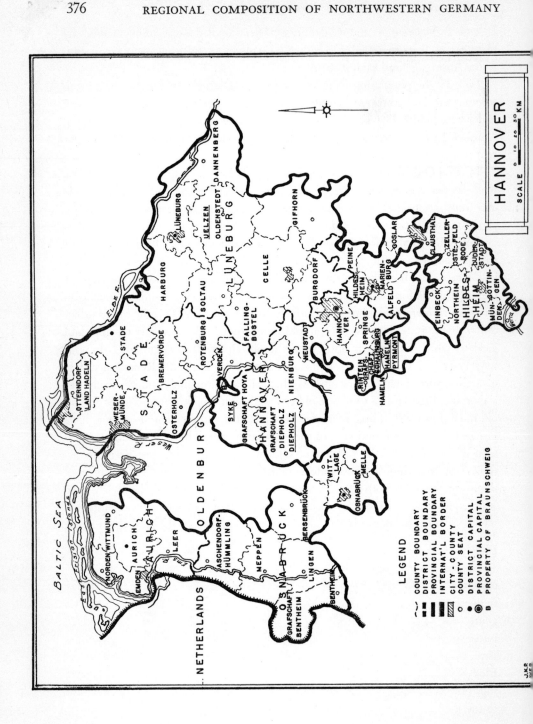

Chapter 15

THE PROVINCE OF HANOVER*

The Province of Hanover lies in northwestern Prussia, bordering the Netherlands on the west. Its coastline on the North Sea is broken by the relatively small Bremen-Oldenburg area, while to the east lie the Prussian provinces of Schleswig-Holstein and Saxony, and the states of Hamburg and Mecklenburg. The southern portion, from which the district of Hildesheim is almost severed by the narrow portion of the state of Brunswick, is bordered by the provinces of Saxony, Hesse-Nassau, and Westphalia, the larger portion of Brunswick, the Lippes and Westphalia.

Four principal types of landscape predominate in Hanover: coastal and river marshlands in the north, lowland geestlands, loess border, and upland hills and mountains in the south. The North Sea coast is marshland, except for a tiny portion in the Cuxhaven area where the geestland juts into the sea. The marshes, frequently protected from the sea by dykes and drainage channels, are separated from the open sea by extensive *Watten* or tidal flats. Along the northwestern section of the coast the tidal flats terminate in the sandy islands of Borkum, Norderney, Juist, Baltrum, Langeoog, Spiekeroog, and the tiny island of Neuwerk (off Cuxhaven). All these islands except Neuwerk are known as the East Frisian Islands (*Ostfriesische Inseln*). The Ems, Weser, and Elbe have cut deep channels through the tidal flats on their way to the sea.

Inland, along the lower courses of these rivers, the coastal marshes are replaced by extensive river marshlands, where dykes and drainage channels are required to keep them free of standing water. The geestland, which rises gently out of the marsh, is covered by heath and moors, and may be divided into two distinct areas: in the west the narrow strip between Oldenburg and the Ems, and in the east the broad *Lüneburger* (*Heide*) heath extending to the Elbe River. The heath has a relatively flat surface, rarely more than undulating, but its edges are frequently steep, particularly when the heath gives way to the lowland valleys of the Elbe, Aller, and the Weser rivers. Only the north-

* German spelling—Hannover.

377

west and northeast sections of the heath are marked by glacial deposits. Westward, the lower geestlands are covered by extensive stretches of bog and moor, which occur in two forms—the elevated dry-top type and the low wet bog. Near the river valleys wide alluvial belts encroach upon the infertile geestland. To the southeast the geest gives way to the rich border zone extending along the southern edge of the geest, which begins just to the north of the forested Weser hills and widens out eastward into the lowland bay of Magdeburg. This area, which constitutes one of the richest agricultural belts in Germany, is level and well drained. Southward from the border area lies southern Hanover which is characterized by rolling country, dominated by the Harz Mountains.

The Province of Hanover had only a moderate population density, with 3,236,868 occupying 38,705 sq. km., the density being 83 per sq. km. There was a remarkable agreement between the landscape and population patterns. The geest of the interior possessed a lesser population ranging from 50 to 75 in the better areas, but frequently under 25 per sq. km. in the poorer regions of western Hanover. The river and coastal marshlands had the relatively dense population of 75 to 100 per sq. km. and frequently over 100 near the urban centers. The southern border area, however, was the most densely settled area ranging between 100 and 200 per sq. km. The higher upland had a very sparse population.

Hanover was probably settled by West Germanic folk as early as 500 or 600 B.C. Since the time of the Roman Empire all of Hanover was occupied by the Low Saxons, whose dialect, Low Saxon, has many varieties. During the fifth century the Frisians, speaking a language now halfway between English and Low Saxon, pushed eastward from their homeland in the northern Netherlands to occupy the northwestern portion of Hanover. They survive on the East Frisian Islands, and evidence of their earlier occupation of the mainland is found in the folkways and folklore of northwest Hanover. Standard German is spoken in most of the cities of the area. The Province of Hanover is largely Lutheran (2,785,000 in 1933), although there is a large Catholic bloc (486,000) in the southwestern portion of the province. The total Jewish population was small, 12,611, in comparison with the other provinces and states of the Reich.

Hanover experienced a slow but steady increase in population during the present century, but the great urban centers, notably the city of Hanover, have grown more rapidly than the rural areas. The population increase, even in the rural parts, was characterized by regional variation; the geestland population expanded more or less uniformly, except for the areas adjacent to Hamburg and along the Lower Weser; the border area population increased much more rapidly.

The early history of the Province of Hanover and the state of Brunswick are merged, for both once formed constituent parts of the ancient Duchy of

Saxony. The descendants of the kings of the Saxons, who had struggled in vain against Charlemagne, were later elevated to the status of dukes. One of the Saxon rulers in 936 became Emperor Otto I of the Holy Roman Empire. The Saxon holdings were then invested with another Low Saxon noble who had extensive holdings in the southern and eastern parts of modern Hanover. Dynastic interchanges brought the lands in Hanover under the rule of the Guelf (Welf), Heinrich of Bavaria, whose son was invested with the Duchy of Saxony in the early twelfth century. As indicated above his son, Henry the Lion (Heinrich der Löwe), fell upon evil days, for he was outlawed in 1180 and deprived of the duchies of Bavaria and Saxony. The latter was divided and its name transferred to the Margraviate of Meissen, which was later to evolve into the modern kingdom and republican state of Saxony. The descendants of Henry the Lion retained family estates in the Lüneburg and Brunswick areas. During the later Middle Ages, the holdings of the family slowly increased. In 1235, they received the Duchy of Brunswick. Otto, the leader of the family of this day, managed to add the cities of Hanover, Göttingen, and the earldom of Stade. His sons divided the inheritance in 1267, one becoming the ancestor of the ducal house of Braunschweig-Wolfenbüttel (modern Brunswick), the other, the ancestor of the reigning house of Braunschweig-Lüneburg, which was destined to evolve into modern Hanover.

The Braunschweig-Lüneburg inheritance took many strange turns, with ramifications which were important not only for Germany but also for England and America. There were many divisions of lands until the seventeenth century, when the Duchy of Lüneburg came under the rule of Duke Ernst August. He married Sophia, daughter of the Elector Friederich V of the Palatinate, son-in-law of King James I of England. Duke Ernst was made an Elector of the Holy Roman Empire in 1692. After his death in 1698, his son Georg Wilhelm, who was the second Elector of Hanover, became George I of England (1714). From this time until the accession of Queen Victoria in 1837, the history of Hanover is merged with that of the reigning family of Great Britain.

The period between 1715 and 1813 was one of considerable aggrandizement for this land whose rulers were now styled Electors of Hanover. During this period the holdings of the Electors consisted of the principality of Calenberg centering about the city of Hanover, the earldom of Hoya (1543), the earldom of Diepholz (1585), the principality of Lüneburg consisting of old family estates, the territory of Hadeln (1689), and the mining district of Clausthal in the Harz area. The duchies of Bremen and Verden, both formerly ecclesiastical states, secularized in 1648 and later acquired by Sweden, were added to Hanover by the Peace of Stockholm (1720). The next substantial increase came in 1803, when Hanover took over the principality of Osnabrück, an archbishopric which had been partly secularized and placed partly under Hanoverian control in 1648. Hanover took the side of the Allies against the French during the Revolutionary period until its neutralization in 1795. Prussia, jealous of the growing power of Hanover and its advantage as an English outpost on the continent, occupied the Electorate for a few months in 1801 at the instigation of the French. The state was again defeated by the Prussians in 1803. After Napoleon's defeat of Prussia in 1806, southern Hanover was made a part of the Kingdom of Westphalia, while northern Hanover was added to the French Empire. The victory of the Allies brought the restoration of Hanover. At Vienna (1815), Hanover received East Friesland, the secularized bishopric of Hildesheim, and the city of Goslar in return for the surrender of most of the Duchy of Saxe-Lauenburg to Prussia. The Electorate of Hanover was elevated to the status of a kingdom.

The remaining nineteenth century history of the area was turbulent and filled with constitutional struggles. In 1837, the close political ties of Hanover and Great Britain separated after a union of 123 years, for Queen Victoria could not, under the traditional Salic law, ascend the throne of Hanover. Ernst August, Duke of Cumberland, became King of Hanover. The new King managed to save his position in 1848 by restoring the liberal constitution of 1833. This last phase of Hanoverian history is colored by its jealousy of Prussia and its leaning to the side of Austria. The difficulties between Austria, Denmark, and Prussia over the duchies of Schleswig and Holstein brought the issue to a head in 1864. Despite a Prussian request for neutrality in the Seven Weeks' War, Hanover joined with Austria. In 1866, following Austria's defeat, Prussia occupied Hanover and incorporated it as a province. There was a strong *"Welf"* (Guelph) underground opposition to Prussian overlordship that continued during the rest of the nineteenth century, and the traditions of an independent Hanover have survived until recently in the Hanoverian party of republican days, which insisted upon states' rights in general and the reconstruction of Hanover in particular. However, most of the citizens of the state seem to have given in to the inevitable and to have become loyal subjects of the Prussian Kingdom and later of the Prussian Republic.

The advent of Prussian control brought several administrative changes. The basic Prussian pattern of provincial administration was not introduced until the Provincial Constitution of May 1884. This ordinance was modified by the liberal republican and later reactionary Nazi laws.

Hanover presented a heterogeneous political picture. In imperial times the southern Göttingen-Hildesheim area, which had strong industrial and manufacturing interests, went Social Democratic, while the agrarian north turned either to the unimportant German Farmer Union party or the Guelph Hanoverian party (*Hannoversche Partei*). The German Farmer Union party, which represented the conservative agrarian interests, was strong in the southern

Lüneburg and northern Stade areas. The Hanoverian party, which stood for the re-establishment of the old Kingdom of Hanover, had its major strongholds in the districts of Hanover, Stade, and Lüneburg. An interesting feature of the political situation was the fact that the northwest district of Aurich followed the Liberal Progressive party or the other small independent political groups. The Catholics of the southwestern part of Hanover, naturally, voted for the Center party.

In republican days the Province of Hanover as a whole gave first place in its elections to the Social Democratic party. In four of its six administrative districts this party's position was strong, especially in the urban areas. But in the other two districts, Osnabrück and Aurich, the Catholic and the Nationalist parties respectively, took top positions. With the rise of National Socialism in 1930, the province began to drift toward this party, and by 1932 every one of its administrative districts except Catholic Osnabrück went over strongly to the Hitler column. In the presidential elections of 1932 only two of the province's districts, Catholic Osnabrück and Social Democratic Hildesheim, voted for Hindenburg against Hitler. Interestingly enough, the local Hanoverian party secured nearly 200,000 votes in the province as late as 1928—more than half of them in the two districts of Lüneburg and Stade. In the following elections, however, most of these votes went to the Nazis. Similarly, the nationalist and liberal voters, who were quite strong throughout the province, gave many of their votes to the Nazis. Only the administrative district of Osnabrück consistently opposed Hitler by supporting the Catholic party strongly in every election.

Under the Republic there was an extension of direct national administration to finance, railways, unemployment insurance and employment, and labor welfare. There was the usual pattern of national control of finances carried out through the State Finance Office of Hanover and the State Finance Office of Weser-Ems (Bremen) and their local finance offices and main customs offices. The National Construction Offices at Hanover, Lüneburg, and Osnabrück were under the State Finance Office of Hanover, while the Construction Director at Emden was under the office at Bremen. The nationalized railways of the province were operated by the National Railroad Directorate of Hanover. Problems relating to labor were handled by the State Labor Office of Lower Saxony (Hanover) and the main Welfare Office of Hanover. Those departments of welfare, social insurance, health, trade and industry, and labor, which were subject to national legislation, were administered upon delegation by the province. The economic life of the province, which was subject to limited provincial control, was organized in national agricultural, industrial, commercial, and labor associations and organizations.

Under the Nazis, the province of Hanover was organized under the following party districts: Weser-Ems (Oldenburg), East Hanover (Lüneburg), and South Hanover (Hanover). Each of the party district headquarters included the usual party offices which exercised control over the appropriate offices of provincial administration. The Elite Guard in Hanover was under the Nordsee (Hamburg) and West (Düsseldorf) commands, while the Storm Troops worked under the Nordsee (Bremen) and Lower Saxony (Hanover) commands. The N. S. Motorcorps was under the control of regional offices at Hamburg and Frankfort. The Hitler Youth was under the Nordsee (Oldenburg) and Lower Saxony (Hanover) commands. The affiliated organizations of the Nazi party—associations for civil servants, jurists, teachers, physicians, welfare, war victims, and technicians—maintained offices at each party district headquarters. This dense network of party controls guaranteed the political stability of the state.

Territorially, the Nazi regime made some minor changes. Near Hamburg, the county of Harburg-Wilhelmsburg and some adjacent territory were ceded to Greater Hamburg, in exchange for the former Hamburg area of Cuxhaven. The city county of Bremerhaven, which had been under the jurisdiction of Bremen, was merged with Wesermünde, a Hanoverian city; the Bremerhaven dock installations, however, remained under Bremen's jurisdiction. Hanover, in turn, gave up the city county of Vegesack to Bremen. The territorial reorganization of Brunswick in 1942 brought several changes in south Hanover. The city county and county of Goslar and the eastern part of the county of Marienburg were lost in exchange for the county of Holzminden, giving the province a new corridor to link its central and southern sections.

Under the Nazis, the administration of the Province of Hanover was headed by a Chief President who resided in the city of Hanover. He was vested with broad political and supervisory control of administrative, social, economic, and cultural activities, although much of the actual administration was carried out by the District Presidents.

The Chief President, with his supervisory and political powers, was aided by an Advisory Provincial Council which replaced the old Provincial Legislature and Provincial Committee. It is important to note that the Chief President of Hanover was not a Nazi party leader as was usual in most Prussian provinces. This may be due to the fact that Hanover was divided into three party districts for purposes of party administration.

The work of the general provincial administration was supplemented by special and technical services under direct national control. During the imperial period only the state administered courts, railways, and mining offices and the nationally operated postal system lay outside the scope of the general administration of the Province of Hanover. Justice, as usual, was administered by the Prussian Ministry of Justice and was handled by the Superior State Court of Celle, the Collegiate Courts of First and Second Instance of Aurich, Göttingen, Hanover, Hildesheim, Lüneburg, Osnabrück, Stade, and Verden, and the numerous local Courts of First Instance. The national postal system within the province was under the National Postal Directorates (Empire) or National Postal Directorates (Republic and Third Reich) of Hanover, Bremen, Brunswick, Hamburg, and Oldenburg. Typically, national regulations for trade and industry, weights and measures, social insurance and welfare, public health, and the collection of imperial revenues were administered upon delegation from the Reich.

The Nazi regime brought an extension of national administrative controls. Direct national administration was extended to justice, air matters, and labor relations. Many of the traditional fields of state administration were brought under tight national control.

Hanover was the most important governmental and administrative center for it was the provincial capital and the seat of many of the special administrative services, as well as the district administrative center for the central Hanover governmental administrative district. Hildesheim in the southeast, Osnabrück in the southwest, and Lüneburg, Stade, and Aurich in the north ranked next in importance because of their status as district administrative centers. The small town of Celle was the administrative center of the Hanoverian courts.

RURAL ASPECT

Agriculture and forestry in the marshlands, geestlands, uplands, and the rich border areas of the Province of Hanover provide for the support of 30 per cent of its population. About 50 per cent of the population of the province dwells on farms and in villages and small towns close to the soil. The general administration of rural Hanover centered in the city of Hanover, the provincial capital, and the six district capitals, Hanover, Hildesheim, Lüneburg, Stade, Osnabrück, and Aurich. The day to day administration of rural Hanover was carried out through the forty-seven counties into which the administrative districts were divided. These counties were headed by County Managers who served both as the agents of the central government and the local self-government. The county administration and self-government were regulated by the County Constitution of 1884 which was modified by the liberal laws of the Republic and by the reactionary laws of the Third Reich. The villages, which were once governed by the old Hanoverian Law for the Towns (*Gesetz für die Landgemeinden*) of 1859, followed the German Municipal Code after 1935.

Under the Nazis, each village or town administration consisted of a Mayor, the Party Agent, two or three administrative assistants, and a town council.

Village and town self-government were once more important. The county and its villages and towns handled welfare and public works; some owned a forest and managed a local market; occasionally they operated their own utilities.

Despite the excellent soils of the border area, Hanover does not constitute one of the better agrarian regions of the Reich. Approximately 56 per cent of the land is devoted to agrarian activities: 31 per cent to crops, and 25 per cent to stock raising. The character of agriculture varies widely throughout the province, owing to the soil and climatic conditions. The climate of the province varies considerably from north to south and from east to west. The marshes of the north have a mild North Atlantic climate with an average January temperature of 3 degrees C. and an average July temperature of 17 degrees. Although the winters are somewhat milder to the west of the Weser, the average summer temperature is much the same throughout the northwest lowlands. The uplands of the southeast, however, have cold winters and milder summers, accompanied by a greater amount of rainfall. The frost dates are important for agriculture. In the marshes the first frost comes in early November, while the last frost occurs about the second week in April. In the geest, the first frost arrives earlier, about the middle of October. The upland summer is very short.

The salty soil areas of the cool, humid marsh or polder area along the coast are largely occupied by meadowland devoted to cattle and horse raising. The age-long peasant effort to reclaim the marshes from river and coastal flats was aided by the government during the period of the Empire and the Republic. The Nazi government put the Labor Service to work at this task. The non-salty portions of the marshlands, which constitute about one-half of the area, are devoted to crops of oats, wheat, horse bean, and barley. Market garden and dairying become more important near the larger cities of the coast.

The slightly elevated geest, which shares the cool and humid climate of the marshlands, supports only a scant agrarian population owing to its infertile soils. The moors and bogs have been partly reclaimed for crop cultivation by means of the "Dutch System"; that is, by drainage and the enrichment of the underlying soils. This work has led to the formation of new agricultural settlements known as Finn Colonies. These colonies are most numerous in the Ems valley of western Hanover, where extensive reclamation work was carried out by the Labor Service. The best farmland of the northwest is to be found in the shallow valleys intersecting the fen and moors of the geestland. It is the geest area, however, which has made Hanover important for its livestock. Excellent horses are raised in the northern districts of Aurich and Stade, while the Lüneburg Heath is famous for its *Heidschnucken* breed of sheep. Although farmers frequently supplement their income by raising hogs, their chief support is cattle raising and dairying.

The border zone of degraded chernozem soils extending from the Weser uplands to the Bay of Magdeburg forms the real tillage area of the province. This treeless, hedgeless zone, being far from the sea, has a drier and warmer climate than the geestland or marshland. It is a crop country, important for wheat, barley, and particularly for sugar beets which are rotated with the cereal crops. Some cattle are raised and are fed from the beet pulp released by the sugar beet industries. Many of the farmers are rich enough to own farm machinery. Southward, the border area gives way to the foothills of the Harz Mountains. This upland country is famous for its orchards which produce quantities of apples, plums, pears, and cherries. The valleys are rich and fertile, supporting a variety of crops.

LAND UTILIZATION (1933)

(HECTARES)

Cultivated Land		1,195,000
Grain	775,000	
Legumes	23,000	
Root Crops	329,000	
Green Vegetables	9,000	
Industrial Crops	7,000	
Fodder Crops	52,000	
Small Gardens		48,000
Houses and Barns		64,000
Meadow		433,000
Pasture		550,000
Orchards		8,000
Forests		745,000
Moorland		180,000
Waste Land		346,000
Total Land Area		3,569,000

PERCENTAGE OF LAND-USE

Agrarian Land		56%
Cultivated Land	31%	
Meadowland	25%	
Forest and Woods		19%
Other Types of Land		25%

Nineteen per cent of Hanover is given over to woods and forests, the smallest amount of any of the provinces in Prussia except Schleswig-Holstein. Less than 10 per cent of the northwestern marsh, heath, and moorland has a forest cover, and here it consists of only oases of beech and oak. There are quantities of bush and shrub, but this cannot be counted as forest land. Along the eastern margin of the province, the North German pine slowly begins to replace the heath and moorland flora. Another belt of pine extends along the Weser and sweeps southward into the northern part of Westphalia. In these areas, woodland will frequently account for 14 to 21 per cent of the area. The border region, as has been indicated, is almost devoid of trees and bushes, but the hilly lands to the south are covered with a forest which frequently occupies from 30 to 40 per cent of the land, deciduous trees in the lower hills and extensive forests of larch and fir in the higher areas. Almost a third of the forests of Hanover are held in the seventy-nine state forest reserves. The cities, towns, and villages of Hanover hold only a very limited portion of the forest land. Beginning in 1877, a large land reclamation project centered in the Lüneberg Heath area, which involved breaking up the hard pan of the extensive waste heathlands and planting oak and pine.

The sober, outwardly unemotional Low Saxon peasants of the geest and marshland form a distinct cultural bloc. The peasants of the river and coastal marshlands dwell in a village of the *Marschhufendorf* type. The houses of these villages in northwestern Hanover are of the East Frisian type reflecting the earlier occupation of the Frisians. Today, the Frisians occupy the isles off the coast, where they make their living by fishing and trade with the tourists. They are a gruff, stolid, slow moving lot, whose rationalistic turn of mind has produced some of Germany's leading intellectuals. The Low Saxon farmers of the geest are not as well off economically as their brothers of the marshlands. They dwell in the typical Lower Saxon house—long rectangular structures housing a barn and living quarters. To the west of the Weser River, these houses occupy the center of the farm, while in the Lüneburg Heath area between the Weser and the Elbe, the Low Saxon houses of the peasants are always found grouped in villages of the agglomerated type. To the southeast, the politically conservative, patriarchal Low Saxon peasant gives way to the richer, more sophisticated farmer of the border area.

The extreme southern part of Hanover is occupied by Germans of an East Middle German type, speaking a variety of Thuringian dialect. They dwell in agglomerated villages in houses of a Middle German "Frankish" type which consist of living quarters and a number of barns built about a farm yard, all enclosed by walls. The peasants of this part of Hanover, living by means of subsistence farming, have strong nationalistic interests; they were among the first to adopt Nazism. They are famous for their colorful folk art and varied folk songs. The contrasts between the Frisians of the coastal islands, the poor peasants of the geest, the rich farmers of the border area, and the simple folk of the southern uplands reveal the varied character of economic, political, and cultural interests within rural Hanover.

URBAN ASPECT

Hanover was one of the less densely settled of the Prussian provinces. It was a predominantly rural area, for about 50 per cent of its population dwelt in villages of less than 2,000 inhabitants. Another 36 per cent lived in towns ranging from 2,000 to 100,000, while only 13 per cent of the population was centered in the large city of Hanover. This city was the only large urban center, for each of the other cities, Emden and Osnabrück in the west, Wesermünde and Lüneburg in the north, and Celle, Hameln, Hildesheim, Goslar, and Göttingen in the south and east, had a population of less than 100,000. Only three of these cities had a population in excess of 50,000. The cities were the centers of the industrial and commercial life of the province. Osnabrück, Hanover, and Hildesheim, which are situated in richer southern Hanover, were important not only as centers of economic activity, but as the foci of administrative life in their districts. Hanover had a position of special importance, thanks to its greater population and its status as the provincial capital. It should be noted that the administrative centers of the two northern districts, Aurich and Stade, did not correspond with the economic centers of Emden and Wesermünde. The Hanoverian cities provided the homes of the million workers engaged in industries and crafts and the half million workers engaged in trade and transportation. About 48 per cent of the working population of the province derived its living from nonagrarian pursuits.

The ten larger cities of Hanover constituted city counties, each of which was headed by a Chief Mayor directly responsible to the District President. After 1935 their government and administration followed the national pattern laid down by the German Municipal Code of that year. The democratic features of city government, which were provided by the City Constitution of 1858 and the liberal measures of the Weimar era, were swept away by the Nazis.

Low Saxony constitutes a distinct administrative, political, economic, and cultural bloc. It is interrupted only by the economic-cultural area of the Lower Weser which centers in Bremen and is cut into only by the Lower Elbian area focused upon Hamburg. Its agrarian support comes from the dairying and livestock zone of the marshes and geest and the crop zone of the border area of the southeast. Its industries are based upon the minerals of the Harz, the lignite fields of the southeast, and the iron ore of the Osnabrück area. The industrial and manufacturing activities of southern and eastern Hanover are served by an east-west and north-south transportation system making use of water, rail, and road facilities. The city of Hanover is the natural center of this area as well as the administrative and economic capital of the province. The smaller district economic and administrative units of Hildesheim and Osnabrück in the south, Lüneburg in the east, and Emden and Wesermünde-Bremerhaven in the north, are similarly centers of their respective areas. They are integral parts of the province, and they also serve as peripheral areas of transition to adjacent Nordmark (Hamburg-Schleswig-Holstein), Rhineland-Westphalian, Central German, and Eastern German economic regions. An attempt will be made to indicate the character of these integrating and decentralizing forces for each of the major economic activities of the province.

The Province of Hanover has a rich economic potential. Although north Hanover has few mineral resources, unless one includes the rock quarries along the lower Elbe, there are considerable mineral resources extending in a belt from the middle Weser to the middle Elbe. Around the city of Hanover and to the east there are deposits of lignite and potash, which have led to the development of important chemical industries at Hanover, Lüneburg, Goslar, and Celle. The iron and other mineral resources of the Harz area have provided the basis of the metal industries of Goslar and Hildesheim. Manufacturing industries making use of iron and steel developed naturally in southeastern Hanover.

The city of Hanover was important for the production of railway locomotives and railway cars, and the center of the Hanomag auto works and a number of machinery companies. Near-by Hameln presented a marked contrast, for it was the center of a number of household industries manufacturing furniture, leather goods, textiles, and pottery. Goslar, important for iron, machinery, and chemicals, also produced a number of stone, paper, and wood products. Göttingen, aside from its aluminum works, was mainly interested in the production of fine mechanical goods and scientific instruments. The rich agricultural resources of this area have encouraged the growth of important sugar beet refineries at Hanover and Hildesheim. Most of the cities of the area are engaged in textile manufacturing.

To the west lies the Osnabrück manufacturing area with its coal and iron deposits, the center of a small iron and steel industry. Osnabrück is also the center for textile, celluloid, and paper manufacturing. The port cities of the north, Emden and Bremerhaven-Wesermünde, were mainly supported by their commerce and trade; however, each had some industry. Bremerhaven, as indicated previously, had shipbuilding firms and a number of companies interested in the metal and wood industry. Fishing played a role in the economic life of Wesermünde and Emden.

The basic road network of Hanover is the product of a long historical development going back to the Middle Ages. The key junctions in the pattern are Osnabrück, Hanover, and Lüneberg. Major roads link Emden to the Ruhr and Osnabrück, Hanover to Westphalia, Bremen, and Hamburg. The uplands of the southeast are served by an intricate maze of roads, while the plains of the northern part of the province are cut by numerous east-west and north-south highways. Road maintenance was under the Provincial Corporation and the County Construction Master (*Kreisbaumeister*) and the Road Master of each county. During the Nazi regime, the normal road system was partly supplemented by the construction of the modern national super-highway. The original plans called for the following roads in Hanover: the Ruhr-Hanover-Berlin national super-highway, the Hamburg-Hanover-Göttingen super-highway, the Hanover-Bremen-Oldenburg-Emden super-highway, and the Münster-Osnabrück to Oldenburg and Emden super-highway. The two last named roads were not completed.

The railroads of the state were operated by the National German Railways through the National Railroad Directorate at Hanover, which had the jurisdiction of railway matters in the Province of Hanover, the state of Brunswick, the Hanseatic City of Bremen, and the state of Oldenburg. One of the main rail lines of the Reich—the Ruhr-Hanover-Berlin line—runs through the southern part of the Province of Hanover. The next most important line is the Frankfort (Main)-Hanover-Hamburg line. Another main railroad line extends from the Ruhr northeastward across Hanover to Bremen and Hamburg. A minor line links Wesermünde, Bremen, and Hanover. The latter city is the key point of the rail system within this province and is one of the great rail centers of the Reich.

The important natural water transportation facilities of the province include the Ems, Weser, and Elbe rivers. The famous Weser-Elbe and Ems-Weser or Mittelland canal, which links the Rhineland with the canal system of eastern Germany, connects the cities of Osnabrück, Hanover, and Hildesheim with both western and eastern Germany. The north-south Dortmund-Ems canal, which carries coal northward to the port of Emden from the Ruhr and provides for the transportation of Swedish iron ores to the furnaces of the Rhineland, is linked to the rest of Hanover by the Mittelland canal, the Küsten-Leda canal (Ems-Oldenburg-Bremen), and the Ems-Jade canal (Emden-Wilhelmshaven). These canals and rivers are linked either to the ports of Hamburg, Bremen, Bremerhaven, Wilhelmshaven, or to Emden. The two ports within the Province of Hanover, Wesermünde-Bremerhaven and Emden, are small in contrast to the greater ports of Hamburg and Bremen. The port of Emden is located on the estuary of the Ems. After the construction of the Dortmund-Ems and Ems-Jade canals, the port was deepened so that it might accommodate the larger sea-going vessels. The old inner and the new outer basins were well equipped with warehouses, cranes, and railway facilities. The trade of the port normally involved the importation of iron ore, cereals, and timber and the exportation of coal, coke, and industrial products. The only major commercial airport in the entire province was at the city of Hanover. It was an important air traffic center for both domestic and international air travel in normal times.

The commercial centers of Hanover, Hildesheim, Goslar, Lüneburg, and Osnabrück in the south and Emden and Wesermünde-Bremerhaven in the north were the focal points of trade and commerce in the province. The banking and credit enterprises of the province included branches of the *Reichsbank* and the great commercial banks of Berlin as well as provincial and county financial and banking institutions. The stock exchange at Hanover served most of northwest Germany.

The urban population of the province, constituting about one-half of the total, was largely engaged in industry and crafts (31 per cent). Trade and transport enterprises employed only about 16 per cent of the population. The rural character of the province accounted for a large independent upper class, while the industries and crafts of the cities account for the large number of workers and the relatively small number of white collar people.

The cities of Osnabrück, Hanover, and Hildesheim in the southern part of the state have evolved from old market towns on the strategic east-west trade route which skirts the northern edge of the Central German uplands. Hanover's original status as the center of the Electorate and the then Kingdom of Hanover was obscured by its modern industrial life. Like Hanover, Hildesheim and Osnabrück were basically industrial towns. The cities of the north, Emden and Wesermünde-Bremerhaven, are recent developments, whose evolution must be dated to the era of the industrial revolution. Hanover, which is the largest city of the province, grew up at the junction of the Leine and Ihme rivers.

Hameln, well known for the legend of the Pied Piper, is located thirty-three miles to the southwest of Hanover. Hildesheim, on the northern slopes of the Harz, occupied an important position in the economy of central Hanover. Its Old City (*Altstadt*) is surrounded by promenades, which were once the site of city walls. Goslar, a former imperial capital in early Saxon times, is located in the corridor which once linked central and southern Hanover. This city was designated by Hitler as the National Peasants City (*Reichsbauernstadt*), and it was the national headquarters of the National Food Estate (*Reichsnährstand*). Göttingen, on the river Leine, is famous for its old university. Lüneburg, the major city of northeast Hanover, has been called the Nuremberg of the North. Its old city bears witness to the days when it was a prosperous member of the Hanseatic League. Celle, to the south of Lüneburg, is the court center for Hanover. The Weser river port of Wesermünde, which was established by the Nazis in 1939, served as the outport of Bremen. Cuxhaven, which was acquired by Hanover as a result of the territorial reorganization of Hamburg, is of minor importance in the economy of Hanover. Osnabrück, the most important city of southwest Hanover, is a Catholic city famous for its Gothic and Renaissance architecture.

Chapter 16

THE STATE OF BRUNSWICK*

The small state of Brunswick was divided into two main parts by the isthmus connecting Hildesheim with the southern portion of Hanover. There were six smaller parts or exclaves imbedded in the surrounding Prussian provinces. Brunswick, the capital of the state, was in the larger northern portion, which is surrounded by the Prussian provinces of Saxony and Hanover. The southwestern section, which contains the towns of Holzminden and Gandersheim, adjoined the provinces of Saxony and Westphalia, and the southeastern (Blankenburg) section of the state, which is situated in the Harz Mountains, was bounded by the provinces of Saxony and Hanover, and the state of Anhalt. Only three of the exclaves were large enough to have any importance. The Thedinghausen exclave is situated on the Weser near Bremen in the Province of Hanover, while the Harzburg exclave is located between the provinces of Hanover and Saxony. The small exclave of Kalvörde is embedded in the Province of Saxony. The entire state was quite small, with a total land area of 3,672 sq. km.

The state of Brunswick, which lies between the Harz Mountains and the Aller and Weser rivers, has an extremely varied landscape. The northern part, which is the most important economically, is relatively low and flat, belonging for the most part to the fertile border area that extends eastward from the northern foothills of the Harz into the Middle Elbe Basin. The few hills of the northern portion are low, with a maximum elevation of 300 m. In the southeastern or Blankenburg portion, the lower hills are covered with deciduous forests and contain many clearings for agriculture and settlement, while the higher portions of the Harz are rugged and heavily forested. The southwestern Holzminden and Gandersheim area, which is bordered on the west by the Weser River, is dominated by the Solling uplands.

The people of the state of Brunswick are Low Saxons who have occupied this area since the beginning of our era. Today, the Low Saxon or *Plattdeutsch*

* German spelling—Braunschweig.

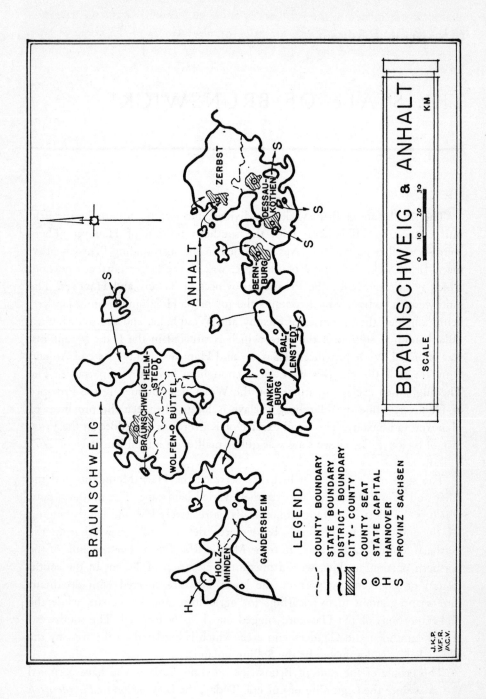

dialect is still spoken in the rural areas, although standard German is common in the towns and cities. There are no cultural cleavages of the religious type, for over 88 per cent of the people are Lutheran Protestant. The Catholic population numbered 21,900 in 1933, while the Jewish population, which was largely concentrated in the city of Brunswick, numbered only 1,174. In 1933 the total population of Brunswick was 512,900. It was not a densely settled state, based on western European standards, for the average population density was only 134 individuals per sq. km. The fertile northern section is the most densely settled; it supports 100 to 200 per sq. km. as compared with the other two major sections of the state, which are hilly or mountainous, and support only 50 to 100 per sq. km. The population of the state, like that of most of Central Germany, has grown rapidly since 1870 under the impact of the industrial revolution. Between 1875 and 1925 an increase of 75 per cent occurred in the northern section while in other portions of the state there were slight increases ranging up to 25 per cent. While there has been little emigration from this area to lands outside the Reich, the industries and rich farm lands of the state have long attracted workers not only from the poorer East Elbian area, but also from lands in eastern Europe. In 1933 there were 2,000 foreign residents, over 50 per cent of whom were Poles.

The lands of Brunswick formed a part of the Duchy of Saxony at the beginning of German history. In the tenth century they were ruled by the family of Brunos, the Counts of Nordheim, and the Counts of Supplinburg. Later, in the twelfth century, these lands were inherited by Heinrich the Proud, Duke of Saxony. When his son Henry the Lion (Heinrich der Löwe) was placed under the imperial ban in 1181, his duchy was dismembered, with only the territories of Brunswick and Lüneburg remaining under his jurisdiction. In 1235 Henry's grandson Otto was made Duke of Brunswick and Lüneburg. It was not until 1267 that the duchy was divided between the sons of Otto, Albert becoming Duke of Brunswick, and Johann, Duke of Lüneburg. From the thirteenth to the sixteenth century, the history of the state of Brunswick is closely tied to that of the Duchy of Lüneburg, which occupied the southwestern part of what is now the Province of Hanover. During this period these lands were held by various branches of the family.

In 1596, after all but one of the branches had died out, the two sons of Ernst of Lüneburg, who had acquired most of Brunswick, divided the lands and established the lines of Dannenberg and Lüneburg-Celle. The latter line later took the name of Hanover and became the ancestors of the Kings of Hanover, while the Dannenberg family took the name of Braunschweig-Wolfenbüttel in 1635. This family ruled Brunswick until 1735 when it was supplanted by the Braunschweig-Bevern family, which had split off from the direct Dannenberg line in 1666. This state has never played an important part in German politics. It suffered from religious division during the Reformation and the Thirty Years' War. In the days of Frederick the Great of Prussia, Brunswick sided with the Prussians and was ravaged by the French. The mercenaries from Brunswick served with the English army in the American Revolutionary War in order to pay off some of the indebtedness the state had accumulated during the expensive wars of the eighteenth century in Germany. During the Napoleonic era, Brunswick sided with Prussia against France. In 1806 Napoleon dissolved the duchy and annexed it to the Kingdom of Westphalia.

After the Treaty of Vienna in 1815 there was a change for the better in Brunswick. Revolution and disorder swept the state in 1820 and 1830; but during the reign of Duke Wilhelm (1831-1884), order was restored and constitutional reforms were instituted. In 1844 the state joined the Prussian Customs Union. While Duke Wilhelm took very little part in the war between Austria and Prussia in 1866, Brunswick joined the North German Confederation in 1867 and became a member state of the German Empire in 1871. Under the Empire, the government of the state, which was regulated by the Constitution of 1832, continued with a unicameral State Assembly, composed of delegates elected on the basis of a complicated class system of suffrage, and a Ministry of State. State administration was carried out by the Interior Affairs Authorities (*Landesverwaltungsbehörden*), the Justice Administration (*Justizverwaltung*), the Finance Administration (*Finanzverwaltung*), and a Commission of Examiners (*Prüfungskommission*). Economic, public health, welfare, transportation, surveying, church, and educational affairs were handled by separate groups of offices and authorities. Duke Wilhelm died childless in 1884, and according to existing conventions Brunswick would have passed to Georg, who had been deposed as King of Hanover in 1866. His son Ernst, Duke of Cumberland, pressed the claim of Hanover. The Brunswick Council of Regency and the Imperial Federal Council rejected their claims and appointed the Prussian prince, Albert. After Albert's death in 1906, Duke Johann Albert of Mecklenburg-Schwerin was made regent. This arrangement lasted until 1913 when Ernst, the grandson of Georg of Hanover, was made Duke of Brunswick following his reconciliation with Kaiser Wilhelm II which was cemented by his marriage to the Prussian Princess Victoria Louisa.

In 1918 Brunswick became one of the constituent republics of Germany. Under the constitution of 1922 it was governed by a Minister President and a Ministry of State which was responsible to an elected, representative State Assembly. State administration was carried out under a Ministry of State by ministries for Interior, Justice, Finance, and Education and by an Auditing Office (*Rechnungskammer*) and an Administrative Court (*Verwaltungsgerichtshof*).

During the Weimar period direct national administration was extended to finance, railways, unemployment insurance and employment, and labor welfare. Supervision of finances within the state was carried out through the local finance offices and the main customs offices (*Hauptzollämter*) which were under the State Office at Hanover. The National Construction Office at Brunswick was also under the State Finance Office of Hanover. The nationalized railways of the province were operated by the National Railroad Directorate of Hanover. Labor and unemployment problems were handled by the State Labor Office and the main Welfare Office at Hanover. Welfare, social insurance, health, trade and industry, and labor were partially under national control, but were administered by the state. Limited state supervision was also imposed on the economic life of the state, which was organized under national associations for agriculture, industry, trade, and labor.

The state of Brunswick was not unlike other parts of Northwest Germany in its political beliefs up to the election of 1930. Under the Empire, it supported two parties—the Social Democrats who captured the votes of the urban area in all national elections, and the conservative German Farmers Union party, which was second in national elections and first in state elections, owing to the system of class suffrage which gave the rural areas a definite advantage over the cities. Under the Republic, the state gave more than a third of its votes to the Social Democratic party to make it the leading party in the state as it was in the nation. The two bourgeois parties—the German People's party and the German National People's party—were second and third in order of popular strength. But with the 1930 election, the Nazis became the second party in the state, increasing their total vote from 19,000 to 83,000 in one election. In the county of Wolfenbüttel, the National Socialists became the leading party. When the presidential elections came along in the spring of 1932, the state of Brunswick made Hitler a governmental councilor thereby automatically conferring German citizenship on him so that he could become a candidate for the presidency. Hindenburg carried the state by less than 6,000 plurality. Wolfenbüttel voted for Hitler. In the two National Assembly elections which followed in the same year, the Nazis became the leading party with just short of a clear majority of all the votes cast. All districts in the state without exception gave more votes to the National Socialists than to any other party, and in Wolfenbüttel the party received an absolute majority.

The State of Brunswick formed a part of the Nazi party district of South Hanover, which had its headquarters at Hanover. As in all other parts of Germany, the complicated party organizations reached down into all aspects of life and controlled every activity.

Changes under the Nazi regime were drastic. Like the other German states,

Brunswick lost its federal status and its rights were transferred to the Reich. A National Governor was placed in charge of the states of Brunswick and Anhalt. He was directly responsible to the national Minister of the Interior, but also subject to directives coming from other national ministers. The actual administration was under the Minister President, head of the State Ministry, which latter was responsible for the coordination of government and administration. There were three other state ministries: the Ministry of Finance *Finanzministerium* (personnel; state taxation, credit, and finance; state utilities and enterprises; state forests; and construction); the Ministry of the Interior (local government and administration; police affairs; health, welfare, and social insurance; and agricultural, industrial, and commercial affairs); and the Ministry for Educational and Cultural Affairs (*Ministerium für Volksbildung*). These ministries must be regarded as national agencies carrying out national orders and functioning for state purposes.

The administrative changes of 1942 were accompanied by extensive territorial changes, which grew out of the establishment of the new industrial city county of Watenstedt-Salzgitter. Northern and southwestern Brunswick were joined together through the absorption of the city county and county of Goslar and the eastern part of the county of Marienburg of the Province of Hanover and through the annexation of part of the county of Wernigerode. In turn, Brunswick lost the county of Holzminden to the Province of Hanover and the exclaves of Bodenburg and Ölsberg and a few villages to the Province of Saxony.

The work of the state government and administration was supplemented by special and technical services under direct national control. During the imperial period only the nationally operated postal system lay outside the scope of state administration. In this state, justice was administered by the Justice Administration through the Superior State Court, the Collegiate Court of First and Second Instance at Brunswick, and the local Courts of First Instance. The national postal system within the state was under the Chief Postal Directorate (under the Empire) or the National Postal Directorate (under the Republic and the Third Reich) of Brunswick. National regulations for trade and industry, weights and measures, social insurance and welfare, public health, and the collection of imperial revenues were administered upon delegation from the Reich.

In the Nazi regime, national administrative controls were greatly extended. In addition, many of the traditional fields of state administration—police, health, welfare, education, and certain aspects of social insurance—were brought under tight national control. Here, too, the services and functions of the general and special administrative systems were supplemented by an extensive system of corporate administration.

Rural Aspect

Agriculture and forestry play only a moderate role in the life of the people of the state of Brunswick. Only 18 per cent of the population or 96,200 individuals were engaged in these rural pursuits. The economic structure of this state was much like that of Anhalt and Thuringia, although a greater percentage of the population lived closer to the soil, for here over 41 per cent of the population dwelt in villages of less than 2,000 in population. Under the Nazis the local administration of the state was under the state Ministry of the Interior at Brunswick, which was ultimately subject to the supervision of the national Ministry of the Interior in Berlin. Much of the day-to-day administration in rural areas, however, was under the County Managers of the counties and their subordinates, the Mayors of the villages and towns which make up the counties. County government and administration in the area were very much like that of Prussia. The pattern of county administration was based upon the laws of 1924 and their modification with the advent of the Nazi regime in 1933. The County Manager was the leader of the county administration and self-government. He was assisted by a County Advisory Committee, which before 1936 was responsible, together with an elected County Assembly, for county self-government. Under the Nazis the municipal government of the 12 towns over 2,000 population and the 433 villages of the state followed the pattern laid down in the German Municipal Code of 1935.

In Brunswick over 59 per cent of the land is used for crops and stock raising. The larger northern portion of the state constitutes the best agricultural area. It is a level region forming a part of the extensive fertile border zone of Central Germany. The climate is dry and warm with an average July temperature of 17-18 degrees C. and an average January temperature of 0 degrees C. The average yearly rainfall ranges between 600 and 800 mm. The rich chernozem soils of the northern part of the state are intensively farmed; the major crops include wheat, sugar beets, and potatoes. The beet waste has been utilized to build up an extensive cattle industry. Market gardening is common near the large city of Brunswick. The counties of Blankenburg, Gandersheim, and Holzminden, which are dominated by the Harz Mountains in the southeast and by the Weser-Solling uplands in the southwest, have a cooler, moister climate. The higher areas of the county of Blankenburg in the Harz Mountains become extremely cold and moist. The agricultural land of this part of the state is devoted to forage crops and grain, which are grown on soils of mixed type ranging from sandy loams to clays. The main rural industry of the south is, however, cattle and sheep raising. Horse breeding is of importance in the county of Blankenburg. The higher parts of the uplands are almost entirely given over to pasture and woodland.

The greater part of the state falls within the real tillage zone of the Reich. The major crops for the state as a whole are wheat and sugar beets. Livestock is important only in the south. The figures for land utilization indicate the amount and types of land available for agriculture (figures in hectares):

Cultivated Land		166,700
Grain	101,800	
Legumes	2,900	
Root Crops	48,500	
Green Vegetables	3,500	
Industrial Crops	1,100	
Fodder Crops	8,900	
Small Gardens		5,300
Meadow		30,700
Pasture		13,800
Orchards		690
Vineyards		
Forests		111,500
Waste Land		7,100
Houses and Barns		6,300
Roads and Parks		22,100

About 59 per cent of the land is devoted to agrarian activities, 46 per cent being under cultivation, while over 13 per cent is used for meadow and pasture. Forests (32 per cent) and waste and urban land (9 per cent) account for the remainder.

The main forest areas are located in the southwestern and southeastern sections. The northern part is open treeless plain with the total woodland averaging less than 10 per cent of the area. The lower hills of the south are covered with high broad-leafed beech forests which account for from 29 to 37 per cent of the area. The higher parts of the southeast, in the Harz mountain area, are heavily forested with spruce, fir, and beech. About 64 per cent of the forest land is owned by the state. It was administered through thirty forest reserves which are under the section for State and Private Forests (*Staats- und Privatforsten*) in the state Ministry of Finance at Brunswick. The remainder of the forest land is largely held by private interests. County and municipal forest holdings are extremely small.

The rural population of the state has declined rapidly during the last hundred years under the impact of the industrial revolution. Today, the peasants still retain much of their old folkways, although the traditional ways of the past are more strongly entrenched in the southern uplands than in the northern section of the state, where agriculture has been modernized. They dwell in agglomerated *Hufendorf* villages, many of which go back to the beginning of our era. These villages are composed of houses of the Central German type, consisting of a dwelling and barns surrounding a court or farm yard. Most of the villages, which range between 600 and 1600 in population, are large enough to support a school and church. There are also a number of larger settlements with populations ranging between 1600 and 4500, which serve as market towns. In the uplands to the south, the small village with a population of 200 to 600 is most common. The farms which are situated outside the villages tend to be small in the south, averaging between 5 and 20 hectares in size, while those of the fertile northern section are medium sized, averaging between 20 and 100 hectares. The Low Saxon peasants of Brunswick are independent farmers. Their outlook is politically conservative and socially patriarchal.

Urban Aspect

The state has only one large city, Brunswick, the capital. The other important towns include Holzminden and Gandersheim in the southwest, Wolfenbüttel and Helmstedt in the north, and the Harz mountain town of Blankenburg. These towns are all county places and serve as regional market centers. Founded in Carolingian times (although their sites may well have been occupied since the Neolithic period), much of their development came during the period between the fifteenth and the eighteenth centuries. This statement is particularly true of Wolfenbüttel, Brunswick, and Blankenburg, which served as the residences of the princes of Brunswick during this period. The industrial revolution was felt throughout the state, but only the city of Brunswick underwent rapid change, although numerous industries were introduced into the other towns.

The city of Brunswick, which had a population of 166,800, is the only city-county in the state. Its government and administration followed the pattern laid down by the German Municipal Code of 1935, which replaced the liberal code of 1924. There was a Chief Mayor, who was directly responsible to the state Minister of the Interior.

The state of Brunswick formed a part of the Northwest German economic region. Its economic life is oriented toward the important city of Hanover. The state should be regarded not as a distinct unit within northwestern Germany but as a component part of southern Hanover, which for purposes of economic planning in recent years was a part of the territory of the Regional Planning Association of Hanover.

The industrial development of the state is based upon mineral resources which are located in the foothills and foreland of the Harz Mountains. The extensive lignite deposits near Helmstedt, the salt and oil deposits near Brunswick, and limited quantities of iron, lead, copper, and quarry products from the southern part of the state and particularly from the Harz area, constitute the major natural resources. Brunswick, Helmstedt and, in Nazi times, Salzgitter, were the major industrial centers. Automobiles (*Büssing*), railway signal equipment, machinery, textiles (linen and wool), and leather goods were the main industries. Helmstedt, which is mainly a mining center, has plants for manufacturing machinery, textiles, and glass. Sugar refining is carried on in both towns. Holzminden in the southwest and Blankenburg in the southeast have a few factories, but these have little importance compared with those of Brunswick. Refined sugar and agricultural products are manufactured in most of the larger towns of the state. The heavy and light industries dependent upon iron and coal are largely limited to Helmstedt and Brunswick. The Nazis erected the huge Hermann Göring steel works and furnaces at Salzgitter south of Brunswick; automobile plants were also constructed near-by. In terms of the number of plants and employees, the industries had the following order of importance: food products, machinery, and quarrying. Power needs were met by the important lignite power station south of Helmstedt and by power brought in from the water power plants on the tributaries of the upper Weser. These plants were supplemented by numerous local utility works operated by municipal and county authorities.

Brunswick is the key point of the road systems. Main highways radiate from this city to Magdeburg, Hanover, Kassel, Erfurt, and Hamburg, and it is situated on the main national super-highway extending from the Rhineland to Berlin. The rest of the state is served by an excellent network of local roads. The construction and maintenance of the main state roads were handled by the Ministry of Finance at Brunswick, while local roads were under the county administration. The city of Brunswick is situated on a major rail line running from Berlin via Magdeburg to Hanover and Hildesheim. River transportation facilities are important; the capital city is on a branch canal connecting with the important Mittelland canal which links the Rhineland with eastern Germany. Southwestern Brunswick is served by the Weser River, which permits the shipment of goods overseas via the port of Bremen. The state has an important domestic airport at the city of Brunswick.

Although the economic life of the state is oriented toward the city of Hanover, Brunswick is a major commercial and financial center, while the smaller towns like Wolfenbüttel, Helmstedt, Blankenburg, and Holzminden are local market towns. Branches of the great commercial banks as well as the local county and municipal mortgage and savings banks supplemented branches of the *Reichsbank* at Brunswick and Helmstedt. The state financial institutions —*Braunschweigische Landessparkasse* and *Braunschweigische Staatsbank* at Brunswick—were under the state Ministry of Finance. The state government operated three insurance organizations—life, fire, and accident.

The urban population was largely engaged in industry and crafts. Thirty-eight per cent of the total population or 195,400 individuals were dependent upon industrial, manufacturing, and craft activities. In terms of the numbers of persons employed, the mining and machinery industries are the most important. Another 16 per cent of the population or 85,700 individuals were engaged in trade and transportation activities. The remaining part of the population may be classified as follows: 8 per cent in the professions and civil service, 2 per cent as household servants, and 18 per cent as independent or retired. The remaining 18 per cent were employed in agriculture or forestry. An examination of the class structure shows that there was a relatively large working class, which embraced over 44 per cent of the population, whereas the upper class and the white collar class were unusually small in comparison with those of adjacent areas.

The city of Brunswick is an ancient city going back to the beginnings of the Middle Ages. During the later medieval period it was an important commercial center and served as an inland port for the Hanseatic League. Its rich Gothic and Renaissance buildings reveal its importance in early times. In the seventeenth century it became the residence of the Dukes of Brunswick. One of the ducal palaces built in the early nineteenth century became an *SS Führerschule*. The museums of the city were numerous. The state was the birthplace of the mathematician Gauss and the last home of the poet Lessing, who was for many years the librarian of the famous collection of books at Wolfenbüttel, a charming garden town which lies to the south of the capital city. The only real industrial center is Helmstedt. Although it was a university town in early modern times, it was interested mainly in mining. Holzminden, Gandersheim, and Blankenburg are merely small provincial towns. Brunswick is the only city in the state which is of importance from the national point of view.

BIBLIOGRAPHY

Auswärtiges Amt, *Bismarck und die nordschleswigische Frage, 1864-1879* (Berlin, 1925).

Beuermann, A. *Die Provinz Hannover* (Berlin, 1910).

Brandt, O. *Geschichte Schleswig-Holstein* (Kiel, 1925).

Great Britain, Foreign Office, *Schleswig-Holstein,* in Peace Handbook, Vol. VI, No. 5 (London, 1920).

Haas, H. *Deutsche Nordseeküste* (Bielefeld & Leipzig, 1900).

Hamburgs neue Verfassung (Hamburg, 1921).

Hayman, E. *Danish-German Relations in Schleswig* (London, 1940).

Heberle, Rudolf "The Political Movements among the Rural People in Schleswig-Holstein, 1918 to 1932," *The Journal of Politics,* Vol. 5, No. 1, February, 1943, pp. 3 ff; Vol. 5, No. 2, May, 1943, pp. 115 ff.

King, W. *Chronicles of the Three Free Cities, Hamburg, Bremen, and Lübeck* (London, 1914).

Linde, R. *Die Lüneburger Heide* (Bielefeld & Leipzig, 1921).

Linde, R. *Die Niederelbe* (Bielefeld & Leipzig, 1913).

Prior, W. R. *North Sleswick under Prussian Rule, 1864-1914* (London, New York, 1914).

Reissert, O. *Das Weserbergland und der Teutoburger Wald* (Bielefeld & Leipzig, 1925).

Schmarje, J. *Die Provinz Schleswig-Holstein* (Berlin, 1904).

Scholz, O. *Landeskunde der Provinz Schleswig-Holstein* (Breslau, 1917).

Schrepfer, H. *Der Nordwesten, Landeskunde von Deutschland* (Leipzig, 1935).

Schulz, B. *Die Deutsche Nordsee* (Bielefeld & Leipzig, 1928).

Steilen, D. *Die Niederweser* (Bielefeld & Leipzig, 1928).

Tacke, B. and Lehmann, B. *Die Nordseemarschen* (Bielefeld & Leipzig, 1924).

Tacke, B. and Lehmann, B. *Die Norddeutschen Moore* (Bielefeld & Leipzig, 1912).

Verfassung der Freien Hansestadt Bremen (May 18, 1920) (Berlin, 1920).

Chapter 17

INTRODUCTION TO
WESTERN GERMANY

Western Germany is the most heavily industrialized region in the Reich, the richest in mineral resources, and important also for its agricultural produce. It includes the Prussian provinces of Westphalia, Hesse-Nassau, the Rhine Province, the state of Hesse, and the Saar territory. The Rhine River cuts through the center of this region, serving as its chief artery of transportation. On the west of the valley are the Eifel-Hunsrück ranges, and on the east the Sauerland, Westerwald, and Taunus uplands. The higher portions of these ranges are characterized by a village economy which is supported by dairying and forestry, while the larger villages and small towns of the lower hills and upland valleys depend upon grain and livestock. To the north lie the great Köln and Münster plains of the northern Rhine Province and Westphalia, whose extensive coal and lignite fields support the industries of Aix-la-Chapelle (Aachen), Cologne, Düsseldorf, Essen, Dortmund, and Hamm. The demand for food by the large cities of the Rhine-Ruhr area has drawn the farmers of the north into the integrated economy of the lower Rhineland. The dairy and livestock farms of the lower Rhine and the Münster area and the crop farms and market gardens of the rolling country skirting the northern foothills of the Mittelgebirge, provide the immediate rural background for the highly urbanized and industrialized Rhine-Ruhr. The uplands along the Rhine constitute a transitional area, which falls partly under the influence of the great cities of the north and partly under the influence of the cities of the Rhine-Main area, which borders the highlands on the south. The cities along the middle Rhine and Main rivers—Mainz, Wiesbaden, Frankfort, and Darmstadt—have evolved in a rich valley area, characterized by small farms interested in the cultivation of market gardens, vineyards, and orchards. The life of the western German area is also conditioned by the economic influence of the urban centers in the Saar, which have had extensive commercial ties with the southern Rhine Province and the Rhine-Main area, and by the great city of Kassel, which occupies a position that is transitional between the economic foci of the Lower Rhineland, southern Hanover, and the Rhine-Main area.

The people of Western Germany are mostly descendants of the Low Saxon and Franconian tribes which settled in this part of the Reich at the beginning of our era, driving out or subduing and then intermarrying with the older Keltic population. Later when they pushed across the Rhine to conquer the Roman holdings in Western Germany, other peoples, mainly Keltic, but with some Mediterranean admixture brought in by the Romans, were absorbed by the Germanic tribes. The gradual differentiation of the Franks and Low Saxons during the medieval era led to the formation of several distinct peasant groups, each speaking a separate dialect. The Low Saxon tongue survives in the north, whereas a Westphalian variety is spoken in the northern Rhine Province and northern Westphalia. A Low Franconian dialect, akin to the languages of the Low Countries, is spoken in the northern tip of the Rhine Province, while the dialect of the Cologne–Aix-la-Chapelle (Köln-Aachen) area is known as Riparian Frankish or Franconian. The Rhine and Mosel dialects of Franconian are spoken in the southern Rhine Province, while Hessian, a variety of Franconian, is common throughout the rural areas of Hesse-Nassau and the northern part of the state of Hesse. The people of the villages and small towns of the Rhine-Main area speak a dialect closely related to Rhine Franconian. The differences, which are reflected in these modern dialects, are also apparent in the customs, usages, and folkways of the people. However, while the dialects still survive in the rural areas, they have been replaced in the larger towns and cities by standard German. The mixed character of the peoples of Western Germany is also revealed by the racial composition of the area. The people of the north belong to a basic Nordic type, strongly conditioned by ancient racial types, which have survived from the Stone Age. To the south and west, where Keltic and Roman occupation played an important role, the basic Nordic solution is increasingly affected by Alpine and Mediterranean racial elements.

Historically, Western Germany begins with the formation of the tribal kingdoms of the Franks and the Low Saxons. By the fifth century, most of what is now the Rhine Province, Hesse-Nassau, and Hesse was under the control of the Franconian tribes, while Westphalia formed a southern outpost of Low Saxon power which had its major stronghold on the plains of Northwestern Germany. By the sixth century, the Merovingian leaders of the Franks had brought most of France and southern Germany under their control. The Carolingian leader Charlemagne added the Low Saxon area to his empire in the late eighth century. With the disintegration of Carolingian power, the old tribal leaders once again gained control, and Western Germany fell under the rule of three tribal dukes: the northeastern area, which included Westphalia and all

of the modern Rhine Province lying to the east of the Rhine, was under the
dukes of Saxony; while the lands situated to the west of the Rhine fell to the
dukes of Lower and Upper Lorraine. The Rhine-Main area formed a part of
the early medieval Duchy of Franconia. During the era of the empire of the
Saxons, Franconians, and Hohenstaufens, there were few significant territorial
changes, except for the emergence of the Landgraviate of Hesse.

After the destruction of the medieval empire of the Germans, which was
accompanied by the break-up of the tribal duchies, the lands of Western Germany fell into the hands of a great number of lay and ecclesiastical rulers. The
Westphalian area was ruled by the bishops of Münster and Paderborn, the
counts of Ravensberg and Mark, and the dukes of Westphalia, who were vassals
of the archbishops of Cologne. The tiny Lippes were already in the hands of
their stable dynasty, which was to rule until the end of World War I. The Rhine
Province area was subject to the archbishops of Cologne and Trèves and a number of lay rulers including the dukes of Kleve, Berg, and Jülich. The Rhine-
Main area of southern Hesse-Nassau and Hesse was largely subject to the
Archbishop of Mainz and the Electors of the Palatinate (Kurpfalz), while the
Hesse uplands were held by the Counts of Nassau and the Landgraves of
Hesse. Western Germany during the era of the aristocratic confederation was
ruled largely by ecclesiastics. This contrasts strongly with Eastern Germany,
where the Habsburgs, Wettins, Wittelsbachs, and Hohenzollerns were laying
the foundations of the territorial states which were to dominate the development of eighteenth and nineteenth century Germany.

Prussia gained her first holdings in Western Germany during the era of
the Reformation, when the duchies of Jülich, Berg, Kleve, and the county of
Mark fell under the control of the Hohenzollerns. During the period of the
Thirty Years' War, they lost control of the duchies of Berg and Jülich to
the Electors of the Palatinate. The only other important territorial change of the
seventeenth century was the emergence of the Landgraviate of Hesse-Darmstadt, which was to provide the basis for the gradual evolution of the state of
Hesse. It should also be noted that the cities of Cologne, Dortmund, and Frankfort had gained the status of free and imperial cities during the late medieval
era.

The Napoleonic era brought the next basic territorial changes in Western
Germany. By 1803 all of the old lay and ecclesiastical states situated to the west
of the Rhine had been conquered and absorbed into France. The legacy of
ecclesiastical rule had not prepared the west for its defense. To the east, Napoleon allowed the duchies of Berg, Nassau, Kurhessen (Hesse), Hesse-Darmstadt, and the Imperial City of Frankfort to survive. The old ecclesiastical states
disappeared, while Prussia gained temporary control of most of northern Westphalia. In 1807 Napoleon placed most of the Westphalian area under the ephem-

eral Kingdom of Westphalia, which lasted until the defeat of the French at Leipzig (1813).

With the Treaty of Vienna (1815), Prussia became the dominant power in Western Germany. The greater part of the area was ceded to Prussia, which organized it as the Rhine Province and the Province of Westphalia. The two Lippes and the little state of Waldeck managed to survive on the margins of the Westphalian area. In the southeast the reorganized states of Nassau, Hesse-Kassel, and Hesse-Darmstadt and the Imperial City of Frankfort continued to rule. Prussia held the tiny exclave of Wetzlar, which was embedded between Hesse-Darmstadt and Nassau, while Oldenburg ruled the small exclave of Birkenfeld in the southern Rhine Province.

The next changes in Western Germany came in 1866, when the independent states of the west joined with Austria in an attempt to prevent the further expansion of Prussian power. The defeat of Austria and her allies in the Seven Weeks' War gave the Prussian victors the opportunity to seize the states of Nassau and Hesse-Kassel and the Imperial City of Frankfort. These territories together with the exclave of Wetzlar and a small portion of the state of Hesse-Darmstadt were joined together to form the modern province of Hesse-Nassau. The modern territorial configuration of Western Germany had been fixed, except for Birkenfeld and Waldeck. The independent state of Waldeck was absorbed into the Prussian Province of Hesse-Nassau in 1929, while the Oldenburg exclave of Birkenfeld was transferred to the Rhine Province by the Nazis.

The territorial structure of Western Germany is a recent creation. Prussian control on an extensive scale dates from 1815 and 1866. Unfortunately, the divided character of political organization during medieval and early modern times, when the area was ruled by numerous lay and ecclesiastical states, did not leave a legacy of political stability. Governmental and administrative unity was provided or rather imposed by the Prussians. Although the area lacks a traditional spirit of political unity, the economic changes of the nineteenth century industrial revolution gave Western Germany a new orientation. The growth of the heavy industrial and manufacturing Rhine-Ruhr area, the development of the manufacturing cities of the Rhine-Main area, and the emergence of the industrial Saar gave the west a new basis for economic life. Although these three urban areas are separated by the Rhine uplands, they are tied together by the ease of Rhine transportation. The development of numerous industrial and commercial ties in the course of the last hundred years has given the west an economic unity, which transcends the medieval legacy of cultural and political disunity.

Chapter 18

THE RHINE PROVINCE*

The Rhine Province, which is the most westerly of the Prussian provinces, adjoins the Netherlands, Belgium, Luxemburg, and France on the west, the Saar Territory and the Bavarian Palatinate on the south, and the Prussian provinces of Westphalia, Hesse-Nassau and Hesse on the east. The territory of the province remained stable from its formation in 1815 until the end of World War I. The Treaty of Versailles detached the Eupen and Malmedy areas from the western margins of the province and gave them to Belgium; and in the southwest, territory was detached from the province and from the Bavarian Palatinate to form the Saar Territory. When the Saar was returned to the Reich in 1935, it remained a separate administrative area. The Eupen and Malmedy areas were retaken by the Nazi Reich in 1940.

The Rhine River, which traverses almost the entire length of the province, divides it into a larger western portion and a smaller eastern section. In the south lie the Rhenish Slate Mountains, through which the river cuts a deep, eighty-mile gorge, extending from Bingen to Bonn. The Eifel and Hunsrück ranges, which are only 300 to 600 meters in height, extend in a southwesterly direction from the Rhine and are divided by the meandering valley of the Mosel (Moselle) River. The major towns of this upland area are Koblenz and Trèves. In the east, spurs of the Westerwald and the Sauerland hills extend from the east bank of the Rhine into Central Germany. The southern upland slopes northward from a low plateau, which is transitional between the lowlands and the surrounding hills of the Cologne Bay. North of Aix-la-Chapelle (Aachen) and Bonn the province is flat and forms an integral part of the North German Plain. This section of the province is famous for its rich coal and lignite deposits, which have made possible the development of the great, heavily industrialized cities of Essen, Duisburg, and Düsseldorf. This is the area of the important manufacturing towns of München-Gladbach, Wuppertal, Krefeld, Aix-la-Chapelle, and Cologne.

* German spelling—Rheinprovinz.

407

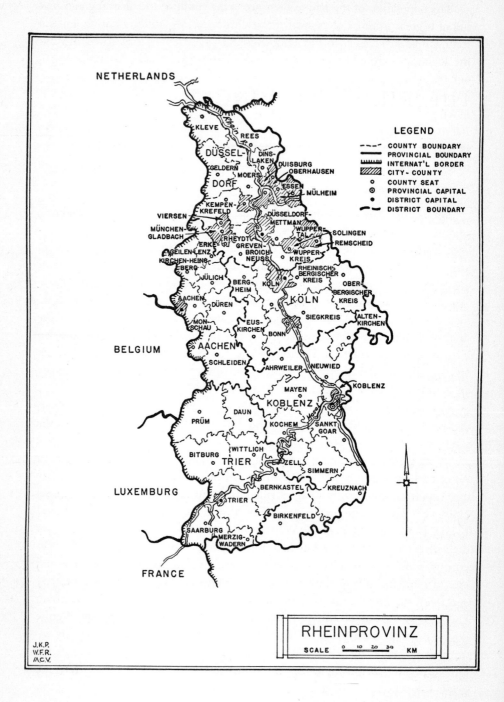

NETHERLANDS

KLEVE
REES
DÜSSEL-
DINS-
LAKEN
DUISBURG
GELDERN
OBERHAUSEN
DORF
MOERS
ESSEN
MÜLHEIM
KEMPEN-
KREFELD
VIERSEN
DÜSSELDORF-
METTMAN
MÜNCHEN-
WUPPER-
SOLINGEN
GLADBACH
RHEYDT
TAL
ERKE
REMSCHEID
GREVEN-
GEILEN-LENZ
BROICH
WUPPER-
KIRCHEN-HEINS
NEUSS
KREIS
BERG
RHEINISCH-
JÜLICH
BERGISCHER
BERG-
KREIS
HEIM
KÖLN
OBER-
AACHEN
BERGISCHER
DÜREN
KÖLN
KREIS
MON-
EUS-
SIEGKREIS
ALTEN-
SCHAU
KIRCHEN
BONN
KIRCHEN
BELGIUM
AACHEN
SCHLEIDEN
AHRWEILER
NEUWIED
MAYEN
KOBLENZ
KOBLENZ
PRÜM
DAUN
KOCHEM
SANKT
GOAR
WITTLICH
BITBURG
ZELL
TRIER
SIMMERN
LUXEMBURG
BERNKASTEL
KREUZNACH
TRIER
BIRKENFELD
SAARBURG
MERZIG-
WADERN
FRANCE

LEGEND
----- COUNTY BOUNDARY
——— PROVINCIAL BOUNDARY
▨▨▨ INTERNAT'L BORDER
▨▨▨ CITY-COUNTY
o COUNTY SEAT
⊙ PROVINCIAL CAPITAL
• DISTRICT CAPITAL
-••- DISTRICT BOUNDARY

RHEINPROVINZ
SCALE 0 10 20 30 KM

J.K.P.
W.F.R.
M.C.V.

The population of the Rhine Province is the result of the blending and mixing of a great number of peoples. Palaeolithic and Mesolithic hunting and collecting folk survived to blend with Neolithic agrarian peoples spreading into the Rhineland from southeastern Europe during the third millennium before our era. During the Bronze Age (1800-1000 B.C.) this population was supplemented by nomadic invaders coming from the northeast and by Alpine folk moving down the Rhine Valley from southern Germany. The Iron Age (1000-200 B.C.) brought Keltic peoples to the Rhineland. Then came Germanic (Frankish) peoples from Northwest Germany who pushed into the Rhine area to settle among the Kelts. The western Rhine Province was under Roman rule during the first four centuries of our era. This period, which was characterized by the introduction of Mediterranean civilization into Western Germany, was marked by the foundation of towns, the construction of roads, and the introduction of the hillside vineyard. Jewish traders and merchants from the Levant found their way to the various Roman settlements on the left bank of the Rhine. The internal collapse of the Roman Empire and the barbarian invasions left the territory of the province under the control of the Frankish tribes. Standard German is generally spoken, although it is conditioned by the local dialects of the country folk and the lower classes of the cities. The northern Low Franconian and the southern Middle Franconian dialects as well as the Westphalian Low Saxon dialect of the most northern part of the province go back to the time of the Frankish settlement of the Rhineland. The Rhinelanders are mainly Catholic, although Lutheran groups are irregularly distributed in the northern and eastern portions of the province. In 1933 the Catholics numbered 5,126,000, the Protestants 2,283,000. The former Jewish population of 52,000 was large in comparison with that of other provinces.

The Rhine Province constitutes one of the most densely settled portions of Germany. In 1933 the population numbered 7,631,000 and occupied 24,477 square kilometers; the average population density was 314 individuals per square kilometer. Only the state of Saxony has a greater density. There is, however, great regional variation in density, for in the northern industrial and manufacturing areas the population density averages over 400 per square kilometer, while in the upland agrarian areas it ranges between 25 and 75 per square kilometer. There has been a steady increase in the Rhenish population since 1816, when it was but 1,739,000. The greatest increase accompanied the main phase of Ruhr industrialization, 1890-1910. Unlike the people in other parts of the Reich, few Rhinelanders have left their homes for new lands. Although the industrial areas have long attracted the worker and peasant from all parts of the Reich, the Nazi munitions boom greatly increased this movement. The war brought many foreign workers to the northern part of the Rhine Province.

The first well organized government along the Rhine came with the Roman occupation, which lasted from the first to the late fifth century. During the Merovingian and Carolingian eras, the Rhineland formed the geopolitical core of the Frankish realm. After the death of Charlemagne and the division of his kingdom, it was divided between the short-lived Kingdom of Lotharingia and the duchies of the Franks and Low Saxons. During the period of the early medieval Holy Roman Empire, under the Saxon, Franconian, and Hohenstaufen dynasties (911-1254) the western Rhineland was ruled by the dukes of Upper and Lower Lorraine, the eastern Rhineland by the dukes of Saxony, while the dukes of Franconia held the southeastern corner of the province. The late Middle Ages brought the disintegration of these so-called Stem Duchies and the subdivision of the Rhenish territory into a number of tiny states and principalities. The southern part of the Rhine Province fell under the control of the Archbishop and Elector of Trèves (Trier), the Elector of the Palatinate, and the Duke of Luxemburg. The northern Rhine Province was under the Archbishop and Elector of Cologne, the duchies of Jülich, Berg, and Kleve, and the free and imperial cities of Cologne and Aix-la-Chapelle.

The first Prussian holdings in the Rhineland were acquired in 1614, when the Electors of Brandenburg inherited the Duchy of Kleve. During the later seventeenth century, the Hohenzollerns of Brandenburg acquired the territories of Upper Gelderland and Mörs. At the same time, the Wittelsbach line of the Palatinate acquired the duchies of Berg and Jülich by right of inheritance. The wars of the French Revolutionary and Napoleonic periods brought the next basic reorganization of the territories within the Rhineland. By 1803 all of the Rhine Province west of the Rhine had been absorbed into France. The remaining lands east of the Rhine were held by Prussia and the Duchy of Berg. In 1806 the lands to the east were organized under the French Confederation of the Rhine.

The Napoleonic reorganization eliminated most of the old principalities and prepared the way for the settlement at Vienna (1815) which placed the entire area under Prussian control. The Prussian government organized the Rhineland territory into the Rhine Province which they subdivided into the five governmental administrative districts of Düsseldorf, Cologne, Aix-la-Chapelle, Koblenz, and Trèves. The provincial administration reached its final form under the Empire in the Provincial Constitution of 1887. The dominant movement of the nineteenth century was the industrialization of the northern portions of the province. This movement was accompanied by widespread political liberalism.

The defeat of Germany in 1918 was followed by the Allied occupation of the left bank of the Rhine. Bridgeheads on the right bank at Cologne, Koblenz, and Mainz gave the Allies access to the interior of the Reich. The northern part of the Rhine Province was held by Belgian and British troops, while the southern portion of the province was under American troops, based upon the strategic town of Koblenz. The French were at Mainz. The occupation was beset from the start by the problem of Rhenish Separatism, which had grown out of a desire for freedom from Prussia rather than from Germany. The Separatist movement, backed by France, continued by fits and starts until 1924. Difficulties over reparations in 1921 resulted in the occupation of the Duisburg-Düsseldorf area from March to August 1921. Further troubles over reparations, which came at the height of the German inflation, resulted in the French and Belgian occupation of the Ruhr from January 1923 to August 1925. The gradual evacuation of the Rhineland, which came with the stabilization of internal conditions, was completed in 1930, the Americans having left much earlier in 1923.

When the Nazi regime came to power there began an immediate agitation for the military re-occupation and re-militarization of the Rhineland. On March 8, 1936, Hitler denounced the Locarno Treaty, which guaranteed the western frontiers of Germany, France, and Belgium, and on the same day German troops crossed the Rhine. By the end of 1936 the control of the Rhine returned to Germany through the denunciation of the waterways clauses of the Versailles Treaty, which had provided for international control of river navigation. This same year marked the beginning of the construction of the Siegfried line, which extended from the Dutch to the Swiss frontier. By 1939 the Rhine Province was prepared for World War II.

The national and provincial politics of the province have long been conditioned by the attitudes of its two major groups—the Catholics and the industrial proletariate. Under the Empire the industrial area turned to the Social Democratic party, while the agrarian and Catholic portions of the province voted consistently for the Catholic Center party. In the major national and provincial elections of the twenties and early thirties, the province gave consistently strong support first to the Catholic party, second to the Social Democratic party, and third to the Communist party, which gained a strong position in the Ruhr area after World War I. Within the province, the Catholic party was strongest in the administrative districts of Aix-la-Chapelle, Cologne, Koblenz, and Trèves, and also in the western part of the Düsseldorf district. Only in the eastern part of the governmental administrative district of Düsseldorf, namely in the large Ruhr cities like Düsseldorf, Wuppertal, Remscheid, and Solingen were the Communists stronger than the Catholics. Essen, however, gave first place to the Catholic Center party. In the days of the Republic, therefore, the principal question was the size of the Catholic vote.

In the southern part of the Rhineland in the two administrative districts of Koblenz and Trèves, the Catholic vote was close to a clear majority over all other parties. It was also above a third in the other districts except in the Ruhr.

With the rise of the Nazis, a relatively small shift took place in Duisburg, Mülheim, and Wuppertal, and also in the Upper Berg (*Oberbergischer*) County. Elsewhere the previous political lines held, and the Nazi vote was consistently lower than elsewhere in Germany excepting only Berlin, South Germany, and Westphalia. Cologne for many years after Hitler's accession to power remained an opposition center to the Nazis. Even in the Nazi controlled election of March 5, 1933, only the few following counties and cities in addition to the four mentioned above went into the Hitler column: Kreuznach, Simmern, Dell, Wittlich, and Bernkastel of the counties, and Düsseldorf, Krefeld, Koblenz, and München-Gladbach of the cities. In the straight contest between Hitler and Hindenburg for President in 1932, Hindenburg won by a two to one majority, Hitler carrying only a few cities like Remscheid and Solingen where the Communist candidates split the Hindenburg vote. When the Nazis took over the administration of the province, all important Catholic, Socialist, and Communist officials were removed from office, and all other political parties were abolished. The province, however, was predominantly Catholic and proletarian and was never a Nazi stronghold.

The administration of the province was organized under a Chief President who resided at Koblenz. He was vested with broad political and supervisory control of administrative, social, economic, and cultural activities, although much of the actual administration was carried out by the District Presidents of the governmental administrative districts of Aix-la-Chapelle (Aachen), Düsseldorf, Cologne, Koblenz, and Trèves. The work of the general provincial administration was supplemented by special and technical services under direct national controls.

During the imperial period only the state-administered courts, railways, and mining offices and the nationally operated postal system lay outside the scope of the general administration of the Rhine Province. The Superior State Court of Düsseldorf and its Collegiate Courts of First and Second Instance at Duisburg, Kleve, Krefeld-Uerdingen, München-Gladbach, and Wuppertal, the Superior State Court of Cologne (Köln) and its collegiate courts at Aix-la-Chapelle, (Aachen), Bonn, Koblenz, Cologne, and Trèves, and the Superior State Court of Hamm (Westphalia) and its collegiate courts of Essen and Siegen (Westphalia) conducted all judicial matters. The national postal system within the province was under the Chief Postal Directorate (under the Empire) or National Postal Directorates (under the Republic and the Third Reich) of Düsseldorf, Cologne, Aix-la-Chapelle, Trèves, and Koblenz. Such matters of trade and industry, weights and measures, social insurance and welfare, public health, and the collection of imperial revenues that were under national control were administered upon delegation from the Reich.

The Republic brought the further extension of direct national administration to finance, railways, unemployment insurance and employment, and labor welfare. There was the customary pattern of national control of finances with the State Finance Offices of Düsseldorf and Cologne and their local finance offices and main customs offices supervising these matters. The construction office at Düsseldorf was under the State Finance Office in that city, while those of Aix-la-Chapelle, Cologne, Koblenz, and Trèves were under the office at Cologne. The nationalized railways of the province were operated by the National Railroad Directorates at Essen, Cologne, Wuppertal, Saarbrücken, and Mainz. Affairs of labor were handled by the State Labor Office of the Rhineland (Cologne) and the main Welfare Office of the Rhineland (Koblenz). Areas of welfare, social insurance, health, trade and industry, and labor which were subject to national legislation, were administered upon delegation by the province. A number of national agricultural, industrial, commercial, and labor associations guided the economic life of the province.

A further extension of national administrative controls occurred under the Nazi regime. The Nazis organized the province under the following party districts: Essen, Düsseldorf, Cologne, and Koblenz. As in other Prussian provinces Nazi party organization was complete and detailed and reached down to the smallest villages, including everyone in its control. Direct national administration, which was continued for finance, posts, labor and labor welfare, and railways, was extended to justice, air matters, propaganda and labor relations. Furthermore, fields normally under state administration—police, health, welfare, education, and certain aspects of social insurance—were now conducted under national control.

Here, as in the other provinces, a system of corporate administration, in addition to the general and special administrative systems guaranteed complete national supervision within the province.

The greatest concentration of governmental and administrative agencies was focused upon Koblenz, the provincial capital. Düsseldorf was important not only as a district administrative seat, but as the headquarters of the Provincial Corporation and as the center of economic agencies serving the northern Rhine Province. Cologne, a district administrative center, served as the center for economic administration in the southern part of the province. Aix-la-Chapelle and Trèves were also centers of district administration.

Rural Aspect

The pattern of rural settlement in the Rhine Province goes back to the Neolithic period, when the Rhine and Mosel valleys were occupied by Danubian peasants who had migrated from southeastern Europe. During the Bronze Age with its mild dry climate there was a further extension of agrarian settlement, which was continued through the Iron Age with the settlement of the Keltic farmers. The Roman legions brought more than Roman governmental control. Mediterranean ways of cultivation were introduced. The steep sides of the Rhine and Mosel valleys were terraced and grape vines were planted, establishing the first of the Rhenish vineyards. The occupation of the Rhine area by the Frankish tribes brought about only a temporary delay in the development of the rural settlement. After Carolingian times, the German peasants began to extend the available agricultural land through the exploitation of the forests of the uplands and the draining of the marshes of the north. The modern period has only intensified the development of agriculture and forestry to meet the needs of the growing urban population. The improvement of agricultural methods involving the introduction of the system of crop rotation and better agricultural tools and implements accompanied the German industrial revolution.

The impact of industrialization on the rural Rhine Province was severe, for it was marked by a drastic occupational shift. At the beginning of the nineteenth century, over 90 per cent of the population was engaged in agriculture and forestry, while in 1933 only 12 per cent of the total provincial population derived its living from these rural pursuits. Nevertheless approximately 18 per cent of the population of the area dwells in small villages with populations of less than 2,000, while another 17 per cent lives in villages and small towns with population ranging between 2,000 and 20,000.

The general administration of the Rhine Province centers in the city of Koblenz, the provincial capital, and in the five district capitals of Düsseldorf, Aix-la-Chapelle, Cologne, Koblenz, and Trèves. The day-to-day administration of the rural part of the province is carried out through the forty-two counties into which the administrative districts are divided. These counties were headed by County Managers who served as agents both of the central government and of local self-government. The county administration and self-government were regulated by the County Constitution of 1872/1881, which was modified by the liberal laws of the Republic and the reactionary laws of the Third Reich.

Each village or town administration which was governed by the Town Constitution of 1845 until the Nazi Municipal Code of 1935, consisted of a Mayor, two or three administrative assistants, usually in honorary service, an appointed town council, and under the Nazis, a Party Agent. The elected town and village councils and assemblies were abolished by the Nazis. The communities handled public welfare and poor relief, roads and streets, drainage, public works, and a few enterprises, such as, town forest, market, and an occasional utility plant.

The Rhine Province also had a number of Unions of small rural villages (*Ämter*) for the management of common affairs (drainage, roads, health, etc.) of several adjoining hamlets. This form of local administrative organization permits each member village to retain its status as a town. The Union was headed by a Mayor who was assisted by two or three administrative department heads, a council of Union Elders (*Amtsälteste*), and under the Nazis the inevitable Party Agent.

Although the Rhine Province is not a rich agrarian region, the proportion of land under cultivation is about average for Germany. The character of agriculture varies greatly from north to south within the province. The northern portion, which may be subdivided into a Lower Rhine and a Cologne, Aix-la-Chapelle (Köln-Aachen) area, has mild winters, dry springs, cool summers, and warm autumns. The average July temperature is about 17 degrees C., while the average January temperature is about 1 degree C. The last frost occurs about the 18th of April, while the first frost comes about the 28th of October. The Lower Rhine area, which lies to the north of Düsseldorf and München-Gladbach, consists of lowland country which is best adapted to pasture, hay, and forage crops. It supports an important dairying and livestock industry. Market gardens increase in number near the larger cities of the Ruhr industrial region. The Cologne, Aix-la-Chapelle area, which enjoys a drier and warmer climate, is devoted chiefly to wheat, barley, sugar beets, and livestock raising. Although this area is best adapted to crop cultivation, which is frequently mechanized, dairying is important in the vicinity of the larger cities.

The southern upland portion of the Rhine Province contrasts strongly with the north. It has cold winters, cool moist springs, and dry summers. The last frosts come very late in the year, occurring toward the end of May, while the first frosts come early, striking in the middle of October. The uplands of the Eifel, Hunsrück, Westerwald, and Sauerland are largely devoted to livestock and grain. Dairying is the dominant activity in the higher upland areas; it involves the production of butter and cheese rather than milk because of the distance from urban markets and the lack of adequately developed transportation facilities. The field crops are largely cultivated for home consumption. The sheltered valley land of the Rhine and Mosel has one of the mildest and most equable climates of Germany. The valley slopes are covered with vineyards and orchards, while the river bottoms are planted with grain, green corn, and tobacco, interspersed with vineyards and fruit trees.

The major proportion of agricultural production for market in the province comes from farms ranging in size between 15 and 20 hectares. The smaller farms tend to consume most of their production at home. The area ranks third in fodder, fourth in cattle and wheat, and fifth in barley production among the provinces and states of Germany. Naturally, fruit and wine are important Rhineland products. The following figures give a statistical summary of the agriculture of the province for the year 1933.

LAND UTILIZATION (HECTARES)

Cultivated Land		919,000
Grain	531,000	
Legumes	6,000	
Root crops	246,000	
Vegetables	13,000	
Industrial Crops	4,000	
Fodder Crops	119,000	
Small Gardens		42,000
Meadow		218,000
Pasture		182,000
Orchards		8,000
Vineyards		15,000
Forests and Woods		703,000
Houses and Barns		66,000
Moorland		2,000
Waste Land		75,000
Roads, Parks, Water Surface		139,000

The Rhine Province has a moderate forest cover occupying approximately 30 per cent of the land. While there are relatively few trees in the most northern part of the area, where the Cologne–Aix-la-Chapelle plains support scattered oak groves, 30 to 40 per cent of the lower highland is covered by heavy beech forests. The highest parts of the uplands have a pine and sub-alpine flora. A variety of interests own the forest land. The state owns about 133,000 hectares, or 18 per cent of the total forest area, which is administered through thirty-five state forest reserves. The remainder of the forest land is held by private interests and by the municipal and county governments.

The contrast between the northern and southern Rhine Province holds true for the pattern of rural life and settlement. The Low Franconians of the northern Rhine lowlands live on isolated farms centering about houses of Low Saxon type. In this area where livestock raising and dairying are the main rural economic pursuits, the scattered homestead form of settlement, allowing free access to fields and meadows, is best adapted to the life of the peasants. The farms tend to be of moderate size, averaging from 5 to 20 hectares. To the south in the Middle Franconian portions of the province, where crop cultivation provides the basis of the rural economy, the rural population dwells in irregular villages of the Haufendorf type. In the rich Cologne–Aix-la-Chapelle plains area, these villages, consisting of dwellings of the Middle German type, formed by a house and barns arranged about a square, range from 600 to 1600 in population. The upland villages of the Eifel, Westerwald, and Hunsrück tend to be smaller with populations ranging between 200 and 600, while in the highest portions of the Eifel and Hunsrück, the tiny hamlet with 15 to 70 inhabitants is most common. The large Middle Franconian type of village extends southward from the Cologne, Aix-la-Chapelle area along the valleys of the Rhine and Mosel.

The Rhinelanders are generally a musical people with a vivacious temperament. They love carnivals and festivals. Their interest in things artistic and musical manifests itself in the varied architecture of their villages and in their many folk songs. Their diet is light, and wine is more common than beer, sodden drunkenness is uncommon. The Rhinelanders are relatively cordial to strangers. They are not as militaristic as the northeastern Germans, but there is, however, a strong feeling of national loyalty throughout the Rhineland.

Urban Aspect

Most of the larger cities of the Rhine Province are concentrated in the north. Although many of the cities and towns of this area go back to Roman times, and although they grew and prospered on the basis of Rhenish river trade and commerce during the Middle Ages, the development of the modern pattern of settlement did not come until the nineteenth century when the Rhinelanders and Westphalians turned to the exploitation of the extensive coal deposits along the Ruhr. The Ruhr industrial area, which is shared by the Rhine Province and the Province of Westphalia, was not only the largest German industrial region, but also the greatest in continental Europe, as a result of its coal, its proximity to the iron ore deposits of the Siegerland and Lorraine, and its cheap water transportation. Considerable iron ore also is imported from Sweden and Spain. The growth of the large Rhenish cities during the past hundred years has led to the creation of a gigantic urban zone in which there is hardly a break in the continuity of houses, mines, blast furnaces, steel mills, and factories. To the west of the Rhine-Ruhr industrial area there are several manufacturing towns which derive their raw materials from the Ruhr coal fields—such as München-Gladbach, Viersen, Rheydt, Neuss, and Krefeld. The manufacturing towns of Wuppertal, Remscheid, and Solingen, which are located in the foothills of the Sauerland, are also dependent for raw materials on the heavy industries of the Ruhr.

The Rhine Province possesses two other significant manufacturing and industrial areas which center around the cities of Aix-la-Chapelle and Cologne. The towns of Trèves and Koblenz in the southern part of the province are provincial cities, more interested in commerce than manufacturing. Over 50 per cent of the population of the province lives and works in the twelve large cities with populations of over 100,000, while another 14 per cent lives in the thirty towns with populations between 20,000 and 100,000. Eighteen larger cities of the Rhine Province are organized as city-counties. The democratic features of city government, which had been provided by the City Constitution of 1856 and the liberal measures of the Weimar era, were swept away by the Nazis. After 1935, their government and administration followed the German Municipal Code.

Economically, the Rhine Province may be divided into two distinct economic regions. The northern portion of the province has an urbanized economy based upon industry and manufacturing, made possible by its great coal and lignite fields, the adjacent iron mines of the Siegerland, and the transportation facilities of the Rhine and Ruhr rivers. The uplands of the province have a rural agrarian economy, based upon livestock, wine, fruit, and commerce. It constitutes a transitional economic area caught between the industrialized Lower Rhineland and the manufacturing centers of the Rhine-Main area, which is oriented toward the city of Frankfort. Again, the Nazi government demonstrated its knowledge of economic structure; it placed the heavy industrial area of the Rhine and Ruhr under the Ruhr Planning Association and the rest of the province, which has an economy based upon light manufacturing and agrarian pursuits, under another regional planning association. The sharp differences between the economy of the northern and southern portions of the area were further recognized through the establishment of an Economic Office (*Wirtschaftskammer*) at Cologne for the south, and an Economic Chamber at Düsseldorf for the north.

The basis of the great economic development of the Rhine Province is formed by the Ruhr coal fields, which have a greater output and greater reserves than any other coal field in Europe. There are coal mines also in the Aix-la-Chapelle area, while lignite is mined north and west of Cologne. Iron ores are found scattered through the uplands (Prüm and Altenkirchen). There are extensive rock quarries along the Rhine and Mosel. The Ruhr area, which has a fifth of the blast furnaces of the Reich, has an adequate coal supply, but must depend upon iron imported from Sweden, Lorraine, and Spain.

The manufacturing industries are largely located near the centers of heavy industry. Iron and metal working industries are found south and east of the Rhine and Ruhr, while there are important textile industries at and near Krefeld and Wuppertal.

Most of the gas, electricity and water consumed locally in the Rhine Province is produced or provided by plants owned by cities, associations of cities, or by mixed enterprises. The provincial power grid is linked to Osnabrück (Westphalia) and Frankfort (Hesse-Nassau) by high tension lines. Other lines run to the great plants of the Saar and the Nahe waterpower plant of the Pfalz. The Cologne–Aix-la-Chapelle area had four main plants: coal plants at Kohlscheid and lignite plants at Zukunft, Fortuna, and Goldenburg; in addition, there were other plants at Essen. High tension lines link these plants to a transformer station at Koblenz. A Mosel River line connects Koblenz with a small plant at Trèves. There is a partial gas grid in the province. The area north of the Mosel is dependent on the Ruhr, while the southeast gets its gas from the Saar. The eastern Runsrück is dependent on the Frankfort area.

The road pattern of the Rhineland is determined by the northern plain and by the valleys of the Rhine and Mosel. Aside from the network of roads in the north and the major roads running along the Rhine and Mosel valleys, there is an extensive system of minor roads within the province. The major provincial roads were maintained by the Provincial Corporation, while the local county roads were under the supervision of the county Road Master. Under the Nazi regime, the normal road system was supplemented by the national super-highways.

The railroads of the Rhine Province follow almost the same basic patterns as the road system. The heaviest traffic is carried by the two double track lines along the Rhine, while the heaviest traffic centers are Cologne and Düsseldorf. The Ruhr industrial area has an extremely intricate rail network. The railroads, which were owned by the national government, were operated by the German Railroad Company, an integral part of the national Ministry of Transportation. In the province, they were under the National Railroad Directorates of Essen, Cologne, Mainz, Saarbrücken, and Wuppertal.

Economically, the Rhine River is vastly more important than the road and rail systems. This most important of German rivers flows for over 200 miles through the Rhine Province. Until 1935, the traffic was regulated by the International Commission for Navigation on the Rhine at Strasbourg. Navigation matters were also under the Ministry of Transportation. In the Rhine area, river transportation enterprises were organized in the Ship Operators Corporation of the Rhine (*Schifferbetriebsverband Rhein*), which was located at Duisburg. The Rhine is joined by the Mosel at Koblenz, the Sieg at Bonn, the Lippe at Wesel, the Ruhr at Duisburg, and the Lahn at Koblenz. Major canals connect it with eastern France and northern Germany. The main port of the river in the Rhine Province is Duisburg, but minor ports are located at Cologne, Düsseldorf, Wesel, Wesserling, Leverkusen, Ober-Lahnstein, Koblenz, and Krefeld. The traffic on the Rhine derives from the industries of the Ruhr-Rhine area, the potash of Alsace, and the trade of the riparian states. The three main peacetime commodities were coal and lignite, iron, and cereals, which constituted four-fifths of the traffic. The heaviest traffic was between the Netherlands and Mainz with coal going upstream from Duisburg to Mainz and Mannheim and cereals traveling from the North Sea to Duisburg. The chief international air center of the province was located at Düsseldorf; domestic air centers were situated at Essen and Cologne.

The commercial and financial life of the province centers in the cities of

Düsseldorf, Essen, Cologne, Aix-la-Chapelle, Koblenz, and Trèves. The major goods produced in and shipped from the Rhine Province included coal, lignite, coke, iron, and steel, while iron ore, cereals, and other industrial raw materials constituted the major imports of the province. The coal of the Ruhr fields in normal times finds its way up the Rhine as far as Mannheim and Karlsruhe. It was shipped eastward into Central Germany and southward to the Main Valley region of northern Bavaria. The heavy industries of the Ruhr have long supplied a great proportion of Germany's industrial and manufacturing enterprises with needed materials. The numerous textile mills of the Lower Rhineland furnished most of Western Germany with its needs.

The banking and credit institutions of the Rhine Province ranged from branches of the great commercial banks of Berlin, which were mainly interested in investments of the industrial type, to the local county and municipal mortgage and savings banks. The provincially owned *Landesbank der Rheinprovinz, Rheinische Girozentrale und Provinzialbank,* and the *Rheinischer Sparkassen- und Giroverband* were located in Düsseldorf, the major financial center of the province. The operations of these banks were supplemented by the services of the main branches of the *Reichsbank.* The provincial government operated a life insurance and a fire insurance organization. These institutions, like the provincially operated banks, were under the Provincial Corporations. The Rhineland was served by the stock exchanges at Düsseldorf and Cologne.

The urban population of the Rhine Province was largely engaged in industry and crafts, for while over 3,570,000 individuals were supported by these pursuits, only 1,395,000 individuals were engaged in trade, finance, and transportation. A distinctive class structure is noticeable. First, there was a large working class, constituting about 46 per cent of the population. Secondly, the upper class, which accounted for another 15 per cent of the population, was rather large in view of the character of Rhineland economy. And finally, the white collar and civil servant groups were small in comparison with those of other Prussian provinces.

The urban centers of the Rhine Provinces vary from the heavy industrial complexes like Essen and Duisburg to the small provincial trading centers like Koblenz and Trèves. Between these two extremes one finds the manufacturing towns like Wuppertal and München-Gladbach and the commercial cities of Cologne and Düsseldorf. The northern part of the province belongs to the large cities (*Grossstädte*), which were created by the German industrial revolution. Cologne, which was founded in Roman times, has long held a commanding position in the life of the lower Rhineland because of its position on the Rhine at the point where the important east-west trade route of north Central Europe crosses this river. In the early days of the German industrial revolution the wealth of the Cologne merchants and bankers was used to open up the Ruhr coal fields. The development of lignite mining near Cologne has enabled this city to maintain its economic development. Düsseldorf, the successful rival of older Cologne, is also located on the Rhine, but nearer to the industrial cities of Neuss, Krefeld, Essen, Mülheim, and Duisburg. In more recent times Düsseldorf has taken from Cologne a sizable portion of its commercial and financial activity. This shift from Cologne to Düsseldorf is further emphasized by the fact that the latter city, and not Cologne, is the center of much of the economic administration for the lower Rhineland. Cologne, however, retains those administrative services oriented toward the southern Rhineland. The manufacturing city of Aix-la-Chapelle, which has developed in the course of the past seventy-five years because of local coal deposits, is isolated from the main Rhine-Ruhr industrial area by the Cologne plains. Away from the industrialized areas of the Rhineland the towns are more colorful. Life in the smaller provincial centers like Koblenz and Trèves goes on at a slower pace. There are universities at Bonn and Cologne.

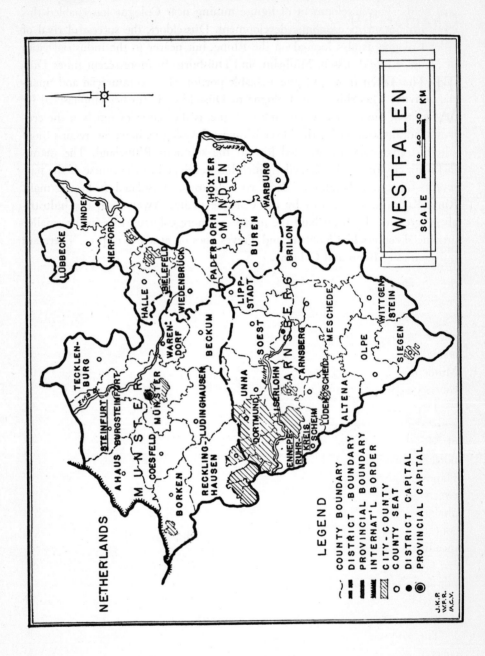

Chapter 19

THE PROVINCE OF
WESTPHALIA* AND THE LIPPES

The province of Westphalia is bounded on the north and east by the province of Hanover and the states of Schaumburg-Lippe, Lippe-Detmold, and Brunswick. The southeastern and southwestern portions of Westphalia adjoin the province of Hesse-Nassau and the Rhine Province; while the northwestern frontier borders the Kingdom of the Netherlands. Lippe and Schaumburg-Lippe, often referred to as the two Lippes, are located at the northeastern corner of Westphalia. Lippe consists of the counties of Detmold and Lemgo and a small bit of territory in Westphalia at the junction of the districts of Arnsberg, Minden, and Münster, while Schaumburg-Lippe, which is situated to the north, consists of the counties of Bückeburg and Stadthagen.

The northern part of the province of Westphalia, which constitutes an extension of the great North German Plain, is frequently called the lowland bay of Münster. Transitional between the uplands of Middle Germany and the northern plain, it forms a triangular area, cut off from the infertile lowlands of Hanover by the Teutoburger Forest (*Wald*), which forms an upland block between the upper Ems and the middle Weser. The uplands of northeast Westphalia and the two Lippes, which have sometimes been called the Weser hill country, reach up to a mean elevation of 1,150 feet. In the portion of the province in the far northeast, the upland country gives way to the great northwestern German plain. To the east, the Egge Mountains (*Eggegebirge*) effectively put an end to the lowland. The southern boundary of the Westphalian plains is formed by the Haarstrang Hills which divide the basins of the Lippe and Ruhr rivers.

The Münster Basin, which is underlaid with extensive coal deposits, is partly covered by glacial deposits washed out of the Central German upland. While outcroppings of the underlying cretaceous chalk beds are common in the south-

---

* German spelling—Westfalen.

ern and eastern margins of the plains, later tertiary marls (crumbly soil, chiefly clay and calcium carbonate) predominate in the central part of the basin of Westphalia. The northern and western plains of the province are sandy with frequent fens and bogs. The triangular southern part of Westphalia, lying to the south of the Haarstrang and the Ruhr River, is dominated by the rugged slate hills and the wooded valleys of the Sauerland. The Rothaar Mountains (Rothaargebirge) and the Egge Mountains form the highest areas of the hilly Sauerland, which is drained by the Ruhr and its affluents, the Lenne and Möhne in the north and by the Sieg and Eider rivers in the south. The Rothaar Mountains of the Sauerland, the Egge Mountains of eastern Westphalia, and the Teutoburger Forest of the northeast form the watershed between the basins of the Weser and Rhine rivers. The Province of Westphalia may be divided into two basic areas, a northern agrarian area dominated by Bocholt, Münster, Bielefeld, and Herford and a west central industrial area, containing some of the great cities of the Ruhr. The uplands of the south have several minor manufacturing towns.

The Province of Westphalia is the second most densely settled of the Prussian provinces. In 1933, the population was 5,039,000 individuals occupying 20,214 sq. km. The density was 249 individuals per sq. km. Although there is agreement between the landscape and demographic patterns, the heavy concentration of population in the western part of the province between the Lippe and the Ruhr rivers is accounted for by the great Rhine-Westphalian industrial development. The Ruhr-Westphalian zone of this western industrial area is one of the most densely settled parts of the Reich. Even outside the numerous cities of this area the density exceeded 200 per sq. km. The marginal areas have a density ranging between 100 and 200 individuals per sq. km. The northern, eastern, and southern portions of the area are characterized by a moderate density, averaging between 40 and 100 per sq. km. Only the higher reaches of the Sauerland have a sparse population.

Lippe and Schaumburg-Lippe have a relatively dense population. In 1933, Lippe had a population of 175,000, occupying a territory of 1,215 sq. km., while Schaumburg-Lippe had a population of 49,000, occupying an area of 340 sq. km. The Lippes are predominantly rural lands of small towns and villages.

This part of the Reich was probably settled by West Germanic folk as early as 200 or 300 B.C. Although in Roman times only the northern part of the province was in the hands of the Low Saxons, by Carolingian days (800 A.D.) they had gained control of most of the territory of the modern province. Today, most of the lands of Westphalia and all of the Lippes are occupied by a Low Saxon folk speaking a Westphalian variety of the Low Saxon dialect. South of the Lenne River, one finds peasants speaking a number of West Middle German dialects, such as Riparian and Rhine Frankish in the areas adja-

cent to the Rhine Province and a Hessian variety of Frankish in the parts near
to the province of Hesse-Nassau. The population of Westphalia is about equally
divided between Lutheranism and Catholicism. The Catholics, who in 1933
numbered 2,517,000, are located in the northwestern and eastern portions of the
province. The Protestants, located in the industrial Ruhr and the northeastern
agrarian areas, numbered 2,357,000. The total Jewish population was small,
about 18,800. In comparison with other states and provinces of the Reich, the
province had only a moderate Jewish population. The two Lippes are predominantly Protestant.

The population of Westphalia has increased very rapidly since the industrial revolution. In 1910 the population numbered 4,088,000, while today it has
reached a total of 5,039,000. Since 1870 the provincial population increase has
not been characterized by wide regional variations, except for the extremely
rapid growth of the urban centers along the Ruhr. The rest of the province
sustained from 75 to 150 per cent increases. The population characteristics of
the two Lippes are like those of the non-industrial portions of Westphalia.

As a political unit, Westphalia is a creation of modern times, dating from
the period of Napoleon and the Congress of Vienna (1815). The term *Westfalen* (Western Plain) was first applied to the western province of the ancient
Duchy of Saxony. During the period of the Saxon Emperors of the Holy Roman Empire, it consisted of the western part of the modern province and
extended northward to Friesland. After the fall of Henry the Lion of Saxony
in 1180, the Duchy of Saxony was subdivided four ways, segments going to the
bishopric of Münster, which had been instituted in 802 A.D.; the bishopric of
Paderborn, the archbishopric of Cologne, and to Philip of Heinsberg, who received the Sauerland and other lands which were to become the Duchy of Westfalen. Within the Duchy several secular territories were held as fiefs from the
archbishops and later Electors of Cologne. During the later Middle Ages the
Duchy fell more and more under the control of Cologne, and after 1480 it was
ruled for the Electors by their Marshal (*Landdrost*) until 1803.

Prussia obtained her first holdings in Westphalia by acquiring the territories
of Mark and Ravensberg from the Electors in 1614. The Peace of Westphalia
(1648) added the bishopric of Minden to Prussia. The next reorganization of
territory came in 1803, when the church lands were secularized. Prussia received the bishopric of Paderborn and the eastern part of Münster, while Hesse-
Darmstadt obtained the electoral Duchy of Westfalen.

The settlement of 1803 was short-lived, for in 1807 Napoleon established the
Kingdom of Westphalia, which embraced most of the modern province and a
large section of Hanover. After Napoleon's defeat at Leipzig (1813), the Kingdom was dissolved and the old order restored. At the Congress of Vienna in
1815, Hesse-Darmstadt gave up the electoral Duchy of Westphalia to Prussia,

which was already in possession of a large part of the area. The result was the formation of the modern province of Westphalia. Territorially, it was divided into three districts: Münster, based upon the old lands of the bishopric of Münster; Minden, constituted out of the ancient bishoprics of Paderborn and Minden; and Arnsberg, formed from the county of Mark and the old electoral Duchy of Westphalia.

The history of the Province of Westphalia after its formation shortly after 1815 merges with that of Prussia. The provincial administration did not, however, receive its final form until the passage of the Provincial Constitution of 1886. The exploitation of its rich coal deposits after the middle of the nineteenth century transformed the entire life of the province. The small market towns along the Lippe and Ruhr rivers rapidly developed into mighty industrial centers. The zone of urban settlement and industrial establishments expanded within the space of the last seventy years to convert the entire Ruhr area into one vast urban agglomeration. The conservative Westphalian peasant became a worker with social and democratic interests.

The two Lippes have a history characterized by traditional territorial and dynastic stability. Both Lippes were ruled by petty barons from early medieval times until 1613, when a division of inheritance invested Lippe-Detmold in one son and a few bailiwicks in another, whose descendants built them into the principality of Schaumburg-Lippe. The territory of the two states did not change hands or increase or decrease in size from the settlement of 1613 down to Nazi times.

During the nineteenth century, the two Lippes were hereditary and constitutional principalities. Lippe, which was governed under the Charter of Rights of 1836 and the Electoral Law of 1876, was under a unicameral State Assembly, composed of delegates elected on the basis of a three class system of suffrage. Administration was carried by a State Ministry which supervised the active departments of government. In Schaumburg-Lippe the government of the hereditary and constitutional principality was regulated by the Constitution of 1868. It consisted of an assembly, composed of delegates partly appointed by the prince, the clergy, and the nobility, and partly elected by the people. The administration, which was carried out under the authority of the prince, was carried out by a single ministry.

The two states of the Lippes did not undergo any drastic changes until World War I, and then the occasion, which marked their transition to republics, was hardly violent. The two princes merely packed up and disappeared from public life. During the period of the republic a proposal to unite Schaumburg-Lippe with Prussia was rejected by the people in a referendum in 1926. Under the Republic, the government of Lippe, which was regulated by the Constitution of 1920, consisted of a unicameral assembly, composed of democratically elected delegates, and a Provincial Presidency (*Landespräsidium*), consisting of three members. In Schaumburg-Lippe, the Constitution of 1922 (modified in 1924 and 1927) provided for a democratically elected assembly and a provincial government composed of a Council of State and four deputies.

POLITICAL ASPECT

The Province of Westphalia, being predominantly urban and industrial, has given its political support principally to the parties of the Left and the Center. Under the Empire, the Catholic portions of the province, which are located in agrarian Münster and in the southern portion of the district of Minden, voted for the Catholic Center party. The northern portion of Minden, which was largely Lutheran in its religious faith, followed the National Liberal and the Liberal Progressive parties. The industrial portions of the district of Arnsberg voted for the Social Democrats, while the agrarian portions of this district followed the National-Liberal party. Under the Republic, the Catholic Center and Social Democratic parties were strongest, with the Communists occupying a strong third position in the Ruhr area. The non-Catholic areas in rural Westphalia and the Lippes turned to either the German People's party or the conservative German National People's party. As Hitler's strength grew after 1930, the Socialist vote dropped, but the Communist vote increased, and the Catholic vote remained quite constant. In northern Westphalia, in the administrative districts of Münster and Minden, the Catholic vote was always highest. In southern Westphalia, in the Arnsberg administrative district, the Catholic vote until the rise of the Nazis was also highest, but the votes of the two proletarian parties, Socialist and Communist, when combined outnumbered other parties.

The Nazi party never dominated any part of the province in public elections until after Hitler's accession to power. In fact, the province was one of the areas in Germany in which Hitler was relatively weak. When he ran for President in 1932 he carried only four relatively small voting districts in the whole province, Hindenburg's vote being two and one-half to three times greater than Hitler's. There was always a very sizable Communist vote in the province, especially in the Ruhr portion of the district of Arnsberg, rising to 23 per cent in 1932. The Nazi vote averaged less than 25 per cent in the four elections preceding the consolidation of Hitler's power. The traditionally conservative and even reactionary Lippes gave Hitler a sizable vote as early as 1930, but the other parties including the Socialists, Communists, and the strong Nationalists, together outnumbered Hitler's party until 1933. Lippe gave stronger support to Hitler than did Schaumburg-Lippe.

During the imperial period, the Prussian administered courts, railways, and mining offices and the nationally operated postal system lay outside the scope of

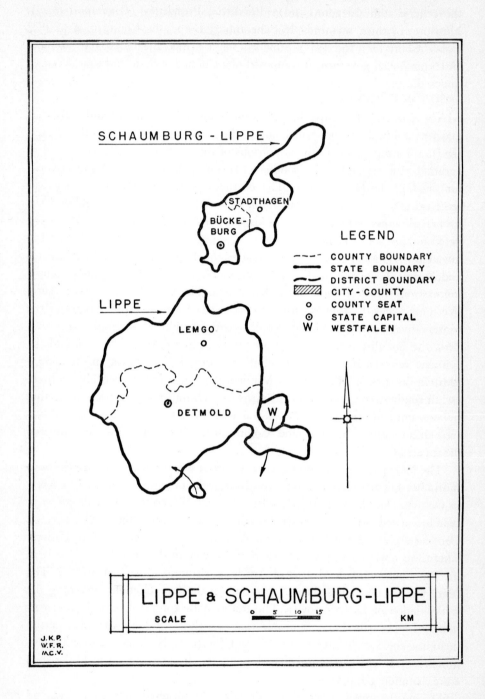

LEGEND

- - - - COUNTY BOUNDARY
——— STATE BOUNDARY
——— DISTRICT BOUNDARY
▨ CITY - COUNTY
o COUNTY SEAT
⊙ STATE CAPITAL
W WESTFALEN

LIPPE & SCHAUMBURG-LIPPE

SCALE   0   5   10 15   KM

J.K.P.
W.F.R.
M.C.V.

the general administrations. Justice, which was administered by the Prussian Ministry of Justice, was under the Superior State Court of Hamm and the Collegiate Courts of First and Second Instance of Arnsberg, Bielefeld, Bochum, Dortmund, Essen, Hagen, Münster, Paderborn, and Siegen in Westphalia and under the Superior State Court of Celle (Hanover) and the collegiate courts of Bückeburg and Detmold in the two Lippes. The national postal system within Westphalia and the two Lippes was under the Chief Postal Directorates (under the Empire) and the National Postal Directorates (under Republic and the Third Reich) of Dortmund and Münster. National regulations for trade and industry, weights and measures, social insurance, welfare, public health, and the collection of imperial revenues were administered upon delegation from the Reich.

In republican times there was a further extension of direct national administration to finance, railways, unemployment insurance and employment, and labor welfare. National control of finances within Westphalia and the two Lippes was carried out by the State Finance Office of Münster and its *Finanzämter* and *Hauptzollämter*. *Reichsbauämter* were located at Dortmund, Minden, and Münster. The nationalized railways of the province were operated by the *Reichsbahndirektionen* Essen, Hanover, Münster, Cologne, and Wuppertal. Labor and unemployment problems were handled by the *Landesarbeitsamt* Westfalen (Dortmund) and the *Hauptversorgungsamt* Westfalen (Münster). Certain aspects of welfare, social insurance, health, trade and industry, and labor, which were subject to national legislation, were administered upon delegation from the Reich. The economic life of the province was organized in a number of national agricultural, industrial, commercial, and labor organizations.

The Westphalia-Lippe area was organized under the Nazi party district of North Westphalia (districts of Münster and Minden, Lippe, and Schaumburg-Lippe) and South Westphalia (district of Arnsberg), which had their headquarters at Münster and Bochum respectively. As in the other parts of Germany, Nazi party organizations covered the whole area with their all-embracing system.

The administration of the province was headed by a Chief President who resided in the city of Münster. He was vested with broad political and supervisory control of administrative, social, economic, and cultural activities, although most of the actual administration was carried out by the District Presidents located in each of the three administrative districts into which the province is divided—Münster, Minden, and Arnsberg, and by the other special administrative services. During the Nazi regime the Chief President was also a Nazi party leader.

In 1934, the Nazis liquidated the federal status of the two Lippes, transferring their rights to the Reich. One National Governor was placed in charge of the government and administration of both states. He was directly responsible to the Minister of the Interior, but he also carried out the instructions of other national ministers. The Governor for Lippe and Schaumburg-Lippe, who maintained his headquarters at Detmold in Lippe, was also the Nazi party district leader for North Westphalia (Münster). Although there was joint national political control for both states, their internal administration was quite separate. The center of administration for the state of Lippe was at Detmold. The actual head of the administration was also the Governor, but the work of administration was carried out through the State Government (*Landesregierung*). It consisted of three governmental sections (*Abteilungen*). One dealt with personnel, police, welfare, health, and interior administration, while a second handled finance, accounts, construction, agriculture and industry, forests, and banking. The third managed the schools, archives, and libraries of the state. The administration of Schaumburg-Lippe, which had its center at Bückeburg, was headed by a State President, who was assisted by a deputy. This small state had no ministries or departments with independent status for administration, all work being carried out by the Office of the State Government. The work of the provincial administration of Westphalia and the state governments of the Lippes was supplemented by special and technical services under direct national control.

Under the Nazi regime, direct national administration was extended to justice, air matters, propaganda, and labor relations. Many traditional fields of state administration—police, health, welfare, education, and certain aspects of social insurance—were also brought under strict national control. In addition, there were the usual corporate administrations, which added further to the regimentation.

The most important general administrative center was Münster, the provincial capital and a center for district administration. The next two most important centers of general administration were located in the small towns of Minden and Arnsberg. The chief center of economic administration was located at Dortmund. While the offices of general administration for Lippe and Schaumburg-Lippe were located in the capitals of the two states, economic problems were handled from Dortmund, finance from Münster, and justice from Celle.

Rural Aspect

Westphalia was almost wholly agricultural until the discovery of the underlying coal measures, when it became predominantly an urban industrial region. In 1933, only 12 per cent, or 644,000 individuals, were supported by agriculture and forestry. Only 15 per cent of the population of the province dwelt on small farms and in villages and towns close to the soil. The people of the Lippes lived in small towns and villages, the largest town, Detmold, having had a population of less than 18,000. Their interests were essentially agrarian. The day-to-day administration of rural Westphalia was carried out by the thirty-two counties into which the administrative districts were divided. These counties were headed by County Managers who served both as the agents of the central government and of the local self-government. The county administration and self-government were regulated by the County Constitution of 1886, which was later modified by the Republic and the Third Reich. The villages of Westphalia, which were governed under the Constitution for Rural Villages and Towns of 1856, followed the German Municipal Code after 1935. Each village or town administration consisted of a Mayor, Party Agent, two or three administrative assistants, and an appointed town council. Village and town self-government were once more important. Small hamlets occasionally joined to form local *ad hoc* districts *(ämter)* for the administration of common affairs.

The villages of Lippe, which were governed by the Municipal Code (*Gemeindeverfassungsgesetz*) of 1927, were ruled by a Municipal Executive (*Gemeindevorstand*) and Municipal Representatives (*Gemeindevertretung*). Their government and administration was supervised by the County Manager. The union of counties (*Ämter*) or Nazi counties, which were under an Executive Committee (*Amtsausschuss*) and a Council (*Amtsrat*) (eliminated by the Nazis), formed a unit of state administration and local self-government. The County Manager, as head of administration and self-government, was responsible to the state government. In Schaumburg-Lippe, the two counties and villages, which served as units of state administration and local self-government, were governed under the County Constitution of 1923 and the Constitution for Rural Villages and Towns of 1870 until the Nazi regime. The county government and administration consisted of a County Manager, County Committee, and a County Assembly, while village government was under a Representative Body (*Bürgervorsteherkollegium*), a Magistry, and a Mayor. The Nazis drastically altered the form of county government by strengthening the position of the County Manager in both the Lippes. After 1935 village government in the Lippes followed the pattern laid down by the German Municipal Code.

The agriculture of Westphalia is varied and important despite the great and predominating industries of the province. Over 62 per cent of the land is devoted to agrarian activities: 36 per cent to crops and 26 per cent to stock raising and dairying. The plains of the northwestern part of the province have much in common with Northwestern Germany. The plains area enjoys a mild moist Atlantic climate with an average January temperature of 1 degree C. and an average July temperature of 17 degrees C. There are approximately 745 mm. of rainfall each year. Dairying and beef are the main agrarian interests. The major crops are largely grown to support the livestock industry. Together with the Low Saxon area, Westphalia, Oldenburg, and Western Hanover supply the Ruhr industrial area with most of its beef and dairy products. Swine are also grown in great numbers on the plains. The hams of this area are famous throughout Germany.

The Haarstrang or Hellweg area, between the Lippe and Ruhr rivers, which borders the southern plains of Westphalia, constitutes the best agricultural land in the province. Its climate is warmer and drier than that of the plains to the north or the hills of the Sauerland to the south. The plains and rolling hills of the Hellweg are largely devoted to the cultivation of wheat, oats, and rye. Near the large cities of the Ruhr area, dairying and market gardening are more important. Although many of the farms are small, they are frequently mechanized. The higher portions of the Sauerland, which have a moist cold climate, are largely devoted to dairying, pasture, and forage crops. The lower parts of the Sauerland, the Teutoburger Forest, and the Egge Mountains of eastern and northeastern Westphalia enjoy a drier and warmer climate. This hilly country is largely devoted to forage crops, grain, and livestock. The cultivation of hemp plays an important role in the northeastern part of the province and in the Lippes.

To generalize, one might say that the humid and cool plains and higher uplands are largely devoted to cattle raising and related crops, while the Hellweg and the lower hills to the east and northeast are dominated by dairying and cereal crops with intensive crop cultivation playing a greater role near the larger cities. The following figures of land utilization for the year 1933 give the detailed picture.

WESTPHALIAN LAND UTILIZATION (HECTARES)

Cultivated Land		714,500
Grain	460,000	
Legumes	11,000	
Root Crops	166,000	
Green Vegetables	3,000	
Industrial Crops	4,500	
Fodder Crops	70,000	
Small Gardens		41,000
Houses and Barns		60,000
Meadow		188,000
Pasture		280,000
Orchards		3,300
Forests		535,000
Moorland		7,000
Waste Land		55,000

PERCENTAGE OF LAND-USE

Agrarian Land 62%	
Cultivated Land 36%	
Meadowland 26%	
Forests and Woods 26%	
Other Types of Land 12%	

THE STATE OF LIPPE—LAND UTILIZATION (HECTARES)

Cultivated Land		52,750
Grain	34,000	
Legumes	1,000	
Root Crops	12,000	
Green Vegetables	400	
Industrial Crops	350	
Fodder Crops	5,000	
Small Gardens		2,700
Houses and Barns		2,400
Meadow		5,800
Pasture		11,000
Orchards		460
Forest		33,000
Moorland		74
Waste Land		4,500

PERCENTAGE OF LAND-USE

Agrarian Land 62%	
Cultivated Land 46%	
Meadowland 16%	
Forests and Woods 27%	
Other Types of Land 11%	

THE STATE OF SCHAUMBURG-LIPPE—LAND UTILIZATION (HECTARES)

Cultivated Land		14,097
Grain	9,700	
Legumes	300	
Root Crops	3,300	
Green Vegetables	37	
Industrial Crops	60	
Fodder Crops	700	
Small Gardens		960
Houses and Barns		950
Meadow		3,600
Pasture		1,900
Orchards		66

Forest   6,600
Moorland   180
Waste Land   180

PERCENTAGE OF LAND-USE

Agrarian Land 61%
   Cultivated Land 43%
   Meadowland 18%
Forests and Woods 19%
Other Types of Land 20%

Twenty-six per cent of Westphalia is given over to woods and forests. The plains of the Münster Bay are famous for their oak groves. The beech forests of the southern upland cover from 30 to 40 per cent of the land. The beech forests of the eastern hills are not so dense, covering from 29 to 37 per cent of the land. Only a small portion (10 per cent) of the forests of the area is included within the sixteen State Forests. Another 10 per cent of the forest land is owned by the cities, towns, and villages of the province. The private owners hold the greatest portion of the forests of the province of Westphalia. The forests of Lippe, which cover 27 per cent of its land, are under the control of a forestry service subject to the control of the forestry office of the Second Section of the state government. There is less forest land in Schaumburg-Lippe (19 per cent).

The peasants of Westphalia north of the Sauerland form a distinct cultural block with important cultural traditions going back to the migration period. The Westphalians, who are the most southern of the Low Saxon peoples, have an intensely peasant point of view. They are patriarchal and politically conservative. One finds them to be a reserved, restrained people, not strikingly subservient to authority. For the most part, they dwell in isolated farm houses of rectangular type sheltering a barn and living quarters. Although this peasant house type is architecturally related to those of Northwest Germany, it has a distinctive Westphalian style. In the northeast, east, and south, the peasants dwell in agglomerated villages; they are composed of typical Low Saxon houses in the northeast and Middle German houses of the Frankish type in the east and southeast. South of the river Lenne of the Sauerland, the Low Saxon-Westphalian peasant gives way to the Frankish peasant of the Rhine Province and Central Germany. Although the Westphalian and Frankish peasants possess different dialects, costumes, and folkways, they are both essentially interested in the land. Both groups are composed largely of independent farmers living on small farms which they own. It is interesting to note that while the farms of the plains and the lower upland areas are medium sized, those of the upland Frankish peasants are very small, averaging less than five hectares in size. The conservatism of the Westphalian peasant has done much to temper the folk character of this otherwise highly industrialized province of the German worker.

URBAN ASPECT

The Prussian province of Westphalia is second only to the Rhine Province in population density. Over 31 per cent of the population lives in cities of over 100,000: Gelsenkirchen, Münster, Recklinghausen, Bielefeld, Minden, Bochum, Dortmund, and Hagen. All of these great centers of population, except Münster, Minden, and Bielefeld, which are located in the northern and northeastern portions of the province, are integral parts of the great Ruhr industrial area. Another 53 per cent of the population dwells in towns ranging from 2,000 to 100,000. Those over 25,000 include the cities and towns of Bottrop, Gastrop-Rauxel, Hamm, Herne, Iserlohn, Lüdenscheid, Lünen, Wanne-Eickel, Wattenscheid, and Witten of the Ruhr industrial area; Bocholt, Gladbeck, and Herford of the north; and Siegen of the far south. The cities are the centers of the industrial and commercial life of the province. Most of the cities of the Ruhr urban complex, which occupies the northwestern corner of the governmental administrative district of Arnsberg and the southwest part of the district of Münster, are located in the area between the Lippe and Ruhr rivers. Within this zone, there is an almost complete continuity of industrial establishments, workers' houses, and apartments.

The administrative center at Arnsberg is to the east of this "Black Country." Münster is situated in an isolated position on the Westphalian plains. It serves as the provincial capital and the center of administration for the district of Münster, while Minden, which is not a city county, is the administrative center of northeastern Westphalia. The other cities of the north are the economic centers of predominantly agrarian areas. Industrial Siegen serves as the economic center of southern Westphalia. There are no large cities in the two Lippes.

The 21 larger cities of Westphalia constitute city counties, each of which is headed by a Chief Mayor directly responsible to the District President of his district. Their government and administration followed the pattern laid down by the German Municipal Code of 1935. The democratic features of city government, which had been provided by the City Constitution of 1856 and the liberal measures of the Weimar era, were swept away by the Nazis.

The northern portion of the Rhine Province and the western part of Westphalia constitute a distinct economic block within the Reich. The basis of the economy of this region is the extensive coal and lignite fields extending from Aix-la-Chapelle to the eastern part of the Ruhr Valley. The Rhine, Lippe, Ruhr and their related canal systems provide excellent transportation facilities, which are supplemened by an intricate railroad network. The agrarian activity of the plains of the Münster Bay and the Lower Rhine, as well as the upland to the south, provides for the feeding of this gigantic urban complex. The total industrial area may be subdivided into smaller integral units. The Ruhr zone of heavy industries, which extends across the northern part of the Rhine Province and eastward across Westphalia occupying a zone between the Lippe and the Ruhr rivers as far as the city of Hamm, forms one of the most significant economic areas in Europe. Southward, the uplands of the Sauerland with their iron resources and extensive dairy and cattle industries, constitute another small economic area oriented toward the Ruhr, while the land to the east and north of the Ruhr zone forms an important agrarian belt also oriented in terms of trade and economic interest toward the great Rhine-Westphalian industries. The northeastern cities of Westphalia, Bielefeld and Herford, although interested economically in the affairs of the Ruhr, are oriented toward Low Saxony and the cities of Osnabrück and Hanover.

The real basis of economic life for Westphalia is the Ruhr coal field which extends northwards from the Ruhr Valley and westward into the Rhine Province. It maintains a greater production and has greater reserves than any other coal area in continental Europe. The coal measures are tilted and in some places coal actually out-crops into the valleys. The coal deposits sink gradually farther beneath the surface as one moves northward. While very poor coal comes from the northern Sauerland, the coal of the Ruhr Valley is better in quality and can be used for the production of coke, essential for the steel mills of the Ruhr area. Farther to the north, one finds the deep coal measures which yield the excellent hard "long-flame" Emscher coal. The mines of the Münster area still farther to the north often are at a depth of 4,900 feet. The more important mining centers are at Bottrop, Gelsenkirchen, Recklinghausen, Bochum, Castrop-Rauxel, Dortmund, Wanne-Eickel, Wattenscheid, and Witten.

Iron ore for the Ruhr industries has to be imported from Lorraine, Sweden, Spain, and North Africa, since the ores of the Siegerland are insufficient and expensive. The coal, coke, and ore are used by the iron and steel industries of Bottrop, Gelsenkirchen, Recklinghausen, Bochum, Dortmund, Hamm, Wanne-Eickel, Wattenscheid, and Witten. The Westphalian heavy industrial complex of mine shafts, blast furnaces, steel mills, rolling mills, coke ovens, and chemical plants is tied together by a network of railroads, rivers, and canals. Manufacturing is carried on in a number of adjacent towns: Hamm (steel products and machinery), Iserlohn (small metal goods), and Lüdenscheid (aluminum). Dortmund, Bochum, Recklinghausen, and other cities of the Ruhr area are not devoted exclusively to heavy industry, for they produce a number of manufactured products of a lighter type. The industrial town of southern Westphalia is Siegen, an old iron mining center. The manufacturing towns of Bielefeld and Herford in northeastern Westphalia are famous for their textiles, especially linen, which is made from the flax that is grown throughout the northeastern region of the province. Both cities also have important food industries. Münster and Bocholt of western Westphalia have textile mills, but they are more significant as market towns than as centers of manufacturing. Münster is also important for brewing, agricultural machinery, and food products.

The industries of western Westphalia are supported by a well developed power network. Within the province, there are large coal power plants at Hattingen, Dortmund, Herdecke, and Siegen. These plants are linked to the great lignite plants of the Rhine Province by three great high tension lines: the Rhine Province-Münster-Osnabrück line, the Düsseldorf-Ruhr line, and the Cologne Siegerland line. These larger plants are supplemented by numerous municipally owned power stations.

The basic pattern of roads in Westphalia was set during the Middle Ages. Major roads running east-west follow the Ruhr and Lippe valleys linking eastern Westphalia and Paderborn to the Rhine area. The major road junction in the north is Münster from which roads lead to Paderborn and the cities of the Ruhr industrial area. The Sauerland uplands are crossed by two major east-west roads. North-south communication in the hilly areas is difficult except in the east and northeast. Road maintenance was under the Provincial corporation, the County Construction Master, and the Road Commissioner (*Strassenmeister*) of each county. When the Nazis came to power, the normal road system was supplemented by the construction of the modern national super-highway. The original plans called for the following super-highways in Westphalia: Dortmund-Münster-Osnabrück, Dortmund-Paderborn, with branch roads leading southward to Kassel, and three roads westward from Dortmund into the Rhine Province. Several of these roads were completed.

The railroads of Westphalia were operated by the National German Railways through the National Railroad Directorates of Essen, Hanover, Münster, Cologne, and Wuppertal. Although most of the railroads of the province were operated out of Münster, some of the roads in the northeast were under Hanover, while the lines of the Ruhr industrial area were under Essen, Cologne, or Wuppertal. These offices and service centers operated one of the best developed rail networks in the world, the railroad system serving the Ruhr industrial area. The main rail lines of the province include the east-west Berlin-Hanover-Dortmund-Rhine Province line and the Dortmund-Münster-Osnabrück-Bremen-Hamburg line. The Ruhr area might be said to form one gigantic rail junction.

The important natural water transportation facilities of Westphalia are provided by the Ems, Lippe, and Ruhr rivers, which are supplemented by the great canals of the province. The important Dortmund-Ems canal, which extends northward via Münster along the Ems River to the port of Emden, is important for the export of Ruhr coal and the importation of Swedish iron ores. It is linked to the eastern part of northern Germany by the famous Mittelland canal which joins the Ems-Dortmund canal in Hanover and extends eastward via Minden and Hanover to the Elbe. The Ruhr area is linked to the Rhine by the canalized Ruhr, Lippe, and Emscher rivers and by the Rhine-Herne canal. Almost all of the important Ruhr industrial towns maintain city operated canal ports for the shipment and importation of coal, coke, ore, and grain. The major airports at Münster and Dortmund once provided connections for all parts of the Reich and Europe.

Outside the Ruhr-Westphalian urban area, the cities of Bocholt, Münster, Herford, Bielefeld, and Paderborn serve as the focal points of trade and commerce in northern Westphalia, while Siegen is the important trade center of the south. Many of the small economic enterprises of the province and the two Lippes feared the effects of cartelization. Their fears had foundation, for many small enterprises, particularly in the retail trades, have been closed down, while others have been practically cartelized through the agency of the Nazi National Association of Commerce (*Reichsgruppe Handel*). The German businessman, concerned with production; the commercial man, interested in management and finances; and the business bureaucrat with legal, economic, and technical training in the operation and administration of great enterprises, were the important cogs of Germany's war economy. The financial enterprises of the province ranged from the local savings banks (*Sparkassen*), mostly municipal, to the branches of the great commercial banks in the larger cities. The latter type of bank plays a great role in industrial and commercial finance. There were very few private banks doing other than stock brokerage business. To these institutions must be added the provincial bank, largely interested in the mortgage business, and the local offices of the *Reichsbank*, concerned with discount operations and the usual government services.

The urban population of Westphalia, which constitutes well over 64 per cent of the province, is largely engaged in industry and craft activities. While manufacturing enterprises employed over 2,554,000 workers, trade and transportation engaged only 716,000 individuals. The resultant class structure in percentages was as follows in 1933:

Independent Status	13%	Civil Servants	5%
Family Dependents	6%	Workers	51%
White Collar Employees	9%	Servants	2%
Occupationless	14%		

The industries of the province accounted for the large number of workers, while the minor significance of trade accounted for the small class of white collar employees. The absence of large cities and large scale industrial enterprises in the Lippes might lead one to believe that these states were predominantly rural and agrarian, but it should be noted that only 21 per cent of the population of each state derived its living from agriculture and forestry, while 12 to 13 per cent of the population of the Lippes was engaged in trade and transportation. About 45 per cent of the population of Lippe was engaged in industry and crafts, while 40 per cent of the population of Schaumburg-Lippe lived by industry and craft activity. The class structure of the Lippes is interesting. While the labor class has about the same proportion as that of other states and provinces of the Reich, the upper class is proportionally slightly larger and the white collar class is definitely smaller.

The great industrial cities of the Ruhr, Bochum, Gelsenkirchen, Dortmund, Recklinghausen, and Hagen, developed rapidly during the past hundred years in the course of the German industrial revolution through the exploitation of the rich coal deposits of the area. Once they were small commercial towns with only minor industrial and manufacturing interests, serving the adjacent agrarian population and oriented northward toward the great Hansa cities of the North Sea coast. Today, their rapid industrial expansion has created a great "Black Country" of mines, factories, and workers' houses. Although the Ruhr towns are now oriented toward the Rhineland, their older interest in the north is still apparent. The provincial cities of Siegen, Bocholt, Münster, Herford, and Bielefeld represent the more normal industrial development of the old German market town.

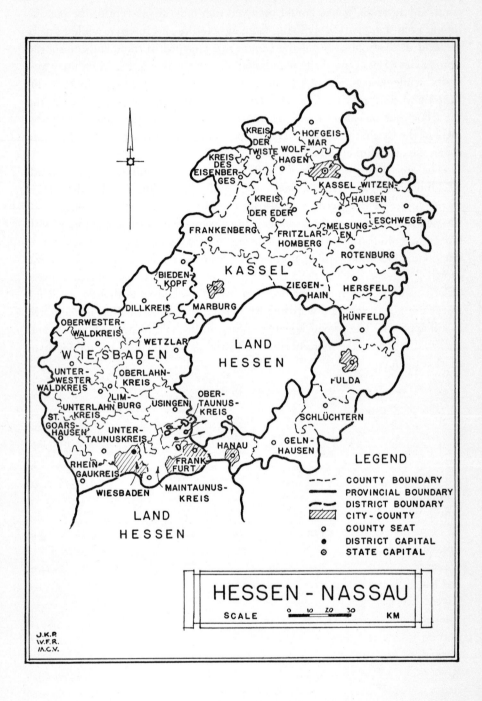

LEGEND

‐ ‐ ‐ ‐ COUNTY BOUNDARY
━━━━ PROVINCIAL BOUNDARY
━ ━ ━ DISTRICT BOUNDARY
▨ CITY - COUNTY
○ COUNTY SEAT
● DISTRICT CAPITAL
◎ STATE CAPITAL

HESSEN - NASSAU

SCALE 0 10 20 30   KM

Chapter 20

THE PROVINCE OF HESSE-NASSAU AND THE STATE OF HESSE*

The Prussian province of Hesse-Nassau and the state of Hesse are contiguous areas located in the central part of Western Germany. The Rhine Province lies across the Rhine to the west, Westphalia and Hanover are to the north, Saxony and Thuringia lie to the east, and Bavaria (Bayern) and Baden to the southeast and south. The state of Hesse is made up of two parts, separated from each other by the province of Hesse-Nassau. The southern part lies to the south of the Main River and constitutes the greater part of the so-called Rhine-Main Basin. The northern part is a kind of large exclave within the province of Hesse-Nassau.

The general frontiers of the two Hessian areas have been the result of a long historical development; they are not delineated by natural geographical barriers. The land slopes gradually upward from the Hessian Hills in the north, through the Westerwald and Vogelsberg uplands to the Taunus Mountains in the southwest, which continue across the Rhine as the Hunsrück ranges. This highland country with its ruined castles constitutes the most scenic part of the Rhine Valley. South of the rivers Rhine and Main, the southern part of the state of Hesse in the Rhine-Main Basin is hemmed in by the Taunus, Odenwald, Spessart, and Hardt Hills. The northern and eastern parts of the province of Hesse-Nassau are dominated by the valley of the River Fulda, which joins with the River Werra in the northeastern part of the province to form the Weser River. The Fulda flows north through the hills of eastern Hesse, a region of forested uplands and narrow but fertile valleys. The landscape of the northern portion of Hesse-Nassau is the result of complicated faulting and folding accompanied by the usual volcanic activity, plus the erosive action of the Eder River and the Fulda River, which rises in the Wasserkuppe (3117 ft.), an eminence of the Rhön Mountains (Rhöngebirge) dominating the southeastern part

---

* German spelling—Hessen-Nassau, Land Hessen.

of the province. In the central part, the meandering Lahn River cuts through the Rhine Plateau between the Westerwald and the Taunus, flowing westward into the Rhine just south of Coblenz. Farther to the south, the Main, likewise flowing westward, joins the Rhine south of the Taunus near Wiesbaden and Mainz. The Wetter River, which rises in the heights of the Vogelsberg, flows southward through the undulating plains of the Wetterau district, separating the Vogelsberg from the Taunus, into the Main River near Frankfort. The vital urban portion of the Hesse and Hesse-Nassau area, lying largely within the Rhine-Main Basin, includes the cities of Frankfort, Hanau, Wiesbaden, Mainz, and Darmstadt. The other cities—Kassel, Fulda, Giessen, and Marburg—are isolated urban centers.

The Province of Hesse-Nassau is the third most densely settled of the Prussian provinces. In 1933, the region had a population of 2,584,000 occupying 16,-845 sq. km. The density was 153 per sq. km. The state of Hesse is even more heavily settled, for over 1,429,000 individuals occupy 7,961 sq. km., a density of 185 per sq. km. There is a remarkable agreement between the landscape and demographic patterns of distribution, for the areas of dense population (more than 200 per sq. km.) are located along the valleys of the Rhine and Main, while the zones of moderate density (100 to 200 per sq. km.) are to be found in the valleys of the Lahn, Wetter, and Fulda. Though the hills of the Taunus have a very sparse population with less than 25 per sq. km., the Westerwald is rather well settled with a density of 75 to 100 per sq. km. The hills and uplands of northern and eastern Hesse and Hesse-Nassau have only a slight population varying with local conditions from 25 to 75 individuals per sq. km.

This part of Germany was occupied by Keltic folk until the second century before our era. By the time of the Roman occupation of the Rhineland, the Germanic tribes had pushed as far west as the Rhine, and in the far southwest they had crossed the Rhine and Main to take possession of the Rhine-Main Basin. The end of the migration period (A.D. 600) found most of Hesse and Hesse-Nassau in the possession of the Rhine Frankish and Hessian tribes. A small portion of the northern part of Hesse-Nassau was in the hands of the Low Saxon Westphalian peoples. These basic groups developed through the Middle Ages to form the three dialect groups which distinguish the modern peasants, that is, Rhine Frankish, Hessian, and Low Saxon. Standard German, however, is spoken in most towns and cities.

The Protestant population, which is the largest religious group, numbered about 1,776,000 in the province of Hesse-Nassau and about 933,000 in the state of Hesse. In both areas, it constituted between 65 and 68 per cent of the total population. The Catholics, who numbered 709,000 in Hesse-Nassau and 439,000 in Hesse, were located chiefly along the Rhine and Main rivers. There is another rather large Catholic group in southeastern Hesse-Nassau centering about the town of Fulda. The total Jewish population of Hesse-Nassau once numbered 46,000. Most of these were in the larger cities and particularly in the Frankfort area. The smaller Jewish population of Hesse once numbered 17,000. The total Jewish population of this part of the Reich was quite large in comparison with other areas.

Both the Province of Hesse-Nassau and the state of Hesse have experienced a steady increase in population during the present century. Since 1875, the great urban centers, particularly Frankfort and Wiesbaden, have grown rapidly under the impetus of industrialization. Most of the rural areas have grown slowly during the last seventy years, but a few, for example, the upland region of eastern North Hesse, lost population. Relatively few Germans left for other countries during the twenties and early thirties. In the late thirties, almost 1,900 left for other lands, while only about 690 returned to the province of Hesse-Nassau. These figures, which are proportionately the same for Hesse, are in contrast with those for the rest of the Reich, for nationally emigration was greater in the twenties and early thirties and then decreased, with the result that the number of Germans returning to the Reich actually exceeded the number leaving.

This region was originally settled by the Chatti, who are identified with the later Hessi, but political history does not begin until the time of the migration period (A.D. 400). Although many of the Hessi later pushed westward, enough remained behind to give their name to the area. The Hessian District (*Hessegau*) first appears in the region of the Werra, Fulda, and Lahn during the Merovingian and Carolingian periods. During the early Middle Ages in the time of the Saxon and Franconian Emperors most of what is now Hesse and Hesse-Nassau was under the dukes of Franconia. Much of the land, however, was under the suzerainty of practically independent dukes and counts. The dynastic history of Hesse begins under Heinrich I with his investiture as a Landgrave of Hesse (1263). He had come by this inheritance after a long and involved series of dynastic marriage alliances. His successors and descendants made frequent partitions of the land and occasionally added a few bits of territory.

In 1504, Wilhelm II reunited all the constituent parts of the Landgraviate and bequeathed it to his son Philip the Generous, who played an important role in the Reformation. Though most of Hesse and Hesse-Nassau remained under the firm rule of the dukes of Franconia until the thirteenth century, thereafter this area, like most of the Reich, fell into the hands of several independent petty princes. While the Landgraviate of Hesse was developing in northern Hesse-Nassau, the Duchy of Nassau was taking shape in the southwest under the Earls of Nassau. The petty state of Waldeck gradually gained status as an earldom. The remainder of the area was ruled by the Bishop of Mainz, the dukes of Westphalia, who were subject to the archbishops of

Cologne; the bishops of Würzburg, and the Bavarian Wittelsbach rulers of the Palatinate. The city of Frankfort, which goes back to Roman times, was an important commercial town. In 1254, it was made an imperial city and after 1356 it was the center for the election of the Emperors of the Holy Roman Empire. After 1562, all German Emperors were crowned at Frankfort until the dissolution of the Holy Roman Empire by Napoleon.

The death of Philip the Generous in 1567 was significant for the history of this part of the Reich. The youngest son, Georg, received the Earldom of Katzenellenbogen comprising the city of Darmstadt. His successors became the landgraves of Hesse-Darmstadt. The eldest son received the largest share, the greater part of the district of Kassel. His successors made appropriate additions. The small territory of Hesse-Homburg developed as a fief of Hesse-Darmstadt. There was little in the way of significant territorial change until the time of Napoleon.

The Bavarian rulers of the Palatinate, the Bishop of Mainz, the Bishop of Würzburg, and the Archbishop of Cologne still held considerable portions of what is now modern Hesse and Hesse-Nassau. French expansion to the Rhine under Napoleon brought drastic changes. Between 1801 and 1813, Hesse-Darmstadt, which had consisted of spotty bits of territory on both sides of the Rhine and Main, lost all its possessions on the west side of the Rhine River and received as indemnification the ancient Duchy of Westphalia.

The Landgraviate of Hesse-Kassel, with territories situated in the northeastern part of modern Hesse-Nassau, received the towns of Fritzlar and Amöneburg for losses of territory to the west of the Rhine to the French. At the same time the Landgrave of Hesse was promoted to the dignity of Elector. After the battle of Jena (1806), the new Elector was forced to leave his state, which was made a part of the French Kingdom of Westphalia. In 1813, Hesse-Kassel was restored and the lands of the ancient bishopric of Fulda were added to its territory.

The old Earldom of Nassau, which had gained the dignity of a principality in 1688, was again united under the rule of one prince. In 1806, Nassau lost its lands west of the Rhine but gained the dignity of the title of duchy. The petty state of Waldeck, which had been raised to the rank of a principality after the addition of the Earldom of Pyrmont and after other dynastic arrangements in 1712, was not disturbed to any great extent by the Napoleonic Wars. It joined the Rhenish Confederation and gave in to the French. The Free and Imperial City of Frankfort was occupied by the French in 1806, and in 1810 it was made the center of the French Grand Duchy of Frankfort. The period of French rule in western Germany had done its work well; the ecclesiastical states had disappeared and the more important secular states had been consolidated and unified.

The Treaty of Vienna in 1815 left the region included within the present province of Hesse-Nassau and the state of Hesse divided into the Grand-Duchy of Hesse, the Electorate of Hesse, the Duchy of Nassau, Hesse-Homburg, the principality of Waldeck, and the Free and Imperial City of Frankfort. The latter city was particularly important during this period as the capital of the German Confederation. The Electorate of Hesse, which is better known as Hesse-Kassel, passed through periods of conservative reaction, liberal attempts, constitutional troubles, palace revolutions, and struggles against the growing might of Prussia. The Duchy of Nassau had similar difficulties. The real issue lay in the choice of an alliance with Austria or with Prussia. In the War of 1866, Hesse-Kassel, Hesse-Homburg, the Duchy of Nassau, and the city of Frankfort sided with Austria. In a matter of days they were overrun by Prussian armies. The Prussian government soon gave these territories the status of a province, making the old Duchy of Nassau and the city of Frankfort into the district of Wiesbaden and the lands of Hesse-Kassel and the territory of Hesse-Homburg (which had been ceded by Hesse-Darmstadt as a part of indemnity for her part in the War of 1866 when she sided with Austria) into the district of Kassel. The provincial administration received its final form under the Empire in the Provincial Constitution of 1885.

Hesse-Darmstadt, which later came to be called the state of Hesse, and the tiny principality of Waldeck survived the storm of 1866. They joined the North German Confederation and later became members of the German Empire (1871). Under the Empire, the Grand Duchy of Hesse was governed by the liberal constitution of 1820 (modified in 1856, 1862, 1872, 1900, and 1911). Its government consisted of a bicameral legislature, composed of a House of Lords (*Herrenhaus*), much like the Prussian one, and a Chamber (*Kammer*), with delegates elected by all taxpayers, and an executive, which consisted of a State Ministry, acting for the Grand Duke. State administration was carried out by Ministries for Interior, Finance, and Justice. The State Ministry was responsible for foreign affairs and the administration of matters pertaining to the ducal house.

After World War I both of these areas became constituent units of Weimar Germany, Hesse-Nassau as a Prussian province, the state of Hesse as a state. Under the Republic, the state of Hesse, which was governed under its Constitution of 1919, had a democratically elected assembly and a responsible State Ministry. Administration was carried out by Ministries for Interior, Justice, Finance, Labor and Economics, and Religion and Education. Waldeck history came to an end in 1928 when the Pyrmont section was added to Hanover and the rest of the land absorbed into the province of Hesse-Nassau. These territorial consolidations were effectuated first by a treaty between Prussia and Waldeck dated March 23, 1928, and second by a law of the *Reichstag* dated December 7, 1928.

Politically, the state of Hesse and province Hesse-Nassau present a diverse picture. Under the Empire, the southern portion of the state of Hesse gave its votes to the Social Democrats along with the industrial cities of Frankfort and Hanau. The industrial and manufacturing areas of the districts of Wiesbaden and Kassel also followed the Socialist cause. The northern portion of the state of Hesse, the western agrarian section of the southern part of the state along with the parts of the district of Wiesbaden voted for the National-Liberals. The agrarian portions of the district of Kassel, with the exception of the Fulda area which voted for the Catholic Center party and the industrial areas followed the Economic Union party. The reform party and the German Farmer's Union party had only limited holdings. Under the Republic the Social Democrats continued to hold a strong position in the Hesse and Hesse-Nassau area thanks to their strong position in the larger cities. The rural areas supported either the German National People's party or the German People's party, while the Catholic area about Fulda gave strong support to the Center party.

As early as the 1930 *Reichstag* election, the state of Hesse cast 18.5 per cent of its votes for the Nazi party. By the election of July 1932, the Nazi percentage rose to 43 per cent, then dropped a little to 40.2 per cent in the November 1932 election, and rose again to 47.4 per cent in the March 1933 election. Thus the Nazis were the strongest party in the state of Hesse during the critical period of 1930-1933. The party was particularly strong in the agrarian portion of Upper Hesse (Oberhessen), where it secured clear majorities over all other parties combined. Only in Offenbach, a city close to Frankfort-on-the-Main, and in Mainz were the Socialists strong. The province of Hesse-Nassau was also a center of strong Nazi support, between 35 and 45 per cent of its vote being cast for the Hitler party in the critical elections. The province also gave Hitler a big vote when he ran for President in 1932. The only part of the province which consistently voted a majority against Hitler was the county and city county of Fulda where the Catholic party was in control.

During the imperial period the Prussian administered courts, railways, and mining offices of Hesse-Nassau, and the nationally operated postal system of the Hessens lay outside the scope of the administration of the province and state. Justice was administered by the Superior State Court of Frankfort and the Collegiate Courts of First and Second Instance of Frankfort, Limburg, and Wiesbaden and by the Superior State Court of Kassel and the Collegiate Courts of Hanau, Kassel, and Marburg in Hesse-Nassau and by the Superior State Court of Darmstadt and the Collegiate Courts of Darmstadt, Giessen, and Mainz in the state of Hesse. At Frankfort and Kassel, the Chief Postal Directorates operated the postal system under the Empire; the National Postal Directorates operated it under the Republic and the Third Reich. National regulations for trade and industry, weights and measures, social insurance, welfare, public health, and the collection of imperial revenues were administered upon delegation from the Reich.

Under the Republic direct national administration was extended to finance, railways, unemployment insurance and employment, and labor welfare. National control of finances was carried out in Hesse-Nassau by the State Finance Office of Kassel and in Hesse by a similar office in Darmstadt. The Construction Offices at Darmstadt and Mainz were under Darmstadt, while the ones at Frankfort and Kassel were under Kassel. The nationalized railways of the area were under the National Railroad Directorates of Frankfort, Kassel, and Mainz. Labor and unemployment problems were handled by the State Labor Office of Hesse (Frankfort) and the main Welfare Office of Hesse (Kassel). Delegated from the Reich to the state were specific aspects of welfare, social insurance, health, trade and industry, and labor, which were subject to national legislation. The economic life of the area was organized in a number of national agricultural, industrial, commercial, and labor organizations.

The Hesse and Hesse-Nassau area was organized under the Nazi party district of Hesse-Nassau (Frankfort) and Kurhesse (Kassel). As in the other districts of Germany, Nazi party organization was complete and all-pervasive reaching down in a variety of ways to every citizen in every hamlet.

The Province of Hesse-Nassau was a Prussian province headed by a Chief President who resided in the city of Kassel. Under the Nazis, he was vested with broad political and supervisory control of administrative, social, economic, and cultural activities, although much of the actual administration was carried out by the District Presidents of the governmental administrative district of Wiesbaden and the district of Kassel and by the other special administrative services. It should be noted that in the case of the province of Hesse-Nassau provincial self-government was not organized on the basis of the provincial area, but by the administrative district in the District Corporations of Hesse (Kassel) and Nassau (Wiesbaden).

In contrast, the state of Hesse became a federal state under the Weimar Republic, having the same legal status, if not the power of Prussia. In 1934 the Nazis liquidated the federal status of the state of Hesse and transferred its rights to the Reich. A National Governor with headquarters at Darmstadt was placed in charge of the government and administration. He was directly responsible to the National Minister of the Interior, but was also subject to directives from other national ministers. The National Governor for Hesse was also the party leader for the party district of Hesse-Nassau (Frankfort-on-the-Main). The imposition of the control of the Governor upon the government and administration did not produce any vital change in the structure of the

Hessian State Government (*Hessische Landesregierung*) which was headed by a deputy of the Governor.

The work of the provincial administration of Hesse-Nassau and the state administration of the state of Hesse was supplemented by special and technical services under direct national control.

Following its custom, the Nazi regime further extended national administrative controls to include justice, air matters, propaganda, and labor relations. Many of the traditional fields of state administration—police, health, welfare, education, and certain aspects of social insurance—were brought under tight national control.

Economic planning was carried out by the Rhine-Main Planning Association (Hesse, district of Nassau, and the southern part of the district of Kassel) and the Kurhesse Planning Association (Northern Kassel District). Spatially, they were equivalent to the party districts of Hesse-Nassau and Kurhesse. The usual corporate administrations were created to complete the control within the area.

The cities of Darmstadt and Kassel, the state and provincial capitals, were the important centers of general administration. Frankfort was the vital center for special and particularly economic administration. Wiesbaden was of importance as a center for district administration.

RURAL ASPECT

Agriculture and forestry are matters of secondary importance in both Hesse and Hesse-Nassau, for only 21 per cent of their populations make their living by means of rural activities. However, about 43 per cent of the population of the province of Hesse-Nassau dwells in small villages of less than 2,000, while 35 per cent of the population of the state of Hesse is located in small villages of this size. The general administration of rural Hesse-Nassau centers in the city of Kassel, the provincial capital, and the two district capitals of Wiesbaden and Kassel. The day-to-day administration of rural Hesse-Nassau was carried out through the thirty-six counties into which the administrative districts are divided. After the elimination of the three provinces of the state of Hesse, the county, which had much the same status as the Prussian county, was directly responsible to the official in charge of interior administration (*Abteilung Ib*), who was a high official without the title of minister. Prussian counties were headed by County Managers who served both as the agents of the central government and local self-government. County administration and self-government were regulated by the County Constitution of 1885, which was modified by the liberal laws of the Republic and the reactionary acts of the Third Reich.

Under the Empire, the villages and small towns were regulated by the Constitution for Rural Villages and Towns of 1897, which was later modified by the

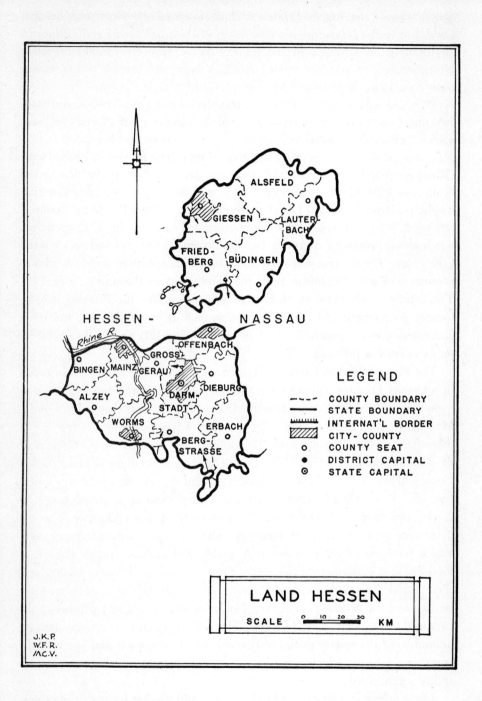

LEGEND

– – –	COUNTY BOUNDARY
———	STATE BOUNDARY
⊞⊞⊞	INTERNAT'L BORDER
▨	CITY- COUNTY
○	COUNTY SEAT
●	DISTRICT CAPITAL
⊙	STATE CAPITAL

LAND HESSEN

SCALE   0   10   20   30   KM

J.K.P.
W.F.R.
/AC.V.

liberal laws of the Republic. After 1935, it followed the German Municipal Code. Under the Nazis, the administration of the small towns and villages of the counties consisted of a Mayor, a Party Agent, two or three administrative assistants, and an advisory town council. Village and town self-government were once more important. The county and its villages continued to handle public works and welfare. Some of the counties owned a county bank and operated utility works of various types. Some of the towns owned a forest and managed a local market. Occasionally, they operated their own utilities.

The state of Hesse was originally divided into three provinces, Rhine Hesse (Rheinhessen), Upper Hesse (Oberhessen), and Starkenburg, which served as units of state administration and self-government. The state administration was headed by a Provincial Director, who was assisted by a Provincial Committee, while self-government, which was organized in a Provincial Corporation, was under a Provincial Assembly and the Provincial Director and a Provincial Committee. The director was responsible for the supervision of county administration and self-government until the elimination of the provinces in 1937. The county in the state of Hesse was very much like the Prussian county. County government and administration, as well as provincial, city, and town government, was regulated by the Laws of 1874 and 1911 and by the liberal republican laws of 1919 and 1922.

The Nazis introduced several vital changes. The Hesse county was headed by a County Director who served as the agent of both central and local government. The title of the County Director (*Kreisdirektor*) was changed to County Manager in 1938. He was assisted by a County Advisory Committee which was thereafter appointed by the state. The duties, functions, and responsibilities of the County Manager of the Hesse county are much like those of the Prussian County Manager. The direct administration and supervision of county institutions and affairs were frequently vested in commissions or commissioners who carried out their work under the direction of the County Director. The old democratic processes of government and administration in the Hessian county which were vested in the County Assembly and included public control of local finances, personnel policies, welfare matters, and other county affairs, have disappeared. The once important county committee, which administered the decisions of the assembly, under the Nazis became an advisory adjunct to the County Director or County Manager. The committee and the county manager administered the county public works and welfare programs and operated the county's enterprises which range in character from farm or forest to a complex utility organization.

Hesse originally had a special law for cities and another for rural communes. These codes were scrapped at the time of the promulgation of the new municipal code in 1935. Under the Nazis, the administration of the towns and villages of the Hesse counties followed the national pattern.

Agriculturally, Hesse and Hesse-Nassau are moderately important areas within the Reich. In Hesse over 61 per cent of the land is devoted to agrarian activities, while only 51 per cent of the province of Hesse-Nassau is agriculturally important. The state of Hesse has the advantage of holding extensive territories in the fertile Rhine-Main Basin. The character of agriculture varies widely throughout this area owing to the widely differing conditions of relief and soil previously described.

The fertile valley plains and the immediate hilly land of this basin constitute the most important agricultural area of the Hessens. Its rich chernozem soils bordered by rather fertile brown forest soils are excellent for agriculture. The plains of the Rhine-Main area present a mosaic of vineyards, orchards, and fields of grain, potatoes, and tobacco. The climate is characterized by mild winters with an average January temperature of 0 degrees C. and warm summers with an average July temperature of 18 degrees C. Warm summers are also characteristic of the valleys of the Lohn, Wetter, and Fulda. The climate of the Rhine-Main area is also noted for its dryness. The average annual rainfall is only 500 mm. The warm sunny climate and fine soil are particularly good for the cultivation of wheat, barley, and green corn for fodder. Near the large cities of the basin, market gardening plays an important role. The adjacent hills have been terraced for the cultivation of the vine and fruit trees. Noteworthy, however, is the fact that the growing of grapes and fruit generally constitutes only one part of the activities of a farm. This type of agriculture extends northward up the Wetter River Valley from the Main into the Wetterau, and is also characteristic of the agrarian life of the lower Lahn Valley.

The hilly lands of the southern, central, and northeastern parts of the province of Hesse-Nassau and the northern part of the state of Hesse enjoy a dry warm climate which rapidly becomes moist and cool with marked increases in elevation. This is a land of alternating upland and valley which favors the three-field farming of rye, oats, and potatoes. The raising of livestock is far more important than the cultivation of crops in the hills, while grain, sugar beets, and fruit play an important role in the drier, warmer, more fertile river valleys. The higher portions of the Taunus, eastern Westerwald, the Vogelsberg, and the Rhön Mountains enjoy a cool humid climate and are characterized by a forest podzol soil which is hardly good for farming. Much of the land is forested, but the valley meadowland and the occasional upland pasture are excellent for livestock. This is not a milk producing region owing to the distance from markets, but the production of butter and cheese is important. Sheep raising plays an important role. Small fields in the hills are used for the cultivation of oats, rye, and potatoes for home use and fodder for the livestock.

To generalize, the lowland basin of the Rhine-Main area is important for wine, fruit, and grain, while the lower uplands are significant for their production of grain and livestock. The higher uplands are important for the production of hay and dairy products. In terms of significance for Germany as a whole, the state of Hesse is counted on for vegetables, tobacco, fruit, and grapes, while the province of Hesse-Nassau is important for the production of grain and dairy products.

LAND UTILIZATION (HECTARES)

THE PROVINCE OF HESSE-NASSAU

Cultivated Land		573,000
Grain	348,500	
Legumes	7,200	
Root Crops	147,000	
Green Vegetables	3,600	
Industrial Crops	5,100	
Fodder Crops	61,600	
Small Gardens		16,000
Meadow		202,900
Pasture		53,100
Orchards		3,800
Vineyards		3,500
Forests		678,200
Waste Land		27,200
Houses and Barns		22,500
Roads and Parks		96,700

PERCENTAGE OF LAND-USE

Agrarian Land		51%
Cultivated Land	34%	
Meadowland and Pasture	15%	
Forests and Woods		41%
Other Types of Land		8%

THE STATE OF HESSE

Cultivated Land		324,900
Grain	168,500	
Legumes	2,300	
Root Crops	105,000	
Green Vegetables	6,200	
Industrial Crops	2,000	
Fodder Crops	40,900	
Small Gardens		9,400

Meadow	97,000
Pasture	12,200
Orchards	3,500
Vineyards	16,700
Forest	240,500
Waste Land	6,000
Houses and Barns	11,000
Roads and Parks	40,300

PERCENTAGE OF LAND-USE

Agrarian Land		61%
Cultivated Land	43%	
Meadowland and Pasture	18%	
Forests and Woods		32%
Other Types of Land		7%

Forty-one per cent of Hesse-Nassau and 32 per cent of Hesse are given over to woods and forests. Hesse-Nassau is the most heavily forested of all the Prussian provinces or German states, while Hesse ranks as the fifth most heavily forested province or state. The dominant tree of the forests of Hesse-Nassau and Hesse is the West German beech, but there are important growths of spruce, pine, and oak. In Hesse-Nassau over 40 per cent of the forest land is held in 118 state forest reserves. The cities, towns, and villages of the province own a slightly larger share of the forest land. In the state of Hesse almost one-third of the forest land is held in sixty state forests. These forests were managed by the agents of the Forest and Construction Administration of the state government.

The people of rural Hesse and Hesse-Nassau are chiefly the Rhine Franks (Rheinfranken) of the south and the Hesse or Hessians of the center and north. North of Kassel, one finds peasants of the Low Saxon Westphalian type. The Rhine Franks, who have much in common with the Rhinelanders of the Rhine Province and the Eastern Franconians of Northern Bavaria, are a vivacious and somewhat temperamental folk with definite musical and artistic abilities. For the most part they dwell in agglomerated villages of the *Haufendorf* type consisting of Middle German Franconian houses of brick and timber surrounding a farm yard. In upland parts of the eastern zone of the northern section of Hesse, the *Haufendorf* gives way to the *Strassendorf* in which the Frankish house type is found in small groups scattered along a valley road. This village has also been called the *Waldhufendorf*. The farms of the Franconian peasants dwelling in Rhine-Main Basin are of moderate size (5 to 20 hectares), while those of the uplands are very small. The system of land inheritance calling for the frequent subdivision of a farm among all the heirs has resulted in a large number of tiny farming plots. Festivals and carnivals play an important role in the life of these Franconian peasants. Their food is light and varied. Wine is far more important than beer. The rural people are not as militaristic as the north-eastern Germans, but strong national loyalty is a common trait.

The Hessians located in the northern part of the Hesse and Hesse-Nassau area speak a dialect which is considered to be a variety of Rhine Frankish, but owing to long separate cultural development, they have evolved a distinctive culture, characterized by distinctive folkways and folklore. They dwell in villages of the agglomerate type consisting of houses quite like those of the South. Their living comes from subsistence farming and home industry. Many of the peasants have left the land, attracted by the industries of Kassel. The Hessian peasant is famous for his ability as a wood carver, and this interest, first exploited for amusement and home decoration, has led to the development of an extensive handmade toy industry. The costumes, folk art and music, and temperament of the Hessian are the things which really distinguish him from the Rhine Frankish peasant of the South. Once the Hessian mercenaries were renowned for their military spirit, but today they are not a markedly militaristic people.

Urban Aspect

Hesse-Nassau and Hesse are moderately settled areas. While 42 per cent of the population of Hesse-Nassau and 34 per cent in Hesse dwell in small towns of less than 2,000, over 22 per cent in Hesse-Nassau and 47 per cent in Hesse live in towns and cities of 2,000 to 100,000. The only large city is Frankfort-on-the-Main in the Province of Hesse-Nassau, one of the more important cities of Europe. The other large cities are also located in the Rhine-Main Basin. On the northern bank of the Rhine, one finds the city of Wiesbaden which is important as a health resort, manufacturing town, and administrative center of the governmental district of Wiesbaden of the Province of Hesse-Nassau. The only other city with a population of over 150,000 is Hanau, located on the north bank of the Main just east of Frankfort.

In the state of Hesse, there are only two cities with a population over 100,-000: Darmstadt, the state capital; and Mainz, a manufacturing town located at the junction of the Main and Rhine rivers. Offenbach, on the south bank of the Main across the river from Hanau, forms an integral part of the Frankfort industrial area. The small city of Worms is located in the southern part of Hesse on the Rhine. The small university towns of Marburg in Hesse-Nassau and Giessen in Hesse are situated in the central part of this area, and in the eastern part of the province, the old Hessian ecclesiastical center of Fulda leads an isolated existence. Kassel, which is, undoubtedly, the most important city of the upland area, is the provincial capital of Hesse-Nassau and the center of the administration of the governmental district of Kassel. The cities in Hesse and Hesse-Nassau provide the homes for about a million and a half workers engaged in industry and crafts and about three-quarters of a million workers engaged in trade and transportation. About 55 per cent of the working population of this area derives its living from nonagrarian pursuits.

The eleven larger cities of Hesse and Hesse-Nassau constitute city-counties, each of which was headed by a Chief Mayor who was directly responsible to the District President in Hesse-Nassau and to the Interior Administration in Hesse. In the Province of Hesse-Nassau, city-county government and administration followed the pattern laid down by the German Municipal Code after 1935. The democratic features of city government, which had been provided by the City Constitution of 1897 and the liberal measures of the Weimar era, were swept away by the Nazis. In the state of Hesse, older forms of city government, which followed the mayoral pattern, disappeared under the Nazis.

The Rhine-Main region, which is sometimes referred to as the Middle Rhine District, is essentially a manufacturing area with its traditional center at the city of Frankfort. This whole area constitutes a distinct political, economic, and cultural block embracing the state of Hesse, the governmental administrative district of Wiesbaden, and the southeastern part of the district of Kassel. These latter governmental units break up its administrative unity, but it is significant that the Nazis established for the purposes of total planning a Rhine-Main Regional Planning Association which includes this entire area. There are no heavy industries and only a few extractive industries, which consist of some lignite fields and a few salt mines up the Main River from Frankfort, to support the industries of the Middle Rhine. The great chemical, leather, machinery, and engineering industries are the result of the development of old traditional undertakings under the impetus of Rhenish trade. Today, these industries are dependent on coal, lignite, iron, and steel shipped up the Rhine from the heavy and extractive industries of the Ruhr.

The Rhine-Main cultural and economic area has important external connections and interrelationships. It has long played an important role in terms of foodstuffs, raw materials, and manufactured goods in the life of the Saar, except for the period when the external trade interests of the Saarland were forcibly oriented to the west. It has important ties with the transitional Koblenz area. The northern part of the two Hessens and the district of Kassel, with its mixed industrial life mainly interested in light manufacturing, form a definite transitional area partly oriented toward the industrial area of Hanover and Hildesheim and partly toward the Rhine-Main region. Its distinctive economic position, undoubtedly, led the Nazis to establish the separate Kurhesse Planning Association for the governmental administrative district of Kassel.

The Hesse and Hesse-Nassau area has significant natural resources. The adjacent iron mines of the Taunus produce a low grade ore and have not led to the development of any heavy industry, despite the ease and cheapness of the Rhine water transportation for coal. The other two resources of importance include the salt mines near Fulda and around Kassel and the lignite fields to the east of Frankfort and of the Kassel area. These resources supplemented by materials brought in from the North by the Rhine have been important for the development of the extensive chemical industries of Frankfort, Wiesbaden, Darmstadt, Offenbach, Worms, and Mainz. The basic factor for the industries of the southern part of the area is the Rhine waterway, for it makes possible the cheap transportation of raw materials from the great Ruhr industrial area. The machinery and metalware plants of Frankfort, Hanau, Wiesbaden, Darmstadt, Mainz, Offenbach, and Worms are essentially connected with this Rhine trade. The other industries of the south represent specialized development.

The intensive agriculture of the Rhine-Main Basin with its output of grapes, fruit, vegetables, and tobacco supports an extensive food processing industry. Wiesbaden, Mainz, and Worms are important centers for the fruit and wine trade. The isolated towns of central and eastern Hesse and Hesse-Nassau were characterized by mixed industries of the light manufacturing type: Fulda (rubber, wax, textiles, and enamel ware), Marburg (tobacco, pottery, carpets), and Giessen (textiles, rubber, and machinery). As has been pointed out, the Kassel industrial area constitutes a distinct development based first upon the adjacent salt and lignite resources and secondly upon raw materials coming by water up the Weser and Fulda rivers. Kassel is important for the production of locomotives, machinery, airplanes, textiles, chemicals, scientific instruments, and food products. Like the rest of the area, it is interested in mixed light manufacturing. The industries of northern Hesse-Nassau are supported by an extensive and well-developed power network. There are two important lignite plants and three water power electrical plants in the immediate vicinity of Kassel. High tension lines link the plants of the Kassel area with those of Hanover in the north and Frankfort in the south. The latter area is well supplied with electrical power facilities. There are eight lignite and four water power plants in the Rhine-Main area. These are linked by high-tension lines to the electrical plants of Mannheim on the south, the Ruhr on the north, and Nuremberg on the east. These larger power plants are supplemented by the local municipal plants.

The roads along the Rhine and Main rivers undoubtedly go back to Roman times. The major Rhine road runs along the west bank from Worms via Mainz to Bingen, while the major road along the Main extends along the north bank of the river from Mainz via Wiesbaden to Frankfort and Hanau. The main road east of the Rhine River in the Rhine-Main Basin skirts the foothills of the Odenwald, passes through Darmstadt, and ultimately ends at Frankfort. A major road links Darmstadt with Mainz. A number of roads fan out to the north and east from Frankfort to connect with Giessen and central Hesse and with Fulda and the valley of the Fulda. A major road extends northward along the river Fulda to Kassel which is the key road junction of the North whence roads radiate northward to Hanover, eastward into the Province of Saxony, and westward toward the Rhine Province. Other roads link Giessen with Cologne and Hanover. The key junctions of the road system are Mainz, Frankfort, Fulda, Giessen, and Kassel. Road maintenance was under the Provincial Corporation and the two District Corporations in the Province of Hesse-Nassau, while the Forest and Construction Administration handled road affairs for the government of the state of Hesse. Local roads were taken care of by the county authorities. During the Nazi regime, the normal road system was supplemented by the construction of the modern national super-highway which linked Darmstadt, Frankfort, Kassel and Cologne with magnificent limited access super-highways.

The railroads of Hesse and Hesse-Nassau were operated by the National German Railways through the National Railroad Directorates of Frankfort, Kassel, and Mainz. There are several main rail lines. A double track line coming from the north follows along both banks of the Rhine River to Mainz, an important rail junction. An important line continues southward along the west bank of the Rhine from Mainz, while other lines follow both sides of the Main from Mainz to Frankfort, the most important rail center in this part of the Reich. One major line runs south from Frankfort to Darmstadt and thence southward along the east bank of the Rhine. Other lines radiate eastward from Frankfort to Würzburg and to Fulda, whence they connect with Erfurt and the great cities of the state of Saxony. Another major line connects Frankfort via Giessen and Kassel with Hanover.

The Rhine, Main, and the lower portion of the Fulda constitute the major natural water transportation facilities of Hesse and Hesse-Nassau. It must be noted that river transportation on the Fulda, which connects with the important Weser artery, stops at Kassel and that the Main River traffic east of Frankfort is insignificant though it continues eastward to connect with the Ludwig canal which links the Danube and Main rivers. Traffic on the Lahn River is unimportant. The significance of the Rhine and Main rivers for the industrial life of the Main area has already been discussed in an earlier section. It should be noted in conclusion that the river cities of Mainz, Wiesbaden, Frankfort, Hanau, Offenbach, and Worms operate municipally owned ports. The only major civil aviation airport in this area was at Frankfort. It was an important center for both domestic and international air travel in normal times. The air service and air lines were operated by the German Airways Corporation, although the airports were owned and operated by city governments.

The commercial centers of Frankfort, important for trade in chemicals and metals; Offenbach, famous for leather goods; Darmstadt, a general commercial center; and Worms, Mainz, and Wiesbaden, all significant in the wine trade, are the focal points of the commercial life in the Middle Rhine area. Frankfort is the predominating commercial city. The towns of Giessen, Marburg, and Fulda are significant as market towns catering to an agricultural trade, while Kassel in the north is the important commercial town of that region. The small business enterprises of this area, which originally expected to profit at the expense of big business under the Nazis, have suffered greatly, for all small enterprises were forcibly organized for purposes of control. A great many of the small retail firms have disappeared in the last years.

The banking and credit institutions of Hesse and Hesse-Nassau ranged from the branches of the great commercial banks of Berlin, which are mainly interested in industrial investments, to the local municipal savings banks. Frankfort is not only the important banking center of Hesse and Hesse-Nassau, but ranked as one of the more significant finance centers of the Reich. In Hesse-Nassau, the District Corporations of Hesse (*Regierungsbezirk* Kassel) and Nassau (*Regierungsbezirk* Wiesbaden) maintained provincial banks, while the Hesse State Bank at Darmstadt served this purpose in the state of Hesse. These institutions were mainly interested in the mortgage business and were supplemented by the branches of the *Reichsbank,* a central bank of issue, doing the usual discount operations and governmental services. The only stock exchange of this area was located at Frankfort.

The urban population of Hesse and Hesse-Nassau forms about 55 per cent of the total population of the area. While industry and crafts engage about 1,559,000 workers, trade and transportation employ another 676,000. The class structure is characterized by a large independent upper class, amounting to 18 per cent of the population. The number of civil servants, which amounts to 6 per cent of the population, is only slightly above the national average. The number of white collar employees (9 per cent) and workers (40 per cent) is not as large in proportion as in the heavily industrialized areas, but it measures up to the average for the manufacturing regions. The existence of a large upper class in the two Hessens cannot be accounted for in terms of landed wealth and must be due to the great number of small privately owned manufacturing establishments.

The cities to the north of the Main River and the Taunus Mountains are widely separated from one another. Giessen and Kassel developed from small agricultural market towns which once had the dignity of being the capitals of small sovereign states. Kassel took the industrial way of expansion, while Giessen along with Marburg have remained cultural centers famous for their universities. Fulda, long an important ecclesiastical center, remains essentially a small market town. The number of towns is much greater in the Rhine-Main area, where they developed because of the richness of the soil, cheap river transportation, their location near mineral deposits, and the consequent industrial activity. However, many owe their original status to the political conditions of the past when Germany was divided into a vast number of sovereign states each requiring a capital, which accounts for Darmstadt, Mainz, and Worms. Today, there may be too many cities in view of the economic potentialities of the area under modern conditions. Frankfort seems to be in a more favorable position. This once important governmental center, whose life as a free city was cut short in the middle of the last century, is typically German. In type, it is transitional between the cities of northern and southern Germany, but some of its old and characteristic ways disappeared under the impact of Nazification. Its key location in Germany and in Europe will always give it a pre-eminent position.

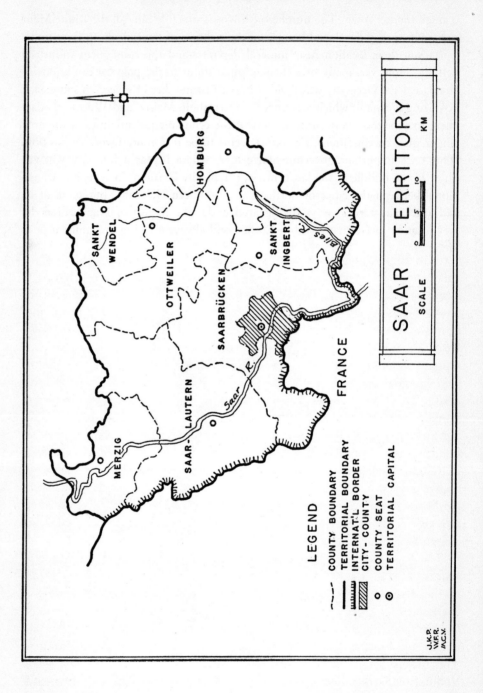

Chapter 21

THE SAARLAND

The Saarland is a mining and industrial district located on the Franco-German frontier. It is bordered on the south and west by French Lorraine, on the north by the Prussian province of Rheinland, and on the east by the Bavarian Palatinate. Geographically, it embraces most of the basin of the middle Saar River, which rises in the Vosges Mountains and flows north and northwestward through the western part of the Saar and the southwestern tip of the Rhine Province to join the Mosel River upstream from ancient Trèves. The Saar Basin, a region of wooded hills and open rolling country underlaid by ancient resistant rocks, forms a transitional area between the Rhine plateau of Western Germany and the west Rhine scarplands consisting of the Vosges and Hardt ranges. To the north lie the forested foothills of the Hunsrück, which form the southernmost part of the Rhine Plateau. In the east a westward extension of the Saar-Nahe upland (Bergland) separates the Hunsrück ranges from the Hardt upland of the Bavarian Palatinate to the south. The Prims River, rising in the Hunsrück Hills, flows southward through the rolling and hilly lands of the western portion of the basin, to enter the Saar River, which drains most of the basin. The Köllerbach, Fischbach, and Sulzbach in the central basin area are relatively unimportant streams, while the Blies River drains most of the eastern Saar.

The Saar Basin is divisible into six geographical areas, the northwestern Saargau on the lower Saar, the southern Bliesgau along the Blies River, the northeastern Saar-Nahe uplands, the industrialized Saar Valley, the famous Saarkohlen Forest, and the central Saar agricultural zone. The overwhelmingly German population is concentrated in the Saar River Valley and along its tributaries, the Fischbach and Sulzbach, in the southern portion of the territory. They dwell in the several large industrial and mining towns like Dillingen, Völklingen, Saarbrücken, St. Ingbert, and Neunkirchen, which have developed as a result of their proximity to the adjacent coal deposits and the evolving iron, steel, and glass industries. These towns grew up on the major road connecting

461

eastern France with the vital Rhine-Main area of Western Germany. The Saar Basin, which has been held in the past by both France and Germany, occupies a strategic position on the invasion route to Metz, the military key to eastern France and the Middle Rhine.

The valley and basin of the middle Saar have been occupied by agrarian peoples since the Neolithic period, which dates back some five millennia. Many centuries before the beginning of our era, this region was taken over by Keltic-speaking agriculturists, who were subjected to the rule of the Romans for the first five centuries A.D. During the last years of Roman imperial rule, German Franks from beyond the Rhine were slowly infiltering the Saar area. With the breakdown of Roman rule, the Franconians came in great numbers to the Saar Basin via the Mosel Valley and the Palatinate, converting the area to the German language. Today the Saarland is a German area speaking a Franconian dialect, although standard German is spoken in most towns and cities. The Saarlanders are also of mixed religious persuasion. Although there were 588,000 Catholics, constituting 72 per cent of the population, the Protestant group numbered over 215,000. The Catholic group was concentrated in the western and central portions of the basin, while the Protestants lived in the eastern area adjacent to the Palatinate. There were a few Protestant sections in the districts of Saarbrücken and Völklingen. The Jewish population, which numbered 3,118 in 1933, was surprisingly small in view of the urban character of the Saar.

Excluding Hamburg, Bremen and Berlin, the Saar is the most densely settled German territorial unit. In 1933 it had a population of 812,200 individuals occupying an area of 1,924 sq. km. The population density was 422 individuals per sq. km. In addition to the densely settled southern portions of the basin, there are minor concentrations of population around Merzig in the northwest and St. Wendel in the northeast. The population of the Saar has increased rapidly during the past century and a half under the impetus of increasing industrialization. It quadrupled between 1871 and 1935. The rate of growth has been steady since 1870, owing to the rapid expansion of mining and industry under the impact of the late nineteenth century industrial revolution. The population composition of the Saar has been characterized by an excess of males, which was due to the industries of the area which had long attracted male workers from adjacent areas within the Reich. The number of foreign residents living in the Saar was not unusually large in 1933 in view of the heavy industries and mining works. In that year the foreign residents numbered only 6,700, consisting mostly of French. These figures do not take into account the so-called Saar French (*Saarfranzosen*) who must be counted as natives of the area. This group is quite small, accounting for less than 5 per cent of the total population.

The Saar Basin has had the status of a frontier district since Roman times, for it forms a part of the old Lothringen (Lorraine) territory lying between the

Upper Maas and the Middle Rhine. The history of the Saar has long been intimately connected with that of Lorraine, for this basin occupies a strategic position on the major highway connecting the Paris Basin, the traditional seat of French power, with the Rhine-Main Basin, one of the traditional centers of German strength. From the Saar the Mosel Valley and the Zaberner depression (*Senke*) between the Hunsrück and the Hardt have long given the forces of France access to the Middle Rhine and the Germans entry to eastern France. In Roman times this basin formed a part of the imperial province of Germania Superior which served as one of the bastions of the Roman Empire against the barbarian Germans. Evidences of Roman rule survive in traces of ancient roads and the ruins of once prosperous villas and towns. The Migration era brought the conquest of the middle Saar area by the Franks, who held it throughout the period of Merovingian (481-768) and of Carolingian (768-843) rule.

Upon the division of the Carolingian realm at Verdun (843), it became a part of the much disputed possessions of Lothar, lying between the holdings of the French and German Carolingian families. After the establishment of relatively stable political conditions in Germany under the Saxon (919-1024) and Franconian (1024-1125) families, the Saar formed a part of the frontier duchy of Upper Lorraine. With the breakdown of the larger duchies after the fall of the Hohenstaufen Emperors, the Saar fell into the hands of many petty rulers: the Wittelsbach line of the Kur Palatinate (Kurpfalz), the bishops of Trèves and Metz, the counts of Lower Saargau, and the enfeebled dukes of Lorraine. After 1381 the counts of Nassau-Saarbrücken became a factor in the politics of the area. During the later Middle Ages, the Reformation, and the Thirty Years' War, these local rulers jockeyed for power and influence in the Saar area.

After the sixteenth century, French influence became more and more important. In 1552 Metz, Toul, and Verdun fell to France, and by the end of the seventeenth century, the conquests of Louis XIV brought the French into the western margins of the Saar. There were few frontier changes from the beginning of the eighteenth century until the armies of Revolutionary France swept eastward to the Rhine. The Saar along with the rest of German territory west of the Rhine was absorbed into France and organized into departments. With the defeat of Napoleon, the Saar was restored to Germany. The Napoleonic wars, which had brought the dissolution of the small principalities of the Saar, ended with Prussia and Bavaria in control of the area. Prussia received the larger western portion, which it added to the Rhine Province, while Bavaria obtained the smaller eastern section, which it added to the Bavarian Palatinate. Prussian and Bavarian control lasted until the end of World War I.

After the defeat of Germany in 1918, French troops occupied the Saar area. It remained under French military control until January 1920, when the Saar

Territory was formed under Section IV of the Versailles Treaty. Under this section Germany ceded to France the coal mines of the Saar basin as compensation for the destruction of coal mines in northeastern France and as part payment of the reparations. The district containing the mines was roughly defined by the treaty and subsequently established by an international boundary commission. The counties of Ottweiler, Saarbrücken, Saarlautern, Sankt Wendel and almost half of the county of Merzig along with the county cities of Saarbrücken were detached from the Rhine Province and the city county of Homburg and Sankt Ingbert from the Bavarian Palatinate to form the Saar Territory.

This territory, without the status of a state with sovereign rights, was placed under the trusteeship of the League of Nations for the period between 1920 and 1935. The treaty specified that a plebiscite should be held in 1935 to determine whether the territory or certain sections of it should continue under the League, be united with France, or given back to Germany. The voters consisted of all persons above twenty years of age who were resident in the territory at the date of the signing of the treaty. Under the League it was governed by a commission, which was appointed by and responsible to the League, consisting of one Frenchman, one Saar resident, and three "neutral" members chosen from citizens of countries other than France and Germany. The Commission was assisted by a consultative council of thirty members elected every three years by the popular vote of the inhabitants of the Saar. The council had only an advisory capacity without the power of initiative, although all laws were submitted to it before promulgation. The League Commission was further assisted by an appointed Technical Committee of nine for advice on special problems. The League Commission controlled public works, railroads, waterways, communications, agriculture, social insurance, education, trade and industry, finance, public welfare, and foreign relations, while inhabitants retained their assemblies for local affairs. Matters affecting religion, language, and nationality remained untouched.

Under the treaty the Saar was included within the French customs regime after 1923 and the French were allowed to use their own currency in financial matters pertaining to the operations of the mines. After 1923 the French franc became the legal currency of the Saar. During this period, the mines, as property of France, were operated by the French Ministry of Public Works. The first years of the rule of the League Commission were not easy, for the pro-French Commission allowed French military forces to remain, which was productive of a number of disagreements and troubles. International pressure brought the partial reduction of the French garrison and the establishment of a local gendarmerie. After 1925 affairs in the Saar went smoothly until the time for the plebiscite approached. The plebiscite was held January 13, 1935, after an extensive propaganda campaign from Nazi Germany. The vote was overwhelmingly (90 per cent) for reunion with Germany. Later, the Nazi Reich purchased the coal mines from the French government.

Under the Empire the Saar area supported first the Catholic Center party and secondly the National Liberal party. Its religious persuasion was stronger than its economic interests. This strongly industrialized area gave only a small vote to the proletarian Social Democratic party. Since the Saar was under an international governing commission until the plebiscite of 1935, public elections were limited to the choice of a Consultative Council. Little can be gained from these elections to show the political views of the population. After the plebiscite, the area was incorporated into Nazi Germany, and the inhabitants were forced into a one-party mold. For that reason, no recent election data since World War I are available to explain the political outlook of the Saarlanders. Nevertheless, it is known that there were two major political groups in republican times, the Catholic Center party and the Social Democratic party. There was some Communist strength, and a little Nationalist party support. As a working class area, however, the Saar citizens were quite naturally oriented toward the left, except where the influence of the Catholic Church held them within the Catholic Center party. In the eastern Lutheran areas, middle class politics prevailed in local affairs.

After the plebiscite, the League returned the Saar to Germany. On January 30, 1935, the Saarland was placed under a Nazi National Commissioner appointed by the Führer and responsible to the national Minister of the Interior. The temporary character of this administrative decision was evidenced by the fact that the law setting up the Saar administration stated that the Saarland would remain in charge of the Commissioner until the territory was united with an adjacent national district. This arrangement, however, lasted until after the conquest of France in 1940, when the Saar was combined with the Bavarian Palatinate and French Lorraine to form the district of Westmark.

An administrative organization was set up immediately after the Nazis took control in 1935. The National Commissioner, who was the permanent representative of the Reich government in the Saarland, was placed in charge of the government and administration of the territory. As the head of the Saarland administration, he was charged with the general supervision of all Saar officials and the execution of orders from national ministries and authorities. He also had general supervision over the county and city-county administrations. In Nazi party affairs, he was the leader for the party district of the Saar-Palatinate (*Gau Saar-Pfalz*).

Immediately after the Reich took over the Saar, Hitler appointed eight deputies to the Nazi *Reichstag*. In 1936 and 1938 they were elected by the inhabitants of the Saar. By this method, the Saar area, important for its resources and industries and its strategic position on the French-German frontier, was rapidly absorbed into the Nazi Reich. The administrative reforms of 1941 brought several drastic changes. The new district of Westmark (formerly French Lorraine, the Saar, and the Bavarian Palatinate), which was headed by a Governor who was also the party leader, was given a new administration, consisting of seven departments: Administration, Finance, Health and Welfare, Economics, Education, Construction, and Self-Administration.

The work of the general administration of the Saar was supplemented by special and technical services under direct national control. During the imperial period, special administrative services of the national, Prussian, and Bavarian governments functioned in the area in the same fashion that they worked in other parts of the Reich. During the period when the Saar was under International control, all connections with the Reich and its administrative apparatus were cut. The Saar government and administration provided for all needs within the territory.

The Nazi regime brought the re-establishment of the old imperial special administrative services and the introduction of new services, which had been developed in the Reich during the republican and early Nazi periods. The Nazi administrative pattern for the supervision of police, education, health, welfare, and other fields of administration, which were once handled by the state governments, was extended to the Saar. To the services and functions of the general and special administrative systems was added the usual system of corporate administration; life within the Saarland was completely regimented. Under the Nazis, Saarbrücken, the logical capital of the Saar territory, was the major administrative center, but as has been pointed out, in the case of certain special and technical services as well as of corporate administration, the main regional headquarters were located outside the Saarland.

RURAL ASPECT

The rural life of the Saarland, based upon agriculture and forestry, is of relatively minor importance in contrast to the extensive mining and industrial developments of the area. The Saar Basin is, nevertheless, one of the oldest settled areas in north Central Europe. The open country along the Saar River, which was first settled by peasants from the middle Danube region, has been cultivated for the last four or five thousand years. Toward the middle of the second millennium B.C., it was occupied by Keltic peasant cultivators who held the area until Roman times. The conquest of the lands on the left bank of the Rhine by the Roman legions brought the Saar under Roman imperial control. With the waning of Roman power on the Rhenish frontier, Franconian German settlers pushed up the Mosel River Valley and up the Saar Valley to settle and occupy the good agricultural lands. The German villages established between

the ninth and eleventh centuries are located with few exceptions in the Saar
Valley. Between the eleventh and fifteenth centuries, the Franconian peasants
began the conquest of the lands to the east of the Saar River. Much of the land
was first cleared by the process of burning off the timber to obtain temporary
clearings for agricultural purposes. The woodland during this period was used
chiefly as forest pasture. This eastward movement of peasants completed the
basic pattern of village settlement. During the early modern period, which
was marked by the growth of the glass and iron industries in the Saar, more of
the forest areas were cleared for the production of charcoal and small industrial-
craft towns expanded into markets for agricultural products. The nineteenth
century with the extensive development of mining and industry in the Saar,
and the consequent growth of urban agglomerations in the southern part of
the territory, brought increasing emphasis upon crop cultivation and the introduction of dairying. Despite the great changes of the past century, much of
the Saar retains its rural look, although today only 16 per cent of the population dwells in small villages (less than 2,000) and only 7 per cent of the
population makes its living from agriculture and forestry.

The general administration of the Saarland centered in the city of Saarbrücken, the capital. The day-to-day administration of rural Saarland was carried on in the seven counties into which the territory was divided. These counties were headed by County Managers who served both as agents of central
government and of local self-government.

Under the Nazis, each village or town administration of the county followed
the national pattern laid down by the German Municipal Code of 1935. The
Saar also had several unions of small rural villages for the management of common affairs (drainage, roads, health, ec.) of several adjoining hamlets. This
was a form of local administrative organization of self-governing type, which
permitted each member village to retain its status as a town. The Union was
headed by a Mayor who was assisted by two or three administrative department
heads, a council of Elders, and a Party Agent.

The open rolling country and the forested uplands and hills of the Saar
Basin are moderately good for agriculture, although it plays a relatively unimportant part in the total economy of the Saarland. The soils of the Saar are of
two types, the alluvial soils of the Saar Valley and the degraded mountain and
forest soils of the rolling plain and uplands. The climate of the Saar Basin is of
the dry-warm western German type, characterized by an average yearly temperature of 8-9 degrees C. with an average January temperature of 1.5 degrees
C. and an average July temperature of about 20 degrees C. The lower western
Saar area tends to be warmer and drier than the hilly eastern portion. The
western portion has an average yearly rainfall of about 600 to 800 mm., while
the eastern section has from 800 to 1000 mm. of precipitation. The distribution

of crop land is conditioned by the location of the mines and industrial plants, areas of intensive urban settlement, topography, and forest. The industrial-urban zone along the Saar, Fischbach, and Sulzbach rivers is used only to a limited extent for agriculture, for less than 25 per cent of the land of this zone is devoted to crop cultivation. Nevertheless, some rye, wheat, oats, and fruit are grown here, but the major crop is potatoes, which are raised in the numerous small gardens of the miners and workers.

The best crop area is to be found in the central Saar area just north of the industrial zone, where over 40 per cent of the land is used for crops, with an-other 20 per cent used for pasture and the rest in forests and waste. The chief crops of this central area include rye, oats, and potatoes. Garden crops also play a considerable role in the rural economy. The main wheat areas of the Saar are located in the southern Saar and just to the west of Saarlouis, while the main areas for rye are situated in the western and northwestern parts of the basin. Fruit is grown mainly in the northwestern portion of the Saar along the Saar River and in the south central area. Livestock raising and dairying are comparatively important activities owing to the urban market demand. The major areas of good pasture and meadow are located in the northern and south-ern parts of the basin, which were once heavily forested. Cattle are raised in the northern hilly section, while swine are more common on the farms along the Saar, Fischbach, and Sulzbach rivers in the industrialized portion of the Saar-land.

Most of the hilly Saar Basin with its varied landscape of valleys and heights is devoted to grain and livestock. Three-field farming with the rotation of rye, oats, and potatoes is common throughout the area. Similar land is elsewhere given over to livestock raising, but here the demands of the workers of the towns and cities of the Saar have caused it to be devoted to potatoes, garden crops, and dairying. The dry, warm Saar Valley presents an interesting con-trast to the hilly agricultural land of the basin, for here the emphasis is upon the cultivation of fruit and grain. The wide Saar Valley, outside the industrial and urban areas, is a checkerboard of vineyards, orchards, and fields of grain and potatoes. The figures for land utilization (given below in hectares) indi-cate the amount and types of land available for agriculture.

Cultivated Land	71,300
Grain	33,900
Legumes	700
Root Crops	25,800
Green Vegetables	600
Industrial Crops	100
Fodder Crops	10,200

Small Gardens   4,200
Meadow and Pasture   37,700
Orchards   713
Vineyards   3

Nearly 60 per cent of the land area of the Saar Basin is given over to agrarian activities, with about 39 per cent of the land used for crop cultivation and 21 per cent for livestock raising and dairying. Of the remainder 30 per cent is forest land and 10 per cent is used for houses, industrial establishments, roads, and parks.

The Saar Basin, away from the valley of the Saar River, was once heavily forested, with broad-leafed oak growing in the lower areas and beech in the higher portions. Some of the land was cleared for temporary cultivation by burning. By 1800 much of the forest land had been depleted through cutting for wood which was used in making charcoal required by the ceramic and iron industries of the early modern Saar. The forests, although now relatively unimportant, have had the greatest long-run influence on the economy of the region. Since the beginning of the nineteenth century, there has been little reduction in the total amount of forest land. Extensive areas have been cleared to make way for the expansion of industrial-urban agglomerations and agriculture; the planting of spruce and pine has adequately compensated for losses in the industrial sections. The forest land is owned by a variety of interests. The state owns approximately 48 per cent of the forests, or 27,000 hectares, which is administered through ten state forest reserves. Another 30 per cent is held by county and municipal governments, while the remainder is owned by private interests.

The land is largely held in small farms of less than five hectares which are worked by Franconian peasants. A number of farms range in size from 5 to 20 hectares, but very few in excess of this size. The typical rural settlement is the small village with a population of between 200 and 600. Large enough to support a school, it is typically of the open *Haufendorf* type, consisting of houses containing the living quarters and barn arranged along two or three parallel streets or roads. In the western, southern, and eastern portions of the Saar Basin, the agglomerated *Mehrstrassendorf* with its intricate street pattern is most common. The houses are of the same type, though there is a marked difference in the style of peasant home architecture between the eastern and western parts of the basin. Most of the houses, except in the north and east, are built of stone. In the more heavily forested northern and eastern portions of the Saar, the brick and timber type of house is more common. In and near the industrial areas along the Saar, Fischbach, and Sulzbach rivers, urban architecture has strongly influenced rural construction.

Many of the villages of the mining areas have changed drastically under the impact of industrialization, for the old village is now surrounded by a belt of modern miners' houses. In the heart of the industrial zone, there are a number of villages built along modern lines without attention to traditional themes. The traditional folkways of the predominantly Protestant Franconian peasants have largely given way and survive only to a limited extent in the northern and eastern portions of the area. The people are highly musical and artistic, and in contrast with the peoples of northern and northeastern Germany, they are light-hearted and vivacious. They are not as militaristic as the Prussians, but they have a strong national loyalty and feeling, which was intensified by their exile from the Reich.

Urban Aspect

The industrialized urban area along the Saar and between the Fischbach and Sulzbach rivers, although surrounded by forests, fields, and small villages, is characterized by mines, slag heaps, factories, and urban settlement. The beginnings of the major cities and towns of the Saar go back to the early Middle Ages, when Saarbrücken was the cross-roads of trade between Lorraine and the Rhine, Flanders and Italy. During the later Middle Ages, Merzig, Lebach, St. Wendel, Ottweiler, and Saargemünd grew to importance as market towns, while Saarbrücken in western Saarland and Homburg and Blieskastel in the east were important fortifications and residence cities. The beginning of the seventeenth century marked the establishment of the glass industry in the Saar area, which in that day utilized local clays, flints, and ash obtained from the extensive woodland. The utilization of the limited iron ores, which have long since been exhausted, began in the seventeenth century and reached its height in the eighteenth. These pre-nineteenth century industrial developments were accompanied by a rapid increase in the settlement of the Saar, Fischbach, and Sulzbach river area. Over twenty "industrial-craft" villages were established in this region during the seventeenth and eighteenth centuries.

Although these developments had laid the foundations for the industrial urbanization of the Saar, the real growth of the urban agglomeration of the southern Saarland came in the nineteenth century with the opening of the Saar coal fields and the improvement of transportation resulting from the introduction of the railroad. Towns like Dillingen and Völklingen on the Saar River and Dudweiler, Sulzbach, Friedrichstal, St. Ingbert, Neunkirchen, and Wiebelskirchen in the Saarkohlen-Forest area developed from small agrarian towns with a limited amount of craft-industries into important coal mining or metallurgical centers with populations ranging between 20,000 and 30,000 inhabitants. Saarbrücken, the capital of the area, increased rapidly in size and population to become the major center of the basin with a population of over

129,000 inhabitants. In 1933 over 84 per cent of the population dwelt in the larger towns and cities of the Saar. Saarbrücken was the only Saar city which had the status of a city-county. Under the Nazis, municipal government and administration followed the national pattern laid down by the German Municipal Code of 1935.

The Saar Basin forms a part of the important Southwest German economic area which includes the Bavarian Palatinate, Baden, and Württemberg. Before World War I, the Saar was economically tied to the Rhine-Main Basin as well as the Southwest, furnishing these areas with coal and metal products. During the late nineteenth and the early twentieth centuries when Germany possessed the iron ores of Lorraine, an intimate association developed between Saar coal and Lorraine iron, which made possible the rapid expansion of the Saar iron and steel industry. This industrial development came after the exhaustion of the scanty local Saar iron ores and with the change from charcoal to coke. The traditionally important glass and ceramic industry coupled with less important industries such as chemicals, lumbering, leather, and textiles have long supplemented the coal mining and steel industries, giving the basin a well rounded industrial structure. The temporary internationalization of the Saar after World War I brought the complete re-orientation of the whole Saar economy toward France, although its old German markets still played a significant role. The return of the Saar to the Reich brought with it the problem of the re-absorption of the coal basin into the economy of Germany.

The reunion of the Saar raised several important economic problems, for the Saar had lost its easy access to Lorraine ores, and Lorraine was cut off from the needed Saar coal; in addition the Saar was now cut off from its extensive French coal market. Economically, the Saar would find many advantages through the maintenance of its relations with French Lorraine which had formed the basis of much of its development between 1871 and 1935. Although the Saar is culturally oriented toward Germany, its economic interests are tied to Lorraine. From the point of view of economic regionalism, the Saar Basin is a transitional border area, locked between eastern France and western Germany. After the Saar was united with the Reich, the Nazis joined it to the Palatinate to form the Saar-Palatinate Planning Association, because of the potential economic ties between these two adjacent areas. With the fall of France and the reconquest of Lorraine, the Nazis were able to restore, at least temporarily, the unity of the Saar-Lorraine area by the establishment of the national district of Westmark.

The major natural resource of the Saar is coal, which occurs in four major seams running in a southwest-northeasterly direction along the Fischbach and Sulzbach rivers. The most southern seam consists of fat coal, which lies too deep for mining by present techniques. The next two seams, lying to the north, are mined for steam and gas coal, while the northern seam yields coal of poor quality. The Saar coal, which has been mined for the past hundred and fifty years and intensively since 1871, has long been shipped to the coke plants of the Lorraine iron ore fields, which contain the most important iron deposits of Europe. Unfortunately the Saar coal does not make good coke and must be mixed with other coals, which come from the Ruhr, Aix-la-Chapelle, Belgium, Valenciennes (France), and even English fields. Its nearness to Lorraine, however, has led to its increasing use in the French furnaces.

The Saar coal is used extensively for the production of industrial and domestic gas and electricity. There are major gas-producing plants along the Saar and Fischbach rivers which furnish gas to Kaiserslautern, Mannheim, and Ludwigshafen by means of underground pipe lines. Branch lines service the greater portion of the Palatinate area. Saar coal is shipped to most of the small city gas works in the southern Rhine Province, the Palatinate, Baden, and Württemberg. The domestic coal supply of most of southwestern Germany comes from the Saar fields. The Saar coal also supports ten large coal electrical plants which are interconnected by a dense power network. High tension lines link the Saar electrical stations with Trèves, Koblenz, and the Ruhr, while another line running through Kaiserslautern, connects with the power stations at Mannheim, whence lines radiate to Stuttgart and southern Baden.

The metallurgical industries of the Saar began on the basis of local supplies of iron ore and the extensive forest reserves of the area, which made possible the cheap production of charcoal. The local iron industry goes back to the seventeenth and eighteenth centuries, when Saar iron products were exported to all parts of Central Europe. With the exhaustion of local iron ores and the conversion from charcoal to coke in the middle eighteenth century, the iron industries, which were established at Dillingen, Völklingen, Saarbrücken, and Neunkirchen in the course of the nineteenth century, produced Thomas steel on the basis of Lorraine ores. After World War I and the loss of Lorraine, the German-owned mills of the Saar, facing increased prices for Lorraine ores, turned to the production of Martin steel, which is made from scrap. Although the French had hoped to curb competition of the German-owned Saar steel mills by increasing the price of Lorraine ore, the Saar iron industry managed to adjust itself to this artificial situation by turning to quality products which enabled it to establish a considerable market in Germany. The advent of Nazi control resulted in further orientation of the Saar iron industry toward the Reich.

The glass industry is the second traditional enterprise of the Saar Basin. The glass factories of modern Saarlouis, Völklingen, Saarbrücken, Merzig, and St. Ingbert now depend upon clays and flints imported from the Rhineland, France, England, and Sweden. Although the industrial life of the Saar Basin began with the glass and iron industries, which were based upon local supplies of ore, clay, and charcoal, today, these resources are exhausted or have been replaced by others, such as coal and iron ore imported from Lorraine. They did, however, make possible much of the Saar's industrial development, since they tended to localize industry in the basin and created a pool of initial manpower for the exploitation of coal and iron. The local production of gas and coke in the Saar has led to the development of a sizable local chemical industry at Merzig, Saarlouis, Saarwellingen, Saarbrücken, and Ottweiler, while the iron from the blast furnaces of the Saar is absorbed to a considerable extent by local steel mills and metal fabrication plants, which are located at Dillingen, Völklingen, Saarbrücken, St. Ingbert, Rohrbach, and Homburg. During the last two decades the metallurgical industries of the basin have placed increasing emphasis on machinery and construction steel.

The other industries of the Saarland are of secondary importance. They include several pottery, leather, and textile plants that are located in towns surrounding the Saarkohlen-Forest. It must be noted that the core of the Saar industrial area lies at Saarbrücken. The coal mining district extends northeastward and southwestward in a broad zone lying just north of this city. The important heavy industrial centers of Merzig, Dillingen, and Völklingen are situated downstream on the Saar River from Saarbrücken, while the smaller industrial towns of St. Ingbert and Neunkirchen are located northeastward from Saarbrücken and to the south of the coal fields. Saarbrücken is, therefore, not only the administrative and governmental capital, but also the natural center of Saar industry and transportation.

The origins of the modern transportation pattern go back to pre-Roman times when a Keltic salt route from Lorraine crossed the Saar at Saarbrücken and continued eastward to the Rhineland. During the Roman period it became an important military highway. Medieval Saarbrücken was the junction of trade routes connecting the Rhine and Lorraine, and Flanders and the Vosges area. Today the Saar Basin is served by an adequate road and rail network, which is supplemented by a moderately good canal system.

The modern road system of the Saar centers upon the city of Saarbrücken, whence roads radiate eastward to Mannheim via Homburg and Kaiserslautern, northeastward to Neunkirchen and St. Wendel, via the mining area, and northwestward along the Saar River to Trèves via Völklingen, Saarlouis, Dillingen, and Merzig. The construction and maintenance work on these major roads was under the Saarland Road Construction Office, while the local county roads were under the county administrations. Under the Nazis a Mannheim-Kaiserslautern-Saarbrücken super-highway was built to supplement the previous road system.

The major rail lines of the Saar Basin follow the same routes as the major roads. One runs from Metz in Lorraine via Saarbrücken and Neunkirchen to

Bingerbrück and Frankfort in the Rhine area, while other rail lines connect with Trèves and Mannheim. These major lines, which were constructed during the fifties and sixties of the last century, have been supplemented by numerous east-west lines linking the Saar coal fields with the Rhine and the Palatinate and the iron ore fields of Lorraine. The railroads of the Saar were under the National Railroad Directorate of Saarbrücken, which also served the southwestern corner of the Rhine Province. In addition to this central office, Saarbrücken had an Operations Office, a Traffic Office (*Verkehrsamt*), and a Machine Shop (*Maschinenamt*).

The water transportation facilities of the Saar are not adequate. Before World War I, the Saar's trade in coal and iron ore was oriented toward Lorraine. The traffic problem was met in that day through the canalization of the Lorraine sections of the Saar and Mosel rivers, which connect with the Rhine-Marne canal running from Strassburg to the Paris Basin. This round-about waterway gives Saar coal access to the Rhine and to the ore fields of Lorraine, but these canals, which were built during the nineteenth century, are shallow and inadequate. The French have long proposed a Mosel-Saar canal as a solution, while the Germans have desired a Saar-Rhine canal. This would improve the Saar outlet to the South German market, which has fallen to a considerable extent under the influence of the Ruhr coal area. The canal problem will certainly be present in the reconstruction period which lies ahead. The Saar area was served by one major national airport at Saarbrücken which provided connections with Mannheim, Frankfort, and Cologne.

The Saar has occupied an excellent commercial position since early modern times when it was at the crossroads of trade between the Rhineland and Lorraine and between Flanders and Italy. During this period iron, glass, and lampblack were traded in Flanders for fish and cloth. Today coal is the basis of commerce. Before World War I, Germany took about 60 per cent of the exported coal, while France received only 6 per cent. German Alsace-Lorraine absorbed another 18 per cent, while Italy and Switzerland took the remaining 16 per cent. Within Germany most of the coal was shipped to the Rhine-Main and South German areas, where it was used for railroads, Rhine town gasworks, and domestic heating. In terms of the total prewar production, about two-thirds of the coal was exported. The World War and the internationalization of the Saar brought a complete reorientation of the coal trade, for the amount of exported coal shipped to France increased to 45 per cent, while the German trade dropped to 16 per cent. Aside from the artificial restrictions set up by the French, the increasing use of lignite and the growing importance of Aix-la-Chapelle coal in Germany tended to drive the Saar coal out of its traditional coal markets in the Hessian and Main areas. In the field of iron and glass commerce, the shift was not great, for after World War I, although the Saar gained some markets in France, there was only a minor reduction in the German market.

The reunion of the Saar with the Reich brought a restoration of the trade and commercial relations which had prevailed before World War I. Today, in terms of freight traffic carried by rail, iron products and coal are the major commodities produced in the Saar and shipped to adjacent parts of the Reich, while Lorraine iron ore, Ruhr coal for coke mixtures, clays and flints for ceramics, and food products are shipped in from adjacent areas. The commerce of the Saar faces several distinct handicaps, for it is not close to either the Paris or the Frankfort markets and lacks good water transportation. Any settlement of the Saar economic problem must recognize the unique juxtaposition of Lorraine ore and Saar coal and it must attempt to bring about a restoration of both the French and German markets. The Saar is bound to occupy a key position in the future economic relations between France and Germany.

The banking and credit institutions of the Saarland ranged from branches of the great commercial banks in Berlin, which were mainly interested in investments of the industrial type, to the local municipal savings banks. The *Reichsbank,* which served as the banker's bank for Germany, handling Reich payments and receipts, placing of issues, credit, and controlling money and the capital markets, had a branch office at Saarbrücken.

The population of the Saarland was largely engaged in industry and crafts. The large urbanized population was occupationally divided as follows: in 1935 industry and crafts 53 per cent, trade and transportation 18 per cent, agriculture and forestry 7 per cent, public and professional service 6 per cent, servants 6 per cent, and occupationless 13 per cent. The Saar had the largest industrial and craft group in the Reich. On the other hand, the upper class and their dependents, which accounted for about 14 per cent of the population, was the smallest in the Reich: a class distribution to be expected in an industrial area where the enterprises were owned and operated by large corporations. The white collar group, which handled the affairs of the large industries, was quite small, accounting for only 9 per cent of the population. The laboring class was large, constituting 52 per cent of the population. The civil service group was about average for the Reich, accounting for about 5 per cent of the population.

The Saarland is essentially urban, with 84 per cent of the population dwelling in the cities. It is concentrated along the Saar, Fischbach, and Sulzbach rivers near the mines and factories. A surprisingly large number of workers, however, live in the outer margins of the Saar industrial area, commuting to work each day. Industrial workers constituted 50 to 65 per cent of the population in most of the eastern and northern portions of the Saar. Essentially rural areas are limited to the northeastern and northwestern corners of the basin. This pattern of settlement and the interrelation of industrial occupation and rural life has given the Saar its particular character. It is predominantly an area of workers with rural ways of living in an environment in which the factories and mines are largely hidden by the fields and forests of rolling Saar landscape.

The larger cities and towns of the Saar are unpleasantly industrial. Saarbrücken, which has long been the political and administrative focus of the area as well as the major commercial and industrial center, is oriented about its Old City on the Saar River. Its greatest development came in the late nineteenth and early twentieth centuries, when it spread westward along the Saar River and penetrated into the surrounding forests. The towns of Dillingen, Dudweiler, Friedrichstal, Wiebelskirchen, Sulzbach, and Neunkirchen are industrial centers, built about the core of a medieval village which has been modernized to form the business and commercial section of the town. Merzig in the northwest and Ottweiler and St. Wendel in the northeast still retain their position as market towns. Aside from Saarbrücken, only the towns of Homburg and Blieskastel in the eastern Saar were originally residence cities. The population of these Saarland cities cannot be regarded as a rootless proletariat, for most of the people of the cities are natives of the Saar or the adjoining Rhenish areas.

BIBLIOGRAPHY

Calker, W. van *Das Staatsrecht des Grossherzogtums Hessen* (Tübingen, 1913).

Capot-Rey *La region industrielle sarroise* (Paris, 1934).

Florinsky, M. T. *The Saar Struggle* (New York, 1934).

Follmann, O. *Die Eifel* (Bielefeld & Leipzig, 1912).

Fox, N. *Saarländische Volkskunde* (Bonn, 1927).

Geschichtlicher Atlas der Rheinprovinz (Bonn, 1894).

Geschichtlicher Atlas der Rheinprovinz (Bonn, 1894-1923).

Guyot, Y. *La Province rhénane et la Westphalie;* étude économique (Paris, 1915).

Hanson, J. *Preussen und Rheinland um 1815-1915* (Bonn, 1918).

Hardenburg, B. von. *Hessenland* (Bielefeld & Leipzig, 1934).

Kerp, H. *Am Rhein* (Bielefeld & Leipzig, 1912).

Kerp, H. *Die Rheinprovinz* (Berlin, 1911).

Kuske, B. *Die Volkswirtschaft des Rheinlandes in ihrer Eigenart und Bedeutung* (Essen, 1925).

Mackinder, Sir H. J. *The Rhine* (New York, 1908).

Mielert, F. *Westfalen* (Bielefeld & Leipzig, 1925).

Mielert, F. *Westfalen,* 2d ed. (Bielefeld & Leipzig, 1925).

Most, O., Kuske, B. and Weber, H. *Wirtschaftskunde für Rheinland und Westfalen,* 2 vols. (Berlin, 1931).

Osborne, S. *The Saar Question* (London, 1923).

Overbeck, H. & Sante, G. W. (ed.) *Saar-Atlas* (Gotha, 1934).

Pollock, James K. "The Saar Plebiscite" in *American Political Science Review,* Vol. 29, No. 2, pp. 275-282 (1935).

Preuss, V. "Die Volksabstimmung im Saargebiet," in *Beiträge zum ausländischen öffentlichen Recht und Völkerrecht,* vol. 22 (Berlin, 1934).

Reinhard, R. and Voppel *Land und Volk an der Saar* (Breslau, 1934).

Royal Institute of International Affairs, *The Saar Problem,* 4th rev. ed. (London, 1934).

Russell, F. M. *The International Government of the Saar* (Berkeley, University of California Press, 1926).

Schrepfer, H. *Der Nordwesten, Landeskunde von Deutschland* (Leipzig, 1935).

Spethmann, H. *Die Grosswirtschaft an der Ruhr* (Breslau, 1925).

Stephanblome, J. *Die Provinz Westfalen* (Berlin, 1912).

Techter, W. *Die Provinz Hessen-Nassau* (Berlin, 1914).

Truck, V. *Das Verwaltungs- und Verfassungsrecht des Grossherzogtums Hessen* (Darmstadt, 1874).

Wambaugh, S. *The Saar Plebiscite* (Harvard University Press, 1940).

Chapter 22

INTRODUCTION TO
CENTRAL GERMANY

The Central German region, consisting of the Prussian province of Saxony and the states of Anhalt, Saxony, and Thuringia, occupies the heart of the Reich. It is dominated by the fertile plains of the loess border area, extending along the Elbe-Saale Valley from Magdeburg to Leipzig. This fertile loess area, which enjoys a dry, warm climate, is agriculturally important for the production of sugar beets, wheat, and barley and the raising of livestock. Its lignite and salt deposits have made possible the industrial development of the modern cities of Magdeburg, Halle, Merseburg, and Leipzig. The northern part of the Central German area, which is known as Altmark, forms a part of the plains of northern Germany. Its sandy glacial soils, coupled with a dry-warm climate, make it an ideal region for the cultivation of rye and potatoes. It must be regarded as an integral part of the East Elbian plain, although its economic orientation is toward the Central German city of Magdeburg. While the northern portion of Central Germany gives way to the North German Plain, the central core of plains is bordered by the Hessian, Thuringian, and Saxon hills on the west and south, while the Fläming upland divides the lands along the Elbe and Saale from the ancient river valleys and moraines of Brandenburg. To the west the rolling country rises rapidly into the ancient Harz massif, while to the southwest, the hilly lands of the Thuringian Basin, where lie the small cities of Erfurt, Weimar, and Jena, rise into the Thuringian Forest. To the east are the manufacturing cities of Plauen, Zwickau, and Chemnitz, and the capital city of Dresden, beyond which rises the Ore Mountains, which separate Central Germany from Czechoslovakia.

Central Germany is occupied by peoples whose ancestors first settled on the fertile plains lying along the Elbe during the first millennium before our era. They drove out the earlier Keltic population, which had settled on the rich

478

loess soils of the border area at the end of the Neolithic period. Toward the end of the Roman Empire, the strong Thuringian tribe held control over the lands between the Weser and Elbe. During the sixth century, however, the Thuringian tribal state was destroyed, for they lost the area to the east of the Elbe-Saale line to the westward moving Slavs; the Low Saxon tribes conquered the Altmark region, while the rest of their tribal holdings were conquered by the Merovingian leaders of the Franks. After the Carolingian era, the Thuringians, reinforced by peoples from western Germany, pushed eastward to occupy and settle the lands lying beyond the Elbe and Saale rivers. They intermarried with the Slavic pastoralists, and evolved to form the Upper Saxon stock of the medieval and modern state of Saxony and the southeastern part of the Prussian Province of Saxony.

The northern part of the Province of Saxony, embracing the Magdeburg and Altmark areas, remained in the hands of the Low Saxons, while the Thuringians retained control of their ancient homeland, the Thuringian Basin. These three groups, the Slavs, the Low Saxons, and the Thuringians, which are differentiated by contrasting speech, folkways, customs, and usages, have tended to coalesce in modern times. From the point of view of race, the peoples of Central Germany are also highly mixed, consisting of a blend of Alpine, Nordic, and Mediterranean stocks. But the economic unification of Central Germany during the past hundred years has tended to eliminate the particularistic ways of the Central German peoples. Although the dialects and folkways survive in many of the backward rural areas, the towns and cities share a common German language and culture.

The political history of Central Germany begins with the tribal kingdom of the Thuringians, which was inherited by the Franks and Low Saxons in the course of the sixth century. By the beginning of the ninth century all of Central Germany, lying to the west of the Elbe-Saale line, was under the control of Charlemagne. After the collapse of Carolingian power, the old tribal leaders of Low Saxony and Thuringia regained control and under the Saxon Emperors, the lands beyond the Elbe-Saale river line were brought under German control and organized as the *Thüringer Mark*. These political divisions held until Hohenstaufen times when the Central German area was ruled by the Landgraves of Thuringia, and the Margraves of Landsberg and Meissen. The Altmark area had been annexed by the new Margraviate of Brandenburg.

The destruction of the medieval Empire of the Germans, which came after the fall of the Hohenstaufen dynasty, resulted in several new territorial arrangements. During the fourteenth and fifteenth centuries, the Wettin family gained control of most of the southern upland area: the Landgraviate of Thuringia, the Margraviate of Meissen, and the Electorate of Saxony. The lands along the

Elbe and the Saale had fallen under the powerful archbishops of Magdeburg, while the princes of Anhalt obtained a small group of scattered territories at the junction of the Saale and Elbe. Altmark was already under the firm rule of the electors of Brandenburg. Only the cities of Nordhausen and Mühlhausen had managed to gain the status of free and imperial cities. It is important to note that the stage was set for the modern struggle for the lands along the Elbe-Saale rivers, for the Wettin and Hohenzollern families were already entrenched in Central Germany.

The Reformation brought the first retraction in the Wettin territories. The Duchy of Saxony, which embraced most of what is now Thuringia, fell to the Ernestiner line of the Wettins, while the small feudal states of Henneberg, Reuss, and Erfurt managed to strengthen their position. The Thirty Years' War brought further changes. The Wettin rulers of the Albertiner line, who were now the electors of Saxony, expanded their territorial holdings through the acquisition of Habsburg Ober- und Nieder-Lausitz and Vogtland. After the Peace of Westphalia (1648), the Hohenzollern electors of Brandenburg acquired the lands of the archbishops of Magdeburg. On the eve of the French Revolution, Central Germany was under the rule of the electors of Saxony, the electors of Brandenburg, the princes of Anhalt, and the now numerous Saxon dukes of Thuringia.

The Napoleonic era brought about the next basic territorial changes in Central Germany. The petty states of Thuringia, and the electors of Saxony, who received the rank of king owing to their cooperation with the Napoleonic cause, continued to rule in the southern part of the area. The north continued under the princes of Anhalt and Preussen until the formation of the ephemeral Kingdom of Westphalia, which absorbed all of the Prussian holdings situated to the west of the Elbe River. The Treaty of Vienna (1815) defined the modern territorial configuration of Central Germany. The state of Saxony lost all of its holdings in the Torgau, Merseburg, and Naumburg areas to Prussia for its aid to Napoleon. These territories were combined with the Prussian holdings near Nordhausen, Halle, Magdeburg, and Stendal to form the modern Province of Saxony. The territories of the numerous Thuringian states and the state of Anhalt remained intact, as did the boundaries of the modern states of Thuringia, Anhalt, and Saxony and the Prussian Province of Saxony, except for a few minor changes such as that involved in the cession of the Koburg area of Thuringia to Bavaria in 1920 and the exchange of inclaves and exclaves between the Province of Saxony, the state of Anhalt, and the state of Brunswick.

While the political division of the Central German area was settled at Vienna in 1815, the economic, social, and cultural unity of the lands along the Elbe and Saale developed during the nineteenth century industrial revolution. The old market towns of Magdeburg, Halle, Erfurt, Gotha, Leipzig, and Chemnitz, which had been important craft and trading centers since the medieval era, evolved into important centers of modern industry and commerce. This development was accompanied by the evolution of an integrated transportation network which gave the area a closely knit economic unity.

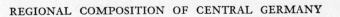

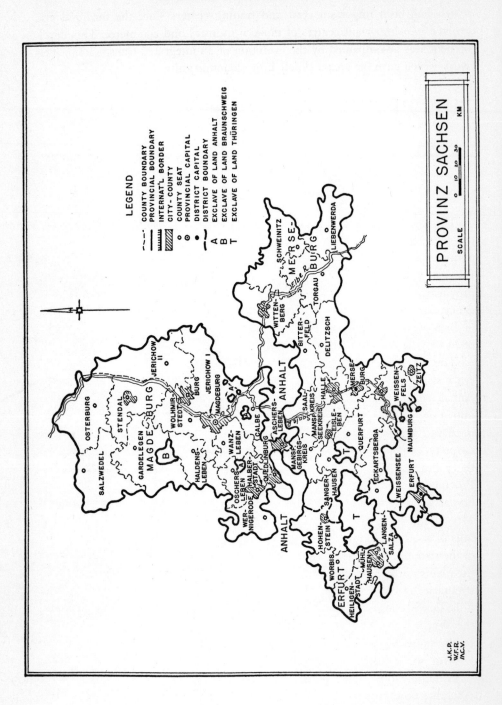

Chapter 23

THE PROVINCE OF SAXONY*

The Prussian Province of Saxony constitutes the northern section of Central Germany. Formed through the cession of the northern part of the Kingdom of Saxony and other lands to Prussia in 1815, it is bounded by the Prussian Province of Brandenburg, the states of Thuringia and Saxony, and the Prussian provinces of Hesse-Nassau and Hanover and the state of Brunswick. Its territory surrounds small territorial exclaves of the state of Thuringia, the state of Brunswick, and the state of Anhalt, while various exclaves of the Province of Saxony lie embedded in the territory of the state of Thuringia.

The northern district of Magdeburg, whose only connection with the southern districts of the province is a small corridor separating the main portion of Anhalt from its largest exclave in the Province of Saxony, can be subdivided into several minor landscape areas. The northern portion, known as Altmark, is characterized by ancient glacial moraines, waterways, and heaths like the *Letzlinger Heide*. The western part of the district of Magdeburg gives way to the valley of the Aller which is transitional to the *Lüneburger* heath of the Province of Hanover. Southward from the glaciated plains area lies the rich border zone beyond which lie the northern foothills of the Harz Mountains. Merseburg, the southeastern district, is bordered on the north by the Fläming hills of southern Brandenburg, on the south by the plains of the northern part of the state of Saxony and the rolling hills of the Thuringian Basin. To the west the plains of the Merseburg district, which are drained by the Saale and Mulde, tributaries of the Elbe, give way to the uplands of the district of Erfurt. The hilly southwestern district of Erfurt is located between the Thuringian Basin, the Werra River, and the southern foothills of the Harz Mountains and is a rough upland area through which run the unusually fertile valleys of the Unstrut and *Goldene (Aue)* plains.

Although most of the province has been settled by agrarian peoples since Neolithic times, the Germans did not reach the middle Elbe area until the sec-

---

* German spelling—Provinz Sachsen.

ond half of the first millennium B.C. During the Germanic migration period, following the southeastward movements of the Vandals and Goths, pastoral Slavic peoples pushed westward to the Elbe-Saale river line. The western portion of the Province of Saxony was settled in the first centuries of our era by Low Saxon folk, who occupied the northern district of Magdeburg, and by Thuringians, who took over the area of the two southern districts. After the Carolingian period, these two peoples pushed eastward across the Elbe and Saale to colonize East Elbian Germany. Most of the Province of Saxony east of the Elbe-Saale line was in the hands of the Low Saxon and Thuringian colonists by the eleventh century. During the Middle Ages they formed the two main dialect groups which distinguish the modern peasants of north and south province of Saxony. It should be noted that the Thuringians, reinforced by peoples from Western Germany, slowly differentiated and evolved into the mixed Upper Saxons of our day. Standard German, however, is spoken in most towns and cities and is becoming increasingly common in the rural areas. The province is predominantly Protestant. In 1933 there were 3,001,000 Lutheran Protestants, and 251,000 Roman Catholics. The latter religious group is widely scattered throughout the province. The Jewish population was extremely small, numbering about 7,146 in 1933.

In that year the Province of Saxony ranked seventh in size and population among the provinces and states of the German Reich. Its population numbered 3,400,600 with a density of 133 individuals per sq. km. Excluding the Hansa cities and Berlin, the Province of Saxony was the eleventh most densely settled territorial unit in Germany. This population did not have a uniform spatial distribution. The most heavily settled areas were located in the border zone extending west of Magdeburg, and in the region of Halle and Merseburg along the river Saale, where the average density exceeded 200 per sq. km. The whole plains area bordering the Elbe and Saale in the northern and southeast districts had a density of 100 to 200 per sq. km. Even the uplands of the district of Erfurt, which had a density of 75 to 100, were relatively heavily settled in comparison with similar areas of the Reich. The only sparsely settled areas were located in the foothills of the Harz, which protrude into Saxon territory. The Province of Saxony had long been one of the more heavily settled areas of the Reich. In the last century and a half, the population has steadily increased, although its greatest period of expansion came between 1870 and 1910 and was due to the rapid industrialization of this part of Germany in the late nineteenth century. Between 1875 and 1925 the population of the eastern section of the province increased by almost 75 per cent, while that of the more hilly western areas increased by only 25 per cent. More recently population movement has been very feeble, for during the period 1933 to 1939 the percentage of population increase was but 0.2 per cent. Population migration in terms of immigration overseas was hardly a factor in the region. In comparison with southern or northwestern Germany very few individuals left the province for lands outside the Reich. There has been, on the other hand, a moderate movement of peoples into the province from the agrarian areas of Prussia east of the Elbe.

The Province of Saxony has been a Prussian territory since 1815 when it was created through the amalgamation of the northern half of the Kingdom of Saxony, old Prussian Altmark, the territory of Magdeburg, the principality of Halberstadt, and lands belonging to the old electorate of Mentz. The political history of this area goes back for several centuries. Although it was a part of the tribal kingdom of the Thuringians during the fifth century, and later a frontier district in the Empire of Charlemagne, its history as a part of the German state began in the period of the Saxon Dynasty of the eleventh and twelfth centuries when it was divided between the Duchy of Saxony of northwest Germany, Thuringia, and the Thuringian Mark. After the Hohenstaufen period of the thirteenth century, when Germany disintegrated into a loose feudal federation, this area broke up into a number of states and principalities. Altmark, which forms the northern part of the district of Magdeburg, was by this time already a constituent part of the ancient Margraviate of Brandenburg; Magdeburg, which had been an archbishopric since 967, gained independent status. The southeastern portion of the district of Magdeburg was ruled in medieval times by the bishops of Halberstadt; the southern part of the modern province was held by several rulers. The Archbishop of Magdeburg owned a strip of territory along the Saale, while Erfurt was in the hands of the Elector of Mainz. The remainder of the area was largely under the Wettin family, who were to become the electors of Saxony. This territorial arrangement survived until the conclusion of the Thirty Years' War. At the Treaty of Westphalia (1648) the bishopric of Halberstadt was secularized and ceded to the electorate of Brandenburg, while the archbishopric of Magdeburg, which was also secularized, was not annexed by Prussian Brandenburg and the Hohenzollerns until 1680. The territory of Magdeburg on the Saale was likewise ceded to the Elector of Brandenburg.

By the eve of the French Revolution all of what is now the Province of Saxony was held by Brandenburg and Saxony except for the free and imperial cities of Nordhausen and Mühlhausen. During the Napoleonic period, all of Prussia's holdings in the Province of Saxony west of the river Elbe were incorporated into the short-lived Kingdom of Westphalia which had its capital at Erfurt in the heart of the old territory of the Elector and Archbishop of Mainz. This territory, which had been given to Prussia by the Napoleonic settlement of 1803, was returned to Prussia in 1815. At the Treaty of Vienna (1815), Prussia was given the Saxon holdings in the Province of Saxony area because of the alliance of Saxony (elevated from an electorate to a kingdom by Napoleon in 1806) with the French throughout the Napoleonic period. The Saxon holdings were combined with the older Prussian holdings along the Elbe to form the Province of Saxony. In point of fact the southern portion of the old electorate, which now forms the state of Saxony, escaped Prussian rule only through the support of Prussia's rival, Austria. After 1815 the history of the Province of Saxony merges with the history of Prussia. The provincial administration was first established by the Provincial Constitutions of 1815 and 1826. Under the Empire, the Provincial Constitutions of 1875/1881 established a greater degree of self-government. The Weimar Republic laws accomplished a further liberalization of provincial government and administration.

The administration of the Province of Saxony followed the regular pattern of Prussian administration and was headed by a Chief President who resided in the city of Magdeburg. He was vested with broad political and supervisory control of administrative, social, economic, and cultural activities, although much of the actual administration was carried out by the District Presidents of the administrative districts of Magdeburg, Merseburg, and Erfurt.

The Nazis subdivided the Province of Saxony into two new provinces, the Province of Magdeburg (administrative district of Magdeburg) and the Province of Halle-Merseburg (administrative districts of Merseburg and Erfurt).

The work of the provincial administration of Saxony was supplemented by special and technical services under direct national control. During the imperial period, the Prussian administered courts, railways, and mining offices and the nationally operated postal system lay outside the scope of general provincial administration. Judicial matters, which were administered by the Prussian Ministry of Justice, were under the Superior State Court at Naumburg and the Collegiate Courts of First and Second Instance of Erfurt, Halberstadt, Halle, Magdeburg, Naumburg, Nordhausen, Stendal, and Torgau. The courts of the counties of Schleusingen and Ziegenrück were transferred to the Superior State Court at Jena after 1933. The national postal system within the Province of Saxony was under the Chief Postal Directorates (Empire) or National Postal Directorates (Republic and Third Reich) of Erfurt, Magdeburg, and Leipzig. National regulations for trade and industry, weights and measures, social insurance, welfare, public health, and the collection of imperial revenues were administered upon delegation from the Reich.

Under the Republic direct national administration was extended to finance, railways, unemployment insurance and employment, and labor welfare. Within Saxony national control of finances was carried out by the State Finance Office of Magdeburg and its local finance offices and main customs offices. National Construction offices were located at Erfurt, Halle, and Magdeburg. The National Railroad Directors of Erfurt, Halle, and Hanover operated the national railways. Labor and unemployment problems were handled, as usual, by a State

Labor Office for Central Germany (Erfurt) and the main Welfare Office for Central Germany (Magdeburg). Some features of welfare, social insurance, health, trade and industry, and labor, which were subject to national regulation, were administered upon delegation from the Reich. As to economic life, it was organized under a number of national agricultural, industrial, commercial, and labor organizations.

Under the Empire the Province of Saxony was a strong Social Democratic area. The industrial and manufacturing areas along the Elbe and Saale voted for the Social Democratic party, while the northern agrarian area of Altmark gave its support to the Conservative party and the National Liberals. The hilly Erfurt area was heterogeneous in its political outlook supporting the Catholic Center, National Liberal, Conservative, and Liberal Progressive parties. The National Liberals and the Liberal Progressives also had some support in the eastern part of the district of Merseburg. Under the Republic, the province also cast its votes for several parties, but without giving an outstanding lead to any one of them. The Social Democrats came first in the order of voters' preference; the German National People's party was second; the Communist third, and the German People's party fourth.

With the rise of the National Socialists in 1930, the second place was taken by them. Not until the July 1932 *Reichstag* election, however, did the Nazis assume first place in the order of political parties. In that election their vote exceeded the combined vote of the Socialists and Communists, but due to a strong Nationalist vote, the Nazis did not get a majority of all the votes. In the November 1932 election, the Nazi vote dropped, but the party remained the strongest single party in the province. The Nationalists, quite significantly, still secured over 200,000 votes in the province in this election. In the presidential elections of 1932, Hindenburg carried the province against Hitler, but he did not receive a majority because a substantial vote was cast for both the National-Socialist and the Communist candidates for President. Of the three administrative districts in the Province, the district of Merseburg always cast a sizable Communist vote, and the district of Magdeburg always gave strong support to the Social Democrats. Zeitz was a strong Socialist city, and in Halle, Erfurt, and *Saalkreis* the Communists were strong. The county of Salzwedel was a Nationalist center which finally went over to the Nazis. The counties of Heiligenstadt and Worbis in the district of Erfurt regularly voted for the Catholic Center party. Other cities such as Naumburg, Quedlingburg, Halberstadt, Stendal, and Eisleben gave strong support to the Nazis throughout the critical period in their rise to power. The city county of Magdeburg favored the Social Democrats. The northern counties in the province were, in general, Nationalist and Nazi.

The Province of Saxony was organized under the Nazi party districts of

Magdeburg-Anhalt (Dessau), Halle-Merseburg (Halle), and Thuringia (Weimar). Within these party districts the multifarious Nazi organizations spread out in every functional way and controlled individuals and groups minutely and completely. National administrative controls were extended at the expense of state and local administration through general, specific, and corporate administrations.

RURAL ASPECT

The soil of the Middle Elbian portions of the Province of Saxony has long been exploited by the peasant. The wooded uplands of the western part of the province, however, were not extensively cultivated until the Middle Ages, when German peasants began to clear them for agrarian activities. Although industry and manufacturing are the major interests of the modern Province of Saxony, over 21 per cent of the population is engaged in agriculture and forestry. Taking the province as a whole, a surprisingly large proportion of the population still lives in small villages close to the soil. In 1933 about 38 per cent of the population lived in villages with a population of less than 2,000, while 30 per cent lived in towns ranging in size from 2,000 to 20,000. While agricultural activity is common throughout the province, in comparison with other economic activities, agriculture and related rural activities are more extensive in the district of Magdeburg than in the two southern districts of Merseburg and Erfurt, where industry and manufacturing are the dominant activities. The general administration of the Province of Saxony centered in the city of Magdeburg, the provincial capital, and in the three district capitals—Magdeburg, Merseburg, and Erfurt. The day-to-day administration of rural Saxony was carried on in the thirty-six counties into which the administrative districts are divided. These counties were headed by County Managers who served both as agents of central government and of local self-government. County administration and self-government were regulated by the County Constitutions of 1825, 1872/1881, which were later modified by the liberal laws of the Republic and by the reactionary laws of the Third Reich. Under the Nazis, each village or town administration of the county followed the national pattern laid down by the German Municipal Code of 1935. Village and town self-government were once important. The villages were governed under the Constitution for Rural Villages and Towns of 1872 and the liberal laws of the Weimar Republic.

Saxony is the most fertile of the Prussian provinces. The plains of the districts of Magdeburg and Merseburg along the Middle Elbe contain the famous Magdeburger border loess zone of rich fertile chernozem (dark brown to black) soils extending from Halle and Leipzig northward to Magdeburg and the area adjoining the northern foothills of the Harz. This rich agricultural zone, which enjoys warm, dry summers with an average summer temperature of over 16 degrees C. and an average summer rainfall of less than 275 mm., is important for wheat, barley, and sugar beets. Livestock raising has been developed through the utilization of beet-waste, while dairying has become important near the larger manufacturing centers. The farms of the loess area tend to be large, averaging over 100 hectares in size. There are a few widely scattered large estates, once manors. This region is one of the few in Germany where agriculture is almost universally mechanized, but the large numbers of day laborers required at harvest time constitute an important rural labor problem. Northward, the rich loess area with its profitable agriculture gives way to the sandy glaciated plains of Altmark, while eastward from the Elbe in the district of Merseburg infertile sandy soils again replace the rich chernozem of the border area. Although the valley of the Middle Elbe, which runs through or borders this eastern and northern portion of the province, is given over to livestock raising and dairying, supported by the rich valley meadows and pastures; away from the valley the infertile soils support a typical East Elbian agriculture.

The northern Altmark and the southeastern Merseburg area, which enjoys somewhat cooler and moister summers than the border area, is dominated by rust-colored forest soils. The major crops are rye and potatoes. The farms of this poorer agricultural area, where crop yields are scanty in comparison with those of the loess zone, are smaller, ranging from 20 to 100 hectares in size. The western part of the Province of Saxony is dominated by the foothills of the Harz Mountains and the uplands and fertile valleys of the district of Erfurt. While the higher portions of western Saxony enjoy cool moist summers with an average summer rainfall of over 400 mm. and an average summer temperature of about 14 decrees C., drier warmer conditions set in as one approaches the loess zone to the east. The mixed sandy loams and clay soils of this area support crops of oats, rye, potatoes, and forage crops. Flax, hops, oilseeds, and fruit are also important crops in the foothills of the Harz and in the valleys of the Unstrut and the *Goldene (Aue)* plains. Market gardening is important near the larger towns like Erfurt and Quedlinburg. In the higher areas livestock raising, dairying, and subsistence crop cultivation are more characteristic. This is an area belonging to the small independent peasant.

The greater part of the Province of Saxony forms a part of the real tillage zone of the Reich. The rich Middle Elbe loess zone produces one of the largest sugar beet crops in Germany. It is also important for surpluses of wheat and rye. The province as a whole, however, is not self-sufficient in potatoes, oats, or barley, and it is dependent upon other areas of the Reich for livestock needs. The diversified crops of the western upland area are not sufficient to produce surpluses for other parts of the Reich. The figures for land utilization (given below in hectares) indicate the amount and type of land available for agriculture.

Cultivated Land		1,416,900
Grain	847,100	
Legumes	32,900	
Root Crops	398,300	
Green Vegetables	17,100	
Industrial Crops	9,900	
Fodder Crops	111,600	
Small Gardens		31,200
Meadow		179,000
Pasture		77,700
Orchards		9,000
Vineyards		260
Forests		576,300
Waste Land		48,000
Houses and Barns		47,400
Roads and Parks		145,400

Agrarian activity utilized about 68 per cent of the land of the province, with 57 per cent devoted to crop cultivation and 11 per cent to pastoral activities. The remaining land was divided between forests (22 per cent) and waste land (10 per cent).

The forests of the Province of Saxony are comparatively small in comparison with those of other provinces and states of the Reich. The loess zone of the Middle Elbe is an open almost treeless area where the forest cover ranges between 4 and 12 per cent of the area. Northern Altmark has a few scattered forests made up of north German pine, which occupy about 16 per cent of the area, while the eastern Merseburg district, also characterized by growths of north German pine, has a slightly heavier cover occupying from 31 to 39 per cent of the area. The uplands of the district of Erfurt, which were relatively heavily forested in the early Middle Ages, still have a relatively good woodland cover (29 to 37 per cent of the area) of beech of the west German type that give way northwards to the heavy Hercynian (Central German) spruce, fir, and beech forests of the Harz foothills and the alpine spruce of the Harz Mountains. The land was owned by a variety of interests. The state owned about 191,500 hectares or about 33 per cent of the total. There were 44 state forest reserves. About one-half of the remaining forest land was held by private interests, while the remaining areas were owned by county and municipal governments.

The people of rural Saxony may be divided into a northern Low Saxon group and a southern Thuringian group. The area west of the Elbe-Saale line, which once divided the Slavs and the Germans, is occupied by villages of the agglomerated *Hufendorf* type, which are common throughout Western and Central Germany, while to the east the colonial *Strassendorf* type, built along a road, and the *Rundling* (round) type, evidencing the earlier Slavic occupation, are common. The *Waldhufendorf* villages of the Harz Mountain area were founded during the early Middle Ages when the forests were first cleared and settled by the Germans. The division between the Low Saxon and Thuringian group is clearly revealed by the typical Low Saxon house (*Niedersächsisches Haus*) of the Magdeburg area which is characterized by a single building of brick and timber sheltering the barn and living quarters, and by the Middle German farms (*Gehöfte*) of the two southern districts which are characterized by a separate dwelling and two or three barns situated on a farmyard square. Most of the villages of the southern Thuringian area embracing the districts of Merseburg and Erfurt were fairly large, ranging in size from 600 to 1600 inhabitants. There were a few larger market villages with a population between 1600 and 4500. The smaller village with a population between 200 and 600 was more common in the northern Low Saxon Altmark area and the eastern part of the district of Merseburg. This area is hard to characterize from the point of view of folk culture because the impact of mechanized agriculture in the great loess area and the growth of industry and manufacturing in the numerous towns and cities of the province have done much to modernize the rural way of living. Old customs, traditions, and folkways survive to a limited extent in the uplands west of the border area. The greater proportion of the modern rural population, however, has given up its old local and particularistic ways for what might be called the German way.

Urban Aspect

Almost all of the cities of the Province of Saxony were established by Germans during or just after the Carolingian period. Many of the towns, like Magdeburg, Halle, and Erfurt, were already important market towns in the Middle Ages. The salt of Stassfurt and Halle and the copper and silver of the Harz Mountains have been exploited for the last six hundred years. The modern development of the area as one of the vital industrial-manufacturing zones of the Reich began with the late nineteenth century industrial revolution. The cultivation of the sugar beet in the border area since the latter part of the last century has made Magdeburg the major sugar market and refining center of Germany and reinforced its position as the leading city of the northern part of the province. Halle, the age-old rival of Magdeburg, is the major city of the southeastern section of the province. Its growth in modern times came with the exploitation of the important lignite and potash resources of the province. The only other large provincial town is Erfurt in the southwestern part of the province.

Today, 20 per cent of the population of the Province of Saxony dwells in these three cities, which serve as the regional centers of the area. Another 12 per cent of the population dwells in smaller cities and towns with a population ranging between 20,000 and 100,000. The sixteen larger cities of the province constitute city counties. Under the Nazis, municipal government and administration followed the national pattern laid down by the German Municipal Code of 1935.

The Province of Saxony formed a part of the Central German economic area consisting of the state of Saxony, the state of Thuringia, the state of Anhalt, and the Province of Saxony. The economic interdependence was greater between these territorial units than between any two of them or with any adjacent area. The development of the industrial-manufacturing complex, which occupied most of the basin of the Middle Elbe, was due in part to the natural wealth of the area in good soil, lignite, and potash, and in part to its position on major north-south and east-west transportation arteries. The province did not form a distinct socio-economic area. This fact was realized by the Nazis when they placed the governmental districts of Magdeburg and Merseburg, and the state of Anhalt under one State Planning Association, and attached the district of Erfurt to the planning association of Thuringia because of its close economic and cultural ties with that state.

Many of the industries of the Middle Elbe area owed their remarkable development to the introduction of the briquetting press in the middle of the last century which made possible the extensive use of lignite. The lignite deposits of the region, which are covered by a thin mantle of glacial material and are easily mined by surface stripping, are located in a wide zone extending from Bitterfeld and Magdeburg to Halle and Leipzig. The Saxon lignite with its high bitumen content is especially useful to the chemical industry for the production of oil, tar, gas, and wax. It is also used as a substitute for coal by the Middle Elbian industries.

The real development of the lignite came in the twentieth century and particularly after World War I, when improvements in methods of transmitting electricity and demands for resources and raw materials, after the loss of coal in the Silesian area to Poland, brought a more extensive exploitation of the lignite fields for the production of electrical power. The lignite mining area of the Province of Saxony became the largest in the world. Important lignite power stations, vital to the industries of Central Germany, were located at Zschornewitz, Bitterfeld, Halle, Gross-Kayna, Bleicherode, and Magdeburg. These plants were linked together by high tension lines to form an electrical power network not only for this province but also for the state of Saxony, the Province of Brandenburg, and the city of Berlin. Many of these plants are owned by mixed private and public interests; a few are operated by the provincial government.

Salt deposits of the Province of Saxony, produced by evaporation from saline water over many thousands of years, provided raw materials for the salt and soda industries; and potassium salts for agriculture, which made possible cultivation of submarginal lands to the east of the Elbe and in many other locations, the deposits are mined chiefly at Stassfurt, Halle, and Schönebeck. Germany maintained a world monopoly of potassium salts until other sources of usable potassium salts were found in France and America. Other natural resources include copper minerals of the Mansfield area in the Harz, some silver, and a small amount of hard coal.

Despite the absence of coal and iron resources, the Province of Saxony had an important metallurgical and machine industry which was dependent upon raw materials obtained from the Ruhr. Magdeburg and Halle are the major centers of this branch of industry; Magdeburg in the north developed important machinery plants and metalware works. Other centers were located at Stendal, Schönebeck, Stassfurt, Halberstadt, and Burg in northern Saxony, at Bitterfeld, Merseburg, Zeitz, and Wittenberg in southeastern Saxony, and at Erfurt, Mühlhausen, and Nordhausen in the southwestern part of the province. The chemical industry developed into one of the most important of the Reich on the basis of the salt and lignite deposits. Merseburg, with the near-by *IG Farben Leunawerke,* was a most important center, but plants were to be found also at Halle, Erfurt, Magdeburg, Schönebeck, Stassfurt, Bitterfeld, Stendal, and Nordhausen. The products of the chemical industry of the province were chiefly dyes, fertilizers, caustic soda, and nitrogen products. The large agricultural production of the border area made possible numerous agricultural industries.

Magdeburg owed much of its modern development to the cultivation of sugar beets. It was the sugar market and sugar refining center of Germany. Quedlinburg, Halle, Weissenfels, and Zeitz constituted the other important sugar marketing and processing centers. The leather industry was of minor importance in comparison with other industries; its centers included Burg, Halberstadt, Merseburg, Erfurt, and Nordhausen. Although the textile industry of the province was never as well developed as in the state of Saxony, there were numerous clothing manufacturing plants and a few cotton and wool textile mills at Halberstadt, Aschersleben, Magdeburg, Weissenfels, Zeitz, Erfurt, Mühlhausen, and Nordhausen. Nordhausen and Erfurt were also important for linen textiles. In addition to these major industries, there was a great variety of other types of manufacturing. Chocolate was made at Magdeburg, Halberstadt, Halle, and Wittenberg; rubber products at Halberstadt and Erfurt; and paper and wood products at Nordhausen, Weissenfels, Merseburg, Halle, and Burg.

This brief survey of the types of industries and their distribution clearly indicates that while lignite and salt led to the development of an important chemical industry, the agricultural industries and the leather industry were likewise important. The metal and machinery industry which had developed to meet the needs of the above industries was of unusual significance in view of the necessity of importing the essential raw materials.

Owing to its central location the Province of Saxony has long played an important role in the national transportation system. The backbone of the road transportation pattern is the north-south road between Halle and Magdeburg. Just south of Halle it connects with the major east-west road connecting Frankfort-on-the-Main, Eisenach, Erfurt, Leipzig, Dresden, and Breslau, while at Magdeburg it connects with another major east-west road linking Cologne, Dortmund, Hanover, Magdeburg, and Berlin. Aside from these major national arteries, there is an extensive network of roads within the province. The major provincial roads were maintained by the Provincial Corporation. In this province as elsewhere under the Nazi regime, the normal road system was supplemented by the super-highway. One national highway running from Hanover to Berlin cuts across the northern part of the province, while another which runs from Leipzig to Halle divides at the latter place, with one branch going to Magdeburg and another to Hildesheim. Erfurt is located on the national super-highway running from Leipzig to Eisenach.

The major rail lines follow almost the same basic pattern as the road system. The railroads, owned by the state, were operated by the German Railroad Company, an integral part of the national Ministry of Transport. In the Province of Saxony the railroads were under the National Railroad Directorates of Erfurt, Halle, and Hanover.

River and canal transportation was extremely important for the province. The Elbe, with its important river ports of Magdeburg, Schönebeck, Wittenberg, and Torgau, and the Saale, with its river ports of Halle, Weissenfels, and Merseburg, provide these important industrial and manufacturing towns with cheap transportation to the port of Hamburg and the North Sea. This river system connects at Magdeburg with the Mittelland canal, the great east-west canal which connects the industries of this province with the markets of Berlin to the east and the important heavy industries of the Ruhr to the west. Magdeburg from the point of view of rail, road, river, and canal transportation is the key junction of the province and served as its major distributing center. Although Magdeburg had some national importance as a center for air transportation, Halle, its industrial and commercial rival, was the major center for domestic and international aviation in the area. The airlines of the Reich were operated by the German Airways Corporation, while the airports were owned and administered by the municipalities.

Magdeburg was the capital of the Province of Saxony and the center for much of the economic administration within the province. It was an important market for sugar, grain, potash, wood products, and fodder and a key transport center. Halle, however, its age-old rival, served as the financial and commercial capital of the district of Merseburg, while Erfurt, which is commercially and financially oriented toward Thuringia, served the northern Thuringian area as well as the southwestern district of the Province of Saxony. Lignite, salt, fertilizer, and some metal products were the main commodities produced and shipped by rail from the region, while coal and metal to support the metallurgical and machine industry were the main products brought in from adjacent areas.

The lignite of the Province of Saxony was shipped to the state of Thuringia, the state of Saxony, the western Province of Brandenburg, the eastern Province of Hanover, and the state of Bavaria. There was also an extensive trade in machine goods, but most of this trade was between the industries of the Province of Saxony and the state of Saxony. The clothing industry of the province was dependent upon the textile mills of Thuringia and the state of Saxony. The overseas trade of the province went by rail or river to Hamburg and thence overseas. The banking and credit institutions of the province ranged from branches of the great commercial banks of Berlin, which were mainly interested in investments of the industrial type, to the local county and municipal mortgage and savings banks. The provincially owned banks and financial institutions were about equally divided between Halle and Magdeburg. The operations of these banks were supplemented by those of the main branches of the National Bank at Magdeburg, Halberstadt, Halle, Nordhausen, and Erfurt. The provincial government operated a life insurance and two fire insurance organizations. These institutions, like the provincially operated banks, were under the Provincial Corporation. The province also had two stock exchanges, one at Magdeburg and another at Halle.

The urban population of the Province of Saxony was largely engaged in industry and crafts. Of the total population, 40 per cent, or 1,358,000 individuals, were in the industries, manufacturing establishments, and crafts, while only 16 per cent, or 542,900, were occupied in trade and transportation activities. Another 6 per cent were engaged in professional work or public service. Worthy of attention is the class structure. The working class, which constituted about 48 per cent of the population, was one of the largest in the Reich, while the upper class was one of the smallest. The white collar and civil servant group was unusually small in comparison with those of other Prussian provinces.

The vital portion of the Province of Saxony is located in the basin of the Middle Elbe along the Elbe and Saale rivers. This is the area of the rich loess soil supporting an intensive agriculture and of the salt and lignite deposits which have made possible the vast urban and industrial region extending from Halle to Magdeburg. The northern district of the province is dominated by the city of Magdeburg, the capital of the province. Its history goes back to the Carolingian era, and it was one of the important departure points for East Elbian colonization during the early Middle Ages. During the later Middle Ages and the early modern period, it was the major market town of old Altmark. Although Magdeburg has long been a significant transportation point and commercial center, its real development did not come until the development of the sugar beet industry in the late nineteenth century. The industrial revolution brought the addition of important machinery and chemical plants. The smaller towns, Halberstadt, famous for its old medieval brick buildings, Quedlinburg, an agricultural town, and Aschersleben to the south, and the towns of Stendal and Burg which are situated to the north, are economically and culturally oriented toward Magdeburg.

Southeastern Saxony centered about the city of Halle on the Saale. Modern Halle, the commercial, industrial, and financial rival of Magdeburg and of near-by Leipzig, the greatest city of Central Germany, has been a market center since the medieval period, when it was commercially tied to the Hansa cities of the north. The coming of the railroad and the impetus of the industrial revolution have converted it into one of the major industrial centers of Germany. Its culture is Protestant. It has long been the center of the Martin Luther University. Intimately tied to Halle were the cities along the Saale—Merseburg, important for its chemical industry; Naumburg, once a charming residential town with a large retired class; Weissenfels, significant for its mixed industries; and Zeitz in the far south. Eisleben, an old mining town, which was the birthplace of Martin Luther, and Wittenberg on the Elbe, which is traditionally important as the center of many of Luther's activities, constituted the remaining towns of the southeastern part of the province. Southwestern Saxony, which is oriented toward Thuringia rather than the Middle Elbian part of the province was dominated by the city of Erfurt. This city, which is the economic center of the area, has long been an important commercial and transport center. The old market towns of Mühlhausen and Nordhausen were oriented toward this important town.

Chapter 24

THE STATE OF ANHALT

The state of Anhalt, which was a small irregularly shaped territory in Central Germany, consisted of two major portions and five exclaves in the adjoining Prussian Province of Saxony. The larger eastern portion, situated along the Elbe, was almost completely enclosed by the districts of Merseburg and Magdeburg of the Province of Saxony, while its eastern frontier adjoined the Prussian Province of Brandenburg. The smaller western portion of Anhalt, which was separated from the eastern section by the Province of Saxony, was also largely enclosed by this province, although on the west it bordered the state of Brunswick. The entire state was very small with a total area of 2,314 sq. km.

For its size, Anhalt has an extremely varied landscape. The western portion of the state consists of rolling hill country rising to the Harz Mountains in the southwest. The eastern section, which is traversed by the Elbe and its tributaries, the Mulde and Saale, consists of level plains country. The land between the Saale and the Elbe, which forms a part of the Central German loess border area extending from Halberstadt and Magdeburg to Halle and Leipzig, is extremely fertile. Most of the land to the east of the Elbe forms a flat sandy plain with extensive pine forests and numerous bogs and marshes. The more heavily settled eastern portion of the state supports the cities of Bernburg, Köthen, Dessau, and Zerbst, which form a part of the vast Central German urban and industrial complex.

The people of Anhalt belong to two different German tribal groups, which had driven out the older Slavic occupants and effectively occupied the state by the end of the Carolingian times. The Low Saxons settled the northern portions of Anhalt, the Thuringians the southern. The latter group, reinforced by peoples from all parts of western Germany, evolved into the mixed Upper Saxons of modern times. There were no significant cultural cleavages of the religious type, for over 88 per cent of the population is Lutheran Protestant. Out of a total population of 364,400, the Catholic population numbered 13,000 in 1933, the Jewish population about 900.

497

Although Anhalt was one of the smaller territorial units of the Reich, it had a relatively large population density because of its location within the Central German industrial area. The most densely settled part of the state was located between the Saale and the Elbe, where the population density frequently exceeded 200 per sq. km. The hilly western section had a density of 60 to 80 per sq. km. The average population density for the state was 157 per sq. km. The population of this small state, like that of most of Central Germany, grew rapidly under the impact of the industrial revolution. Between 1875 and 1925 it increased over 75 per cent. There was little emigration to lands outside the Reich since its industries tended to attract workers not only from the poorer East Elbian area, but from lands beyond the Reich. In 1933 there were 1,600 foreign residents.

The political history of Anhalt begins in the sixth century when it was a part of the ephemeral kingdom of the Thuringians. During the subsequent two centuries it was under the Saxon rulers of Northwest Germany. After the conquest of the Saxons by Charlemagne in the late eighth century, it formed a part of the Duchy of Saxony. The dukes of Saxony ruled the Anhalt area until the twelfth century, when it came under the rule of the Margrave of Brandenburg. In 1170, Bernhard, the son of Albert the Margrave of Brandenburg and a descendant of the earls of Ascania, became Count of Anhalt. His son Heinrich received Anhalt as a separate inheritance and must be regarded as the real founder of the House of Anhalt. Upon his death in 1252, his three sons partitioned the lands of Anhalt, founding the lines of Aschersleben, Bernburg, and Zerbst. The lands of the Aschersleben line were lost in 1315 when the line became extinct, and the inheritance passed to the bishopric of Halberstadt. In 1468 the lands of Anhalt-Bernburg were inherited by the Anhalt-Zerbst line, which in the meantime had undergone various divisions. By the sixteenth century, however, the family had been narrowed down to the branches of Anhalt-Köthen and Anhalt-Dessau. By 1570 the branch of Anhalt-Dessau had managed to control all the lands of Anhalt, but not for long; in 1603 the lands were again divided, re-establishing the lines of Dessau, Bernburg, Plötzkau, Zerbst, and Köthen.

During the Thirty Years' War, when Anhalt was severely ravaged, the various princes chose the eldest member of the family to act as the authority for Anhalt. In the seventeenth and eighteenth centuries the processes of extinction and inheritance eliminated the lines of Plötzkau and Zerbst, while the establishment of the principle of primogeniture prevented the further subdivision of the land. During the Napoleonic era, when the three princes of Anhalt—Bernburg, Dessau, and Köthen—were elevated to the rank of duke, they joined the Confederation of the Rhine and supported the French until 1813, when with the downfall of Napoleon they joined the Allies. In 1815 they became members of the German Confederation and, after its founding, they joined the Prussian Customs Union. The next important change came in 1847 when the line of Anhalt-Köthen became extinct, and its lands were divided between the Bernburg and Dessau lines. In 1863 the Dukes of Anhalt-Dessau inherited the troubled Duchy of Bernburg, which had suffered under the feeble rule of its last duke.

The united Duchy of Anhalt took the side of Prussia during the Seven Weeks' War against Austria and joined in with all of Germany in the Franco-Prussian War. In 1871 the Duchy became a state of the German Empire. During the period of the Empire, the state of Anhalt was an hereditary and constitutional duchy. The Duke, who served as the executive, governed through a State Ministry. The administration of the state's affairs was carried out by administrative departments for justice, finance, interior, and church affairs. Legislative power was vested in an assembly which consisted of delegates appointed by the Duke, the highest taxed landowners, the highest taxed owners of industrial and commercial enterprises, and by the cities and rural communes.

In 1918 the last duke was swept away by the German Revolution and Anhalt became one of the constituent states of the Weimar Republic. The constitution of 1919 gave Anhalt a democratic government with an assembly elected on the basis of universal suffrage.

The state of Anhalt was a strong Social Democratic area. Under the Empire and Republic, the state consistently supported the socialists. It was, however, one of the first German states to turn to National Socialism. Although the Social Democratic party remained the strongest party in the state up to the early elections of 1932, the National Socialists then became the second strongest party. In the presidential elections of 1932 Hindenburg carried the state only by a very small plurality over Hitler. Similarly, in the elections to the state legislature in the same year, the Nazis received the largest number of seats. In the *Reichstag* elections which followed in November 1932, the party of Hitler came close to receiving an absolute majority of all the votes cast. The Nationalists and the German People's party, which had formerly occupied second and third place respectively in the state's political constellation, were almost eliminated. Bernburg was the only district in which the Communist party had any strength. After 1932 the Nazis were the leading political party in all the counties and city counties into which the state was divided, and in Zerbst they had a clear majority. In the cities, the Nazi lead was not so great as in the rural areas.

The work of the state administration of Anhalt was supplemented by special and technical services under direct national control. During the imperial period only the nationally operated postal system lay outside the scope of the general administration. Justice, which was under the state, was administered by the

Collegiate Court of First and Second Instance at Dessau from which appeals went to the Superior State Court at Naumburg. The national postal system within Anhalt was under the Chief Postal Directorate (under the Empire) or the National Postal Directorate (under the Republic and Third Reich) of Magdeburg. Trade and industry, weights and measures, social insurance, welfare, public health, and the collection of imperial revenues, in so far as they were nationally regulative, were administered upon delegation from the Reich.

With the Republic came a further extension of direct national administration to finance, railways, unemployment and employment, and labor welfare. Within Anhalt national control of finances was carried out by the State Finance Office of Magdeburg, while the nationalized railways were under the National Railroad Directorate of Halle. Problems concerning labor were handled by the State Labor Office for Central Germany (Erfurt) and the main Welfare Office for Central Germany (Magdeburg). Welfare, social insurance, health, trade and industry, and labor, matters which were subject to national regulation, were administered in the customary way by delegation from the Reich. The economic life of the state was organized under a number of national agricultural, industrial, commercial, and labor organizations.

The advent of the Nazi regime brought drastic changes in the government and administration of Anhalt. Like the other German states it lost its federal status, and its rights were transferred to the Reich. The Nazis placed one National Governor in charge of the two states of Brunswick and Anhalt. The National Governor was directly responsible to the national Minister of the Interior, but was also subject to the directives coming from other national ministers. The actual state administration was carried out by the Anhalt State Ministry which was headed by a Minister of State. It was a national agency carrying out national orders and functioning for state purposes.

Anhalt formed a part of the National Socialist party district of Magdeburg-Anhalt. It was organized, as all districts were, from the top down, and it included every kind of party group, functional, territorial, and professional.

National administrative controls were extended to justice, air matters, and labor relations under the Nazi regime, while propaganda affairs were handled by the Ministry of Propaganda. Also many traditional fields of state administration—police, health, welfare, education, and certain aspects of social insurance—were brought under tight national control. These services and functions of administration were supplemented by an elaborate system of corporate administration, which resulted in complete regimentation of life within Anhalt.

Rural Aspect

Anhalt was situated in the heart of one of the traditionally important agrarian zones of Germany, the Central German loess-chernozem zone of black earth soils. Agriculture and forestry were, however, of secondary importance in the economy of the state, for only 63,100 individuals or about 17 per cent of the population were engaged in rural pursuits. About 26 per cent of the population dwelt in villages of less than 2,000 in population. Although the local administration of the state, after 1933, was under the Department of the Interior of the Anhalt State Ministry, which was administratively under the national Ministry of the Interior in Berlin, much of the day-to-day rural administration was under the County-Managers of the counties.

County government and administration in Anhalt were very much like that of Prussia. Under the Empire, county administration was based upon the County Constitution of 1870 which provided for a State Administration and a county assembly and county executive committee. After World War I, the pattern of county administration was based upon the laws of 1921 and their modification with the advent of the Nazi regime in 1933. Under the Nazis, the county committee survived as an appointed advisory committee. Municipal government of the 305 towns and villages of Anhalt in Nazi times followed the pattern laid down in the German Municipal Code of 1935. Before 1935 it was governed by the Town, City, and Village Constitution of 1882.

Over 65 per cent of the land of Anhalt was used for crops and stock raising. The rich agricultural plains area in the eastern portion of Anhalt enjoys a dry, warm climate. The average July temperature is over 18 degrees C., while the average January temperature is near 0 degrees C. The average yearly rainfall is less than 500 mm. per year. Eastward beyond the Elbe, cooler and drier conditions prevail, while to the west, in the county of Ballenstedt, the climate becomes progressively more cool and moist as one approaches the foothills of the Harz Mountains. The plains area is extremely fertile; it has been cultivated for at least four thousand years. The east and west portions of the state have less fertile soils of mixed types. The major crops of the plains area include wheat, sugar beets, potatoes, and barley. The waste from the sugar beets has been used as fodder for an extensive cattle industry. The common crops of the uplands to the west include flax, hops, and fruit. The rich meadowland along the banks of the Elbe, Mulde, and Saale is used for raising cattle of excellent quality. Beyond the Elbe to the east, the land is used for rye, potatoes, and livestock, although this sandy area is largely given over to pine forests and bogs.

The greater part of Anhalt formed a part of the real tillage zone of the Reich. The central area produced significant quantities of cereals and sugar beets, while the sandy plains to the east and the rolling hills to the west were mainly devoted to livestock. The figures for land utilization indicate the amount and types of land available for agriculture (figures in hectares):

Cultivated Land		128,300
Grain	76,200	
Legumes	2,800	
Root Crops	36,000	
Green Vegetables	2,300	
Industrial Crops	700	
Fodder Crops	10,300	
Small Gardens		4,100
Meadow		15,000
Pasture		2,000
Orchards		800
Vineyards		0
Forests		58,400
Waste Land		2,000
Houses and Barns		4,500
Roads and Parks		14,800

Sixty-five per cent of the land of Anhalt was devoted to agrarian activities. Fifty-six per cent of the land was under cultivation, while over 9 per cent was used for meadow and pasture. The remaining land area is devoted to forests (25 per cent) and waste and urban land (10 per cent).

The central part of Anhalt is almost treeless with forest areas covering less than 10 per cent of the area, whereas the hills to the west are rather well forested with beech and oak (29 to 37 per cent of the area), and the sandy plains to the east of the Elbe support extensive pine forests (31 to 39 per cent of the area). About 50 per cent of the forest land was owned by the state of Anhalt. It was administered through eleven forest reserves under the Forest Administration of the State Ministry at Dessau. The remainder of the forest land was divided almost equally between private owners and county and municipal governments.

The rural population of Anhalt does not possess a distinctive rural culture. The Low Saxons of the north and the Thuringians of the south have merged to form a nondescript Central German peasant group of Upper Saxon type. They dwell in houses of Central German type, consisting of a house and one or two barns about a farmyard. In the western part of Anhalt these houses are grouped together in agglomerated villages of the *Haufendörfer* type, while in eastern Anhalt the occasional round village reflects the age when this part of the Reich was occupied by Slavic folk, while the long *Strassendörfer* goes back to the days of German colonization. The villages west of the Elbe in the more fertile section tend to be large, with populations ranging between 600 and 2,000, while those to the east of the Elbe are small, with populations ranging between 70 and 600. The farms, which are situated outside the villages, tend to be large, averaging over 100 hectares in size. There are a few small farms in western Anhalt.

Urban Aspect

The four largest cities of Anhalt—Bernburg, Dessau, Köthen, and Zerbst —go back to the beginning of the Middle Ages. They are German foundations originally established in the colonial era when the Germans were pushing eastward to settle Slavic territory. Their main development came during the period between the fifteenth and eighteenth centuries when these cities were the centers of the four main principalities of Anhalt. The next period of growth came in the late nineteenth century under the impact of the German industrial revolution. The four cities—Bernburg with a population of 38,300, Dessau with 91,423, Köthen with 26,700, and Zerbst with 20,100—are city-counties. Under the Nazis their government and administration followed the pattern laid down by the German Municipal Code of 1935. There was a Chief Mayor, who was directly responsible to the Anhalt State Ministry at Dessau.

Anhalt formed a part of the Central German economic area consisting of the states of Anhalt, Saxony, and Thuringia and the Province of Saxony. This area was characterized by an intensive type of economic interdependence. Anhalt's industries and commerce were of minor significance in comparison with those of the three other component areas of Central Germany. It could not be regarded as a distinct unit within this greater area.

The industrial and manufacturing enterprises of Anhalt were based upon the local lignite and salt deposits and the cultivation of the sugar beet. Bernburg was the major center for the mining of lignite and salt, which are among the basic activities of the Middle Elbian area. The chemical industry was also important at Dessau and Köthen. The sugar industry, which is common throughout the Saxony-Anhalt area, had its major centers in Anhalt at Bernburg, Dessau, and Köthen. The machinery industry, which developed to supply the needs of the above industries, was dependent upon raw materials shipped in from the Rhine-Ruhr area. Dessau, Köthen, Bernburg, and Zerbst had small machinery manufacturing establishments. Dessau was the major center, important for machinery works and the Junkers airplane plant. While Bernburg, Köthen, and Dessau had the typical Middle Elbian combination of sugar, chemical, and machinery manufacturing, Zerbst, which is located in northeast Anhalt, was mainly interested in the production of food products, leather goods, and its famous bitter beer. The power needs of Anhalt are met by electrical power stations using lignite for fuel. These stations are connected by high tension lines to the great lignite power stations of the province of Saxony.

Although all of Anhalt is linked together by local roads, there is no major east-west road to link the four major cities of the state. These towns are, however, situated on secondary roads radiating from Magdeburg to points south of Anhalt in the Province and the state of Saxony. The construction and maintenance of the main state roads were handled by a department of the State Ministry at Dessau, while local roads were under the county administrations. While the road system of Anhalt has not been supplemented by the Nazi superhighway, two of these new national highways cross the state, passing near Bernburg and Dessau. Anhalt is crossed by two major rail lines, one running from Magdeburg via Zerbst and Dessau to Dresden, and another running from Halle via Köthen to Magdeburg. River transportation facilities are important in Anhalt, for the state is traversed by the navigable Elbe and its tributary, the Saale. Bernburg on the Saale and Dessau on the Elbe are the important river ports. There were no major airports in Anhalt. It was served by those at Halle and Magdeburg.

The economic life of Anhalt was oriented toward the city of Magdeburg. Dessau, the state capital, was the major commercial and financial center of the state. The chief commercial products of Anhalt for export to other parts of Germany included lignite, salt, fertilizer, chemicals, and some machinery, while coal and metal, the raw materials for the local metallurgical and machinery industry, were brought in from Western Germany. The banking and credit institutions of Land Anhalt ranged from branches of the great commercial banks of Berlin, which were mainly interested in investments of the industrial type, to the local county and municipal mortgage and savings banks. The operations of these banks were supplemented by those of the branches of the *Reichsbank* at Dessau, Köthen, and Bernburg. There were no state banking institutions. The state government of Anhalt owned and operated only one insurance enterprise, a fire insurance company. Anhalt was served by the stock exchanges at Halle and Magdeburg.

The urban population of Anhalt was largely engaged in industry and crafts. Of the total population, 44 per cent or 162,000 individuals were dependent upon industrial, manufacturing, and craft activities. In terms of numbers of persons employed, the mining, chemical, and machinery industries were the most important. Another 14 per cent of the population or 51,800 individuals were engaged in trade and transportation. The remaining part of the population was employed as follows: 6 per cent in the professions and civil service, 2 per cent as household servants, while 17 per cent are independent or retired. The remaining 17 per cent of the population were employed in agriculture or forestry. There was a large working class, which constituted over 50 per cent of the population. This was typical for Central Germany; but the upper class and the white collar class were unusually small, even in comparison with those of the adjacent provinces and states of Central Germany.

The urban portion of Anhalt was situated largely between the Saale and Elbe rivers, except for an extension northward which included the city-county of Zerbst. The rest of eastern Anhalt and all of the western portion of the state, consisting of the county of Ballenstedt, had a decidedly rural character. The four major cities of Anhalt—Bernburg, Dessau, Köthen, and Zerbst—follow the same pattern of growth and development. They were founded in the early Middle Ages by German colonists from the west. All four cities owed their earliest prosperity to the rich loess and chernozem soils and to their position on Saale-Elbe north-south trade routes. Their development in early modern times was largely due to the fact that all four served as centers for the major principalities of Anhalt. The renaissance and baroque buildings of the four cities evidence their prosperity before and after the Thirty Years' War.

The modern development of Bernburg, Dessau, and Köthen came with the industrial revolution. Dessau grew from a small town of 17,500 in 1871 to a city of 91,400 in 1933. Although salt mining has long been a factor in the economy of Bernburg and Köthen, lignite mining did not become common until after the middle of the nineteenth century. The latter part of the nineteenth century and the twentieth century brought the chemical and machinery industries to the three western cities of Anhalt. Zerbst in the east has had a more normal development, for it remains even today a market town with extensive agrarian interests which are reflected in its food industries. With the exception of Dessau, the state capital, the cities or towns of Anhalt are small and provincial. They are not important from a national point of view.

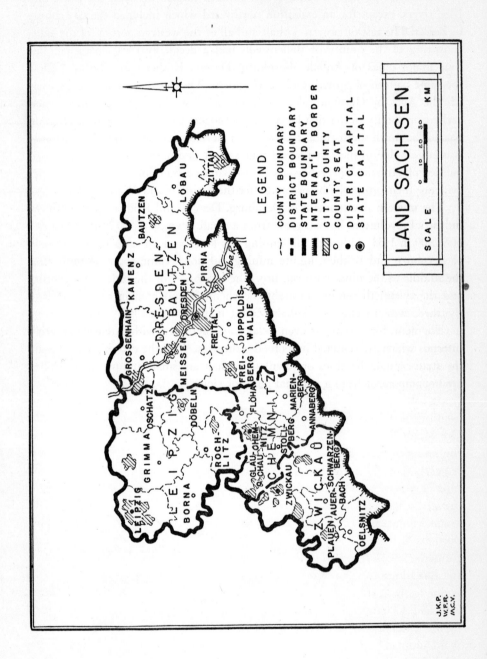

Chapter 25

THE STATE OF SAXONY*

The state of Saxony is situated in southeast Central Germany. To the south lie the Ore Mountains, the natural barrier separating Germany from Czechoslovakia. To the west were the states of Bavaria and Thuringia, to the north the Prussian Province of Saxony, and to the east the Prussian Province of Silesia. The state of Saxony was a compact territory whose frontiers had a circumference of 1900 kilometers. The frontiers before World War II were established by the Treaty of Vienna in 1815.

The state of Saxony is mostly hilly or mountainous, although the districts around Leipzig and along the northern frontier are level, constituting as they do a part of the North German Plain. These plains constitute a loess-covered area supporting an intensive agricultural economy important for its industrial crops oriented about the industrial cities of Leipzig, Wurzen, and Oschatz. Southward the plains give way to the gradually rising German foreland of the Ore Mountains, extending in a northeasterly direction for 225 kilometers along the southern border of the state of Saxony, from the Fichtel Mountains (*Fichtelgebirge*) in northeast Bavaria and the hilly Vogtland to the mountains and hills of Upper Lusatia (*Oberlausitz*) and the Saxon Switzerland (*Sächsische Schweiz*), lying between the northeastern ranges of the Ore Mountains and the Giant Mountains (*Riesengebirge*) of the Sudeten (*Sudetic*) chain. The higher portions of these uplands were once rich in silver, copper, and lead ores which formerly attracted the German miner, while the lower areas have been cleared for agriculture since the early Middle Ages. The modern wealth of the uplands is due to the textile and metallurgical manufacturing establishments at Plauen, Zwickau, Chemnitz, and Freiberg, which are situated in the southwest portion on the Elster and Mulde. These rivers rise in the Ore Mountains and flow northward ultimately to join the Elbe River. The latter river, which rises in Czechoslovakia, cuts through the southern Saxon uplands and divides the Ore Mountains from the hills of Upper Lusatia. The hills along the Elbe, after it enters

* German spelling—Land Sachsen.

507

the state of Saxony, are composed of sandstone which has been weathered into picturesque and fantastic forms. They form a riparian upland that is important for the commercial and industrial towns of Dresden, the capital of the state —Meissen, Bautzen, and Zittau.

Peasants have cultivated the fertile loess plains of the northern part of the state since the Neolithic period. Illyrian peoples dwelt in the nonforested portions of Saxony during the Bronze and Iron ages, while just before the beginning of our era most of Central Germany was occupied by the Germanic Thuringians. After the migration period (A.D. 450-750), pastoral Slavic tribes pushed into Central Germany, settling in Saxony and eastern Thuringia. The Saale and Elbe rivers formed the frontier dividing the Germans and Slavs. In the tenth century German peoples began to re-colonize the area between the Saale and the upper Elbe. Franks from the Upper Main area and Thuringians from the land west of the Saale occupied the Saxon area. They mixed with the Slavic population to form the Middle German Upper Saxon folk of modern Saxony. Evidence of the earlier Slavic occupation survives in round villages of the valley and lowland, and in place names like Leipzig and Dresden, with the Slavic endings "zig" and "en." The group of Slavic Wends living south of Bautzen constitutes living evidence of the Slavic character of early Saxony. The Upper Saxons, who must not be confused with the Lower Saxons of Northwest Germany, form a distinct group of people with a common territory and a similar set of cultural values. Much of the unity of the Upper Saxons is a product of their political history, which is marked by the evolution of the Saxon state. The cultural unity of the area is not seriously affected by religious division. The Lutheran Protestants in 1933 numbered 4,522,000, constituting 87 per cent of the population; the Roman Catholics, 196,000; and the Jewish population, which was concentrated in the larger cities, 20,584. The latter group was of only moderate size in comparison with other parts of the Reich.

The state of Saxony ranked third among the German states in population. In 1933 it had a population of 5,196,000 inhabitants, occupying an area of 14,994 sq. km. The population density, which was the greatest for any comparable German state or province, was 346 individuals per sq. km. The population of Saxony has grown more rapidly in the course of the past hundred years than that of any other large German state. In 1815 the population numbered 1,178,000 and in 1875, 2,760,000. Under the impetus of the industrial revolution in the latter 19th century, it increased to 4,808,000 by 1910. Though the whole state was relatively densely populated, most of the population was concentrated in the large cities and towns. From the point of view of structural density, there were two main urban zones: the Leipzig, Chemnitz, and Plauen triangle in western Saxony, and the Elbe River zone extending from Meissen through Dresden to the Czech frontier. In these regions the average population density ranged between 300 and 500 per sq. km. Even the predominantly agrarian portions of the state had a relatively dense population, 80-130 per sq. km.

The Saxon area remained under Slavic control until the tenth century of our era. In 930 the forces of the Saxon Emperor Heinrich I of the Holy Roman Empire drove eastward from the Saale-Elbe line of Carolingian times and established a fort at Meissen on the Elbe to protect eastern Germany from raids by the Slavs. The fort at Meissen became the center of the Thuringian March (*Thüringer Mark*), extending from the Saale beyond the Elbe into western Silesia. This area was established as the Margraviate of Meissen. In 1046 the Franconian Emperor Heinrich III invested Earl Dedo II of Wettin with the Margraviate of Meissen. Dedo's successors gradually enlarged their territory. Events in other parts of Germany were meanwhile shaping the destinies of the Wettins. In 1179 the powerful Duchy of Saxony, which embraced most of northwestern Germany, was dismembered. The northeastern portion of the duchy and the electoral privileges of the dukes of Saxony were invested in Duke Bernhard of Ascania, the ancestor of the House of Anhalt. In 1422 the electoral line of the House of Ascania became extinct and the Emperor Sigismund invested the Margrave Friedrich of Meissen with the Ascanian portion of old Saxony and with the electoral rights. The title of Margrave of Meissen gradually became obsolete and was replaced by the title of Elector of Saxony. During the period between 1000 and 1433 the Franconians and Thuringians from the west had successfully colonized most of the Saxon area. The older Slavic population was slowly disappearing through intermarriage.

The year 1464 is important in Saxon history, for Friedrich II died leaving his lands to his sons Ernst and Albert. Ernst became Elector and gained the lands about Wittenberg, while Albert received the Margraviate of Meissen and eastern Thuringia. Ernst's grandson, Johann Friedrich, was deposed as Elector in 1547, for his part in the wars of the Reformation, by Charles V, Emperor of the Holy Roman Empire. Albert's grandson, Moritz, was invested with the electorate, but was obliged to cede to the deposed Elector and his descendants lands which became the Saxon Grand-Duchy and the duchies of Thuringia. This exchange of dignities and territories marked the establishment of the younger Albertiner line in Saxony, whose lands then included the southern portion of the modern Province of Saxony and a corner of the Province of Brandenburg.

Moritz, Elector of Saxony, although a Protestant, aided the Catholic Emperor Charles V in the wars of the Reformation in order to secure his power and prestige in Saxony. Internally, his reign was important for advances in education, tax reform, and the beginning of coal mining. His successor, August I, followed a wise domestic policy. Mining and agriculture were strongly encouraged. Finer breeds of sheep and cattle were imported from other lands. Foreign weavers were brought in to found the textile industry. During the first phase of the Thirty Years' War, Saxony sided with Sweden and was ravaged by the Catholic forces of Wallenstein, while the latter part of this war saw Saxony at the side of the Emperor and brought the ravages of the Swedes. The land had suffered severely during the long war and, as a result of its alliance with Catholic German states, it found after the treaty of Westphalia (1648) that its place as a leader of Protestant Germany had been taken by the state of Brandenburg. Saxon fortunes did not revive with the reign of August the Strong (*der Starke*) (1694-1733), whose connections with Poland were disastrous for Saxony. August was elected King of Poland in 1697 and immediately involved Saxony in the Polish wars against the Swedes. His successor Friedrich August (1733-1763), Elector of Saxony and King of Poland, managed to involve the state in the Silesian War and the Seven Years' War. Saxony gained nothing.

The long reign of the Elector Friedrich August III (1763-1827) opened with a period of internal reconstruction and reform. In 1791 he wisely declined the offer of the Polish crown, rightfully fearing Russia's intentions toward the Poles. Friedrich August managed to keep out of the struggle between France and Prussia until 1796 when he concluded a treaty with the French. In 1806 Saxony joined with Prussia against Napoleon and suffered defeat at Jena. In the same year, however, Friedrich August revived his alliance with France and entered the Confederation of the Rhine. In December 1806, he became King of Saxony as Friedrich August I. The state continued to back the Napoleonic cause. At Leipzig in 1813 the French and Saxon forces were decisively defeated by the Allies. Friedrich August was taken prisoner at Leipzig, and Saxony was occupied by the Russians. At the Congress of Vienna (1815), Prussia, backed by Russia, demanded all of Saxony, while Austria, backed by Great Britain, sought to maintain the region as a buffer state between herself and Prussia. The Congress assigned the northern portion of the Kingdom of Saxony to Prussia, leaving the southern portion with Friedrich August, who was permitted to retain his title of king.

In 1815 Saxony joined the German Confederation. In the politics of the Confederation it was overshadowed by Prussia. Shortly after King Anton came to power in 1827, the pressure of the revolutionary movement of 1830 brought the establishment of the constitution of 1831, which was to serve as a basis of government until 1918. The old feudal estates and privy council were replaced by a two-chamber legislature and a responsible ministry. The pressure of the revolutionary movement of 1848 resulted in further reforms. In 1854 Johann succeeded his brother Friedrich August II who had ruled since 1836. Johann, the scholar and translator of Dante, followed a federalistic and pro-Austrian policy in the difficult sixties. When war broke out between Austria and Prussia in 1866, Saxony sided with Austria and was immediately occupied by Prussia. Although Saxony lost no territory, she was compelled to pay an indemnity and join the North German Confederation. She also lost the control of postal, railway, military, and foreign affairs to Prussia. In 1870 the troops of this state fought with those of Prussia against France.

In 1871 Saxony joined the German Empire. Under the Empire, the Kingdom of Saxony, an hereditary and constitutional monarchy, had a bicameral legislature, consisting of an upper chamber (*Herrschaft*) (delegates from the nobility, the churches, the large towns, the University of Leipzig, etc.) and a lower chamber (*Kammer*) (deputies from towns and rural areas). The executive consisted of the King and a State Ministry (*Gesamtministerium*). State administration was carried out by Ministries for Interior, Justice, Finance, Education and Church Affairs, Foreign Affairs, and War. There was a separate Ministry for the affairs of the royal house, as well as several top administrative courts with independent status. In 1873 Albert, son of Johann, became King of Saxony. His reign was marked by the rapid growth of the Social Democratic party. The conservative opposition attempted to block its growth with the election law of 1896, which mitigated against a correct representation of the mass of people, thereby eliminating the Social Democrats from the Diet. The strength of the Social Democrats was shown in the 1903 elections for the German Imperial Parliament, when all but one of the twenty-three Saxon members were Social Democrats. Although this brought the minor reforms of 1904 and 1907, the conflict over the election system and the constitution continued until 1918. Meanwhile, in 1904, Friedrich August III had ascended the Saxon throne. Highly industrialized Saxony suffered severely during World War I. In 1917 the Socialist and left-wing parties, which had managed to gain some representation in the Saxon Diet after the minor reforms of 1904 and 1907, began to demand an early conclusion of peace.

In November 1918, revolution broke out and Friedrich August III abdicated. During the following months there was violent street fighting in Leipzig, Dresden, and Plauen, which culminated in the formation of a Soviet Republic at Leipzig in April 1919. It was dissolved by the national army in May. Although all the political parties, except the Communist at first, accepted the constitution of 1920, political disturbances continued, especially in western Saxony. Sporadic street fighting lasted into 1923, when a coalition of the German People's party, the Democrats, and the Social Democrats took over the government. In April 1928, an exchange of certain territory was made with Thuringia, eliminating the three exclaves of the Saxon territory. The constitution of 1920 provided for a one-chamber assembly elected by the people on the basis of equal, secret, direct, universal suffrage and proportional representation. This body elected the Minister President, who in turn nominated the rest of the Ministry. The State Ministry was responsible to the assembly.

During the Empire and the Republic, the state of Saxony was a Social Democratic stronghold. Densely populated and highly industrialized, the state was a
natural center for both Socialist and Communist activity. The great cities of
Dresden and Leipzig were administered by Socialist mayors, and the state legislature was oriented toward the left. The state ministries were held in most cases
by Socialist ministers, although the German People's party and the German
National People's party exercised an influence in state affairs out of all proportion to their voting strength. Communism also was a force in Saxony in republican times, and the party regularly elected its members to city councils, to the
state legislature, as well as to the *Reichstag.* During the republican period eight
to ten Communist deputies sat in the *Reichstag* representing Saxon districts.
With the great upsurge of the National Socialist strength in the 1930 elections,
Saxony lifted Hitler's party to second place in two of its three electoral districts,
namely in Dresden and the Chemnitz-Zwickau districts. In the Leipzig district
the Socialists and Communists still retained first and second places respectively.
By 1932 the district of Chemnitz-Zwickau gave Hitler 47 per cent of its vote
in the second presidential election, thus making the district the second strongest Hitler district in all of Germany at that particular time. In the July 1932
Reichstag election, the Nazis became the most numerous party in all of Saxony,
although their vote did not yet equal the votes of the Social Democratic and
Communist parties together, except in the Chemnitz-Zwickau district where
the Nazi vote far exceeded the vote of both of the proletarian parties. The cities
of Plauen and Zwickau were always the greatest Nazi strongholds, giving clear
majorities to Hitler's party. In Chemnitz, Bautzen, and Dresden the Nazis had
become the most numerous party in 1932, although in these cities the Socialists
and Communists together outnumbered them. The great city of Leipzig held
firm to Socialist leadership and led the whole Reich in voting participation, but
the district in which it was located put the Nazis in the lead. It is perhaps
significant that the Chemnitz-Zwickau district, which was the district in which
the Communists were strongest, was the one in which the Nazis rolled up such
impressive majorities. In the crucial elections of 1932 and 1933, a drop in the
Nazi vote in the November 1932 election was accompanied by a rise in the Communist vote, while a rise in the Nazi vote in the following election of March
1933 was accompanied by a drop in the Communist vote. Indubitably, large
numbers of Communists entered the Nazi party at this time. "Red" Saxony,
especially the Chemnitz-Zwickau districts, somewhat strangely perhaps supported Adolf Hitler. Whether the reason was unemployment or whether it was
the revolutionary appeal of Hitler, it is difficult to say.

The modern administrative subdivision of the state of Saxony into districts
goes back to the five early modern provinces. Though there were some changes
in the early nineteenth century, after 1871 the state was divided into the follow-

ing five administrative districts (*Kreishauptmannschaften*) similar to the Prussian Governmental Administrative Districts: Bautzen, Chemnitz, Dresden, Leipzig, and Zwickau. These in turn were subdivided into twenty-two city-counties (*Bezirksfreie Städte*), each headed by a Chief Mayor, and twenty-seven counties (*Amtshauptmannschaften*) similar to the Prussian counties, each headed by a County-Manager (*Amtshauptmann*) who was responsible for the administration of the municipality (*Gemeinde*) within his county. The five administrative districts, each under a District Director (*Kreishauptmann*) lasted until 1933 when the number of districts was reduced to four through the consolidation of Dresden and Bautzen. Under the Republic, the district, which served as an area of state administration, was headed by a District Director, who was assisted by a district committee, composed of delegates from the County Diets and City Councils.

The Third Reich brought the replacement of the county committee by an appointed Advisory Committee and the strengthening of the position of the District Director. Under a decree of 1938, when the designation for administrative areas and officials was made uniform in the Reich, the *Kreishauptmannschaft* and the *Kreishauptmann* were renamed *Regierungsbezirk* (*Rgbz.*) and *Regierungspräsident*, while the *Amtshauptmannschaft* and the *Amtshauptmann* became *Landkreis* and *Landrat*.

OLD AND NEW TITLES AND DESIGNATIONS

Designation and Official	Old Designation and Official	New Designation and Official
Administrative District	*Kreishauptmannschaft*	*Regierungsbezirk*
District President	*Kreishauptmann*	*Regierungspräsident*
City County	*Bezirkfreie Stadt*	*Stadtkreis*
Chief-Mayor	*Oberbürgermeister*	*Oberbürgermeister*
County	*Amtshauptmannschaft*	*Landkreis*
County-Manager	*Amtshauptmann*	*Landrat*

Each *Bezirksfreie Stadt* became a *Stadtkreis*. These changes left four administrative districts under District Presidents, who were responsible to the state Minister of the Interior at Dresden. It is important to note that the Saxon districts were intermediate areas of decentralized state administration and that they had no self-governing functions. The District Presidents had prime responsibility for the local government and administration in the areas under their jurisdiction and supervisory authority over special national services. They were responsible for health and police affairs, agricultural, commercial, and industrial matters, and the supervision of schools. As direct national officials with general supervisory powers in their respective districts, they served as the district

authority for the rural police and the Order Police. The District President maintained administrative relationships with medical and veterinarian officials, industrial inspectors, and public works authorities of their districts. They were
also responsible for the technical, commercial, and industrial schools, and they
served as inspectors of county school authorities. Each served as the head of the
district Price Supervisory Office (*Preisüberwachungsstelle*), the Food Office
(*Ernährungsamt*), and the Economic Office (*Wirtschaftsamt*). They were also
the supervisory authority for the county Land Registration Offices (*Katasterämter*). In January 1943, the four Saxon District Presidents were suspended for
the duration of the war and their functions transferred to the state ministries.

The work of the state administration was supplemented by special and technical services under direct national control. During the imperial period only
the nationally operated postal system lay outside the state administration. The
national uniform court system, which was administered by the state Ministry
of Justice, consisted of the Superior State Court of Dresden and the Collegiate
Courts of First and Second Instance of Bautzen, Chemnitz, Dresden, Freiberg,
Leipzig, Plauen, and Zwickau. As usual, the national postal system within Saxony was under the Chief Postal Directorates (Empire) or National Postal
Directorates (Empire and Third Reich), located, in this instance, at Chemnitz,
Dresden, and Leipzig. Following the normal procedure, national regulations
for trade and industry, weights and measures, social insurance, welfare, public
health, and the collection of imperial revenues were carried out upon delegation
from the Reich.

In the Republican period there was a further extension of direct national administration to finance, railways, unemployment insurance and employment,
and labor welfare. State Finance Offices in Dresden and Leipzig with their local
finance and customs offices supervised the finances. The National Construction
Office at Dresden and Leipzig functioned under these State Finance Offices. The
nationally operated railways operated under the National Railroad Directorate
at Dresden. In Saxony, the State Labor Office and the main Welfare Office in
Dresden took care of labor's problems. Specific features of welfare, social insurance, health, trade and industry, and labor, which were subject to national legislation, were administered here, as in other states, upon delegation from the
Reich. A number of national agricultural, industrial, commercial, and labor
organizations managed the economic life of the state.

The state of Saxony was constituted as the Nazi party district of Saxony.
Its headquarters were at Dresden and included offices which dealt with every
aspect of party organization reaching down to the lowest citizen and the smallest village.

The advent of the Nazi regime brought rapid and sweeping changes in the
government of the state. In 1934 the Nazis liquidated its federal status. Its

rights were transferred to the Reich, and a National Governor, directly responsible to the national Minister of the Interior, but also subject to the supervision of other national ministers, was placed in charge of the government and administration at Dresden, the capital of the state of Saxony. The conversion of the state into a Reich administrative district was accompanied by a number of other important changes. The State Ministry headed by the Minister President was replaced by a State Chancellery under a Ministerial Director, while the Ministry of Justice and the Labor and Welfare Ministry (*Arbeits- und Wohlfahrtsministerium*) were eliminated. Under the Nazis the *Landesregierung* or central administration was headed by the National Governor, who was also the party leader for the party district of Saxony. He was assisted by a Ministerial Director who headed the State Chancellery which was immediately responsible for the coordination of the work of the following state ministries: Interior, Finance, Economics and Labor, and Education. These ministries served as agents of the Reich and for the state, issuing decrees, and directing, supervising, and executing the affairs of the state. They were, however, subject to the Reich Cabinet and could only carry on their business in the name of the Reich and after clearance with the competent national ministers. The Saxon ministries were separate from the office of the National Governor, and the state cabinet must be regarded as a separate national authority carrying out national orders and at the same time functioning for state purposes. All state officials were indirect national officials.

In the Nazi period national administrative controls were extended to justice, air matters, and labor relations. Most of the customary fields of state administration—police, health, welfare, education, and certain aspects of social insurance—were controlled nationally. Economic planning was carried out by the State Planning Association of Saxony, which was under the leadership of the National Governor. Administrative services and functions of a general and special nature were supplemented by a system of corporate administration which provided for complete supervision of life within the state.

Dresden was the major administrative center of Saxony. It was the state capital and the state headquarters for most of the national special and technical services. It was also the center for district administration. Of the three remaining district centers, Zwickau, Chemnitz, and Leipzig, the latter was the most important for it was not only a center for administration of national finance and justice (*Reichsgericht*), but was the largest Saxon city and its greatest transportation center.

RURAL ASPECT

The loess area of northwest Saxony has been a settled cultivated area for more than five thousand years, and village life and agrarian and forestry activities were the main supports of rural life until the nineteenth century industrial revolution. The upland areas of southern and eastern Saxony, however, were not settled until relatively recent times, when in the tenth to twelfth centuries of our era Thuringian and Franconian peasants from the west cleared the forested highland. In recent years agriculture and forestry have had little real significance in comparison with industrial and commercial activity, for only 431,-000 individuals, or 8.3 per cent of the population, live and work close to the soil, although over 20 per cent of the population live in small villages of less than 2,000 population.

The advent of the Nazi regime resulted in several changes. The features of democratic control were eliminated, although the district committee managed to survive as an appointed advisory council. The interior administration of rural Saxony was under the Ministry of the Interior at Dresden and the four District Presidents at Chemnitz, Dresden, Leipzig, and Zwickau. The day to day rural administration was carried out by the twenty-seven county managers who headed the twenty-seven counties into which the administrative districts were divided. Locally the administration was under the Mayors of the towns which made up the counties.

After the reforms of 1933 and 1938, the county of the state of Saxony was very much like the Prussian county. Before the Nazis, each county (*Amtshauptmannschaft,* later *Landkreis*) was headed by a County Manager (*Amtshauptmann,* later *Landrat*), appointed by the state government, who served as the head of both state administration and local self-government. In his capacity as the head of local self-government, which was organized under a District Union—a public law corporation (*Bezirksverband*) he served as the chairman of the District Committee, which was an administrative board elected by the District Council. The latter legislative organization was elected by the communal representatives of the District Union. The latter organization was responsible for the administration of welfare, public health, public assistance, and the care of the sick, infirm, and insane. It was also responsible for public buildings, road construction and maintenance, and flood control. Institutions of higher and technical education fell under its jurisdiction. It administered the county savings banks and other economic enterprises, including transportation concerns. It also granted financial aid and credit to needy towns within the District Union. The County Manager, in his capacity as head of the county, that is, as the head of state administration, supervised the administrative activities of the District Union and carried out the business of the state at the county level.

Under the Nazi administration of the small towns and villages, the Saxon counties followed the German Municipal Code of 1935. This code replaced the Saxon Municipal Codes of 1823 and 1923/1925. Under the Code of 1923/1925 the municipal governments had consisted of a Mayor and an executive council elected by the Municipal Councilors (*Gemeindeverordneten*), who, in turn, were elected by the citizens of the town or village. Although the work of the municipalities was severely restricted by the Nazis, they still continued to handle public works and welfare, and managed to operate a few enterprises.

Agriculture was of secondary importance in comparison with other economic activities in the state of Saxony. Most of the agricultural land, which constituted about 64 per cent of the total area of the state, lies in the northwest and in the foothills of the Ore Mountains while the forested area, which accounts for 25 per cent of the land area, is largely restricted to the southern uplands. These two areas formed the two main rural and agrarian regions of the state.

Geographically, the lowland zone consists of the fertile plains east of Leipzig. It forms a part of the loess zone which dominates most of Middle Germany, extending from Hanover and Magdeburg to Erfurt and Leipzig. The black and brown soils of steppe type, which are naturally fertile, have been cultivated since Neolithic times. This level area enjoys a dry, warm climate with an average July temperature of 18-19 degrees C. and an average January temperature of 0 to —1 degrees C. The average yearly rainfall is low, averaging between 500 and 600 mm. per year. Climatically, the Saxon lowland, because of its cold winters and warm somewhat more moist summers, belongs to the sub-Sarmatian zone of East Elbian Germany. The good agricultural land of northwestern Saxony is largely divided into medium-sized farms with from 20 to 100 hectares of land, and a number of large estates. This area was devoted to the intensive cultivation of industrial crops. The cash income of the farmers came from rye, wheat, barley, potatoes, and sugar beets. Malt barley which requires a dry winter was also grown widely in this area. Livestock raising, although of secondary importance, had become profitable because of the use of sugar beet waste for fodder. Dairying was of some importance near the large cities.

This was one of the few areas in Germany where agriculture had been mechanized, and here the mechanization was due to the large and medium-sized farms and the productivity of the area, which made it economically possible. The large estates of the lowland centered about a manor house surrounded by the houses and small garden plots of the farm laborers, who received most of their wages in kind, although some of the estates employed seasonal day laborers. The owners of the medium-sized farms dwelt in villages of the round type, going back to the days of Slavic occupation, and the road type, dating back to the days of German colonization. These villages are small, ranging in size from 200 to 1600 inhabitants, but large enough to support a school and church. The houses of the village, which consist of a house and barns arranged about a farmyard, constitute the base for agricultural operations which are carried out in the fields surrounding the village.

The Saxon upland, which rises gradually from the plains to the Ore Mountains, consists of hilly lands extending from Plauen to the river Mulde, the Saxon Switzerland (*Sächsische Schweiz*), and the hills of *Oberlausitz*. In the lower hills to the north of the Ore Mountains, the climate is similar to that of the lowland, although the summers are somewhat cooler and more moist, while the winters are colder. Only the higher parts of the Ore Mountains on the Czech frontier have a typically sub-alpine climate with cool, humid summers and cold, snowy winters. Sandy loams and clays replace the rich loess soil of the lowlands in the upland area, while these give way to the infertile mountain soils of the higher, more heavily forested Ore Mountains.

Agrarian activity began in this part of Saxony less than a thousand years ago. Prior to settlement by the Thuringian and Franconian peasants, the wooded uplands of the area were given over to the hunter and the pastoral nomad. During the first centuries of the present millennium, German peasants cut down much of the forest and cleared the land for cultivation. Copper, lead, and silver mining in the uplands in the later Middle Ages encouraged the further development of the agrarian village despite the poor soils of the hills. In recent years the agricultural land of upland Saxony was held in small (2-5 hectares) and medium-sized (5-20 hectares) farms on which grain, forage crops, and livestock are raised. Buckwheat and flax are common crops in the foothills of the Ore Mountains, while wheat is the main crop in the *Oberlausitz* area. The vineyards, which flourished in Saxon Switzerland during the Middle Ages, are of little importance today. Market gardening and dairying are important near the industrial and manufacturing cities of Plauen, Zwickau, and Freiberg. The heavily forested Ore Mountain area, however, is devoted to livestock and dairying. The small farmers obtain their cash from butter and cheese, and cultivate only enough land to supply their fodder and food needs. In the uplands of Saxony, family labor is the backbone of agriculture, and only the largest farms can afford a farm hand. Agricultural machinery is not common. The peasants dwell in villages of the *Waldhufendorf* type, which consists of houses and barns built about a farmyard and scattered irregularly along a road. The farm land extends from the house and garden into the hills, giving each farmer his strip of arable land, pasture, and woodland. Most of the upland villages are large, with a population ranging between 600 and 1600 inhabitants. An even larger type of village with a population between 1600 and 4500 and capable of supporting a weekly market is common in southwestern Saxony.

Most of the agricultural production of the state comes from the northwestern loess zone. It constitutes a part of the most productive agricultural land of Germany. The uplands are not important for the production of crop surpluses, although their livestock and dairy products are important. The major crop is potatoes, followed by rye, wheat, sugar beets, and finally barley.

LAND UTILIZATION (HECTARES) 1933

Cultivated Land		709,700
Grain	423,000	
Legumes	4,400	
Root Crops	156,000	
Green Vegetables	4,800	
Industrial Crops	4,500	
Fodder Crops	117,000	
Agrarian Land		246,700
Small Gardens	41,300	
Meadow and Pasture	200,800	
Orchards	4,500	
Vineyards	100	

Almost 25 per cent of the land surface of the state of Saxony was covered by forest, leaving 64 per cent for agriculture, which was mostly devoted to crop cultivation, and 11 per cent to waste, roads, and urban construction. Although the amount of forest land was far less than that in the southern and western German states and provinces, it was, nevertheless, about average for the Reich and certainly greater than that of the northeastern Prussian provinces. The actual distribution of the forest area is subject to wide variations. The loess area is now very sparsely wooded, although it may once have been a parkland with scattered stands of deciduous type. The uplands are covered with a combination of spruce, fir, and beech which give way in the higher Ore Mountains to typical alpine spruce forests. These forest lands were owned by a variety of interests. The state of Saxony owned 174,000 hectares of forest land which it administered through seventy-nine state forest reserves. These reserves, which constituted about 47 per cent of the forest area, were under the Saxon State Forest Administration (*Sächsische Landesforstverwaltung*) at Dresden. The work of the forest administration, however, was not restricted to state properties, for it also supervised the management of the municipal forests, which formed about 15 per cent of the forest land, and of the private forests, which included the remaining 38 per cent of the woodland. This work was carried out through the county Forest Office.

The dominant rural group of the state is known today as the Upper Saxon (*Obersachsen*) group. It is a blend resulting from the mixture of Thuringian and Franconian settlers with the old Slavic population. The unification of the area under political and economic pressures is revealed by the uniformity of the lilting and rhythmical modern Saxon speech, which is one of the most distinctive of all German dialects. Its musical quality has given rise to the designation, the "singing Saxon." The widespread and long industrialization of the state has done much to change the ways of rural living. The modern Saxon peasant is a liberal; conservative and old-fashioned ways survive only in the more remote rural areas. The Upper Saxons are alert, convivial, talkative people, and have the reputation of being courteous and cordial to strangers.

URBAN ASPECT

The state of Saxony was one of the most highly urbanized of the German states or provinces. With the Province of Saxony and Thuringia it formed the second most important industrial and manufacturing area in Germany. Although it was settled later than western Germany, its position on trade routes connecting Western Germany with Poland, and northern Germany with Bohemia, its once abundant natural resources, and its rich agricultural potential, resulted in the rapid development of towns and cities in the later Middle Ages. Although most of the major cities of Saxony are Slavic in origin, their real growth did not come until the German settlement of the twelfth and thirteenth centuries. With this more than adequate foundation for urban life, the cities of Saxony mushroomed rapidly under the stimulus of the German industrial revolution. Prior to World War II over 35 per cent of the population of the area dwelt in the four large cities of Leipzig, Dresden, Chemnitz, and Plauen, while another 12 per cent of the population lived in the 25 smaller cities which had a population of more than 20,000.

Leipzig, situated in northwestern Saxony, was not only the commercial and financial center of the state, but one of the important economic centers of the Reich. The area between Chemnitz and Plauen, the "Saxon Manchester," formed a heavily urbanized and industrialized area, studded with numerous large and small manufacturing towns, such as Zwickau, Aue, Glauchau, and Döbeln. Northeastern Saxony was dominated by the city of Dresden, the cultural and political capital of the area, and the smaller Elbe River towns of Oschatz, Meissen, and Pirna. Eastern Saxony was somewhat less urbanized and industrialized than the west, but it did support the towns of Bautzen and Zittau.

The state of Saxony formed an integral part of the Central German industrial area which embraces the state of Thuringia, the Province of Saxony, and the state of Saxony. The development of this area as the second most important German industrial area was based upon the varied mineral resources of the Harz and Ore mountains, supplies of coal, timber, and lignite, and commercial advantages accruing from its position astride vital north-south and east-west trade routes. Although mining in the Harz and Ore mountains and the metal and textile industries of many of the Central German cities goes back to the late Middle Ages, the rapid development of the present industrial complex characterized by a strong economic interdependence, came during and following World War I. The state could be regarded as a distinct economic sub-region, although much of the industrial and commercial life of Saxony was intimately linked with that of Central Germany. The distinct socio-economic character of the area as a real unit of human activity and organization was fully recognized and exploited by the Nazis when they placed this administrative unit under one state planning organization, and coordinated its agriculture under one state peasants' group and its industry under a separate economic unit. They recognized the economic interdependence of the Central German area in terms of trade and particularly transportation, vital for the movement of raw materials, when all of Central Germany was placed under one section of the National Traffic Groups (*Reichsverkehrsgruppen*) with headquarters at Magdeburg.

The state of Saxony has had a varied supply of natural resources. In earlier days the mining of silver, nickel, lead, copper, and other minerals was economically important. Silver mining at Freiberg and Johanngeorgenstadt and the mines of Schneeberg go back to the early Middle Ages. The medieval mining operations in the forested uplands led to the relatively dense settlement of that region, but the deposits were so limited that, even with the primitive mining methods of earlier days, the ores had become exhausted by the late nineteenth century, and the forests had become depleted by the demands for raw material and fuel. The next mining boom came in relatively modern times with the opening of the coal fields near Dresden and in the Zwickau-Chemnitz area; but these veins were small, and today the Saxon coal reserve is very low. The lignite fields near Leipzig and in the Oberlausitz, Dresden, and Zittau areas represent extensions of deposits which have their greatest reserves in the provinces of Brandenburg and Saxony. Hence, Saxon industry is dependent upon outside sources for its major supplies of coal, metal, and lignite.

The only major resources lying within Saxony include clays for brick, which was made in great quantities throughout the state, Elbe sandstone for building material, and the fine porcelain clays of Meissen. The vital power needs of the state are, however, still partly met by local resources. The remaining coal deposits of the Zwickau area supported a number of small coal electrical power stations, and the deposits near Dresden at Pirna, a relatively important coal power station. The only major lignite power station was located in Oberlausitz at Zittau, though other minor lignite plants were situated near Leipzig and Dresden. Most of the power needs were met by the great lignite power stations at Zschornewitz in the Province of Saxony and at Lauta and Trattendorf in the Province of Brandenburg. The latter two stations supplied eastern Saxony, while the former plant supplied western Saxony. The Plauen-Zwickau-Chemnitz area was served by a small power line network which was linked to eastern Saxony by a high tension line running from Plauen to Dresden and Zittau.

Some electrical power was also obtained from the water power stations in Bavaria, for high tension lines connected western Saxony with the water power plants on the Isar River in southern Bavaria.

With the decline of the traditional metal industry, Saxony has turned more and more to the textile field. Textiles were not a relatively new thing, for Zwickau and Chemnitz were already important wool centers in late medieval times, and the production of yarns and cloth had long been a home and village industry. The western portion of Saxony has become the center of cotton manufacturing, thanks to its moister climate and water power potential made possible by the nature of the tributaries of the Mulde River. Chemnitz turned from wool to cotton textiles as long ago as the seventeenth century. The textile industry was mechanized in the eighteenth century, and it soon made Saxony one of the most important European textile centers. Other important textile centers included Zwickau, Plauen, Werdau, Glauchau, Crimmitschau, Mittweida, Meerane, and Wurzen. Although most of these cities still retained some of the traditional wool industry, it developed more extensively in the northeastern part of Saxony.

The machinery and engineering industries were next in importance and had developed to meet the needs of the extensive textile, mining, and paper industries. The major center of the machine industry in western Saxony was located at Chemnitz. Although it must import all its iron by railway, it produced locomotives, automobiles, textile machinery, and other metal products. Other important machinery and metal products manufacturing centers in the area were located at Aue (Wellner silverware and machine tools), Crimmitschau, Freiberg (gold and silverware and machinery), Plauen, and Zwickau. The machine and metal industries made up a part of the mixed industries of the Leipzig and Elbe-Dresden area.

Leipzig developed the manufacturing of printing presses and equipment to meet the needs of its large printing trade. It became an important center for all types of machinery and electrical equipment. Most of the cities of northeastern Saxony had a small interest in the machine industry. Dresden was important for sewing machines, while railway cars and automobile bodies were produced at Bautzen. Meissen and Zittau also had some machinery industry. The city of Riesa on the Elbe had the only important steel works (*Mitteldeutsche Stahlwerke*) in the state, but it could not meet the needs of the industries listed above. Paper manufacturing was almost as important as the machinery, major centers being located in western Saxony near the textile plants. Publishing and printing firms at Leipzig were world famous and constituted the largest center of their type in Germany. The food products and wood products industries ranked next in importance, for which Dresden, Leipzig, and Meissen were the major centers. Other industries were of minor significance in terms of the number of plants and workers. Chemicals were made at Dresden, Chemnitz, and Pirna, while glass and optical goods were important products at Dresden (Zeiss-Ikon), Chemnitz, and Leipzig. Stone and earthenware were made at Chemnitz, Zwickau, and Bautzen, while the world famous "Dresden" china came from Meissen.

The traditional home and village industries of Saxony, which were "carefully" cultivated by the Nazis, still retained some importance. Linen is still made on hand looms in Oberlausitz, while lace making, which was introduced among the villages of the western Ore Mountains in the sixteenth century, still survives on an important scale at Plauen. Toys for export were widely made by home craftsmen in the central Ore Mountain area. Musical instruments and excellent watches came from the Vogtland. In normal times these home-made products were in great demand.

The position of the state in Central Germany gave it easy access to Bavaria on the southwest, to the central uplands on the west, to the northern plains and Prussia on the north, and to Czechoslovakia on the south. A triangular road system linked Plauen, Zwickau, Leipzig, Dresden, and Chemnitz. Other roads connected Plauen with Nürnberg and Augsburg, Stuttgart, Munich, and Passau on the south; Leipzig with Erfurt, Magdeburg, and Berlin; and Dresden with Erfurt, Prague, and Berlin. The construction and maintenance of the main state roads were handled by the state ministry at Dresden, while local roads were under the county administrations. Under the Nazi regime the normal road system was supplemented by the national super-highway connecting Dresden and Leipzig; Dresden, Chemnitz, and Plauen; and Plauen, Gera, and Leipzig.

The major railroad lines had a pattern of distribution much like that of the roads. The key points included Leipzig, Dresden, Chemnitz, Zwickau, and Plauen. The heaviest traffic was borne by the line linking Munich, Regensburg, Hof, Plauen, and Leipzig, which is a major rail junction. The railroads of the state were under the National Railroad Directorate at Dresden, although railroad affairs in northwestern Saxony fell under the directorate at Halle.

The only important water transportation in the state is provided by the river Elbe, which is navigable from Prague in Czechoslovakia to the port of Hamburg on the North Sea. While relatively few finished goods were shipped from Saxony by way of the Elbe, the river was of importance because it provides cheap transportation for coal, lignite, ore, and other raw materials needed by the industries of the region. The small canal linking Leipzig to the river Saale is a recent creation. There were three major international air centers in Saxony, at Leipzig, Dresden, and Chemnitz. Although the air service was operated by the German Airways Corporation, the airports were owned and operated by the municipalities.

Dresden was the political and administrative center of the state of Saxony, but Leipzig was the main commercial and financial center. Dresden, Zwickau, and Plauen, however, played important commercial and financial roles locally. Though all of these cities have been important centers of trade since the Middle Ages, Leipzig has always had the dominant position. It arose at the junction of some of the most important trade routes in Europe. Owing to the enlightened mercantile policies of the Wettins, it rose rapidly to prominence in the commercial field. The great commercial fairs of Leipzig, which have been held yearly since the fifteenth century, attracted businessmen from all over Europe.

The general commercial interests of Saxony reflected its agrarian, forestry, and industrial activities. Coal and iron were brought in by rail and canal from the west to meet the needs of industry. The only important raw materials produced and shipped from the area were stone and clays. Although the light manufactured goods produced by the Saxon industries did not bulk large in traffic statistics, they were nevertheless important. They included wool and cotton textiles, machinery, china and ceramic products, wood products and furniture, and cigarettes. The specialization of the textile industry in the state led to an extensive trade in textiles between the cotton mills of the west and the woolen mills of the east. These in turn carried on an active trade in yarns with Northern Bavaria, Thuringia, and Silesia. The Saxon textile and cloth industries supplied the needs of most of Germany east of the Elbe. The economic interdependence of the Middle German area was also shown by the extensive trade in machinery between the plants of the state of Saxony and those of Thuringia and the Province of Saxony. The state also carried on a large machinery trade with Silesia, Brandenburg, and Berlin. The agricultural machinery needs of the southern part of Central Germany were met by the merchants of Leipzig.

The banking and credit institutions of the state of Saxony had their main centers at Leipzig and Dresden. They ranged in type from branches of the great commercial banks of Berlin, which were mainly interested in investments of the industrial type, to the local county and municipal mortgage and savings banks. The important state banking institutions were located at Dresden. The operations of these banks were supplemented by those of the branches of the *Reichsbank* at Dresden, Leipzig, Plauen, and Zwickau. State insurance companies, with headquarters in Dresden, were under the state Ministry of the Interior. The state of Saxony was served by stock exchanges at Chemnitz, Dresden, Leipzig, and Plauen.

The urban population of Saxony was largely engaged in industry, trade, and transportation enterprises. Of the total population of the state, 2,610,000 individuals, or about 50 per cent of the working population, made their living in industry and crafts, while 936,000 individuals, or about 18 per cent of the working population, were engaged in trade and transportation enterprises. This class structure resulted in several interesting features. The working class of the state was the second largest in the Reich in comparison with other states or provinces. The upper class was relatively small, while the white collar class was large, owing to the need for a large managerial and commercial class. The number of civil servants was about average for the Reich.

The vital urban centers of Saxony were situated in the western Plauen-Zwickau-Chemnitz area, in the northwest Leipzig area, and along the Elbe. Although the level and fertile land of the northwest supported an industrious farming population, and while the partly forested uplands of the south were relatively heavily populated, thanks to traditional industries of the village and craft type, Saxon life centered above all in the larger cities. Dresden on the Elbe was not only the capital of the state, but one of the important German cultural centers. It was called the "German Florence." It owed much of its fame as a cultural and architectural center to the rulers of Saxony, for its real growth came in the baroque period when the Wettin rulers turned their attention to the task of amassing art collections and splendid buildings at their capital. Although royal patronage had gone, the two state theaters, the state opera, the numerous museums, and the state art academy officially carried on the cultural traditions of Dresden. And while it was a city of gardens and parks, it was supported by considerable industry and commerce. It was the main German market center for Greek and Turkish tobacco, the home of numerous food industries, and a center for photographic equipment, straw hats, and machinery.

Down the Elbe from Dresden lies Meissen, the home of Europe's oldest porcelain works, while Freiberg, which is located west of Dresden in the foothills of the Ore Mountains, is the oldest mining center in Saxony. It was well known for its mining academy. The city of Pirna, on the Elbe above Dresden in the heart of the picturesque Saxon Switzerland, was mainly important for its sandstone quarries and art silks. It is also a point of departure for the resorts of the Saxon Switzerland—Bad Schandau and Königstein. Bautzen and Zittau in the hills of Oberlausitz were the only important cities of the northeast.

Leipzig, the commercial and financial center, was originally a Slavic village. Germanized in the eleventh century, by the fifteenth it was already an important trading center holding its first fairs which have continued to attract people from every branch of industry and trade. It was the fifth city of Germany, and owing to its strategic position, it was one of the great transportation points of Central Europe. From an industrial point of view, Leipzig was important for its printing and publishing houses and its metallurgical, textile, and machine plants. Its cultural history is equally remarkable. The University of Leipzig, which was established in 1409, has been an important center of learning for the past two hundred years. In the eighteenth century Leipzig was the residence of Bach, Leibnitz, and Schiller. Goethe was a student at the University. The musical traditions of the city, which was the birthplace of Richard Wagner, continue in the famous Gewandhaus concerts and the work of the St. Thomas' Church Choir. Chemnitz, Zwickau, and Plauen were the important cities of western Saxony. Chemnitz, the third largest city, was mainly a textile and machinery center, while Zwickau was a flourishing mining and industrial town, not without historical and cultural importance for it was the home of Robert Schumann and one of the foci of the Reformation Anabaptist movement. Plauen, in the heart of the Vogtland hills, was another textile town of some importance. Although the state of Saxony had its points of cultural and historical interest for the traveler, it was primarily a densely populated industrial and manufacturing area studded by numerous cities of considerable importance in the economy of the Reich.

Chapter 26

THE STATE OF THURINGIA*

The state of Thuringia occupies the geographical heart of Germany. Technically, the term "Thüringen" was long used to designate a district in the Province of Saxony that is bound by the river Werra, the river Saale, the Harz Mountains, and the Thuringian Forests (*Thüringer Wald*). The name has frequently been used, however, to designate the group of small duchies and principalities lying between the Province of Saxony, the Province of Hesse-Nassau, the state of Saxony, and the state of Bavaria. Although the formation of the state of Thuringia at the end of World War I brought the consolidation of these territories and their subdivision for purposes of administration into ten city-counties and five counties, and one sub-district, the problem of enclaves and exclaves was not settled. Down to the end of World War II various exclaves of the Province of Saxony and the Province of Hesse-Nassau were embedded in Thuringian territory and parts of Thuringia were found within the area of the Province of Saxony and the state of Bavaria.

Thuringia is a hilly land of meadows and forests. In the southwestern portion of the state are the Thuringian Forests and the valley of the Werra River which rises in the southern portion of this upland area and flows northwestward to the west of the forest to join the river Fulda at Münden in the Province of Hanover. The confluence of the two rivers forms the river Weser. The rest of Thuringia which lies to the north and east of the uplands of the Thuringian Forests consists of the Thuringian Basin, the economic and cultural center of the state. The rolling lands of the basin country are drained by the Gera, Ilm, Saale, and Elster rivers, flowing in a north or northeasterly direction, all tributaries of the river Elbe. The Thuringian Basin is surrounded on the north and east by plateau lands which give way northward to the valley of the Goldene Aue plains and to the Harz Mountains, and eastward to the Vogtland and the plateau country of southeast Saxony. While the Thuringian Forest (average elevation of 2460 feet) is heavily forested and sparsely populated, the

* German spelling—Thüringen.

527

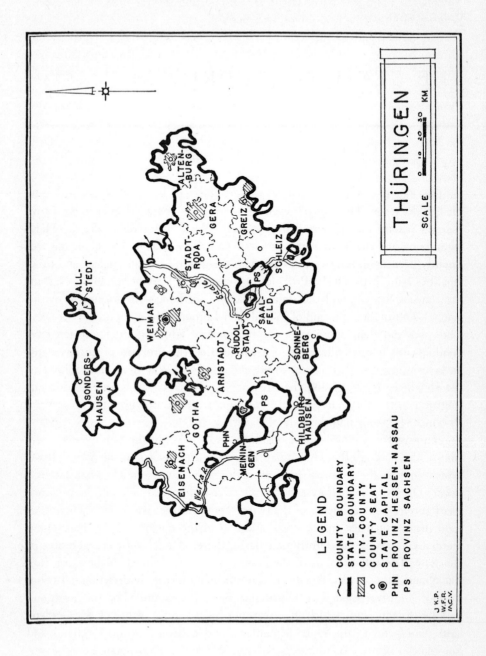

Thuringian Basin is a lower fertile area supporting several cities of fair size—
Weimar, Gotha, Jena, Rudolstadt, and Gera.

The greater part of the state of Thuringia has long been occupied by the
Thuringian peoples, although they did not appear historically until A.D. 420.
This part of Germany had been occupied by Germanic tribes as far back as 200
B.C., when they drove the older Keltic population southward into Bavaria. The
Thuringians were in complete control of the area during most of the fifth and
sixth centuries, when they ruled an area extending from the Oker and Ohre to
the Main and from the Mulde and Elbe to the Werra River. In 531 the Thuringian Kingdom fell to the Franks, and their lands were incorporated into the
Merovingian Empire. Since that time the Thuringian group has slowly lost
ground. During the great period of German settlement, the *Rodungszeit* (750-
1250), the eastern Franks pushing up the valley of the Main occupied the southernmost part of the state of Thuringia, while Low Saxon peoples from northwestern Germany intruded into northern Thuringia. The Thuringians moved
into eastern Thuringia to subdue and mix with the Slavic peoples who had settled between the Ilm and Gera rivers. Today, they are the smallest of the German basic groups (*Stämme*). The modern dialect belongs to Middle German
and is akin to dialects of the Frankish Rhineland and the state of Saxony.
There are no cultural cleavages of the religious type. More than 1,485,000 individuals (over 89 per cent) in 1933 were Lutheran Protestant. There were,
however, numerous Catholic pockets in the southeastern part of the state. The
Jewish population was relatively small in comparison with other parts of the
Reich.

Thuringia ranked seventh in size among the German states, in 1933, and
stood sixth in point of population, with 1,659,500 inhabitants occupying 11,-
762 sq. km. The population density was 141 per sq. km. Excluding the Hanse
cities and Berlin, this made Thuringia the eighth most densely settled of the
twenty-seven German states and Prussian provinces. There was a marked agreement between the pattern of population density and that of distribution. The
most densely settled areas were to be found along the Werra and Saale where
the density in the valley proper was over 200 per sq. km., while the population
density of the hilly areas adjacent to the river valleys ranged between 120 and
200. The basin portion of Thuringia also had a density between 120 and 200 per
sq. km., with the average 145 per sq. km., while the surrounding plateau areas
had a lighter population, with a density ranging between 60 and 80. The uplands of the Thuringian Forests had a relatively heavy population in comparison with other upland areas in Germany. The population density of the
higher portions of the forest ranged between 40 and 60 individuals per sq. km.,
but the average for the forest area as a whole was 91 per sq. km. Since earliest
times this state has been one of the more heavily settled portions of the Reich.

In the last century and a half, the population steadily increased, although the greatest period of increase came between 1870 and 1910. This expansion was due to the rapid industrialization of this part of Germany in the late nineteenth century. Between 1875 and 1925, the population of Thuringia increased by almost 75 per cent. This increase was due to the extensive growth of numerous small towns which added some industry in the course of the last seventy-five years. Migration was hardly a factor in the Thuringian population problem. In comparison with southern or northwestern Germany very few individuals left Thuringia for lands outside the Reich.

The state of Thuringia was established on April 30, 1920, through the union of the territories of Saxe-Weimar-Eisenach, Saxe-Meiningen, Saxe-Altenburg, Saxe-Coburg-Gotha, Reuss, Schwarzburg-Rudolstadt, and Schwarzburg-Sondershausen. At this time the union was recognized by a law of the German Reich based on Article 18, Section 2, of the Constitution of the German Republic. The history of these small duchies and principalities, whose particularistic dynasties were swept away by the revolutions of November 1918, goes back to the Middle Ages. The first known political-administrative organization in the Thuringian area was the tribal kingdom of the Thuringians which lasted from about 400 to 531 when it was conquered by the Franks. During the early Merovingian times it was ruled directly by the Frankish Kings. Later it was placed under the control of a duke. In Carolingian times the dukedom was abolished and the land divided among several Frankish counts. In 804 Charlemagne founded the Thuringian Mark to defend the Saale line against the Slavs. The rule of the frontier Margraves lasted until 908 when Thuringia was annexed by the powerful dukes of Saxony, who controlled all of Northwest Germany. In 930 the Emperor of the Holy Roman Empire established a fort at Meissen to defend the Empire against the inroads of the Slavs. In 1046 the Margraviate of Meissen was given to Earl Dedo II of Wettin, who was the ancestor of the ruling house of the Old Kingdom of Saxony as well as the reigning houses of the Grand-Duchy and duchies of Saxony. In the thirteenth century the holdings of the Wettin family were enlarged by the addition of the Landgraviate of Thuringia. In 1422 the electoral dignity was conferred upon the Margrave Friedrich of Meissen. Since that time the lands of the Margrave have been designated as the electorate of Saxony.

Thuringia formed a united territorial unit ruled by the Electors of Saxony until 1464. As indicated above, upon the death of Friedrich II of Saxony the lands were divided between his sons Ernst and Albert, and the latter obtained by concession the ancient Margraviate of Meissen and part of Thuringia. After John Friedrich, the grandson of Ernst, was deposed as Elector and Albert's grandson Moritz was invested with the electorate, he ceded to the deposed Elector and his descendants the territories of Weimar, Jena, Eisenach, and Gotha, to which in 1554 was added Altenburg. As the Saxon Grand-Duchy and the duchies of Thuringia, these territories were ruled by the descendants of Ernst until World War I.

HISTORICAL DEVELOPMENTS

The Grand-Duchy of Saxe-Weimar-Eisenach.—Johann Friedrich ruled much of what is now known as Thuringia. After his death in 1554 and a series of complicated inheritance settlements, his three sons divided the lands, founding the principalities of Saxe-Weimar, Saxe-Eisenach, and Saxe-Gotha. The dukes at Saxe-Weimar inherited a group of territories about Jena in 1690 and the dominion of Eisenach in 1741. The most brilliant period of the history of this duchy came in the reign of Duke Karl August when Goethe, Schiller, and Herder dwelt at Weimar. The small state managed to maintain its independent status during the early Napoleonic period. In 1807 it joined the Confederation of the Rhine (*Rheinbund*). In 1813 Saxe-Weimar-Eisenach deserted Napoleon for the Allies. At the Congress of Vienna (1815) it received several small territories from the Kingdom of Saxony and the electorate of Hesse, and was elevated to the status of a Grand-Duchy. In 1817 a liberal constitution was granted by the Grand Duke which, except for the revisions of 1850 and 1906, remained in force until 1918. In 1866 Saxe-Weimar-Eisenach joined with Prussia against Austria. The Grand-Duchy became a sovereign and constituent member state of the German Empire in 1871.

The Duchy of Saxe-Meiningen.—This duchy was established by Duke Bernhard, the third son of Ernst the Pious, Duke of Saxe-Gotha, in 1681. His lands consisted of the Meiningen territory, whose history went back to the ancient Earldom of Henneberg, which had been inherited by the Wettin house in 1583. In the eighteenth and early nineteenth centuries, the Duchy was plagued by the evils of the Seven Years' War and later the disruption attendant upon the Napoleonic struggle. During the latter wars Saxe-Meiningen joined the Confederation of the Rhine in 1807 and then turned to the side of the Allies in 1813. In 1815 the Duchy became a member of the German Confederation. Although Saxe-Meiningen had received no territorial additions at the time of the Congress of Vienna (1815), the extinction of the house of Saxe-Gotha in 1825 brought the addition of the Duchy of Hildburghausen and the principality of Saalfeld. The constitution, which remained in effect until 1918, was promulgated in 1829 and revised in 1871, 1873, and 1896. Unlike the other states of Thuringia, Saxe-Meiningen sided with Austria in 1866. Prussian troops occupied the small duchy and forced the abdication of the Duke. His son quickly made peace and joined the North German Confederation. In 1871 the Duchy became a sovereign and constituent member of the German Empire.

The Duchy of Saxe-Coburg-Gotha.—This duchy was established by Albert, a son of Duke Ernst the Pious. In 1699 Albert's line became extinct and the lands of Saxe-Coburg became the object of a violent struggle between the Saxon Dukes. It was eventually assigned to another son of Ernst the Pious, Duke Johann Ernst of Saalfeld, who after this inheritance styled himself the Duke of Saxe-Coburg-Saalfeld. During the eighteenth century there were no territorial changes. The Napoleonic period brought the occupation of Saxe-Coburg-Saalfeld, for its Duke had sided with Prussia against France. The next territorial change came not at Vienna (1815), but upon the extinction of the line of Saxe-Gotha. In 1826 the reigning Duke Ernst II (1818-1893) exchanged Saalfeld for Gotha and assumed the title of Duke of Saxe-Coburg-Gotha. Ernst's brother Albert became the husband of Queen Victoria of England, and, therefore, when Ernst died without heirs in 1893, Prince Alfred, the son of Victoria and Albert, became the ruling Duke of Saxe-Coburg-Gotha. He also died without heirs and the succession passed to Charles Edward, H.R.H. Duke of Albany, who ruled until 1918.

The Duchy of Saxe-Altenburg.—Altenburg was inherited by Duke Ernst the Pious in 1672. His son Duke Friedrich of Saxe-Gotha came into possession of Altenburg in 1680. Altenburg and Gotha remained united until the extinction of the Saxe-Gotha line in 1825. The Duchy of Saxe-Altenburg was established in 1826 when Duke Friedrich of Saxe-Hildburghausen gave his duchy to the Duke of Saxe-Meiningen and took instead the Altenburg portion of the old Duchy of Saxe-Gotha-Altenburg. In 1871 the Duchy became a sovereign and constituent state of the German Empire.

The Principalities of Reuss.—The two principalities of Reuss, which lasted down until the end of World War I, go back to the early Middle Ages when Earl Heinrich I of Glitzberg, descended from the House of Luxemburg, was given the vogtships of Gera and Weida in Thuringia. The lands which later became known as Reuss because of relationships of this family with Russian affairs were gradually enlarged. In 1564 the family divided the lands into three parts—Reuss-Schleiz, Reuss-Gera, and Reuss-Greiz. The Gera branch died out in 1616 and its lands were inherited by the Reuss-Schleiz lines. These two lines flourished until 1918. Both principalities joined the Confederation of the Rhine in 1807, the German Confederation in 1815, and the German Empire in 1871.

The Principalities of Schwarzburg.—These two principalities, like those of Reuss, were of non-Wettin origin. The Schwarzburg line goes back to the twelfth century earls of Schwarzburg and Käfernburg. After many aggrandizements and divisions the lands fell to Earl Günther, establishing the line of Schwarzburg-Sondershausen, and Albert Anton, founding the line of Schwarzburg-Rudolstadt. Both principalities joined the Confederation of the Rhine in 1807, the German Confederation in 1815, and the German Empire in 1871.

Constitutional Developments

Under the Empire, each of the small Thuringian states was governed by a separate constitution, which had been granted between 1816 and 1867. They were ruled by hereditary rulers who carried out the administration of their respective states through a State Ministry. Legislation was cleared through a unicameral assembly, which consisted of delegates appointed by the rulers or elected on the basis of a limited suffrage, except in the truly democratic state of Coburg-Gotha.

All the small dynasties with the exception of Schwarzburg-Rudolstadt, where a republic was established through an agreement between the Prince and the Diet, were swept away by revolutionary methods. The merger of the seven Thuringian states came after much negotiation which began in May 1919. Already before this, the two principalities of Reuss had merged to form one state of Reuss in April 1919, while the personal union between Saxe-Coburg and Gotha had been dissolved. On November 30, 1919, Saxe-Coburg declared for Bavaria. This was effected by the Reich law of April, 1920. Although a movement for the unification of Thuringia was under way, all the states except Gotha, which was in the hands of a Communist regime, instituted elections for constituent assemblies to vote new constitutions. Meanwhile, all the states except Saxe-Meiningen and Saxe-Coburg had tentatively agreed on a federated state with a People's Council—Legislative Chamber (*Volksrat*) and a State Council. Later Saxe-Meiningen joined with the others and on January 28, 1920, the newly formed People's Council declared its right to vote a constitution for a united Thuringia. On March 12, 1920, a provisional constitution was voted, and by June 1920, the first assembly (*Landtag*) had been elected. It accepted the constitution with revisions on March 11, 1921.

The republican government of Thuringia consisted of a single chamber assembly and a ministry responsible to it. The president of the ministry was chosen by the ministry and was its chairman. The republican constitution did not provide for a formal head of state. Administration was carried out by a State Ministry and by the Ministries of Interior, Finance, Education, Justice, and Economics. The old divisions of Thuringia were retained until March 31, 1922, when the land was divided into ten city counties and fifteen counties and one Sub-District (*Kreisabteilung*). Naturally, the newly formed state of Thuringia became one of the constituent republics of Weimar Germany.

Under the Empire and under the Republic the state of Thuringia was a Social Democratic stronghold. The National Liberals and the Liberal Progressives had only small holdings in the Thuringian Forest. In republican times the state strongly supported the Socialists and Communists. Together these parties cast about 40 per cent of the total popular vote. A political party of the Right of local importance known as the Christian National Peasant and Farmers' party (*Christlichnationale Bauern- und Landvolkpartei*), was a factor until 1932 when most of its supporters jumped on the Nazi bandwagon. Receiving some 125,000 votes in 1928 as the second strongest party, the farmers' party vote was cut in half by the July election of 1932, and thereafter practically disappeared in the huge vote given to the Nazis. The National Socialist vote increased phenomenally, rising from 30,000 votes in 1928 to 180,000 in 1930, and to 424,000 in the July 1932 election, in the latter year exceeding the Socialist and Communist vote together. Unlike most other districts of the Reich, Thuringia voted for Hitler for President against Hindenburg in the second presidential election of 1932, an additional proof of its Nazi leanings. Dr. Frick, a leading Nazi, became a member of the Thuringian cabinet as early as 1930. Thuringia was also the first of the German states to install a Nazi state cabinet in the days of the Republic. This occurred in 1932 following the state elections of that year which swept the party into power. With the exception of its few cities, Thuringia throughout its length and breadth supported Hitler. Several of its areas were outstanding strongholds of National Socialism, namely Gotha, Weimar, Meiningen, Sondershausen, and Arnstadt. Hitler always made a point of visiting Weimar, the capital of Thuringia, as often as possible, and since his party acquired its first administrative experience in Thuringia, and there achieved some of its early political victories, the state always played an important part in Nazi party politics.

The state of Thuringia formed a part of the Nazi party district of *Gau* Thuringia, which included the state of Thuringia and the administrative district of Erfurt. The headquarters of the party district at Weimar included offices which dealt with every aspect of party activity and which served as the organizational center for a dense network of party controls.

The advent of the Nazi regime brought drastic changes in the government and administration of Thuringia. Like the other German states, it lost its status as a Federal Republic, and its rights were transferred to the Reich. The Nazis placed a National Governor with headquarters at Weimar, the state capital, in charge of the government and administration. He was directly responsible to the national Minister of the Interior, but was also subject to the directives from other national ministers. It must be noted that the Governor of Thuringia was also the Nazi party leader for the party district of Thuringia. The state administration of Thuringia was headed by a Minister President and consisted of five ministries: a State Ministry, Finance Ministry, Ministry of the Interior, Ministry of Education (*Volksbildungsministerium*), and Economics Ministry. The Minister President headed all of the ministries except the Ministry of the Interior.

The work of the state administration was supplemented by special and technical services under direct national control. During the imperial period only the nationally operated postal system lay outside the state administration. The nationally uniform court system, which was administered by the state under the Empire and by the unified state under the Republic, was under the Superior State Court of Jena and its Collegiate Courts of First and Second Instance at Altenburg, Gera, Eisenach, Gotha, Meiningen, Rudolstadt, and Weimar and the Superior State Court of Naumburg and the Collegiate Court at Erfurt. The national postal system within Thüringia was under the Chief Postal Directorates (under the Empire) or National Postal Directorates (under the Republic and the Third Reich) at Erfurt and Leipzig. National regulations for trade and industry, weights and measures, social insurance, public health, and the collection of imperial revenues was carried out upon delegation from the Reich.

A further extension of direct national administration to finance, railways, unemployment insurance, employment, and labor welfare had occurred during the Republic. The State Finance Office of Thuringia (Rudolstadt) and its finance and customs offices managed the national finances. There was a National Construction Office at Rudolstadt. The nationally operated railways operated under the National Railroad Directorate at Erfurt. Here, too, labor and unemployment problems were handled by a State Labor Office for Central Germany at Erfurt and a main Welfare Office for Central Germany at Magdeburg. Where national legislation affected welfare, social insurance, health, trade and industry, and labor, these services were administered upon delegation from the Reich. The economic life of the state was organized under a number of national agricultural, industrial, commercial, and labor organizations.

National administrative authority was extended to justice during the Nazi regime. Police, health, welfare, education, certain aspects of social insurance, and other customary fields of state administration were brought under national control. Economic planning was carried out by the State Planning Association of Thuringia and the district of *Rgbz.* Erfurt which was under the leadership of the Governor of Thuringia. Again, many corporate administrations added to the general and special administrations secured complete Nazi control throughout the state.

RURAL ASPECT

The open lands of the central and eastern basin of Thuringia have been settled and cultivated since Neolithic times. During the early Middle Ages, the peasants pushed into the woodlands of the surrounding plateau and the Thuringian Forests to clear the land for agrarian activities. Although light manufacturing was the major interest of modern Thuringia, 18 per cent of the population was engaged in agricultural and forestry activities. While rural pursuits were relatively unimportant in the basin area, rural activities predominated in the plateau and the Thuringian Forest areas. Considering the state as a whole, a surprisingly large proportion of the population lived close to the soil. Close to 44 per cent of the population dwelt in villages with a population of less than 2,000, while 31 per cent of the population lived in towns ranging in size from 2,000 to 20,000.

Although the "interior" administration of Thuringia in Nazi days was under the Ministry of the Interior at Weimar, which was subject to the national Ministry of the Interior in Berlin, much of the day-to-day rural administration was under the County Managers of the county and their subordinates, the Mayors of the towns which made up the counties. County government and administration in Thuringia came to be very much like that of the Prussian county. This arrangement has not always been the case. When the sixteen counties were formed out of the old duchies and principalities under the Town and County Constitution of 1922, the local self-administration was organized under an elected county council, which chose each year from its membership a Chairman (*Kreisdirektor*). It was responsible for welfare, insurance, youth, school, road, and unemployment affairs, and managed the enterprises of the county. State supervision was carried out by the County Office which was headed by a County Manager. The Town and County Constitutions of 1926 and 1930 brought the gradual reduction of the functions of the County Council through their transfer to the County Office.

The last change in the organization of county administration came with the advent of the Nazi regime in 1933. The County Manager became the leader of county administration and self-government. The County Council was reduced in size and became an appointed advisory council assisting the County Manager. In 1938 the term County Council was replaced by County Advisory Committee in order to conform with the Prussian designation. The County Manager had the supervision of the government and administration of the towns and villages of the county. He was the administrative authority for all county Order Police. He had control over all officials of Registration Offices for Vital Statistics (*Standesamtbeamte*) and maintained close working relationships with the County Health Office and the local Town Health Offices. He worked with the County School Office (*Kreisschulamt*) and local school officials. In veterinarian affairs, he was assisted by the Veterinarian's Office (*Veterinäramt*). He also worked with the officials of the County Youth Office (*Kreisjugendamt*) the Construction Office, the Office for Supervision of Industry and Trade (*Gewerbeaufsichtsamt*) and the Mining Offices (*Bergämter*) of the State Ministries. Insurance affairs were handled by the county Insurance Office while the non-state forests of the county were under the county Forest Office. The County

Manager was responsible for the operations of the Land Registration Office and worked with the local Revenue Office (*Rentamt*) of the state Ministry of Finance. The County Manager administered the county roads, welfare and relief and other activities which were once under the county self-government. He also operated the county enterprises which frequently included a bank, one or two utilities, a forestry or agricultural establishment, and sometimes an airport.

The system of town and village government and administration which prevailed until 1935 was established by the Town and County Constitutions of 1922, 1926, and 1930. The government of the city centered in the Municipal Council which was elected for a four-year period. The Mayor and his assistants, who formed the Town Executive, were appointed for a period of six years. The Mayor was eligible for election as the chairman of the Town Council. Under the Nazis, municipal government and administration followed the pattern laid down in the new German Municipal Code of 1935. Under this code the management and control of municipal activities were under the effective supervision of the Mayor and the higher authorities. The towns and villages continued to handle public works and welfare, and a few enterprises (town forest, market, and an occasional utility plant).

Although 57 per cent of the land was devoted to agrarian activities, Thuringia as a whole was of secondary importance in agriculture in comparison with similar areas of the Reich. Within Thuringia there are two contrasting agricultural areas—the Thuringian Forest and the Thuringian Basin. The Thuringian Forest consists of the uplands extending from the Saale River northwestward to Eisenach and the valley of the upper Werra, which borders the uplands on the west. The upland area has a cool and humid climate. The average temperature for January is between —3 and —4 degrees C. in the hills, while that of the Werra Valley ranges between —2 and —3 degrees C. The average July temperature is between 14 and 16 degrees C. with lower temperatures prevailing in the uplands. The average July temperature for the higher parts of the forest region is well under 13 degrees C. The average yearly rainfall varies considerably from the Werra Valley (600-800 mm.) to the lower upland (800-1000 mm.) and to the higher portions of the forest (1000-1200 mm). The gray leached podzol soils of the uplands support heavy forests, while the sandy loams and clays of the foothills and the Werra Valley, which have long been cleared for agriculture, have a crumbly structure and are fairly good for cultivation. The chief crops of the valleys and level areas include wheat, oats, rye, and potatoes. Tobacco, hops, and flax are grown in the Werra Valley. Fruit is important in the lower part of the Werra Valley.

The clearings in the forest area are given over to livestock raising and dairying, although there is some subsistence farming based upon the cultivation of cereals and potatoes for home consumption. Although iron, copper, cobalt, and salt mining once played an important role in the highlands, today most of the mineral resources are nearly exhausted. Many of the small towns of the upland and valley turned to light manufacturing which provided part-time work for the impoverished farmers of the upland. The farmers also supplemented their incomes with home industries based upon wood carving. The tourist trade played an important role in the life of the hills. The farms of south-western Thuringia were small to medium sized, ranging from 5 to 20 hectares in area. The farmers of the valleys dwell in agglomerated villages of the *Hau-fendorf* type which are fairly large in size, averaging between 1000 and 4000 in population. The upland village is generally of the *Waldhufendorf* (houses scattered along a road) type. The smaller villages generally center about a cross-roads dominated by a church, while the larger ones are oriented about a market place. These villages are linked together by a maze of winding forest roads which were established at the beginning of the Middle Ages when the forests were first colonized by the Thuringian folk expanding westward from the cen-tral basin area and by Franconian peoples pushing northward from the Main Valley.

Central and eastern Thuringia, which is situated east and north of the Thu-ringian Forest, consists of a central basin area and surrounding plateau country. The Thuringian Basin enjoys a warmer and drier climate than the uplands to the west. The average July temperature is about 17.5 degrees C. while the aver-age January temperature is —1 degree C. There is also considerably less rainfall, about 500 to 600 mm. per year. The growing season of this warmer drier area is much longer. The rich chernozem (black earth) and open loess soils have been cultivated for at least four thousand years. Today, the plains and rolling hills of the basin are used to raise wheat, barley, and sugar beets. The farms of the basin tend to be of the larger type, ranging in size from 20 to 100 hectares, although in the more level areas they frequently exceed 100 hectares, while in the more hilly portions of the basin they are generally smaller than 20 hectares. About two-thirds of the land is cultivated by tenant farmers; the rest is held by independent peasants.

The rural population of the central basin area dwells in large villages of the agglomerated type ranging in size from 600 to 1600 population, while the peo-ple of eastern Thuringia live in small villages with a population ranging be-tween 200 and 600. The occasional round village of the eastern part of Thu-ringia reflects the age when this part of the Reich was occupied by Slavic folk. While the hills of Western Thuringia possessed an occasional large village with a few light industries and a few declining mining centers, the open lands of cen-tral and eastern Thuringia are studded with several important cities of fair size —Gotha, Weimar, Jena, Arnstadt, Greiz, Gera, and Altenburg.

The greater part of Thuringia forms a part of the real tillage zone of the

Reich. It has been particularly important for the whole Central German economic area for its production of cereals and sugar beets. The uplands of western Thuringia furnish the cities of the plains and valleys with dairy products, while the Werra Valley, although not as important as the Rhine or Main valleys from an agrarian point of view, does produce some fruit and tobacco. The figures for land utilization (given below in hectares) indicate the amount and types of land available for agriculture:

Cultivated Land (1933)		511,600
Grain	303,000	
Legumes	12,900	
Root Crops	120,100	
Green Vegetables	1,500	
Industrial Crops	3,100	
Fodder Crops	71,000	
Small Gardens		14,100
Meadow		115,200
Pasture		14,600
Orchards		4,000
Vineyards		14
Forests		392,300
Waste Land		21,800
Houses and Barns		20,200
Roads and Parks		66,300

Of the land area of the state about 57 per cent has been devoted to agriculture; four-fifths of this land is utilized for crops and the rest for pastoral activities. The remaining land area was divided between forests (33 per cent) and urban and waste land (10 per cent).

The forest cover of Thuringia is of the Central German type. Although the loess and black earth portions of central and eastern Thuringia are relatively free from forest, the plateau area of the southeast and the uplands of the southwest are well forested. In the lower parts of the upland, one-third of the area was forested, while in the higher parts of the forest, where the spruce predominates, the forests occupy from 90 to 100 per cent of the area. The forest land was owned by a variety of interests; the state owned about 169,000 hectares, or about 43 per cent of it. This land was administered through 79 state forest reserves which were ultimately under the forest administration of the state Ministry of Finance at Weimar. Another third of the forest land was held by private interests, while the remaining forest lands were owned by county and municipal governments. The work of the state administration at Weimar was not entirely restricted to state-owned forest areas. It supervised, through county forest offices, forestry affairs of the counties, towns, and private interests.

The Thuringians constitute the dominant rural group of Thuringia. This group of people are divided from the Franconians to the south and west by the crest of the Thuringian Forest. The few pockets of Low Saxons in northwestern Thuringia are unimportant. Although the influence of the Franconians of the Main Valley has been great, the culture of the Thuringian as revealed in his dialect, customs, costumes, and traditions, is distinctive. These people are still well known for their varied and colorful folk art which is based upon wood carving. They are a musical people famous for their religious songs. Many of the well-known Christmas songs of Europe and America came originally from this state.

URBAN ASPECT

All the cities of Thuringia have a Germanic origin. Almost all have a medieval city plan involving a market place and fortifications. Some are dominated by an old castle, others by a church. They consist of colorful brick houses with red tile roofs. Many of the towns—Altenburg, Greiz, Gera, Rudolstadt, Gotha, and Weimar—had their main development between the fifteenth and eighteenth centuries when they were established as the centers of the various small Thuringian duchies and principalities. The late nineteenth century saw the addition of manufacturing to the economy of many of the towns, but this did not lead to the growth of great cities. In 1933 only 25 per cent of the population dwelt in cities ranging in size from 20,000 to 100,000. Gera, an important transportation point on the Saale, was the largest with a population of 83,775. Weimar, the capital of Thuringia, Altenburg, at the frontier of industrial Saxony, Eisenach, the industrial town, Gotha, the map center of Germany, and Jena, the center of the German optical industry, were small cities with populations between 40,-000 and 50,000. The ten largest cities of Thuringia were established as city counties in 1922 when the present administrative subdivision replaced one of the old duchies and principalities. The system of city administration, which prevailed until 1935, consisted of a mayor, a city executive committee (*Stadtvorstand*), and a city council. Under the Nazis municipal government and administration followed the pattern laid down by the German Municipal Code of 1935. There were mayors, who were directly responsible to the state Minister of the Interior at Weimar.

Thuringia formed a part of the Central German economic area consisting of the state of Saxony, the state of Thuringia, and the Province of Saxony. This area was linked together by intimate economic relations. The economic interdependence was greater than any economic relation between either Thuringia, the Province of Saxony, or the state of Saxony and any adjacent area. The economic life of Thuringia was almost entirely dependent upon the Province of Saxony and the state of Saxony, for most of its heavier raw materials came from these neighboring areas. Regionally within Thuringia, industry and commerce are concentrated in the cities of the Thuringian Basin. The enterprises of the uplands consisted of old established home industries, only occasionally concentrated in factory establishments. In terms of relationships with immediately adjacent areas, Thuringia looked first toward the Erfurt district of the Province of Saxony and then to the rest of Saxony and the state of Saxony. The distinct social-economic character of the party district of the Thuringian area (Thuringia and the administrative district of Erfurt) as a real unit of human activity was utilized by the Nazis when they made this area into a separate planning association.

The mineral resources of Thuringia are limited. Although local iron and copper ores have been worked in the forest area since the beginning of the Middle Ages, today these deposits are largely exhausted except for the iron ore deposits near Grosskamsdorf. Some lignite is still obtained in the Altenburg and Meiningen areas, while salt mining is common along the Werra and in the central basin area. The power needs of the numerous manufacturing plants of the state were met by numerous small power stations. The large lignite plant in the county of Meiningen was oriented toward Hesse, while the stations located in northern Thuringia were isolated, for the state was without an adequate power line network. The fuel needs of the power plants were met by supplies of lignite from the Province of Saxony; since World War I this substitute largely replaced the coal from the Ruhr.

Despite the absence of coal and iron, Thuringia had a limited metallurgical and machine industry. Machine manufacturing establishments were developed in the course of the later nineteenth century on the basis of metallurgical traditions going back to the Middle Ages. There were centers for this industry at Ruhla, Gotha, Greiz, Gera, Apolda, Arnstadt, and Zella-Mehlis. They were interested in the production of light manufactured items. Ruhla has been famous for its cutlery since the fifteenth century, while Apolda was an historical center of clock manufacturing. In Zella-Mehlis typewriters and business machines were produced. Despite the salt mines and the nearness of lignite, the chemical industry was poorly developed. The only important plants were located at Rudolstadt and Gera. The pottery and glass industries were represented by a great number of plants widely scattered throughout western Thuringia.

The textile industry was the most important one in Thuringia. It had its major centers at Apolda (plants for manufacturing rope), Arnstadt (silk textiles), Eisenach (wool textiles), Gera (wool textiles), Greiz (wool textiles), and Weimar (wool textiles). Apolda, Greiz, and Gera were the main textile manufacturing centers. Altenburg was more interested in the clothing and hat industry. The leather industry was limited in Thuringia, though there were a few plants at Eisenach, Arnstadt, and Gera. While the food industry was widely scattered and uniformly important in the basin area, Gotha (sausage) and Saal-feld (chocolate) stood out as important centers. Thuringia ranked particularly high in two other manufacturing fields, thanks to the printing presses of Justus Perthes at Gotha and the Carl Zeiss optical works at Jena. Most of the industries discussed above are located in the Thuringian Basin. The home industries and an occasional factory in the heavily forested area were not without importance. This upland area supported a considerable population which was mainly engaged in industries requiring skill and patience. The main products in order of importance are dolls, toys, and Christmas ornaments, glass work, wood carving, and fine metallurgical products. While much of the work was done at home, there were many small plants at Meiningen, Hildburghausen, and Sonneberg.

Owing to its central position Thuringia has long played an important role in the national transportation system. The basic road transportation system pattern has been determined by the valleys of the Werra, Gera, Ilm, Saale, and Elster and the open country of northern Thuringia. Major roads run from Sonneberg to Eisenach via the Werra Valley, to Arnstadt and Erfurt via the Gera Valley, and to Jena and ultimately Merseburg via the Saale Valley. Another north-south road in eastern Thuringia follows the Elster Valley connecting Hof, Schleiz, Gera, and Leipzig. A major east-west road extends across northern Thuringia linking Eisenach with Gotha, Erfurt, Weimar, Apolda, Jena, Gera, and Altenburg. The construction and maintenance of the main state roads were handled by the Ministry of the Interior in Weimar, while local roads were under the county administrations. Under the Nazi regime, the normal road system was supplemented by the super-highway. One national high-way running from Nuremberg via Gera to Leipzig crosses eastern Thuringia, while another also starting at Nuremberg runs northward via the Werra Valley to Eisenach. A third national highway crosses northern Thuringia running from Kassel via Eisenach to Weimar, where it branches into two roads, one going to Leipzig, the other to Dresden.

The major rail lines follow almost the same basic pattern as the road system. The major line from the point of view of traffic is the one running from Kassel via Eisenach, Gotha, Weimar, and Apolda to Leipzig. The next most important line connects Nuremberg via Rudolstadt, Jena, and Apolda, with Leipzig and Halle. The rail line along the Elster connecting Leipzig with Gera and Hof (Bavaria) is of secondary importance. The railroads were owned by the German Railroad Company and were operated by its National Railroad Directorate at Erfurt.

River and canal transportation are unimportant in Thuringia. All shipping on the Saale, which connects with the Elbe and ultimately with the port of Hamburg, stops just short of this state. There were no major national or international air centers in Thuringia, although the municipal airports of this state had connections with the important airport at Erfurt. The airlines in the state were operated by the German Airways Corporation while the airports were owned and operated by the municipalities.

Weimar was the commercial and financial capital of modern Thuringia; however, towns like Gotha, Gera, and Altenburg retained something of their former importance as commercial and financial centers when they were capitals. The contemporary importance of Weimar was due to its position as the state governmental and administrative capital. The commercial interests of Thuringia appear in its agrarian, forestry, and industrial activities. In terms of freight traffic carried by rail, textiles, pottery and ceramic products, wood, and metal products were produced and shipped from the state, while coal, lignite, and metal were the main commodities brought in from adjacent areas. The concentration of a large portion of the textile industry in Central Germany led to an extensive trade in yarns among Thuringia, Saxony, and northern Bavaria. There was also an active trade in machine goods between Thuringia and Saxony, which dominated the machine industry of Central Germany. Thuringia had some trade with the Ruhr, sending machine goods in exchange for heavier items. Within the state, Eisenach dominated the trade of the northwest, while Gotha, Weimar, Apolda, Jena, and Arnstadt served the central basin. Eastern Thuringia was served by Altenburg, Gera, and Greiz, while the Thuringian Forest and the southwest turned to Meiningen and Sonneberg. The overseas trade of western Thuringia went out via the Werra-Weser and Bremen, while that of the east moved via the Saale-Elbe and Hamburg.

The banking and credit institutions of Thuringia ranged from the branches of the great commercial banks in Berlin, which were mainly interested in investments of the industrial type, to the local county and municipal mortgage and savings banks. Weimar was the main banking and finance center. The state banking institutions were located at Weimar. They were under the state Ministry of Finance. The operations of these banks were supplemented by those of the branches of the *Reichsbank* at Apolda, Arnstadt, Gotha, and Weimar, doing the usual discount and governmental services. All banks were subject to the supervision of the Thuringian State Bank (*Thüringische Staatsbank*) and ultimately to the National Credit Supervisory Office (*Aufsichtsamt für das Kreditwesen*) in Berlin. The state-owned Thuringian State Insurance Association (*Thüringische Landesbrandversicherungsanstalt*) at Gotha was under the state Ministry of the Interior at Weimar. Gotha was the headquarters for several Central German insurance companies.

The urban population of Thuringia was largely engaged in industry and handicrafts. Of the total population, 48 per cent or 791,000 individuals were engaged in industry and handicrafts, while only 13 per cent or 216,000 were occupied by trade and transportation. Another 6 per cent was engaged in professional work or public service. The working class, which constituted about 49 per cent of the population, was one of the largest in Germany. The upper independent class was about average for the Reich, forming about 17 per cent of the population. The civil servant and white collar class was relatively small in comparison with that of other German areas.

The vital portions of Thuringia are situated to the east of the Thuringian Forest. The central and eastern portions of the state are densely settled from both the rural and urban points of view. The rich rolling farm lands of the basin are studded with comfortable old towns. Weimar on the Ilm, the capital of Thuringia, had its greatest period in the late eighteenth century, when it was an important cultural center. Although the nineteenth and twentieth centuries brought the addition of industry and manufacturing, the city remained the traditional center of German Classicism. The National Constituent Assembly met at Weimar in 1919 to draft the constitution for the new republic and to govern Germany during the transitional period. Hence, the German republic which was created here was called the Weimar Republic. Jena, which is located to the east on the Saale, was by contrast the traditional center of German Romanticism, for it was the nineteenth century home of Hegel, Fichte, and Schilling. In the later nineteenth century it became a world famous center for the optical industry as well as the center for important work in the natural sciences and medicine; it is the home of the University of Jena.

In northwestern Thuringia the city of Eisenach, important for industry and manufacturing, has been the traditional center of Lutheranism, for this was the school town of Luther. In the Wartburg castle near Eisenach, the famous Luther reportedly threw an ink pot at the devil. Gotha, a beautiful old city surrounded by modern construction, was an important eighteenth and nineteenth century center of court culture. Today, it is important for more practical contributions—sausage, rubber, and insurance. Gera, the largest and most industrialized of the Thuringian cities, goes back to the early Middle Ages when it was a center for immigration into eastern Germany. The towns and cities of the Thuringian Forest and the Werra are small. Sonneberg and Meiningen, which are located in the foothills of the forest, have been the main centers for the home industries. In the uplands are many popular spas and winter sports centers.

BIBLIOGRAPHY

Brandt, B. *Der Nordosten, Landeskunde von Deutschland* (Leipzig, 1931).

Graefe, T. *Sachsen, Land der Vielfalt, Werkstatt Deutschlands, Mittelpunkt Deutscher Kultur* (Dresden, 1936).

Günther, F. *Der Harz* (Bielefeld & Leipzig, 1924).

Liersch, H. *Die Provinz Sachsen* (Berlin, 1901).

Mayer, O. *Das Staatsrecht des Königsreichs Sachsen* (Tübingen, 1909).

Ruge, S. *Dresden und die Sächsische Schweiz* (Bielefeld & Leipzig, 1903).

Schotte, F. *Die Produktionsgrundlagen der Provinz Sachsen 1907-1927* (Inaugural Dissertation, Halle, 1932).

Scobel, A. *Thüringen* (Bielefeld & Leipzig, 1923).

Zander, A. *Die wirtschaftliche Entwicklung der Provinz Sachsen im 19. Jahrhundert* (Inaugural Dissertation, Halle, 1934).

Chapter 27

INTRODUCTION TO
SOUTH GERMANY

South Germany includes the territories of the states of Bavaria, Württemberg, Baden, and the district of Hohenzollern. To the south are the High Alps, to the west is the Rhine, across which lie Alsace and the Bavarian Palatinate, and to the east are the Bohemian Forest (*Böhmer Wald*) of Czechoslovakia and the hills of Austria. Internally, South Germany may be divided into five basic ethnographic regions: (1) The Franconian area, based upon the Main Valley and oriented toward the important urban centers of Nuremberg and Wurzburg, has a dry, warm climate, making it ideal for wheat and livestock. (2) Southern and eastern Bavaria is marked off from the Franconian area by the Franconian Jura. Here east of the Jura scarplands are humid, cool uplands consisting of the ranges of the Bavarian and Bohemian Forest and the hills surrounding the valley of the Nab River, which rises in the Fichtel Mountains (*Fichtelgebirge*). (3) The Swabian area, embracing most of the state of Württemberg, and lying to the south of the Main Valley area, is based upon the valley of the Neckar, which is bordered by the Black Forest (*Schwarzwald*) and the Swabian Jura, a western continuation of the Franconian Jura. It is divided from the Franconian area by the uplands forming the divide between the Main and Neckar basins. The agrarian activities of the dry, warm Neckar Basin are oriented toward the city of Stuttgart. (4) To the west beyond the Black Forest lies the Rhine Valley zone with the important Badenese cities of Mannheim, Heidelberg, Karlsruhe, and Freiburg. (5) The north Alpine foreland to the south of the river Danube, bordering the southern slopes of the Swabian and Franconian Jura and the Bavarian Forest, is an agrarian region dominated by the ancient cities of Ulm, Augsburg, Ingolstadt, Regensburg, Munich, and Passau. The political divisions of South Germany do not coincide with the ethnographic areas, for the essentially rural district of Hohenzollern straddles the Swabian Jura, while the southern part of the state of Württemberg extends beyond the Swabian Jura to

Lake Constance (*Bodensee*). The western Rhine Palatinate holdings of Bavaria are an integral part of Western Germany, although they were long under the rule of the Wittelsbachs of Bavaria.

The population of southern Germany is composed of four distinct groups of Germans, the Bavarians, the Franconians, the Swabians, and the Badenese. The Bavarians are found in the southeastern portion of South Germany, which had been under Keltic occupation even after the collapse of Roman power. The Franconians to the northwest of the Bavarians settled in the valley of the Main during the Migration period. The Swabians and Badenese are descendants of the Alemanni who had penetrated into the Rhine and Neckar valleys by the first century, although they did not take over control of these areas until the disintegration of Roman military power in the fifth century. Owing to the isolation afforded by the highlands surrounding the Neckar Basin, the Swabian groups gradually separated from the Alemannic tribes and achieved a variety of cultural independence. The Badenese, in like manner, gradually differentiated along the eastern bank of the Rhine. The Bavarians and Swabians have retained much of their old solidarity, thanks to their geographic isolation until relatively modern times and to the political fortunes of their rulers, who created the states of Bavaria and Württemberg. The Badenese and Franconians, however, have lost much of their old particularism, owing to their position along the Rhine and Main rivers, which exposed them to diverse cultural movements and influences. Of interest is the fact that the Franconian lands were absorbed by the Bavarians, while the Badenese dwell in a state which was an artificial creation of the Napoleonic era.

The political history of South Germany begins with the tribal kingdoms of the Alemanni and Bavarians which emerged after the collapse of Roman power in South Germany. These tribal states were conquered by the Merovingian rulers of the Franks in the course of the sixth century. After the collapse of Carolingian power, the old tribal areas re-emerged under the leadership of the dukes of Swabia, Bavaria, and Franconia, three duchies which held undisputed sway over southern Germany during the era of the Saxon, Franconian, and Hohenstaufen emperors.

The collapse of the medieval empire of the Germans in the thirteenth century was marked by the disintegration of the old tribal duchies. The Duchy of Bavaria, which had embraced all of the lands between the Lech River and modern Linz in Austria and between the Tyrol and Nuremberg, fell apart. The Wittelsbach family, however, managed to obtain control of the vital core duchies of Bavaria-Munich, Bavaria-Landshut, and Bavaria-Straubing. The Palatine line of the Wittelsbach family obtained the Upper Palatinate (Oberpfalz) area, while the archbishops of Salzburg gained control of western Austria. The Tyrol fell to the Habsburgs. The bishops of Passau, Regensburg, Eichstätt, and

Freising emerged as feudal rulers in the heart of the Bavarian area. The city of Nuremberg became a free and imperial city. The Duchy of Franconia (*Franken*), which had dominated the valley of the Main and most of the territory of northern Württemberg and Baden, fell under the control of the Archbishop of Mainz, the bishops of Würzburg and Bamberg, and the Burgrave of Nuremberg. The cities of Schweinfurt, Hall, Rothenburg, and Weissenburg gained the status of free and imperial cities. The southwestern Duchy of Schwaben was inherited by the counts of Württemberg, the bishops of Augsburg, and the free and imperial cities of Gmünd, Ulm, Augsburg, Reutlingen, Stuttgart, and Lindau. The Habsburgs managed to obtain several small blocks of territory in the Freiburg and Konstanz areas. The Palatinate of the Elector (*Kurpfalz*) on the Rhine was largely held by the electors of the Palatine line of the Wittelsbach family.

By the time of the Reformation, the dukes of Bavaria had consolidated their holdings in the southeast, and the burgraves of Nuremberg had given way to the princes of Ansbach and Bayreuth, who were of the Franconian line of Hohenzollerns. In the southwest, the dukes of Württemberg had extended their territories, while the margraves of Baden had obtained several holdings along the Rhine. The numerous free and imperial cities and the strong ecclesiastical states had extended their territorial holdings and strengthened their political positions.

Though the eighteenth century witnessed the gradual improvement of domestic conditions, there was little change in the chaotic territorial organization of South Germany until the Napoleonic era. The basic Napoleonic solution, which had been worked out by 1812, had effected the following changes. Bavaria had received the territories of the bishoprics of Würzburg, Bamberg, Augsburg, Eichstätt, Freising, and Passau, the free and imperial cities of Nuremberg, Ulm, Regensburg, Augsburg, and Kempten, and the principalities of Ansbach and Bayreuth for her aid to Napoleon and in compensation for the loss of territories west of the Rhine. The dukes of Württemberg, who were given the status of kings by Napoleon, were allowed to extend their territories through the absorption of the numerous holdings of the Imperial Knights and the free and imperial cities of southwestern Germany. The margraves of Baden, who were elevated to the rank of Electors, expanded their holdings along the Rhine. The settlement at Vienna (1815) recognized the Napoleonic solutions. Only a few changes were made. Bavaria lost the Tyrol to the Habsburgs, but regained the Rhine Palatinate and received the holdings of the ephemeral Napoleonic Grand Duchy of Würzburg. The territorial acquisitions of the grand dukes of Baden and the kings of Württemberg were also recognized at Vienna.

Although the political division of southern Germany was settled for the nineteenth and early twentieth centuries, the impact of the industrial revolution brought about new orientations in the economic life of the region. Southern Bavaria turned more and more toward Munich, and the Franconian north to Nuremberg. These two areas, except for the Swabians in southwestern Bavaria, constitute distinct cultural and economic units. To the west the economic life of the Baden-Württemberg area tended to coalesce, giving new life to the old cultural unity of the Alemannic peoples, the Badenese and Swabians.

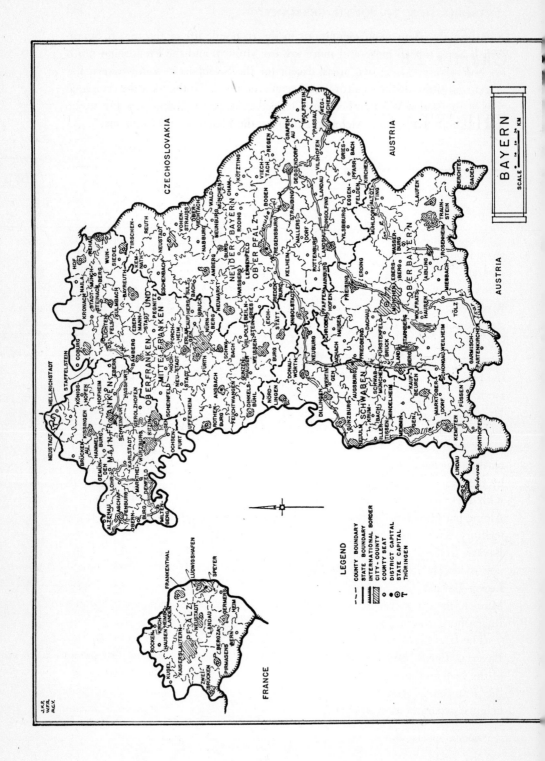

BAYERN

SCALE

LEGEND

COUNTY BOUNDARY
STATE BOUNDARY
INTERNATIONAL BORDER
CITY - COUNTY
COUNTY SEAT
DISTRICT CAPITAL
STATE CAPITAL
THÜRINGEN

Chapter 28

THE STATE OF BAVARIA*

The state of Bavaria includes the greater part of southern Germany, and is second only to Prussia in area and population. It consists of two completely separated and unequal portions, Bavaria proper and the Bavarian Palatinate. The latter, which is much smaller in area, is situated to the west of the Rhine River, and is hemmed in by the Saarland, the Rhine Province, Hesse, Baden, and Lorraine. The larger portion is located in the southeastern part of southern Germany and is bounded on the south by the lower ranges of the Alps, which have been called the Northeast or Bavarian Pre-Alps (extending from the Bodensee to Vienna). The upland gives way northward first to the moraine lands of the East Alpine margins and then to the Bavarian plateau country. North of this lie the Northern Danubian plains extending to the river Danube and occupying the area south of the Danube from the river Lech in the west to the river Enns in Austria. West of the Lech, the Bavarian plateau country reaches northwards to the Danube. This southern Bavarian region is drained by the Iller, Lech, Isar, and Inn rivers flowing northward to the Danube, all with their sources in the high Alps. Across the river Inn the Pre-Alps, the Alpine marginal lands, and the Danubian plains continue eastward on Austrian territory. To the west, the river Iller, which joins the Danube at Ulm, separates Bavaria from the state of Württemberg. The zone lying to the south of the Danube is largely included within the districts of Upper Bavaria (Oberbayern), Lower Bavaria (Niederbayern), and Swabia, and contains the capital city of Munich, the commercial city of Augsburg, and the riparian cities of Ingolstadt, Regensburg, Straubing, and Passau, the latter at the Austrian frontier.

The land between the Danube and the Bohemian Forest is occupied by the Bavarian Forest, while the central part of Bavaria is dominated by the valley of the Nab and its tributaries, draining the Upper Palatinate area. To the west, the Franconian Jura (*Fränkische Alb*), famous for its rocky valleys and heights, separates the Upper Palatinate from the Central Franconian Basin

* German spelling—Bayern.

551

(*Mittelfranken Becken*) which contains the important cities of Nuremberg, Fürth, Bamberg, and Bayreuth in the districts of Upper Franconia (Oberfranken) and Central Franconia (Mittelfranken). It is actually more nearly a plateau than a basin, with its surface of broken resistant scarplands worn down by the erosive action of the tributaries of the Main. To the east and south lie the Franconian Jura, the Eichstadter Jura (*Eichstädter Alb*), the Swabian Jura (*Schwäbische Alb*), and the Frankenhöhe, and to the west the Steiger Forest (*Steigerwald*), the Hassberge, and Koburger uplands. The Steiger Forest and Frankenhöhe hills constitute a natural barrier between this part of Bavaria and Württemberg. The northern portion of Upper Franconia and Central Franconia is drained by the upper reaches of the river Main and surrounded by the Upper Franconian upland (*Oberfränkisches Bergland*) and the Franconian Forest (*Frankenwald*), beyond which lie the lands of the state of Saxony and the Thuringian Forest, marking the southern frontier of the state of Thuringia.

To the west and north of the Franconian basin are the Steiger Forest, the Hassberge, and Koburger uplands, beyond which lies the Bavarian district of Lower Franconia straddling the lower course of the Main, along the banks of which lie the cities of Aschaffenburg, Würzburg, and Schweinfurt. The greater portion of the area consists of the Lower Franconian Plateau (*Unterfränkische Platte*), which is a product of the erosive action of the Main. Northward, these plains give way to the Werra depression which marks the westward continuation of the frontiers of Thuringia, while to the west they become the Rhön and Spessart uplands which are located on the frontiers Bavaria has in common with the state of Hesse and the Province of Hesse-Nassau. Southward the Lower Franconian plains continue into the northeastern part of the state of Baden.

The external frontiers of Bavaria and the internal boundaries of its districts are well defined by natural geographical barriers. The three districts north of the Danube tend to center about a basin, valley, or plains area, while the two southern districts are alike in their basic geographic characteristics—rolling plateau country giving way in the south to the foothills of the Alps. The upland portions of Bavaria are well forested and famous for their unspoiled primeval character. The mountains and hills are intersected by an unusual number of beautiful valleys ranging in type from those given over primarily to rolling meadowland to deep clefts with crevassed and rocky sides. The plains of the Main and Danube, the open country of central Upper Franconia, and the plateau country of southern Bavaria are largely free from forest and available for agriculture. The climate of the entire region is subject to wide variations, for the mountains and uplands have a cold climate accompanied by abundant rainfall, while the plains of the Danube and Main have a much warmer climate with much less rainfall. Taken as a whole, Bavaria has colder winters and warmer summers and autumns than Western Germany.

The isolated Bavarian Palatinate on the Rhine contains the cities of Kaiserslautern, Ludwigshafen, Landau, and Speyer, and shares the culture of the surrounding Rhineland provinces and states. The eastern part of the Palatinate is occupied by the broad upper valley of the Rhine. The southern frontier is formed by the northern ranges of the Low Vosges and the hills of the Lorraine plateau of France. Westward, the hills of the Palatinate Forest (*Pfälzerwald*) or Hardt give way to the uplands of the Saar. Northwestward lie the high hills of the Hunsrück occupying the southeastern corner of the Prussian Rhine Province. Northeastward, the hills of the Palatinate continue for a distance into the state of Hesse, while across the Rhine to the east, the Rhenish plains are within the state of Baden.

Racially, the population of Bavaria is extremely mixed, as the result of the ebb and flow of peoples along the Danube and Main since prehistoric times. Although the Alpine physical type predominates, the division of the peoples of Bavaria in terms of differences of customs, beliefs, and folkways is far more significant than any racial differentiation. These distinctions are reflected in the three dialects of the land. The Upper German Frankish dialect group occupies most of the districts of Lower Franconia, Central Franconia, and Upper Franconia, while the Bavarian or *Bajuwarisch* group dwells in the districts of Upper Bavaria, Lower Bavaria and the Upper Palatinate. The district of Swabia bears the name of the predominant dialect group which extends westward to occupy most of Württemberg.

Although one is apt to associate dialects only with the peasants, this is not true in Bavaria, for standard German is spoken only in the larger cities. The several dialect groups can be considered as distinct cultural or tribal units. Although the differences are products of long historical development, the boundaries of the dialect or cultural groups are vague and seldom coincide with political or administrative divisions. The picture is made more complex by the fact that these dialect groups tend to fuse and mix along their margins. Each group is bound together by a unity of folklore and folkways reflected in common group feelings, attitudes, and aspirations, a condition which is significant in South Germany, in contrast with most other parts of the Reich, where as a rule the consciousness of the local group has been absorbed by a more universal German spirit.

While the Franks of northwestern Bavaria in their transitional position between central and southern Germany have lost much of their group solidarity, the Bavarians and Swabians have retained much in the way of local spirit and loyalty, which has political as well as social significance. Each of these two groups possesses what might be regarded as a political and cultural center—the

Bavarians looking toward Munich, as previously noted, and the Swabians toward Stuttgart. Most of the other cultural or tribal groups of Germany are without a rallying point. Religious division between Catholicism and Protestantism in Bavaria is culturally significant, for the Swabians and Bavarians are almost exclusively Catholic, while the Franks of the northwest lack religious as well as cultural unity. The southern portion of the district of Upper Franconia and Central Franconia is mainly Protestant, while the region along the Main in the northern part of this district and in the district of Lower Franconia is predominantly Catholic. Taking the state of Bavaria as a whole the largest religious group is Catholic, numbering 5,372,000. The Protestant group is, however, quite large, numbering 2,202,000. The total Jewish population, numbering 41,900 in 1933, was not large in comparison with other parts of the Reich. The Jews were chiefly concentrated in the larger cities of the state.

There is a remarkable agreement between the landscape and population patterns. Though the population of Bavaria stood at 7,682,000 in 1933 and occupied 76,089 sq. km., giving a population density of 101 per sq. km., there were significant variations of density among the various administrative districts. The areas of dense population are to be found along the Main and Danube rivers where the density ranges between 100 and 200 individuals per sq. km. The two most densely settled of the older regions of Central Bavaria, Upper Franconia and Central Franconia, which were combined in 1933 to form one governmental administrative district, owe their greater density to the more heavily settled plains of the Central Franconian Basin. The relatively smaller population of the Upper Palatinate and Lower Bavaria, which were combined to form one district in 1932, can be explained in terms of the more sparsely settled uplands of the Franconian Jura, the Upper Palatinate Forest, the Bohemian Forest, and the Bavarian Forest. The population density of the higher parts of this area was frequently below 25 individuals per sq. km., and between 25 and 75 per sq. km. in other portions outside of the Danube Valley. The patterns of population density for Swabia and Upper Bavaria are much the same: a dense population along the Danube (100 to 200 per sq. km.); a moderate population on the Bavarian Plateau (25 to 75 per sq. km.); and the very sparse population in the Alpine foothills and mountains (less than 25 per sq. km.). The greater population density of the Upper Bavarian area is due to the great urban concentration at Munich. Strangely enough, the district of Lower Franconia is not so densely settled as one might expect in view of its position on the Main. This might be accounted for by the extensive upland areas surrounding the Main plains. The Palatinate is very densely settled, but it is important to note that the bulk of its population is concentrated in the area adjacent to the Rhine River and in the zone bordering the Saarland.

The population of Bavaria has increased steadily during the past century.

The urban centers, like Munich and Nuremberg, have sustained great increases in population owing to the impetus of rapid industrialization. All of the districts of the state, except the Upper Palatinate, have had marked population increases. In contrast with the rest of the Reich only a moderate number of Germans left Bavaria for other countries during the twenties and early thirties. In the late thirties, over 1,800 left for other lands each year. The national migration picture was characterized by a decrease in the number of Germans leaving the Reich and an increase in the number returning. This was due to the attractions of the munitions boom.

The characteristic pattern of settlement in Bavaria involving valley farming and upland grazing goes back to the Neolithic period when peasants from southeastern Europe pushed north and westward to settle in the valleys of the Danube and Main. The second millennium B.C. brought the introduction of metal and improved methods of agriculture, while the first was marked by the great Keltic Hallstatt and La Tène iron cultures. The lands south of the Danube fell under Roman control at the beginning of our era. The first towns of any importance (for example, Augsburg, the Roman town of Augusta) were established at this time. Mediterranean ways of living, although strongly modified by local conditions, dominated the scene.

After five centuries of control in southern Bavaria, the Romans gave way before the onslaught of the Swabians and Bavarians (Baja, corruption of Bojer derived from Bojerland or Bohemia), while Frankish tribes pushed eastward along the Main to occupy northern Bavaria. The Franks were the main political factor, for it was the Frankish Agilolfing family which ruled the region after the Romans. Though this was an age of disorder marked by Slavic, Avar, and Magyar inroads from the east, civilization was slowly asserting itself. Christianity, which had lingered on after Roman times, developed rapidly after the first phase of the migrations. The first laws were committed to writing and the land was divided into districts which were placed under counts.

At the end of the eighth century the Agilolfing Dukes were replaced by Carolingians, who ruled until the early days of the Saxon Kings and Emperors when the Bavarian Welfs gained power (1070). In 1180, the Duchy of Bavaria consisting of the modern districts of Lower Bavaria, Upper Bavaria, and the Austrian Tyrol, passed to the Wittelsbach family who were destined to rule Bavaria until 1918. During the age of the Franconian (1024-1125) and Hohenstaufen (1138-1254) Emperors, the Duchy of Bavaria developed rapidly. There were great improvements in trade; the towns were slowly increasing in importance. Although the Tyrol was lost in Hohenstaufen times, Bavaria was adequately compensated with lands to the north. The year 1255 marks the beginning of a period of territorial division. In 1329, the Pfalz or Palatinate branch of the Wittelsbach family gained control of lands on the Rhine. In 1356 they were elevated to the ranks of electors. In Bavaria, the lands of the Bavarian Wittelsbachs underwent a number of divisions. The duchies of Bavaria-Straubing, Bavaria-Landshut, and Bavaria-Munich arose in the South. The North fell under the rule of a number of bishops and free cities backed by increasing wealth and trade. Interestingly enough, representative institutions involving the formation of an assembly developed in this period of growing feudal disorder.

Bavaria proper was not reunited until the beginning of the sixteenth century when primogeniture was established in 1506. Wilhelm, who came to power on the eve of the Reformation, continued the traditional policy of opposition to the growing power of the neighboring Austrian Habsburgs. He did much to discourage the Protestants and took an active part in the Catholic Counter-Reformation. Duke Maximilian I, who came to power in 1596, prepared Bavaria for an active part in the Thirty Years' War through his reform of the financial, judicial, and administrative systems and by his establishment of a militia. During the first phase of the war, he acquired the electorate of the Upper Palatinate from the Palatinate branch of the Wittelsbach family which had held this area since 1329. Though the northern parts of Bavaria suffered in the last phases of the war, Bavaria had gained an electoral vote which enabled it to play a more important role in the politics of the Holy Roman Empire.

During the later seventeenth and the eighteenth centuries, Bavaria managed to play at least a minor role in most of the European wars. The attempt to challenge the succession of Maria Theresa of Austria through the seizure of Austrian lands ended in failure, and Habsburg troops occupied Bavaria. The Duke of Bavaria was saved only by the intervention of Prussia. The death of Maximilian III in 1777 brought an end to the line of Bavarian Wittelsbachs. Bavaria fell to the Palatinate branch of the Wittelsbach family of the Rhenish Palatinate. The first ruler of the new line, Duke Karl of Zweibrücken, finally established his rights after the War of the Bavarian Succession which ended successfully for the Wittelsbachs in 1779, thanks again to Prussia. In spite of all these efforts, Karl was not greatly concerned about Bavarian affairs, for he attempted to trade Bavaria to Austria for the Netherlands and the title of King of Burgundy.

On the eve of the French Revolution, Bavaria was still backward and medieval. In 1792, the French revolutionary armies conquered the Palatinate of the Elector and by 1795 they had reached Munich. Austrian forces were advancing into Bavaria to attack France. Bavarian sympathies were for France, and in 1801, Bavaria entered an alliance against Austria, her traditional enemy. In compensation for losses west of the Rhine, Bavaria received a number of ecclesiastical territories and several cities to the north. The Bavarians profited from their association with the French, for in 1805 they received additional lands mostly at the expense of Alpine Austria. During this period, Bavaria was under the rule of the enlightened Maximilian IV (1795-1825), successor of Karl, and his able minister Montgelas, who sought for every advantage that could be obtained from the French. Under French influence, a new constitution was established which wiped away the last vestiges of medieval ways. In 1806, Maximilian IV became the first King of Bavaria (Maximilian I). The administration of the enlarged Kingdom of Bavaria was completely reorganized under the leadership of Montgelas in 1808, when the land was divided into the following seven districts, eight including the Palatinate.

Upper Bavaria (*Oberbayern*) consisting of the southern part of the Duchy of Bavaria, the bishopric of Freising, the provostship of Berchtesgaden, and a few towns which once belonged to the Austrian archbishopric of Salzburg.

Lower Bavaria (*Niederbayern*) consisting of the northern portion of the Duchy of Bavaria and the bishopric of Passau.

Upper Palatinate (*Oberpfalz*) comprising the former Imperial and Free City of Regensburg, Neuburg-Sulzbach and the Duchy of Leuchtenberg.

Upper Franconia (*Oberfranken*) consisting of the principality of Bayreuth, the bishopric of Bamberg, and a number of lands belonging to Franconian nobles.

Central Franconia (*Mittelfranken*) consisting of the principality of Ansbach, the lowland of Bayreuth, and the Imperial and Free City of Nuremberg, and the free and imperial cities of Rothenburg, Dinkelsbühl, Windsheim, and Weissenburg. Other territories included lands of the Teutonic Order, the bishopric of Eichstätt, and a number of tiny principalities.

Lower Franconia—now Mainfranken (*Unterfranken*) included the bishopric of Würzburg and principality of Aschaffenburg.

Swabia (*Schwaben*) included the free and imperial cities of Augsburg, Kempten, Memmingen, Lindau, and Donauwörth, the bishopric of Augsburg, the Margraviate of Burgau, the principality of Oettingen, lands of the princes and earls of Fugger, the earldom of Pappenheim, and the principality of Neuburg.

Bavaria continued to back France until 1812 when it was apparent that Napoleon's days were over. In 1813, she switched to the Allies. After the Peace of Paris (1814) and the Congress of Vienna (1815), the territories acquired from Austria were returned, but the final settlement did not actually come until 1818 when Bavaria was assured about Austria's ambitions in southern Germany.

The revolutionary liberalism was short-lived because the revolutions of 1830 in Europe brought a firm conservative reaction. From 1815 to 1848, Bavaria sought to hold the balance of power within Germany in an effort to protect the smaller states and her own position against Austria and Prussia. The revolutions of 1848 in Europe resulted in the abdication of Ludwig I (1831-1848) in favor of his son Maximilian II (1848-1864). Mild reforms brought pacification. After 1848, the Bavarians were quick to realize that Prussia, not Austria, required watching; hence Bavaria backed Austria in the dealings with Prussia, opposing the Prussians in Schleswig-Holstein and backing Austria in the Seven Weeks' War of 1866 which secured for Prussia hegemony in Germany. The shrewd policies of Bismarck after 1866 led to a complete revolution in the attitudes of Bavaria; for when the test came in 1870, Bavarian troops marched with the Prussian armies against France. In 1871, the state became an integral part of the German Empire but retained its own system of law and administration. It was also granted certain *Sonderrechte* or special rights within the Empire. Nevertheless, the new status was not well received at home, and the liberal pro-Prussian ministries were only kept in power by the support of the royal house which was now headed by Ludwig II (1864-1886). The days which followed were not easy ones for the Wittelsbachs, for Ludwig II went insane and finally committed suicide in 1886, when he was succeeded by his equally insane brother Otto I. The land was placed under the regency of Prince Luitpold (1886-1912).

Though Bavaria had joined the Empire, this did not end Bavarian separatism. The Bavarian political groups stood in constant opposition to Bismarck's efforts for nationalization at the expense of federalism, while the Catholic Bavarians feared the religious policies of the Lutheran Prussians. Every effort was made to retain the slowly vanishing rights of the small German states. During the period of the Empire, Bavaria continued under the constitutional arrangements of 1818, which provided for an hereditary and constitutional monarchy. All executive power was a prerogative of the King, although his ministers assumed responsibility for his acts. Legislative power was vested in a Chamber of Councilors (*Kammer der Reichsräte*), consisting of royal princes, crown dignitaries, clergymen, noblemen, and appointed life members, and a Chamber of Representatives (*Kammer der Abgeordneten*), consisting of deputies, elected by secret, direct, and universal suffrage. Executive affairs were carried out by a Council of State—Ministers, nine State Dignitaries, one Royal Prince and a State Ministry. Administration was carried out by ministries for the Royal House and Foreign Affairs, Interior, Justice, Education and Ecclesiastical Affairs, Finance, and War. There was a General-Director of the Royal State Railway (*General-Direktion der Königlichen Staats-Eisenbahn*) and a General-Director of the Post and Telegraph (*General-Direktion der Posten und Telegraphen*), which had a separate status within the national postal system. The state administrative court also had independent status.

Bavarian troops fought with great valor for German nationalism in World War I. Bavaria, despite her particularism, backed the German national war effort. At the end of the war, events in this state followed the same pattern as in other German states. Rioting broke out in Munich, and Ludwig III (1913-1918), who had been Otto's regent since 1912, fled the land. On November 8, Bavaria was proclaimed a democratic and socialist republic. The first socialist leader, Kurt Eisner, lasted until his assassination by reactionary elements in February 1919. The consequent disorders were firmly dealt with by Berlin. Thereafter Bavaria adopted a democratic and republican constitution and became one of the federal states of the Weimar Republic. The constitution of 1919 provided for a democratically elected assembly, and a responsible State Ministry. Administration was carried out by ministries for Foreign Affairs, Interior, Justice, Education and Ecclesiastical Affairs, Finance, and Agriculture. The Administrative Court (*Verwaltungsgericht*) and the Supreme Auditing Court (*Oberster Rechnungshof*) had independent status. In 1920 the neighboring Saxe-Coburg was added to Bavaria, as a consequence of the fact that the territory of Saxe-Coburg and Gotha had fallen apart after the departure of its duke in 1918. Gotha was made a part of the state of Thuringia.

Under the Empire, Bavaria had been dominated by the Catholic Center party and the Social Democratic party. The Catholics held most of southern Bavaria, the districts of Swabia, Upper Bavaria, Lower Bavaria, and the Upper Palatinate. The Social Democrats, however, were strong at Munich, while the Bavarian Farmer's Union held portions of Lower Bavaria. The urban portions of northern Bavaria voted for the Social Democrats, while the rural portions were dominated by the Catholic Center party. The Conservative party obtained a few votes in the Franconian Jura. The Rhenish Palatinate was largely Social Democratic, although the Catholic Center party and the National Liberal party had extensive followings in the small towns and villages. Under the Republic, prior to Hitler's accession to power, Bavarian politics were controlled principally by two strong political parties, namely the Bavarian People's party and the Social Democratic party. The former was the local counterpart in Bavaria of the Catholic Center party in the other sections of the Reich. The latter was Germany's strongest party up to the July, 1932, election when the National Socialists took the lead. There was a third party, known as the *Deutsche Bauernpartei* or German Peasant's party which was also influential until it was pretty largely absorbed into the Hitler movement after the 1930 elections.

Since Bavaria was the birthplace of the Nazi party and Munich was its main headquarters, one might have expected Bavaria to have been a Nazi stronghold. But such was not the case. At no time prior to 1933 were the Hitlerites able to secure more than a third of the total votes cast in all of the four districts into which the state of Bavaria was divided for electoral purposes. The Bavarian People's party, the Catholic party of Bavaria, held its leading position right up to its dissolution after Hitler came to power. This party was strongly organized and astutely led. Even in the 1930 upsurge of Nazi strength only 10 Nazi members of the National Assembly out of a total Nazi representation of 107 were elected from Bavaria, and in the November 1932 election—the last regular election—only 21 seats out of a Nazi total of 230 in the *Reichstag* were held by delegates from Bavaria.

Within the Bavarian state, the Palatinate and Franconia were areas in which Hitler received most of his votes, as much as 43 per cent of the total vote in Franconia going to Hitler in the July 1932 election. Within the Franconian district the area around Bayreuth known as Upper Franconia, and the area around and west of Nuremberg known as Central Franconia showed a rather strong disposition in favor of the Nazis. Contrariwise Lower Bavaria and the Upper Palatinate constituting one election district, the twenty-fifth, always gave large majorities to the parties which opposed Hitler, principally the Bavarian People's and Social Democratic parties. In the crucial July 1932 election, for instance, 48 per cent of the voters of this district supported the Bavarian People's party. Only the Cologne district in all of Germany outranked Bavaria in its opposition to Hitler. The districts of Upper Bavaria-Swabia, and Lower Franconia were two other parts of Bavaria which never supported Hitler in free elections.

It is evident that Bavaria was not a unit politically, its various districts differing from each other considerably. And yet it nurtured its own political party, the Bavarian People's party, and as a state it never gave Hitler the necessary support to put him in power.

The modern district administrative subdivision of Bavaria into eight districts goes back to 1808 when the land was divided into eight *Kreise* (in Bavaria the *Kreise* were administrative districts similar to the Prussian *Regierungsbezirke*). This division lasted until 1932-1933, when the *Kreise* were renamed administrative districts and reduced to six in number: Upper Bavaria, Lower Bavaria and Upper Palatinate (each a separate district until January 1932), Swabia, Upper and Central Franconia, Lower Franconia Mainfranken (formerly called Unterfranken), and the Palatinate. Each district was subdivided into: a number of city counties; a few small but historically important towns directly under the district but not in a county (*Kreisunmittelbare Städte*); and counties which included a number of smaller municipalities or towns.

Each of the six administrative districts was headed by a District President who was responsible to the State Minister of the Interior. They were located as shown in the following table:

Governmental Administrative Districts	Seat of Administration
Upper Bavaria	Munich
Lower Bavaria and Upper Palatinate	Regensburg
Palatinate	Speyer
Upper and Central Franconia	Ansbach
Lower Franconia	Würzburg
Swabia	Augsburg

The district president was assisted by an administrative body composed of departments for Interior (education, church affairs, health, police), Finance (taxes, budgetary affairs, and financial control of public property), and Forests (state forests and game preserves, and supervision of the management of forest properties of lower units of government). It should be remembered that the district was both an area of decentralized state administration and of local self-government. The latter involved the maintenance of medical, charitable, and educational institutions, economic establishments, and other enterprises.

Although their actual operation was always in the hands of the District Administration headed by the District President, in pre-Nazi days the administration was supervised by an elected assembly and committee. Only the committee, which was appointed and advisory, survived in Nazi Bavaria. It must be emphasized that the administration at the district level was subject to the general supervision of the Ministry of the Interior and that special activities were under the supervision of the proper national authority or ministry. Legally the administrative functions of the Bavarian district were regulated by the laws of 1808, the County Constitution of 1927, and the reactionary Nazi laws.

During the imperial period, Bavaria retained quasi-independent control of its postal system and administered its court system, which followed the national pattern. Justice under the Bavarian Ministry of Justice, was administered by the Superior State Court of Munich and the Collegiate Courts of First and Second Instance at Augsburg, Deggensdorf, Eichstätt, Kempten, Landshut, Memmingen, Munich, Munich II, Passau, and Traunstein, the Superior State Court at Nuremberg and the collegiate courts at Amberg, Ansbach, Nuremberg, Regensburg, and Weiden, the Superior State Court at Bamberg and the collegiate courts at Aschaffenburg, Bamberg, Bayreuth, Coburg (after 1918), Hof, Schweinfurt, and Würzburg, and the Superior State Court at Zweibrücken and the collegiate courts at Frankenthal, Kaiserslautern, Landau, and Zweibrücken. The postal system, which was under the Bavarian General-Director of the Royal Post and Telegraph until 1920 when it passed under the National Postal Ministry, was under the Chief Postal Directorates (Empire) or National

Postal Directorates (Republic and Third Reich) of Augsburg, Bamberg, Landshut, Munich, Nuremberg, Regensburg, Speyer, and Würzburg. National regulations for trade and industry, weights and measures, social insurance, public health, and the collection of imperial revenues were carried out upon delegation from the Reich.

The Republic extended direct national administration to finance, railways, unemployment insurance, employment, and labor welfare. National regulation of finances within Bavaria was carried out by the State Finance Offices of Munich, Nuremberg, and Würzburg and their local finance and customs offices. National Construction offices were located at Munich, Nuremberg, and Landau. The nationalized railways were operated by the National Railroad Directorates of Nuremberg, Munich, Augsburg, Regensburg, and Ludwigshafen. Labor and unemployment problems were handled by the State Labor Office of Bavaria, (Munich) and the Main Welfare Office of Bavaria (Munich). Many services which were subject to national legislation were carried out upon delegation from the Reich. Economically, the state was organized in a number of national agricultural, industrial, commercial, and labor organizations.

Under the Nazis, Bavaria was organized under the following Nazi party districts: Munich-Upper Bavaria (Munich), Swabia (Augsburg), Bavarian Ostmark (Bayreuth), Lower Franconia (Würzburg), and Saar-Palatinate (Neustadt). The headquarters for each party district included offices which dealt with all aspects of party activity, and reached down to every citizen and village.

The advent of the Nazi Third Reich brought rapid and sweeping changes in the status and character of the government of Bavaria. In 1934, the Nazis liquidated its federal status. Its rights were transferred to the Reich, and a National Governor, directly responsible to the National Minister of the Interior, but also subject to the supervision of other national ministers, was placed in charge of the government and administration. The conversion of the state into a Reich administrative district was accompanied by a number of other important changes. The Bavarian Assembly and the state ministries for justice and foreign affairs were eliminated, while the old General Ministry (*Gesamtministerium*) was replaced by a State Chancellery.

The liquidation of Bavaria as a state within a federal republic had many significant administrative consequences. The central administration, though headed by a Minister-President, was subject to the political control of the Governor. The Minister President, however, headed the Bavarian State Chancellery (*Bayrische Staatskanzlei*) which coordinated the work of the various state ministries and handled press and legal affairs, relations with the army, and state and local utility matters. The Minister President was also head of the Bavarian State Forest Administration (*Bayrische Landesforstverwaltung*). The Bavarian

Cabinet at this time consisted of four ministries: Interior, Education and Culture, Finance, and Economics. The state cabinet and its ministries served as agents for the Reich and for the state, issuing decrees and laws, and directing, supervising, and executing the affairs of the state. They were, however, subject to the Reich Cabinet and could carry on their business only in the name of the Reich and after clearance with the competent national ministers. Although the Bavarian Cabinet was separate from the office of the Governor, it must be regarded as a separate subordinate national authority carrying out national orders and at the same time functioning for state purposes. All state officials were indirect national officials.

Direct national administration under the Nazis was extended to justice, air matters, propaganda, and labor relations. Former fields of state administration such as police, health, welfare, education, and certain aspects of social insurance, were brought under close national regulation. Economic planning was carried out by the State Planning Association of Bavaria, which was under the leadership of the Governor. The Palatinate, however, after 1935 was under the State Planning Association of the Saar-Palatinate. Services and functions of a general and special administrative nature were supplemented by an elaborate system of corporate administration.

RURAL ASPECT

Rural pursuits, based upon agriculture and forestry, play a significant role in the life of Bavaria, for over 31 per cent of its population lives and works close to the soil. This proportion is large in contrast with the rest of the Reich except for the northeastern part of Germany. Rural Bavaria is occupied by four distinct ethnic groups of German type. The Bavarians have been settled in the southeastern portion of the state for many centuries. Today, they are found chiefly in the district of Upper Bavaria and the district of Lower Bavaria and the Upper Palatinate. Southwestern Bavaria is the home of the Swabian folk whose distribution more or less coincides with the administrative district of Swabia. The Franconian or Frankish peoples, who are characterized by a lack of cultural coherence, dwell in northern and western Bavaria, primarily in the districts of Upper Franconia, Central Franconia and the district of Lower Franconia. The detached Bavarian Palatinate, which is located on the Rhine, is inhabited by Rhenish Franks.

The general administration of Bavaria centered in the state capital at Munich and the six district capitals: Munich (Upper Bavaria), Regensburg (Lower Bavaria and Upper Palatinate), Ansbach (Upper Franconia and Central Franconia), Würzburg (Lower Franconia), Augsburg (Swabia), and Speyer (Palatinate). While much of the rural general administration was carried out by the county administrations into which each of the districts was divided, a number of offices and agencies handle special and technical services under direct national control at the district and county levels. The county, which was known as the district (*Bezirksamt*) until 1938, served as both an area of state administration and local self-government. It was headed by a County Manager, who was formerly known as a district chairman (*Bezirksoberamtmann*). The pattern of county government and administration was established by the laws of 1852, 1919, and 1928. These laws provided for a district committee and a district assembly which assisted the district chairman. The Nazis eliminated the elected District Assembly, converted the District Committee into an appointed advisory committee, and strengthened the position of the County Manager. The most important function of this official was the supervision of the administration of the villages and towns of his county. He also served as the administrative authority for all county Order Police. He maintained close working relationships with the County Physician and the town physicians of the local town health offices. He also worked with the local officials and agencies for schools, construction and road affairs, price and rationing control, and welfare matters. As head of the local county organization for self-government, he managed and supervised the establishments, institutions, and enterprises of the county.

The village and town administrations of the counties of Bavaria, consisting of a Mayor, a Nazi Party Agent, two or three administrative assistants, and an appointed Advisory Council, followed the pattern laid down in the new German Municipal Code of 1935, which replaced the Bavarian Municipal Code of 1927. Though the management and control of village public life was under the effective supervision of higher authorities, the small towns and villages continued to handle public works and welfare, and a few enterprises—the town forest, the market, and an occasional utility plant.

Agriculturally, Bavaria is one of the important areas of the Reich. Over 57 per cent of the land is devoted to agrarian activities, while another 33 per cent of the total land area is occupied by forest. The character of agriculture varies widely throughout this area owing to widely differing conditions of relief and soil, but these factors account for only a part of the strong regional contrasts in rural life. Many of these contrasts are rooted in the differences distinguishing the peasants and foresters of Bavaria, the Bavarians of the southeast, the Swabians of the southwest, the Franks of the north and west, and the Rhenish Franks of the Palatinate.

Southeastern Bavaria, although occupied by a single peasant group, the Bavarians, presents numerous geographical and cultural contrasts which are important for an understanding of agriculture and rural life. Over 31 per cent of the population of this area makes its living from agriculture and forestry. The truly rural character of this part of the Reich is best revealed by the character of settlement, for over 52 per cent of the population dwells in villages of less than 2,000, while another 18 per cent dwells in villages and towns ranging from 2,000 to 20,000 in population. The hilly northern portion of this area is more predominantly rural than the southern part which centers about Munich.

The most southern portion of the district of Upper Bavaria is dominated by the sub-Alpine mountain ranges which are transitional to the high eastern Alps of Austria. The higher portion in the south, consisting of limestone heights often of the karst type and cut by the narrow gorge-like valleys of the rivers leading northward to the Danube, is largely given over to pasture and forests. Northward, these uplands give way to an area of irregular relief, whose origin goes back to the last extension of the Alpine glaciers. This is a land of small lakes, moraines, bogs, and moors characterized by an extremely poor soil. The climate is severe with very cold, snowy winters and cool, humid summers. The heavy rainfall hardly encourages agriculture; pastoral and forestry activities are almost universal in these regions. The scant population, which dwells on isolated farms or in tiny valley villages which seldom have a population of more than 70 or 80 persons, works farms ranging in size from 5 to 20 hectares, although farm establishments ranging up to 100 hectares are not infrequent in the more open valleys. The farms utilize the rich grass of the valley meadowland and the short grass and herbage of the upland pastures for cattle raising and dairying and the production of butter and cheese. Sheep grazing also plays an important role in the highlands. The stony valley fields do not produce good crops, although oats, rye, and potatoes are raised for home use and fodder.

In the lower valley areas where land is better for cultivation, cereals are grown for cash. The farms of this part of the sub-Alpine region tend to be of the larger type. Here the villages are also larger, ranging from 70 to 200 inhabitants in some cases. Occasionally, one will find villages of the more average type in the Reich with a population of 200 to 600 inhabitants. This is a land of hardy independent farmers everywhere dwelling in picturesque rectangular dwellings, housing their living quarters and barn. Their deep religious convictions are revealed in the landscape by the numerous wayside shrines of the area. All of the larger villages support a church; their curious mushroom domes can be seen far out over the valley.

In the southern part of the district of Upper Bavaria the sub-Alpine zone gives way to the Bavarian Plateau. The geological basis of the plateau area is the old morainic material pushed down during the glacial age. Today, the land is mostly covered by out-wash gravels and sands cut and dissected by rivers whose erosive action has led to the formation of numerous valley terraces and hilly areas. While the higher portions are well forested, the lower valley areas are frequently swampy, although some are now being reclaimed for pasture. This area enjoys a milder climate than the uplands to the south, but the annual rainfall is still quite heavy. Cattle raising, dairying, and the cultivation of fodder crops, grown on a fertile but heavy soil, are still the dominant rural activities, aside from forestry, although the cultivation of cereals, barley for brewing, and rye, is much more important than in the sub-Alpine uplands. The rural population dwells in widely scattered villages of the agglomerated *Haufendorf* type, which are of normal size ranging from 200 to 600 in population. This village type gives way to the small village with 70 to 200 people or the tiny hamlet with 15 to 70 inhabitants in the eastern part of the plateau area. The farms of the area tend to range from 5 to 20 hectares in size with larger farms (20 to 100 hectares) more common than in the uplands to the south. There are significant variations in field systems. While the sub-Alpine area is made up chiefly of pastures and small irregular cultivated areas, the plateau area is farmed by means of the three-field system. The farmers and villagers of the area still use the typical old-fashioned rectangular Bavarian peasant dwelling for housing.

The area between the Bavarian Plateau and the Danube River, occupying the southern portion of the district of Lower Bavaria and Upper Palatinate, consists of level plains extending from Augsburg eastward along the southern side of the Danube into Austria. Its loess soil has been worked for the last five thousand years, and the warmer and drier climate of these lower elevations makes it an excellent agricultural zone. Cereals, particularly wheat, are cultivated, frequently with mechanized equipment. Hops constitute an important cash crop, while livestock raising is a significant secondary activity. The farms of this area tend to be large (20 to 100 hectares), although the smaller farm of 5 to 20 hectares is still common. Most of the farms of the plains are likewise handled by means of the three-field system. Throughout the Bavarian plains and particularly to the east, one finds numerous isolated farm houses of the square Bavarian type serving as the center for a larger farm. A few large peasant villages of 600 to 1600 population, generally centering about a main square, are located along the banks of the Danube and the lower Isar. Away from the river, the small hamlet and village are as common as in the Bavarian plateau area.

The territory of the districts of Lower Bavaria and the Upper Palatinate to the north of the Danube River, lies in the hilly country where the Franconian Jura, the Upper Palatinate Forest, the Bohemian Forest, and the Bavarian Forest surround the valley of the Nab. The Franconian Jura, which forms the easternmost part of the Main-Neckar scarplands, is a high limestone upland where summer pastures alternate with bleak unproductive areas. It has only a scant rural population. It is the natural barrier separating the Bavarians from the Frankish peoples to the northwest, while the Upper Palatinate Forest, the Bohemian Forest, and the Bavarian Forest to the east beyond the valley of the Nab serve as the natural barrier separating the Bavarians from the Czechs of

Bohemia. These upland areas, running from northwest to southeast, are heavily forested, and the only open areas, the valleys, are often occupied by moors and bogs. The lowlands between the uplands, which are traversed by the River Nab, enjoy a warm, dry climate which contrasts with the cooler and moister climate of the surrounding uplands. The hilly central portion of the Upper Palatinate with its mixed soils ranging from sandy loams to clays is largely devoted to grain, fodder, and livestock which are raised on small farms ranging in size from 5 to 20 hectares. Larger farms (20 to 100 hectares) occur only in the occasional wide valleys. The farms of the surrounding uplands are quite small, many averaging less than 5 hectares. Although a number of isolated farm houses dot the landscape, the typical settlement in the more open areas is the agglomerated village with a population which seldom exceeds 600. In the Franconian Jura to the west, the smaller village (70 to 200 population) and the tiny hamlet (15 to 70) are more common. The hamlet predominates in the Bohemian Forest and the Bavarian Forest. The typical house of the area is the rectangular Bavarian type, although the square Bavarian variety common on the plains to the south is characteristic in the forests while the Franconian type becomes increasingly frequent as one proceeds to the west and north.

Southwestern Bavaria, consisting of the district of Swabia, is occupied by the Swabian folk, whose major area of settlement lies to the west in Württemberg. They extend eastward from the Iller, which forms the boundary between Württemberg and Bavaria, to the Lech River, holding the lands lying between the Swabian Jura and the Alps. Swabians who make their living from agriculture and forestry constitute the largest occupational group, accounting for 36 per cent of the population. Most of them dwell in small villages and towns. About 53 per cent live in hamlets and small villages of less than 2,000 while another 25 per cent dwell in small towns ranging in size from 2,000 to 20,000.

Geographically, the land of the Swabians may be divided into three landscape areas. The southern portion of the area is dominated by the ranges of the sub-Alps. The upland valley pastures and stony fields support cattle raising and a limited amount of crop cultivation. The same general conditions of settlement and agriculture which prevail in the southern portion of the Bavarian area extend westward across southern Swabia. The main land area of Swabia consists of the westward continuation of the Bavarian Plateau. Rural life is still dependent upon cattle raising, dairying, and fodder crops with the cultivation of cereals and hops playing a secondary role. The contrast between the Bavarian and Swabian portions of the plateau lies in the character of settlement. In Swabia, the larger village with a population ranging between 600 and 1,600 is very common along the Lech and Danube. In the central portion of the plateau the villages are of normal size (200 to 600 population), while the hamlet and small village become more frequent as one approaches the Alpine foothills. The character of the landscape and agriculture of the Swabian Jura has much in common with that of the Franconian Jura.

Northern and western Bavaria, the district of Upper Franconia and Central Franconia and the district of Lower Franconia, belong to the Franconians. Although more highly urbanized than southern Bavarian, 35 per cent of the people still make their living from agriculture and forestry. The southern Upper Franconian and the western Lower Franconian areas, where 62 per cent of the population dwells in villages of less than 2,000 and another 18 per cent in small towns of 2,000 to 20,000, contrast strongly with the more urbanized Central Franconia area dominating northeast Franconia, where only 37 per cent of the population lives in small villages and only 11 per cent in small towns. These varying conditions of settlement reflect important differences in economic conditions.

The districts of Upper Franconia and Central Franconia in northeast Bavaria occupy the scarplands of the Main Valley. The Central Franconian Basin, an elevated plateau area worn down by the erosive action of the Main and its tributaries, is broken here and there by small scarps running from northeast to southwest that continue eastward to rise up into the Franconian Jura. On the west, the Frankenhöhe and the Steiger Forests (*Steigerwald*) scarplands divide the Central Franconian Basin from Württemberg. Northward, the basin is bound by the Hassberge and Koburger uplands beyond which lie the Upper Franconian uplands and the Franconian Forest. Most of the surrounding uplands are of no great elevation, but the higher sandstone scarplands and uplands are less fertile. Although the entire area enjoys a typical Central German climate, there is a considerable natural variation with elevation, for while the Central Franconian Basin enjoys a relatively warm, dry climate, the higher upland areas tend to have cold, snowy winters and mild, damp summers. The pattern of soil distribution follows the relief and climatic patterns. The lower basin area has a fertile sandy soil, while the uplands possess soils of mixed type consisting of sand and clay. All the farms of the eastern Franconian area are small, ranging in size from 5 to 20 hectares.

The only large farming establishments are located in the better farming areas of the Franconian Basin. The lower more level portions of this area are devoted to grain and fruit. Here, too, the sequence of farm activities follows the three-field system involving the rotation of rye, oats, and potatoes. The cultivation of grain and the raising of fruit tend to be emphasized in the warm, dry valleys and basins. The rich valley meadowland is devoted to grazing, while the gentle slopes of the valleys are used to raise barley, oats, spelt, and hops. The valley and sloping basin land is generally separated from the higher uplands by a zone of forests. Beyond the forestland, the uplands are used for grazing and the growth of forage crops. The upland cattle are used for milk, meat, and transportation. There are few horses in this part of Germany. Most of the farmers of the valley and basin land dwell in large villages (200 to 1,600 population) of the agglomerated type consisting of Middle German Frankish houses. In the uplands, the tiny village or hamlet (15 to 200 population) predominates, though in the very poor upland areas to the east one can find many isolated upland farm houses of Frankish type. While the farmers of the valley are prosperous, those of the uplands are poor and must frequently supplement their income by work on larger valley farms or in the industries of neighboring towns.

Western Franconia centers about the plains of the lower Main. These lower Franconian plains open up west of the Steiger Forest, the Hassberge, and Koburger uplands and extend westward along both sides of the Main to the granite Spessart and Rhön uplands, which separate the lower Franconian area from the Rhine-Main Basin. Southward, they give way to the hills of Württemberg. Climatically, this area is transitional between the more severe climate of Franconia and the milder one of the Rhineland. The climate and soil of the plains are quite like those of the Rhine-Main Basin. Agriculture in this region of valleys, plains, and hills is based upon wine, fruit, and grain. The sunny slopes of the narrower valleys are covered with vineyards, the open plains with orchards, fields of grain, potatoes, Indian corn, and extensive vineyards. Grain growing becomes more important in the hilly areas. The farmers of the valleys dwell in large agglomerated villages (600 to 1,600 in population) with their small farms, which seldom exceed 5 hectares in size, situated outside the village complex. In the higher areas, where grain growing is more important, the farms tend to be larger, ranging between 5 and 20 hectares. The villages decline rapidly in size after one leaves the plains, but nowhere within this area does one find the numerous small villages and hamlets of less than 200 people which are so common in eastern and southern Bavaria. Both village and farm houses of Western Franconia are typically Frankish.

The Rhine Palatinate, situated on the Rhine to the south of the state of Hesse, constitutes one governmental administrative district, the district of the Palatinate. The population belongs to the Rhenish Franconian (Rheinfranken) group which also dominates the state of Hesse and much of the Province of Hesse-Nassau. Geographically, it occupies the plains bordering the western side of the Rhine, the central Palatinate Forest, or Hardt, and the Lorraine Hills which intrude into the western part of the district. Agriculture and forestry are only of secondary importance since the Palatinate forms a part of the industrialized Rhenish area. While 61 per cent of the population is engaged in industry, trade, and transportation, only 25 per cent makes its living from agriculture and forestry. This is an area of large villages with populations ranging from 600 to 1,600. Although in the higher upland areas villages are of the smaller type (population 200 to 600), in the northern part of the Palatinate Forest one can find a large number of isolated farm establishments. The small farms of the Rhenish plains, which are generally smaller than 5 hectares, are devoted to the cultivation of grain, fruit, and tobacco. Though this type of agriculture extends into the foothills of the Palatinate Forests, the uplands of central and eastern Palatinate are given over to grain, livestock, and forage crops. Here the farms are slightly larger ranging from 5 to 20 hectares in size. The villages and houses of the rural area are much like those in Franconia.

The most productive areas include only the Bavarian plains and the Middle Franconian Basin, while the least productive ones consist of the Franconian and Swabian Jura, the Bohemian Forest, the Bavarian Forest, the sub-Alpine area, and the Bavarian Plateau. The rest is moderately good for various types of agrarian activity. The southern part of the state, which enjoys a humid, cool climate, is best for dairying, forage crops, and pasture, while the bulk of central and northern Bavaria, enjoying a warmer, drier climate, is good for grain and livestock. The western portions of the state, including the Lower Franconian and Palatinate areas, have long been regions of intensive agriculture, specializing in grain, fruit, and wine. The uplands throughout Bavaria are given over to cattle raising and dairying.

LAND UTILIZATION (HECTARES)

Cultivated Land		2,623,351
Grain	1,586,294	
Legumes	22,910	
Root Crops	542,386	
Green Vegetables	16,577	
Industrial Crops	23,010	
Fodder Crops	388,419	
Small Gardens		57,432
Meadow		1,439,392
Pasture		212,965
Orchards		17,830
Vineyards		22,305
Forests		2,519,718
Waste Lands		311,861
Houses and Barns		97,971
Roads and Parks		296,688

PERCENTAGES OF LAND-USE

Agrarian Land	59%
Cultivated Land	35%
Meadowland and Pasture	22%

Small Gardens, Orchards,
     Vineyards 2%
     Forests and Woods 34%
     Other Types of Land 7%

Though 34 per cent of Bavaria is covered by woods and forests, the local distribution is subject to wide variation. The most densely forested areas, where
the forest cover amounts to over 45 per cent of the total land area, are located
in the sub-Alpine upland, the Bohemian Forests, parts of the Franconian Jura,
the Spessart and Rhön areas, and the western uplands of the Palatinate. The
regions of sparse forest cover, where the woodland occupies less than 25 per
cent of the land, are located in the Central Franconian Basin and on the plains
of the southern part of the district of Lower Bavaria. The rest of the land is
rather well forested. Conifers account for 80 to 90 per cent of the forest cover
everywhere in the state except for the district of lower Franconia and the district of the Palatinate, where the forests are composed of equal proportions of
conifer and broadleaf trees. There is great diversity in the types of forests to be
found in the region. In the far south, the sub-Alpine area, one finds extensive
spruce forests and some larch and pine. Northward, there is a transitional belt
of spruce, fir, and beech. The Bavarian forest interests utilize the heavy rainfall and soils for growing spruce and in some areas planted spruce forests have
replaced the original mixed forestland. The Bavarian Plateau is largely occupied
by broadleaf forests with the beech predominating in the south and the oak in
the north. Especially sandy areas support pure stands of pine. The plains area,
which lies between the plateau and the Danube, is occupied by only occasional
patches of forest. The forest of the Bohemian area is much like that of the sub-
Alpine area, while the lower Upper Palatinate Forest and the Bavarian Forest
support extensive growths of fir, beech, and Central German spruce. The Franconian Jura, the Swabian Jura, and the Upper Palatinate hills are dominated by
the pine and oak. Much of the oak has been cut in this region and new growths
of birch, aspen, and alder are now important.

The forests of Franconia, which occupy the Central Franconian Basin and
the plains and hills of the lower Main area, were originally composed of beech
growing in the higher areas and oak in the plains and valleys. Today, these
broadleaf forests are partly giving way to pine forests. Spruce is grown widely
in this area. In the Rhenish Palatinate area, the western hills were once covered
by extensive forests of oak and beech, but today, the pine plays an important
role. These forest lands are owned by a variety of interests. The state of
Bavaria owns about 937,000 hectares of forest area, administered through 327
state forests reserves, which were managed by the State Forest Administration.
In the eastern and southern portions of Bavaria, the district of Upper Bavaria,

the district of Lower Bavaria and the Upper Palatinate and the district of Central Franconia and Upper Franconia, the state owns between 20 and 30 per cent of the forest area, while private interests hold from 60 to 70 per cent. The municipalities possess only a limited amount of the forest land, about 10 per cent in this general area. The character of forest ownership is quite different in the district of Lower Franconia and the district of the Palatinate, for here the municipalities own approximately 40 per cent of the forest area, while the state owns from 30 to 40 per cent of the forests. Private interests have only a small stake in the woodland, owning 12 per cent of the forest land in the Palatinate and 20 per cent in Lower Franconia.

The four dominant rural groups of Bavaria are the Bavarians of the southeast, the Swabians of the southwest, the Franconians of the center, north, and northwest, and the Rhenish Franconians of the Palatinate. They are distinguished from one another by a variety of factors: dialect, religion, food and drink habits, agricultural practices, and attitudes. While one cannot accurately define in a scientific manner the exact characteristics of an average rural type, such as the Bavarian or Franconian, it is worthwhile to give a few of the dominant characteristics for each type. Physically, the Bavarian may be of the tall, dark, round-headed Dinaric racial type, or the blond blue-eyed Alpine-Nordic racial blend. He tends to dwell in small villages and to work a small to medium-sized farm. His interests run to cattle raising and dairying rather than crop cultivation. He has a reputation for taking life in a lighthearted manner. His humor is coarse, and frequently he gets rid of his anger by cursing and gesticulation. He is noted for his love of fighting, a quality which makes him a good cold-steel fighter and often leads to crimes of violence. He drinks beer in quantity and is fond of meat. He likes the rougher sports, wrestling and hunting. Music and folk dancing play an important role in the life of the Bavarian. Back of this rustic and sometimes crude way of life is a devout Catholic faith.

The Swabian, who lives to the west of the Bavarian in southwest Bavaria, is physically much like the Bavarian. Although his villages are much like the ones found in the Bavarian area, his house is typically Swabian. Dialect and temperament are the real things which set the Swabians off from the surrounding peoples of this part of Germany. Their language has a certain primitive roughness and a distinctive phonetic quality. They are a difficult people to know well because of their reserve with strangers, although once an acquaintanceship has been established, one will find the Swabians friendly and good humored. They are a shrewd, tenacious, astute people.

The Franconians of central, north and northwestern Bavaria are difficult to characterize because of their divided and scattered distribution. Those of the Main River area possess a culture which can only be considered as transitional between northern and southern Germany. They have lost their old group feeling. It has given way to the consciousness of a more universal Germany. They are a practical and domestic folk who have the important quality of being adaptable. The historical reasons for this lack of a unified group feeling may lie partly in the fact that the Franconian area has suffered from political and cultural disunity since the late Middle Ages. Although they are, today, divided by religious faith, attitudes, folkways, and even dialect (for in Franconia a dialect does not exist for any broad area), those with similar ways of speaking tend to cluster about important towns. The universal distribution of the Frankish house reflects the day when they formed a unified cultural group. The Rhenish Franconians and the Eastern Franconians have much in common. Festivals and carnivals play an important role in the life of both groups. Wine and light food are more important in the Rhenish area, while beer and more starchy meals are common to the east. The Rhenish Franconians have much more in common with the Rhinelanders than the Franconians of northern Bavaria. After all, their home, the Palatinate, is on the Rhine and it has long traditions which are only understandable in Rhenish terms.

URBAN ASPECT

The state of Bavaria is not densely settled. The eastern part of the state, comprising the district of Lower Bavaria and Upper Palatinate, does not support anything in the way of an urban complex. There are a few small cities—Landshut, Straubing, Passau, Amberg, and Weiden—ranging in size from 20,000 to 30,000 population, which have long been market towns serving their agrarian environs. Today, each has some industry. The only city of any importance is Regensburg on the Danube, which has a population of 82,000. Southern Bavaria, consisting of the districts of Upper Bavaria and Swabia, has two important urban centers, Augsburg and Munich. The market towns of Ingolstadt on the Danube and Kempten in southern Swabia, both with a population of about 25,000, are the only other centers of importance. Southern Bavaria, like the eastern part of the state, has a predominantly rural, agrarian, social-economic structure.

Northern Bavaria, which is included within the district of Central Franconia and Upper Franconia and the district of Lower Franconia, has an essentially agrarian-industrial, social-economic structure that is oriented about two urban complexes. One centers about the industrial city of Nuremberg which occupies the heart of the Central Franconian Basin, the other about the much less important city of Würzburg on the plains of the Main. The other cities of Franconia—Bamberg, Bayreuth, Coburg, Hof, Ansbach, Erlangen, Aschaffenburg, and Schweinfurt—all with a population less than 45,000, are, again, old market towns with some added industry. The more purely industrial towns of Aschaffenburg and Schweinfurt, which are located on the lower Main are

oriented along with Würzburg toward the Rhine-Main economic area. Nuremberg is by all odds the dominating economic and cultural center of Northern
Bavaria. The cities of the Palatinate belong to the Rhineland. The main metropolitan area, which centers about the important river port and industrial city
of Ludwigshafen and the smaller towns of Frankenthal, Kaiserslautern, Pirmasens, Speyer, and Zweibrücken is oriented economically not toward the
Rhine-Main focus to the north, but westward to the Saar and east and southward toward Baden and Württemberg. The culture of this strongly industrialized agrarian area is Rhenish.

Only a portion of the fifty-nine city-county administrations in Bavaria rank
as city counties under the German Municipal Code, although thirty of the
smaller towns are classified as cities on a Bavarian basis in so far as they have
no affiliations with a county administration and are directly responsible to a
District President. They are known as cities outside county jurisdiction (*Kreisunmittelbare Städte*) but do not have the national status of city-counties.
Many of these cities have acquired this special status by reason of their once having been free and imperial cities of the older Holy Roman Empire. Twenty-nine
of the larger cities have the status of city counties. Prior to the Nazis, the government of the municipalities followed first the pattern provided by the Law of
1808 and later the Constitution for Towns of 1927. They provided for a Municipal Council Constitution (*Gemeinderatverfassung*) form of government. The
Nazis put an end to the democratic ways provided by these laws.

The cities of Bavaria tend to group themselves into three economic regions,
each of which constitutes a more or less distinct social-economic and cultural
bloc, that serves as a real unit of human activity and organization. Southern
Bavaria, consisting of the districts of Swabian and Upper Bavaria, and the old
district of Lower Bavaria plus the southern portion of the old district of Upper
Palatinate, forms one of these economic regions, while northern Bavaria made
up of the districts of Lower Franconia, Upper Franconia and Central Franconia, and the northern part of the old district of Upper Palatinate constitutes
another distinct economic unit. The Rhenish Palatinate is a third unit, with its
Rhineland relationships. The dominant focal points from the urban point of
view of these regions are Munich, Nuremberg, and Ludwigshafen.

The economic life of southern Bavaria under the Nazis was subject to the
plans of the State Planning Association which served all of Bavaria and was
organized under the Economic Chamber at Munich. Although Munich is the
dominant center of southern Bavaria, the other smaller cities have important
local significance serving as focal points of smaller economic areas. It must be
emphasized that Munich, which is the largest city of southern Germany, and
Augsburg, which is second in importance to Munich in southern Bavaria, are
the dominant urban centers of this area, and that the other smaller cities of

Landshut, Straubing, Regensburg, Ingolstadt, and Kempten are primarily small market centers with some added industry serving their immediate rural environs.

The industries of southern Bavaria are faced with a drastic shortage of raw materials and power. The lignite fields to the west of Munich and to the north of Regensburg do not satisfy industrial needs. These power needs are met by a number of important water power plants, located on the Lech, Isar, and Inn rivers. The three largest power stations, which produce from 100 to 200 million kwh. per year, are situated on the upper Isar (*Walchensee-Werke*), the middle Isar near Munich (*Mittelisar-Werke*) and the lower Inn (*Innwerke*). Small plants, producing from 50 to 60 million kwh. per year, are located on the Lech near Augsburg, the lower Inn (*Alzwerke*), and the Danube near Passau. These plants are linked together by a number of high tension lines. One runs northward along the Isar River to Regensburg and thence north to Saxony, while another line links Munich to Augsburg, from where lines run westward into Württemberg and northward to Nuremberg. The Passau plant connects with the Isar power line at Regensburg. These larger power plants are supplemented by a number of municipally owned water power and lignite plants. Added supplies of lignite for power in a raw and bricked form and coal are brought in by rail from Central Germany and the Rhineland. Local raw materials largely consist of stone and clay, agricultural products, and wood.

Although southern Bavaria does not support an iron and steel industry, metal is brought in from central and western Germany for its moderately developed machinery industry. Munich was an important center for the production of machinery, locomotives, and automobiles (*Krauss, Maffei,* and *Bayrische Motorenwerke*), while Augsburg has the important *Maschinenfabrik-Augsburg-Nürnberg-MAN*—machine works which produced the first Diesel motors. The *Bayrische Flugzeugwerke* was located at Augsburg, and other small machine plants at Regensburg and Landshut. The chemical industries of Munich, Augsburg, and the few other cities of the south were of minor significance in comparison with those of other parts of the Reich. The manufacture of textiles is of some importance in the southwestern part of the state. Augsburg, where the tradition of weaving goes back to the original Fugger weavers of the late Middle Ages, is the important center, although there are plants for both linen and cotton at Kempten, Lindau, and Munich. Food products and the wood industries have a real importance in southern Bavaria. All cities and towns of any size at all have firms engaged in these industries. The manufacture of beer ranks high in the area. Munich (*Hofbräu, Löwenbräu, Spatenbräu,* and *Häckerbräu*) beers are famous beyond the borders of Germany. Other important breweries are located at Augsburg, Landshut, Regensburg, Ingolstadt, and Passau. Southern Bavaria is also important for furniture and house furnishings. The clays and iron-free sands of the Bavarian Forest have led to the growth of the porcelain and glass works at Nymphenburg and Regensburg. In relation to the rest of the Reich, southern Bavaria is important for the production of wood and timber products, food products, and water power. Its machinery, chemical, and textile industries have only minor significance.

The main roads of southern Bavaria have been traveled since the Middle Ages. They include the route from Passau along the Danube via Regensburg to Nuremberg, the road from Salzburg in Austria via Munich and Augsburg to Ulm in Württemberg, the Munich-Ingolstadt-Nuremberg road, and the Munich-Kempten-Lindau route. Munich is the key to the road system, which has been supplemented under the Nazi regime by the national super-highway, for roads radiate from this city to Nuremberg, Salzburg, and Stuttgart.

Southern Bavaria is also served by an excellent railroad network which was under the jurisdiction of the National Railroad Directorates in Munich, Augsburg, and Regensburg. Most of the heavy rail traffic is borne by the Munich-Würzburg-Frankfort, the Munich-Nuremberg-Leipzig, and the Vienna-Regensburg-Nuremberg lines. While a number of small lines run southward from Munich into the Alpine foothills, only one is important—the one penetrating the valley of the Inn to reach the Brenner Pass and Italy.

The only important waterway in southern Bavaria is the Danube (*Donau*) which is navigable upstream as far as Regensburg, where it connects with the poor Ludwig Canal which winds northward to connect with the Main at Bamberg. There are important river ports at Regensburg, Straubing, and Passau. The only major civil aviation airport in this area was at Munich, an important center for both domestic and international air travel. Although the air service in Bavaria as in all Germany was operated by the German Airways Corporation, the airports were owned and operated by the municipalities.

The city of Munich is the predominating center of trade and finance in southern Bavaria. Augsburg ranks next in importance. The smaller towns of Passau, Straubing, Regensburg, Ingolstadt, and Landshut in the northern and eastern part of this area are oriented mainly toward Munich, while Donauwörth, Kempten, and Lindau look first to Augsburg, but ultimately to Munich. Neu-Ulm in western Schwaben, on the other hand, looks westward to the city of Ulm in Württemberg. Munich rose to importance as a commercial center during the nineteenth century. Augsburg's commercial importance is traditional, dating back to the days of the great Fugger and Welser trading families who flourished during the fifteenth and sixteenth centuries. Munich's commercial power was due to the redistribution of trade alignments, which came with the introduction of the railroad, and its paramount position as the modern capital of Bavaria. Towns like Regensburg and Ingolstadt have retained their position in southern Bavarian trade owing to their strategic commercial positions on rail lines and rivers. The trading interests of the state reflect its agrarian and industrial activities. Internally, trade in cattle, wood and timber, food products, and paper were important. Machinery and textiles played a secondary role. In terms of freight traffic, agricultural products, wood and timber, stone, and clay were important.

Although Bavaria did not play a great role in the import-export trade of the Reich, it is hardly self-sufficient. Southern Bavaria, because of the needs of the large Munich metropolitan area, was not even self-sufficient in foodstuffs, for grain from overseas was brought in via the Rhine River through the port of Mannheim, which also served as the distributing point for oil. Wheat flour was also shipped from the mills of Central Germany. The trade in coal, lignite, and iron has already been mentioned. The specialization and concentration of the textile industry in Germany led to an active trade in yarns between the mills of western and southern Bavaria and those of Württemberg and Baden. Augsburg was the main center for the distribution of finished cloth in southern Bavaria. Trade relations in the machine industry were even more complex. While the exchange of machine goods between Augsburg and Nuremberg in northern Bavaria was about equal, Augsburg was heavily dependent upon the plants of Württemberg for many of its machine tool needs. Munich, on the other hand, was mainly dependent upon the heavy machine industries of the Saxon area. The agricultural trade of the south, which was mostly in cattle and meat, was oriented toward Saxony. The limited overseas exports were shipped out largely through the ports of the Weser and Elbe.

The banks of the more important towns and cities of southern Bavaria ranged from branches of the great commercial banks of Berlin, which were mainly interested in industrial investments, to the local municipal savings banks. The main state banks, the *Bayrische Staatsbank, Bayrische Landeskultur-Rentenbank* (Credit for rural settlement), *Bayrische Siedlungs- und Landbank* (Agricultural credit), the *Bayrische Gemeindebank* (Central bank for local municipal savings banks) had their headquarters at Munich for the whole state. The operations of these banks were supplemented by branches of the *Reichsbank* at Munich, Ingolstadt, Regensburg, and Augsburg. Southern Bavaria was served by the stock exchange at Munich.

Economically, northern Bavaria forms a distinct regional unit dominated by the city of Nuremberg; Würzburg on the lower Main has economic importance in the western part of this region. While northern Bavaria is subject to the State Planning Association for the state of Bavaria at Munich, the regional economic character of the area is reflected in the general organization for nonagrarian enterprises. There is a branch of the Economic Chamber for Bavaria at Nuremberg to handle the economic organization of northern Bavaria. The cities of Bayreuth, Coburg, Nuremberg, and Würzburg, and the town of Bamberg, are the important industrial centers in Franconia. The numerous other smaller, and perhaps more beautiful towns, are mainly significant as local market and cultural centers.

The industries of this area are better off than those of southern Bavaria, for power and raw materials are more accessible. There are large iron ore deposits east of Nuremberg in the Franconian Jura near Amberg. Although the largest proportion of this ore is shipped by rail to the Ruhr industrial area, some is sent southward to the heavy industrial center at Linz in Austria, while enough is kept at Amberg to support a small iron and steel industry. Amberg obtains the necessary coal and coke from the fields and coke plants of the Rhineland and Central Germany. The heavy industries of Amberg have made possible the real development of the scattered iron and metal manufacturing industries of Franconia, whose real center, however, is to be found at Nuremberg. This city along with its industrialized suburb, Fürth, has important manufacturing plants producing machinery, bicycles, motors, automobiles, and other metal wares of a lighter type such as bells, brasses, toys, and small machine parts. The only other center for the machine industry in the central and eastern portions of northern Bavaria is at Bayreuth. To the west, however, along the lower Main, there were important metal manufacturing plants at Würzburg (mechanical presses of König and Bauer), Aschaffenburg (motors and machinery), and Schweinfurt (Fichtel and Sachs automobiles, torpedoes, and bearings). These plants receive their raw materials from the Ruhr via the Rhine-Main waterways. The most important industry of northeast Franconia is textile manufacturing. There are important cotton textile plants at Bamberg, Bayreuth, Kulmbach, Erlangen, and Nuremberg, knitting mills at Aschaffenburg and Nuremberg, and linen mills at Weiden and Nuremberg. The only important chemical plants are to be found at Nuremberg and Fürth. The clay and stone resources of the Franconian Jura have led to the growth of several specialized industries, such as the glass industries which are scattered through the Upper Palatinate and the porcelain plants at Coburg, Hof, and Bayreuth.

Food and wood products have real importance in the industrial life of Franconia. The manufacturing of beer, sausage, and other food products is of importance at Nuremberg, Bamberg, Bayreuth, and a number of smaller towns in eastern Franconia. Nuremberg is the world market center for hops. The cities along the lower Main, like Würzburg and Aschaffenburg, are more interested in wine and fruit. Throughout Franconia, industry, except for that of Amberg, is of the lighter type because of the absence of coal and raw materials. Franconian industry is interested in manufacturing articles which take little in the way of raw materials and have a high value when finished—textiles, leather, machinery, watches, optical goods, toys, musical instruments, and food products. The power needs of these industries are partly met by the great water power plant (*Grosskraftwerke* Franken) just south of Nuremberg. Power lines link this plant to Amberg, Bamberg, Würzburg, Aschaffenburg, and Schweinfurt within northern Bavaria. This power network is linked by high tension lines to the lignite plants of the Rhine Province, the water power stations of southern Bavaria and Central Germany, and the extensive coal and lignite power stations of the Saxon area.

Nuremberg, like Munich, is a key road junction, for roads radiate from this city to Würzburg, Bamberg, Coburg and Erfurt, Bayreuth, Plauen, and Leipzig, Prague, Regensburg, Munich, Augsburg, and Stuttgart. It is the center of a spider-web road pattern which spreads out all over Franconia. The national super-highways of northern Bavaria have the same pattern of distribution. This city is also the key junction of the rail net of Franconia. The administration of railway facilities of northern Bavaria was under the National Railroad Directorate at Nuremberg.

Water transportation on the Main River played a very active part in the commercial life of medieval and early modern Franconia. In the days of smaller river ships, goods were carried up the Main as far as Bamberg. Schweinfurt and Würzburg were important river ports. The advent of the railroad and the coming of the industrial revolution requiring the larger river boats capable of carrying heavier cargoes put an end to navigation on the upper Main. Today, Aschaffenburg stands at the head of navigation of the Lower Main and serves as the distributing point for goods coming into Franconia by the Rhine-Main waterway. It is true, however, that small boats can still travel as far upstream as Bamberg, where they can connect with the Ludwig canal that leads southward to the Danube. Traffic on this route is unimportant. Northern Bavaria is mainly dependent upon its roads and railways, for there are no canals or waterways of importance. Nuremberg had the same status in air transportation that Munich has in the south. It had the only large airport for civil aviation.

Nuremberg is also the important commercial and financial center of Franconia. Würzburg, which occupies second place, has a transitional economic position, for it is partly oriented toward Frankfort and the Rhine-Main area and partly toward Nuremberg and Franconia. The smaller towns of Bamberg, Coburg, Amberg, Bayreuth, Ansbach, and others in north and east Franconia are primarily small market towns with some added industry. They are oriented toward Nuremberg. Schweinfurt and Aschaffenburg, however, look toward Würzburg. Würzburg, Nuremberg, and Bamberg have long been important commercial centers. Nuremberg, the most famous of the three, was the medieval distributing point for luxury products (spice, silk, ivory) from Italy. In early modern times, the merchants of this city did business in Bohemia, Poland, Austria, Hungary, France, and the Low Countries. A primitive iron industry, which was under way by the sixteenth century, added to its wealth and fame as a center of crafts. Bamberg and Würzburg, which did not fare so well as Nuremberg in the industrial revolution, originally owed their fame and fortune to traffic on the main route linking Frankfort to the cities of Saxony.

The contemporary commercial interests of the Franconian cities reflect their agrarian and manufacturing interests. They export some agricultural products, wood products, light manufactured goods, and metal wares to other parts of Germany. The major import was coal from the Ruhr and Rhineland. It should be noted that the area was not agriculturally self-sufficient, owing to the large population of its important cities. Grain was brought in by the Rhine-Main waterway to Aschaffenburg, from which it was distributed by rail to eastern Franconia. The trade relations of the machinery industry of the Nuremberg and Würzburg areas were oriented in two directions, northward toward Saxony with the balance of trade in favor of the latter and southward toward Augsburg. Relations with the Rhine-Main area were not significant. The textile industries of northeast Franconia were closely tied to those of Thuringia and Saxony. The distributing point for finished cloth, however, was at Aschaffenburg. From the point of view of trade in agricultural, forest, and manufactured products most of northern Bavaria was oriented toward the great Saxon industrial area, although the Lower Main area centering about Würzburg looked westward toward Frankfort and was partly tied to the Ruhr-Rhineland industrial centers. The two main banking and finance centers of Franconia, Nuremberg, and Würzburg, were dependent upon Munich. The types of banking institutions were the same as those in the south, branches of the great Berlin commercial banks, offices of the state banks, municipal savings banks, plus the usual branches of the *Reichsbank*.

The Rhenish Palatinate, where over 45 per cent of the population makes its living from industry and crafts, is situated between three important industrial areas: the Saar, famous for its heavy and extractive industries, is located to the west; the Main-Rhine area centering about Frankfort and Darmstadt lies to the north; while the industries of northern Baden are just across the Rhine. Although the Palatinate is bound by industrial and commercial ties to all three, its most intimate connections are with the Saarland. Cognizance of this factor was taken when the German authorities set up a separate planning association for the Saar-Palatinate (Saarpfalz) area. The important industrial towns of Pirmasens, important for leather and shoes; Zweibrücken, for ceramic and leather industries; and Kaiserslautern, for leather, shoe, tobacco, and textile industries, are embraced physically within the eastern margins of the Saar industrial area. The western Palatinate and its industries are linked by a number of east-west roads, by the Saarbrücken-Kaiserslautern-Ludwigshafen-Mannheim railroad, and by the national super-highway route to the cities of the Rhine

Valley. The railroads are under the National Railroad Directorate at Ludwigshafen.

The other industrial cities of the Palatinate include Ludwigshafen, the largest city of the area and one of the great chemical centers of the Reich (*IG Farben*), and Speyer, the district capital and an important center for the manufacture of textiles, shoes, and airplanes. Both cities are located on the Rhine; cheap
water transportation has made possible their development through the importation of raw materials by water from the Ruhr industrial area to the north.
The Rhine River transportation is supplemented by important rail lines running along both banks of this river.

Commercially and financially, the cities of the Palatinate look either westward to the Saar or southeastward toward Baden and Württemberg, but the
commercial significance of the Rhine and the financial importance of Frankfort cannot be overlooked. The commercial and financial ties of Baden and the
Saar-Palatinate area led the German authorities in Nazi times to place the foreign trade of these three areas under one Foreign Trade Office at Mannheim
in northern Baden. It is important to remember that the Palatinate, despite its
isolated position, is an integral part of the state of Bavaria. The banking and
financial institutions of the area are subject to the supervision of the State Bank
in Munich, which serves as the intermediate authority for the National Ministry
of Economics in Berlin.

The urban population of Bavaria is largely concentrated in the fifty-nine
towns and cities. It forms about 47 per cent of the total population. In Bavaria
as a whole, in 1933 over 2,583,000 individuals were engaged in mining, industry, and crafts, while 1,023,000 were employed in trade and transportation.
About 7 per cent made its living in the civil service and professions. Another
unusual class structure is presented in this state. For Bavaria had a very small
laboring class in comparison with other parts of the Reich; it included about
35 per cent of the population. The upper class, which accounted for 24 per cent
of the population, was the largest for any province or state in Germany. This
fact cannot be accounted for in terms of landed wealth or independent peasant
farmers. It must be partly due to the great number of small privately owned
business enterprises. The result was a small white collar class (7 per cent), for
much of the supervisory work of the small enterprises was carried out by their
owners.

The larger cities of southern Bavaria are supported by an industrious and
independent Bavarian and Swabian peasantry. Economically, politically, and
culturally, the rural Bavarian area, with the exception of the northern part of
the administrative district of the Upper Palatinate, and the rural Swabian area
are oriented toward Munich. This city, which was long the residence of the

Wittelsbach rulers of Bavaria, blossomed out into the Hellas of modern Germany, thanks to the lavish gifts of the ruling family. It has always attracted artistic and intellectual settlers from all parts of the Reich, each bringing his own cultural contribution. It is well known for its museums (*Deutsches Museum, Alte* (Old) *Pinakothek, Glyptothek,* and a number of others), state theaters, summer Wagner and Mozart festivals, and monuments and parks including the English Garden (*Englischer Garten*) and the Monument of Bavaria. The educational institutions of Munich, the University and the academies for art and music, are world-famous. These and other universities, theological seminaries, and normal schools in Bavaria are subject to the supervision of the State Ministry for Education and Culture (*Staatsministerium für Unterricht und Kultus*). The technical High-School (*Technische Hochschule*) of Munich is under the District President of Upper Bavaria, while the local elementary and secondary schools, as in all parts of the Reich, are managed by the local municipal school authorities of Munich.

Munich is the seat of the Archbishop who has jurisdiction over the Catholics of the administrative districts of Swabia, Lower Bavaria and the Upper Palatinate, and Upper Bavaria. Munich and the latter district fall largely under the Bishop of Freising. The economic support of this city of innkeepers, scholars and professors, artists, officials, workers, and technicians has derived from its light manufacturing industries, financial and commercial operations, and tourist trade. Although the burghers of Munich have built the world famous *Deutsches Museum* for technology and science, they have long objected to commercialization and industrialization, proclaiming Munich the center of German culture. Before World War I, it stood in opposition to Berlin, the Kaiser, and the industries of the north and central parts of Germany, but after the end of the last war it took to politics and Pan-Germanism. Nazism received strong support from the conservative urban elements, who tried to sell Germanism to the rural Bavarian and Swabian separatists. Munich remains, despite its veneer of culture, a mundane Catholic and Bavarian city of burghers who have acquired an interest in things intellectual and artistic.

The smaller city of Augsburg is the only other large center in southern Bavaria. Until the nineteenth century, it was the major city of southern Germany. Although Munich has captured its commercial position in the economic life of this part of Bavaria, Augsburg has retained its old traditions going back to the days of its independence and the times of the Fugger merchants, when it was the political and economic center of the Holy Roman Empire. Today, its economic support comes from its machine and textile industries and local trade. Augsburg is the seat of the Catholic bishop who has jurisdiction over the Swabian district of southern Bavaria. A Catholic theological school, which is supported by the state, is located here. Augsburg remains a city of traditional significance, important today as the administrative center of the district of Swabia, and the religious and economic center of western southern Bavaria.

The city of Regensburg (Ratisbon), located to the north on the Danube, is the religious and administrative center of the administrative district of Lower Bavarian and Upper Palatinate. It is the center for the Bishop of Regensburg and for a Catholic theological school. Traditionally, it is famous as the home of the painter Albrecht Altdorfer (1537) and the astronomer Kepler (1517).

The other towns and cities of southern Bavaria are small commercial and trading centers. Some have political and cultural significance. Passau at the junction of the Danube and the Inn is the seat of a bishop of the Catholic Church. The only teachers' normal school for southern Bavaria is at Passing, and there is a theological school at Freising. The charming mountain village of Garmisch-Partenkirchen at the foot of the Zugspitze, the highest peak in Germany, is a favorite tourist resort, while the Alpine village of Oberammergau is known throughout the world for its Passion Play. The small village of Berchtesgaden in the most southern and eastern part of Bavaria has symbolic significance since the country home of Adolf Hitler was located in the mountains above it, and the village itself had a branch National Chancellery which served the Führer when he was in residence at Berchtesgaden.

The Bavarians, burghers and peasants, owe much of their cultural unity to the Wittelsbachs. Until the Napoleonic era which brought the rapid expansion and the formation of the modern state of Bavaria, there was a remarkable agreement between the territories of the Wittelsbachs and the lands of the Bavarians. The cultural coherence of this area was not disrupted by the religious disunity following the Reformation. Politically, as well as culturally, the Bavarian burgher and peasant look first to Munich and then to Berlin. The Swabians are culturally tied to Swabian Württemberg, as has been pointed out, but politically and economically they must turn to Munich. They lack the political and cultural traditions of the Bavarian, for until relatively modern times, they dwelt in a land divided against itself.

Although rural Franconia includes only the districts of Lower Franconia and the district of Central Franconia and Upper Franconia, the economic area dominated by the great city of Nuremberg includes a slightly larger area; for the economic life of the northern part of the administrative district of the Upper Palatinate, which from the point of view of rural culture belongs to the southern Bavarian area, is tied intimately to that of Franconia. It is a land of many small and beautiful walled towns, like Dinkelsbühl and Rothenburg, which have changed little since the end of the Middle Ages. Here and there these small towns have been transformed under the impact of the railroad and the industrial revolution into industrial centers. Nuremberg and its suburb, Fürth, are outstanding examples. Nuremberg, which retained the spirit of the time when it was a free and imperial city of the German Reich and the memory of the days of Hans Sachs of the *Meistersinger,* and Albrecht Dürer, has developed from a trade and commercial center, once dominated by patrician merchants, into a thriving industrial center now in the hands of workers, technicians, commercial men, and business bureaucrats. Intellectually, it does not have the status of Munich, although the school for humanistic studies founded by Melanchthon in 1526 still survives. It has the Bavarian state schools for Applied Arts and Commerce.

The smaller cities of the north are oriented toward Nuremberg. Bamberg grew up on the basis of the trade between the Rhine and Saxony, while Coburg, a small market and industrial town, used to be the center of the Grand Duchy of Saxe-Coburg-Gotha. Amberg is important for its iron and steel industries. The small town of Erlangen, the center of one of the important state Universities, and the town of Eichstätt, the seat of a bishopric and the center for a Catholic theological school, lie to the south of Nuremberg.

The life of western Franconia tends to center about the old commercial and university town of Würzburg. This town, the center for a state normal school and the seat of a Catholic bishop, has retained its traditional economic status owing to its favored position in terms of transportation and agricultural resources. The smaller industrial towns of Aschaffenburg and Schweinfurt are oriented first toward Würzburg. These three cities occupy a transitional cultural and economic position, partly oriented toward Nuremberg and partly toward Frankfort. Franconia is utterly lacking in the cultural coherence which characterizes the Bavarian part of southern Bavaria.

The densely populated Palatinate supports a number of industrial towns. Those along the Rhine: Ludwigshafen, famous for its chemical industry; Speyer, the religious and administrative center of the Palatinate, famous for its cathedral—the greatest Renaissance structure in Germany; and Frankenthal, an industrial center, reaped their riches from the cheap Rhine transportation by turning to industrialization. Economic life is on the decline in these Rhineland cities. However, those to the west of the Hardt upland, Kaiserslautern, Zweibrücken, and Pirmasens, are in a more favorable position, for their economic affiliations are with the thriving heavy industrial centers of the Saarland. The economics, politics, and culture of the Palatinate are essentially Rhenish.

Chapter 29

THE STATE OF WÜRTTEMBERG AND HOHENZOLLERN

The state of Württemberg in southwest Germany lying between Bavaria and Baden is roughly oval in shape, with an area somewhat smaller than the state of Massachusetts. The southwestern portion almost entirely surrounds the Prussian Hohenzollern Territory which is likewise known as the district of Sigmaringen. Württemberg is divided into two unequal portions by the upper Danube. The much smaller southern portion extends southward from the Danube across the rolling Danubian plateau country to Lake Constance on the border between Germany and Switzerland. On the west is the state of Baden, and across the Iller River to the east is Bavaria. North from the Danube the state may be divided into two regions: the central and the northern basins. The Neckar River flows north and northwest through the central basin. Within this basin and to the west are the rich cultivated upper and lower districts beyond which lie the north-south ranges of the Black Forest, in which the Neckar rises. To the south are the southwest-northeast ranges of the Swabian Jura, which extend from the southeastern corner of the state of Baden across Württemberg north of the Danube into Bavaria. Though the Swabian Jura is lower than the Black Forest, in some places it rises to an altitude of 3,000 feet. The district of Hohenzollern straddles the Jura (Alb), extending northward into the central Neckar Basin and southward across the Danube. The northern basin of Württemberg is drained by the Neckar and its two main tributaries, the Jagst and Kocher rivers. To the west is the hilly Odenwald and the Neckar *Bergland* (Upland) of northern Baden. In the north center, the Hohenloher plains occupy the main portion of this fertile elevated area, and give way northward to the plains of the lower Main. To the east, the Frankenhöhe uplands separate northern Württemberg from the Franconian portion of Bavaria. Generally speaking, Württemberg is a hilly land, for less than 30 per cent of its territory can be char-

LEGEND

– – – –	COUNTY BOUNDARY
———	STATE BOUNDARY
⊥⊥⊥⊥	INTERNAT'L BORDER
▨	CITY - COUNTY
○	COUNTY SEAT
●	DISTRICT CAPITAL
◉	STATE CAPITAL
▤	HOHENZOLLERN
B	TERRITORY OF BADEN

WÜRTTEMBERG

SCALE   0 10 20 30   KM

J.K.P.
W.F.R.
IAC.V.

acterized as plain. Most of the level country is to be found in the north (Hohen-loher plains) along the upper Neckar.

The greater part of the state of Württemberg and all of Hohenzollern were occupied by the Swabian peoples. Until the second century before Christ most of this part of Germany was occupied by Keltic-speaking folk, who made their living by cultivating the limited valley lands or herding in the uplands. Although the Roman occupation of southwestern Germany seems to have put an end to extensive tribal movement until the third century of our era, the Germanic Alemanni certainly penetrated into the Württemberg-Baden area by the first century. Their position remained stabilized until the fourth century when, under the pressure of Gothic and Burgundian tribal movements, they expanded westward across the Rhine into Alsace and southward into northern Switzerland. The Swabians or *Schwaben,* who were slowly beginning to separate from the Alemanni after A.D. 400, gained a kind of cultural independence owing to the protection and isolation afforded by the highlands surrounding the Neckar Basin. They were not recognized in name until the eleventh century, when the term Swabia replaced that of Alamannia as a designation for what is now central Württemberg.

The modern distribution of the Swabians, whose rough dialect is classified as a variety of Alemannic, is largely restricted to the Neckar Basin, though they also extend southward across the Danube to occupy the northern part of the Danube Plateau country of Württemberg and the Swabian district of Bavaria. Within the southernmost part of Württemberg one can find an Alemannic folk dwelling in the plateau country adjacent to Lake Constance. Their dialect is akin to that spoken in northern Switzerland and southern Baden. A small portion of the northern part of Württemberg is occupied by southern Franconians, whose earlier leaders provided the first rulers of Germany. However, the dominant cultural group of Württemberg is Swabian. The cultural unity of these people is not seriously affected by the religious division within Württemberg where over 67 per cent of the population is Protestant. The Catholics, who constitute about 31 per cent of the population of the state, are largely concentrated in the Franconian north, although large numbers of Catholics dwell in the Swabian portions of the Swabian Jura and the Danubian Plateau. Swabian Hohenzollern is almost entirely Catholic. However, the Swabian core of Württemberg centering about Stuttgart in the Neckar Basin is Protestant. The total Jewish population of Württemberg, which once numbered about 10,-000, was quite small in comparison with other areas of the Reich. Most of the Jews were concentrated in the larger cities like Stuttgart, Ulm, and Heilbronn.

Württemberg ranked third in area among the German states, but it had only a moderately large population in comparison with others. In 1933 it had a population of 2,696,000, which occupied an area of 19,507 sq. km.—a population density of 138 per sq. km. The Prussian district of Hohenzollern, most of which was surrounded by Württemberg, was the smallest administrative unit of Prussia, and aside from Berlin, the Hansa cities, and Schaumburg-Lippe, it was the smallest territory within the Reich. In 1933 it had a population of 72,900 occupying an area of 1,142 sq. km. It was the most sparsely settled area in Germany, except Pomerania, for its population density exceeded 100 persons per sq. km. along the upper Neckar and upper Danube, while the northern Hohenloher and southern Danubian plains-plateau areas were only moderately densely settled (60 to 80 per sq. km.). The uplands, the Swabian Jura, Frankenhöhe, and the Steiger Forest (Steigerwald) had a population density of about 50 persons per sq. km. The intensity of settlement in the Württemberg uplands was much greater than in similar areas in the eastern part of southern Germany.

The population of the state of Württemberg has increased steadily since 1816, although the greatest periods of increase came between 1816-1849 and 1880-1910. The first phase of population expansion came with the economic recovery which followed the Napoleonic wars, while the second, which was marked by the growth of the main urban centers of Württemberg, was due to the German industrial revolution of the latter part of the nineteenth century. This fact is illustrated by the evolution of modern Stuttgart, which has grown from a small "provincial" capital of 92,000 in 1872 to a large industrial city of 420,000 in 1933. Most of the other prominent towns of modern Württemberg had a population of less than 5,000 in 1860, while today they are double or treble that size. The rapid growth of the urban areas of Württemberg, which are located about Stuttgart and in the south along Lake Constance about Friedrichshafen and Ravensburg, has been at the expense of the upland regions and the northern plains area, which have actually undergone a decline in population. From a rural point of view, the only areas which have sustained a moderate population increase are located along the valley of the upper Neckar and on the Danubian Plateau. One other area of population growth deserves mention, namely the area around the thriving manufacturing center of Rottweil in the upper part of the Neckar Valley. The tiny district of Hohenzollern had a population of 61,000 in 1834, as compared with 72,900 in 1933. After World War I, over 700 left each year for other lands, while very few returned to this part of the Reich. Most of these emigrants were drawn from the northwestern and southeastern parts of Württemberg. Very few left the northeastern and southwestern parts of Hohenzollern.

The beginnings of history in this part of the Reich go back to the days of the Kelts, Alemanni, and Romans, but political developments which point more definitely to our own day began in the fifth century with the tribal state of the Alemanni, which occupied most of southwestern Germany. As noted above, its career was short lived, for in 496 the whole Alemannic area was conquered by the Franks under Clovis. It remained a part of the Merovingian and Carolingian Frankish empire until the ninth century when the territory of modern Württemberg was incorporated into the Duchy of Swabia and the Duchy of Franconia. It was ruled by the famous Hohenstaufen family during the period of the Saxon (919-1024) and Franconian (1024-1125) emperors of the Holy Roman Empire. It was one of the sources of strength of the Hohenstaufen family when they served as emperors (1138-1254). After the fall of the Hohenstaufen family from power, the central portion of modern Württemberg (about 1265) went to the Count of Württemberg, who was already in possession of a considerable amount of territory in the Neckar Basin. His successors rapidly increased the territories by purchase or marriage alliances. After a period of constant division of territory within the family, the lands of Württemberg were declared indivisible and united under Count Eberhard V (1482). This arrangement was confirmed by the German Emperor and Imperial Diet in 1495, when Württemberg was elevated to the status of a duchy.

The first rulers of the territory of Hohenzollern appear in Carolingian times. In 980, Earl Friedrich erected the famous Hohenzollern castle, which has since become the family name of this dynasty. Just after the middle of the twelfth century, the eldest son of Earl Rudolph II of Hohenzollern, Friedrich IV, inherited the territories of Hohenzollern, while the younger son, Konrad, was appointed Burgrave of Nuremberg, and became the ancestor of the house of Brandenburg. The lands of Hohenzollern remained intact until 1576 when they were divided between the sons of Earl Karl I. One became Earl of Hohenzollern-Hechingen, while the other became the Earl of Hohenzollern-Sigmaringen. In the early seventeenth century, both earldoms were elevated to principalities.

The beginnings of constitutional liberties in Württemberg go back to the settlement of the Peasants' War in 1514 when Duke Ulrich (1498-1550) made certain political concessions in exchange for money. The Duke soon quarreled with the Swabian League of Cities which was backed by the Duke of Bavaria, who invaded Württemberg, expelled Ulrich, and sold his lands to the Austrian Habsburgs. Duke Ulrich was restored thanks to the backing of the Count of Hesse and other Protestant princes, but he was forced to accept his lands as an Austrian fief. His Protestant connections had immediate results, for he proceeded to introduce Protestantism on a wide scale. His son completed the task of converting the Württemberg Swabian to Protestantism and set up the system of church government which has survived to the present day. In 1599 Württemberg freed herself from Austria by the payment of a large sum of money and once more became a direct fief of the Holy Roman Empire. The duchy suffered severely during the Thirty Years' War, although its dukes took part only in the latter phases of the war. The land was depopulated and impoverished and had no time to recover, after the peace of Westphalia (1648), before it was attacked and ravaged by the French in 1688, 1703, and 1707.

Württemberg slowly recovered from the disasters of the seventeenth and early eighteenth centuries, despite the extravagance of Duke Karl Eugen (1728-1793). His Catholic faith and that of his father and predecessor, Karl Alexander, had been unpopular, as had his arbitrary methods of raising money, his defiance of even the few constitutional limitations of his state position, and his insistence upon fighting Prussia, a Protestant power. He died without issue in 1793 and was succeeded by one brother and then by a second, during whose short reign Württemberg was plunged into the Napoleonic Wars. Friedrich II (1797-1816) was a model ruler considering the stormy era in which he lived. At first he fought against the French, but after the peace of Luneville (1801) and a private treaty in 1802, he sided with the French until the Battle of Leipzig (1812). Through the treaties the Duke of Württemberg received the territories of nine imperial towns together with some smaller bits of land which had once been under ecclesiastical jurisdiction, in exchange for a small bit of territory which Württemberg held to the west of the Rhine. With the waning of Napoleon's power, Duke Friedrich, who had been elevated to the status of a king by Napoleon in 1806, made a treaty of alliance with Austria, and his armies marched with the Allies into France. The Treaty of Vienna (1815) recognized his royal title and his recent territorial acquisitions.

In 1815, the new Kingdom of Württemberg joined the German Confederation. One of the last acts of Friedrich, who died in 1816, was the presentation of a constitution to an assembly of the people. Although it was rejected, a new constitution, which was to survive until 1918, was granted in 1819 by the new King Wilhelm I (1816-1864). The administrative reorganization of the land was achieved in 1817; Württemberg was divided into four *Kreise* (equivalent to Prussian districts), which were subdivided into eighty-two county districts (*Oberamtsbezirke*), equivalent to the Prussian counties.

The long reign of Wilhelm I was one of marked progress in education, in the arts, and in culture generally. Trade and industry grew and prospered. The constitution of 1819 did not completely satisfy the desire for political freedom, but it was much more liberal than those of the other German states, and made Württemberg one of the leading states of the German Reich for liberal constitutional developments. The Constitution, which set the pattern of government until 1918, provided for a bicameral legislature, consisting of an Upper Chamber (princes, nobles, knights, clergymen, and appointed representatives of universities, commerce and industry, agriculture, and handicrafts) and a Lower Chamber (delegates elected on the basis of proportional representation by universal, secret, and direct suffrage). The executive consisted of a Privy Council (*Geheimer Rat*) and a State Ministry, which carried out the administration of the land through Ministries for Foreign Affairs, Interior, Justice, Church Affairs and Education, War and Finance. State railways were under the Ministry for Foreign Affairs. The State Court (*Staatsgerichtshof*), which served as the guardian of the constitution, had independent administrative status.

Minor political disturbances occurred after 1830, but Württemberg was never seriously affected by the revolution of 1848. In 1864 Wilhelm was succeeded by his son Karl I (1864-1891). Throughout the long struggle between Austria and Prussia for hegemony in Germany, Württemberg sided with the Austrian Habsburgs. In 1866 Württemberg went to the aid of Austria in the Seven Weeks' War. The defeat of Austria brought the Prussian occupation of northern Württemberg. Karl saved his state by paying a moderate indemnity to Prussia. Although Württemberg continued to follow an anti-Prussian policy, the land was swept by nationalistic feelings when the war broke out between France and Prussia in 1870, and Württemberg fought on the side of Prussia. In 1871 this kingdom became a part of the German Empire, although she retained control of her own postal and railway affairs. The last years of the Kingdom of Württemberg were beset with problems of succession, for after the death of Karl I (1891) and his successor King Wilhelm (1891-1910), the throne of Württemberg fell to the Catholic branch of the family, to the Roman Catholic Duke Albert. These difficulties were accompanied by a movement for constitutional reform which eventuated in the revision of the old constitution in 1906.

The history of the two Hohenzollern territories during the eighteenth and early nineteenth centuries was most uneventful. In 1848 the two Hohenzollern princes were forced to resign because of political difficulties, and in consequence of an agreement made in 1695 the two principalities passed to the King of Prussia in 1850. The two princes were restored and placed under the protection of Prussia. In 1869 the family of Hohenzollern-Hechingen died out, and this territory fell to the Prince of Hohenzollern-Sigmaringen. It is interesting to note that the Prussian proposal to make the Prince of Hohenzollern King of Spain was the immediate cause of the Franco-Prussian War of 1870. This prince of Hohenzollern finally managed to find a throne, for he became King of Rumania in 1881.

The transition from Empire to Republic after World War I was accomplished without violence in Württemberg and Hohenzollern. Württemberg's royal family departed, and the state became one of the constituent republics of Weimar Germany. Tiny Hohenzollern's fate was in the hands of Prussia, for its prince had departed, leaving it to become a separate administrative territory with the status of a governmental administrative district designated as the Hohenzollern State.

Republican Württemberg, under its constitution of 1919, had a State Diet (*Landtag*) consisting of eighty members elected every four years. They, in turn, elected the Minister President who headed the state ministry which served as the chief administrative authority. Administration was carried out by ministries for the Interior, Justice, Education, Finance, and Economics. A Superior Auditing Court and the Administrative Court had independent status. The year 1924 brought a significant reorganization of local administration in Württemberg, for the four districts and the eighty-two county districts were abolished and replaced by sixty-one counties directly responsible to the state Ministry of the Interior. The functions of the old districts were transferred to the counties.

Württemberg, famous for its tradition of liberalism, supported the Social Democratic and Catholic Center parties. Under the Empire southern Württemberg and Hohenzollern voted for the Catholic Center party, while the industrialized Neckar Valley area supported the Social Democratic party. The western part of the state gave its support to the Liberal Progressive party, which also had several strongholds about Ulm, which voted for the National Liberal party. The agrarian northeast supported various independent candidates. The politics of Württemberg were decidedly liberal during the period of the Weimar Republic. In addition to the powerful Social Democratic party which received the strongest electoral support, there was also the Catholic Center party in second position, the *Landbund* or Peasants' party, and finally the German Democratic party—a genuinely liberal group.

The principal cities such as Stuttgart, Heilbronn, Esslingen, Reutlingen, and Ravensburg gave their votes principally to the Social Democratic, Communist, or Catholic parties. Ulm, however, went Nazi in 1930 and remained a Nazi stronghold. For the state as a whole, Nazi strength averaged only 27 per cent in the four crucial *Reichstag* elections from 1930 to 1933. The Nazis became the leading party of Württemberg in July 1932, but the other parties held the majority of the votes among them until they were all dissolved in 1933. The Hohenzollern district included within the state of Württemberg always supported the Catholic party very strongly and went over to the Nazis only after Hitler's accession to power. The votes of the Peasants' party were gradually absorbed into the Nazi party, and the small Liberal parties of the middle, like the Democratic and People's parties, were gradually squeezed out between the extremes of the Right and Left.

During the imperial period, the state of Württemberg retained quasi-independent control over its postal system and administered its court system which followed the national pattern. In this case, justice was administered by the Superior State Court at Stuttgart and the Collegiate Courts of First and Second Instance at Ellwangen, Heilbronn, Ravensburg, Rottweil, Stuttgart, Tübingen, Ulm, and the Collegiate Court of Hechingen, which served the territory of Hohenzollern. It should be noted that the district of Hohenzollern, although a

Prussian territory, was generally served by regional offices concerned with affairs in Württemberg. The postal system of Württemberg was under the Chief Postal Directorate (Empire) or National Postal Directorate (Republic and Third Reich) at Stuttgart, while the postal service in Hohenzollern was under the National Postal Directorate at Karlsruhe (State of Baden). National regulations for trade and industry, weights and measures, social insurance, public health, and the collection of imperial revenues was carried out upon delegation from the Reich.

The Republic brought the further extension of direct national administration to finance, railways, unemployment insurance, employment, and labor welfare. There were the usual national controls over finances; these were carried out by the State Finance Office at Stuttgart and its local finance and customs offices. National Construction Offices were located at Ludwigsburg, Stuttgart, and Ulm. The nationalized railways were operated by the National Railroad Directorate at Stuttgart. All matters of labor and unemployment were under the State Labor Office for southwestern Germany (Stuttgart) and the Main Welfare Office of southwestern Germany (Karlsruhe). Where welfare, social insurance, health, trade and industry, and labor were subject to national legislation, they were carried out upon delegation from the Reich. The economic life of the area was organized under national agricultural, industrial, commercial, and labor organizations.

The state of Württemberg and Hohenzollern were organized as the party districts of Württemberg-Hohenzollern with party headquarters at Stuttgart. A dense network of party machinery radiated from headquarters and guaranteed the political stability of Württemberg and Hohenzollern during the Nazi period.

The advent of the Nazi regime brought drastic changes in the government and administration of Württemberg. It lost its status as a federal Republic, and its rights were transferred to the Reich. The Nazis placed a National Governor with headquarters at Stuttgart, the state capital, in charge of the government and administration. He was directly responsible to the national Minister of the Interior, but was also subject to the directives from other national ministers. The Governor of Württemberg was also the Nazi party leader for the party district of Württemberg-Hohenzollern. Nazi administrative changes in the Prussian territory of Hohenzollern State followed the pattern of those which took place in all Prussian districts. The administration of this small territory was headed by a District President, not by a provincial Chief President.

When the Nazis came to power in Württemberg, the State Diet, which was elected by the people, was eliminated along with the procedure calling for the election of the central administration by this legislature. The Ministry of Justice was dissolved, and its powers were transferred to the national Ministry of

Justice in Berlin. The state ministries were subordinated to the national cabinet. They could act only in the name of the Reich and after clearance with or the consent of the competent national minister. The Nazi administration of Württemberg was headed by a Minister President, who became the deputy of the Governor.

The territory of Hohenzollern, which had the status of a governmental administrative district, the district of Sigmaringen, was headed by a District President with headquarters at Sigmaringen. He was vested with broad supervisory and political powers. One of his main functions was the supervision of local government. He was the district authority for the Order Police and the rural police. Agricultural, industrial, commercial, and financial affairs and the relations between the district and the various Nazi economic estates were under his office.

The Nazi regime extended national administrative services to justice, air matters, propaganda, and labor relations. Customary fields of state administration—police, health, welfare, education, and certain aspects of social insurance—were now directed by national authorities. Economic planning, an essential of the Nazi system, was under the State Planning Association of Württemberg-Hohenzollern, which was under the leadership of the Governor. Corporate administrations were inaugurated, which gave the state further opportunity for control.

RURAL ASPECT

Agriculture and forestry, the main supports of rural life, are of secondary importance in Württemberg and Hohenzollern. Little more than 27 per cent of the population of this area makes its living from rural activities. There are, however, significant regional variations. The old Jagst area, which occupies the Hohenloher plains and the Frankenhöhe in northeastern Württemberg, and the old Danube area, the zone embracing the Swabian Jura and the Danubian plateau country in southeastern Württemberg, are mainly devoted to agriculture and forestry. Most of the people dwell in small villages of less than 2,000 in population, but about 44 per cent live in small towns and cities ranging in size from 2,000 to 100,000. Western and northwestern Württemberg are more dependent on industry and commerce than agriculture and other rural pursuits. The plains of the Neckar Basin are studded with small cities and towns.

The old Black Forest administrative area in southwestern Württemberg, however, still retains much of its former agrarian status. It is still a land of peasants and small villages, although in many of the towns ranging in size from 2,000 to 20,000 small manufacturing enterprises are located. To the north, the old Neckar area, centering about the modern industrialized cities of Heilbronn and Stuttgart, has turned to industry and commerce. Agriculture is relatively unimportant; only 29 per cent of the population dwells in villages of less than 2,000, while 37 per cent lives in towns and cities ranging in size from 2,000 to 100,000, and over 33 per cent of the population is concentrated in the large urban complex of Stuttgart. Hohenzollern, whose population has remained almost static for the last hundred years, is entirely devoted to agriculture and forestry. Over 83 per cent of its population dwells in villages of less than 2,000. The few towns of the territory are small in size, ranging from 2,000 to 20,000. Taken as a whole, the Württemberg-Hohenzollern area in comparison with other states and provinces of the Reich is not of great importance from the point of view of agriculture and forestry.

The "general" or "interior" administration of Württemberg was under the Ministry of Interior in Stuttgart; however, much of the day-to-day rural administrative work was carried out by county administrations which were responsible to Stuttgart. The general administration of Hohenzollern was entirely of the rural type, for this land was divided into two county administrations which were directly responsible to the District President in Sigmaringen. Even though much of the administrative work in Württemberg and Hohenzollern was carried out by the counties, their work was supplemented by a number of offices and agencies at the county level which handled special and technical services under direct national control, generally working under the direction of a regional office located at Stuttgart.

Under the Nazis the county in the state of Württemberg was very much like the Prussian county. This similarity has not always been the case for there have been two major reorganizations of rural administration in the last thirty years. The first took place in 1924. Under this reorganization Württemberg was subdivided into sixty-one chief counties, each headed by a Chief Executive of County (*Oberamtsvorstand*) who served as the head of state administration and as the leader of local self-government. In matters of local self-government, which included public safety, public health, public welfare, construction and maintenance of highways, flood control, and education, he was assisted and controlled by a County Administrative Board and a Representative Assembly (*Amtsversammlung*).

The second reorganization came with the advent of the Nazi regime in 1933-34, which brought about the elimination of the democratic control of county government, although the County Administrative Board managed to survive as an advisory council. The next changes in Württemberg county administration came in 1938. At this time the number of counties was reduced to thirty-four through the consolidation of a number of the sixty-one chief counties.

THE ADMINISTRATIVE AREAS, BODIES, AND OFFICIALS

	Area	*Official*	*Council*	*Assembly*
1924	Chief County	Chief Executive of County	County Admin. Board	Representative Assembly
	(*Oberamtsbezirk*)	(*Oberamtsvorstand*)	(*Bezirksrat*)	(*Amtsversammlung*)
1933	"	"	"	Eliminated
1938	County (*Landkreise*)	(*Landrat*)	County Committee (*Kreis-ausschuss*)	

Also in 1938, the Prussian designations of *Landkreis, Landrat,* and *Kreisaus-schuss* replaced the Württemberg designations of *Oberamtsbezirk, Oberamts-vorstand,* and *Bezirksrat* respectively. The Nazi County Manager, who was assisted by an appointed county advisory committee, had the supervision of the government and administration of the towns and villages of the county.

The administration of the small towns and villages followed the pattern laid down in the Württemberg Municipal Code of 1930. Under this code the towns and villages were organized on the basis of communal self-administration which centered in an elected municipal assembly under the chairmanship of a popularly elected director or mayor, who was responsible for the administration of the affairs of the municipality. The assembly and director were supervised by the old Executive Committee (*Amtsvorstand*). Under the Nazis, the Municipal Code of 1935 placed the management and control of municipal activities under the effective supervision of higher authorities. The small towns continued to handle public works and welfare, and a few enterprises (town forest, market, and an occasional utility plant).

The territory of Hohenzollern consisted of the counties of Hechingen (population 37,600) and Sigmaringen (population 35,300). They were headed by County Managers who were responsible to the District President at Sigmaringen. The County Manager, who served as an agent of both state administration and local self-government, was assisted by an appointed county committee and a county secretary (*Kreissekretär*). County government and administration followed the Prussian pattern and after the advent of the Nazis were regulated by the German Municipal Code of 1935.

Agriculturally, Württemberg and Hohenzollern are only moderately important areas. In Württemberg more than 60 per cent of the land is devoted to agriculture, while in the more forested territory of Hohenzollern only 56 per cent of the land is used for crops or pasture. This area can be subdivided into three rural or agrarian regions, each characterized by a contrasting type of agriculture and a differing set of cultural conditions growing out of past traditions plus the attempt to meet the local requirements set up by widely varying natural conditions.

The Neckar Basin region consists of the Hohenloher plains, the rolling hills of the upper and lower districts, which are traversed by the upper Neckar River, and the Swabian upland. It has a typical scarpland type of relief, for the Neckar and its tributaries have worn the marls and limestones down into plateaus, leaving the more resistant sandstones to rise into scarps which are usually about 500 to 700 feet higher than the plateau area. In general, this area of river bottoms and hilly lands has one of the driest and warmest climates of Germany. The average yearly rainfall is between 600 and 800 mm., while the average winter temperature is —1.8 degrees C. (January), and the average summer temperature is about 17 degrees C. (July). The brown forest soils of the Neckar Basin, which have long been cleared for agriculture, have a crumbly structure and are fairly good for cultivation of wheat, summer barley, and fodder crops, supplemented by small vineyards and orchards in the valley areas. Livestock are kept on a limited scale and only for home needs. The farms of this area are seldom larger than 5 hectares. The few which range in size from 5 to 20 hectares are largely located in the hilly areas and are almost entirely devoted to cereal crops. Land values are relatively high in this area owing to the specialization in fruit and grapes, but the small size of the average farm forces many of the peasants to seek part-time employment in the industries of the small towns of the Neckar Basin.

Another factor in the land value situation is the constant effort of the peasants to increase the size of their holdings by purchase of adjacent land in order to have a farm that is large enough to support a family. The great number of small farms is the result of the system of inheritance prevalent in southern and western Germany, calling for the real division of land among all the heirs. In one village, for example, 540 peasants owning a total of 3,000 acres of farm land cultivated approximately 24,000 plots. For the past seventy years the government has made an effort to solve this problem by regrouping the lands of a village. Progress has not been rapid, and even now over one-half of the farm land of Württemberg stands in need of reorganization. The Nazis made some progress by abolishing the old majority consent and ordering a regrouping by decree. The Farm Inheritance Act of 1933 did not have much effect in southwestern Germany, for here most of the farms fall below the minimum 15 acre limit of this law which was designed to check the division of land, to prevent the accumulation of debts, and to insure a "German" peasantry. Most of the farmers of the Neckar Basin dwell in agglomerated villages of the *Haufendorf* type, which are fairly large in size, averaging between 600 and 1600 in population. These villages composed of Frankish type houses generally center about a crossroads dominated by the village church.

The uplands of the Swabian Jura and the Frankenhöhe are elevated sandstone scarpland with infertile soils, which support extensive deciduous and coniferous forests. In contrast with the Neckar Basin, the climate is much more humid and cool. The average yearly rainfall is between 800 and 1400 mm. The average temperature for the month of January is about —3.6 degrees C., while the average temperature for the month of July is about 16 degrees C. The growing season is much shorter, for while the first frost strikes in the Neckar area in late October, it comes to the uplands in late September. The same difference applies to the last frost, which comes in early April in the plains, but may strike as late as the last part of May in the uplands. Economically, the peasants of the upland are dependent upon forestry and dairying. The extensive upland meadowland and pasture is excellent for livestock. This area is particularly important for its milk cattle. In the more remote areas, the milk is converted into butter and cheese, but fortunately most of the farms of the Swabian uplands can ship their milk directly to the industrial towns of the Neckar Basin. Crop cultivation (oats, rye, and potatoes) is limited and largely for home consumption. In the Frankenhöhe uplands, however, there are large farms given over to the raising of cereals for cash. The farms of this area, though still small from an American point of view, average from 5 to 20 hectares in size. Regrouping is not needed so much here as in the Neckar Basin area. Most of the farmers of the uplands live in small villages of the agglomerated type ranging in size from 200 to 600 in population. There are a few larger villages in the better parts of the upland.

The Danubian plateau area south of the Swabian Jura and extending to Lake Constance in Württemberg consists of the Danubian plateau country which extends from eastern Baden eastward across Württemberg and southern Bavaria to Austria. The area can be divided into three zones, one formed by the low Danube valley plains, which have a relatively dry and warm climate, a second consisting of the lowlands adjacent to Lake Constance, with a similar climate, and a third zone, the plateau between the Danube and the lake. The plateau lands enjoy a fair amount of rainfall (800-1000 mm. per year), and the climate is humid and cool in comparison with that of its margins to the north and south. Soils are remarkably similar throughout this region, but the marked differences in climate make for contrasting types of agriculture. In the Danube Valley grain, livestock, and forage crops are important, while wine, fruit, and grain are common in the Lake Constance area. The plateau region is largely devoted to livestock and dairying. Crop cultivation, which is restricted to cereals and hops, plays a secondary role. The three zones of this region are also characterized by contrasts in settlement; while the farmers of the Danube Valley and the Lake Constance area tend to live in villages of the larger type which range in size from 600 to 1600 in population and are capable of supporting a church and school, the peasants of the plateau area frequently live in isolated farmhouses, although many have their homes in relatively small villages of 200 to 600 inhabitants. In the southern part of the plateau, there are a number of tiny hamlets (17 to 70 inhabitants) and small villages (70 to 200 inhabitants). The characteristic house of these villages is of the Alemannic or Swiss type.

The Württemberg and Hohenzollern area is particularly important within the Reich for the production of fruit, hops, and dairy products. The figures for land utilization (given below in hectares) give a broad picture of the amount and types of land available for agriculture:

Cultivated Land		644,663
Grain	381,794	
Legumes	9,400	
Root Crops	123,280	
Green Vegetables	4,729	
Industrial Crops	6,569	
Fodder Crops	118,891	
Small Gadens		14,998
Meadow		450,092
Pasture		40,505
Orchards		11,345
Vineyards		11,765
Forests		606,865
Waste Land		42,038
Houses and Barns		26,457
Roads and Parks		90,346

Of the land area of Württemberg and Hohenzollern about 60 per cent is devoted to agrarian activity with a third of this devoted to crops and the rest to pastoral activities. The remaining land area is divided between forests (30 per cent) and urban and waste land (10 per cent).

The forest cover of this part of Germany is extremely varied in type, but fairly uniform in terms of surface distribution. Although there are extensively open areas in the Neckar Basin and in the far south, generally about 30 per cent of the land is covered by woodland. The forests of the hills of the Neckar area are of the deciduous type, being composed largely of beech and oak; there is some elm and ash, however. Following the upland scarp area from the Black Forest north and eastward along the Swabian Jura to the Frankenhöhe, one first finds stands of fir, beech, and spruce. These are replaced in the lower Swa-

bian Jura by broadleafed trees (beech forests), which in turn give way northward to the spruce and beech forests of the Frankenhöhe uplands. South of the
Danube there is an extensive zone of deciduous forests (beech and oak) extending across southern Württemberg and southern Bavaria. The forest land is
owned by a variety of interests. In Württemberg the state owns about 202,000
hectares of forest land, about one-third of the forested area. This land was administered through 137 state forest preserves, each under a Forest Office which
was responsible to one of the 34 Chief Forester's Centers (*Oberförsterstellen*).
These centers were under the Forest Direction (*Forstdirektion*) in the Ministry of Finance at Stuttgart. Another third of the land was held by private interests, while the remaining forest area was owned by county and municipal
governments. In Hohenzollern only 20 per cent of the forest area was owned by
private interests, while another 20 per cent was in the hands of local municipalities. The remaining 60 per cent was administered by the state through the office
of the district Chief Forest Master (*Oberforstmeister*) at Sigmaringen.

The Swabians constitute the dominant rural group in Württemberg and
Hohenzollern. The Alemannic peoples in the far south and the Franconians in
the far north can only be regarded as minority cultural groups in comparison
with the Swabians. Dialect and temperament are the real things which set the
Swabians off from the other peoples of southern Germany. Their language has
a certain primitive roughness and a distinctive phonetic quality. Being a people of natural reserve, they make friends slowly, but they are good-natured and
friendly once they accept a stranger. Keen perception and firm determination
are qualities often found among the Swabians. The folk art of rural Swabia is
famous; this land is well known throughout Germany for its folk songs and
wood carvings. The common folk have the reputation for honesty and straight-
forwardness, though their manners are characterized by a certain bluntness.
Their military abilities are excellent, and in modern times Swabians have been
frequently used as shock troops. This is a survival of the mercenary soldier
(*Landsknecht*) tradition. They love to be brave, although their exploits may be
frequently foolhardy.

Urban Aspect

The state of Württemberg is slightly more densely settled from the urban
point of view than other areas of the Reich. The main urban centers are almost
entirely located in the moderately industrialized Neckar Basin. Stuttgart, which
has a population of 420,500, is the most important city of Württemberg and is
located centrally within the Neckar Basin. The only other large cities of the
basin are Heilbronn (population 68,900) and Ludwigsburg (population 34,100),
which lie to the north of Stuttgart on the Neckar, and Esslingen (population
43,000), on the Neckar to the south of Stuttgart. Most of the remaining towns

of Württemberg, Gmünd, Göppingen, Heidenheim, Reutlingen, and Tübingen, which range in size from 20,000 to 28,000, are also located in the Neckar Basin. Stuttgart, the capital of Württemberg, serves not only as the political and administrative center of this state, but as the vital point in its economic and cultural life. Ulm on the Danube, a city of 62,400 inhabitants, although traditionally more important and economically significant as the center for the Danubian lands of Württemberg, is of minor importance in comparison to Stuttgart. Hohenzollern does not possess an important urban center.

Until the reorganization of local administration in 1938, all of the municipalities of the state of Württemberg were incorporated in one of the sixty-one chief counties, except for the city of Stuttgart, which constituted a separate city-district. It must be pointed out, however, that large and medium-sized towns were supervised by the Interior Ministry at Stuttgart, while the smaller towns and villages fell under the chief county authority. In 1938 the number of counties was drastically reduced from sixty-one to thirty-four. Under this reorganization, which came at almost the same time as the adoption of Prussian administrative designations, two of the larger cities, Heilbronn and Ulm, were given the same status as Stuttgart, that is, a city-county status. The smaller cities also had the status of city counties under the German Municipal Code. But in Württemberg they were still joined with the neighboring counties, although their administrations were directly under the Ministry of Interior in Stuttgart. Württemberg always laid stress upon the idea that rural and urban areas should be joined together and not separated. Hence the above middle-sized cities were still a part of their neighboring county, even though the form of their government after the advent of the Nazis followed the uniform pattern laid down in the Municipal Code. Until the Nazi regime, these cities were governed by the council form constitution (*Stadtratsverfassung*) type of government, which involved a council composed of elected members supplemented by important professional administrative officers. The council served as the administrative agency, while the mayor was the presiding officer who directed and supervised the municipal administrative affairs in terms of the decisions and directives of the council. Under the Nazis, these city counties followed the basic pattern of administration laid down in the German Municipal Code of 1935.

The economic life of Württemberg and Hohenzollern centers about the city of Stuttgart, which is the main center of economic activity in the whole of southwestern Germany. The Württemberg-Hohenzollern area tends to form a more or less distinct social-economic and cultural bloc that serves as a real unit of human activity and organization. This was fully recognized by the Nazis when they made this area into one State planning association. The economic organization for this area was also under one Economic Chamber at Stuttgart.

The natural resources are limited, for there is neither coal nor lignite. There is, however, a limited amount of iron ore in the eastern Swabian Jura. The few blast furnaces at Ellwangen in eastern Württemberg, making use of coal shipped in from the Ruhr and Saar, produce some iron which is largely consumed by the local machine industry. Other resources include the salt mines at Heilbronn, Rottweil, and Hall. Small amounts of silver, gold, and copper are obtained in the Göppingen area. One of the most developed industries, despite the few resources, is the metallurgical and machine industry. Important plants are located at Heilbronn, Esslingen, Stuttgart, Göppingen, Aalen, Ulm, Ravensburg, Rottweil, and Tuttlingen. Stuttgart is particularly important, for it contained the *Daimler-Benz* automobile factories, the *Hirth-Werke* (airplane motors), and the *Bosch-Werke*. Locomotives are manufactured at Esslingen, and other automobile plants are located at Ulm. Friedrichshafen was the center for the *Dornier* airplane plant. Gmünd is famous for its small plants which deal in rare metals. The textile industry is also important. Wool and cotton mills are found extensively in a zone extending from Freudenstadt in the west through Stuttgart, Göppingen, and Esslingen to Heidenheim. Important cotton mills are located elsewhere at Swabian-Hall, Rottweil, Tuttlingen, and Ravensburg. Linen weaving is common in the Rottweil, Reutlingen, and Ulm zone bordering the northern foothills of the Swabian Jura. The salt deposits in northern Württemberg provide the basis of the chemical industries of Heilbronn and Stuttgart. Leather industries are located at Aalen, Calw, Esslingen, and Backnang, the smaller manufacturing cities of Württemberg. Pottery and glass works are situated in the southwestern part of the state at Rottweil, while Göppingen is an important center of the wood and paper industry. Ulm and Stuttgart are important places for furniture. Food industries are particularly important in the Neckar Basin area. In general, one might say, that throughout Swabia, industry is interested in manufacturing articles which take little in the way of raw materials of the heavy type. This area is a region of mixed light manufacturing—machinery, textiles, glass, pottery, furniture, and clothing.

The power needs of these industries are partly met by small coal plants supplied by Saar and Ruhr fuel, but major power needs are met by water-power stations like the one at Esslingen which produces from 50 to 60 million kwh. per year. This plant is linked by a major high tension line, which runs via Ulm to Augsburg, where it connects with the Bavarian power lines that are supplied by numerous Alpine water power stations. The southern part of Württemberg and Hohenzollern is supplied with power by the great Rheinfelden plant in southern Baden. Southeastern Württemberg is electrically linked by small high tension lines to the Esslingen-Augsburg line.

The road pattern of southwestern Germany goes back to the Middle Ages. The main east-west road running from Augsburg to Ulm, Stuttgart, and Karlsruhe has been used for centuries. The Freiburg (Baden)-Stuttgart-Ansbach (Bavaria)-Nuremberg road and the Stuttgart-Heilbronn-Frankfort (Hesse-Nassau) road became important in modern times. Stuttgart is the obvious key road junction. The construction and maintenance of the ordinary roads were carried out by the local county administrations, while the major roads were under the Road and Water Construction Offices (*Strassen- und Wasserbau-ämter*). During the Nazi regime, national super-highways were built here as in the other states. Today these roads radiate from Stuttgart to Karlsruhe and Munich.

The road network is supplemented by an excellent railroad network. The railroads of Württemberg and Hohenzollern were under the National Railroad Directorate of Stuttgart. The major lines include the Konstanz-Stuttgart-Nuremberg line, the Augsburg-Ulm-Stuttgart-Karlsruhe line, and the Ulm-Stuttgart line. Most of the rail traffic is borne by the line connecting Stuttgart with Karlsruhe, Mannheim, and Ludwigshafen, which are the main centers for the importation of supplies into Württemberg.

Although the Rhine is outside the Württemberg area, it is vital to the industries of the Neckar Basin, because it provides cheap transportation, enabling coal and iron to be shipped to the Swabian industries. The Neckar River, which joins the Rhine at Mannheim, is not important for transportation because only small vessels can navigate upstream from the Rhine to Heilbronn and Stuttgart. The Danube in southern Württemberg is not navigable. Most of the larger river vessels go only to Regensburg in Bavaria, and only a few small ones reach as far upstream as Ulm, on the Bavarian frontier. The major center for air transportation was located at Stuttgart. Friedrichshafen on Lake Constance had only minor importance as an air center, but it was well known for its Zeppelins. Although the air service in Württemberg, as in all of Germany, was operated by the German Airways Corporation the airports were owned and operated by the municipalities.

The city of Stuttgart is the financial and commercial capital of the Württemberg-Hohenzollern area. Heilbronn in the north and Ulm in the southeast are important in their immediate areas, but they, in turn, are oriented toward Stuttgart. The smaller towns occupy a definitely secondary place in commercial life. Stuttgart, like Munich, arose to importance as a commercial and industrial center during the nineteenth century. In earlier times, Ulm, famous for its wool and linens, and Heilbronn, for its salt, played a greater role in the trade of southwestern Germany. Stuttgart in these days was famous for its wine. Its modern growth and development as the commercial and industrial center of Württemberg was due to the railroad and the consequent redistribution of trade alignments. The trading interests of Württemberg reflect its agrarian and industrial activities. In terms of freight traffic, agricultural products, finished metal goods and machinery, wood products, and ceramic materials were the important products of the area. The industries of Württemberg were heavily dependent upon imported raw materials, brought in by means of the Rhine and the great river port of Mannheim-Ludwigshafen. About 60 per cent of the traffic at this port was coal, two-thirds of which came from the Ruhr area, the rest from the Saar. Raw metal was also imported into Württemberg. It should also be noted that Mannheim-Ludwigshafen was the distributing point for oil and grain in southwestern Germany.

The trade relations of the Swabian machine industry were complex. Württemberg supplied the needs of many of the small plants of Augsburg and southwestern Bavaria. It was also the source for the machine tools used in the Palatinate. The exchange of machinery products between Württemberg and the Ruhr and Saxony, though not large, was about equal. The specialization and concentration of the textile industry in Germany led to an active trade in yarns between the mills of Württemberg and those of southern Bavaria and Baden. Stuttgart was the commercial center for the textile trade in southwestern Germany. Most of the business establishments, industrial and commercial, were small in size. They had originally expected to profit at the expense of big business under the Nazi regime. This, however, was not the case, for they suffered greatly from regimentation and governmental control. A great many of the small enterprises, especially small retail firms, disappeared in the last years of the Nazi regime. The larger corporations, capable of meeting the big orders placed by the Nazi war machine, flourished.

The banking and credit institutions of Württemberg and Hohenzollern ranged from branches of the great commercial banks of Berlin, which were mainly interested in industrial investments, to the local municipal savings banks. Stuttgart was the important center. The state banking institutions—*Landeskreditanstalt, Landesversicherungsanstalt,* and the *Württembergische Hypothekenbank*—had their headquarters at Stuttgart. The operations of these banks were supplemented by those of the branches of the *Reichsbank* at Stuttgart, Esslingen, Göppingen, Heilbronn, and Gmünd, which did the usual discount operations and governmental services. The financial institutions of Hohenzollern were limited in number. A *Landesbank* and Fire Insurance Agency (*Feuerversicherungsanstalt*) for this area were located at Sigmaringen. The supervision of the banking business in Württemberg fell under the Ministry for Economics (*Wirtschaftsministerium*), while in Hohenzollern it was under the District President, though in both cases it was ultimately subject to the national National Credit Supervisory Office (*Aufsichtsamt für das Kreditwesen*). The Württemberg-Hohenzollern area was served by a stock exchange at Stuttgart. Stuttgart was by all odds the main financial center of southwest Germany.

While 42 per cent of the population dwelt in villages of 2,000 or under in population, and another 31 per cent lived in small towns of 2,000 to 20,000, the remaining 27 per cent dwelt in the city counties, 17 per cent in cities from 20,000 to 100,000, and 10 per cent in cities of over 100,000 population. Taking Württemberg as a whole, over 1,086,000 individuals were employed in mining, industry, and crafts, while 343,000 were engaged in trade and transportation. The working class, which formed about 35 per cent of the total population, was relatively small in comparison with other areas of the Reich. The upper class, which accounted for about 24 per cent of the population, was one of the largest in the Reich. This class distribution cannot be accounted for in terms of landed wealth or independent peasant farmers of moderate wealth; it must be, in part, due to the great number of small privately owned business enterprises in this state. Another result of this structural pattern was a relatively small white collar class, which accounted for only 8.5 per cent of the population. The number of civil servants was about average for the Reich, while the number of professional people was well below that of other states and provinces. The occupational composition and class structure of the small territory of Hohenzollern, which had an essentially rural basis, contrasts strongly with that of Württemberg. Over 49 per cent of its inhabitants were engaged in agrarian pursuits, while only 35 per cent of the population was employed in industry, crafts, trade, and transportation. Hohenzollern, though small in size, had the largest upper class in Germany. Its laboring class was the smallest. The professional, civil service, and white collar groups were extremely small in number, all well below the average for the Reich.

The vital portion of Württemberg is situated in the Neckar Basin, which is dominated by the city of Stuttgart and dotted with numerous small industrial centers. This land of fields, orchards, and vineyards, hemmed in on all sides by wooded uplands, has been tied culturally and economically to the Rhine since Roman times, while the Danube and the ancient trade route from Stuttgart and Ulm to Munich have brought in influences not only from southeastern Germany, but from the lands of eastern Europe. Stuttgart, previously described as an economic center, was also the political, administrative, and cultural center of Württemberg and one of the large important South German cities. It was a handsome city, famous for its modern architecture. Culturally, it is important as the home of the philosopher Hegel and the poets Hauff and Schwab. Schiller wrote his play "The Robbers" (*Die Räuber*) while he was studying medicine there. During the later Middle Ages it was made the capital of the lands of the Counts of Württemberg. It remained a small market town important only for political reasons until the nineteenth century. In 1800 its population stood at 20,000. The industrial revolution in Germany brought rapid changes, for by 1883 its population had increased to 120,000. The real period of industrializa-

Chapter 30

THE STATE OF BADEN

The state of Baden occupies the southwestern corner of the German Reich. It is an L-shaped territory about the size of the American state of Connecticut. It is bounded on the south and west by the upper Rhine, the only significant natural international frontier in Western Germany. Across this river from Baden lies Switzerland to the south, and French Alsace and the Bavarian Palatinate to the west. The Rhine delimits the boundary except in the south about Schaffhausen and at Basel where Swiss territory extends northwards across the Rhine in four places. On the north, Baden adjoins the southern portion of the state of Hesse and the western Lower Franconia district of Bavaria, while on the east it is bordered by the state of Württemberg, except in the southeast where the Prussian territory of Hohenzollern interrupts the continuity of the Baden-Württemberg frontier. In the southeast the Rhine widens into Lake Constance, which forms the frontier between Baden and Switzerland. The greater proportion of the state of Baden is dominated by mountains, whose foothills extend eastward into the state of Württemberg.

The state of Baden consists of two physiographic regions: the western portion along the east bank of the Rhine, the only level land, constituting about 20 per cent of the land area, and the eastern uplands and plains which extend the full length of the state from Lake Constance in the south to the boundaries of Hesse and Bavaria in the north. The Rhine area consists of the wide rift valley, a deep-faulted trough, now covered to a great depth by water-borne deposits. The upper Rhine River after leaving Lake Constance flows westward through a narrow valley until it reaches Basel, where it turns sharply to the north to enter the deep rift valley extending from Basel to Mainz. It follows a meandering path through a wide flood plain which is bordered on both the French and German sides by pine-covered terraces composed of infertile sands and gravels. On both sides of the Rhine beyond the terrace zone one finds a series of small marginal plateaus and hills, covered with a loess mantle. This

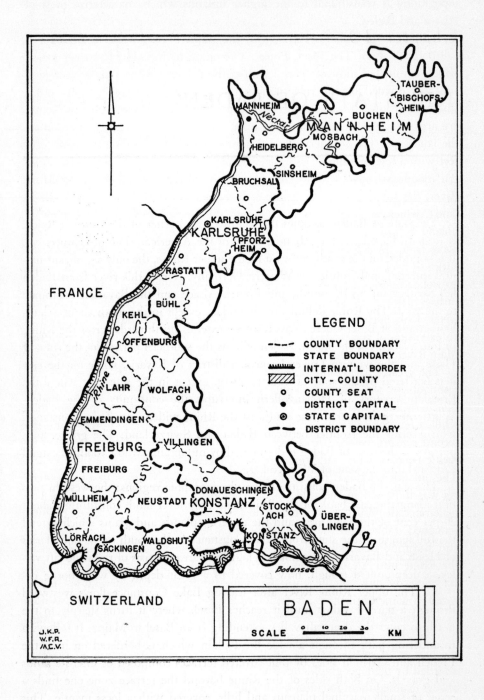

FRANCE

SWITZERLAND

LEGEND
COUNTY BOUNDARY
STATE BOUNDARY
INTERNAT'L BORDER
CITY - COUNTY
COUNTY SEAT
DISTRICT CAPITAL
STATE CAPITAL
DISTRICT BOUNDARY

BADEN
SCALE   0   10   20   30   KM

J.K.P.
W.F.R.
/AC.V.

topography is transitional to the higher uplands which characterize most of Alsace and Baden.

In Baden, the upland is known as the Black Forest, while in Alsace it is called the Vosges. The Black Forest, a remnant of the old Hercynian massif which dominated most of central and southern Germany in remote geological times, is divided by the river Kinzig into a higher southern portion and a smaller and lower northern area. Although rejuvenated valleys give the southern area a rugged look, the rounded hills of the old Hercynian massif dominate the landscape. The southern Black Forest has a mean elevation of about 3,100 feet with a few mountains rising above the 4,000-foot tree line, while the northern mountains have a mean elevation of only 2,100 feet. North of the Murg River, the forest gives way to the hilly Kraichgau or Neckar upland (Bergland), which, in turn, gives way, beyond the Neckar River, to the Odenwald upland occupying the southern portion of the state of Hesse. Before turning away from the Rhine and its adjoining uplands, one should take note of the curiously isolated Kaiserstuhl, an independent volcanic formation, occupying an isolated position on the Upper Rhine flood plain near Freiburg. The northeastern plains, to the north and east of the Neckar upland and the lower Neckar River, look northward toward the river Main, for they must be regarded as an extension of the lower Franconian lowland, which is traversed by the lower Main River.

The greater part of the state of Baden is occupied by the Badenese folk, descendants of the Alemanni, who once ruled all of southwestern Germany. Northern and eastern Baden, however, is settled by southern Franconian folk, while a few Swabians live in the eastern foothills of the Black Forest. Until the second century before Christ most of this part of the Reich was occupied by Keltic peoples, who made their living by cultivating the fertile Rhine Valley. The uplands remained primeval land, only occasionally penetrated by hunters. As was indicated in the study of Württemberg, the Germanic Alemanni had penetrated the Württemberg-Baden area by the first century A.D. Their position remained stable until the fourth century, when under the pressure of Gothic and Burgundian tribal movements, the Alemanni expanded westward across the Rhine into Alsace and southward into modern Switzerland. The modern Badenese did not emerge until the later Middle Ages. They were not recognized in name until the nineteenth century, although the term Baden was used in a restricted sense after the thirteenth century. The people of Baden must, however, have constituted a separate cultural group within the larger Alemannic bloc from relatively early times owing to the relative degree of isolation afforded by their geographic location, although their position on the Rhine has always exposed them to cultural influences borne by traders and merchants from Italy and the Low Countries who were using the important Rhenish routes.

Their cultural unity is seriously affected by religious division: 58 per cent of the population is Catholic, but there is a large Lutheran minority and a considerable number of Calvinists. The former Jewish population of Baden in 1933 numbered 20,600 or approximately 0.86 per cent of the population. Most of the Jews were concentrated in the Rhenish towns of Freiburg, Karlsruhe, and Mannheim.

The state of Baden ranks fifth in size and population among the German states. In 1933 it had a population of 2,412,000, occupying an area of 15,069 sq. km.; the population density was 160 individuals per sq. km. The distribution of this population is strongly conditioned by the natural and economic features of the area. The population is most thickly clustered in the north about the industrial towns of Karlsruhe, Pforzheim, and Mannheim. The entire valley of the Rhine is more or less densely settled with an average density varying between 100 and 200 per sq. km. The northern part of the valley within the state of Baden about Mannheim which is located at the junction of the Rhine and Neckar, is heavily settled. The Black Forest has a very sparse population, the density varying between 50 and 75 individuals per sq. km. In the southernmost part of the forest the density is frequently less than 25 per sq. km., while in the extreme north and in the Neckar upland, some of the lower areas are relatively densely settled. The population of the state of Baden has increased steadily since 1816, when the average population density for all of Baden stood between 50 and 100 per sq. km. The first phase of population expansion came with the economic recovery following the Napoleonic Wars, but the real growth of the population of Baden came in the period of the German industrial revolution, 1880-1910. By 1871 the average density of northern Baden had increased to 125 per sq. km., although there was little change in the south. After 1871 the population of the entire state was on the upgrade, but the greatest increase was in the northern industrialized area about Mannheim and Karlsruhe.

The present state of Baden is a relatively modern creation, dating only from the time of the Napoleonic Wars. Before that time the lands which now form the territory of Baden were ruled by a number of counts and dukes. The history of settlement in the Rhenish part of Baden, however, goes back to the Neolithic age when peasants from southeastern Europe pushed westward to penetrate and settle the upper valley of the Rhine. The second millennium before our era brought the increasing use of the Rhine Valley as a trade route linking northern and central Europe with the more civilized Mediterranean world. This period witnessed the introduction of improved methods of agriculture and metal-working. Human activity was still restricted to the flood plains of the Rhine. By the first millennium before Christ this area was occupied by Keltic folk. Although the Romans brought the Keltic peoples dwelling to the west of the Rhine under their control by the time of Caesar, Baden was not

fully subjugated by Rome until A.D. 83. During the period of Roman occupation, when Baden formed a part of *Germania Superior,* Mediterranean ways
of living, though strongly modified by local conditions, dominated the scene.
Already before the beginning of our era, the Germanic Alemanni had been
filtering into southwestern Germany, and certainly by the second century A.D.
they had merged with the local basic Keltic population, and with the Romans
they created a Germanic-Celtic-Roman culture. The presence of the Romans
is witnessed, today, by the chance survival of bits of road and the ruins of
Roman settlements and forts. The beginnings of Christianity and the first settlement of the Jews in Germany date back to this age.

The decline of Roman power and prestige was marked in southwestern Germany by extensive Germanic tribal movements. Alemannic folk dwelling outside the Roman *limes* filtered steadily into the lands along the Rhine. After
the fourth century, they expanded farther to the west and south under Gothic
and Burgundian pressure and at the same time asserted their control in southwestern Germany. Shortly after the fall of the Roman Empire in the west
(A.D. 476), the Alemanni created a tribal kingdom which embraced most of
Switzerland and Alsace in addition to southwestern Germany. This kingdom
fell to the conquering Franks during the sixth century. The Alemannic area
was placed under a duke, and the land was divided into counties ruled by
Counts. When the Merovingian Emperors of the Franks were replaced by the
Carolingian rulers, Alemannia played an increasingly important role in the
affairs of that day.

After the collapse of the realm of Charlemagne, the southern part of Baden
fell under the rule of the dukes of Swabia, while the northern portion was ruled
by the dukes of Franconia. This division prevailed throughout the age of
the Saxon (925-1024), Franconian (1024-1125), and Hohenstaufen (1138-1254)
Emperors. The independent history of Baden began in this period with the acquisition of territory in Baden by Hermann, the son of Berthold of Zährin-
gen, the Duke of Carinthia, and the Margrave of Verona. Hermann, who had
acquired the lands in Baden by marriage arrangements, was succeeded by his
son, Hermann, who was the first to style himself the Margrave of Baden (1130).
He ruled as a vassal of the Duke of Swabia. In 1200 the lands were divided
and the lines of Baden-Baden and Baden-Hochberg were established. After the
collapse of the large duchies in the period following the Hohenstaufen Emperors, the margraves gained greater and greater independence within their respective lands. In 1503 Margrave Christoph I reunited the lands of both lines, but
his death brought renewed division, for the lands of Baden were now divided
between the lines of Baden-Baden and Baden-Durlach. The two houses were
not the sole rulers of the territory of modern Baden, for various lands were
held by the electors of the Palatinate (Mannheim Area), the bishops of Mainz

and Würzburg (Northeast Baden), the bishops of Speyer and Strassburg (Rhenish Lands), and the Habsburgs (the Breisgau area in southern Baden). During the periods of the Reformation and the Thirty Years' War, the Baden family was divided against itself. After the Treaty of Westphalia (1648), the family rivalry tended to weaken under the pressure of the French attack on the Rhineland under the leadership of Louis XIV. In 1771 the family of Baden-Baden died out and the lands of Baden were reunited under Karl Friedrich of Baden-Durlach.

Although the lands of Baden had been reunited, they did not constitute a compact territory. Instead they consisted of isolated areas near Freiburg, Kehl, and Karlsruhe, and a few bits of territory on the west bank of the Rhine. The long reign of Karl Friedrich (1746 to 1811) was marked by agricultural and commercial development. Baden's opportunity for territorial aggrandizement came during the Napoleonic Wars. In the opening phases of the wars Baden suffered, for she sided with Austria against France. Baden lost all of the lands on the west side of the Rhine in 1801, but Karl Friedrich was adequately compensated in 1803, thanks to the intervention of his relative, the Emperor Alexander I of Russia. Baden received the lower Rhenish Palatinate, the bishopric of Konstanz, and several smaller territories, and Karl Friedrich was elevated to the dignity of an elector. In 1805 Baden changed sides and supported Napoleon. Karl Friedrich was made a Grand Duke in 1806, and was awarded the Breisgau and other lands at the expense of the Habsburgs. Karl died in 1811, having quadrupled the size of Baden. His grandson and successor supported Napoleon until the Battle of Leipzig (1813) and then turned to the Allies.

The Treaty of Vienna (1815) recognized the territorial acquisitions of the Napoleonic period. Baden, which had now achieved its full territorial growth, entered the Germanic confederation as a Grand Duchy. The Congress of Vienna had not, however, decided the question of succession in Baden, which involved the rival claims of Bavaria and Austria. This affair was settled in 1819 when Austria, Prussia, and Bavaria accepted the decision of the Grand Duke Karl Ludwig Friedrich (1811-1818) which made the Counts of Hochberg, who were the issue of an earlier morganatic marriage, capable of succession. This established the Hochberg dynasty which reigned until 1918.

A liberal constitution had been granted to Baden in 1818, but reaction soon set in and by 1825 the constitution ceased to have any active existence. In 1830 Leopold became Grand Duke of Baden. His reign brought liberal reforms in constitutional, civil and criminal law, and in education. In 1832 Baden joined the [Prussian] Customs Union. The state, however, did not escape the revolutionary movement of 1848, and, although concessions were made, there were a number of insurrections by radicals. In May 1849, the Grand Duke fled from Karlsruhe and sought the aid of Prussia. The revolution was over by August of the same year as a result of Prussian military intervention. In 1852 Leopold died and was succeeded by his eldest son, Ludwig, who was incapable of ruling; Friedrich, his second son, served as regent until he became Grand Duke in 1858. After 1848, all of the South German states were quick to realize that Prussia, not Austria, required watching. Baden backed Austria against Prussia in the period before 1866. After only a very brief contest with Prussia, Baden gave in, signing a treaty of peace and alliance. In 1870 the troops of Baden played a conspicuous role in the war against France, and in 1871 Baden joined the German Empire.

During the imperial era, Baden, which was governed under the Constitution of 1818 (modified in 1841, 1849, 1862, 1867, 1868, 1869, 1870), had a legislature, consisting of an Upper House (princes, nobles, clergymen, and representatives of agriculture, commerce, trades, and towns), and a Lower Chamber (delegates elected by towns and rural districts). The executive consisted of a State Ministry, which carried out the administration of the state through ministries for Royal House and Foreign Affairs, Interior, Justice, and Education, and Finance. A Chief Auditing Chamber (*Oberrechnungskammer*) had independent status.

The internal politics of Baden in the period following 1871 were dominated by the struggle over education and the Catholic church. The Grand Duke followed a course of moderation and won the esteem of his subjects. He had not secured the rights of Baden upon her entry into the German Empire, for the control of the army, railways, postal service, and the conduct of foreign affairs were placed under Prussia. The Grand Duke Friedrich I died in 1907 after a reign of fifty-one years. His successor, Friedrich II, ruled until the revolution following World War I.

The passing of the Grand-Duchy in 1918 was not accompanied by violence. The liberalism of its nineteenth and twentieth century rulers is, even today, well remembered by the citizens of Baden. In November 1918, the last Grand Duke abdicated and the provisional government proclaimed Baden a republic. The state adopted a democratic and republican constitution and became one of the federal states of the Weimar Republic. The constitution of the Republic of Baden provided for a one-chamber assembly elected on the basis of equal, secret, direct, universal suffrage. The State Ministry, consisting of the State President and four other members, was elected by and made responsible to the assembly. In additon to the State Ministry, there were ministries for Interior, Justice, Education, and Finance. The Auditing Court (*Rechnungshof*) and Administration Court (*Verwaltungsgericht*) at Karlsruhe had independent status.

The state of Baden has been traditionally the seat of strong liberal sentiments. Many of the outstanding liberals at the Frankfort convention of 1848 came from Baden. In the days of the Empire, it furnished support to the Catho-lics and the Social Democrats in their struggles against Bismarck. The south-ern part of the state was strongly Catholic and voted for the Catholic Center party, except around Freiburg where the Liberal Progressive and the National Liberal parties had a considerable following. The people of northern Baden sup-ported a variety of liberal parties, the Social Democrats, National Liberals, and Liberal Progressives. The Social Democrats had a strong following at Mannheim, while the Catholic Center party was strong in the rural northeast. The Conservatives had a small following in the upland area, east of Karlsruhe. Under the Republic, Baden voted most strongly for the parties of the center and the left. After the rise of Hitler, Baden gave the Nazis a sizable vote, but at no time prior to his accession to power was Hitler able to corner more than a third of the total vote of the state. In the presidential elections of 1932, Baden voted almost two to one for Hindenburg against Hitler. Compared to the state of Württemberg, however, Baden was stronger for Hitler, and in several districts, the Nazis were very strong. For instance, the County of Kehl, opposite Strassburg on the Rhine, was a Nazi stronghold, and the other districts along the Rhine boundary gave Hitler considerable support. Also the cities of Karls-ruhe, Heidelberg, and Pforzheim went over to the Nazis before they came into power, and remained in this party's column. On the other hand, the State Commissary District of Konstanz voted regularly for the Catholic party, and in both of the crucial *Reichstag* elections of 1932, not a single precinct in the whole district went for Hitler. Another Catholic stronghold was the north-eastern precinct of Tauberbischofsheim. In Mannheim, the state's largest city, there was a strong Socialist and Communist vote. On the whole, however, the moderate parties like the Democrats, the German People's party, and the Cath-olics were stronger in Baden than the proletarian parties.

During the imperial era only the nationally operated postal system lay out-side the scope of the state administration. It was operated by the Chief Postal Directorate (Empire) or National Postal Directorate (Republic and Third Reich) at Karlsruhe. The courts of Baden, which followed a uniform national pattern, were administered under a state Ministry of Justice. They included the Superior State Court of Karlsruhe and the Collegiate Courts of First and Second Instance at Freiburg, Heidelberg, Karlsruhe, Konstanz, Mannheim, Mosbach, Offenburg, and Waldshut. National regulations for trade and in-dustry, weights and measures, social insurance, and the collection of imperial revenues was carried out upon delegation from the Reich.

Following customary procedure, the Republic extended direct national ad-ministration to finance, railways, unemployment insurance, employment, and labor welfare. Financial controls within Baden were carried out by the State

Finance Office at Karlsruhe and its local finance and customs offices. Labor and unemployment problems were handled by the *Landesarbeitsamt Südwest-deutschland* (Stuttgart) and the *Hauptversorgungsamt Südwestdeutschland* (Stuttgart). Certain aspects of welfare, social insurance, health, trade and industry, and labor, which were subject to national legislation, were carried out upon delegation from the Reich. The economic life of the state was organized under national agricultural, commercial, industrial, and labor organizations.

Under the Nazis, Baden was organized as the party district of Baden. The party district offices at Karlsruhe included every phase of party activity and carried the party work down to the lowest citizen and the smallest hamlet.

The advent of the Nazi regime brought rapid and sweeping changes in the government of Baden. In 1934 the Nazis liquidated its federal status. Its rights were transferred to the Reich, and a National Governor directly responsible to the National Minister of the Interior, but also subject to the supervision of other national ministers, was placed in charge of the government and administration at Karlsruhe, the capital of Baden. The conversion of the state of Baden into a Reich administrative district was accompanied by a number of other important changes. The assembly and the state ministry of justice were eliminated.

Under the Nazis, the central administration was headed by the State Ministry which was under the Minister President, who in turn was subject to the political control of the Governor. The Minister President, however, headed the State Chancellery in the State Ministry, which coordinated the work of the present state ministries. The Baden cabinet consisted of three other ministries: Interior, Culture and Education, and Finance and Economics. They served as agents of the Reich and for the state, issuing decrees and laws, and directing, supervising, and executing the affairs of the state. They were, however, subject to the Reich Cabinet and could only carry on their business in the name of the Reich and after clearance with the competent national ministers. Although the Baden ministries were separate from the office of the Governor, the state cabinet was a separate national authority carrying out national orders and at the same time functioning for state purposes. All state officials were indirect national officials. The work of the general state administration was supplemented by special and technical services under direct national control.

With the Nazis direct national administration was extended to justice, air matters, propaganda, and labor relations. Many of the traditional fields of state administration—police, health, welfare, education, and certain aspects of social insurance—were brought under tight national control. The services and functions of the general and special administrative systems were supplemented by an extensive system of corporate administration.

Rural Aspect

Agriculture and forestry, the main supports of rural life, have only moderate significance in the life of Baden. Only 604,000 individuals (about 25 per cent) lived and worked close to the soil. This number is the smallest percentage for any state in southern Germany. Only the southeastern section centering about Konstanz and the eastern uplands were dominantly rural from an economic point of view, while the northern part of Baden, around Mannheim and Karlsruhe, was highly industrialized and the southern area, near Freiburg, was more interested in the lighter industries and crafts than in agriculture. During the Nazi period, the interior administration of most of rural Baden was under the County Managers of the counties and their subordinates, the Mayors of the towns which made up the counties.

Under the Nazis, the county of Baden was very much like the Prussian county as a result of the reforms of 1934, 1936, and 1939. The first administrative subdivision of Baden was made in 1832 when the land was divided into seventy-nine counties, which were supervised by four State Commissioners (*Landeskommissäre*) in charge of the State Commissioner's districts of Konstanz, Freiburg, Karlsruhe, and Mannheim. It should be emphasized that the State Commissioner was not an official of general administration at the intermediate level like the Prussian District President, but was merely the representative of the central authority in residence in the district. The law regulating the counties was issued in 1863; it also provided for the reduction of their number of counties to fifty-three. The financial and economic troubles which followed the last war brought a further reduction of counties to forty. Each county was headed by a County Manager, who served as the head of both state administration and local self-government. He was assisted by an Administrative Board, and was subject to a Representative Assembly in matters of self-government.

The advent of the Nazi regime brought several changes. The features of democratic control were eliminated, although the Administrative Board and the Executive Committee managed to survive as appointed advisory councils (1934). The real change in local government came with the gradual replacement of the county by the County Organizations for Self-Administration (*Landkreisselbstverwaltungskörper*) through the transformation of the old Town Corporations, whose origin dates back to 1892. The reorganization of 1936 brought a still further reduction, leaving only twenty-seven counties. In 1938 the name *Amtsbezirk* was changed to conform with the Prussian designation, *Kreis*.

As a result, the Nazi County Manager (*Landrat*) was the head of all state administration and all local self-government within the state county under his jurisdiction. He was assisted by an administrative board consisting of six to ten County Advisers, half of them local mayors and half of them citizens of the county. This board also served as a lower administrative court. The Citizen Advisers could also be appointed by the County Manager to assist in special administrative services. This official had prime responsibility for the supervision of the government and administration of the towns and villages of his county.

Village and county administration was regulated by the Baden Municipal Codes of 1831, 1874, and 1921. Under these codes municipal governments consisted of two bodies, an elected Citizens' Committee (*Bürgerausschuss*) and a Town Council, made up of members appointed or elected by the former, both with equal power to make decisions. The Mayor who was appointed by the Citizens Committee headed both. Under the Nazis, the management and control of Municipal activities was placed under the effective supervision of higher authorities.

Agriculturally, Baden is of only moderate importance in comparison with other areas of the Reich. Most of the agricultural land, which constitutes about 54 per cent of the total area of the state, is concentrated in the Rhine Valley and in the area adjacent to Lake Constance, while the forested area, which accounts for 40 per cent of the land surface, is largely restricted to the Black Forest and Neckar uplands. These two areas, which are largely occupied by the Badenese, form the two main rural and agrarian regions of the state of Baden.

Geographically, the Rhenish zone can be divided into two distinct portions; the narrow winding section of the Rhine Valley between Lake Constance and Basel and the wider Rhine valley zone between Basel and Mannheim in northern Baden. The Rhine, originating in the high central Alps, flows northward to Lake Constance. After flowing through the lake it turns westward to cut its way through the moraine lands of the Rhine-Rhône Plateau which extends from Lake Geneva into southwestern Germany. This is an area characterized by a variety of land forms and soils and covered by an alternation of fields, meadows, and woods, but in the immediate area of the Rhine Valley agricultural activity is much like that farther downstream. At Basel the Rhine turns northward and flows in a general northerly direction until it reaches the Rhenish uplands of western Germany. Proceeding from the Rhine River to the uplands of the Black Forest, the valley is divided into three distinct zones: the Rhine flood plain, the terrace zone, and the foothills and marginal plateaus which are transitional to the Black Forest uplands. Between Basel and Karlsruhe, the flood plain of the Rhine is wide, and because of its gradient it is frequently wet, a factor which is responsible for extensive moors. Even after years of reclamation work, most of this portion of the Rhine Valley is pasture, whereas north of Karlsruhe the flood plain is drier and is more widely used for crop cultivation. The terrace lands which adjoin the flood plain are dry and infertile. In many parts they are given over to pine forests.

The next land zone, the foothill and marginal plateau region, is exceptionally fertile, although like most of the rift valley, it has a very low average yearly rainfall, 600-800 mm. per year. Its southerly latitude and low sheltered position give the Rhine Valley the warmest climate in Central Europe. The winters are mild and the summers hot. Throughout the valley, the growing season is long, for the last frost comes as early as the end of March and the first frost does not strike until late October. To return to the real agrarian zone of the valley, the marginal plateaus and foothills are important for the cultivation of wheat, fruit (peaches and apricots), industrial crops (chicory, beet, and tobacco), and grapes. Some of the most important vineyards of Central Europe are to be found in this area. The farms of the valley tend to be small, averaging less than 5 hectares in size. These small agricultural plots constitute a distinct problem. Most of them have originated through the system of inheritance common in this area which provides for the real division of the land. The attempt of the farmer to increase the size of his holdings in order to have enough land to support his family has not only increased the amount of farm indebtedness, but forced all land values up to uneconomic heights. In the past century, the government of Baden has made an effort to correct the situation by the long and expensive process of regrouping the plots and strips of a village into farms of reasonable size. In earlier days this was done with the majority consent of the village; the Nazis did it by decree. However, the Nazi effort to curb the division of land through the Farm Inheritance Act of 1933 failed in Baden, since most of the farms fall below the limitations of the law. Today, over one-half of the farm land of Baden still stands in need of regrouping.

In respect to land tenure, there is still another interesting feature in Baden. Some land is still owned in common, and the peasants of a village have a right to it for their lifetimes. In Baden the common land is not restricted to pasture, and sometimes crop land will go with a certain house or with a certain length of stay in a village. Since the common land is redistributed after a peasant's death, the land is frequently worked hard without regard to the preservation of its fertility. Many of the farmers of this area supplement their income by working in the light manufacturing industries of the Rhenish towns. It is estimated that over 40 per cent of the farmers of the Rhine Valley are employed part-time in industry. Most of the rural Badenese dwell in small agglomerated villages which range in size from 200 to 1600 inhabitants. The smaller villages are able to support a school, the larger ones generally center about a church. They are composed of rectangular plastered houses of the Rhenish type.

The peasants of the Black Forest and the Neckar upland are mainly interested in dairying and cattle raising, since the deep valleys of the forest and the heavily forested upland areas allow little room for crop cultivation. In the Black Forest, the higher land, which occasionally rises above the timber line, enjoys considerable rainfall and has mild summers and cold snowy winters. Much of the higher upland consists of rough pasture, which is used for cattle grazing between May and October. Cheese is the chief dairy product. The lower parts of the forest are densely covered with spruce and fir, which have given the name to this area. Crop cultivation is extremely limited. Some oats, rye, and potatoes and occasionally fruit trees are raised in the valleys, but the main economic support of this area is forestry. There is more open land for cultivation in the lower Neckar upland, but again forestry is the main activity.

The uplands of Baden are not densely settled, and most of the present settlements date from relatively recent times. The forest hamlet, consisting of a few houses built about irregular junctions of roads and with a population ranging between 15 and 70 inhabitants, and the isolated farmstead are the common forms of settlement. The slightly larger village with a population ranging from 70 to 200 inhabitants becomes common only in the lower areas of the upland. The typical house is made of wood and is characterized by a rectangular form, two stories in height, with a great overhanging roof. It is ideal for the humid climate of the upland. The small farms, which average less than 5 hectares in size, are not capable of supporting the upland peasants. They are largely dependent upon auxiliary earnings made from catering to the extensive tourist trade or from home industries and crafts (clock making, toy making, and wood carving). The Nazis always showed particular concern for the home industries. Their efforts to regulate and organize these industries met with some opposition, for the peasant worker values his independence more than his security.

To generalize about agrarian production in Baden, the most productive agricultural zone is formed by the Rhine Valley. Its dry, warm climate coupled with fertile soils, particularly in the foothill areas, has made it one of the important fruit-producing areas of the Reich. The cultivation of grain and industrial crops is important. The upland agriculture is much less valuable in comparison with the intensive valley agriculture, but it supplies the industrial cities of the valley with dairy products. The cheese produced in the upland is shipped throughout Germany. The importance of the forest land and home industries cannot be overlooked.

LAND UTILIZATION (HECTARES)

Cultivated Land	454,600
Grain 231,000	
Legumes 4,400	
Root Crops 109,000	

Green Vegetables	. . . . . .	5,200
Industrial Crops	. . . . . .	10,300
Fodder Crops	. . . . .	94,700
Agrarian Land .	. . . .	341,500
Small Gardens	. . . . . .	11,500
Meadow and Pasture	. . . .	313,000
Orchards	. . . .	5,600
Vineyards	. . . .	11,400

Approximately 40 per cent of the land surface of the state of Baden is covered by forest. The actual distribution of the forest area is subject to wide variations. The valley of the Rhine, except for the pine-covered forest area, is almost treeless. The foothill and marginal plateau area is partly covered by broadleafed forests, consisting of oak at the lower elevations and stands of beech, elm, and linden in the higher areas. The forests of the above regions are not extensive. Most of the forest land of the state is concentrated in the Black Forest and Neckar upland. The forest cover of the former consists largely of fir, beech, and spruce. In the higher parts of the forest there are occasional pure stands of fir, while in the highest areas are pure stands of spruce and a flora of alpine type. The forests of the lower Neckar upland are largely formed of oak and beech. These forest lands are owned by a variety of interests. The state of Baden owns 98,790 hectares of forest land which is divided between 74 state forest reserves. The state forests, which constitute 17 per cent of the total forest area, are administered by the Forest Section (*Forstabteilung*) in the Finance and Economic Ministry at Karlsruhe. It works through the forest offices which are located in each county. Municipal forests held about one-half of the forest land in Baden, while private forest interests owned about 33 per cent of the forest land.

The dominant rural group of the state is of Alemannic origin. Today, they are known as the Badenese. Their culture, which is characterized by a distinct complex of dialect, attitudes, and folkways, can only be understood in Rhenish terms. It has developed on the Rhine, one of the main highways of Europe. Influences from Switzerland, France, and even Italy have played an important role in the development of the culture of the Badenese. They have much in common with the Rhenish Franconians and the Swabians who surround them on the north and east, although their dialect and many of their customs reveal intimate connections with the Alsatians living on the west side of the Rhine. Their love of festivals, carnivals, and dress pageants depicting episodes of local history and tradition, like their preference for wine and light food, is typically Rhenish. The Badenese, like the Swabians, have long been stereotyped as typical German peasants.

Urban Aspect

The state of Baden is the most densely settled of the South German states and has the largest urban population in southern Germany, although it does not possess any large metropolitan areas that can be compared with Stuttgart, Munich, or Nuremberg. While only 41 per cent of its population dwelt in villages and hamlets of less than 2,000 population, over 18 per cent lived in the two great cities each of which had a population of over 100,000: Karlsruhe and Mannheim, which are located on the Rhine in northern Baden. Of the remaining larger cities, including Heidelberg, Pforzheim, and Freiburg, only the last is located in southern Baden. The northern Rhine Valley portion of Baden is studded with numerous large and small manufacturing towns which have developed in the course of the last hundred years under the impetus of the German industrial revolution and cheap Rhine transportation. Southern Baden has a more rural character. Its main cities, Freiburg and Konstanz, can be regarded only as old market towns with some added industry.

Under the Nazis, the seven larger cities of Baden constituted city counties with separate territorial status; their administrations were directly under the Ministry of the Interior at Karlsruhe. Baden, like Württemberg, has always laid stress upon the idea that rural and urban areas should be joined together and not separated. Hence the Nazi change marked another departure from old traditions. The larger cities, like the smaller towns and villages, were once administered under the Baden Municipal Codes of 1831, 1874, and 1921. Under the Nazis, they were administered under the new German Municipal Code of 1935.

The economic life of Baden is almost entirely dependent upon the Rhine, for almost all of the heavier raw materials have to be imported from the Saar or Ruhr industrial areas. Economically, the area forms a part of the southwestern German economic region, which embraces the Saar, the Bavarian Palatinate, Baden, Württemberg, and Prussian Hohenzollern. Although much of the industrial and commercial life of this area is dominated by Stuttgart in Württemberg, the state of Baden tends to be a distinct economic sub-region, owing to its position on the Rhine and to its partial isolation from the industries of Swabia on the east which is afforded by the Black Forest. From the point of view of trade in basic industrial materials, Baden is oriented more toward the Saar and Ruhr than toward Württemberg. The distinct social-economic character of the Baden area, as a real unit of human activity and organization, was fully recognized by the Nazis when they made the state of Baden into a separate planning association. The organization of economy is also under one Economic Chamber. Regionally within Baden, industry is concentrated in the cities of the densely settled northern portion of the Rhine Valley extending from Karlsruhe to Mannheim. The manufacturing and commercial activities of southern Baden are relatively unimportant in comparison with those of the north. The economic enterprises of this state tend to be of the small type; only Mannheim can be regarded as a center of large corporations engaging in the heavier types of industry and manufacturing.

Natural resources are extremely limited, consisting only of salt deposits used by the chemical industries. These deposits are found in the Rhine Valley, near Lörrach and Freiburg. The power needs of the many small manufacturing plants are partly met by numerous small-scale hydroelectric plants in the Black Forest. The only major water power station in northern Baden, the *Murgwerk,* is near Pforzheim. It is connected with Mannheim by a high tension line. It does not, however, provide for all the power needs of the Mannheim industries, for this city is linked by high tension lines to the great coal electrical works of the Saar. The power needs of many of the industries of northern Baden are met by coal shipped in, largely from the Ruhr. About one-third of the coal, however, comes overland from the Saar. Southern Baden is supplied by electrical power made at the great *Rheinfelden Werke,* near Lörrach.

Despite the absence of the essential resources for modern industry—coal and iron—an active metallurgical and machine industry has developed at Mannheim, Bruchsal, Pforzheim, Karlsruhe, Offenburg, Freiburg, and Lörrach. Mannheim is the most important of these centers. Its long importance as a machine center is emphasized by the fact that the first German locomotive was constructed here. Benz also invented the first automobile in this city. Pforzheim is important as the center of the German ornament and jewelry industry. It has been a center for gold and silver smiths since the middle eighteenth century. These interests and traditions support the goldsmith and industrial arts schools at Pforzheim. The machine manufacturing plants at Freiburg, Offenburg, and Lörrach are very small in comparison with those of the north, and cater to the extensive textile industries of southern Baden. Some cotton manufacturing is done at Pforzheim in northern Baden, but most of the textile industry is concentrated in the south at Offenburg, Freiburg, Lahr, and Lörrach. These textile plants are mainly interested in cotton, although wool is important at Offenburg and Freiburg, and silk textiles are made at Lörrach. The main centers of the Baden chemical industry are located at Mannheim and Freiburg. Mannheim had one of the large *IG Farben* plants, which made use of coal shipped in by the Rhine and salt brought down the Neckar from Heilbronn in Württemberg. Leather, wood and furniture, and pottery manufacturing enterprises, making use of locally available resources, are found in almost all of the moderate sized towns of Baden. Aside from Mannheim, one might say that industry in Baden, like that in Württemberg, mainly produces light manufactured articles requiring few raw materials of the heavy type. This is a region of mixed manufacturing: light machinery, paper, textiles, pottery, and wood products.

The Rhine Valley provides the chief artery of water, road, and rail transportation in Baden. Although there are some routes across the high Black Forests, they are few in number. Since earliest times the Rhine Valley has been used for road and water transportation, the first real roads having, undoubtedly, been built by the Romans. Today a modern highway links Konstanz with Basel, where the road turns northward to follow the Rhine Valley to Freiburg, Baden-Baden, Karlsruhe, Heidelberg, and Mannheim. Roads go from both Karlsruhe and Mannheim across the Neckar upland to Stuttgart. The construction and maintenance of the main state roads were handled by the Section for Water and Road Construction (*Abteilung für Wasser- und Strassenbau*) in the Finance and Economic Ministry at Karlsruhe, while local roads were under the county administrations. Here, too, the Nazi regime built national super-highways. One highway has been built along the east bank of the Rhine to link Frankfort with Karlsruhe, while another runs from Karlsruhe via Stuttgart, Augsburg, and Munich to the Austrian frontier.

The major railroad line also follows the Rhine Valley. There are branch lines linking Mannheim with Würzburg, Karlsruhe with Stuttgart, and Offenburg with Konstanz. The railroads of Baden were under the National Railroad Directorate at Karlsruhe. The main traffic is born by the double track line along the Rhine, the center for which is Mannheim.

The Rhine is the most important artery of commerce because it provides cheap transportation for coal, metal, and grain to be shipped from ports on the North Sea and river ports in the Ruhr to the industries of Baden. Mannheim, located at the junction of the Rhine and Neckar, is one of the great river ports of Germany, ranking with Berlin and Duisburg. It is the distributing point for grain, coal, metal, and even oil for all of southern Germany. The amount of traffic on the Rhine diminishes somewhat south of Mannheim, although it is still substantial as far south as Karlsruhe. Even above Karlsruhe, there is some traffic on the Rhine to the port of Kehl in Baden and as far south as Basel, but most of its stops at Strassburg in Alsace or takes the Rhine-Rhône canal; this canal has been built along the western side of the Rhine in Alsatian territory to connect with Mulhouse (Alsace) and Basel and ultimately with southern France. Strasburg is also the junction point for another canal, the Marne-Rhine canal, which connects with the canal system of northern and eastern France. There were no major international air transportation centers in Baden. Minor airports were located at Freiburg, Karlsruhe, and Mannheim. Although the air service in Baden, as in all of Germany, was operated by the German Airways Corporation, the airports were owned and operated by the municipalities.

While Mannheim, before World War II, was the undoubted industrial capital of Baden, Karlsruhe, in addition to being the capital of the state, is its main financial and commercial center. Mannheim and Pforzheim always played important financial and commercial roles in their immediate areas. Freiburg and Konstanz have much the same function in southern Baden. The smaller towns definitely play a secondary role in the commercial life of Baden. The modern commercial and financial importance of Karlsruhe is due to its position as the state governmental and administrative center.

In terms of freight traffic carried by rail, agricultural, stone and clay, textile, and wood products were produced and shipped from southern Baden, while chemicals, metal products, fertilizer, and agricultural products were important in northern Baden. Part of the requirements of the industries of northern Baden (Mannheim, Pforzheim, and Karlsruhe) were met by rail transportation which brought in some of the coal and iron required by the heavy industries. In southern Baden, coal and iron also had a high priority. Most of these needs, however, were met by water transportation. Mannheim and the adjacent port centers of Rheinau and Ludwigshafen are the key points. Mannheim is the best place for the transshipment of goods from overseas coming in via the North Sea ports, or for goods from the Ruhr bound for southern Germany or Switzerland. Even though Strasbourg has become important in this respect in recent times, Mannheim still retains its economic importance and its commerce with the markets in southern Germany. The trade of Mannheim was not restricted to coal and iron, for it is also the chief distributing point for oil and grain in southern Germany.

Trade in machine goods within southern Germany was extremely complex. While northern Baden and the Mannheim area were heavily dependent upon the machinery industries of Swabia, the similar industries of Karlsruhe and Pforzheim found an outlet for their products in Württemberg. The alignment of the trade in machinery was further conditioned by commercial relations with the Saar and Ruhr areas. The specialization and concentration of the textile industry in Germany led to an extensive trade in yarns between the mills of southern Baden and those of Württemberg. Most of the textile industries of Baden were oriented economically toward Stuttgart, the textile capital of southwest Germany. As a rule, the business enterprises, industrial and commercial, are small in size.

The banking and credit institutions of Baden ranged from branches of the great commercial banks of Berlin, which were mainly interested in investments of the industrial type, to the local county and municipal mortgage and savings banks. Karlsruhe was again the important center where the state banking institution, the *Badische Bank,* had its headquarters. The operations of these banks were supplemented by those of the branches of the *Reichsbank* at Karlsruhe, Bruchsal, Bühl, Lahr, Offenburg, Rastatt, Freiburg, Emmendingen, Konstanz, Lörrach, Säckingen, Triberg, Villingen, Waldkirch, Mannheim, Heidelberg, and Weinheim. The state insurance companies—*Öffentliche*

Lebensversicherungsanstalt Baden, *Badische Gebäudeversicherungs-Anstalt,* and the *Badischer Gemeinde-Versicherungsverband*—were under the state Ministry of the Interior. The Baden area was served by a stock exchange at Karlsruhe.

The urban population of Baden is largely engaged in industry, trade, and transportation enterprises. Of the total population, 937,000 individuals, or 40 per cent of the population, made their living in industry and crafts, while 382,-000, or 16 per cent, were engaged in trade and transportation. Another 8 per cent was engaged in professional work or public service. The working class, which formed about 37 per cent of the total population, like that of the other south German states, was relatively small in comparison with other areas of the Reich. Although Baden had a relatively smaller upper class than either Bavaria or Württemberg, it was still one of the largest in the Reich. This larger upper class, like that of Württemberg, is the result of the addition of owners of small, private, manufacturing and commerical enterprises to the upper income group. A small white-collar class, 9.7 per cent of population, is the result here, too. The number of civil servants was well above the average for the Reich.

The vital portion of Baden is situated along the Rhine valley between the river and the uplands of the Black Forest and Neckar upland. The valley area is densely settled both from the urban and rural points of view. There are hundreds of picturesque small villages of peasants who are supported by their work on small farms where they raise fruit, vegetables, grapes, and some grain. Some of the large villages and smaller towns have a machine shop or small textile mill. The life of the valley area contrasts strongly with that of the forested upland with its sparse population of conservative peasants making a living from dairying and home industries.

Much of the life of the valley centers in the larger cities. Mannheim, frequently mentioned as one of the important industrial, commercial, and transportation centers of the Reich, is of relatively recent origin. It was founded in 1606 and owes its growth almost entirely to the German industrial revolution and the modern development of Rhine transportation. The town of Heidelberg, which lies up the Neckar River from Mannheim, has long been a cultural center; its famous university, founded in 1386, is the oldest in Germany. The picturesque ruins of Heidelberg castle and the thermal springs of the town have attracted tourists from all over the world. Karlsruhe, which is situated at the junction of the Paris-Stuttgart-Munich and the Amsterdam-Cologne-Basel main railroad lines, was founded as the capital of Baden in 1715. The fan-like plan of the city and its extensive gardens and parks, which date back to the time of the city's foundation, were developed during the neo-classical period. The modern industrial portion of Karlsruhe is centered around the port area.

The city of Pforzheim, which is situated to the east of Karlsruhe in the foothills of the northern Black Forest, has long been one of the main centers of the German jewelry and ornament industry since its founding by the Romans. The only important town between these cities of northern Baden and Freiburg in the south is Baden-Baden, the world famous spa. Freiburg, which is located on one of the marginal plateaus adjacent to the Rhine Valley, is the center of Catholicism in Baden, the seat of a Catholic archbishop, and the home of the Catholic University of Freiburg. It's ideal geographic location makes it one of the favorite residential cities of Germany. The only other important city in Baden is Konstanz, located in the far southeast on Lake Constance. Once a free and imperial city of the Empire, it is today only a city with an illustrious past.

BIBLIOGRAPHY

Beer, K. *Der Böhmer Wald und Bayerische Wald* (Bielefeld & Leipzig, 1925).

Dittmar, W. R. *The Government of the Free State of Bavaria,* Ph.D. Thesis, Columbia University (New York, 1939).

Doebert, M. *Bayern und Deutschland* (Munich, Berlin, 1922-1926).

Doebert, M. *Entwicklungsgeschichte Bayerns,* 2 vol. (Munich, 1916-31).

Forstdirektion, *Die forstlichen Verhältnisse Württembergs* (Stuttgart, 1880).

Glötz, W. *Frankenland* (Bielefeld & Leipzig, 1924).

Göz, K. *Das Staatsrecht des Königsreichs Württemberg* (Tübingen, 1908).

Gradmann, R. *Süddeutschland* (Stuttgart, 1931).

Great Britain, Foreign Office *Bavarian Palatinate,* Handbook No. 37 (London, H. M. Stationary Office, 1920).

Haas, H. J. *Schwabenland* (Bielefeld & Leipzig, 1925).

Haushofer, M. *Bayerns Hochlands und München,* 2nd ed. (Bielefeld & Leipzig, 1911).

Haushofer, M. *Oberbayern, München, und Bayerisches Hochland* (Bielefeld & Leipzig, 1900).

Kiechbaum, E. *Baiernland, Landschaft und Volkstum* (Munich, 1938).

Kohl, G. *Die Organisationsgewalt in Württemberg* (Inaugural Dissertation, Tübingen-Stuttgart, 1933).

Krebs, N. *Der Südwesten, Landeskunde von Deutschland* (Leipzig, 1931).

Lämmle, A. *Die Reise ins Schwabenland* (Stuttgart, 1943).

Mattern J. *Bavaria and the Reich* (Baltimore, 1923).

Neumann, L. *Der Schwarzwald* (Bielefeld & Leipzig, 1923).

Piloty, R. F. *Hundert Jahre bayerischen Verfassungsleben* (Würzburg, 1918).

Riezler, S. von *Geschichte Baierns,* 8 vol. (Gotha, 1878-1914).

Schneider, E. *Württembergische Geschichte* (Stuttgart, 1896).

Seydel, M. von *Bayerisches Staatsrecht* (Tübingen, 1913).

Trampler, K. *Bayerische Ostmark* (Munich, 1934).

Völter, J. L. *Geographische Beschriebung von Württemberg* (Stuttgart, 1836).

Walz, E. "Das Staatsrecht des Grossherzogtums Baden," in *Das öffentliche Recht der Gegenwart,* Bd. V (1909).

Wolter, E. *Die Bevölkerungsverteilung in den einzelnen Landschaften Württembergs von 1834-1925* (Tübingen, 1934).

Zahn, F. *Bayern und das Reich,* 2nd ed. (Munich, 1925).

Appendix

1

Cabinets under the Weimar Republic

1. Scheidemann . . . . February 13, 1919
2. Bauer . . . . June 21, 1919
3. First Cabinet Müller . . . . . . March 27, 1920
4. Fehrenbach . . . . June 25, 1920
5. First Cabinet Wirth . . . . . . May 10, 1921
6. Second Cabinet Wirth . . . . . October 26, 1921
7. Cuno . . . . November 22, 1922
8. First Cabinet Stresemann . . . . . August 13, 1923
9. Second Cabinet Stresemann . . . . October 6, 1923
10. First Cabinet Marx . . . . . . November 30, 1923
11. First Cabinet Luther . . . . . . January 15, 1925
12. Second Cabinet Luther . . . . . January 20, 1926
13. Second Cabinet Marx . . . . . . May 16, 1926
14. Third Cabinet Marx . . . . . . January 29, 1927
15. Second Cabinet Müller . . . . . June 28, 1928
16. Brüning . . . . April 1, 1930
17. Von Papen . . . . May 31, 1932
18. Von Schleicher . . . . November 17, 1932
19. Hitler . . . . January 30, 1933

2

Area and Population of Germany 1910, 1933, and 1938
(1938—after incorporation of Saar, Austria, and Sudetenland)

German Empire 1910	540,857.6 sq. km.	64,925,993 people
Weimar Republic 1933 . . .	470,544.73 sq. km.	66,031,580 people
Hitler Germany 1938	583,279.61 sq. km.	78,790,000 people

Source: *Statistisches Jahrbuch für Das Deutsche Reich,* Vol. 34, p. 1, Berlin, 1913;
   Vol. 57, p. 7, Berlin, 1938.

3

RELIGIOUS GROUPINGS IN GERMANY, 1933

Protestants	. . . .	41,080,161
Catholics	. . . .	21,762,056
Jews	. . . .	502,799
Others	. . . .	2,686,564 (of whom 2,441,714 were registered without any religious affiliation)

Source: *Statistisches Jahrbuch für Das Deutsche Reich,* Vol. 57, p. 22, Berlin, 1938.

4

CHRONOLOGY OF GERMAN REGIMES SINCE A.D. 800

Carolingians	800-911
Konrad	911-918
Saxonian Emperors	919-1024
Franconian Emperors	1024-1125
Lothar III of Sachsen	1125-1137
Hohenstaufen Emperors	1138-1254
Wilhelm of Holland	1247-1256
Interregnum	1254-1273
Emperors of different Houses:	
Rudolf I of Habsburg	1273-1291
Adolf of Nassau	1292-1298
Albrecht I of Austria	1298-1308
Heinrich VII of Luxemburg	1308-1313
Ludwig IV of Bayern	1314-1346
Friedrich III (The Fair) of Austria	
Karl IV of Luxemburg	1346-1378
Wenzel	1378-1400
Ruprecht of the Palatinate	1400-1410
Sigismund of Luxemburg	1410-1437
Habsburg Emperors	1438-1806
Rheinbund (Confederation of the Rhine)	1806-1813
Deutscher Bund (German Confederation)	1815-1866
Norddeutscher Bund (North-German Confederation)	1866-1871
Hohenzollern Emperors	1871-1918
German Republic	1918-1933
Hitler Germany	1933-1945

5

ELECTIONS FOR THE REICHSPRESIDENCY

1925 and 1932

	March 29, 1925	April 26, 1925
Jarres	10,416,658	
Held	1,007,450	
Ludendorff . . .	285,793	
Braun	7,802,497	
Marx	3,887,734	13,751,605
Hellpach	1,568,398	
Thälmann	1,871,815	1,931,151
Hindenburg . . .		14,655,641
Participation	68.9%	77.6%

	March 13, 1932	April 10, 1932
Düsterberg	2,558,900	
Hindenburg . . .	18,654,670	19,359,983
Hitler	11,341,360	13,418,547
Thälmann	4,982,939	3,706,759
Winter	111,486	
Participation	86.2%	83.5%

6

SELECTED PROVISIONS FROM THE CONSTITUTION
OF THE GERMAN EMPIRE*
(April 16, 1871)

PREAMBLE

His Majesty the King of Prussia in the name of the North German Confederation, His Majesty the King of Bavaria, His Majesty the King of Württemberg, His Royal Highness the Grand Duke of Baden and His Royal Highness the Grand

* From Otis H. Fisk, *Germany's Constitutions of 1871 and 1919* (Cincinnati, 1924).

Duke of Hesse and Rhenish Hesse for the parts of the Grand Duchy of Hesse lying north of the Main, form a perpetual Federation for the protection of the Federation's territory and of the law in force within the same, and also for the fostering of the welfare of the German People. This Federation shall bear the name German Empire, and shall have the following

CONSTITUTION

I. Federal Territory

Article 1

The Federal territory consists of the States of Prussia (with Lauenburg), Bavaria, Saxony, Württemberg, Baden, Hesse, Mecklenburg-Schwerin, Saxe-Weimar, Mecklenburg-Strelitz, Oldenburg, Brunswick, Saxe-Meinigen, Saxe-Altenburg, Saxe-Coburg-Gotha, Anhalt, Schwarzburg-Rudolstadt, Schwarzburg-Sondershausen, Waldeck, Reuss of the Elder Line, Reuss of the Younger Line, Schaumburg-Lippe, Lippe, Lübeck, Bremen and Hamburg.

Article 5

The Imperial legislative power is exercised by the Bundesrat and the Reichstag. The concurrence of the majority votes of both bodies is necessary and sufficient for an Imperial statute.

In cases of bills concerning the military system, the navy, and the revenues mentioned in Article 35, if a disagreement exists in the Bundesrat, the vote of the presiding officer shall decide the matter, if such vote is for the maintenance of the existing order of things.

Article 11

The Presiding Officer of the Federation appertains to the King of Prussia, who bears the name *German Emperor*. The Emperor has to represent the Empire in the Law of Nations, in the name of the Empire to declare war and conclude peace, to enter into alliances and other treaties with foreign states, to accredit and to receive ambassadors.

For a declaration of war in the name of the Empire the consent of the Bundesrat is required, except in case of an attack upon the territory of the Empire or its coasts.

In so far as the treaties with foreign states relate to such matters as, according to Article 4, belonging in the domain of the Imperial legislation, the concurrence of the Bundesrat is required for their conclusion and the approval of the Reichstag is required for their validity.

Article 12

The Emperor summons, opens, prorogues and closes the Bundesrat and the Reichstag.

Article 15

The presiding chair in the Bundesrat and the conduct of business appertain to the Imperial Chancellor, who is to be appointed by the Emperor.

The Imperial Chancellor can let himself be represented, by virtue of written substitution, by any other member of the Bundesrat.

Article 20

The Reichstag shall proceed from universal and direct elections with secret voting.

Until the statutory regulation which is reserved in S5 of the Election Statute of May 31, 1869 (Federal Gazette, 1869, page 145), there shall be elected in Bavaria 48, in Württemberg 17, in Baden 14, in Hesse South of the Main 6, in Alsace-Lorraine 15 deputies, and accordingly the total number of deputies shall be 397.

Article 24

The legislative period of the Reichstag lasts five years. For the dissolution of the Reichstag during this period a resolution of the Bundesrat with the concurrence of the Emperor is required.

Article 28

The Reichstag acts with an absolute majority vote. For the validity of its action the presence of a majority of the legal number of the members is required.

Article 76

Controversies between different members of the Federation, so far as they are not of a private-law nature and therefore to be decided by the competent tribunals, shall be disposed of by the Bundesrat upon application of one of the parties.

Constitutional controversies in members of the Federation in whose Constitutions no authorities to decide such controversies are designated, the Bundesrat has to settle amicably, upon application of one of the parties, or, if that is not successful, to bring them to settlement by way of Imperial legislation.

Article 78

Amendments of the Constitution are had by way of legislation. They shall be considered as rejected if they have fourteen votes against them in the Bundesrat.

Those provisions of the Imperial Constitution by which certain rights of individual members of the Federation in their relations to the whole are determined, can be amended only with the consent of the member of the Federation entitled to said rights.

7

Selected Provisions from the Weimar Constitution*
(August 11, 1919)

PREAMBLE

The German People, united in all their branches, and inspired by the determination to renew and strengthen their Commonwealth in liberty and justice, to preserve peace both at home and abroad, and to foster social progress, have adopted the following Constitution.

Article 1

The German Commonwealth is a republic.
Political authority is derived from the People.

Article 13

The laws of the Commonwealth are supreme over the laws of the States which conflict with them.

If doubt arises, or difference of opinion, whether State legislation is in harmony with the law of the Commonwealth, the proper authorities of the Commonwealth or the central authorities of the States, in accordance with more specific provisions of a national law, may have recourse to the decision of a supreme judicial court of the Commonwealth.

Article 17

Every State must have a republican constitution. The representatives of the People must be elected by the universal, equal, direct and secret suffrage of all German citizens, both men and women, according to the principles of proportional representation. The State Cabinet shall require the confidence of the representatives of the People.

The principles in accordance with which the representatives of the People are chosen apply also to municipal elections; but by State law a residence qualification not exceeding one year of residence in the municipality may be imposed in such elections.

Article 20

The National Assembly is composed of the delegates of the German people.

Article 21

The delegates are representatives of the whole People. They are subject only to their own consciences and are not bound by any instructions.

* Translated by William Bennett Munro and Arthur Norman Holcombe (published by the World Peace Foundation).

Article 25

The President of the Commonwealth may dissolve the National Assembly, but only once for the same cause.

The new election occurs at the latest on the sixtieth day after such dissolution.

Article 41

The National President is chosen by the whole German People.

Every German who has completed his thirty-fifth year is eligible for election.

The details will be regulated by a national law.

Article 48

If any State does not perform the duties imposed upon it by the Constitution or by national laws, the National President may hold it to the performance thereof by force of arms.

If public safety and order in the German Commonwealth is materially disturbed or endangered, the National President may take the necessary measures to restore public safety and order, and, if necessary, to intervene by force of arms. To this end he may temporarily suspend, in whole or in part, the fundamental rights established in Articles 114, 115, 117, 118, 123, 124 and 153.

The National President must immediately inform the National Assembly of all measures adopted by authority of Paragraphs 1 or 2 of this Article. These measures shall be revoked at the demand of the National Assembly.

If there is danger from delay, the State Cabinet may for its own territory take provisional measures as specified in Paragraph 2. These measures shall be revoked at the demand of the National President or of the National Assembly.

The details will be regulated by a national law.

Article 52

The National Cabinet consists of the National Chancellor and the National Ministers.

Article 53

The National Chancellor and, on his proposal, the National Ministers are appointed and dismissed by the National President.

Article 54

The National Chancellor and the National Ministers require for the administration of their offices the confidence of the National Assembly. Each of them must resign if the National Assembly by formal resolution withdraws its confidence.

Article 56

The National Chancellor determines the general course of policy and assumes responsibility therefor to the National Assembly. In accordance with this general policy each National Minister conducts independently the particular affairs intrusted to him and is held individually responsible to the National Assembly.

Article 60

A National Council will be organized to represent the German States in national legislation and administration.

Article 68

Bills are introduced by the National Cabinet or by members of the National Assembly.

National laws are enacted by the National Assembly.

Article 73

A law enacted by the National Assembly shall be referred to the People before its promulgation, if the National President so orders within a month.

A law whose promulgation is deferred at the demand of at least one-third of the National Assembly shall be submitted to the People, if one-twentieth of the qualified voters so petition.

A popular vote shall further be resorted to on a measure initiated by the People if one-tenth of the qualified voters so petition. A fully elaborated bill must accompany such petition. The National Cabinet shall lay the bill together with a statement of its attitude before the National Assembly. The popular vote does not take place if the desired bill is enacted without amendment by the National Assembly.

A popular vote may be taken on the budget, tax laws, and laws relating to the classification and payment of public officers only by authority of the National President.

The procedure in connection with the popular referendum and initiative will be regulated by national law.

Article 76

The Constitution may be amended by process of legislation. But acts of the National Assembly relating to the amendment of the Constitution are effective only if two-thirds of the legal membership are present, and at least two-thirds of those present give their assent. Acts of the National Council relating to the amendment of the Constitution also require a two-thirds majority of all the votes cast. If an amendment to the Constitution is to be adopted by the People by popular initiative, the assent of a majority of the qualified voters is required.

If the National Assembly adopts an amendment to the Constitution against the objection of the National Council, the President may not promulgate this law, if the National Council within two weeks demands a popular vote.

8

IMPORTANT NAZI DECREES*
LAW TO COMBAT THE NATIONAL CRISIS
(The Enabling Act)
(March 24, 1933)

The Reichstag has enacted the following law which, with the consent of the Reichsrat and after determination that the requirements for laws changing the constitution have been complied with, is hereby promulgated:

Article 1. National laws can be enacted by the national cabinet as well as in accordance with the procedure established in the constitution. This applies also to the laws referred to in article 85, paragraph 2, and in article 87 of the constitution.

Article 2. The national laws enacted by the national cabinet may deviate from the constitution insofar as they do not affect the position of the Reichstag and the Reichsrat. The powers of the president remain undisturbed.

Article 3. The national laws enacted by the national cabinet are prepared by the chancellor and published in the Reichsgesetzblatt. They come into effect, unless otherwise specified, upon the day following their publication. Articles 68 to 77 of the constitution do not apply to the laws enacted by the national cabinet.

Article 4. Treaties of the Reich with foreign states which concern matters of national legislation do not require the consent of the bodies participating in legislation. The national cabinet is empowered to issue the necessary provisions for the execution of these treaties.

Article 5. This law becomes effective on the day of its publication. It becomes invalid on April 1st, 1937; it further becomes invalid when the present national cabinet is replaced by another.

LAW CONCERNING THE HEAD OF THE GERMAN REICH
(August 1, 1934)

The national cabinet has decided upon the following law which is hereby proclaimed.

1. The office of the national president is united with that of the national chancellor. In consequence, the former powers of the national president pass to the leader and national chancellor, Adolf Hitler. He appoints his deputy.

2. This law becomes effective from the moment of the death of the National President von Hindenburg.

* From Rappard et al., *Source Book on European Governments* (New York, 1937), Part IV, *passim.*

Law Prohibiting the Formation of New Political Parties
(July 14, 1933)

1. The National Socialist German Workers' party is the only political party in Germany.

2. Whoever undertakes to maintain the organization of another political party, or to form a new political party, is to be punished with imprisonment in a penitentiary up to 3 years or with confinement in a jail from 6 months to 3 years unless the act is punishable by a higher penalty under other provisions.

Law for the Protection of German Blood and German Honor
(September 15, 1935)
(Nuremberg Law)

Clearly realizing that the purity of the German blood is the prerequisite for perpetuating the German people, and inspired by an inflexible determination to secure the existence of the German nation for all time to come, the Reichstag has unanimously passed the following law which is hereby proclaimed:

1. (1) Marriages between Jews and citizens of German or kindred stock shall be prohibited. Marriages concluded despite the law shall be considered void even when they were concluded abroad in circumvention of this law.

(2) Only the public prosecutor shall bring suit for annulment.

2. Non-marital sexual intercourse between Jews and citizens of German or kindred stock shall be prohibited.

3. Jews shall not employ in their household female citizens of German or kindred stock under 45 years of age.

4. (1) Jews shall not hoist the Reich and national flag nor display the Reich colors.

(2) They are, however, permitted to display the Jewish colors. The exercise of this privilege is placed under Government protection.

5. (1) Persons acting in violation of paragraph 1 shall be sentenced to jail.

(2) Men acting in violation of paragraph 2 shall be sentenced to prison or jail.

(3) Persons acting in violation of the regulations of paragraph 3 or 4 shall be sentenced to imprisonment up to one year and to a monetary fine or to one of these punishments.

6. The National Minister of the Interior, in agreement with the Deputy Führer and with the National Minister of Justice, shall issue the necessary legal and administrative regulations for executing and supplementing this law.

7. This law shall come into force on the day following its promulgation, excepting paragraph 3 which will not come into force until January 1, 1936.

Nuremberg, September 15, 1935, at the Party Convention of Freedom.

Glossary

A

Abteilung—Section, department.

A. G.—Aktiengesellschaft—Joint Stock Corporation.

Allgemeine Verwaltung—General Administration.

Allgemeines Landrecht—General Land Law.

Amt—Office.

Amtskammern—County Chambers.

Amtsausschuss—Precinct Committee.

Amtsbezirk—Precinct (In Baden similar to a county).

Amtsgericht—Court of First Instance.

Amtsverbände—Communal Unions.

Amtsvorstand—Local Executive Committee.

Amtsvorsteher—Precinct Chairman or Director.

Arbeitsamt—Labor Office.

Arbeitsdienst—Local Labor Service.

Arbeitsgericht—Labor Court.

Arbeitslosenversicherung—Unemployment Insurance.

Arbeitsvermittlung—Employment Implementation.

Aufsichtsamt für Privatversicherung—Supervisory Office for Private Insurance.

Ausländerkartei—Aliens' Register.

Auslandsorganisation—Overseas Organization.

Auswärtiges Amt—Foreign Office.

B

Bahnhof—Railroad Station.

Bauamt—Construction Office.

Bayrische Volkspartei—Bavarian People's Party.

Beamter—Official, Civil Servant.

Beigeordnete—Administrative Department Heads.

Beigeordneter—Professional City Expert, Administrative Department Head.

Beirat—Advisory Councilor.

Bergbehörde—Mining Authority.

Betriebsamt—Railroad Operations Office.

Betriebsräte—Factory Council

Bezirksamt—District Administration Office.

Bezirksausschuss—District Committee.

Bezirkskasse—District Treasury.

Bezirksversammlung—District Council.

Börsenausschuss—Stock Exchange Committee.

Bundesamt für Heimatwesen—Federal Office for Welfare Matters.

Bundesrat—Federal Council.

Bundestag—Federal Diet.

Bürgerliches Gesetzbuch—German Civil Code.

Bürgermeister—Mayor.

Bürgermeisterverfassung—Mayor Plan.

Bürgerschaft—Citizen's Assembly.

Burggraf—Count.

Büro des Reichspräsidenten—Office of the National President.

D

Deutsche Arbeitsfront—German Labor Front.

Deutsche Demokratische Partei—German Democratic Party.

Deutsche Gemeindeordnung—German Municipal Code.

Deutsche Reichsbahngesellschaft—German Railroad Company.

Deutsche Volkspartei—German People's Party.

Deutscher Bund—Germanic Confederation.

Deutscher Gemeindetag—German Municipal League.

Deutscher Industrie und Handelstag—Diet for German Industry and Commerce.

Deutscher Landwirtschaftsrat—German Council for Agriculture.

Deutschnationale Volkspartei—German National People's Party.

Dienststelle—Administrative Office.

Disziplinarhof—Disciplinary Court for Civil Servants.

Disziplinarkammern—Chambers of Discipline.

Dreierausschuss—Committee of Three.

Dreikaiserbund—Three Emperors' League.

E

Eichungsämter—Offices of Weights and Measures.

Eichungsinspektion—Weight Inspection.

Einzelsiedlung—Farmstead.

Eisenbahndirektion—Railroad Directorate.

Engere Versammlung—Narrower Assembly.

Ermächtigungsgesetz—Enabling Act.

Ernährungsamt—Food Office.

Erzieher—Educator.

F

Fachverbände—Trade Associations.

Fehn Kolonien—Finn Colonies.

Finanzamt—Finance Office.

Finanzverwaltung—Finance Administration.

Forstverwaltung—Forest Administration.

Fortschrittliche Volkspartei—Progressive Liberal Party.

Führerrat—Leader Council.

Fürsorgeverbände—Welfare Unions.

G

Gau—Nazi Party District.

Gauhauptmann—Deputy for Local Government.

Gauleiter—Nazi Party District Leader.

Gaurat—Advisory Council for Local Affairs.

Geheime Staatspolizei (Gestapo)—Secret State Police.

Geheimer Rat—Privy Councilor.

Gemeinde—Commune—Villages and Towns.

Gemeinderatverfassung—Mayoral Plan.

Gemeindeversammlung—General Assembly.

Gemeindevertretung—Elected Representative Assembly.

Gemeindevorsteher—Municipal Chairman.

Gemeines Deutsches Recht—German Common Law

Gendarmerie—Rural County Police

G. m. b. H.—Gesellschaft mit beschränkter Haftung—Limited Liability Company.

Gesundheitsamt—Federal Health Office.

Gewerbe—Industry.

Gewerbe-Ordnung—Trade Law.

Gleichschaltung—Coordination.

Gutsbezirk—Manorial Estate.

H

Handel—Trade.

Handelsgesetzbuch—Commercial Code.

Handwerk—Craft.

Handwerks- und Gewerbetag—National Organization for crafts and handicrafts.

Haufendorf—Type of Home-Agglomerated villages.

Hauptamt—Main Office.

Hauptsatzung—City Charter.

Hauptversorgungsämter—Main Welfare Offices.

Hauptverwaltungsamt—Main Administrative Office.

Herrenhaus—House of Lords.

Hochbauamt—Building Office.

Hochbauämter—County Construction Offices.

Hofgericht—Palace Court.

Hofrechte—Manorial Laws.

I-J

Innere Verwaltung—Inner Administration.

Jugendamt—Youth Office.

Justizbehörde—Judicial Authority.

K

Kammer für Handelssachen—Chamber for Commercial Affairs.

Kanalamt—Canal Office.

Kanzleien—Chancelleries.

Kartellgericht—Cartel Court.

Katasteramt—Land Registry Office.

Kommission für Arbeiterstatistik—Commission for Labor Statistics.

Kommunistiche Partei Deutschlands—German Communist Party.

Kreis—County (In Bavaria similar to Prussian administrative district).

Kreisarzt—County Doctor.

Kreisausschuss—County Committee.

Kreiskasse—County Treasury.

Kreisordnung—County Constitution.

Kreistag—County Assembly.

Kreistierarzt—County Veterinarian.

Kulturbauamt—Soil Conservation Office.

Kurfürsten—Electors.

Kurverein von Rense*—Imperial Elections at Rense.

L

Land—State.

Landbezirk—Rural District.

Landbund—Agricultural League.

Landesarmendirektion—State Welfare Office.

Landesausschus—Provincial Committee.

Landeseichungsämter—State Weights and Measures Offices.

Landesfürsorgestellen—Provincial and State Welfare Offices.

Landeshauptmann—Provincial Director.

Landeskommissar—State Commissioner.

Landeskommissarbezirke—State Commissioner's Districts.

Landesplanunggemeinschaft—Regional Planning Association.

Landesrat—Advisory Councillor to Provincial Director.

Landesversammlung—State Assembly.

Landesversicherungsämter—State Insurance Offices.

Landeszolldirektion—State Office for Customs Duties and Excise Taxes.

Landgemeinde—Rural Village or Town.

Landgemeindeordnung—Constitution for rural villages and towns.

Landherr—Rural Administrator.

Landgericht—Collegiate Court of First and Second Instance.

Landkreis—County.

Landrat—County Manager.

Landrecht—Common Law.

Landstände—Territorial Diets.

Landtag—State Diet.
Lehnrechte—Feudal Laws.
Luftämt—Air Office.
Luftämter—Aviation Offices.

M

Magistratsverfassung—Magisterial Plan.
Marschhufendorf—Buildings clustered together.
Maschinenamt—Machine Office and Shop (R. R.).
Mehrstrassendorf—Type of village; agglomerated with intricate street pattern.
Ministerium—Ministry.
Ministerpräsident—Minister President.

N

Nationalsozialistische Deutsche Arbeiterpartei—National Socialist German Worker's Party.
Neuaufbaugesetz—Law for the New Structure of the Reich.
Norddeutscher Bund—North German Federation.
Normal-Eichungskommission—Normal Weight Commission.

O

Oberbürgermeister—Chief Mayor.
Oberförster—Chief Forester.
Oberkommando des Heeres—High Command of the Army.
Oberkommando der Marine—High Command of the Navy.
Oberkommando der Wehrmacht—High Command of the Armed Forces.
Oberlandesgericht—Superior State Court.
Oberpräsident—Chief President.
Oberpräsidialrat—Chief Councilor to Chief President.
Oberregierungsrat—Chief District Councilor.

Oberste Reichsbehörden—Supreme Administrative Authorities.
Oberverwaltungsergericht—Supreme Administrative Court.
Ordnungspolizei—Order Police.
Ortsarmenverbände—Town Welfare Unions.
Ortsbezirk—Precinct.

P

Partei—Political Party.
Parteibeauftragter—Nazi Party Agent.
Parteikanzlei—Party Chancellery.
Patentamt—Patent Office.
Plattdeutsch—Low Saxon.
Plenum—General Assembly.
Polizei—Police.
Polizeipräsident—Police President.
Präsidialkanzlei—Presidential Chancellery.
Preisbildungsstelle—Price-Fixing Office.
Provinzialausschuss—Provincial Committee.
Provinziallandtag—Provincial Assembly.
Provinzialrat—Provincial Advisory Council.
Provinzialverband—Provincial Corporation.
Prüfungskommission—Commission of Examiners.

R

Räte—Councils.
Ratsherr—Councilor.
Rathsmannen—Councilors.
Rechnungshof—Court of Accounts.
Rechnungsprüfungsamt—Controller's Office.
Regierung—Government.
Regierungen—Administrative Offices.
Regierungsassessor—District Technical Adviser and Assistant.
Regierungsbezirk—Governmental Administrative District.

Regierungspräsident—District President.

Regierungsrat—District Councilor.

Reichsamt des Innern—Imperial Office for Interior.

Reichsamt für Landesaufnahme—National Office of Topography.

Reichsarbeitsdienst—National Labor Service.

Reichsarbeitsministerium—National Labor Ministry.

Reichsarbeitsverwaltung—National Labor Administration.

Reichsarchiv—National Archive.

Reichsaufsichtsamt für Privatversicherung—Private Insurance Organization.

Reichsautobahn—National Super Highway.

Reichsbahndirektion—Railroad Directorate.

Reichsdeputationshauptausschuss—Imperial Committee.

Reichseisenbahnamt—Imperial Railroad Office.

Reichsfinanzhof—National Finance Court.

Reichsfürsten—Princes of the Realm.

Reichsgericht—National Supreme Court.

Reichsgesetzblatt—National Law Gazette.

Reichsgesundheitsamt—National Health Office.

Reichshauptstadt—National Capital.

Reichsjustizministerium—National Ministry of Justice.

Reichskammergericht—Court of the Imperial Chamber.

Reichskanzler—National Chancellor.

Reichskanzlei—Office of the National Chancellor.

Reichskohlenrat—National Coal Council.

Reichskuratorium für Wirtschaftlichkeit—National Rationalization Board.

Reichsland—National Territory.

Reichsluftfahrtministerium—National Air Ministry.

Reichsmarineamt—Imperial Marine Office.

Reichsministerium—National Minister for the Interior.

Reichsministerium für Ernährung und Landwirtschaft—National Ministry for Food and Agriculture.

Reichspostamt—National Post Office.

Reichspostdirektionen—Regional Postal Directorates.

Reichsrat—National Council.

Reichsregierung—National Cabinet.

Reichsschatzamt—Imperial Treasury.

Reichsschuldenkommission—National Debt Commission.

Reichsschuldenverwaltung—National Debt Administration.

Reichssicherheitshauptamt—Main Office for the Security of the Reich.

Reichssippenamt—National Office for Ancestry Research.

Reichssportamt—National Sport Office.

Reichsstatthaltergesetz—Law Relating to National Governors.

Reichsstelle—National Office.

Reichsstelle für Aussenhandel—National Foreign Trade Office.

Reichsstelle für Auswanderungswesen—National Office for Emigration Affairs.

Reichsstelle für Raumordnung—National Office for Regional Planning.

Reichstag—National Assembly.

Reichstreuhänder der Arbeit—National Trustee of Labor.

Reichsverband des Deutschen Handwerks—National Union of the German Handicraft.

Reichsverkehrsministerium—National Transportation Ministry.

Reichsversicherungsamt—National Insurance Office.

Reichswehrministerium—National Defense Ministry.

Reichswirtschaftsrat—National Economic Council.

Reichswirtschaftsministerium—National Economic Ministry.

Residenzstädte—Cities where early rulers had residence.

Ritter—Knights.

S

Schule—School.

Schutzstaffel—*S.S.*—Elite Guard of NSDAP.

Schwurgericht—Jury Court.

Seeamt—Sea Office.

Sonderverwaltungen—Special Administrations.

Sparkasse—Saving Bank.

Spitzenverbände—Top Employer's Associations.

Staatsgerichthof—National Constitutional Court.

Staatsministerium—State Ministry.

Staatspartei—State (Democratic) Party (1930).

Staatsrat—Council of State.

Stadtausschuss—City Committee.

Stadtbezirk—City District.

Städteordnung—Constitution for Cities.

Stadtgemeinden—Municipalities.

Stadtkreis—City County.

Stadtrat—City Councillor.

Stadtverfassung—City Charter.

Stadtverordnetenversammlung—City or Town Council.

Statistisches Amt—Office for General Statistics.

Statistisches Reichsamt—National Statistical Office.

Statthalter—National Governor.

Steuer—Tax.

Strafkammer—Chamber for Criminal Cases.

Strassendörfer—Villages with houses in a single row.

Strassenmeister—Road Master.

Sturmabteilung—S.A.—Storm Troops of NSDAP.

T

Tiefbauamt—Road and Canal Office.

U

Überwachungsausschuss—Interim Control Committee.

Untersuchungsausschüsse—Investigating Committees.

Urstromtal—Ancient River Valleys.

V

Verkehr—Traffic.

Verkehrsamt—Traffic Office (railroad).

Versicherungsämter—Insurance Offices.

Versorgungsamt—Welfare Office.

Versorgungsgerichte—Welfare Courts.

Verwaltung—Administration.

Verwaltungsbezirk—Administrative District.

Verwaltungsgerichtshof—Administrative Court.

Verwaltungsrat—General Board.

Vogteien—Bailiwicks.

Volkswohlfahrt—People's Welfare.

Völkischer Führerstaat—Folk Leader State.

Volksbegehren—Popular initiative.

Volksbildungsministerium—Ministry of Education.

Volksentscheid—Referendum.

W

Watten—Tidal flats.

Wehrkreis—Corps Area.

Wirkschaftskammer—Economic Chamber.

Wohlfahrtsämter—Welfare Offices.

Wohlfahrtsministerium—Welfare Ministery.

Z

Zentralausschuss der Unternehmeverbände—Central Committee of Employer's Associations.

Zentrum—Catholic Center Party.

Zollverein—Customs Union.

Zweckverband—Special Union.

Zweikollegienverfassung—Bicameral Constitution.

INDEX